SEVENTEENTH-CENTURY PROSE
MODERN ESSAYS IN CRITICISM

❧

Seventeenth-Century Prose

MODERN ESSAYS IN CRITICISM

Edited by STANLEY E. FISH

The University of California at Berkeley

New York OXFORD UNIVERSITY PRESS 1971

OXFORD UNIVERSITY PRESS

Oxford   London   New York
Glasgow   Toronto   Melbourne   Wellington
Cape Town   Salisbury   Ibadan   Nairobi   Lusaka   Addis Ababa
Bombay   Calcutta   Madras   Karachi   Lahore   Dacca
Kuala Lumpur   Hong Kong   Tokyo

For Abdiel:
"His Loyalty he kept, his Love, his Zeal."

Preface

It is often said that discursive prose has yet to receive the kind of close attention we give to poetry as a matter of course. This collection presents strong evidence to the contrary. One need only glance through the table of contents to realize how many of the twentieth century's best critical minds have applied themselves to our subject; and the reader of the following pages will soon discover that these men and women are not writing with their left hands. Indeed, the quality of this body of criticism is remarkable. The explanation, I think, is to be found not only in the texts that have generated it, but in the continuity of its concerns and methods. In a very real way, Morris Croll is the only begetter of this anthology. The questions he first asked in 1917 are being asked today. The answers he put forward are still themselves the subject of debate. The techniques he employed may have been extended and refined, but they have not been superseded. From Croll to Jones to Williamson, the tradition has passed to a second generation and now perhaps to a third, and it shows no signs of losing its vitality.

That vitality has made the task of the editor particularly difficult, and I make the usual apologies for my selections. Not every reader will like what he finds here or find here what he likes. The balance is weighed heavily in favor of essays whose focus is narrowly analytic. This is so because it is my hope that the collection will be of use both to students of the seventeenth century and to the more general reader who would like to be able to talk about prose (of whatever period) with force and precision.

My principle of organization is simple and obvious. Section I presents some of the major theoretical statements. Section II presents con-

siderations of individual stylists. This division is of course artificial—
there is much valuable criticism in the first section and a great deal
of theory in the second—but it has the advantage of affording the
reader a chronological perspective on what is a yet to be concluded
chapter in the history of criticism.

I am grateful for the advice and counsel of these friends and colleagues, Jonas Barish, Jackson Cope, Thomas Kranidas, Herbert
Mann, Leonard Nathanson, Joan Webber; and for the expert help
of my editorial assistants, Mayhill Anderson and Thomas Stehling.

Stanley E. Fish
Berkeley, California
May 1970

Contents

ix

II INDIVIDUAL STYLES

Theories of Seventeenth-Century Style

MORRIS W. CROLL

✭

Attic Prose: Lipsius, Montaigne, Bacon

Montaigne

THE FOUNDER OF LIBERTINE STYLE

There is a striking similarity between the moral experience of Montaigne at the time of his retirement and that through which Lipsius passed more gradually in arriving at the ultimate form of his thought. He too was touched with the melancholy of the late Renaissance. His confessed aim in his retirement was to study it and come to terms with it; and the method of his study in the first phase of his philosophical development was purely Stoic. The essays which we can prove to have been written during the first five or six years after his retirement are as like in tone and spirit to the Stoical treatises of Lipsius as the writings of two authors working independently are ever likely to be. The essay on Solitude, for instance, is a kind of companion-piece or complement to Lipsius' dialogue on *Constancy*.

Rhetorically, too, Montaigne effected his escape from humanistic orthodoxy through the Stoic doorway; and he asserted his freedom with more boldness and promptitude, perhaps actually became conscious of it at an earlier date, than Lipsius. He is in no doubt, even in the earliest of his Essays, about his distaste for Cicero's style; and indeed is the only Anti-Ciceronian who dares to express his independence with perfect frankness. "Fie upon that eloquence," he says, when speaking of Cicero, "that makes us in love with itself, and not with the thing." The very beauty of Cicero's language, the faultlessness of his oratorical rhythm, is the defect he finds in him, just as Erasmus had found him too perfect. "He will sometimes," he admits, "confound his numbers; but it is seldom." "As for me, I like a cadence that falleth shorter, cut like Iambics."[1] He may make his opposition more particular and varied in his later writings; he cannot make it more clear and positive than it is in the period between 1572 and 1576.

But he has not yet attained the characteristic independence of his matured opinions. Like Lipsius', his opposition to Cicero's sole authority is that of a school. The terms of his polemic are all Stoic terms; the books that he reads, he says, in words that are almost identical with a later phrase of Lipsius, are only those that will make him "more *wise* and *sufficient,* not more worthy or eloquent";[2] and the authors who have won away his admiration from "the master of those who speak" are also those in whom he has studied the Stoic philosophy which meets his moral need at this time: Seneca and, in a less degree, Lucan. The "soldatesque" style of Cæsar, it is true, also commands his special admiration; for what is it but the language of a great Stoic in action; but he is after all a writer, that is to say, a rhetorician, and as a model for his own imitation Seneca alone could serve his turn. Upon this model, in fact, his style was formed in his early writing, and the general character it took at that time was never radically changed, as he himself observed, even though his theory of style and his tastes passed through more than one phase of development in succeeding years. Pasquier described him as *un autre Sénèque de notre langue,* Père Garasse as *un Sénèque en désordre;* and the careful analysis of his style by many modern critics has but confirmed these judgments of an earlier day. His style, says Sainte-Beuve, is "a tissue of metaphors," and, as regards the other conspicuous trait of a Senecan style, Etienne Pasquier has truly said of his book that it is "un vrai séminaire de belles et notables sentences."

If Montaigne had advanced no further in the development of his moral and rhetorical theory than the stage he had reached in 1576 he would not have become the pioneer in a new phase of modern thought. His talent, his inimitable skill would of course have made his writings more familiar to the world than those of Muret and Lipsius; but he would have occupied a place similar to theirs and about equal to it in the history of the rationalist movement of the age.

Doubtless his freedom from the obligations of a professional consistency was a cause that his influence was not bounded by these limitations; some would prefer to say that it was merely an effect of the native superiority of genius to any circumstances whatever; and perhaps the truest statement of all would be that his preference of an unrelated freedom to the embarrassments of a defined career was in and of itself the decisive manifestation of his genius, including all the rest as its natural consequence. At all events, he passed beyond the limits of the "new kind of learning," even at the time when Muret and Lipsius were still seeking its exact academic formulæ and definitions. By the time his first volume appeared, in 1580, he had already renounced systematic stoicism—though he never moved out of the zone of intellectual and literary interests into which his stoic study had introduced him—and had found his way to the main highway of modern thought, which leads directly from Petrarch and Erasmus to the liberal skepticism of the eighteenth century. He had discovered that the progress of rationalism meant much more than a change of orthodoxies, meant nothing less in fact than the full exercise of curiosity and the free play of individual differences.[3]

A change of literary tastes kept pace with this philosophic development. Students of Montaigne's *Essais* have discovered that the publication of Amyot's translations of Plutarch's works, and particularly of *Les Œuvres Morales et Meslees* in 1572, had a decisive effect in this respect upon all his later work. The full meaning of the extraordinary delight he always took thenceforth in the reading of this work cannot be discussed here: we need only observe that it was quite as much an effect as a cause of the progress that was going on in his literary opinions. In an addition to his last volume, in the edition of 1588, he said that of all the authors he knew Plutarch was the one who "best mingled art with nature,"[4] and the phrase exactly describes the literary ideal toward which he was tending throughout his career. He was always in quest of the natural man in himself, the free individual self who should be the ultimate judge of the opinions of all the sects and schools; and as the natural complement of this philosophic enquiry he was always feeling his way at the same time toward a theory of style which should allow the greatest possible scope to the expression of differences of individual character, or, in other words, the greatest possible naturalness of style that is consistent with the artificial limits necessarily imposed upon all literary composition. We can observe through all the stages of his development a steady approximation to such a theory; but in the latest editions of his *Essais* he has worked out its formulæ with surprising definiteness, and has become, both as teacher and model, the initiator of a particular tendency within the general bounds of the Anti-Ciceronian movement which is destined to have even greater consequences in literary history than the Stoic model of style described by Lipsius. To this tendency we are justified in giving the name "Libertine"—though the term is new in *literary* criticism— because it not only indicates the connection between the kind of prose-style which it produces and the philosophy to which it is related, but also exactly describes the character of this prose-style itself.

The freedom of Montaigne's literary opinions was partly due, as we have already observed, to his deliberate choice of a career free from official responsibilities: he became a "man writing for men." But it was also due in large measure to the fact that he was the first of the Anti-Ciceronian leaders to use a vernacular language in his writings; and this is so great a point of difference that it cannot be passed over in a discussion of seventeenth century prose-style.

LATIN AND THE VERNACULAR TONGUES 1575–1625

The last quarter of the sixteenth century was the period when the literary claims and pretensions of Latin and the modern languages were most evenly balanced, when it was easiest to pass from one to the other without a change of subject-matter or style. Before that time there had been a fairly clear, though by no means a deliberate, differentiation of their uses. The chief artistic use of the vernacular in the sixteenth century had been to express the surviving medievalism of the culture of that age. It was the language, for instance, of what had been perhaps the most general medium of medieval literary expression, the sermon; it was the language of a multitude of romantically-retold tales of both antiquities, in which the fading ideals and customs of chivalry were adapted to an age of courtiers; it was the language of courtly ceremonial and show; it was the medium in which the medieval book of etiquette and universal instruction enjoyed a brief revival. It reflected, in brief, the customs of a courtly

life which had not been modified in its essential features by the
intellectual effort of the Renaissance. On the other hand, whatever
was really new and forward-looking in the Renaissance found its
prose-expression in the ancient tongue. Some humanists, it is true,
foresaw the modern uses of their mother-languages: Bembo, Du
Bellay, Ascham, for instance. Yet their writings are not representative of the usual vernacular prose of their time; and there is little
distortion in the statement that in 1550 all serious, modern thought
was expressed in Latin, all that was traditional, or merely popular,
in its character tended to find its way into vernacular prose.

One hundred years after that date the progress of modernism had
reversed these relations in most respects. The usual language of serious criticism, and even of philosophy, had become English, French,
or Italian; and, what is more important, the *subject* of literary criticism had become chiefly the vernacular languages and their usages;
Latin was already the language of a dead literature, whose chief
value was to enrich the native styles with romantic allusion, heroic
images, and far-echoing rhythms.

In these observations there is of course nothing new, and the purpose of reviving them here is to call attention to a fact which scholarship has not yet clearly enough taken account of, that between the
two *termini* that have just been mentioned there was a most interesting period in which the two languages, or the two kinds of languages,
the ancient and the vernacular, were present in the minds of most
well-educated people in relations of almost exact balance and equality,
and there were no real differences whatever between the uses of the
one and the other. This period, which extended over about two generations, one before the turn of the century, one after, was the hinge
on which the great change turned, a quiet revolution, effected unconsciously in the main, it would seem, and participated in by many
who would have regretted it if they had known what they were
doing, but of vastly more importance than most of the changes which
have been the subject of literary controversy. This period should be
more carefully studied by literary historians with reference to the
history of the modern languages than it has yet been; and there are
the two comments on it which are directly suggested by the study of
"Attic" prose.[5]

The first has to do with the effect of the equalization of the languages upon the vernacular literatures, and is to the effect that out
of this passing state of equilibrium emerged a standard form of

literary prose in every modern language, upon which all later forms are founded and out of which they have developed without radical or revolutionary change.

Italian, English and French prose of the preceding periods has various merits which antiquarians love to point out for the reproof or exhortation of writers of the present day. But none of it is quite *standard* prose. Some of it is too popular and crude and violent. Some of it is too highly wrought and fantastically mannered. And a third kind,—the smallest class,—though pure and correct, is too poverty-stricken, thin, and limited in its expressive resources. The explanation of this fact of course is that, as we have just observed, men of ideas reserved all the serious, progressive, and modern uses of their intellects for expression in Latin; they felt that the spoken languages had not been sufficiently conventionalized to carry the definite meanings and logical processes of continued exposition. It was good for *concrete* uses alone. And as long as this sort of differentiation continued in force there could not be a standard prose-style in either Latin or the various vernaculars, for a standard form of prose is determined by the *general* thought of the age which it expresses, its collective wisdom and experience; it is neither remotely and professionally intellectual, on the one hand, nor a simple record of facts and sensations, on the other; its function is rather to relate the varied phenomena of the external life of each period to its dominant ideas and the general philosophic trend of its mind. It is clear that no such style could make its appearance in an age when the intellect spoke one language, the senses another.

On the other hand, when these two languages had become virtually interchangeable in the minds of a great many writers, as they were, for example, in the minds of Montaigne and Bacon, when one and the other came with equal ease and idiomatic freedom from their pens, it made little difference in fact which one they used, for each would have some of the characteristic quality of the other. A writer in Latin would show the colloquial and concrete qualities of his speech in his own language; a writer in French or English would derive from his Latin the rhetorical firmness, the exact use of abstraction, the logical process which the learned language imposes.

This is the phenomenon that we observe in fact in the period of Montaigne and Bacon. These are the first writers in the vernacular languages who employ a style which renders the process of thought and portrays the picturesque actuality of life with equal effect and constantly relates the one to the other; and it is in this sense that we may justify the statement that the Ani-Ciceronian leaders—Montaigne, Charron, and Pasquier in France, Bacon, Hall, Jonson, Wotton in England—are the actual founders of modern prose-style in their respective languages. In the works of these authors, and in none of those that precede them, we can find a style in the popular language which is at once firm, uniform, and level enough to be called a style and also adaptable enough to adjust itself to the changing life of the modern world—a style which may grow and change in later generations without losing its recognizable features.

The second comment to be made in this connection is that the character of the Anti-Ciceronian movement in prose-style—whether we consider its fundamental principles or the models it proposed for imitation—was eminently favorable to the process of leveling and approximation, the virtual blending, in fact, of Latin and vernacular style that was going on during this period. Ciceronian purism had tended to keep the two kinds of speech apart from one another. Not that the Ciceronians had been unfavorable to the study of prose-style in the vernacular. Bembo and Ascham, on the contrary, had studied the subject carefully. But their purism in Latin style begot a corresponding temper in their treatment of the native languages, and they mistakenly attempted to shut up Italian, French and English within the inadequate limits of the literary vocabulary which they had acquired at the beginning of the sixteenth century. Misled by the lack of a proper historical sense which was characteristic of their school, they pretended that the vernacular tongues had already attained their full maturity and were ready to be standardized in grammars, dictionaries, and rhetorics. The central idea of the Anti-Ciceronian movement, on the other hand, was that style should be adapted to the differences of men and times. The great modern principle of unending change and development was implicit in its rhetorical theory; and many of its leaders expressed their new-found joy in freedom by indulging in strange caprices of vocabulary. English and French are suddenly deformed by a riot of freakish Latinisms on the one hand, and expanded at the same time by new and piquant discoveries in the expressiveness of colloquial speech. The Latin of humanist and scholar of course loses its remoteness by the same process, and begins to bristle with strange words picked up from Plautus, or Greek, or medieval Latin, or the living languages.

To discuss the interesting results in the style of seventeenth-century prose that followed this general prevalence of the hedge-breaking custom would require a separate essay, perhaps a volume. We must proceed here merely to point out that there was a more specific way in which Anti-Ciceronianism aided the process of leveling and the transference of the qualities of Latin prose to the various vernaculars, namely, through the character of its preferred Latin models. The Ciceronian style cannot be reproduced in English, or indeed in any modern language. The ligatures of its comprehensive period are not found in the syntax of an uninflected tongue; and the artifices necessary to supply their function must produce either fantastic distortion or insufferable bombast. This is true after all the experiments of four centuries in quest of formal beauty. Certainly in the sixteenth century no modern speech had developed an art of prose adequate to the imitation of so difficult a model, and the best that any of them could do was to reproduce the oratorical style of medieval Latin, in which only the ornaments and the simpler elements of the form of the Ciceronian pattern are employed for the purpose of formal beauty. That these could indeed be transferred with some success into vernacular forms of style had been proved in Spain and England, and even in Italy and France; but it was evident that none of the varieties of *estilo culto* developed by this process was adequate to serve as a vehicle for the advancing thought of the new age or to portray the actualities of any real world. No oratorical prose, indeed, whether based on the pure Ciceronian, or on the derived medieval, pattern, could serve for this purpose. As long as these were the preferred models a normal form of French or English prose could not appear.

But Seneca is easy. There is nothing in his syntax that could prove a bar to the expression of the ideas of a keen-minded critic of the end of the sixteenth century concerning the moral experience of his times or himself; on the contrary, the brevity of his constructions, the resolved and analytic character of his sentences, would provide such a writer with a mold exactly adapted to the character of his mind and the state of his language. Tacitus, of course, is harder reading; but the kind of difficulty that he offers would prove to be no more than a welcome stimulus and challenge to the trained wits of rationalists like Lipsius, Bacon, Malvezzi, Gracian, and Balzac. In brief, ancient Anti-Ciceronianism worked in a *resolved* style, and the perfect success with which its manner was transferred to French, Italian, Spanish, and English style during the early seventeenth century is proof of its fitness to serve as the model on which a standard modern prose could be formed.

Finally, it is to be observed that the equilibrium between the languages determines the sources from which the student of the Anti-Ciceronian movement must draw his knowledge of contemporary opinion. He must learn to disregard linguistic boundary-lines. He must use the Latin discussions of contemporary and ancient Latin style, discussions in Latin of contemporary vernacular style—and these are frequent until the middle of the seventeenth century—and of course, more and more as time goes on, discussions of vernacular tendencies in the vernacular; and he must learn that all of these are of equal value. It has already been seen that the beginnings of the movement were in humanistic Latin prose, in the works of Erasmus, Muret, Lipsius; and naturally the theory and criticism of it are found in the same place. But it is somewhat surprising to discover that a whole generation after the balances have tipped in favor of the literary use of the vernacular, criticism of vernacular tendencies in prose-style continues to appear in Latin. Descartes, for instance, writes to Balzac in Latin an illuminating letter concerning the French style of the time, and Bacon was certainly thinking of English, French, and Italian style in the paragraph concerning recent prose which he added to his Latin translation of the *Advancement of Learning* in 1622. The student must learn, in short, that as far as style is concerned there was no difference in the mind of this period between Latin prose, on the one hand, and English, French, Italian, or Spanish, on the other: Lipsius writes to Montaigne of his style, after reading his first volume of *Essais,* in similar terms to those he had used in writing at an earlier date to Muret of his new manner of writing.[6]

Nor are these facts valuable only as indicating a method of study. They are of first-rate importance in the history of the movement itself as showing that in the minds of most of its leaders it was in the classical and not in the popular tradition. On this point there can be no question. Even when the custom of writing prose in the native languages had become very common, as it did during the decades 1590–1610, most of those who fell in with the new tendency felt that they were following in the train of Politian, Erasmus, and Muret, and ultimately of Seneca and Tacitus. They thought of their vernacular style as having come over to them from the Latin of the humanists or as directly derived from the Latin style of antiquity;

and they seem usually to have been unaware of any relation, either of opposition or evolution, with the vernacular prose of the preceding age.

The only very important exception to this general rule is to be found in the critical utterances of Montaigne and of certain writers, like Pasquier, for instance, who were directly influenced by him. Montaigne was well read in the vernacular literature of the sixteenth century and even of an earlier period; and he was too humane a critic of life to pass by the true mirrors of his age without studying his own features in them too, even though his grand enthusiasms are all for certain of the ancients. His criticisms, it is true, are too few and inexplicit to be satisfying; but they tend to show that he regarded the ornate prose and poetry of the past age with something of the same contempt that he felt for Bembo and other Ciceronianizing Latinists. We wish that he had been more definite in telling us why he scorned Guevara's famous *Golden Book;*[7] but we may be reasonably certain that the poverty of their content and the richness of their stylistic ornament were equal causes of his distaste. We should like to be certain too that he is thinking of the Spanish prosaists and the style of Guevara and Mexia when he speaks of "l'affectation et la recherche des fantastiques élévations espagnoles et petrarchistes";[8] for the association of Petrarchanism in verse and the *estilo culto* of Guevara and Lyly in prose as two similar manifestations of the medieval love of rhetoric would be exactly what we should expect in an Anti-Ciceronian and rationalist like Montaigne. But the passage as a whole does not permit us to say with *certainty* that he was thinking of Spanish *prose,* and we must be content to know that he did actually dislike both these kinds of vernacular writing. The *franche naïveté* of Froissart was, on the other hand, wholly to his taste, and if he seems not to understand the real importance of Rabelais he at least enjoyed him.[9]

Bacon

BACON AND TACITUS

There is only one other author of nearly equal importance with Lipsius and Montaigne in the history of the establishment of the Attic tradition—Francis Bacon. He was not quite the first professed Anti-Ciceronian in England. Thomas Nashe and Gabriel Harvey

undertook a vigorous attack during the nineties against both Ciceronian Latin and the ornate vernacular style of Lyly and his school,
each of them seeking an escape from formalism through the method
of extravagance and licentious freedom of style; and there are interesting similarities between their efforts and those of some Continental "libertines" of the same period. But neither of these writers
had philosophy or authority enough to lead his age, and their attack
on tradition was soon lost sight of in the great success of Bacon's
more imposing offensive movement.

As a historian, Bacon offers useful aid to the student of prose-
style. In a passage in the *Advancement of Learning* (most of which
was probably written some years before its publication in 1605), he
has sketched the history of the Ciceronian cult and described the
causes that produced it. He is perhaps following a faulty sketch in
one of Muret's orations (delivered at Rome in 1575, in introducing a
course in Juvenal): but his account is so much more complete and
correct that it may be considered the first attempt to place the Renaissance in historical perspective.—Should we add that his success is
a sign that the Renaissance has already passed or is passing? Perhaps
so—Ciceronianism is his illustration of that distemper of learning
"when words are valued more than matter"; its origin, he finds, was
in the excessive zeal of the scholars of the sixteenth century for an
exact knowledge of the words of antiquity, and he attributes this
in turn—acutely enough but not altogether correctly—to the controversial needs created by the Reformation, and the search for authority
among the Fathers of the Church. He quotes a joke from Erasmus'
Ciceronianus, names as leading Ciceronians since Erasmus' time
Ascham and Car, the Protestant German humanist Sturm, and the
"Portugal bishop Osorius" (the latest exemplar of the pure cult),
describes their style with his usual analytic skill, and closes with the
striking statement, which perhaps is due to hints in Erasmus' dialogue, that if he should have to choose between the "weight" of the
scholastic philosophers and the "copie" of the rhetorical humanists
he would take the former.

The words of this passage are probably familiar to most literary
scholars; but this is not true of the supplement to it which Bacon
added when his work was translated into Latin and published as
De Augmentis Scientiarum in 1622. The new passage provides a
fairly exact measure of the amount of water that has run under
the bridge in three or four decades of literary history, and has an

additonal interest as an illustration of a new kind of curiosity, in
the men of this generation, which enables them to turn upon themselves and recognize their own changes of taste and temper. Their
perception of historical perspectives has made them more observant
of change and progress in their own world; a new intelligence is
emerging from the methods of skeptical inquiry taught by Petrarch,
Erasmus, and Montaigne. In translation, Bacon's words are as follows:

> "Somewhat sounder is another form of style,—yet neither is
> it innocent of some vain shows,—which is likely to follow in
> time upon this copious and luxuriant oratorical manner. It con-
> sists wholly in this: that the words be sharp and pointed; sen-
> tences concised; a style in short that may be called 'turned'
> rather than fused. Whence it happens that everything dealt
> with by this kind of art seems rather ingenious than lofty. *Such
> a style is found in Seneca very freely used, in Tacitus and the
> younger Pliny more moderately; and it is beginning to suit the
> ears of our age as never before.* And indeed it is pleasant to
> subtle and low-ranging minds (for by means of it they conciliate
> the honor due to letters); however better-trained judgments
> disapprove it; and it may be looked upon as a distemper of
> learning, in as far as it is accompanied by a taste for mere words
> and their concinnity."

This passage tells admirably what the Anti-Ciceronian movement
is, and how it arose. It describes the form of the new style, and
provides a motive for its rapid diffusion at the beginning of the
seventeenth century. Not only this, however; it also establishes the
parallel between this contemporary Anti-Ciceronianism and that of
the first century, both in the character of its style and in its relation
to the oratorical prose of the preceding century. The only point we
miss is that Bacon does not clearly say that the new tendency is due
to actual imitation of the ancients; and this defect is easily accounted
for by Bacon's unwillingness to admit the effective survival of the
principle of imitation and authority either in himself or his age; it
is of a piece with the unfortunate, and sometimes mean, reticence he
displays concerning his own great obligations to intellectual masters
of the ancient and modern worlds.

And in fact, notwithstanding the apparent cool detachment of his criticism, Bacon knows very well that he is here describing his own style. He has left sufficient evidence in his own utterances of the truth of his secretary's statement that Tacitus, Cæsar, and Seneca were his favorite authors, and that the order of his preference was that in which these three names are here mentioned. Nor have the critics required the aid of such statements; the resemblance of Bacon's style to that of his masters has often been observed by them. The praise he bestows on Seneca's style, says one of them, *ad ipsum Verulamium haud immerito detorqueri possit*. He was attracted to Seneca and Tacitus, this writer continues, by kinship of talent; and it was in the assiduous reading of these authors that he cultivated his taste for a style of acute and condensed brevity, ornamented, at the same time, with the riches of rhetoric and an almost poetic splendor of words.[10]

How are we to account then for the derogatory, or at least balancing, tone of the passage we have just quoted? Properly interpreted, it may serve as an aid to a more exact description of Bacon's tastes and the character of his literary influence than has yet been attempted, or to a correction of some misconceptions concerning them. It has been the custom to place Seneca first among Bacon's models and favorites, but this is an error. When his words are carefully examined, it is apparent that what he says in discommendation of the style "freely used" by Seneca is all directed toward "vain shows" and verbal ornament, the same fault of undue love of concinnity, in short, which was a cause of the revolt against Cicero's form of rhetoric. This is somewhat puzzling, especially in view of the fact that Seneca himself had made current among Anti-Ciceronian critics the phrases they habitually used to express their contempt for the sensuous beauty of the balanced Ciceronian phrase: *non ornamentum virile concinnitas*, and so forth. But the reader of Seneca can reconcile the contradiction. For that very literary and rhetorical essayist customarily framed his *antitheses* and *argutiæ* in a balanced form, different indeed from that of the copious oratorical style, but yet capable of becoming almost as transparently artificial. At its best an excellent literary form for the insinuation of subtle shades of thought and fine distinctions, at its worst it is indeed no more than "mere words and their concinnity." And it must be added that Bacon has in mind the imitators of Seneca more than Seneca himself: almost certainly Lipsius' Latinity; probably the English style of Bishop Hall's *Epistles* and other moral writings; perhaps also the

Senecan manner of a number of English essayists who had written
since his own first volume of 1597. All these writers had shown how
easily the imitation of Seneca could descend to verbal ingenuity or
mere pun on occasions when the idea was not worthy of the artifice
bestowed upon it.

The faults of Tacitus and his imitators were clear enough to
seventeenth-century critics; but they did not run in this direction.
Obscurity, enigma, contortion are not qualities of style that comport
with concinnity and the study of the abstract charm of words. Evidently Bacon is drawing a vertical line of distinction down through
the area of Anti-Ciceronianism in addition to the other transverse
line that divides it as a whole from the Ciceronian types of prose;
and when this is observed and confirmed by a reference to the
qualities of his own style, his literary comments and judgments
throughout his works become more consistent. It becomes clear that
he has not expressed anywhere a positive approval of Seneca's
subject-matter or style, though he refers to his letters as a model for
the new essay-form and cites his father as skilful in antitheses.
But on the contrary he has directly praised Tacitus in a private letter
to Sir Fulke Greville, as "the first of historians," and again, in the
Temporis Partus Masculus, with the characteristic emphasis of his
laconic style: "Many like the moral doctrines of Aristotle and Plato;
but of Tacitus it may be said that he utters the very morals of life
itself."[11] The former of these passages is worthy of a careful consideration.[12] He says that history is of most use for those who wish
to know only humanity, and continues: "For poets, I can commend
none, being resolved to be ever a stranger to them. Of orators, if I
must choose any, it shall be Demosthenes, both for the argument
he handles, and for that his eloquence is more proper for a statesman
than Cicero's. Of all stories, I think Tacitus simply the best; Livy
very good; Thucydides above any of the writers of Greek matters."
In every respect this is a characteristic Anti-Ciceronian utterance:
in its rejection of poetry from useful studies, in its preference of
Tacitus to Livy (along with which goes a liking for Thucydides),
and in its contemptuous treatment of oratory, partly veiled by the
exaltation of Demosthenes above Cicero. Finally, it is to be noted
that the extraordinary enthusiasm of the writer for history—which
virtually means politics when connected with the influence of Tacitus
—associates him with a particular phase of the Anti-Ciceronian complex which had already declared itself in the programs of Muret and

Lipsius. It is true that at about the same time that Bacon was writing these words he must also have been writing the passage in an early section of the *Advancement of Learning* in which he speaks without qualification of Cicero as the first, or second, of orators, Livy as the first of historians, Virgil and Varro as first in their kinds of all those known to men. But the apparent conflict only gives us the opportunity to note a fact that every student of one subject must take account of: that the Anti-Ciceronian critics, even the boldest of them, always keep an Augustan and Ciceronian orthodoxy in reserve; and even Montaigne will admit that if an abstract literary excellence, independent of the practical and moral uses of the works in which it is displayed, be the basis of one's judgment, the Augustan age and the ages that resemble it are on a higher plane than any others. It is sometimes necessary to surprise them in the more confidential tone of letters and casual notes in order to discover the full range of their heterodoxy.

In Bacon's case, the frequency of his quotation from Tacitus may be accepted as evidence of his preference of that author to all others; for an acquaintance with Tacitus was not in that age to be taken for granted; nor was the citation of his difficult phrases a literary convention, as was that of the Senecan "sentences." On the contrary, it was the mark of an individual taste or a peculiar initiation. Bacon's influence, like his own prose-style, can best be explained in terms of his admiration and imitation of Tacitus; and the point has had to be elaborated at some length for the reason that it has a special bearing upon the development of seventeenth-century English style. The other models of Anti-Ciceronian prose were already known to Englishmen: Hall and the letter-writers were familiarizing them with the Senecan manner of Lipsius, and the intimate whimsical vein of Montaigne was beginning to be domesticated in their own prose. From these sources they could learn most of what Anti-Ciceronianism had to teach concerning the expression of acute wit by ingenious rhetoric. But the desire for wit and ingenuity was only one phase of seventeenth-century taste. Combined with it was a desire for ceremonious dignity, an ideal of deliberate and grave demeanor, which was partly, no doubt, an inheritance from the courtly past, but was modified and indeed largely created by the profound moral experience which the new age was undergoing. A prose-style that should adequately express this age must contrive, therefore, to mingle elements that in any other period would appear oddly contrasted.

It must be at once ingenious and lofty, intense yet also profound, acute, realistic, revealing, but at the same time somewhat grave and mysterious. It must have in short that curious sublimity which is felt in the painting of El Greco, in the sermons and letters of Donne, and in certain sculptures of Bernini.

Seneca—its favorite author—might *suggest* the ideal manner; but he was too superficial, too familiar, to furnish a complete model of it. Lucan's nodosity and rhetorical pomp served better as a guide to the poets; and Tacitus, if he had not been too difficult (and indeed too novel, for he had not been widely read in the sixteenth century) would have been the usual exemplar of English prose-style. Bacon's great service to English prose was that he naturalized a style in which ingenious obscurity and acute significance are the appropriate garb of the mysteries of empire; and by means of his example the Tacitean strain became familiar to many English writers who were not sufficiently trained in Tacitus himself to imitate his style directly.[13]

SCIENCE AND SEVENTEENTH CENTURY PROSE

Besides domesticating the style of Tacitus in English prose, Bacon aided in various technical ways which cannot be described here in the formulation of a new rhetorical program.[14] But of course his greatest service to the prose movement of his time was not directly and expressly a literary one. It is to be found in his contributions to the great intellectual movement of which Anti-Ciceronianism is but the rhetorical and literary expression.

The progress of rationalism during the sixteenth century had been rapid, and it had been increasingly so as the century drew to an end. But the complete triumph which it was to obtain was still adjourned by a partial lack of coöperation among its leaders in the various fields of intellectual endeavor. Many of them were specialists, of course, who failed to understand as clearly as the defenders of orthodoxy in the universities and courts did how closely their various subjects were related to one another in the general interests of progress. Cujas and Alciati, for instance, were jurists; Ramus' studies ranged widely, but he impressed himself on his age as a logician; Montaigne was a moralist pure and simple; and though Muret and Lipsius were both fully aware of the revolutionary implications in their methods of study, they were daunted by the formidable front of orthodoxy. Intellectually free, they were involved in practical relations with the powers of conservatism which compelled them to protect themselves by disingenuous compromises and a shocking Machiavellianism. Of course their hesitations and concealments were only the usual marks of all movements of radicalism and innovation; a forward tendency never presents as solid a front as the established system that it is bound to conflict with, because its aims are partly concealed in the future, and no one can tell how the various elements that coöperate in it will relate and adjust themselves in the final settlement. But reformers had more than the usual reasons for fear and vacillation in the sixteenth century because the orthodoxies of all kinds, religious, political, intellectual, and literary, were more than usually aware at that time of the community of their interests and more effectively united in self-defense. What was needed at the end of the century was such an appraisement of the situation as would give an equal consciousness of their common aims, an equal clearness of purpose, to the champions of the more progressive and positive modes of thought.

This was the most important part of the task undertaken by Bacon in the *Advancement of Learning* and the *Novum Organum.* It is now generally recognized that the materials of which these works were made were most of them old and familiar; many of them had even been worked up by his predecessors into almost the form in which Bacon used them. Aristotelianism, medieval scholasticism, Barthollism, Platonism, Ciceronianism, Euphuism, and whatever other shadowy phantoms of reality had haunted the Renaissance, had already been severally exposed to the criticism of reason. But Bacon gathered them all together within the limits of a single survey, and covered them all over with one narrow *hic jacet.* After that they were as pallid and ridiculous as ghosts astray in the open daylight, they could no longer frighten any one.

But that was not all that he did for the new rationalism. He put the vigorous new natural sciences of his age at the center of all his projects for the progress of knowledge. The program of education announced by Muret and elaborated by Lipsius included only the two branches of moral philosophy (the *sapientia,* or private morality, of the ancient Stoics and Peripatetics, and the *prudentia,* or worldly wisdom, which they studied in Tacitus, Machiavelli, and other ancient and modern politicians), with the rhetoric appropriate to them. The effect of Bacon's writings was to put natural science in a definite place in this program,—not the first place, it is true, because the

century that began with Montaigne and ended with La Bruyère and
Halifax was above all else the century of moral philosophy,—but
yet in a recognized position of authority, from which it could exercise a constant influence upon the moral researches of the age by
clarifying, illustrating, defining their method of procedure. This
modification had such important literary effects that it must not be
passed over here with a mere mention.

The method introduced by Lipsius and Montaigne in the study
of the moral situation of their time was in fact the method of science. It does not appear that these philosophers thought of it in that
way, or were in any profound way affected by the scientific studies
that preceded Bacon's work: their intellectual houses were without
windows, or had very narrow ones. But they were compelled by the
impulse of their positivistic purposes to adopt the same method of
experiment and induction in their own subjects that has since produced such astounding results in natural science. These philosophers
were in revolt, not only against the medieval forms of thought, as
they are often said to have been, but also against the aims of the
Renaissance itself as they had chiefly displayed themselves hitherto.
For the effort of their own century had been devoted, exactly like
that of the more remote past, chiefly to the rearing of conspicuous
philosophic constructions which had no foundations in immediate
observation or experience. "Men have despised," said Bacon, "to be
conservant in ordinary and common matters . . . ; but contrariwise
they have compounded sciences chiefly of a certain resplendent or
lustrous matter, chosen either to give glory to the subtlety of disputa-
tions or to the eloquence of discourses."[15] They themselves took the
humbler task of searching these glorious Houses of Pride to their
sandy foundations. Nor did they pretend to raise other constructions
in their stead, except only such modest shelters as would serve their
immediate moral needs. To be conversant in ordinary and common
matters was their only boast. To distinguish the facts of moral experience with critical and inquiring eyes, to record their observations
with the acuteness and exactness of the new literary style they had
devised for this purpose, this was an intellectual exercise well
adapted to their subtle wits; and it was a task moreover that afforded
them the thrill of novel adventure. In short, the intellectual program
of the seventeenth century was the scientific work of moral observation and delineation; and Montaigne's avowal of his purpose to portray for the first time exactly what the thing is that goes by the name

of a man is echoed at the other end of the century with only a slight difference of tone, in La Bruyère's truly scientific program, "the *description* of man."

Bacon therefore did not have to teach the method of science to the moralists of his age; for they had already learned it. But the new studies in natural history which Bacon helped to make popular were of great aid to them in their own work, because it trained them, and of course their audiences too, in the habit of exact observation, sharp definition, and clear classification which were necessary for their purpose. Bacon himself provides an excellent illustration of scientific method in the realm of moral observation; for the aphorisms, *Antitheta,* "topics," "colours of good and evil," etc., from which, as from a spinner's bottom, he says, he unwound the thread of his essays, are pieces of scientific apparatus used in a moralist's workshop. They are the notes he has taken at the moment when the experiment was on and observation was keenest and then allocated, by a rough-and-ready scheme of classification, among certain headings and sub-headings which will make them available for future reference. To enumerate the works of seventeenth-century morality that were composed by this method would be tedious: Descartes' *Meditations,* Wotton's *Aphorisms of Education,* and countless other works display the method in their form; and it is but slightly veiled by a more elaborate manner in Browne's *Religio Medici;* Pascal, La Bruyère, Temple, and Halifax all employed it.

To distinguish rhetorical from intellectual process in the writings of professed naturalists is to divide between the bark and the tree: whatever the motions of their minds, they will betray themselves in their style. But some of the results of the addition of science to the intellectual program may be traced most clearly in the history of prose-style. They are chiefly of two opposite kinds, which finally came into open conflict in the second half of the century. At first the natural sciences tended to give greater imaginative range and freedom to the new Attic prose. We may observe this phenomenon most clearly in the writings of certain professed men of science who became literary men and stylists through an interesting blending in their thought of the ideas of Bacon and Montaigne, students of medicine especially, like Sir Thomas Browne and Robert Burton or the Parisian doctor Gui Patin, who bring into new and curious relations the results of their physical explorations of man's nature and the moral speculations of their time. Essentially moralists, as all men of their age were, they were able to add to the common stock of ideas and images a wealth of curious detail derived from their professional pursuits and their knowledge of unfamiliar facts. The courageous skepticism of the new kind of morality and the rhetorical audacity that accompanied it appealed equally to their tastes; and they contributed in their turn out of their mastery of physiological research to the effects of curiosity and novelty on which so much of the success of the new prose depended. In two writers in which we may fairly describe the union of scientific and moral interest as perfect and equal—in Sir Thomas Browne and Pascal,— we may observe at their highest development the powers of intellectual imagination which might be born of this union.

As the century advanced, however, it became apparent that science was not to remain on the side of poetry and the imagination; on the contrary, it allied itself more and more closely with the movement for clarity and common sense which was gathering strength from so many different sources. A well-known pronunciamento of the Royal Society in England expressly dissociated the literary aims of that scientific body from the rhetoric of Bacon and aligned them with the new taste for a plain and clear style. At the same time, in France, the influence of Descartes was gradually making itself felt even among those who were not at all willing to accept his philosophy: imagination began to be a word of derision; Malebranche taught an almost geometrical use of reason as a corrective of its evil influence; the teachers of Port Royal found in logic the way to a Christian plainness and purity of style; and the quality that distinguishes the style of La Bruyère, and even the nobler language of Pascal, is a strictly scientific precision rather than those occasional, and as it were accidental, triumphs of revelation which are effected by an ambitious imagination or a roving fancy.

Conclusion

Muret, Lipsius, Montaigne, and Bacon, though the period of their collective activity covers three-quarters of a century, belong to a single generation in the development of Renaissance culture, the generation in which modern rationalism definitely declared itself as the doctrine of the future, and the new, the Anti-Ciceronian, form of prose-style assumed its place in the world of letters. But Muret belongs at the beginning of this generation; he is partly the pioneer, partly the founder of its intellectual program. The three philosophers we have considered in the preceding pages lived in the full flower of its career, when its conflict with the forces of the past was virtually over. Rationalism had now won its victory, and displayed that tendency to divide into various schools or phases which always appears when a general idea mingles with the several elements of a varied intellectual life and takes different color from each of them.

In this phase of its history Attic prose divides into the three main forms, or perhaps we should call them merely tendencies toward distinct forms, which displayed themselves more conspicuously in the generation that followed, and can even be distinguished, though less clearly, in the "classical" prose which developed in a succeeding generation out of seventeenth-century Attic. Lipsius, Montaigne, and Bacon each represents one of these three forms or tendencies, and the discussion of their ideas has perhaps made clear what they are. A specific statement will serve, however, to make more definite what has already been said of them.

I. First in order of importance is a tendency due to the prevalence of Stoic philosophy. The prose in which this tendency is manifest can best be known as prose of the Stoic model. 'Senecan prose' would be more definite; but it would sometimes include too much, and on the other hand it would fail to indicate the full scope of Stoic imitation. Lipsius is as clearly the founder of this style as he is of the Neo-Stoic philosophy which usually accompanied it in the first half of the century.

II. To the student of events beyond the limits of the seventeenth century, a tendency in style associated with the skeptical or "libertine" thought of that century and especially with the influence of Montaigne, would seem worthy of the first place in order of importance. This we can only call "libertine" prose, whether we consider its philosophical implications or its rhetorical theories and form. The groundwork of this style is the Senecan pattern, which is so much more apparent in the Stoic model; but it aims at freedom, and chooses several other writers, ancient and modern, as the models by which it seeks, through the method of imitation, to escape from the method of imitation. Rabelais is the chief of these. Montaigne adds the taste for Plutarch's essays; and the form of Montaigne's own style, from 1600 onward, mingles with that of Rabelais' in almost equal proportions in the prevailing forms of libertine style in the seventeenth century.

III. Next to these in the favor of the age was the prose of "politicians" and students of "prudential wisdom": Bacon, Malvezzi, Gracian, Grotius, and a host of others, who get their rhetorical and often their political ideas chiefly from Tacitus.

To these three major forms must be added a tendency which cannot be separated from any of them, but manifests itself everywhere as the peculiar mark of the genius of the seventeenth century, a tendency observable in writers as normal as Bacon, Browne, and Balzac, but apparent in its full efflorescence in the letters of Donne, the essays of Gracian and Malvezzi and many of their fellow countrymen, the histories of Pierre Mathieu, and many similar works. For this tendency there is unfortunately no convenient name in English. "Metaphysical" is even a less happy term to describe the kinds of prose in which it appears than the related kinds of poetry; and there seems to be no possibility of making a practicable adjective or noun in English from the continental terms *concettismo,* etc. It may be known as the "prose of imaginative conceit" in order that we may keep in line with the terms of current criticism. But I am tempted to make the bold innovation of calling it "the baroque style" in prose; for no other term will so exactly describe its characteristic qualities.

In the three forms enumerated above (with due regard to the *concettistic* tendency in each of them) may be ranged all the Attic prose of the century from 1575 to 1675, and that is to say all its characteristic prose, except the writings of one or two great individualists who escape the influence of their time; and it is upon the lines laid down in this classification that the further study of seventeenth-century prose-style must be conducted. What is now necessary is a thorough survey of Stoic prose, libertine prose, and Tacitean prose separately, each treated with reference to its philosophical theory, its preferred models in antiquity and modern times, its relation to the culture of the age, and its rhetorical forms. Only the outlines of such a survey can be suggested, of course, in the study of individual authors,—even of such representative and influential leaders as Muret, Lipsius, Montaigne, and Bacon.

NOTES

1. I, 40 (*Consideration sur Ciceron*).
2. *Ibid.*
3. The change of Montaigne from Stoicism to Libertinism is well treated in Strowski's work on him and also in his *De Montaigne a Pascal*, vol. I. Professor Villey's *Les Sources et l'Évolution des Essais* provides the exact details necessary.
4. III, 6 (*Des Coches*), near the beginning.
5. Many interesting points concerning the relation of the vernacular languages and Latin in the sixteenth century are brought out by Clément in his work on Henri Estienne (Paris, 1899), pp. 197-304 and elsewhere.
6. Lipsius to Montaigne, 1589, *Epp. Misc. Cent. I* (first published in 1590). See also the correspondence between Mlle. de Gournay and Lipsius of the same year, in which the lady writes in French, the *savant* in Latin; yet the style is of the same mould. Concerning this correspondence see Bonnefon, *Montaigne et ses Amis*, II, 334-352.
7. I, 48 (*Des Destries*).
8. II, 10 (*Des Livres*).
9. See Villey, *Les Sources et l'Évolution*, I, 204.
10. See P. Jacquinet, *Francisci Baconi de re litteraria judicia*, Paris, 1863, pp. 98 ff.
11. *Aristotelis et Platonis moralia plerique admirant; sed Tacitus magis vivas morum observationes spirat.* Spedding ed. (1870), III, 538.
12. I accept Spedding's suggested attribution of this letter to the hand of Bacon, though it was sent in the name of Essex. It seems to me impossible that Essex should have been so familiar with the new trend of thought and studies in the nineties as the writer shows himself to be.
13. On the "sublimity" of Tacitus, see an interesting passage in La Mothe le Vayer, *Jugemens sur Historiens, Works* (1685), III, 208: "Son genre d'ecrire grave (etc.)."
14. To avoid repetition I have omitted several points concerning Bacon's rhetorical theory which are more or less developed in the essay on "Muret and Attic Prose" mentioned above. Most important of these perhaps is Bacon's constant dependence upon Aristotle's *Rhetoric*— often a peculiar sign of Anti-Ciceronian intention. There is need of a thorough and complete study of Bacon's rhetorical teachings.
15. *Adv. of Learning*, II (*Works*, Spedding ed., 1870, III, 418).

MORRIS W. CROLL

The Baroque Style in Prose

I. *Introduction*

In the latter years of the sixteenth century a change declared itself in the purposes and forms of the arts of Western Europe for which it is hard to find a satisfactory name. One would like to describe it, because of some interesting parallels with a later movement, as the first modern manifestation of the Romantic Spirit; and it did, in fact, arise out of a revolt against the classicism of the high Renaissance. But the terms "romantic" and "classical" are both perplexing and unphilosophical; and their use should not be extended. It would be much clearer and more exact to describe the change in question as a radical effort to adapt traditional modes and forms of expression to the uses of a self-conscious modernism; and the style that it produced was actually called in several of the arts—notably in architecture and prose-writing—the "modern" or "new" style. But the term that most conveniently describes it is "baroque." This term, which was at first used only in architecture, has lately been extended to cover the facts that present themselves at the same time in sculpture and in painting; and it may now properly be used to describe, or

From Kemp Malone and Martin B. Ruud, editors, *Studies in English Philology in Honor of Frederick Klaeber* (Minneapolis: University of Minnesota Press), pp. 427-456. Copyright 1929 by the University of Minnesota.

at least to name, the characteristic modes of expression in all the arts during a certain period—the period, that is, between the high Renaissance and the eighteenth century; a period that begins in the last quarter of the sixteenth century, reaches a culmination at about 1630, and thenceforward gradually modifies its character under new influences.

Expressiveness rather than formal beauty was the pretension of the new movement, as it is of every movement that calls itself modern. It disdained complacency, suavity, copiousness, emptiness, ease, and in avoiding these qualities sometimes obtained effects of contortion or obscurity, which it was not always willing to regard as faults. It preferred the forms that express the energy and labor of minds seeking the truth, not without dust and heat, to the forms that express a contented sense of the enjoyment and possession of it. In a single word, the motions of souls, not their states of rest, had become the themes of art.

The meaning of these antitheses may be easily illustrated in the history of Venetian painting, which passes, in a period not longer than one generation, from the self-contained and relatively symmetrical designs of Titian, through the swirls of Tintoretto, to the contorted and aspiring lines that make the paintings of El Greco so restless and exciting. Poetry moves in the same way at about the same time; and we could metaphorically apply the terms by which we distinguish El Greco from Titian to the contrast between the rhythms of Spenser and the Petrarchans, on one hand, and the rhythms of Donne, on the other, between the style of Ariosto and the style of Tasso. In the sculptures of Bernini (in his portrait busts as well as in his more famous and theatrical compositions) we may again observe how ideas of motion take the place of ideas of rest; and the operation of this principle is constantly to be observed also in the school of architecture associated with the same artist's name. In the façade of a Baroque church, says Geoffrey Scott, "a movement, which in the midst of a Bramantesque design would be destructive and repugnant, is turned to account and made the basis of a more dramatic, but not less satisfying treatment, the motive of which is not peace, but energy." [1]

And finally the change that takes place in the prose style of the same period—the change, that is, from Ciceronian to Anti-Ciceronian forms and ideas—is exactly parallel with those that were occurring in the other arts, and is perhaps more useful to the student of the baroque impulse than any of the others, because it was more self-conscious, more definitely theorized by its leaders, and more clearly described by its friends and foes. In some previous studies I have considered the triumph of the Anti-Ciceronian movement at considerable length; but I have been concerned chiefly with the theory of the new style; and my critics have complained, justly, that I have been too difficult, or even abstract. In the present study I hope to correct this defect. Its purpose is to describe the *form* of Anti-Ciceronian, or baroque, prose.

There are of course several elements of prose technique: diction, or the choice of words; the choice of figures; the principle of balance or rhythm; the form of the period, or sentence; and in a full description of baroque prose all of these elements would have to be considered. The last-mentioned of them—the form of the period—is, however, the most important and the determinant of the others; and this alone is to be the subject of discussion in the following pages.

The Anti-Ciceronian period was sometimes described in the seventeenth century as an "exploded" period; and this metaphor is very apt if it is taken as describing solely its outward appearance, the mere fact of its form. For example, here is a period from Sir Henry Wotton, a typical expression of the political craft of the age:

> Men must beware of running down steep hills with weighty bodies; they once in motion, *suo feruntur pondere;* steps are not then voluntary.[2]

The members of this period stand farther apart one from another than they would in a Ciceronian sentence; there are no syntactic connectives between them whatever; and semicolons or colons are necessary to its proper punctuation. In fact, it has the appearance of having been disrupted by an explosion within.

The metaphor would be false, however, if it should be taken as describing the manner in which this form has been arrived at. For it would mean that the writer first shaped a round and complete oratorical period in his mind and then partly undid his work. And this, of course, does not happen. Wotton gave this passage its form, not by demolishing a Ciceronian period, but by omitting several of the steps by which roundness and smoothness of composition might have been attained. He has deliberately avoided the processes of mental revision in order to express his idea when it is nearer the point of its origin in his mind.

We must stop for a moment on the word *deliberately*. The negligence of the Anti-Ciceronian masters, their disdain of revision, their dependence upon casual and emergent devices of construction, might sometimes be mistaken for mere indifference to art or contempt of form; and it is, in fact, true that Montaigne and Burton, even Pascal and Browne, are sometimes led by a dislike of formality into too licentious a freedom. Yet even their extravagances are purposive, and express a creed that is at the same time philosophical and artistic. Their purpose was to portray, not a thought, but a mind thinking, or, in Pascal's words, *la peinture de la pensée*. They knew that an idea separated from the act of experiencing it is not the idea that was experienced. The ardor of its conception in the mind is a necessary part of its truth; and unless it can be conveyed to another mind in something of the form of its occurrence, either it has changed into some other idea or it has ceased to be an idea, to have any existence whatever except a verbal one. It was the latter fate that happened to it, they believed, in the Ciceronian periods of sixteenth-century Latin rhetoricians. The successive processes of revision to which these periods had been submitted had removed them from reality by just so many steps. For themselves, they preferred to present the truth of experience in a less concocted form, and deliberately chose as the moment of expression that in which the idea first clearly objectifies itself in the mind, in which, therefore, each of its parts still preserves its own peculiar emphasis and an independent vigor of its own—in brief, the moment in which truth is still *imagined*.

The form of a prose period conceived in such a theory of style will differ in every feature from that of the conventional period of an oratorical, or Ciceronian, style; but its most conspicuous difference will appear in the way it connects its members or clauses one with another. In the period quoted above from Wotton the members are syntactically wholly free; there are no ligatures whatever between one and another. But there is another type of Anti-Ciceronian period, in which the ordinary marks of logical succession—conjunctions, pronouns, etc.—are usually present, but are of such a kind or are used in such a way as to bind the members together in a characteristically loose and casual manner. The difference between the two types thus described may seem somewhat unimportant; and it is true that they run into each other and cannot always be sharply distinguished. The most representative Anti-Ciceronians, like Montaigne and Browne, use them both and intermingle them. But at their extremes they are not only distinguishable; they serve to distinguish different types, or schools, of seventeenth-century style. They derive from different models, belong to different traditions, and sometimes define the philosophical affiliations of the authors who prefer them.

They will be considered here separately; the first we will call, by a well-known seventeenth-century name, the *période coupée*, or, in an English equivalent, the "curt period" (so also the *stile coupé*, or the "curt style"); the other by the name of the "loose period" (and the "loose style"); though several other appropriate titles suggest themselves in each case.[3]

II. *Stile Coupé*

(A)

One example of the *période coupée* has already been given. Here are others:

> Pour moy, qui ne demande qu'à devenir plus sage, non plus sçavant ou eloquent, ces ordonnances logiciennes et aristoteliques ne sont pas à propos; je veulx qu'on commence par le dernier poinct: i'entends assez que c'est que Mort et Volupté; qu'on ne s'amuse pas à les anatomizer. (Montaigne)

> 'Tis not worth the reading, I yield it, I desire thee not to lose time in perusing so vain a subject, I should be peradventure loth myself to read him or thee so writing, 'tis not *operae pretium*. (Burton)

> No armor can *defend* a fearful heart. It will kill itself, within. (Feltham)

> Oui; mais il faut parier; cela n'est pas volontaire, vous êtes embarqués. (Pascal)

> L'éloquence continue ennuie.
> Les princes et les rois jouent quelquefois; ils ne sont pas

toujours sur leurs trônes, ils s'y ennuient: la grandeur a besoin
d'être quittée pour être sentie. (Pascal)

The world that I regard is myself; it is the microcosm of
my own frame that I cast mine eye on: for the other, I use it
but like my globe, and turn it round sometimes for my recrea-
tion. (Browne)

Il y a des hommes qui attendent à être dévots et religieux
que tout le monde se déclare impie et libertin: ce sera alors le
parti du vulgaire, ils sauront s'en dégager. (La Bruyère) [4]

In all of these passages, as in the period quoted from Wotton,
there are no two main members that are syntactically connected.
But it is apparent also that the characteristic style that they have
in common contains several other features besides this.

In the first place, each member is as short as the most alert intelligence would have it. The period consists, as some of its admirers
were wont to say, of the nerves and muscles of speech alone; it is
as hard-bitten, as free of soft or superfluous flesh, as "one of Caesar's
soldiers." [5]

Second, there is a characteristic order, or mode of progression,
in a curt period that may be regarded either as a necessary consequence of its omission of connectives or as the causes and explanation
of this. We may describe it best by observing that the first member
is likely to be a self-contained and complete statement of the whole
idea of the period. It is so because writers in this style like to avoid
prearrangements and preparations; they begin, as Montaigne puts
it, at *le dernier poinct*, the point aimed at. The first member therefore exhausts the mere fact of the idea; logically there is nothing
more to say. But it does not exhaust its imaginative truth or the
energy of its conception. It is followed, therefore, by other members,
each with a new tone or emphasis, each expressing a new apprehension of the truth expressed in the first. We may describe the progress
of a curt period, therefore, as a series of imaginative moments occurring in a logical pause or suspension. Or—to be less obscure—we
may compare it with successive flashes of a jewel or prism as it
turned about on its axis and takes the light in different ways.

It is true, of course, that in a series of propositions there will
always be some logical process; the truth stated will undergo some

development or change. For example, in the sentence from Montaigne at the beginning of this section, the later members add something to the idea; and in the quotation from Pascal's *Pensées sur
l'Éloquence,* given below it, the thought suddenly enlarges in the
final member. Yet the method of advance is not logical; the form
does not express it. Each member, in its main intention, is a separate
act of imaginative realization.

In the third place, one of the characteristics of the curt style is
deliberate asymmetry of the members of a period; and it is this trait
that especially betrays the modernistic character of the style. The
chief mark of a conventional, or "classical," art, like that of the
sixteenth century, is an approximation to evenness in the size and
form of the balanced parts of a design; the mark of a modernistic
art, like that of the seventeenth, and the nineteenth and twentieth,
centuries, is the desire to achieve an effect of balance or rhythm
among parts that are obviously not alike—the love of "some strange-
ness in the proportions."

In a prose style asymmetry may be produced by varying the length
of the members within a period. For example, part of the effect of
a sentence from Bishop Hall is due to a variation in this respect
among members which nevertheless produce the effect of balance or
rhythmic design.

> What if they [crosses and adversities] be unpleasant? They
> are physic: it is enough, if they be wholesome.[6]

But the desired effect is more characteristically produced by conspicuous differences of form, either with or without differences of
length. For instance, a characteristic method of the seventeenth
century was to begin a succession of members with different kinds
of subject words. In the sentence quoted from Wotton the first two
members have personal subjects, the third the impersonal "steps";
in the quotation from Pascal the opposite change is made.

> Mais il faut parier; cela n'est pas volontaire, vous êtes
> embarqués.

In both of these periods, moreover, each of the three members has
a distinct and individual turn of phrase, meant to be different from

the others. Again, in the period of La Bruyère quoted at the beginning of this section, each new member involves a shift of the mind
to a new subject. (Observe also the asymmetry of the members in
point of length.)

Sometimes, again, asymmetry is produced by a change from literal
to metaphoric statement, or by the reverse, or by a change from one
metaphor to another, as in the last example quoted from Pascal,
where the metaphor of one embarked upon a ship abruptly takes
the place of that of a man engaged in a bet. Or there may be a
leap from the concrete to the abstract form; and this is an eminently
characteristic feature of the *stile coupé* because this style is always
tending toward the aphorism, or *pensée*, as its ideal form. The second passage quoted from Pascal illustrates this in a striking way.
It is evident that in the first three members—all concrete, about kings
and princes—the author's mind is turning toward a general truth,
which emerges complete and abstract in the last member: *la grandeur
a besoin d'être quittée pour être sentie.*

The curt style, then, is not characterized only by the trait from
which it takes its name, its omission of connectives. It has the four
marks that have been described: first, studied brevity of members;
second, the hovering, imaginative order; third, asymmetry; and
fourth, the omission of the ordinary syntactic ligatures. None of these
should, of course, be thought of separately from the others. Each
of them is related to the rest and more or less involves them; and
when they are all taken together they constitute a definite rhetoric,
which was employed during the period from 1575 to 1675 with as
clear a knowledge of its tradition and its proper models as the sixteenth-century Ciceronians had of the history of the rhetoric that
they preferred.

In brief, it is a Senecan style; and, although the imitation of
Seneca never quite shook off the imputation of literary heresy that
had been put upon it by the Augustan purism of the preceding age,
and certain amusing cautions and reservations were therefore felt
to be necessary, yet nearly all of the theorists of the new style succeeded in expressing their devotion to their real master in one way
or another. Moreover, they were well aware that the characteristic
traits of Seneca's style were not his alone, but had been elaborated
before him in the Stoic schools of the Hellenistic period; and all the
earlier practitioners of the *stile coupé*, Montaigne (in his first phase),

Lipsius, Hall, Charron, etc., write not only as literary Senecans, but rather more as philosophical Stoics.

Senecanism and Stoicism are, then, the primary implications of *stile coupé*. It must be observed, however, that a style once established in general use may cast away the associations in which it originated; and this is what happened in the history of the curt style. Montaigne, for instance, confessed that he had so thoroughly learned Seneca's way of writing that he could not wholly change it even when his ideas and tastes had changed and he had come to prefer other masters. And the same thing is to be observed in many writers of the latter part of the century: St. Évremond, Halifax, and La Bruyère, for instance. Though these writers are all definitely anti-Stoic and anti-Senecan, all of them show that they had learned the curt style too well ever to unlearn it or to avoid its characteristic forms; and there was no great exaggeration in Shaftesbury's complaint, at the very end of the century, that no other movement of style than Seneca's—what he calls the "Senecan amble"—had been heard in prose for a hundred years past.

(B)

The curt or serried style depends for its full effect upon the union of the several formal traits that have been described in the preceding section. We have assumed hitherto that these traits are as rigorous and unalterable as if they were prescribed by a rule; and in the examples cited there have been no significant departures from any of them. But of course slight variations are common even in passages that produce the effect of *stile coupé*; and some searching is necessary to discover examples as pure as those that have been cited. This is so evidently true that it would need no illustration except for the fact that certain kinds of period eminently characteristic of seventeenth-century prose arise from a partial violation of the "rules" laid down. Two of these may be briefly described.

(A) In a number of writers (Browne, Felltham, and South, for example) we often find a period of two members connected by *and*, *or*, or *nor*, which evidently has the character of *stile coupé* because the conjunction has no logical *plus* force whatever. It merely connects two efforts of imagination to realize the same idea; two as-it-were synchronous statements of it. The following from Browne will be recognized as characteristic of him:

> 'Tis true, there is an edge in all firm belief, and with an easy
> metaphor we may say, the sword of faith.

Again:

> Therefore I perceive a man may be twice a child, before the
> days of dotage; and stand in need of Æson's bath before three-
> score.[7]

Often, too, in a period consisting of a larger number of members
the last two are connected by an *and* or the like. But this case can
be illustrated in connection with the one that immediately follows.

(B) The rule that the successive members of a *période coupée*
are of different and often opposed forms, are asymmetrical instead
of symmetrical, is sometimes partly violated inasmuch as these members begin with the same word or form of words, for example, with
the same pronoun subject, symmetry, parallelism, and some regularity
of rhythm thus introducing themselves into a style that is designed
primarily and chiefly to express a dislike of these frivolities. It is to
be observed, however, that the members that begin with this suggestion of oratorical pattern usually break it in the words that follow.
Except for their beginnings they are as asymmetrical as we expect
them to be, and reveal that constant novelty and unexpectedness
that is so characteristic of the "baroque" in all the arts.

One illustration is to be found in the style of the "character" writings that enjoyed so great a popularity in the seventeenth century.
The frequent recurrence of the same subject word, usually *he* or
they, is the mannerism of this style, and is sometimes carried over
into other kinds of prose in the latter part of the century, as, for
instance, in writings of La Bruyère that are not included within the
limits of the "character" genre,[8] and in passages of Dryden. It is indeed so conspicuous a mannerism that it may serve to conceal what
is after all the more significant feature of the "character" style,
namely, the constant variation and contrast of form in members that
begin in this formulistic manner.

The style of the "character," however, is that of a highly specialized genre; and the form of the period with reiterated introductory
formula can be shown in its more typical character in other kinds of
prose, as, for example, in a passage from Browne describing the
Christian Stoicism of his age:

Let not the twelve but the two tables be thy law: let Pythagoras be thy remembrancer, not thy textuary and final instructer:
and learn the vanity of the world, rather from Solomon than
Phocylides.[9]

Browne touches lightly on these repetitions, and uses them not too
frequently. Balzac uses them characteristically and significantly. A
paragraph from his *Entretiens* may be quoted both in illustration
of this fact and for the interest of its subject matter:

Nous demeurasmes d'accord que l'Autheur qui veut imiter
Seneque commence par tout et finit par tout. Son Discours
n'est pas un corps entier: c'est un corps en pieces; ce sont des
membres couppez; et quoy que les parties soient proches les
unes des autres, elles ne laissent pas d'estre separées. Non
seulement il n'y a point de nerfs qui les joignent; il n'y a pas
mesme de cordes ou d'aiguillettes qui les attachent ensemble:
tant cet Autheur est ennemy de toutes sortes de liaisons, soit
de la Nature, soit de l'Art: tant il s'esloigne de ces bons exem-
ples que vous imitez si parfaitement.[10]

The passage illustrates exactly Balzac's position in the prose development of the seventeenth century. Montaigne is indeed—in
spite of his strictures upon him—his master. He aims, like Montaigne,
at the philosophic ease and naturalness of the *genus humile;* he
has his taste for aphorism, his taste for metaphor; he is full of
"points," and loves to make them show; in short, he is "baroque."
But by several means, and chiefly by the kinds of repetition illustrated in this passage (*c'est . . . ce sont; il n'y a point . . . il n'y a
pas mesme; tant . . . tant*), he succeeds in introducing that effect
of art, of form, of rhythm, for which Descartes and so many other
of his contemporaries admired him. He combines in short the "wit"
of the seventeenth century with at least the appearance of being
"a regular writer," which came, in the forties and fifties, to be regarded in France as highly desirable. In his political writings, and
especially in *Le Prince,* his iterated opening formula becomes too
evident a mannerism, and on page after page one reads periods of
the same form: two or three members beginning alike and a final
member much longer and more elaborate than the preceding that

may or may not begin in the same way. The effect is extremely rhetorical.

(c)

Finally, we have to observe that the typical *période coupée* need not be so short as the examples of it cited at the beginning of the present section. On the contrary, it may continue, without connectives and with all its highly accentuated peculiarities of form, to the length of five or six members. Seneca offered many models for this protracted aphoristic manner, as in the following passage from the *Naturales Quaestiones* (vii. 31):

> There are mysteries that are not unveiled the first day: Eleusis keepeth back something for those who come again to ask her. Nature telleth not all her secrets at once. We think we have been initiated: we are still waiting in her vestibule. Those secret treasures do not lie open promiscuously to every one: they are kept close and reserved in an inner shrine.

Similar in form is this six-member period from Browne's *Religio Medici*:

> To see ourselves again, we need not look for Plato's year: every man is not only himself; there have been many Diogeneses, and as many Timons, though but few of that name; men are lived over again; the world is now as it was in ages past; there was none then, but there hath been some one since, that parallels him, and is, as it were, his revived self.[11]

What has been said in a previous section of the characteristic mode of progression in *stile coupé* is strikingly illustrated in such passages as these. Logically they do not move. At the end they are saying exactly what they were at the beginning. Their advance is wholly in the direction of a more vivid imaginative realization; a metaphor revolves, as it were, displaying its different facets; a series of metaphors flash their lights; or a chain of "points" and paradoxes reveals the energy of a single apprehension in the writer's mind. In the latter part of the seventeenth century a number of critics satirize this peculiarity of the Senecan form. Father Bouhours, for instance, observed that with all its pretensions to brevity and significance this style makes less progress in five or six successive statements than a Ciceronian period will often make in one long and comprehensive construction. The criticism is, of course, sound if the only mode of progression is the logical one; but in fact there is a progress of imaginative apprehension, a revolving and upward motion of the mind as it rises in energy, and views the same point from new levels; and this spiral movement is characteristic of baroque prose.

III. The Loose Style

(A)

In the preceding pages we have been illustrating a kind of period in which the members are in most cases syntactically disjunct, and we have seen that in this style the members are characteristically short. It is necessary now to illustrate the other type of Anti-Ciceronian style spoken of at the beginning, in which the members are usually connected by syntactic ligatures, and in which, therefore, both the members and the period as a whole may be, and in fact usually are, as long as in the Ciceronian style, or even longer.

It is more difficult to find an appropriate name for this kind of style than for the other. The "trailing" or "linked" style would describe a relation between the members of the period that is frequent and indeed characteristic, but is perhaps too specific a name. "Libertine" indicates exactly both the form of the style and the philosophical associations that it often implies; but it is wiser to avoid these implications in a purely descriptive treatment. There is but one term that is exact and covers the ground: the term "loose period" or "loose style"; and it is this that we will usually employ. In applying this term, however, the reader must be on his guard against a use of it that slipped into many rhetorical treatises of the nineteenth century. In these works the "loose sentence" was defined as one that has its main clause near the beginning; and an antithetical term "periodic sentence"—an improper one—was devised to name the opposite arrangement. "Loose period" is used here without reference to this confusing distinction.

In order to show its meaning we must proceed by means of examples; and we will take first a sentence—if, indeed, we can call it a sentence—in which Bacon contrasts the "Magistral" method of writing works of learning with the method of "Probation" appropriate to "induced knowledge," "the later whereof [he says] seemeth to be *via deserta et interclusa*."

> For as knowledges are now delivered, there is a kind of contract of error between the deliverer and the receiver: for he that delivereth knowledge desireth to deliver it in such form as may be best believed, and not as may be best examined; and he that receiveth knowledge desireth rather present satisfaction than expectant inquiry; and so rather not to doubt than not to err: glory making the author not to lay open his weakness, and sloth making the disciple not to know his strength.[12]

The passage is fortunate because it states the philosophy in which Anti-Ciceronian prose has its origin and motive. But our present business is with its form; and in order to illustrate this we will place beside it another passage from another author.

> Elle [l'Imagination] ne peut rendre sages les fous; mais elle les rend heureux, à l'envi de la raison qui ne peut rendre ses amis que misérables, l'une les couvrant de gloire, l'autre de honte.[13]

There is a striking similarity in the way these two periods proceed. In each case an antithesis is stated in the opening members; then the member in which the second part of the antithesis is stated puts out a dependent member. The symmetrical development announced at the beginning is thus interrupted and cannot be resumed. The period must find a way out, a syntactic way of carrying on and completing the idea it carries. In both cases the situation is met in the same way, by a concluding member having the form of an absolute-participle construction, in which the antithetical idea of the whole is sharply, aphoristically resumed.

The two passages, in short, are written as if they were meant to illustrate in style what Bacon calls "the method of induced knowledge"; either they have no predetermined plan or they violate it at will; their progression adapts itself to the movements of a mind discovering truth as it goes, thinking while it writes. At the same time, and for the same reason, they illustrate the character of the style that we call "baroque." See, for instance, how symmetry is first made and then broken, as it is in so many baroque designs in painting and architecture; how there is constant swift adaptation of form to the emergencies that arise in an energetic and unpremeditated forward movement; and observe, further, that these signs of spontaneity and improvisation occur in passages loaded with as heavy a content as rhetoric ever has to carry. That is to say, they combine the effect of great mass with the effect of rapid motion; and there is no better formula than this to describe the ideal of the baroque design in all the arts.

But these generalizations are beyond our present purpose. We are to study the loose period first, as we did the curt period, by observing the character of its syntactic links. In the two sentences quoted there are, with a single exception, but two modes of connection employed. The first is by co-ordinating conjunctions, the conjunctions, that is, that allow the mind to move straight on from the point it has reached. They do not necessarily refer back to any particular point in the preceding member; nor do they commit the following member to a predetermined form. In other words, they are the loose conjunctions, and disjoin the members they join as widely as possible. *And, but,* and *for* are the ones employed in the two sentences; and these are of course the necessary and universal ones. Other favorites of the loose style are *whereas, nor* (= *and not*), and the correlatives *though . . . yet, as . . . so.* Second, each of the two periods contains a member with an absolute-participle construction. In the loose style many members have this form, and not only (as in the two periods quoted) at the ends of periods, but elsewhere. Sir Thomas Browne often has them early in a period, as some passages to be cited in another connection will show. This is a phenomenon easily explained. For the absolute construction is the one that commits itself least and lends itself best to the solution of difficulties that arise in the course of a spontaneous and unpremeditated progress. It may state either a cause, or a consequence, or a mere attendant circumstance; it may be concessive or justificatory; it may be a summary of the preceding or a supplement to it; it may express an idea related to the whole of the period in which it occurs, or one related only to the last preceding member.

The co-ordinating conjunctions and the absolute-participle construction indicate, then, the character of the loose period. Like the *stile coupé,* it is meant to portray the natural, or thinking, order; and it expresses even better than the curt period the Anti-Ciceronian prejudice against formality of procedure and the rhetoric of the schools. For the omission of connectives in the *stile coupé* implies, as we have seen, a very definite kind of rhetorical form, which was practiced in direct imitation of classical models, and usually retained the associations that it had won in the Stoic schools of antiquity. The associations of the loose style, on the other hand, are all with the more sceptical phases of seventeenth-century thought—with what was then usually called "Libertinism"; and it appears characteristically in writers who are professed opponents of determined and rigorous philosophic attitudes. It is the style of Bacon and of Montaigne (after he has found himself), of La Mothe le Vayer, and of Sir Thomas Browne. It appears always in the letters of Donne; it appears in Pascal's *Pensées;* and, in the latter part of the century, when Libertinism had positively won the favor of the world away from Stoicism, it enjoyed a self-conscious revival, under the influence of Montaigne, in the writings of St. Évremond, Halifax, and Temple. Indeed, it is evident that, although the Senecan *stile coupé* attracted more critical attention throughout the century, its greatest achievements in prose were rather in the loose or Libertine manner. But it must also be said that most of the sceptics of the century had undergone a strong Senecan influence; and the styles of Montaigne, Browne, Pascal, and Halifax, for instance, can only be described as displaying in varying ways a mingling of Stoic and Libertine traits.

(B)

Besides the two syntactic forms that have been mentioned—the co-ordinating conjunctions and the absolute construction—there are no others that lend themselves by their nature to the loose style, except the parenthesis, which we need not illustrate here. But it must not be supposed that it tends to exclude other modes of connection. On the contrary, it obtains its characteristic effects from the syntactic forms that are logically more strict and binding, such as the relative pronouns and the subordinating conjunctions, by using them in a way peculiar to itself. That is to say, it uses them as the necessary logical means of advancing the idea, but relaxes at will the tight construction which they seem to impose; so that they have exactly the same effect as the loose connections previously described and must be punctuated in the same way. In other words, the parts that they connect are no more closely knit together than it chooses they shall be; and the reader of the most characteristic seventeenth-century prose soon learns to give a greater independence and autonomy to subordinate members than he would dare to do in reading any other.

The method may be shown by a single long sentence from Sir Thomas Browne:

> I could never perceive any rational consequence from those many texts which prohibit the children of Israel to pollute themselves with the temples of the heathens; we being all Christians, and not divided by such detested impieties *as* might profane our prayers, or the place wherein we make them; *or that* a resolved conscience may not adore her Creator any where, *especially* in places devoted to his service; *where,* if their devotions offend him, mine may please him; if theirs profane it, mine may hallow it.[14]

The period begins with a statement complete in itself, which does not syntactically imply anything to follow it; an absolute participle carries on, in the second member. Thereafter the connectives are chiefly subordinating conjunctions. Observe particularly the use of *as, or that,* and *where:* how slight these ligatures are in view of the length and mass of the members they must carry. They are frail and small hinges for the weights that turn on them; and the period abounds and expands in nonchalant disregard of their tight, frail logic.

This example displays the principle; but of course a single passage call illustrate only a few grammatical forms. Some of those used with a characteristic looseness in English prose of the seventeenth century are: relative clauses beginning with *which,* or with *whereto, wherein,* etc.; participial constructions of the kind scornfully called "dangling" by the grammarians; words in a merely appositional relation with some noun or pronoun preceding, yet constituting a semi-independent member of a period; and of course such subordinating conjunctions as are illustrated above. It is unnecessary to illustrate these various cases.

(c)

The connections of a period cannot be considered separately from the order of the connected members; and, in fact, it is the desired order of development that determines the character of the connections rather than the reverse. In the oratorical period the arrangement of the members is "round" or "circular," in the sense that they are all so placed with reference to a central or climactic member that they point forward or back to it and give it its appropriate emphasis. This order is what is meant by the names *periodos, circuitus,* and "round composition," by which the oratorical period has been variously called; and it is the chief object of the many revisions to which its form is submitted.

The loose period does not try for this form, but rather seeks to avoid it. Its purpose is to express, as far as may be, the order in which an idea presents itself when it is first experienced. It begins, therefore, without premeditation, stating its idea in the first form that occurs; the second member is determined by the situation in which the mind finds itself after the first has been spoken; and so on throughout the period, each member being an emergency of the situation. The period—in theory, at least—is not made; it becomes. It completes itself and takes on form in the course of the motion of mind which it expresses. Montaigne, in short, exactly described the theory of the loose style when he said: "J'ecris volontiers sans project; le premier trait produit le second."

The figure of a circle, therefore, is not a possible description of the form of a loose period; it requires rather the metaphor of a chain, whose links join end to end. The "linked" or "trailing" period is, in fact, as we have observed, an appropriate name for it. But there is a special case for which this term might better be reserved, unless we should choose to invent a more specific one, such as "end-linking," or "terminal linking," to describe it. It is when a member depends, not upon the general idea, or the main word, of the preceding member, but upon its final word or phrase alone. And this is, in fact, a frequent, even a characteristic, kind of linking in certain authors, notably Sir Thomas Browne and his imitators. The sentence last quoted offers two or three illustrations of it: the connective words *as, especially,* and *where* all refer to the immediately preceding words or phrases; and in another period by the same author there is one very conspicuous and characteristic instance.

As there were many reformers, so likewise many reforma-
tions; every country proceeding in a particular way and method,
according as their national interest, together with their constitution and clime, inclined them: some angrily and with
extremity; others calmly and with mediocrity, not rending, but
easily dividing, the community, and leaving an honest possibility of a reconciliation;—*which,* though peaceable spirits do
desire, and may conceive that revolution of time and the mercies
of God may effect, yet that judgment that shall consider the
present antipathies between the two extremes,—their contra-
rieties in condition, affection, and opinion,—may with the same
hopes, expect a union in the poles of heaven.[15]

Here the word *which* introduces a new development of the idea,
running to as much as five lines of print; yet syntactically it refers
only to the last preceding word *reconciliation.* The whole long passage has been quoted, however, not for this reason alone, but because it illustrates so perfectly all that has been said of the order and
connection of the loose period. It begins, characteristically, with a
sharply formulated complete statement, implying nothing of what
is to follow. Its next move is achieved by means of an absolute-participle construction.[16] This buds off a couple of appositional members; one of these budding again two new members by means of
dangling participles. Then a *which* picks up the trail, and at once
the sentence becomes involved in the complex, and apparently tight,
organization of a *though . . . yet* construction. Nevertheless it still
moves freely, digressing as it will, extricates itself from the complex
form by a kind of anacoluthon (in the *yet* clause), broadening its
scope, and gathering new confluents, till it ends, like a river, in an
opening view.

The period, that is, moves straight onward everywhere from the
point it has reached; and its construction shows ideally what we
mean by the linked or trailing order. It is Browne's peculiar mastery
of this construction that gives his writing constantly the effect of
being, not the result of a meditation, but an actual meditation in
process. He writes like a philosophical scientist making notes of his
observation as it occurs. We see his pen move and stop as he thinks.
To write thus, and at the same time to create beauty of cadence in
the phrases and rhythm in the design—and so Browne constantly
does—is to achieve a triumph in what Montaigne called "the art

of being natural"; it is the eloquence, described by Pascal, that mocks
at formal eloquence.

(D)

The period just quoted serves to introduce a final point concerning
the form of the loose period. We have already observed that the
second half of this period, beginning with *which*, has a complex suspended syntax apparently like that of the typical oratorical sentence.
The Anti-Ciceronian writer usually avoids such forms, it is true;
most of his sentences are punctuated by colons and semicolons. But,
of course, he will often find himself involved in a suspended construction from which he cannot escape. It remains to show that even
in these cases he still proceeds in the Anti-Ciceronian manner, and
succeeds in following, in spite of the syntactic formalities to which
he commits himself, his own emergent and experimental order. Indeed, it is to be observed that the characteristic quality of the loose
style may appear more clearly in such difficult forms than in others.
For baroque art always displays itself best when it works in heavy
masses and resistant materials; and out of the struggle between a
fixed pattern and an energetic forward movement often arrives at
those strong and expressive disproportions in which it delights.
   We shall return to Browne in a moment in illustration of the
point, but we shall take up a simpler case first. In a well-known
sentence, Pascal, bringing out the force of imagination, draws a picture of a venerable magistrate seated in church, ready to listen to
a worthy sermon. *Le voilà prêt à l'ouïr avec un respect exemplaire.*

> Que le prédicateur vienne à paraître, que la nature lui ait
> donné une voix enrouée et un tour de visage bizarre, que son
> barbier l'ait mal rasé, si le hasard l'a encore barbouillé de
> surcoît, quelque grandes vérités qu'il annonce, je parie la perte
> de la gravité de notre sénateur.[17]

   Unquestionably a faulty sentence by all the school-rules! It begins
without foreseeing its end, and has to shift the reader's glance from
the preacher to the magistrate in the midst of its progress by whatever means it can. Observe the abruptness of the form of the member
quelque grandes vérités. Observe the sudden appearance of the first
person in the last member. Yet the critic who would condemn its

rhetorical form would have also to declare that there is no art in those vivid dramatic narratives that so often appear in the conversation of animated talkers; for this period moves in an order very common in such conversation.[18]

In this passage the free and Anti-Ciceronian character of the movement is chiefly due to its dramatic vividness and speed. It follows the order of life. Sometimes, however, we can see plainly that it is the mystical speculation of the seventeenth century that changes the regular form of the period and shapes it to its own ends. Sir Thomas Browne provides many interesting illustrations, as, for instance, in the period quoted in the preceding section, and in the following:

> I would gladly know how Moses, with an actual fire, calcined or burnt the golden calf into powder: for that mystical metal of gold, whose solary and celestial nature I admire, exposed unto the violence of fire, grows only hot, and liquefies, but consumeth not; so when the consumable and volatile pieces of our bodies shall be refined into a more impregnable and fixed temper, like gold, though they suffer from the action of flames, they shall never perish, but lie immortal in the arms of fire.[19]

With the first half of this long construction we are not now concerned. In its second half, however, beginning with *so when,* we see one of those complex movements that have led some critics to speak of Browne as—of all things!—a Ciceronian. It is in fact the opposite of that. A Ciceronian period closes in at the end; it reaches its height of expansion and emphasis at the middle or just beyond, and ends composedly. Browne's sentence, on the contrary, opens constantly outward; its motions become more animated and vigorous as it proceeds; and it ends, as his sentences are likely to do, in a vision of vast space or time, losing itself in an *altitudo,* a hint of infinity. As, in a previously quoted period, everything led up to the phrase, "a union in the poles of heaven," so in this everything leads up to the concluding phrase, "but lie immortal in the arms of fire." And as we study the form of the structure we can even observe where this ending revealed itself, or, at least, how it was prepared. The phrase "like gold" is the key to the form of the whole. After a slow expository member, this phrase, so strikingly wrenched from its logical position, breaks the established and expected rhythm, and is a signal of more agitated movement, of an ascending effort of imaginative realization that continues to the end. In a different medium, the period closely parallels the technique of an El Greco composition, where broken and tortuous lines in the body of the design prepare the eye for curves that leap upward beyond the limits of the canvas.

The forms that the loose period may assume are infinite, and it would be merely pedantic to attempt a classification of them. In one of the passages quoted we have seen the dramatic sense of reality triumphing over rhetorical formalism; in another, the form of a mystical exaltation. For the purpose of description—not classification —it will be convenient to observe still a third way in which a loose period may escape from the formal commitments of elaborate syntax. It is illustrated in a passage in Montaigne's essay "Des Livres," praising the simple and uncritical kind of history that he likes so much. In the course of the period he mentions *le bon Froissard* as an example, and proceeds so far (six lines of print) in a description of his method that he cannot get back to his general idea by means of his original syntactic form, or at least cannot do so without very artificial devices. He completes the sentence where it is; but completes his idea in a pair of curt (*coupés*) sentences separated by a colon from the preceding: "c'est la matiere de l'histoire nue et informe; chascun en peult faire son proufit autant qu'il a d'entendement." [20] This is a method often used by Anti-Ciceronians to extricate themselves from the coils of a situation in which they have become involved by following the "natural" order. A better example of it is to be seen in a passage from Pascal's essay on "Imagination," from which another passage has already been cited.

> Le plus grand philosophe du monde, sur une planche plus
> large qu'il ne faut, s'il y a au-dessous un précipice, quoique sa
> raison le convainque de sa sûreté, son imagination prévaudra.
> Plusieurs n'en sauraient soutenir la pensée sans pâlir et suer.[21]

Nothing could better illustrate the "order of nature"; writing, that is, in the exact order in which the matter presents itself. It begins by naming the subject, *le plus grand philosophe,* without foreseeing the syntax by which it is to continue. Then it throws in the elements of the situation, using any syntax that suggests itself at the moment, proceeding with perfect dramatic sequence, but wholly without logical sequence, until at last the sentence has lost touch with its stated subject. Accordingly, this subject is merely left hanging, and a new one, *son imagination,* takes its place. It is a violent, or rather a nonchalant, anacoluthon. The sentence has then, after a fashion, completed itself. But there is an uneasy feeling in the mind. After all, *le plus grand philosophe* has done nothing; both form and idea are incomplete. Pascal adds another member (for, whatever the punctuation, the *plusieurs* sentence is a member of the period), which completely meets the situation, though a grammatical purist may well object that the antecedent of *plusieurs* was in the singular number.

Pascal is usually spoken of as a "classical" writer; but the term means nothing as applied to him except that he is a writer of tried artistic soundness. He is, in fact, as modernistic, as bold a breaker of the rules and forms of rhetoric, as his master Montaigne, though he is also a much more careful artist. *La vraie éloquence,* he said, *se moque de l'éloquence.*

(E)

Two kinds of style have been analyzed in the preceding pages: the concise, serried, abrupt *stile coupé,* and the informal, meditative, and "natural" loose style. It is necessary to repeat—once more—that in the best writers these two styles do not appear separately in passages of any length, and that in most of them they intermingle in relations far too complex for description. They represent two sides of the seventeenth-century mind: its sententiousness, its penetrating wit, its Stoic intensity, on the one hand, and its dislike of formalism, its roving and self-exploring curiosity, in brief, its sceptical tendency, on the other. And these two habits of mind are generally not separated one from the other; nor are they even always exactly distinguishable. Indeed, as they begin to separate or to be opposed to each other in the second half of the century we are aware of the approach of a new age and a new spirit. The seventeenth century, as we are here considering it, is equally and at once Stoic and Libertine; and the prose that is most characteristic of it expresses these two sides of its mind in easy and natural relations one with the other.

IV. *The Punctuation of the Seventeenth-Century Period*

The "long sentence" of the Anti-Ciceronian age has received a remarkable amount of attention ever since it began to be corrected
and go out of use; and there have been two conflicting views concerning it. The older doctrine—not yet quite extinct—was that the
long sentences of Montaigne, Bacon, Browne, and Taylor were sentences of the same kind as those of Cicero and his sixteenth-century
imitators; only they were badly and crudely made, monstrosities due
to some wave of ignorance that submerged the syntactic area of the
seventeenth-century mind. Their true character, it was thought, would
be shown by substituting commas for their semicolons and colons;
for then we should see that they are quaint failures in the attempt
to achieve sentence unity.

The other view is the opposite of this, namely, that we should
put periods in the place of many of its semicolons and colons. We
should then see that what look like long sentences are really brief
and aphoristic ones. The contemporary punctuation of our authors
is again to be corrected, but now in a different sense. This is the
view urged by Faguet in writing of Montaigne, and by Sir Edmund
Gosse concerning the prose of Browne and Taylor.

The later view is useful in correcting some of the errors of the
earlier one. But, in fact, one of them is just as false as the other;
and both of them illustrate the difficulties experienced by minds
trained solely in the logical and grammatical aspects of language in
interpreting the forms of style that prevailed before the eighteenth
century. In order to understand the punctuation of the seventeenth
century we have to consider the relation between the grammatical
term *sentence* and the rhetorical term *period*.

The things named by these terms are identical. *Period* names the
rhetorical, or oral, aspect of the same thing that is called in grammar
a *sentence* and in theory the same act of composition that produces
a perfectly logical grammatical unit would produce at the same time
a perfectly rhythmical pattern of sound. But, in fact, no utterance
ever fulfils both of these functions perfectly, and either one or the
other of them is always foremost in a writer's mind. One or the
other is foremost also in every theory of literary education; and the
historian may sometimes distinguish literary periods by the relative
emphasis they put upon grammatical and rhetorical considerations.
In general we may say, though there may be exceptions, that be-

fore the eighteenth century rhetoric occupied much more attention than grammar in the minds of teachers and their pupils. It was so, for instance, in the Middle Ages, as is clear from their manuals of study and the curricula of their schools. It was still true in the sixteenth century; and the most striking characteristic of the literary prose of that century, both in Latin and in the vernacular tongues, was its devotion to the conventional and formal patterns of school-rhetoric.

The laws of grammatical form, it is true, were not at all disturbed or strained at this time by the predominance of rhetorical motives. There was no difficulty whatever in saying what these rhetoricians had to say in perfect accordance with logical syntax because they had, in fact, so little to say that only the most elementary syntax was necessary for its purposes. Furthermore, the rhetorical forms they liked were so symmetrical, so obvious, that they almost imposed a regular syntax by their own form.

But a new situation arose when the leaders of seventeenth-century rationalism—Lipsius, Montaigne, Bacon—became the teachers of style. The ambition of these writers was to conduct an experimental investigation of the moral realities of their time, and to achieve a style appropriate to the expression of their discoveries and of the mental effort by which they were conducted. The content of style became, as it were, suddenly greater and more difficult; and the stylistic formalities of the preceding age were unable to bear the burden. An immense rhetorical complexity and license took the place of the simplicity and purism of the sixteenth century; and, since the age had not yet learned to think much about grammatical propriety, the rules of syntax were made to bear the expenses of the new freedom. In the examples of seventeenth-century prose that have been discussed in the preceding pages some of the results are apparent. The syntactic connections of a sentence become loose and casual; great strains are imposed upon tenuous, frail links; parentheses are abused; digression become licentious; anacoluthon is frequent and passes unnoticed; even the limits of sentences are not clearly marked, and it is sometimes difficult to say where one begins and another ends.

Evidently the process of disintegration could not go on forever. A stylistic reform was inevitable, and it must take the direction of a new formalism or "correctness." The direction that it actually took was determined by the Cartesian philosophy, or at least by the same time spirit in which the Cartesian philosophy had its origin. The intellect, that is to say, became the arbiter of form, the dictator of artistic practice as of philosophical inquiry. The sources of error, in the view of the Cartesians, are imagination and dependence upon sense impressions. Its correctives are found in what they call "reason" (which here means "intellect"), and an exact distinction of categories.

To this mode of thought we are to trace almost all the features of modern literary education and criticism, or at least of what we should have called modern a generation ago: the study of the precise meaning of words; the reference to dictionaries as literary authorities; the study of the sentence as a logical unit alone; the careful circumscription of its limits and the gradual reduction of its length; the disappearance of semicolons and colons; the attempt to reduce grammar to an exact science; the idea that forms of speech are always either correct or incorrect; the complete subjection of the laws of motion and expression in style to the laws of logic and standardization—in short, the triumph, during two centuries, of grammatical over rhetorical ideas.

This is not the place to consider what we have gained or lost by this literary philosophy, or whether the precision we have aimed at has compensated us for the powers of expression and the flexibility of motion that we have lost; we have only to say that we must not apply the ideas we have learned from it to the explanation of seventeenth-century style. In brief, we must not measure the customs of the age of semicolons and colons by the customs of the age of commas and periods. The only possible punctuation of seventeenth-century prose is that which it used itself. We might sometimes reveal its grammar more clearly by repunctuating it with commas or periods, but we should certainly destroy its rhetoric.

NOTES

1. *The Architecture of Humanism* (London, 1914), p. 225.
2. "Table Talk," in *Life and Letters,* ed. Logan Pearsall Smith (Oxford, 1907), II, 500.
3. For example, the *stile coupé* was sometimes called *stile serré* ("serried style"), and Francis Thompson has used this term in describing a kind of period common in Browne. For synonyms of "loose style" see section III of this paper.
4. References are as follows: Montaigne, "Des Livres," *Essais* II.x. ed. J.–V. Le Clerc (Paris, 1865), II, 122; Robert Burton, "To the Reader," *The Anatomy of Melancholy,* ed. A. R. Shilleto (London, 1893), p. 24; Owen Felltham, "Of Fear and Cowardice," *Resolves*

1. 71 (London, 1677), p. 110; Pascal, *Pensées*, ed. Léon Brunschvicg (Paris, 1904), II, 146 (section VII in 1670 Port-Royal ed.); *Pensées*, II, 269 (section XXI in Port-Royal ed.); Sir Thomas Browne, *Religio Medici*, Part II, section 11, in *Works*, ed. Simon Wilkin (London, 1846), II, 110; La Bruyère, "Des Esprits Forts," (*Œuvres*, ed. G. Servois (Paris, 1865), II, 239. These editions have been used for subsequent quotations from the authors' works.

5. The phrase comes from a midseventeenth-century work on prose style, and is there applied to *il dir moderno*: Daniello Bartoli, "Dello Stile," *Dell' Uomo di Lettere*, in *Opere* (Venice, 1716), III, 101.

6. Joseph Hall, *Heaven upon Earth*, XIII, in *Works* (Oxford, 1837), VI, 20. Note how exactly this reproduces a movement characteristic of Seneca: *Quid tua, uter* [Caesar or Pompey] *vincat? Potest melior vincere: non potest pejor esse qui vicerit.*

7. *Religio Medici*, 1.10 and 1.42, in *Works*, II, 14, 61.

8. For instance, in the famous passage "De l'Homme," 128, in *Œuvres*, II, 61, describing the beast-like life of the peasants of France.

9. *Christian Morals*, section XXI, *Works*, IV, 107. The period occurs in the midst of a paragraph in which each main member of each period begins with a verb in the imperative mood.

10. No. XVIII, "De Montaigne et de ses Escrits," in *Œuvres*, ed. L. Moreau (Paris, 1854), II, 402–403.

11. 1.6, in *Works*, II, 11. Feltham uses this manner with too much self-consciousness. See, for instance, a passage on the terse style (*Resolves*, 1.20) beginning "They that speak to *children*, assume a pretty lisping."

12. *Of the Advancement of Learning*, Bk. II, in *Works*, ed. Spedding, Ellis, and Heath (London, 1868), III, 403–404; ed. Wright, XVII.3.

13. Pascal, *Pensées*, II, 3 (section XXV in 1670 Port-Royal ed.). There should, rhetorically speaking, be semicolons after *raison* and *misérables*.

14. *Religio Medici*, 1.3, in *Works*, II, 4. Italics are mine.

15. *Religio Medici*, 1.4, in *Works*, II, 5.

16. Observe that the period from Browne quoted on p. 223 begins with movements of the same kind.

17. *Pensées*, II, 4–5 (section XXV in Port-Royal ed.).

18. It may be said that Pascal's *Pensées* should not be cited in illustration of prose form because they were written without revision and without thought of publication. But a good deal of characteristic prose of the time was so written, and the effect at which Bacon, Burton, Browne, and many others aimed was of prose written in that way.

19. *Religio Medici*, 1.50, in *Works*, II, 73.

20. *Essais*, II.x, ed. Le Clerc, II, 127.

21. *Pensées*, II, 5.

RICHARD FOSTER JONES

🖎

Science and English Prose Style, 1650–75

Literary style, like human personality, is a compound exceedingly difficult of analysis, for when its more obvious constituents are made clear, there still remains an illusive element, consciousness of which leaves the analyst with the unpleasant sensation of not having reached the bottom of the matter. As the most complex phenomenon in literature, style is the resultant of all the forces, known and unknown, underlying literary development, and the method and extent of the contribution made by each of these forces are a matter of probable inference rather than of positive demonstration. For that reason, any attempt, however ambitious, to account for the style of a literary epoch must be content with pointing out those more obvious influences that are combined and reflected in speech and writing, and with ignoring other factors which may escape detection. Under the protection of this confession I shall attempt to make manifest what seems to me the most important influence instrumental in changing the luxuriant prose of the Commonwealth into that of a diametrically opposite nature in the Restoration.

To one who is familiar with the writers of the Puritan regime, it would be rash to maintain that the style of this period is homogeneous, but probably every one can agree that the dominating

From *PMLA*, XLV (1930), pp. 977-1009. Reprinted by permission of the Modern Language Association of America.

manner of writing was that revealed in the great figures of Jeremy
Taylor, Sir Thomas Browne, and John Milton, and lesser writers
like Nathanael Culverwell. As is well known, this style is characterized by various rhetorical devices such as figures, tropes, metaphors,
and similes, or similitudes, to use a term of the period. The sentences are long, often obscurely involved, and rhythmical, developing
in writers like Browne a stately cadence, which, in the studied
effect of inversions, is the prose counterpart of Milton's blank
verse. The penchant for interlarding a work with Latin and Greek
quotations is also apparent. The diction reveals a host of exotic
words, many Latinisms, and frequently poetic phraseology of rare
beauty. Against this style there arose a movement which later became an organized revolt, and which in the course of its condemnation of the old developed for itself a new standard of expression. The
spirit animating the revolt had its origin in the scientific movement
that determined the intellectual complexion of the seventeenth century. It is the purpose of this article to show that the attacks on the
old, as well as the formulation of a new, style find consistent expression in those associated with the new science, that the first organized scientific body in England, the Royal Society, definitely adopted
a linguistic platform which exerted a powerful influence on the
style of its members even in writings other than scientific, and that
the foremost exponents of the new style were members of this society and in most cases deeply interested in science.

Since Bacon stimulated and, to a certain extent, determined the
scientific development of this period, one should search first in his
writings for evidence of a stylistic standard. Without insisting upon
a direct connection between his views and the movement that arose
near the middle of the century, it would be foolish to underestimate
the possible influence of one whose words were reverenced by later
scientific reformers of style. At the very outset, however, we may
say that his own style was quite different from that advocated by
the scientists. "Ornamented with the riches of rhetoric," as it is, it
everywhere reveals tropes, figures, and similitudes. For this reason
his followers, though worshiping his ideas, never refer to his manner
of expression as a model. Sprat, it is true, cites him as an example,
but for poets and wits, not for writers of serious prose.[1] Rawley,
Bacon's chaplain and biographer, represents his patron as opposed
to fine writing, and tells us that in composing his works, the philosopher "would often ask if the meaning were expressed plainly

enough, as being one that accounted words to be but subservient or ministerial to matter, and not the principal." [2] Yet even Rawley must have been aware that plainness is not a characteristic quality of Bacon's prose, for he immediately adds the rather meaningless statement, "And if his style were polite, it was because he would do no otherwise." Regardless of his own style, however, Bacon attacks all manner of rhetorical devices because they lead to the first distemper of learning, "when men study words and not matter," and he holds that similitudes and ornaments of speech render the detection and correction of errors very difficult.[3] Moreover, near the beginning of the *Magna Instauratio* he reveals a stylistic attitude which, though not apparent in his own practice, is essentially the same as that later maintained by his followers. "It being part of my design," he says, "to set everything forth, as far as may be, plainly and perspicuously (for nakedness of the mind is still, as nakedness of the body once was, the companion of innocence and simplicity), let me first explain the order and plan of the work." [4] While his antagonism to rhetoric and his advocacy of a naked style may not have inspired the stylistic revolt, they had their origin in the same scientific spirit that animated the later reformers of prose, who express views similar to his.

The immediate influence of Bacon's words must have been slight, for the exuberant prose of the Elizabethans continued on to the more highly developed and poetic style of the Commonwealth. In 1646, however, is heard again the plea for a plain style; this time in John Wilkins' *Ecclesiastes, or a Discourse Concerning the Gift of Preaching*. Wilkins, who later became the prime mover in the establishment of the Royal Society, had been for a number of years deeply interested in science, and was at this moment an enthusiastic member of a small group of men who met weekly in London to put into practice the Baconian experimental philosophy. It was the spirit of the latter that prompted him to say, as regards the "phrase" that should be used in preaching,

> It must be plain and naturall, not being darkned with the affectation of Scholasticall harshnesse, or Rhetoricall flourishes. Obscurity in the discourse is an argument of ignorance in the minde. The greatest learning is to be seen in the greatest plainnesse . . . When the notion it self is good, the best way to set it off, is in the most obvious plain expression . . . And it

will not become the Majesty of a Divine Embassage, to be garnished out with flaunting affected eloquence. How unsuitable it is to the expectation of a hungry soul, who comes unto this ordinance with a desire of spiritual comfort and instruction, and there to hear onely a starched speech full of puerile worded Rhetorick? 'Tis a sign of low thoughts and designs, when a mans chief study is about the polishing of his phrase and words. . . . Such a one speaks onely from his mouth, and not from his heart.

The same opinion is continued in another passage, concerning which we must remember that the epithet "solid" was so consistently applied to the new philosophy as opposed to the old that the expression "solid business" is equivalent to scientific matters. "It must be full, without empty and needlesse Tautologies, which are to be avoided in every solid business, much more in sacred. Our expressions should be so close, that they may not be obscure, and so plain that they may not seem vain and tedious." [5] A glance at Wilkins' own writings discovers a practice consistent with his theory, and William Lloyd, in a funeral sermon on him, truly says,

He spoke solid truth, with as little shew of Art as was possible. He exprest all things in their true and Natural colours; with that aptness and plainness of Speech, that grave Natural way of Elocution, that shewed he had no design upon his hearers. His plainness was best for the instruction of the simple . . . He applied him self rather to their understanding than Affections . . . In his Writings he was Judicious and plain, like one that valued not the Circumstances so much as the substance.

Two years later the same contempt for the superficial fineries of verbal dress appears in William Petty, one of the outstanding members of the little group which, about the middle of the century, met weekly in Petty's lodgings at Oxford for the purpose of carrying on experiments, a group that later merged with a similar body in London to form the Royal Society. Petty was especially interested in the practical aspect of science, devoting much of his time to inventions of various sorts. In communicating some matters of scientific nature to Samuel Hartlib, he says,

> I shall desire you to shew them unto no more than needs
> you must, since they can please only those few that are real
> Friends to the Design of Realities, not those who are tickled
> only with Rhetorical Prefaces, Transitions and Epilogues, and
> charmed with fine Allusions and Metaphors.[6]

The expression "Friends to the Design of Realities" is interesting in
this case, for it means nothing more than subscribers to the new
philosophy, and thus the quotation shows that Petty makes style a
distinguishing mark between the experimental philosophers and those
who held to the old tradition. This remarkable sensitiveness to matters of style on the part of the scientists, which is revealed in their
thinking it necessary to confess, and vindicate, their lack of rhetorical
ornament, appears again in a work by Francis Glisson, a famous
physician of the time, and a prominent member of the London group
of Baconians which was formed in 1645. He concludes his Preface
in the following manner:

> Finally expect no flashes of Rhetorick and Courtly-Language;
> > Nobis licet esse tam dicertis,
> > Musas qui colimus severiores.

> And indeed the conditions of the matter forbids all such paint-
> ing; in such a manner,

> > Ornari res ipsa negat, contenti doceri.[7]

The next opposition to rhetorical ornament is discovered in
Hobbes's *Leviathan*, 1651. Though now chiefly remembered for his
psychological and political philosophy, Hobbes was, according to his
own statement, most interested in natural science.[8] His philosophical
interests were developed in France along with Descartes, Gassendi,
and Mersenne, but in his earlier years he had been a companion
of Bacon, and from the latter he may have caught his scientific
enthusiasm. In his characteristically blunt fashion, Hobbes tells us
that there is nothing he distrusts more than elocution, and that he
has rejected the ornament of classical quotations because there is no
longer any virtue in ancient authority.[9] He permits a counselor to
use only significant, proper, and brief language, and forbids them

"*obscure, confused,* and *ambiguous Expressions, also all metaphoricall Speeches, tending to the stirring up of Passion,*" which are useful only to deceive.[10] In speaking of that antithetical pair dear to the seventeenth-century critic—judgment and fancy—he lays down the law, as the Royal Society did later, that—

> In Demonstration, in Councell, and all rigourous search of Truth, Judgement does all; except sometimes the understanding have need to be opened by some apt.similitude; and then there is so much use of Fancy. But for Metaphors, they are in this case utterly excluded. For seeing they openly professe deceipt; to admit them into Councell, or Reasoning, were manifest folly.

And again, "in a Sermon, or in publique, or before persons unknown, or whom we ought to reverence, there is no Gingling of words that will not be accounted folly." [11] Among the four abuses of speech, he lists the metaphorical use of words, "that is, in other sense than that they are ordained for; and thereby deceive others." [12] He insists that "Metaphors and Tropes of speach" are no true grounds for reasoning, and one of the causes for absurd conclusions he ascribes "to the use of Metaphors, Tropes, and other Rhetoricall figures, in stead of words proper." [13] He concludes by saying:

> The Light of humane minds is Perspicuous Words, but by exact definitions first snuffed, and purged from ambiguity; *Reason* is the *Pace;* Encrease of *Science,* the *way;* and the benefit of man-kind, the *end.* And on the contrary, Metaphors, and sensless and ambiguous words, are like *ignes fatui;* and reasoning upon them, is wandering amongst innumerable absurdities.[14]

The same scientifically induced materialism so characteristic of Hobbes appears in John Webster's *Academiarum Examen,* 1653. Webster was a chaplain in the Parliamentarian army, and an early and ardent follower of Bacon. In the work mentioned above he vehemently attacks the old philosophy, and fervently recommends a reformation of the universities in the way of the substitution of experimental science for the Aristotelianized divinity and natural philosophy dominant there. But he is not content with attacking these only; he would place distinctly below the new science such subjects as rhetoric, oratory, and the like, which, he says,

> serve for adornation, and are as it were the outward dress and attire of more solid sciences; first they might tollerably pass, if there were not too much affectation towards them, and too much pretious time spent about them, while more excellent and necessary learning [i.e., experimental philosophy] lies neglected and passed by: For we do in these ornamental arts, as people usually do in the world, who take more care often time about the goods of fortune, than about the good of the body it self or the goods of the mind, regarding the shell more than the kernel, and the shadow more than the Substance.[15]

A similar dislike for an ornate style and a corresponding approval of plainness in expression may be found in Robert Boyle, a scientist so illustrious it would be impertinent to comment on his connection with the new movement. In his *Some Considerations Touching the Style of the Holy Scriptures,* written about 1653 though not published until 1661, he expresses the view that when verbal ornaments are spared, they are not missed, and that some writings expressed in the plainest language outshine other subjects decked with the gaudiest expressions. Nor does he ascribe any importance to an objection that the Bible is destitute of eloquence and unadorned with the flowers of rhetoric, an objection which, he says, "a philosopher [i.e., a scientist] would not look upon as the most considerable." [16]

We also find the Baconian spirit stirring in out-of-the-way places. In 1660 Joshua Childrey published his *Britannia Baconia,* which is in reality a natural history of England, Scotland, and Wales, and the title of which indicates its connection with the new science. The author worshiped Bacon, and regarded his words with almost superstitious awe, trying in all humility of spirit to put into practice the precepts of the great master. He, too, was imbued with a scorn of fine language, and with a feeling that science demanded a style more suited to its purposes. "I have endeavour'd," he says in the Preface, "to tell my tale as plainly as might be, both that I might be understood of all, and that I might not disfigure the face of Truth by daubing it over with the paint of Language." He then proceeds to emphasize the fact that clear and accurate expression is just as

essential to the communication of truth as careful observation is to
its discovery, and he implies his conviction that the prevailing style
was inimical to its proper presentation. A like attitude continues to
be manifested in this branch of science, if for the moment we may
step beyond the chronological limits of this article. Robert Plot, in
the *Natural History of Oxfordshire,* 1676, says,

> And these [natural and artificial phenomena] I intend to
> deliver as succinctly as may be, in a plain, easie unartificial
> Stile, studiously avoiding all ornaments of Language, it being
> my purpose to treat of Things, and therefore would have the
> Reader expect nothing less than Words.[17]

Ten years later, in the *Natural History of Staffordshire,* he is still
making the same stylistic pronouncement, though the need for it
had long ceased to exist. Certainly hostility to the style of the Commonwealth must have been deeply imbedded in scientists to cause
this one to say in 1686, at a time when rhetoric was no longer in
favor with any one of importance,

> I shall make all *Relations* (as formerly) in a plain familiar
> Stile, without the Ornaments of *Rhetorick,* least the matter be
> obscured by too much *illustration;* and with all the imaginable
> brevity that perspicuity will bear.[18]

The foregoing quotations are sufficiently numerous and emphatic
to indicate that repugnance to the prevailing style and a feeling for
the need of a simpler, more direct manner of expression were a
characteristic feature of the new science from its very inception.
To us it seems quite natural that science should be antipathetic to
rhetoric, but in this period some unique factors tended to accentuate
this antipathy. Above everything else, the experimental philosophy
was characterized by a savage attack upon "Aristotelity," to use
Hobbes's term, in the course of which the chief charge was brought
against the wordiness of Peripateticism.[19] Again and again the new
scientists stigmatized the traditional philosophy for being concerned
only with words having no concrete significance and representing
only figments of the imagination. Thus verbal superfluity became
suspect. Allied to this attitude was the feeling for concrete reality,
which naturally eschewed the verbal luxuriance of figurative lan-

guage and the more subtle effects of imaginative expression. All this led to an insistence upon a direct, unadorned style which should be concrete in idea, and clear and economical in expression, in short, to use a phrase of the period, "the marriage of words and things." [20]

When the experimental philosophers were joined in a royally protected society, 1662, it was inevitable that what had been the more or less sporadic and scattered, but still representative, attacks on prose expression should be combined and strengthened into an organized revolt. So we are not surprised to find that in the statutes of the Royal Society, published in 1728, Chapter V, Article IV, reads:

> In all Reports of Experiments to be brought into the Society, the Matter of Fact shall be barely stated, without any Prefaces, Apologies, or Rhetorical Flourishes, and entered so into the Register-Book, by order of the Society.

But the full importance of this requirement is not revealed until we read Thomas Sprat's *History of the Royal Society*, 1667, in an oft-quoted passage of which the author makes clear the Society's intense opposition to rhetorical prose, and outlines the ideal of a new style which had already crystallized and upon which it was vehemently insisting. Sprat's words throw so much light on the movement which we are tracing that I shall give them in full, even at the risk of bringing before the reader's eye that with which he is already familiar.

> Thus they have directed, judg'd, conjectur'd upon, and improved *Experiments*. But lastly, in these, and all other businesses, that have come under their care; there is one thing more, about which the *Society* has been most sollicitous; and that is, the manner of their *Discourse*: which, unless they had been very watchful to keep in due temper, the whole spirit and vigour of their *Design*, had been soon eaten out, by the luxury and redundance of *speech*. The ill effects of this superfluity of talking, have already overwhelm'd most other *Arts* and *Professions*; insomuch, that when I consider the means of *happy living*, and the causes of their corruption, I can hardly forbear recanting what I said before; and concluding, that *eloquence* ought to be banish'd out of *civil Societies*, as a thing fatal to

Peace and good Manners. To this opinion I should wholly incline; if I did not find, that it is a Weapon, which may be as easily procur'd by *bad* men, as *good*: and that, if these should onely cast it away, and those retain it; the *naked Innocence* of vertue, would be upon all occasions expos'd to the *armed Malice* of the wicked. This is the chief reason, that should now keep up the Ornaments of speaking, in any request: since they are so much degenerated from their original usefulness. They were at first, no doubt, an admirable Instrument in the hands of *Wise Men*: when they were onely employ'd to describe *Goodness, Honesty, Obedience;* in larger, fairer, and more moving Images: to represent *Truth,* cloth'd with Bodies; and to bring *Knowledg* back again to our very senses, from whence it was at first deriv'd to our understandings. But now they are generally chang'd to worse uses: They make the *Fancy* disgust the best things, if they come sound, and unadorn'd: they are in open defiance against *Reason;* professing, not to hold much correspondence with that; but with its Slaves, *the Passions:* they give the mind a motion too changeable, and bewitching, to consist with *right practice.* Who can behold, without indignation, how many mists and uncertainties, these specious *Tropes* and *Figures* have brought on our Knowledg? How many rewards, which are due to more profitable, and difficult *Arts,* have been still snatch'd away by the easie vanity of *fine speaking?* For now I am warm'd with this just *Anger,* I cannot with-hold my self, from betraying the shallowness of all these seeming Mysteries; upon which, *we Writers,* and *Speakers,* look so bigg. And, in few words, I dare say; that of all the Studies of men, nothing may be sooner obtain'd, than this vicious abundance of *Phrase,* this trick of *Metaphors,* this volubility of *Tongue,* which makes so great a noise in the World. But I spend words in vain; for the evil is now so inveterate, that it is hard to know whom to *blame,* or where to begin to *reform.* We all value one another so much, upon this beautiful deceipt; and labour so long after it, in the years of our education: that we cannot but ever after think kinder of it, than it deserves. And indeed, in most other parts of Learning, I look on it to be a thing almost utterly desperate in its cure: and I think, it may be plac'd amongst those *general mischiefs;* such, as the *dissention* of Christian Princes, the *want of practice* in

Religion, and the like; which have been so long spoken against, that men are become insensible about them; every one shifting off the fault from himself to others; and so they are only made bare common places of complaint. It will suffice my present purpose, to point out, what has been done by the *Royal Society,* towards the correcting of its excesses in *Natural* Philosophy; to which it is, of all others, a most profest enemy.[21]

This earnest indictment of the earlier mode of expression does not represent the sentiments of Sprat only. The *History* was written at the instigation and under the auspices of the Royal Society, was closely followed by the members during its composition, and when finished was heartily approved by the same body, so that we may look upon Sprat's attitude as typical of that of his colleagues.[22] Furthermore, in the next paragraph Sprat describes in terse and effective manner the style required by the Society of all papers presented to it.

They have therefore been most rigorous in putting in execution, the only Remedy, that can be found for this *extravagance:* and that has been, a constant Resolution, to reject all the amplifications, disgressions, and swellings of style: to return back to the primitive purity, and shortness, when men deliver'd so many *things,* almost in an equal number of *words.* They have exacted from all their members, a close, naked, natural way of speaking; positive expressions; clear senses; a native easiness: bringing all things as near the Mathematical plainness, as they can: and preferring the language of Artizans, Countrymen, and Merchants, before that, of Wits, or Scholars.[23]

The great importance of this discussion of style relative to other matters canvassed in Sprat's *History* is made clear by comments upon the book itself, in which the manner of expression is the characteristic most remarked. In an ode which was prefixed to the *History,* and which will later be treated more in full, Cowley notices, and with great praise, only the style of the work. In the next year Glanvill thinks it necessary to praise its stylistic qualities in a passage which expresses the desired ideal as elucidated by Sprat and renders a fairly accurate criticism of the latter's prose. The book, he says, is writ in a way of so *judicious* a *gravity* and so *prudent* and *modest* an *expression,* with so much *clearness* of *sense,* and such a *natural fluency* of *genuine eloquence:* So that I know it will both *profit* and entertain you. And I say further, that you may remember to do your self this right, That the *Style* of that Book hath all the *properties* that can recommend any thing to an *ingenious relish:* For 'tis *manly,* and yet *plain; natural* and yet not *careless:* The *Epithets* are *genuine,* the *Words proper* and *familiar,* the *Periods smooth* and of *middle* proportion: It is not *broken* with *ends* of *Latin,* nor *impertinent Quotations;* nor made *harsh* by *hard* words, or *needless terms* of *Art;* Not rendred *intricate* by long *Parentheses,* nor *gaudy* by *flanting* [sic] *Metaphors;* not *tedious* by *wide fetches* and *circumferences* of *Speech,* nor *dark* by too much *curtness* of *Expression:* 'Tis not *loose* and *unjointed, rugged* and *uneven;* but as *polite* and as *fast* as *Marble;* and briefly avoids all the *notorious defects,* and wants none of the *proper* ornaments of Language.[24]

It is remarkable how sensitive the scientists were to the problem of expression. We may say without exaggeration that their program called for stylistic reform as loudly as for reformation in philosophy. Moreover, this attitude was in the public mind indissolubly associated with the Society.[25]

Such, then, was the stand firmly taken by the first scientific society in England as regards expression in prose composition. Naturally its stylistic ideal was reflected in the scientific writings of its members.[26] The question next arises, did it actually influence the style of nonscientific writings of the day? Fortunately we have two examples, one of which is remarkable, of men whose style was radically changed under the pressure exerted by the Society. In 1661 Joseph Glanvill, later the most ardent defender of the Royal Society, published his *Vanity of Dogmatizing,* the contents of which time prevents me from describing, except to say that within its narrow compass it gathered all the new threads of philosophical thought that traversed the mid-seventeenth century. It is written in a highly rhetorical, exuberant, one might even say flamboyant, style, animated by an enthusiasm great enough to justify the charge of its being rhapsodical. The modern note sounded by Glanvill, however, must have brought him into sympathetic contact with some fellows of the

Royal Society, and thus have whetted his desire to become a member of that body. At any rate, when, near the end of 1664, he published a second edition entitled *Scepsis Scientifica*,[27] he prefixed an "Address to the Royal Society," in which he eulogized the new philosophy in general and that company in particular. This composition has all the earmarks of being a bid for an invitation to join the philosophers, and such an inference is borne out by the fact that on December 7, 1664, Lord Brereton presented the book to the Royal Society, and, after the "Address" had been read, proposed the author as a candidate for membership.[28] What especially interests us in the dedication is the following passage found near the conclusion:

> I found so faint an inclination [toward publishing the work again] that I could have been well content to suffer it to have slipt into the state of *eternal silence* and *oblivion*. For I must confess that *way* of *writing* to be less agreeable to my *present relish* and *Genius;* which is more gratified with *manly sense,* flowing in a *natural* and *unaffected Eloquence,* than in the *musick* and curiosity of *fine Metaphors* and *dancing periods.* To which measure of my present humour, I had indeavour'd to reduce the style of these Papers; but that I was loth to give my self that trouble in an Affair, to which I was grown too *cold* to be much concern'd in. And this *inactivity* of temper perswaded me, I might reasonably expect a pardon from the *ingenious,* for faults committed in an immaturity of *Age* and *Judgment,* that would excuse them.[29]

Here we have a man desiring admission to the Royal Society, who with humility of spirit apologizes for his past sins, and with obvious alacrity swears allegiance to a stylistic creed that might otherwise have barred his entrance. I would not wish, however, to insinuate that his conversion was not sincere, for later events prove otherwise. But though he had evidently come under the influence of the scientists, and had experienced a true change of heart in stylistic matters, his open apology was evidently intended to serve a purpose. When we remember that less than four years separated the two editions, the reference to the immaturity of youth provokes a smile. It is significant that a man seeking admission into the Society considered it necessary to place himself in the proper position as to style.[30]

A number of changes are introduced into the *Scepsis,* but, as the author states, very few as regards style, and they are concerned only with the substitution of simpler and more usual words for coined words or unusual Latinisms.[31] This change, however, reveals that he was moving in the direction of the new manner of expression demanded by the scientists. It is a stroke of good fortune for our purposes that in 1676 Glanvill published a third abbreviated version of the *Vanity of Dogmatizing*, as the first of seven essays combined to form a volume with the title, *Essays on Several Important Subjects in Philosophy and Religion*.[32] A comparison of this essay with the first version affords nothing short of a revelation. Under the influence of the Royal Society the author's changed stylistic standards had established complete control over his writing, and had caused him to revise with a ruthless hand work written under the inspiration of the great prose writers of the Commonwealth. Furthermore, though in the second edition he had contented himself with an apology, leaving the style little changed, he would not permit the treatise to go forth again until it had become "quite changed in the way of writing." It is hardly necessary to do more than display parallel passages to show what science was doing to prose.

That all bodies both *Animal*, *Vegetable*, and *Inanimate*, are form'd out of such particles of matter, which by reason of their figures, will not cohære or lie together, but in such an order as is necessary to such a specific formation, and that therein they naturally of themselves concurre, and reside, is a pretty conceit, and there are *experiments* that credit it. If after a decoction of *hearbs* in a Winter-night, we expose the liquor to the frigid air; we may observe in the morning under a crust of Ice, the perfect appearance both in *figure*, and *colour*, of the *Plants* that were taken from it. But if we break the *aqueous Crystal*, those pretty *images* dis-appear and are present[ly] dissolved.

And there is an experiment . . . That after a decoction of Herbs in a frosty Night, the shape of the Plants will appear under the Ice in the Morning: which Images are supposed to be made by the congregated *Effluvia* of the Plants themselves, which loosly wandring up and down in the Water, at last settle in their natural place and order, and so make up an appear-

Now these *airy Vegetables* are presumed to have been made, by the reliques of these *plantal emissions* whose avolation was prevented by the *condensed inclosure.* And therefore playing up and down for a while within their liquid prison, they at last settle together in their natural order, and the *Atomes* of each part finding out their proper place, at length rest in their methodical Situation, till by breaking the *Ice* they are disturbed, and those counterfeit *compositions* are scatter'd into their first *Indivisibles. Vanity,* p. 46.

ance of the Herbs from whence they were emitted. *Essays,* p. 11.

Gone is the Brownesque "swelling" sentence at the beginning of the first passage, and the touch of beauty that adorned the account of the experiment has vanished; while the "vicious abundance of phrase" and "volubility of tongue" that characterize the remainder of the quotation have given way to the "plain and familiar words" and the "close, naked, natural way of speaking" of the latter version.

But this is so largely prosecuted by that wonder of men, the Great *Des-Cartes,* and is a Truth that shines so clear in the Eyes of all considering men; that to goe about industriously to prove it, were to light a candle to seek the Sun. *Vanity,* p. 28.

Upon which position all the Philosophy of *Des-Cartes* stands: And it is so clear, and so acknowledg'd a Truth, among all considering Men, that I need not stay to prove it. *Essays,* p. 5.

For body cannot act on any thing but by motion; motion cannot be received but by quantative dimension; the soul is a stranger to such gross substantiality, and hath nothing of quantity, but what it is cloathed with by our deceived

For *Body* cannot act on anything, but by *Motion; Motion* cannot be receiv'd but by *Matter,* the *Soul* is altogether *immaterial;* and therefore, how shall we apprehend it to be subject to *such Impressions. Essays,* p. 6.

phancies; and therefore how can
we conceive under a passive subjection to material impressions.
Vanity, p. 29.

If we will take the literal evidence
of our Eyes; the *Æthereal Coal*
moves no more than this *Inferior
clod doth. Vanity*, p. 78.

To *Sense* the *Sun stands still* also;
and no Eye can perceive its *Actual*
motion. *Essays*, p. 20.

And thus, while every age is but
another shew of the former; 'tis
no wonder, that Science hath not
out-grown the dwarfishness of its
pristine stature, and that the *Intellectual world* is such a *Microcosm.
Vanity*, p. 138.

And thus while every Age is but
an *other shrew* of the *former,* 'tis
no wonder that humane science is
no more advanced above it's *ancient* Stature. *Essays*, p. 25.

In these passages there is an obvious change from "specious tropes"
and "vicious abundance of phrase" to a "primitive purity and shortness," in which "positive expressions" and "native easiness" are manifest. The reduction of these "wide fetches and circumferences of
speech" to a direct and "natural way of speaking" brings out in vivid
relief not only the way in which the scientific spirit was destroying
the sheer joy in language, but also how the definite linguistic stand
taken by the Royal Society was producing results.[33]

Nor is the composition of our
Bodies the only wonder; we are as
much non-plust by the most contemptible *Worm,* and *Plant,* we
tread on. How is a drop of Dew
organiz'd into an Insect, or a lump
of Clay into animal Perfections?
How are the Glories of the Field
spun, and by what Pencil are they
limn'd in their unaffected bravery? By whose direction is the nu-
triment so regularly distributed
unto the respective parts, and how
are they kept to their specifick uni-

formities? If we attempt Mechanical solutions, we shall never give an account, why the Woodcock doth not sometimes borrow colours of the Mag-pye, why the Lilly doth not exchange with the Daysie, or why it is not sometime painted with a blush of the Rose? Can *unguided matter* keep it self to such exact conformities, as not in the least spot to vary from the *species?* That divers Limners at a distance without either copy, or designe, should draw the same *Picture* to an undistinguishable exactness, both in form, colour, and features; this is more conceivable, then that *matter,* which is so diversified both in quantity, quality, motion, site, and infinite other circumstances, should frame it self so absolutely according to the Idea of it and its kind. And though the fury of that *Appelles,* who threw his Pencil in a desperate rage upon the Picture he had essayed to draw, once casually effected those lively representations, which his Art could not describe; yet 'tis not likely, that one of a thousand such præcipitancies should be crowned with so an unexpected an issue. For though *blind matter* might reach some elegancies in individual effects; yet specifick conformities can be no *unadvised* productions, but in greatest likelyhood, are regulated by the immediate efficiency of some *knowing* agent. *Vanity,* pp. 44 ff.

Blind Matter may produce an elegant effect for once, by a great Chance; as the Painter accidentally gave the Grace to his Picture, by throwing his Pencil in rage, and disorder upon it; But then *constant* Uniformities, and Determinations to a *kind,* can be *no Results* of *unguided Motions.*" *Essays,* p. 11.

Here, indeed, is merciless pruning. The "amplification of style" found in the extended illustrations, touched with beauty, of the composition of bodies, has been unhesitatingly cut away, for Glanvill's changed standard reveals in it only a "trick of flaunting metaphor," "specious tropes and figures," and he now feels that the discussion has been rendered "tedious by wide fetches and circumferences of speech." Certainly condensation could go no further than is manifested in the later version. How completely has vanished the feeling for beauty in language, as well as a spirit of enthusiasm and imaginative activity!

The process that had been inaugurated in the *Scepsis Scientifica* of reducing exotic and unusual words, or "hard words," to more natural terms, as well as a constant striving for a simpler, more direct expression, is carried still further in this last version, as is made clear by the foregoing quotations and may be emphasized by further passages. "Which to us is utterly occult, and without the ken of our Intellects" becomes "to which we are altogether stranger"; "those abstrusities, that lie more deep, and are of a more mysterious alloy" = "the Difficulties that lie more deep"; "those principiate foundations of knowledge" = "the Instruments of knowledge"; "Plato credits this position with his suffrage; affirming" = "Plato affirms"; "is a difficulty which confidence may triumph over sooner, then conquer" = "is hardly to be conceived"; "is but as the Birth of the labouring Mountains, Wind and Emptiness" = "stands yet unresolved"; "preponderate much greater magnitudes" = "outweigh much heavier bodies." [34] And there are many verbal changes, always making for greater simplicity or brevity, which may be represented by the following: "our employed mindes" = "we"; "material εἰδωλα = "material Images"; "bodily distempers" = "diseases"; "doth much confer to" = "makes"; "education-prepossessions" = "first opinions"; "præterlapsed ages" = "past ages"; "world's Grand-ævity" = "greatest antiquity"; "midnight compositions" = "dreams."

Although it is true that Glanvill is reducing a book to the dimensions of an essay, and thus omits many ideas *in toto,* the comparisons placed before us reveal not a change in or omission of ideas, but an alteration in treatment and expression only.[35] In sentence structure the Brownesque inversions, as well as Browne's habit of overloading the first part of a sentence at the expense of the latter, are ironed out and straightened into a natural order in which verb follows subject, and object verb. Exclamatory sentences and rhetorical questions are subdued to direct assertions, the length of sentences is perceptibly decreased, and oratorical cadence has almost disappeared. The verbal reform, begun in the *Scepsis*, is continued in the substitution of simpler, more current words for the unusual Latinisms and exotic terms characteristic of Browne, while emotional and extravagant expressions are greatly tempered. There is general condensation in expression, an economy of words which deflates the verbosities and superfluous terms of the earlier style. Figurative language and poetic imagery, whether extended or brief, are abolished, curtailed, or restrained. Illustrations, in the description of which Glanvill had shown a feeling for beauty, are purged of all qualities except the essential one of expository clearness. All the glories of enthusiastic expression and all joy in beauty have faded into the common light of day. We find in a comparison of the two versions not only a change in style but also a vivid picture of the spirit of one age yielding to that of another.[36]

We have in the essays of Abraham Cowley what I take to be another example of the direct influence which the sentiments and regulations of the Royal Society were exerting upon writers. That there was a decided change in style between his early and later prose has been recognized by more than one scholar. Mr. A. A. Tilley in the *Cambridge History of English Literature* asserts that Cowley furnished a complete transition from the old to the new style in prose, his early work revealing stiff, cumbrous, and involved sentences, nearer to Jeremy Taylor than to Dryden, and unlike the conversational ease of the later essays composed during the last four or five years of his life. Mr. Tilley calls especial attention to the fine example of rhetorical prose in the latter part of *A Vision Concerning Oliver Cromwell,* published in 1661 though composed in 1659, contrasting with that the style of the *Essays,* which is neither stiff nor slovenly, and in which the use of metaphors is restrained, and the sentences are well turned.[37] Dr. A. B. Gough, in his edition of Cowley's prose works, also thinks that the style of the *Essays* reveals a decided advance in clarity and ease over the earlier prose.[38] Cowley's first biographer, in the year after the former's death, pointed out "that in the Prose of them [the *Essays*], there is little Curiosity of Ornament, but they are written in a lower and humbler style than the rest, and as an unfeigned Image of his Soul should be drawn without Flattery." Several passages in the essays themselves bear witness to the author's acquired depreciation of eloquence, in one of which he speaks slightingly of "Figures and Tropes of Speech" as only adorning discourse,[39] and in another he refers scornfully to the "tinckling" of oratory.[40] But the best expression of his changed attitudes appears in "The Garden," composed in 1666 and addressed to John Evelyn, where, after an opening paragraph, which misses much of being as rhetorical as the *Vision,* the author says, "You may wonder, Sir (for this seems a little too extravagant and Pindarical for *Prose*) what I mean by all this Preface." [41]

This change has generally been attributed to French influences, especially Montaigne, but we must remember that when the *Vision* and earlier prose works were written, Cowley had for some years been exposed to French influence without results. What possible factor comes into play between 1659, when the *Vision* was composed, and the composition of the *Essays?* In February 1660, Cowley was proposed for membership in, and in the following March was elected to, the "invisible college" that was soon to become the Royal Society.[42] In 1661 he published a *Proposition for the Advancement of Experimental Philosophy,* which was an elaborate plan for a "Philosophical College," and to which the structure of the Royal Society owed much. Upon his retirement into the country he severed formal relations with the Society, since he could no longer attend the meetings, and was not reckoned a member after the passing of the second charter of April 22, 1663. But his contact with the members was by no means broken nor his interest in science lost. In fact, Sprat says, "This labour about Natural Science was the perpetual and uninterrupted task of that obscure part of his Life." On December 7, 1664, at the same meeting at which Glanvill's *Scepsis* was presented to the Society, a committee was appointed to improve the English tongue, composed of more than a score of men, among then Dryden, Evelyn, Sprat, and Waller.[43] Naturally, Cowley, not being a member, does not appear in the list, but we learn from excellent authority that he met with them. On August 12, 1689, Evelyn wrote to Pepys,

> And in deede such [improving the English tongue] was once design'd since the Restauration of Charles the Second (1665), and in order to it three or fowre Meetings were begun at Grey's Inn, by Mr. Cowley, Dr. Sprat, Mr. Waller, the D. of Buckingham, Matt. Clifford, Mr. Dryden, & some other promoters of it. But by the death of the incomparable Mr. Cow-

ley, distance & inconvenience of the place, the Contagion & other circumstances intervening, it crumbled away and came to nothing.

The important place here granted Cowley in the scheme is borne out by what Sprat says in his *Life* of the poet: "we [Clifford and Sprat] had persuaded him . . . to publish a Discourse concerning Style." At the very time Sprat was writing the *History of the Royal Society* with its pronounced opinions on style, he was conferring with Cowley about improving the language and persuading him to write a discourse on style. Certainly Cowley must have been brought into direct and stimulating contact with the stylistic convictions of the new philosophers. This is made all the clearer by his "Ode to the Royal Society," prefixed to Sprat's history, in which he ardently praises Bacon, the new philosophy, and the Society. One stanza, however, is devoted to praise of Sprat's work,

> And ne're did Fortune better yet
> Th' Historian to the Story fit:
> As you [Royal Society] from all old Errors free
> And purge the Body of Philosophy;
> So from all Modern Folies He
> Has vindicated Eloquence and Wit.
> His candid Stile like a clear Stream does slide
> And his bright Fancy all the way
> Does like the Sun-shine in it play;
> It does like *Thames,* the best of Rivers, glide
> Where the God does not rudely overturn,
> But gently pour the Crystal Urn,
> And with judicious hand does the whole Current guide.
> T'has all the Beauties Nature can impart,
> And all the comely Dress without the paint of Art.

From this stanza we see that the only aspect of Sprat's volume which the poet notices is its style, that he attributed to his future biographer credit for purifying prose as the scientists had purified natural philosophy, and that he evidently approved Sprat's indictment of the traditional prose style and subscribed to the new standard that the scientists had formulated. Thus Cowley must have been keenly and sympathetically aware of the efforts made by the experimental philosophers to discredit the old methods of expression, and he must have come under the same influence that metamorphosed Glanvill. To seek for the cause of his stylistic evolution in any other quarter seems to me farfetched, if not futile.

With the example of Glanvill and Cowley before us, may we not infer that the same pressure toward stylistic reform must have been brought to bear upon all members of the Society,[44] and through them even upon the world outside? Furthermore, when we consider the notable array of men of affairs, noblemen, clergymen, and writers who were members of the Society, we must believe that the influence of the latter was indeed far-reaching. The many-sided Isaac Barrow, divine, mathematician, and classical scholar, by virtue of being professor of geometry at Gresham College, Lucasian professor of mathematics at Cambridge, 1663, and a very early member of the Royal Society, could hardly have escaped being influenced by the stylistic attitude of the Society. John Tillotson, another great exponent of the new style, "whose sermons at Lincoln's inn and St. Lawrence Jewry attracted large congregations," and became a stylistic pattern for the whole nation, was not elected a member of the Society until 1672.[45] Yet in another way he had come under its influence. As a son-in-law of John Wilkins, he was associated with the latter in the composition of *An Essay towards a Real Character and a Philosophical Language,* 1668 [46] This remarkable project had long been in Wilkins' mind, and in 1662 he was prodded to develop it by the Royal Society, the members of which were deeply interested in the matter.[47] The study of language naturally involves consideration of style, and we are not surprised to find the stylistic attitude of science reflected in various parts of the *Essay.*[48] In this way Tillotson must have had impressed upon him the stylistic values of the new philosophy.[49]

Finally, Dryden, who asserted that whatever talent he had for English prose was due to his having often read the works of Tillotson,[50] was in a position to be even more directly influenced by the persistent efforts of the scientists to purify prose expression. He joined the Royal Society the same year in which it received the patronage of Charles II, and the poem addressed to Dr. Charleton bears eloquent testimony to his admiration of and interest in the new science. He, too, was a member of the committee appointed to improve the tongue, at the meetings of which, we may infer, he discussed stylistic matters with Cowley, Clifford, and Sprat. That he was no indifferent listener to the scientific discussions of the Society is revealed in his answer to the charge of being magisterial, preferred against him by Sir Robert Howard: "I must crave leave to say, that my whole discourse was sceptical, according to the way of reasoning which was used by Socrates, Plato, and all the Academics of old . . . and which is imitated by the modest inquisitions of the Royal Society." [51] If he was so influenced in the method of presenting his ideas, would he not likewise be influenced in the manner of his expression, a matter considered no less important by the scientists?

Before concluding this article it may be advisable to distinguish between the revolution in style which we have outlined and another stylistic movement of the century.[52] The Anti-Ciceronian movement was the rhetorical counterpart of the revolt against that body of orthodox ideas, gathered largely from antiquity, in which the Renaissance was complacently resting. The rationalistic spirit of inquiry, especially in moral and political matters, which demanded a turning away from what appeared to be only the forms of knowledge to direct observation and the realities of life, also found it necessary to revolt against the Ciceronian style that was closely associated with orthodox philosophies. In the same way, the scientific movement, in the main engineered by Bacon, represented the abandonment of empty theories of nature for observation and experiment. It also announced a stylistic program, but one distinctly different from the Anti-Ciceronian. In short, the desire to discover knowledge which would more fully satisfy the demand for reality was responsible for both revolutions, but the stylistic movements that accompanied them pursued different and divergent courses. The Anti-Ciceronian style found its theories in Aristotle and its models in such Latin writers as Lucan, Juvenal, Persius, Tacitus, Pliny, and especially Seneca; science renounced Aristotle and all his works, and sought for no models in the ancients. Instead of a conscious literary style, such as the other movement was developing, the new philosophy found in the very nature of its material a manner of expression characterized by the lack of literary qualities. The former style, which was far from denying itself the assistance of rhetoric, made use of aphorism, antithesis, paradox, and especially metaphors; the latter, which eschewed all rhetorical flourishes, laid not the slightest claim to these qualities, and against metaphors, as this article has revealed, carried on constant and uncompromising warfare. Again, neologizing was a distinct characteristic of the Anti-Ciceronians, and freakish Latinisms and strange words were admitted into their works; the scientists, on the other hand, abhorred all such importations, preferring "the language of Artizans, Countrymen, and Merchants" to the "hard" words of scholars. Bacon, Hall, Johnson, and Wotton have been considered the Anti-Ciceronian leaders in England, but there is nothing that relates the last three to the stylistic propaganda of science. Bacon, it is true, attacked the study of style for its own sake, which, he claimed, was fostered by study of the classics, and his own style reveals Anti-Ciceronian characteristics, but in at least one passage in his works [53] he condemns this style—in fact, he considers it one of the distempers of learning—and elsewhere, as revealed near the beginning of this article, he states with approval the characteristics which were later embodied in the stylistic ideal of the scientists, and which do not belong to the other movement. Other examples of Anti-Ciceronianism in England are Donne, Burton, and Browne, with the first of whom the scientists were in no way concerned, while against the style of the latter two they were in open revolt. In fact, the inclusion of these men among the Anti-Ciceronians coerces the belief that one object of the scientific attack was not Ciceronianism but Anti-Ciceronianism. Finally, the absence of any reference on the part of the scientific reformers either to the movement in general, or to single representatives of the movement, strongly argues their indifference to, if not ignorance of, the movement as such.

There are, to be sure, certain resemblances between the two stylistic attitudes. In both "reality" is emphasized, but with the scientists the term generally means a material reality, while the Anti-Ciceronians used it to refer much more widely to rationalistic explanations of human experience. Though in both "things" are preferred to "words," the experimental philosophers had concrete objects in mind, while the others were thinking of intellectual or moral conceptions. Indeed, as has been said, both attitudes had their origin in that element in the Renaissance which turned from reliance on the authority of the ancients and their unsatisfying philosophy to a rationalistic examination of actual experience, but they developed in quite different directions. Neither is it significant that both object to musical phrases and pronounced rhythm in prose, though the Baconians were consistent in their practice, as cannot be said of the Anti-Ciceronians. Likewise, the former constantly emphasize clearness, which together with plainness was the cardinal tenet in their creed, but the latter, though sometimes including the word in their terminology, frequently did not exemplify it in their practice. To the scientist brevity meant the excision of all rhetorical devices; to the others it meant studied brevity such as aphorisms, point, and the like. Again, appropriateness, propriety, is a term so general and common that its use by both parties is hardly indicative of any relationships, and, in fact, it signified one thing in science and another in moral matters, which constituted the most important element in the revolt against Cicero. One must be cautious in arguing a relationship from the mere occurrence of similar terms, for terms have a way of detaching themselves from their use and of becoming common property, a fact which may be illustrated by examples given earlier in this article. Alexander Ross objects strenuously to the "Tullian pigments" in Browne's style, an expression that seems immediately to identify him with the Anti-Ciceronians, but Ross was the most orthodox of the orthodox, vociferously opposed to everything new in science and philosophy, and so by no stretch of the imagination can he be included in that group. Browne, on the other hand, was not a Ciceronian, as the charge would imply, but an Anti-Ciceronian. Another example is revealed in the passage quoted from Samuel Parker, in which the expression "scheme of words" is used, and which thus would seem to place him among the enemies of Cicero, since the latter especially objected to the *schemata verborum* in Ciceronian style. But Parker employs the term with reference to metaphors, which are one of the *figurae sententiae*, and these latter are characteristic of the Anti-Ciceronians.

By far the clearest and most consistent explanation of the attacks of science upon rhetorical prose is discovered in the nature of the scientific movement. Above everything else the new science insisted upon the necessity of abandoning the empty notions of traditional philosophy, which seemed far removed from material objects, and of observing carefully and recording accurately all physical phenomena. In the concrete nature of the experimental philosophy is to be found the secret of the craving for a clear, accurate, plain style and the belief that such a style was essential to the attainment of scientific goals.[54] This obsession with the actual nature and appearance of things caused them to resent the interposing of any possible obstruction between observation and description, and gave rise to a stylistic taste which decreed that a rhetorical style, with its figurative language and musical cadence, was the product of folly, vanity, and immaturity, and was not appropriate to serious discourse. Furthermore, the interest in science, together with the wider growth of rationalism, tended to create a distrust of the imagination, a distrust which in some cases was deepened by the growing feeling that fancy was associated with the passions, and, therefore, was a dangerous faculty of the mind. This latter attitude appears infrequently in the scientific revolt, but plays a great part in the attack on pulpit eloquence. Finally, scientific materialism exerted a distinct influence on ideas regarding the nature of language. A suggestion of this appears in Bacon, but it finds clear and definite expression in Hobbes, who claims that words are only the marks of things.[55] Thus the connotative value of words and their power to invest the creations of the imagination with life and being are summarily cast into the discard. Hobbes's idea is implied in the words of many of the scientists, and in Samuel Parker is again clearly stated.[56] Its most remarkable manifestation, however, is in John Wilkins' *Essay towards a Real Character and a Philosophical Language*, 1668, in which words are literally reduced to marks, and which frankly confesses to making no provision at all for such creatures of the imagination as fairies, fauns, and the like on the ground that they have no existence in nature. With this conception of language in the background, is it strange that science came to grips with imaginative prose?

There were, of course, other factors co-operating with science in the simplification of English prose. Rationalism and the steady growth of the classical spirit made against all extravagancies. In explaining the attacks on intricacies of style, Mr. Spingarn mentions the substitution of general for technical terms, the preference for sceptical as opposed to dogmatic modes of thought and speech, the horror of pedantry, the trend toward precision of word and idea, and the attempt to make literature approximate conversation. In most of these matters the presence of the two factors just mentioned may be noted, but it should be remarked that science also was very much concerned with all but the last. Two characteristics of the scientific revolt, however, distinguish it from other stylistic influences, and justify the opinion that science exerted by far the most powerful force upon prose. First, the thoroughgoing nature of the stylistic reform advocated by the experimental philosophers, which, rejecting any compromise whatsoever with rhetoric, insisted upon an undefiled plainness and caused the issue at stake to be outlined sharply and distinctly. Perhaps of greater importance is the fact that reformation of style was a very significant part of a definite program adopted by a closely organized society of prominent men who were aggressively active in promulgating their views. The extent to which Glanvill's style changed under their discipline is a fair gauge of the influence that must have been exerted upon all members of the society, and, through them, upon the outside world.

NOTES

1. *History of the Royal Society*, pp. 416–17. Earlier in the volume he had found in Bacon's prose traits quite different from those demanded by the Royal Society. See p. 36. See also R. Boyle, *Works*, ed. T. Birch, V, 39.

2. *The Works of Francis Bacon*, ed. Spedding, Ellis, and Heath, (new ed., 7 vols., 1879–90), I, 11.

3. *Ibid.*, III, 282–84. The first reference contains his famous explanation of, and attack on, Ciceronianism. Though his own prose reveals elements that ally him to the Anti-Ciceronians, his emphasis upon a plain style is quite foreign to them; furthermore, as will be noted later, he was so far from approving their style that he considered it one of the distempers of learning.

4. *Ibid.*, IV, 22. In a *Preparative towards a Natural and Experimental History* he lists rhetorical ornaments among the factors which increase the difficulty of, while adding nothing to, the work. "And for all that concerns ornaments of speech, similitudes, treasury of eloquence, and such like emptinesses, let it be utterly dismissed." IV, 254.

5. *Ecclesiastes, or a Discourse concerning the Gift of Preaching as it falls under the Rules of Art*, 1646, p. 72.

6. *The Advice of W. P. to Mr. Samuel Hartlib, for the Advancement of some particular Parts of Learning*, London, 1648; *Harleian Miscellany*, 1810, VI, 2.

7. *A Treatise of the Rickets*, 1651. (This is a translation of the Latin edition which appeared the preceding year.) Mention might here be made of John Dury's *The Reformed School* (c. 1649), a passage from which (p. 49) reads: "Whatsoever in the teaching of Tongues doth not tend to make them a help unto Traditionall knowledge, by the manifestation of Reall Truths in Sciences, is superfluous, and not to be insisted upon, especially towards Children, whence followeth that the Curious study of Criticismes and observations of Styles in Authors and of straines of wit, which speak nothing of

80 RICHARD FOSTER JONES

Reality in Sciences, are to be left to such as delight in vanityes more than in Truths." Dury belonged to that group of educational reformers which centered around Comenius, and to which Samuel Hartlib also belonged. Their philosophy, which is shot through with the spirit of scientific utilitarianism, was largely inspired by Bacon, and properly falls in the scientific movement. Dury's emphasis upon "reality" manifests the same attitude as is revealed in the quotation from Petty, and clearly indicates that the materialistic nature of the new science, with its insistence upon direct sense-observation of natural phenomena, was the chief source of this craving for a plain style. For an extended discussion of the influence of the Baconian philosophy upon educational theory, see Foster Watson, *The Beginning of the Teaching of Modern Subjects in England*, chap. vi.

8. See end of the *Leviathan*.
9. *Leviathan*, ed. A. R. Waller, pp. 526–27.
10. *Ibid.*, p. 185.
11. *Ibid.*, pp. 43–44.
12. *Ibid.*, pp. 14–15.
13. *Ibid.*, pp. 21, 25.
14. *Ibid.*, p. 26.
15. *Ibid.*, p. 88.
16. See Boyle's *Works*, ed. T. Birch, II, 92, 136; III, 2, 512; V, 54.
17. P. 2.
18. P. 1.
19. Numerous references might be given to support this statement, but I shall quote only one writer, who figures in this study. "*Aristotelian Philosophy* is a huddle of *words* and *terms insignificant*." And again, speaking of entities, modes, and formalities, "What a number of words here have nothing answering them? . . . To wrest names from their known meaning to Senses most alien, and to darken *speech by words without knowledge;* are none of the most inconsiderable faults of this *Philosophy* . . . Thus these *Verbosities* do emasculate the Understanding; and render it slight and frivolous, as its objects." Joseph Glanvill, *Vanity of Dogmatizing*, 1661, pp. 150 ff. He also speaks of the verbal emptiness of Aristotle's philosophy.
20. One stylistic vice obviously came under the ban of the experimental philosophers. The latter's violent attack upon the ancients and upon authority in general did much to depreciate the value of Latin and Greek quotations. Glanvill, in the *Vanity of Dogmatizing*, attacks this habit on the ground that reliance on antiquity is no longer to be countenanced, so that appeals to it are impertinent and futile. " 'Twas this vain Idolizing of Authors, which gave birth to that silly vanity of *impertinent citations;* and inducing Authority in things neither re-

quiring, nor deserving it. That saying was much more observable, *That men have beards, and women none;* because quoted from *Beza;* and that other *Pax res bona est;* because brought in with a, *said St. Austin.*" (Pp. 142 ff.) In 1678 he says that "the custom is worn out everywhere except in remote, dark corners." (*An Essay Concerning Preaching,* pp. 18 ff.) See also Hobbes's view of the same matter given earlier in this article.

21. Pp. 111–13.

22. Cf. Thomas Birch, *History of the Royal Society,* II, 3, 47, 51, 138, 161, 163, 197 (hereafter cited as *Hist. Roy. Soc.*).

23. P. 113. Sprat believed that English writers in general were freer from stylistic vices than the French. "There might be," he says, with an eye on France, "a whole Volume compos'd in comparing the Chastity, the newnesse, the vigour of many of our *English* Fancies, with the corrupt, and the swelling Metaphors, wherewith some of our Neighbors, who most admire themselves, do still adorn their books." And again, "We have had many Philosophers, of a strong, vigorous, and forcible judgment, of happy and laborious hands, of a sincere, a modest, a solid, and unaffected expression, such who have not thought it enough to set up for Philosophers, only to have got a large stock of fine words, and to have insinuated into the acquaintance of some great Philosophers of the age." (*Observations on Monsieur de Sorbier's Voyage into England,* 1665, pp. 265, 271. See also Sprat, *History of the Royal Society,* pp. 40–41.) Evelyn expresses the same sentiment, only he makes a luxuriant prose style a characteristic of the whole French nation. "The Reader will find," he remarks in the Preface to his translation of a French treatise on painting, "in this discourse (though somewhat verbose, according to the style of this overflowing nation) divers useful remarks." (*Miscellaneous Writings of John Evelyn,* ed. W. Upcott, 1825, p. 559.) Another sturdy Englishman expresses the same sentiment in more emphatic words: "And indeed however our smoother tongued Neighbours may put in a claim for those bewitcheries of speech that flow from Gloss and Chimingness; yet I verily believe that there is ɳo tongue under heaven, that goes beyond our English for speaking manly strong and full." (Nathaniel Fairfax, *A Treatise of the Bulk and Selvedge of the World,* 1674, "To the Reader.") In view of the common opinion that French influence played a great part in the simplification of English prose, these quotations are worthy of note. Furthermore, not a single stylistic reformer in England, as far as my knowledge extends, ever refers, directly or indirectly, to any influence from across the Channel.

24. *Plus Ultra,* p. 84.

25. The following quotation from Sprat's *History* clearly evinces the im-

portant place granted style in the obligations of the scientists. In fact, it shows that the experimental philosophers considered a reformation in current methods of expression essential to the advancement of science. "Their [members of the Royal Society] purpose is, in short, to make faithful *Records,* of all the Works of *Nature,* or *Art,* which can come within their reach: that so the present Age, and posterity, may be able to put a mark on the Errors, which have been strengthened by long prescription: to restore the Truths, that have lain neglected: to push on those, which are already known, to more various uses: and to make the way more passable, to what remains unreveal'd. This is the compass of their Design. And to accomplish this, they have indeavor'd, to separate the knowledge of *Nature,* from the colours of *Rhetorick,* the devices of *Fancy,* or the delightful deceit of *Fables.*" Pp. 61–62.

26. See P. H. Hembt, "The Influence of Early Science on Formative English, 1645–1675," *Journal of Chemical Education,* III, 1051, and C. S. Duncan, *The New Science and English Literature,* pp. 147–54.

27. This version is accessible in a modern edition by John Owen, 1885. All references are to this edition.

28. See Birch, *Hist. Roy. Soc.,* I, 500. Glanvill's purpose is also suggested by a change introduced in the body of the work. A passage in the *Vanity,* p. 240, reads, "And the sole Instances of those illustrious Heroes, *Cartes, Gassendus, Galileo, Tycho, Harvey, More, Digby;* will strike dead the opinion of the worlds decay, and conclude it, in its *Prime.*" In the *Scepsis,* p. 209, there is substituted for the names given above "that Constellation of Illustrious Worthies, which compose the Royal Society."

29. In an earlier passage he gives another excuse for this style though at the same time suggesting the immaturity of youth as one. After speaking of some ingenious people laboring under the prejudices of education and customary belief, he says, "For Such it was then that the ensuing *Essay* was designed; which therefore wears a dress that possibly is not so suitable to the graver *Geniuses,* who have outgrown all *gayeties of style and youthful* relishes; But yet perhaps is not improper for the persons, for whom it was prepared. And there is nothing in *words* and *styles* but *suitableness,* that makes them *acceptable* and *effective.* If therefore this Discourse, such as it is, may tend to the removal of any *accidental* disadvantages from *capable Ingenuities,* and the preparing them for *inquiry,* I know you have so noble an *ardour* for the benefit of Mankind, as to pardon a *weak* and *defective* performance to a *laudable* and *well-directed* intention." (P. liv.) In still another passage he touches upon this all-important matter: "And 'Tis none of the least considerable expectations that

may be reasonably had of your Society, that 'twill discredit that *toyishness* of *wanton fancy;* and pluck the misapplyed name of the *Wits,* from those conceited Humorists that have assum'd it; to bestow it upon the more *manly spirit* and *genius,* that playes not tricks with *words,* nor frolicks with the *Caprices* of *frothy imagination.*" (P. lxv.) These words clearly indicate the popular association of stylistic reform with the Society, and the important place such a reformation occupied in the scientific movement.

30. This case furnishes strong support to Herford's contention that Browne's style was the obstacle in the way of his joining the Royal Society. Browne had early become notorious for his style. In *The Philosophicall Touchstone, or Observations upon Sir Kenelm Digbe's Discourses,* 1645, an attack on the *Religio Medici,* Alexander Ross says, "Your Rhetoricall descriptions (which are both uselesse in and destructive of *Philosophy*) make the soule sometimes equall with God, sometimes no better than a corruptible body; . . . If you lay the fault of this upon your *Rhetoricall* expressions, I must answer you, that *Rhetorick* in such a subject may be well spared: use your *Rhetorick* when you will work upon the *affections,* but not when you will *informe* the *understanding.* Rhetorick . . . ought not to be used, but with great discretion, especially in abstruse questions . . . If you will dispute like a *Philosopher,* you must lay aside *Rhetorick,* and use *Philosophicall* termes; otherwise you will do as the fish *Sepia,* to wit, you'l so thicken the waters of your discourse, with the *liquor* that cometh out of your mouth, that you will make your self *invisible,* and delude the Reader, which is the fashion of those, who dare not confide in the strength of their arguments; whereas *naked* truth cares not for such *dressings,* nor seeks she after such *corners.*" (P. 92.) Ross has nothing but scorn for "Rhetoricall flourishes" and "Tullian pigments." See C. H. Herford's edition of Browne's works, Everyman's Library, p. xiv.

31. Ferris Greenslet in *Joseph Glanvill,* 1900, pp. 200–201, has listed all such verbal changes, which amount to less than a score. Dr. Greenslet notices the difference between Glanvill's early and later work in the matter of diction, clearness, and simplicity, as well as in the quality of imagination. But since he failed to compare the *Vanity* with the version that appeared in the *Essays,* he did not perceive the extent or fully understand the nature of the author's stylistic evolution. Though he attributes the change in part to the influence of science, he failed to perceive the conscious and decisive nature of the influence which the Royal Society exerted on Glanvill. He is correct in detecting Bacon in the concrete imagery and balanced brevity of sentence structure, but he limits Browne's influence too narrowly to words. Though he accurately characterizes Glanvill's later style as

simple, plain, reasonable, he is not sufficiently aware of the profound change that had taken place.

32. Concerning this essay, "Against Confidence in Philosophy," a passage in the preface to the volume reads: "[It] is quite changed in the way of Writing, and in the Order. Methought I was somewhat fetter'd and tied in doing it, and could not express my self with that ease, freedom, and fulness which possibly I might have commanded amid fresh thoughts: yet 'tis so alter'd as to be in a manner new." A comparison of the two versions reveals that chapters xvi, xvii, xviii, and xix, attacking Aristotle and the Peripatetic philosophy, as well as chapters i, ii, vi, xi, xx, xxi, and xxii, have been omitted almost *in toto*; that there is much beneficial rearrangement of material; and that much other material has been either left out or highly condensed. These changes, together with the compression in style, have caused the treatise to shrink to a fourth or a fifth of its first dimensions. A passage in the "Epistle Dedicatory" again calls attention to a change in his stylistic taste: "They [the essays] were some of them written several years ago, and had trial of the World in divers Editions: Now they come abroad together (with some things that are *new*) reduced to such an Order, as is most agreeable to my present judgment."

33. Likewise, the enthusiastic, exclamatory, and picturesque elements of the following passage are strangely subdued to a quieter level. "What cement should untie [unite] heaven and earth, light and darkness, natures of so divers a make, of such disagreeing attributes, which have almost nothing, but *Being*, in common; This is a riddle, which must be left to the coming of *Elias*. How should a thought be united to a marble-statue, or a sun-beam to a lump of clay! The freezing of the words in the air in the northern climes, is as conceivable, as this strange union. That this active spark, this συμψυτον πνευμα [as the Stoicks call it] should be confined to a Prison it can so easily pervade, is of less facill apprehension, then that the light should be pent up in a box of Crystall, and kept from accompanying its source to the lower world: And to hang weights on the wings of the winde seems far more intelligible." (*Vanity*, p. 20.) "So that, what the *Cement* should be that unites *Heaven* and *Earth, Light* and *Darkness*, viz. Natures of so divers a make, and such disagreeing Attributes, is beyond the reach of any of our Faculties: We can as easily conceive how a thought should be united to a Statue, or a Sun-Beam to a piece of Clay: How words should be frozen in the Air, (as some say they are in the remote North) or how Light should be kept in a Box; as we can apprehend the *manner* of this *strange Union*." *Essays*, p. 4.

34. *Vanity*, pp. 26, 27, 29, 53, 137; *Essays*, pp. 5, 6, 13, 25.

35. It would be easy to quote many more parallel passages illustrating this change, but the reader should compare the two versions himself in order to realize fully the transformation that has taken place. It is hardly necessary to point out that all Glanvill's later works reveal the same stylistic evolution.

36. Later Glanvill joined in the attack on pulpit eloquence, which arose about 1668, and his words show that science was by no means without its influence upon this attack. Furthermore, the terms used by the reformers of the pulpit are startlingly similar to those with which the scientists have made us familiar. (See Glanvill, *Philosophia Pia*, pp. 73, 90–91; the last essay in *Essays on Several Important Subjects*, 1676, and *An Essay Concerning Right Preaching*, 1678, pp. 11–51.) For an account of Glanvill's vigorous defense of the Royal Society, consult the present writer's "The Background of *The Battle of the Books*," *Washington University Studies*, VII, Humanistic Series II (1920), 125–29.

37. VIII, 431–33.

38. P. 310.

39. Abraham Cowley, *The Essays and Other Prose Writings*, ed. A. B. Gough, 1915, p. 143.

40. *Ibid.*, p. 199.

41. *Ibid.*, p. 169.

42. Birch, *Hist. Roy. Soc.*, I, 17.

43. *Ibid.*, I, 499. The late Professor Emerson in "John Dryden and A British Academy" (*Proceedings of the British Academy*, X, 1924) calls attention to the fact that Cowley was not a member of this committee, and thinks that Evelyn's memory had played him false in mentioning Cowley. But we must remember that Evelyn does not say that Cowley and the others were members of the committee, and that there is no reason why both the poet and Clifford, who also was not a member, should not have met with the committee.

44. Another possible example of the influence of the Royal Society in sobering the style of its members is found in Samuel Parker, later bishop of Oxford, who in 1666 published *A Free and Impartial Censure of the Platonick Philosophie*, dedicated to Bathurst, then president of Trinity College, Oxford, and formerly a member of the Oxford group of Baconians, to which reference has already been made. Both in the dedication and in the body of the work (pp. 2, 64) Parker expresses his gratitude to Bathurst for turning him from the unprofitable study of the old scholastic philosophy to the new experimental science. Though disclosing the influence of both Hobbes and Descartes, the *Censure* reveals chiefly the influence of Bacon and his followers. Parker brings to bear upon Platonism the same arguments which the experimental philosophers had used, and were

using, against Aristotelianism, namely, that, as regards natural phenomena anyway, its empty notions could not be tested by sense
observations or experiments, the criteria of truth. From this attack
on a philosophy which presumably is mainly words, he passes naturally to an onslaught upon a wordy and figurative style, which is
fully in keeping with the attitude of the scientists, and in the composition of which he undoubtedly had an eye on the Cambridge
Platonists. These latter, he says, "put us off with nothing but rampant
Metaphors and Pompous Allegories, and other splendid but empty
Schemes of speech . . . true Philosphie is too sober to descend to
these wildernesses of Imagination, and too Rational to be cheated by
them. She scorns, when she is in chase of Truth, to quarry upon
trifling gaudy Phantasms: Her Game is in things not words . . . I
remember I had not long conversed with Platonick Authors, when
I took occasion to set it down as a note to my self, that though a huge
lushious stile may relish sweet to childish and liquorish Fancies, yet
it rather loaths and nauceats a discreet understanding then informs
and nourishes it . . . Now to discourse of the Natures of things in
Metaphors and Allegories is nothing else but to sport and trifle with
empty words, because these Schemes do not express the Natures of
Things, but only their Similitudes and Resemblances." (Pp. 73 ff.)
And he continues his attack on metaphors at great length. But in
spite of this expressed antipathy to rhetorical prose, the style of the
Censure is far from being bare and unadorned. (Note, for instance,
the following: "But when they pretend to be Natures Secretaries,
to understand all her Intrigues, or to be Heavens Privadoes, talking
of the Transactions there, like men lately drop'd thence encircled
with *Glories,* and cloathed with the Garments of *Moses* & *Elias,*"
etc., p. 73.) He had been for only a short time a member of the
Royal Society, and perhaps its influence had not had time to bear
fruit. In his next important works, however, *A Discourse of Ecclesiastical Politie,* 1671, we note a decided toning down of his enthusiastic
language, though he himself claims that he is pursuing a middle way
between a bare and an ornate style. (*A Defence,* pp. 97–98.) Parker
is treated more at length in my article on pulpit eloquence.

45. *Cam. Hist. of Eng. Lit.,* VIII, 346, 423.
46. "His [Tillotson's] joining with Dr. Wilkins in perfecting the scheme
of a *real character and philosophical language,* the *essay* towards which
was publish'd in 1668, led him to consider exactly the truth of language and style, in which no man was happier, or knew better the
art of uniting dignity with simplicity, and tempering these so equally
together, that neither his thoughts sunk, nor style swell'd; keeping
always a due mean between flatness and false rhetoric. Together
with the pomp of words he cut off likewise all superfluities and need-

less enlargements. He said what was just necessary to give clear ideas of things, and no more. He laid aside long and affected periods. His sentences were short and clear; and the whole thread was of a piece, plain and distinct. No affections of learning, no torturing of texts, no superficial strains, no false thoughts, nor bold flights. All was solid and yet lively, and grave as well as elegant . . . he retrench'd both the luxuriances of style, and the length of sermons." Thomas Birch, *The Life of the Most Reverend Dr. John Tillotson,* 2d ed., London, 1753, pp. 21–22.

47. Birch, *Hist. Roy. Soc.,* I, 119; II, 265, 281, 283.

48. In the Dedication a passage reads, "To which it will be proper for me to add, That this design will likewise contribute much to the clearing of some of our Modern differences in Religion, by unmasking many wild errors, that shelter themselves under the disguise of affected phrases; which being Philosophically unfolded, and rendered according to the genuine and natural importance of Words, will appear to be inconsistencies and contradictions. And several of those pretended, mysterious, profound notions, expressed in great swelling words, whereby some men set up for reputation, being this way examined, will appear to be, either nonsense, or very flat and jejune." Later he speaks of "the Common mischief that is done, and the many impostures and cheats that are put upon men, under the disguise of affected insignificant Phrases." On pp. 17-18, he says, "As for the ambiguity of words by reason of *Metaphor* and *Phraseology,* this is in all instituted Languages so obvious and so various, that it is needless to give any instances of it; . . . And though the varieties of Phrases in Language may seem to contribute to the elegance and ornament of Speech; yet, like other affected ornaments, they prejudice the native simplicity of it, and contribute to the disguising of it with false appearances. Besides that like other things of fashion, they are very changeable, every generation producing new ones; witness the present Age, especially the late times, wherein this grand imposture of Phrases hath almost eaten out solid knowledge in all professions; such men generally being of most esteem who are skilled in these Canting forms of speech, though in nothing else." The same values that appear in the previous discussions of style also appear in the use of such terms as brevity, perspicuity, significancy, and facility of expression, and the like. See pp. 319, 443, 447.

49. That the Royal Society looked upon Wilkins as specially qualified for the study of language or style is revealed in the fact that, though he was not appointed on the committee to improve the language, perhaps because he was too busy with the *Essay,* he was ordered to attend the first meeting of the committee and outline to them the proper method of procedure. Birch, *Hist. Roy. Soc.,* II, 7.

50. Congreve's dedication of *Dryden's Dramatic Works,* quoted by Ker, *Essays of John Dryden,* I, xxvii, n.
51. "Defence of an Essay of Dramatic Poesy," *Essays of John Dryden,* ed. Ker, I, 124. Dryden in the Preface to *Religio Laici* called himself a sceptic in philosophy, and Ker, I, xv, speaks of him as "sceptical, tentative, disengaged." How much of this quality was due to the scepticism of science that stretched from Bacon to the Royal Society? See Bredvold's "Dryden, Hobbes, and the Royal Society," *Mod. Phil.,* XXV (1928), 417–38.
52. In discussing this paper, a fraction of which was read before one of the groups of the Modern Language Association at Toronto in 1928, one scholar maintained that there was some relation between the two movements and referred to Professor Morris Croll's very able articles on Anti-Ciceronianism. During my own investigations I had discovered no such relationship, and a close study of the problem has confirmed me in the belief that the two movements were separate and distinct in that the scientific demand for stylistic reform neither had its origin in, nor drew support from, the Anti-Ciceronian revolt. For Professor Croll's theories consult the following: "Juste Lipse et le Mouvement Anti-Cicéronien," (*Revue du Seizième Siècle,* Vol. II [1914]); " 'Attic' Prose in the Seventeenth Century," (*Stud. in Philol.,* Vol. XVIII [1921]); "Attic Prose: Lipsius, Montaigne, Bacon," (*Schelling Anniversary Papers,* 1923); "Muret and the History of 'Attic Prose,' " (*PMLA,* Vol. XXXIX [1924]).
53. See *Schelling Anniversary Papers,* pp. 138–39.
54. Probably the most remarkable example of this passion for concrete, material reality in language as well as in philosophy, is discovered in the startling proposal advanced by Nathaniel Fairfax in the preface to *A Treatise of the Bulk and Selvedge of the World,* 1674. Fairfax displays a violent antipathy to all imported words in the English language, and in his own work he tries as far as possible to substitute English coinages for words of foreign origin, with grotesque results in some cases. Since he was a great admirer of the Royal Society and the experimental philosophy, which impressed him with its practical and utilitarian character, it is not strange to find him proclaiming an interest in things, not words. Thus he advocates the purification and enlargement of the English vocabulary, made necessary by the activities of the new scientists, through the introduction of plain, homely words, gathered from the fields and shops. He wishes to realize literally Sprat's "so many things in the same number of words," not difficult Latinisms but the common words of daily use, "words that answer works, by which all Learners are taught to do, and not make a Clatter." More of his sentiments are worth quoting: "Now the *Philosophy* of our day and Land being so much workful

as the world knows it to be, methinks this of all times should be *the* time, wherein, if ever, we should gather up those scatter'd words of ours that speak works, rather than to suck in those of learned air from beyond Sea, which are as far off sometimes from the things they speak, as they are from us to whom they are spoken. Besides, it may well be doubted, whether Latine can now be made so fit to set forth things the writings of a *Working Philosophy* by, as our own Speech. —For we must know that almost all the old pieces of good Latine that we draw by, have been taken up by that sort of learning that is wont to be worded in the Schools, and spent in the setting to sale of such things as could best be glazed with the froth of ink, by the men of Closets. Whence he that is best skill'd in it, is so hard put to it, in the Kitchin, the Shop, and the Ship; and ever will be, though *Plautus* should be as well understood as *Tully*. For the words that are every day running to and fro in the Chat of Workers, have not been gotten into Books and put aboard for other Lands until this way of Knowing by Doing was started amongst us.—But as Learnings being lockt up in the Tongues of the Schools, or Love's being lickt up in more the womanly simprings of the lips, and the smiling kissing speeches of some others abroad, have been enough to enkindle in us a panting after, and fondness for some of those Outlandish dynns: So if the works of our own men shall be shipt over by words of our own tongue, it may happily make others who have love enough for the things, to seek as much after our words, as we upon other scores have done after theirs; the first draught being *English,* name and thing, doing and speaking." Cf. what Sprat says about the Royal Society's "preferring the language of Artizans, Countrymen, and Merchants, before that of Wits, or Scholars."

55. *Leviathan,* ed. A. R. Waller, p. 14.
56. *A Free and Impartial Censure,* p. 61.

MORRIS W. CROLL AND R. S. CRANE

🖋

Reviews of R. F. Jones's "Science and English Prose Style in the Third Quarter of the Seventeenth Century"

The outlines of the history of seventeenth-century prose style are not obscure. At the beginning of the century, or a little before, the retarded rationalism of the Renaissance won its first *general* success in the victory of the Anti-Ciceronian movement of Muret, Lipsius, Montaigne, and Bacon. The program of this movement included the rehabilitation in literary favor of the Anti-Ciceronians of the first century, especially Seneca and Tacitus; and the form and structure of seventeenth-century English prose is largely determined by the imitation of these two authors and of Lipsius and Montaigne, their modern disciples, though, of course, it derives qualities of its own from the fantastic genius of the age that produced it. Then, about the middle of the century, a movement of clarification and "enlightenment" began to be self-conscious, working, however, within the limits set by the Anti-Ciceronian model, now so well established. In this several elements combined to a single end: the mathematical genius of the Cartesian philosophy, the ideal of *mondanité* emerging in French civilized society, and the "practical" aims of Baconian science.

It is with the later of these two movements that Jones is concerned, and specifically with the part that science played in it. The story he tells is not unfamiliar. It is chiefly an account of the successful attempts of the Royal Society, through its spokesman, Thomas Sprat, to

From *Philological Quarterly,* X (April 1931), pp. 184-186. Reprinted by permission of the University of Iowa.

make the prose of scientific study as bare of imagination, reverie, and eloquence as it is possible for written discourse to be. But if the story is not new, Jones has enriched it with new detail, longer quotations, and revealing illustrations. Best of all there is his illustration by parallel passages of Glanvill's re-writing (in 1676) of his *Vanity of dogmatizing*, "so alter'd as to be in a manner new." This is delightfully illuminating. The citations from the earlier work show that Glanvill, like so many others, was then trying awkwardly and amusingly to shoot in Browne's bow. The parallels from the later version reveal and justify the new vision of a clear, lighted prose. They give the reader the same impression that he may receive when he walks from dark vaulted halls into the Library of Trinity College, which is perhaps a work of Wren's.

Jones's essay is a valuable marshalling of facts; but his readers are likely to be puzzled by his attempts to place them in their relations with the general movement of seventeenth-century prose. His statements on this subject are uncertain and even inconsistent; but his conclusion seems to be that Anti-Ciceronian prose and the bare prose of scientific study run parallel throughout the century unaware of each other's existence and character. The real history is somewhat more complex, but also more understandable. The scientific cult of unrhetorical speech from 1650 onward is a second, later stage in the history of the same naturalistic tendency that shows itself in the Anti-Ciceronian victory at the end of the preceding century. It did not create a new, a rival style to the Anti-Ciceronian; it only introduced certain changes within the *cadres* of that style. It was an attempt, a successful attempt, to take the heat and fever out of the imaginative naturalism of Montaigne, Bacon, and Browne, to prune their conceits and metaphors, to restrain the wild motions of their eloquence. But it did not change the form and structure of the prose of its time. That this is the relation between the Anti-Ciceronians and the clarifiers is made clear and explicit in contemporary French criticism; but it is equally clear in English practice. Glanvill's later style is a *revision* of Browne's; and Sprat's easy periods have almost exactly the form of Bacon's harder and knottier ones. Seventeenth-century prose is and remains Anti-Ciceronian and predominantly Senecan; and Shaftesbury's statement, in the last years of the century, that English ears were so accustomed to the Senecan pace in prose that they were scarcely aware of any other is borne out by the facts.—MORRIS W. CROLL.

I add brief notes on two points not discussed in the preceding review.

1. In describing the program of stylistic reform urged by Sprat and other members of the Royal Society, Jones rightly emphasizes the strong anti-rhetorical bias of these men, their antipathy to "Tropes and Figures," their insistence on "a close, naked, natural way of speaking. . . . bringing things as near the Mathematical plainness, as they can." But he does not, I think, make sufficiently clear that in these and similar declarations they were recommending a special type of style suitable for use primarily in "philosophical," that is in scientific works, and were not attempting to impose a universal model of style to be followed in all kinds of writing. A more complete analysis of their theory would make clear the important rôle played in their thinking by the idea, so prominent in ancient rhetoric, that different audiences and different subjects require different manners of treatment. It was on this idea that they normally based their pleas for unmetaphorical plainness in "philosophical" exposition (see, for example, Bacon, *Advancement of learning,* in *Works,* ed. Spedding, Ellis, and Heath [Boston, 1860-64], VI, 120-21; Boyle, *Works* [London, 1772], I, 304-05, 462; II, 254), and in so doing they were following a tradition as old as Aristotle. But it is a mistake to imply, as Jones seems to do, that they also demanded the same extreme bareness in all other forms of prose writing. Sprat certainly did not, as appears from what he has to say of the value of "experiments" in providing writers with "beautiful *Conceptions,* and inimitable *Similitudes,*" "an inexhaustible Treasure of *Fancy* and *Invention* (*History of the Royal Society* [London, 1722], pp. 413, 416-17); and as for Boyle, his comments on the "eloquence" of the Scriptures (*Works* [London, 1772], II, 301-02), as well as some of his remarks on his own manner of writing (e.g., *ibid.,* I, 462; II, 254), reflect a conception of style that can by no means be confined within the narrow limits of the official program of the Royal Society.

2. In his attempt to show that the development with which he is concerned had no real connection with the earlier Anti-Ciceronian movement, Jones remarks (p. 1004): "The Anti-Ciceronian style found its theories in Aristotle. . . ; science renounced Aristotle and all his works. . . ." To realize how imperfectly this generalization fits the facts one need only recall that an important element in Bacon's discussion of rhetoric springs directly from Aristotle (see *Works* [Boston, 1860-64], VI, 301; IX, 131, 134, 135ff, 219; and cf. Croll, *PMLA,*

XXXIX [1924], 282); that Hobbes, whose plea for a "plain" style is quoted by Jones (pp. 981-82), wrote *The whole art of rhetorick in English, being a translation of Aristotle's*; that Cowley mentioned Aristotle's *Rhetoric* as an authority, along with the works of Cicero and Quintilian, in his *Proposition for the advancement of experimental philosophy*; and that Glanvill, in spite of his many attacks on Aristotle, announced in *Plus ultra* (1668) that he was quite willing "to give chearful Acknowledgments to his *Rhetorick, History of Animals,* and *Mechanicks* and could wish that these were more studied by his *devoted* Admirers." R. S. CRANE

R. F. JONES

Science and Language in England of the Mid-Seventeenth Century

In two previous articles I have attempted to prove the influence which science exerted upon the style of English prose, both secular and religious, during the Restoration.[1] Both treatises were more interested in showing the nature and extent of this influence than in making plain its origin. I did mention the probable source of the stylistic views associated with early science, but with little elaboration or documentation.[2] It is the purpose of the present article to furnish a more substantial basis for the theory that in the attitude of science toward language is to be discovered the most important origin of the stylistic reformation with which the scientists were enthusiastically concerned.

In investigating any matter of a scientific import in England of the seventeenth century, one must always take Bacon into consideration, for from him radiated waves of life-giving power which penetrated the farthest nooks and crannies of the period. While there is implied in his constant opposing of nature to books a certain antipathy to language, we discover more definite information concerning this antipathy in the *Novum Organum*.[3] Of the "Idols" that possess the human mind, he considers the Idols of the Market-place (i.e., language) the most troublesome, maintaining that these alone had "rendered philosophy and the sciences sophistical and inactive." He justifies such a belief on the grounds that since words were invented to satisfy in-

From the *Journal of English and Germanic Philology*, XXXI (1932), pp. 315-331. Reprinted by permission of the University of Illinois Press.

ferior intellects, they either stand for things that do not exist at all, or inaccurately represent the truths of nature. This fact, he holds, was responsible for the violent disputes characteristic of the middle ages and Renaissance, which were really concerned with words rather than with realities.[4] In this connection Bacon stresses, as Hobbes did later, and, like Hobbes, inspired by mathematics, the importance of definitions, but he thinks that in dealing with material things definitions themselves may be of little avail, since they are composed of words, and "those words beget others." The materialistic origin of this depreciation of language is further revealed in his listing, in ascending degrees of faultiness, first, names of substances; second, names of actions; and third, names of qualities. In short, Bacon condemned language because it foisted upon the world ideas that had no basis in reality, or confused and distorted the real truths of nature, so that knowledge of them became impossible.

A somewhat hidden but none the less real reason for the distrust of language felt by the early Baconians lay in the difference between the ways of acquiring knowledge adopted by the old and new sciences. Books were the storehouse of the former, experiment and observation of nature the means of acquiring the latter. To master the traditional science which prevailed during the Renaissance, a study of Latin and Greek was necessary, so that a philological training was, as Huxley pointed out several centuries later, the essential qualification of a scientist of that day; but with the advent of Bacon willingness to experiment and observe was proposed as the prime characteristic of a scientist. Thus the opposition between language and observed phenomena became established, and language, inseparably associated with the erroneous science of the past, attracted the suspicion adhering to the latter. George Thomson, one of many who were trying to introduce the new method into the practice of medicine, sometimes with ludicrous results, indignantly assails Henry Stubbe, a fanatical enemy of the Royal Society, for attacking "all true-hearted virtuous, intelligent Disciples of our *Lord Bacon*," and he assures Stubbe that

'Tis *Works*, not *Words; Things* not *Thinking; Pyrotechnie* [chemistry], not *Philologie; Operation,* not merely *Speculation,* must justifie us Physicians. Forbear then hereafter to be so wrongfully Satyrical against our Noble Experimentators, who questionless are entred into the right way of detecting the Truth of things.[5]

Another upholder of the new medicine declares that the only benefit one may derive from studying Galen is "to manage a discourse about fruitless Notions with Elegancy. With this weapon, the Tongue, tis likely Galen himself prevailed over all other Physicians in the Court of the Emperor Antoninus. . . . And yet for all his height of Eloquence we see his principles to be but streight and shallow."[6]

Another scientist, much greater than those mentioned, but one whose linguistic and stylistic views were sometimes inconsistent, reveals on more than one occasion his low opinion of philological study. Boyle considers rhetoric and deductive logic as matters of small importance, and styles himself "a much greater studier than prizer of languages," though, as may be noted in the quotation given below, he bestowed little enough study upon words. In an autobiographical note found among his papers, he makes clear the reason for his pronounced antipathy to philology:

> . . . those excellent sciences, the mathematics, having been the first I addicated myself to, and was found of, and experimental philosophy with its key, chemistry, succeeding them in my esteem and applications; my propensity and value for real learning gave me so much aversion and contempt for the empty study of words, that not only I have visited divers countries, whose languages I could never vouchsafe to study, but I could never be induced to learn the native tongue of the kingdom, I was born and for some years bred in [Ireland].[7]

So strong indeed was the antagonism to language engendered by the new science, that even those who had devoted their lives to linguistic studies were inclined to depreciate their own profession. In a letter to John Collins, a mathematician and fellow of the Royal Society, Edward Bernard, an orientalist of some note who two years later was to join the society, admits that with the exception of mathematics his

> study is literal [i.e., linguistic], and so beside the fame and regard of this age and inferior, in the nature of the thing, if I may speak as fits the schools, to real learning. I must profess that there is [a] great deal of difference, as I esteem, between what is notional only and what is also useful, between the derivation of a word and the solution of a problem.[8]

The whole tenor of his letter reveals the hope and belief that science will grow and thrive at the universities. His own field of study is totally ignored.

Another example of this depreciation of language under the influence of the scientific movement appears in the vigorous attacks on the teaching of the classics in the schools.[9] Under the lead of Comenius, Dury, and others inspired by the Baconian philosophy, the study of the ancient languages was severely reprehended during the period in which puritanism was triumphant. The spirit of utility, which derived its strength from the new science, and which recommended the latter to the Puritans, demanded that language be considered only a means to an end, and thus insisted upon the easiest possible method of learning it, and upon its subordination to the useful study of nature. John Dury, insisting that the true end of science is "to make use of the Creatures for that whereunto God hath made them," maintains that "Tongues are no further finally useful then to enlarge Traditionall Learning; and without their subordination unto Arts and Sciences, they are worth nothing towards the advancement of our Happiness."[10] This critical attitude toward linguistic study was by no means confined to this age nor to the proponents of the new science. It appears in the essayists and other writers on education and kindred matters.[11] The most vigorous condemnation, however, of the study of languages is found in the *Academiarum Examen*, 1653, of John Webster, a Puritan and an enthusiastic Baconian, who expressly advocated the substitution of the new science for the classical studies in the universities.

> The knowledge of Tongues beareth a great noise in the world, and much of our precious time is spent in attaining some smattering and small skill in them . . . before we arrive at any competent perfection in them, and yet that doth scarcely compensate our great pains; nor when obtained do they answer our longing, and vast expectations. For there is not much profit or emolument by them, besides those two great and necessary uses to read, understand, and interpret or translate the works and writings of other men . . . and thereby we may gather some of their hidden treasure; and also to inable men to converse with people of other nations, and so fit men for foreign negotiations, trade and the like.

Since man's knowledge is in no way increased by the mere knowing of languages, he believed that little time should be spent upon them.

> Now for a Carpenter to spend seven years time about the sharpening and preparing of his instruments, and then had no further skill how to employ them, were ridiculous and wearisome; so for schollars to spend divers years for some small scantling and smattering in the tongues, having for the most part got no further knowledge, but like Parrots to babble and prattle, that whereby the intellect is in no way inriched, is but toylsome, and almost lost labour.[12]

An indirect way of attacking the study of the classical languages is revealed in the effort to show that Latin, generally considered the most perfect of tongues, was exceedingly defective. Boyle, in arguing the virtues of his universal character, takes great pains to point out the inconsistencies, illogicalities, anomalies, irregularities, and complexities of Latin, and he emphasizes the difficulty of learning it because of the unusually large number of rules, which he, daring to differ from Bacon, "that incomparable Man," considered a serious defect. The tendency throughout the comparison of his own invented symbols with Latin is to depreciate and discourage the study of the latter.[13]

It is difficult for us to realize the extremes to which this distrust of language was carried. Its frequent appearance during the formative period of modern science bears conclusive testimony to the fact that all verbal media of communication were considered one of the greatest obstacles to the advancement of learning. Yet even the scientists realized that language was at least a necessary evil, if they wished to share their discoveries with others. This realization inspired in them a desire to reduce language to its simplest terms, to make it as accurate, concrete, and clear an image of the material world as was possible. In no one is this attempt more clearly displayed than in William Petty, a versatile and practical scientist and one of the founders of the Royal Society. Influenced by, though not so materialistic as, Hobbes, Petty manifests a desire for clear definitions, and toward this end seeks to place language on a purely materialistic basis, to curtail all verbal superfluity and insignificancy, in short, to sweep away all the fogginess of words.[14] Believing that, "whereas all writings ought to be description of things, they are now onely of words, opinions, theories,"[15] he attempted to draw up a "Dictionary of Sensible Words" which would show "what sensible Matter, Thing, Motion or Action every word therein doth meane and signify."[16] Speaking elsewhere of this dictionary, he expresses as clear a linguistic counterpart of the mechanical philosophy as one could wish for.

> That Dictionary I have often mentioned was intended to translate all words used in Argument and Important matters into words that are *Signa Rerum* and *Motuum*. But the Treasury of *Sensata* are the many Miscellany papers of my scripture, which I add and subtract, compose and distribute as Printers do their Letters.[17]

Not content with reducing all physical phenomena to matter and motion, scientists desired to impose the limitations of the same terms upon language, since they believed that only by making language correspond more closely to the truths of nature was it possible to advance knowledge.[18]

This latter idea, indeed, lay at the bottom of all their linguistic and stylistic views. In discussing the vague conception of "nature" current in his own day, Boyle says, "On this occasion I must not forbear to take notice, that the unskilful use of terms of far less extent and importance, and also less ambiguous, than the word nature, has been, and still is, no small impediment to the progress of sound philosophy."[19] He amplifies his statement by pointing out that most physicians, chemists, and naturalists were content to explain phenomena by means of such expressions as "real qualities," "natural powers," "faculties," and the like, which do not clearly represent anything in the physical world. Such a quiescence in ignorance sufficiently explains why the Baconians considered a reformation of language as important as a change in philosophy. In this respect Boyle may be again quoted, although confirmative passages could easily be brought from other sources.

> I confess I could heartily wish that philosophers and other learned men (whom the rest in time would follow) would by common (though perhaps tacit) consent, introduce some more significant and less ambiguous terms and expressions in the room of the too licenciously abused word nature, and the forms

of speech, that depend upon it, as much as conveniently they
can; and where they think they must employ it, would add a
word or two, to declare in what clear and determinate sense they
use it.[20]

The position of the scientists was that the truth of ideas regarding nature was dependent upon accuracy of language, and that the advancement of science must necessarily wait upon the introduction of greater
precision and clarity into the use of words. This linguistic reformation
was to be achieved by a constant narrowing of terms through strict
definition, and by the employment of words that would be exactly
equivalent, not to hazy conceptions bred in the minds of men by the
loose usage of the past, but to the objective truths of nature. They
were seeking an objective rather than subjective, materialistic rather
than psychological basis for language.

In his *History of the Royal Society*, Sprat speaks of the attempt of
the new scientists to reduce their style to "a mathematicall plainness,"[21] an expression that is more significant than may be realized.
For certainly the remarkable development of mathematics in the seventeenth century, to which Descartes contributed much, and especially the improved mathematical symbols that were coming into
use,[22] exerted no small influence upon conceptions of what language
should be. Hobbes, in his emphasis upon definition and in his general
deductive method, to say nothing of his unfailing interest in mathematics, reveals how much the latter had influenced him, and, indeed,
the movement toward clear definitions characteristic of this period
drew much of its inspiration from mathematics. The Malmesbury
philosopher considered words only the marks of things, just as mathematical symbols possess no virtue in themselves, but merely stand for
quantities and relationships. Seth Ward, professor of astronomy at
Oxford and an early upholder of the new science, declares that the
change from the traditional verbose mathematical writing to "the
symbolicall way, invented by *Vieta*, advanced by Harriot, perfected
by Mr. *Oughtred* and *Des Cartes*" made him hope

that the same course might be taken in other things (the affections of quantity, the object of universall *Mathematicks*, seeming to be an Argument too slender to engrosse this benefit). My
first proposall was to find whether other things might not as
well be designed by symbols, and herein I was presently re-

solved that Symbols might be formed for every *thing* and *notion*.[23]

The period witnessed frequent efforts to employ the analogy between mathematical symbols and verbal terms. Samuel Parker, an ardent convert to the experimental philosophy who at times reveals the influence of Hobbes, in attacking the cloudy terms used by the Cambridge Platonists, insists that "the use of Words is not to explaine the Natures of Things, but only to stand as marks and signes in their stead, as Arithmetical figures are only notes of Numbers; and therefore Names are as unable to explain abstracted Natures, as figures are to solve Arithmetical Problems."[24] Influenced by the new developments in mathematics, scientists wished to degrade language to the same colorless symbolism which had proved so successful in mathematics, so that words would have no more character than the x, y, z of algebra.

The mathematical spirit is also apparent in the remarkable development of various schemes for a universal language which appeared at this time.[25] Seth Ward was of the opinion that "an Universall Character might easily be made wherein all Nations might communicate together, just as they do in numbers and in species. And to effect this is indeed the design of such as hitherto have done any thing concerning an Universall Character."[26] At first the seeming necessity of a multitude of characters in the schemes that had been proposed made him dubious of their feasibility,

> But it did presently occur to me that by the help of Logick and Mathematicks this might soone receive a mightly advantage, for all Discourses being resolved in sentences, those into words signifying either simple notions or being resolvible into simple notions, it is manifest, that if all the sorts of simple notions be found out, and have symboles assigned to them, those will be extreamly few in respect of the other, (which are indeed Characters of words, such as Tullius Tiro's) the reason of their composition easily known, and the most compounded ones at once will be comprehended, and yet will represent to the very eye all the elements of their composition, and so deliver the natures of things: and exact discourses may be made demonstratively without any other paines then is used in these operations of specious Analytics.[27]

Ward also expresses a firm conviction that such a design would prove of great assistance to the advancement of learning, that is

> reall Learning, by which I understand that *Mathematics* and
> *Naturall Philosophy,* and the grounds of Physick. . . . Such a
> Language as this (where every word were a definition and con-
> tained the nature of the thing) might not unjustly be termed
> a naturall Language, and would afford that which the *Cabalists*
> and *Rosycrucians* have vainely sought for in the Hebrew, and in
> the names of things assigned by Adam."[28]

The effort to create a universal language was in part inspired by the desire to rectify the multiplicity of tongues, the "curse of Babel." With the rise of the new science, men were especially impressed with the need of some common medium whereby the discoveries of one country might be transmitted to another. Owing to the attack on the authority of the ancients, Latin, which had hitherto met the need, was in process of being depreciated and discarded. Furthermore, it was difficult to learn, and scientists resented spending too much time on the study of words.[29] Two other considerations, however, exerted a powerful influence on the movement. One was the desire to discover a language which would avoid the defects, real and supposed, of all established tongues, defects of which the age was acutely conscious. The other was the conviction that words should so match things that a word might not only stand as a symbol of a thing, but should also indicate its nature. The first of these two considerations manifests science's wide dissatisfaction with language in general. One linguistic inventor, who drew his inspiration from Bacon and the Baconians, expressed the belief that a universal character, "if happily contrived so as to avoid all Equivocal words, Anomalous variations, and super-fluous synonomas with which all Languages are encumbred, would be of great aid in propagating all sorts of Learning."[30] Dalgarno, who, assisted by Boyle, Wilkins, Ward, Bathurst, Petty, and Wallis,[31] men who composed the Oxford group of experimenters, produced in 1661 his universal language under the title *Ars Signorum,* claimed that the purpose of his work was to show

> a way to remedy the difficulties and absurdities which all lan-
> guages are clogged with . . . by cutting off all redundancy,
> rectifying all anomaly, taking away all ambiguity and aequivo-

cation. . . . In a word, designing not only to remedie the
confusion of languages, by giving, a much more easie medium
of communication than any yet known, but also to cure even
Philosophy itself of the disease of Sophisms and Logomachies;
as also to provide her with more wieldy and manageable instruments of operation, for defining, dividing, demonstrating etc.[32]

The defects of language were in large part considered responsible for
the confused and false ideas of nature which the old philosophy maintained. It was an authentic sense of the dangers inherent in all known
tongues, ancient and modern, that determined the linguistic and
stylistic views of the early scientists.

The climax of this movement toward a universal language was
reached in John Wilkins' ambitious *Essay towards a Real Character
and a Philosophical Language,* 1668, a work sponsored by the Royal
Society. From our point of view, the *Essay* is, indeed, a quixotic book,
but to his own age it was a noble, if somewhat impractical, achievement. The first part of the treatise is devoted to showing the imperfections which, inherent in all tongues, should be remedied by a language constructed according to the rules of art. A single passage
clearly reveals the author's attitude.

As for the ambiguity of words by reason of *Metaphor* and
Phraseology, this is in all instituted Languages so obvious and
various, that it is needless to give any instances of it; every
Language having some peculiar phrases belonging to it, which
if they were to be translated verbatim into another Tongue,
would seem wild and insignificant. In which our English doth
too much abound, witness those words of *Fall, Hand, Keep,
Make, Pass, Put, Set, Stand, Take,* none of which have less
than thirty or forty, and some of them about a hundred several
senses, according to their use in Phrases, as may be seen in the
Dictionary. And although the varieties of Phrases in Language
may seem to contribute to the elegance and ornament of speech;
yet, like other things of fashion, they are very changeable, every
generation producing new ones; witness the present Age, especially in late times, wherein this grand imposture of Phrases
hath almost eaten out solid knowledge in all professions; such
men generally being of most esteem who are skilled in these
Canting forms of speech, though in nothing else.[33]

More than to any other linguistic defect, scientists objected to a word's possessing many meanings or the same meaning as another word, and especially to the use of metaphors. The desire to make the word match the thing, to be in a strict sense a description of a thing or action explains their exaggerated antipathy to metaphors and such figures of speech.

The chief means whereby the linguistic reformers would obviate the deficiencies of existing tongues was to be found in symbols so constructed as to indicate the exact nature of things. Dalgarno was the first to undertake the task, but it was Wilkins who carried the idea to its farthest application. He attempted to classify everything in the universe, and then by a combination of straight lines, curves, hooks, loops, and dots, to devise for each thing a symbol which would denote its genus and species.[34] For those creations of the imagination, such as fairies, which lie beyond the realm of nature, he frankly made no provision, claiming that since they did not exist, they should not be represented in language. At last Hobbes' conception of words as only the marks of things had been literally realized. Wilkins' undertaking represents the lowest state to which language was degraded. Barred from representing the creations of the imagination and stripped of all connotations from past usage, language was to become nothing more than the dead symbols of mathematical equations.[35]

By way of summary, we may say that the linguistic views of seventeenth-century scientists were characterized by a suspicion of language arising out of its association with the old science, which seemed to depend more upon words than upon nature, and out of a feeling that all instituted languages tended to obscure rather than to describe realities. Linguistic defects were discovered in the imperfect meanings given to words, in the many meanings ascribed to a single word, in the figurative use of words, in the multiplication of words through synonyms, and in the number, irregularities, and inconsistencies of grammatical rules. The vividness with which material reality was conceived filled the scientists with alarm lest that reality should be lost through a faulty medium of communication and lest the manner of expression should usurp an importance belonging to the thing described. The result was a linguistic ideal which reduced language to its simplest terms, a single word being exactly equivalent to a single thing, and which, influenced by the unusual developments in mathematics, sought to degrade words to symbols of the same colorless nature as characterized those of mathematics. The effort to realize this ideal resulted in various schemes for a universal language and real character, in which words finally became marks, but marks which indicated the exact nature of the thing. It is hard to overemphasize the fact that science in its youth considered the linguistic problem as important as the problem of the true scientific method.

What stylistic standards would naturally develop out of this conception of language? Certainly none other than those which almost invariably appear whenever the scientists touch upon style. There should be little figurative language, especially metaphors, which falsely describe actions and things. There should be no verbal superfluity, but rather an economy of words sufficient to match exactly the phenomenon. Words should be the plainest possible, with intelligible, clear, and unequivocal meanings, preferably common words which are closer to material realities. There should be no emphasis upon or interest in the mode of expression for its own sake. Rhetorical ornaments and sheer delight in language represent a pernicious misplacing of emphasis, and in the end destroy the solid and fruitful elements in knowledge. What need is there to bring in Seneca and Aristotle to explain what is so easily explicable without them? As far as I can discover, not a single Baconian in any discussion of style mentions either one. I do not say that the two ancient worthies were without influence on style in the seventeenth century, but I am of the opinion that they had nothing to do with the stylistic views of science, which, as I have shown elsewhere were quite different from Anti-Ciceronianism as described by Professor Croll.[36]

In a recent review of one of my articles[37] Mr. Croll holds that the style advocated and adopted by the scientists was actually the Anti-Ciceronian style modified by some changes. These changes, however, even as described by him, were so important and far-reaching as to justify us in considering the result a new style. If my impression is correct, he implies that language is a minor, and structure or form a major, element in expression, and that the latter remained constant throughout the century. He sees in seventeenth-century prose a homogeneity which would certainly confound most literary historians, who have considered the Restoration an important turning point in the development of prose style. Any theory which places Sir Thomas Browne and John Dryden, Jeremy Taylor and John Tillotson in the same stylistic category is puzzling.[38]

In the same review Professor Crane opposes two objections to my article. The first asserts that the scientists insisted upon plainness of

expression only in scientific works, and that they believed other subjects demanded other styles. One has only to turn to a single familiar
passage in Sprat's *History of the Royal Society* (pp. 111-113), a *locus
classicus* in seventeenth-century opinions on style, to see how Sprat
applies his antagonism to rhetoric and his advocacy of a plain style
to "most other Arts and Professions." Furthermore, in a previous article I have attempted to show how the stylistic ideal of science was
carried over into an alien field.[39] The distinction which the scientific
advocates of plainness were chiefly interested in drawing was that between poetry and prose.[40] That the passage in Sprat's *History* from
which Mr. Crane quotes has poets, dramatists, and satirists in mind
for the most part seems clear to me. Certainly Sprat is not speaking of
argumentative or expository prose. With the exception of Boyle[41]
there is little disposition on the part of scientists to establish categories of prose style.[42]

The second objection denies the truth of my statement that "science
renounced Aristotle and all his works" which Mr. Crane interprets
literally. My position is that science had foresworn allegiance to the
authority of Aristotle, and had renounced all the evil consequences
of such an allegiance. Against this position Mr. Crane's citations resolve themselves into inferences. The first is that since Hobbes translated Aristotle's *Rhetoric,* he subscribed to the latter's views. Is it not,
however, just as permissible to infer that since this translation, made
in the course of his tutoring William Cavendish (1633?) and before
he had revealed any interest in science, was never published, the
translator did not consider it worthy of publication? One has only to
compare Aristotle's and Hobbes' opinions of metaphors to see how
little the latter is indebted to the former. The second inference is that
since Cowley, in outlining the studies of youths entering into an
"Apprenticeship in Natural Philosophy," mentions Cicero, Quintilian,
and Aristotle, he considered these men authorities on prose style.
Though the passage is by no means clear, it seems to refer to Cicero
and Quintilian as aids to poets, while the reference to Aristotle reads,
"For the Morals and Rhetorick *Aristotle* may suffice; or *Hermogenes*
and *Longinus* be added for the latter." The mention of Hermogenes,
whom Mr. Crane fails to notice, as an "authority" destroys whatever
significance there otherwise might have been in the naming of Aristotle, for their rhetorical theories diverged widely. It seems clear that
Cowley is only listing in perfunctory fashion well-known writers on
rhetoric. One could hardly ask for clearer evidence of the fact that

Anti-Ciceronianism meant nothing to the scientists than is revealed
in the assigning of these two men to the study of youths, Aristotle,
the mainstay of the Anti-Ciceronians, and Hermogenes, the rhetorician of the Ciceronians.[43] The complete absence, as far as I can discover, of references to or quotations from Aristotle, in the various
passages in which the Baconians express their stylistic views, renders
me very doubtful of his having influenced them at all. Professor
Crane's failure to cite such references strengthens that doubt.

NOTES

1. *Publications of the Modern Language Association,* XLV, 977-1009;
   and *Journal of English and Germanic Philology,* XXX, 188-217.
2. *PMLA,* XLV, 1008; *Jour. Eng. Ger. Philol.,* XXX, 215.
3. See Aphorisms XLIII, LIX, LX.
4. The emptiness and wordiness of disputatious Peripateticism, which
   departed from all material reality, became, of course, the main charge
   which ardent scientists of the seventeenth century brought against
   the old science.
5. Μισοχυμίας, 1671, pp. 31, 40.
6. Marchmont Nedham, *Medela Medicinae,* 1665, p. 256. In *An Answer to a Letter of Inquiry,* 1671, p. 37, one who signs himself
   W. S., and who was enthusiastic over the new science, declares that
   "Skill in tongues is a more jejune and barren kind of Employment.
   The more we grow towards men, the more we understand that
   Words are invented only to signifie *Things;* and while we are studying the nature of things we grudge the time that is spent in hunting
   the Etymology of a word to its first Theam."
7. *Works,* ed. T. Birch, I, 11, 29; V, 229. Another manifestation of this
   effort to dethrone language in favor of material things is found in
   John Webster (*Academiarum Examen,* 1653, p. 20), who considered
   language as only subservient to true learning, whereas natural philosophy of itself conferred knowledge.
8. Letter dated April 3, 1671, *Correspondence of Scientific Men,* I,
   158-159.
9. For a treatment of Bacon's influence on educational theory in England at this time, see Foster Watson's *The Beginnings of the Teaching of Modern Subjects in England,* chap. VI. Watson shows how the
   study of things was constantly and strongly emphasized in opposition
   to the study of words.
10. *The Reformed School* (1650?), pp. 40, 47. See also *PMLA,* XLV,
    981, note 7, where *Drury* should read *Dury.*
11. See T. C., *Moral Discourses,* 1655, pp. 50 ff., and Francis Osborn,

A Miscellany, 1659, p. 78. The avenue, however, through which the scientists reached their conclusions was different from the approach adopted by the others, especially as regards the emphasis placed upon the materialistic nature of truth.

12. P. 21. The third chapter of Webster's book discusses the study of language, in which the author emphasizes the utilitarian purpose of education, denies the usefulness of all speculative subjects, depreciates linguistic studies, and opposes the teaching of grammar. He would substitute the "symbolic, hieroglyphical, and emblematical ways of writing," with special emphasis upon a universal character.

13. *Essay toward a Real Character and a Philosophical Language*, 1668, pp. 443 ff.

14. See the *Petty Papers*, ed. Marquis of Lansdowne, 2 vols., 1928; and the *Petty-Southwell Correspondence, 1676-1687*, ed. Marquis of Lansdowne, 1927.

15. *Petty-Southwell Correspondence*, p. 324.

16. *Ibid.*, pp. 150-151. He further elaborates upon his purpose as intending to show what words have the same meaning, many meaning, or no meaning at all; what words are the names of other words, are merely auxiliary, or are ornamental.

17. *Ibid.*, p. 324.

18. Petty pays tribute to Boyle as one who "understand[s] the true use and signification of words, whereby to register and compute your own conceptions." See also *Advice of W. P. to Mr. Samuel Hartlib*, 1648, *Harleian Miscellany*, VI, 11-12. This materialistic conception of language finds frequent expression throughout the period, as for instance in *The Displaying of Witchcraft*, 1677, p. 21. John Webster, the author, evidently influenced by Bacon, holds that words are but the making forth of those notions that we have of things, and ought to be subjected to things, and not things to words: if our notions do not agree with the things themselves, then we have received false *Idola* or images of them."

19. *A Free Inquiry into the Vulgarly Received Notion of Nature*, written in 1666 though published twenty years later. See *Works*, ed. Birch, 1744, IV, 419.

20. *Ibid.*, IV, 365.

21. P. 113.

22. See Florian Cajori, *A History of Mathematics*, sec. ed., 1919, pp. 139, 157.

23. *Vindiciae Academiarum*, 1654, pp. 20-21.

24. *A Free and Impartial Censure of the Platonic Philosophy*, 1666, p. 61.

25. For a discussion of these schemes consult Otto Funke's *Zum Weltsprachenproblem in England im 17. Jahrhundert*; Heidelberg, 1929

(*Anglistische Forschungen*, Heft 69). Funke, however, fails to mention Henry Edmunson's *Lingua Linguarum*, 1658, and Samuel Hartlib's *Common Writing*, 1647, the latter antedating by several years the earliest work he discusses. Bacon (*Advancement of Learning*, Bk. vi, chap. 1) did much to stimulate interest in the matter. See Funke, *op. cit.*, pp. 1 ff; Wilkins, *Essay towards a Real Character*, 1668, p. 13; Edmunson, *Lingua Linguarum*, 1658, Dedication; John Webster, *Academiarum Examen*, 1653, pp. 24-5; Cave Beck, *Universal Character*, 1657, "To the Reader," and prefatory poem signed by Jos. Waite.

26. *Vindiciae Academiarum*, pp. 20-21. Boyle had expressed the same idea in a letter to Hartlib dated March 19, 1647: "If the design of the *Real Character* take effect, it will in some part make amends to mankind for what their pride lost them at the tower of *Babel*. And truly since our arithmetical characters are understood by all the nations of *Europe*, though every several people express that comprehension with its own particular language, I conceive no impossibility, that opposes the doing that in words, that we see already done in numbers." *Works*, ed. Birch, I, 22.

27. *Loc. cit.* It is worthy of note that one of the early attempts to construct a universal language advocated the substitution of numbers for letters and syllables. See Cave Beck's *Universal Character*, 1657.

28. *Loc. cit.* John Wallis, a co-worker of Ward's in mathematics and the new science, was somewhat dubious of the practicability of such a language. See *Defence of the Royal Society*, 1678, pp. 16-17. It is beside our purpose to enter into a discussion of the speculations regarding the language Adam spoke in the Garden of Eden, and the names he gave things, which was considered the "natural language," except to say that Ward was not the only one to associate a universal character with this language. See John Webster, *Academiarum Examen*, pp. 18-32.

29. As early as 1638 John Wilkins held that a universal language would "mightily conduce to the spreading and promoting of all Arts and Sciences: Because that great part of our Time which is now required to the Learning of Words, might then be employed in the Study of Things." *Mercury*, 3rd ed., 1707, pp. 55-56.

30. Cave Beck, *Universal Character*, 1657, "To the Reader."

31. Dalgarno paid particular tribute to Ward and Wilkins for assistance rendered. See Funke, *op. cit.*, p. 46. It is interesting to note that Ward, Wallis, and Wilkins were all mathematicians.

32. Quoted in Funke, *op. cit.*, p. 16.

33. Pp. 17-18. Boyle believed that such a design as he was promoting "would exceedingly abbreviate the number of words, prevent much circumlocution, contribute to perspicuity and distinction, and very

much promote the elegance and significancy of speech. (P. 319.) As noted on an earlier page, he discusses at length the imperfections of language, especially Latin, and claims that his invented symbols remove all such defects. (Pp. 443 ff.)

34. In the use of lines and dots Wilkins had been anticipated many years by Samuel Hartlib's *Common Writing*, 1647. Hartlib, however, was only intent on devising a character for international use; he was not concerned with making the symbol display the nature of the thing.

35. The scientists, it is true, influenced largely by the French Academy, were concerned with the improvement of the English language. But it must be noted that they considered such an undertaking much inferior to the true goal of the Royal Society. Sprat devotes several pages to the matter, advocating a society to "set a mark on ill Words; correct those, which are to be retained; admit and establish the good; and make some emendations in the Accent, and Grammar." But he considered such a design of less moment than experimental philosophy. The Royal Society did appoint a committee to reform the mother tongue, but after a few meetings the project came to nought. Even while advocating, largely under the influence of the French, this linguistic undertaking, they were careful to emphasize its inferiority to the more important scientific movement. In the dedication to his *Essay* Wilkins says, "Now if those famous Assemblies [Academia de la Crusca and French Academy] consisting of the great Wits of their Age and Nations, did judge this work of Dictionary-making, for the polishing of their Language, worthy of their united labour and studies; certainly then, the Design here proposed [universal character] ought not to be thought unworthy of such assistance; it being as much to be preferred before that, as *things* are better than *words*, as *real knowledge* is beyond *elegancy of speech*, as the *general good of* mankind, is beyond that of any *particular Countrey* or *Nation*."

36. See *PMLA*, xlv, 1004-1006. I do not wish in any way to depreciate Professor Croll's very valuable articles, which have thrown much light on English prose of the first half of the seventeenth century. I think, however, that he has tried to comprehend too many phenomena within the limits of his theory, with the result that many contradictions have arisen, which are hard to explain away.

37. See *Philological Quarterly*, x, 184-185.

38. It seems hardly conceivable to me that the same spirit or movement which inspired the style of Browne, who is considered a thoroughgoing Anti-Ciceronian, should have incited the scientists to attack that style. Can we believe that when Glanvill, coming under the influence of the Royal Society, apologized for his earlier imitation of

Browne's manner of expression, he was moved by the same spirit that had prompted him to adopt it? That his later prose should reveal some of Browne's characteristics is not surprising. It is hardly to be expected that any revision could have eradicated every vestige of his earlier model.

39. "The Attack on Pulpit Eloquence in the Restoration," *Jour. Eng. Ger. Philol.*, xxx, 188-217.

40. *Ibid.*, xxx, 205-206.

41. Boyle expressed almost every stylistic view known to his age. I have already indicated my intention of publishing an article on him (*Jour. Eng. Ger. Philol.*, xxx, 190). Unfortunately the particular edition of Bacon's works to which Crane refers is not accessible to me; so I am not sure what passages he has in mind. Though Bacon lies outside of the field I am treating, and though in places he expresses stylistic views quite different from those of his followers, in other passages he anticipates their attitude. The chapter in which he formally discusses rhetoric (*Advancement of Learning*, vi, 3) reveals no stylistic classifications, but it does reveal an appreciation of rhetoric which the experimentalists of the mid-century could hardly have approved. In fact, Sprat, in his attack on rhetorical devices (*Hist. of the Roy. Soc.*, 111-113) seems to be answering this very chapter.

42. Toward the end of his life Glanvill weakened in his stand for a plain style in the pulpit, and Barrow would permit rhetoric in sermons as a last resort.

43. In describing the growth of Ciceronianism Bacon says, "Then grew the flowing and watery vein of Osorius, the Portugal bishop, to be in price. Then did Sturmius spend such infinite and curious pains upon Cicero the orator and Hermogenes the rhetorician." *Works*, ed. Spedding, Ellis, and Heath, London, 1887, iii, 283.

GEORGE WILLIAMSON

✍

Senecan Style in the Seventeenth Century

As the reign of Elizabeth drew to a close, English prose style yielded
to the pressure of a new movement. The Ciceronian movement had
no sooner reached its climax in the formal periods of Hooker than the
Anti-Ciceronian movement found a leader in Bacon, whose terse
manner of expression became the hall-mark of style among the later
essay and character writers. In 1610 Bacon wrote to Tobie Matthew:
"They tell me my Latin is turn'd Silver, and become current." By this
time his English had, in fact, taken on a Silver-Latin style and become current among the Senecan essayists. Even Polonius was a
Senecan in theory when he observed that "brevity is the soul of wit,"
and in practice when he recognized Hamlet's "points" by remarking,
"How pregnant sometimes his replies are!" But since this is reading
into Bacon and Shakespeare more than either intended, we may well
ask to what extent the English seventeenth century was critically
aware of the Senecan style.[1] To gather evidence of such awareness,
either in the theory or in the criticism of rhetoric, will be the object
of this essay.

Francis Thompson, who was sensitive to Renaissance style, recognized Silver-Latin imitation in Browne:

> Browne was more idiomatic in structure than the Ciceronian
> Hooker. But the admirable knitting of his sentences was not

From *Philological Quarterly*, XV (1936), pp. 321-351. Reprinted by permission of the University of Iowa.

due merely to a better study of English idiom. He was steeped
in classic models more compact and pregnant than Cicero. Like
his French contemporaries, he was influenced by the great Latin
rhetoricians, Lucan, Ovid, and Seneca; whose rivalry it was to
put an idea into the fewest possible words.[2]

Elsewhere I have dealt with other aspects of the Jacobean cultivation
of Silver-Latin style: on the one hand, with the antithetic wit that
was associated with the terse Senecan style;[3] on the other, with the
development of a cult of obscurity which produced "strong lines" after
the example of Persius and Tacitus.[4] When brevity was the soul of
wit, the points of wit often became so pregnant that "significant darkness" or "strong lines" were the result. In short, in Jacobean times the
cult of brevity in Seneca was not unnaturally associated with the cult
of obscurity in Tacitus. Enigmatic or cryptic expression, which both
Chapman and Bacon allow, reached its extreme development in the
poetry of this time under the form known as "strong lines."

At the close of the seventeenth century Shaftesbury felt that the
Senecan style still prevailed, at least so far as the essayists were con-
cerned. The prevailing style, in Shaftesbury's view, derived from the
Epistles of Seneca:

> He falls into the random way of miscellaneous writing, says
> everywhere great and noble things, in and out of the way, ac-
> cidentally as words lead him (for with these he plays perpetu-
> ally), with infinite wit, but with little or no coherence, without
> a shape or body to his work, without a real beginning, a middle,
> or an end.[5]

The great and noble things, word-play, and wit concern Shaftesbury
less than Seneca's violation of unity and coherence. He remarks that
whole letters or pages may be divided or combined at pleasure; "every
period, every sentence almost, is independent, and may be taken asunder, transposed, postponed, anticipated, or set in any new order, as
you fancy." After this analysis of Seneca, Shaftesbury turns to his
own time:

> This is the manner of writing so much admired and imitated
> in our age, that we have scarce the idea of any other model.
> We know little, indeed, of the difference between one model or

character of writing and another. All runs to the same tune, and
beats exactly one and the same measure. Nothing, one would
think, could be more tedious than this uniform pace. The common amble or *canterbury* is not, I am persuaded, more tiresome
to a good rider than this see-saw of essay writers is to an able
reader.[6]

Thus Shaftesbury disparages the style which not only clothed the
work of the aphoristic essayists and character-writers, but corre-
sponded to the Jacobean taste for mingled wit and *gravitas*. He is not
struck by the aspect of this style which Professor Croll has analyzed
acutely:

A prose-style that should adequately express this age must
contrive, therefore, to mingle elements that in any other period
would appear oddly contrasted. It must be at once ingenious
and lofty, intense yet also profound, acute, realistic, revealing,
but at the same time somewhat grave and mysterious.[7]

Professor Croll, however, holds that Bacon naturalized such a style
in English by imitating Tacitus rather than Seneca. But since Shaftesbury is not unaware that Seneca combined wit and gravity, we may
leave the problem of discriminating between Senecan and Tacitean
imitation to the testimony of the time.

Three tendencies of Anti-Ciceronian style have been associated by
Profesor Croll with three important names: the *curt* with Lipsius,
the *loose* with Montaigne, and the *obscure* with Bacon. The curt and
the loose tendencies, as Professor Croll observes, were both Senecan
in pattern; but the curt and the obscure tendencies, which he is
anxious to discriminate, were commonly confused in seventeenth-
century Senecanism. And this is not unnatural, since the peculiar
quality of Tacitus is brevity pushed to the verge of obscurity; moreover, his style offers more likeness than difference when compared
with "Seneca's own style—disconnected, pointed, antithetic, metaphorical and piquant."[8] Both differed from Cicero's polished and flowing amplitude chiefly in the abrupt terseness and jerky movement of
their sentences. For English criticism, therefore, it will be erring on
the right side to regard Senecan style in its most obvious character—
as the cultivation of sententious brevity and all the qualities that go
with rhetorical *sententiae*. In general, the curt Senecan style is marked

by a cultivation of brevity, gravity, and point in the essay manner; its rhythm is jerky and abrupt; in particular, the Tacitean variety is an extreme development of this style. For both Seneca and Tacitus brevity meant Sallust, and in the seventeenth century all three were distinguished for similar qualities. To the curt Senecan style our investigation will be restricted, since the English writers of this period were much less conscious of the loose Senecan style, though here and there that also may be noticed.

It is necessary to remark, however, that the curt style was generally supplemented or relieved by the loose style. The two were commonly intermingled in the expression of Bacon or Browne. Both styles have been carefully analyzed by Professor Croll in "The Baroque Style in Prose," where he has summarized them as "the concise, serried, abrupt *stile coupé,* and the informal, meditative, and 'natural' loose style":

> It is necessary to repeat—once more—that in the best writers these two styles do not appear separately in passages of any length, and that in most of them they intermingle in relations far too complex for description. They represent two sides of the seventeenth-century mind: its sententiousness, its penetrating wit, its Stoic intensity, on the one hand, and its dislike of formalism, its roving and self-exploring curiosity, in brief, its skeptical tendency, on the other. And these two habits of mind are generally not separated one from the other; nor are they even always exactly distinguishable.[9]

The loose style was the more natural, and the curt style the more artful, for it did have to make its "points" show. While the loose period may suggest the Ciceronian, it avoids or breaks the *concinnitas* or symmetry of structure of Cicero; while it may adumbrate a Latin mould, it follows a more organic order of thought. The curt style preempts attention before the Restoration, and the loose style predominates after, but both forms prepare the way for modern English prose. The separation or opposition of the curt style and the loose style distinguishes the Restoration from the first half of the century.

I

The rise of the Anti-Ciceronian cult which marks the seventeenth century has been traced by Professor Croll to Muretus,[10] and its dissemination to Lipsius, Montaigne, and Bacon. What these men discovered in Seneca and Tacitus, or disliked in Cicero, characterized the new taste in style—a taste that ran to the essay style rather than to the oratorical. In 1580 Muretus had defended Tacitus by going so far as to praise his obscurity and asperity of style. The passage which Professor Croll has quoted from this excellent appraisal of Tacitus found its way into late seventeenth-century English from the work of La Mothe Le Vayer:

> Howsoever it be, it is no wonder if *Tacitus* (having imitated *Thucydides,* and both followed *Demosthenes*) retained something of that roughness and austerity, which is observed in the writings of those Two *Graecians;* and which all the Ancients accounted as a virtue, so far is it from deserving to be imputed as a fault, to him that should propose them to himself for imitation. And as some Wines are recommended to our palates by a little bitterness that is in them; and as many persons find that a dusky and obscure light in Churches is most sutable to their exercise of devotion: so others conceive the obscurity of an Author, mixed with a little roughness of Stile, is rather to be esteemed than otherwise; because it disposes the mind to attention, and elevates and transports it to notions, which it would not arrive at in a more easy composition.[11]

Muretus, as Professor Croll remarks, "stirs the ground about the roots of seventeenth-century style"; for the Jacobean cult of obscurity shares this doctrine with him.

Lipsius first employed the Anti-Ciceronian style in his *Quaestiones Epistolicae,* which appeared just before his edition of Tacitus. The character of his new style is best described by Lipsius himself in a letter to a friend:

> I am afraid of what you will think of this work [the *Quaestiones*]. For this is a different kind of writing from my earlier style, without showiness, without luxuriance, without the Tullian concinnities; condensed everywhere, and I know not whether of too studied a brevity. But this is what captivates me now. They celebrate Timanthes the painter because there was always something more to be understood in his works than was actually painted. I should like this in my style.[12]

Professor Croll remarks that both the critical terms and the style of this passage come from Seneca, but it would be hard to show that the stylistic direction differs from that which Muretus discovered in Tacitus. Although Lipsius, as a Stoic, was eventually associated with the point and brevity of Seneca, he began by admiring the dark implications and studied ellipses of Tacitus. There is one kind of brevity which Seneca disparaged and which was more often associated with Tacitus, and that is obscurity, *obscura brevitas*. Seneca approved *"abruptae sententiae et suspiciosae,"* or (in Lodge's words) "abrupt Sentences and suspicious, in which more is to be understood than heard," so long as they were not carried to the point of obscurity. Although Seneca did not allow *copia* or superfluity, he did allow fluency, because it was unlabored and because it revealed personality.[13] In fact, to him *fundere* meant to avoid affected and labored composition, and to achieve the naturalness which he desired, but which was not without artifice.[14] It was this side of Seneca that encouraged the loose style at the same time that his cultivation of *sententiae* stimulated the curt style.

The difficulty of discriminating between Senecan and Tacitean imitation may be suggested by a contemporary criticism of the neo-stoic Lipsius. In Boccalini's *Ragguagli di Parnasso,* first translated into English in 1626, Lipsius is brought before Apollo for his idolatry of Tacitus, and Muretus is one of those who jealously indict him as follows:

> Hee now loved to discourse with no other learned man: no conversation did more agrade him: he commended no other *Historian:* and all with such partiality of inward affection, namely, for the elegancie of his speech, adorned more with choise conceits, than with words; for the succinctnesse of his close, nervous, and grave sententious Oratorie, cleare onely to those of best understanding, with the envy and hatred of other vertuous men of this dominion, dependents of *Cicero,* and of the mighty *Caesarean faction,* who approve it not. And did with such diligence labour to imitate him, that not onely with hatefull antonomasia, hee dared to call him his Auctor, but utterly scorning all other mens detections, he affected no other ambition, than to appeare unto the world a new *Tacitus.*[15]

However, Lipsius "is in the end by his *Maiestie* [Apollo], not only absolved, but highly commended and admired." In this trial Lipsius,

the great Neo-Stoic, is specifically a Tacitean, but generally an Anti-
Ciceronian. If we were to distinguish Lipsius the Tacitean from Lipsius the Senecan, we should have to distinguish where the seventeenth century often confused; furthermore, as a Tacitean he could
find merit in obscurity, as a Senecan he might condone word-play.
Lipsius was the standard-bearer of Senecan style, but if his Anti-
Ciceronian taste culminated in an edition of Seneca (1605) it had
begun with an edition of Tacitus (1574).

In 1591 the first English translation of Tacitus, the work of Sir
Henry Savile, was recommended to the reader by Anthony Bacon in
these words:

> For Tacitus I may say without partiality, that hee hath writen
> the most matter with best conceyt in fewest wordes of anie His-
> toriographer ancient or moderne. But he is harde. *Difficilia
> quae pulchra:* the second reading over will please thee more
> then the first, and the third then the second.

In the second and enlarged edition of 1598 Richard Grenewey declared in his dedication that there is in Tacitus "no woord not loaden
with matter, and as himselfe speaketh of Galba, he useth *Imperatoria
brevitate:* which although it breed difficultie, yet carrieth great gravi-
tie." Thus the words of Muretus came to partial fulfillment in recom-
mendations to the readers of Tacitus in English, who received the
sixth edition of this work in 1640.

When Thomas Lodge revised his translation of Seneca in 1620, he
apologized to the reader for his own shortcomings:

> My businesse being great, and my distractions many; the
> Authour being seriously succinct, and full of *Laconisme;* no
> wonder if in somthings my omissions may seeme such, as some
> whose iudgement is mounted aboue the Epicycle of Mercurie,
> will find matter enough to carpe at, though not to condemne.[16]

For Lodge Seneca was, above all, "laconic"; but W. R., in his eulogy
of Lodge, found other qualities to commend:

> You are his profitable Tutor, and haue instructed him to
> walke and talke in perfect English. If his matter held not still
> the Romane Majestie, I should mistake him one of Ours; he

> deliuers his mind so significantly and fitly. Surely, had hee
> chosen any other Tongue to write in, my affection thinkes, it
> had beene English; And in English, as you haue taught him in
> your Translation; you expresse him so liuely, being still the
> same Man in other garments . . . retaining still the natiue
> grauitie of his countenance. . . .[17]

Although the praise goes to Lodge, it is for catching the qualities of
Seneca, to whom Lodge becomes the *"Senec-Sybill* (or rather *Mer-
curie*) of his oraculous Discourses." And thus Seneca emerges with
qualities which are difficult to distinguish from those of Tacitus, for
he too is succinct, majestic, grave, and oraculous; moreover, Lodge's
English has taught Seneca a second native language, or so it seems
to W. R. in Jacobean days. Whatever the origin, whether in the pregnant brevity of Seneca or in the obscure brevity of Tacitus, the virtue
of difficulty suggested gravity of style to Anti-Ciceronian ears; weight
rather than *copia* now translated the Roman majesty.

While there is evidence for saying that gravity and obscurity were
more commonly associated with Tacitus, and point and ingenuity
with Seneca, these qualities are not very certain differentia for writers
who were celebrated for their succinctness. It is well to remember
such differentia, but it is more historical to accept the general identity
of the two styles as Anti-Ciceronian or fundamentally Senecan in
character. In Hakewill's *Apologie or Declaration of the Power and
Providence of God*, first published in 1627, we find important confirmation of such a view:

> Sr *Henry Savill* sharply censures [Tacitus] for his style, tak-
> ing occasion from those words in the life of *Agricola, bonum
> virum facile crederes magnum libenter: at te* (saith he) *Corneli
> Tacite bonum historicum facile credimus, bonum oratorem
> crederemus libenter,* were it not for this & some other sayings
> of the like making: *Fuit illi viro,* saith Tacitus, (judging of
> *Seneca* as we may of him) *ingenium amaenum,* & *temporibus
> illius auribus accommodatum:* How that age was eared long or
> round I cannot define, but sure I am it yeelded a kinde of so-
> phisticate eloquence and riming harmony of words; where-
> under was *small matter* in sense, when there seemed to be most
> in appearance, and divers instances he brings out of *Taci-
> tus.* . . .[18]

These very interesting remarks, involving the first English translator of Tacitus, are essentially Bacon's indictment of the Senecan fashion, which we shall consider in due course. But this turning of the tables upon Tacitus, to which Hakewill subscribes, emphasizes the resemblance (even in vices) between Seneca and Tacitus as they sounded to English ears.

II

Seneca, when he spoke of style, always preferred things to words—a preference which the seventeenth century remembered to his credit. And Bacon was the first to sound the seventeenth-century preference for things rather than words. That is the burden of his attack on Ciceronian style in 1605, when he condemns the Ciceronians for hunting "more after the choiceness of the phrase, and the round and clean composition of the sentence, and the sweet falling of the clauses . . . than after the weight of matter."[19] This Renaissance delight in style—"the whole inclination and bent of those times was rather towards copie than weight"—was furthered by hatred of the schoolmen, "whose writings were altogether in a differing style and form." Bacon admits the need to clothe philosophy in eloquence for civil occasions, but believes that "to the severe inquisition of truth, and the deep progress into philosophy" such a dress offers some hindrance, for it gives a premature satisfaction to the mind and quenches the desire of further search.[20]

The question of "vain words" leads Bacon to "vain matter," or the second distemper of learning, under which he attacks the schoolmen for crumbling knowledge into subtle distinctions and "vermiculate questions." Their unprofitable subtlety expressed itself in two ways: in fruitless matter and in a fruitless method of handling knowledge, splitting the "cummin seed"; "whereas indeed the strength of all sciences is, as the strength of the old man's faggot, in the bond."

> For the harmony of a science, supporting each part the other, is and ought to be the true and brief confutation and suppression of all the smaller sort of objections; but on the other side, if you take out every axiom, as the sticks of the faggot, one by one, you may quarrel with them and bend them and break them at your pleasure: so that as was said of Seneca, *Verborum minutiis rerum frangit pondera* [that he broke up the weight

and mass of the matter by verbal points and niceties]; so a man may truly say of the schoolmen, *Quaestionum minutiis scientiarum frangunt soliditatem* [they broke up the solidity and coherency of the sciences by the minuteness and nicety of their questions].[21]

And thus Quintilian's criticism of Seneca, slightly misquoted, is turned by Bacon into a criticism of the schoolmen. It might be concluded that a Senecan style would make a fitting dress for a scholastic habit of mind, and we shall have occasion to recall the suggestion. But for the present this must remain a criticism of the schoolmen rather than of Seneca.

In this connection we may wonder a little at what Bacon has to say of aphorisms, especially when we remember that he certainly knew Seneca as a master of *sententiae,* at which Quintilian had directed his criticism. Bacon's theory of the communication of knowledge is vital to his criticism of style, and revolves about the question of methods. The most real diversity of method concerns method as related to the use of knowledge and method as related to the progress of knowledge, or the delivery of knowledge as it may be best believed (the Magistral way), and as it may be best examined (the way of Probation).[22] Since knowledge is now delivered as it may be best believed, not as it may be best examined, "there is a kind of contract of error between the deliverer and the receiver," because "in this same anticipated and prevented knowledge, no man knoweth how he came to the knowledge which he hath obtained." This is the way of rhetoric and the oratorical style; the way of the essay style is quite different, for "knowledge that is delivered as a thread to be spun on, ought to be delivered and intimated, if it were possible, *in the same method wherein it was invented;* and so is it possible of knowledge induced."[23] Here we have the philosophy which underlies the organic method of the "loose" period found in the way of Probation; in the Magistral way, which merely announces the results of inquiry, one cannot see the thought grow.

This brings us to another diversity of great consequence—"the delivery of knowledge in Aphorisms, or in Methods." Here Bacon begins by condemning the practice of spinning a few axioms or observations into a solemn and formal art; "but the writing in Aphorisms hath many excellent virtues, whereto the writing in Method doth not approach."

For first, it trieth the writer, whether he be superficial or
solid: for Aphorisms, except they should be ridiculous, cannot
be made but of the pith and heart of sciences; for discourse of
illustration is cut off; recitals of examples are cut off; discourse
of connection and order is cut off; descriptions of practice are
cut off; so there remaineth nothing to fill the Aphorisms but
some good quantity of observation: and therefore no man can
suffice, nor in reason will attempt, to write aphorisms, but he
that is sound and grounded. But in Methods,

> Tantum series juncturaque pollet,
> Tantum de medio sumptis accedit honoris

[the arrangement and connexion and joining of the parts has
so much effect], as a man shall make a great shew of an art,
which if it were disjointed would come to little. Secondly,
Methods are more fit to win consent or belief, but less fit to
point to action; for they carry a kind of demonstration in orb
or circle, one part illuminating another, and therefore satisfy;
but particulars, being dispersed, do best agree with dispersed
directions. And lastly, Aphorisms, representing a knowledge
broken, do invite men to enquire farther; whereas Methods,
carrying the shew of a total, do secure men, as if they were at
furthest.[24]

If we recall the passage on the schoolmen, we must conclude that the
vice of the schoolmen becomes a virtue in the realm of style; that
aphorisms, which must be filled with "some good quantity of observation," belong to the method of inducing knowledge; and that a Senecan style represents a knowledge broken, and therefore avoids the
"contract of error between the deliverer and the receiver." Here methods present knowledge as it may be best believed, and aphorisms as it
may be best examined, with a view to further inquiry. They are different styles for different purposes, and so Bacon used them. But the
method of probation is not the same as Methods of persuasion; rather,
it belongs, with Aphorisms, to induction and the Senecan style.

Bacon wrote his severest philosophical work, the *Novum Organum,*
in Aphorisms; but he clothed his popular *Advancement of Learning*
in the rhetoric of persuasion or Methods. And yet it would be a mistake to say that "discourse of illustration," "discourse of connection

and order," and "descriptions of practice" are always cut off in the
former and never in the latter. The habit of aphorism and the urge
to persuade were too strong in Bacon to permit single-minded devotion to one manner of expression. The chief exception to this judgment is, of course, his early essays. They provide the best illustration
of the aphorism in which his thought seems commonly to have been
formulated. His change of style in the *Essays* reflects not so much a
growing disapproval of Senecan style as a change from aphorisms to
methods for a particular purpose. In this instance the change seems to
have derived from his meditation on the function of rhetoric in connection with the Stoic method in moral counsel. In the *Advancement
of Learning* Bacon defends rhetoric by saying that virtue must be
shown "to the Imagination in lively representation":

> for to shew her to Reason only in subtilty of argument, was a
> thing ever derided in Chrysippus and many of the Stoics; who
> thought to thrust virtue upon men by sharp disputations and
> conclusions, which have no sympathy with the will of man.[25]

But in the *De Augmentis Scientiarum* he declares more specifically
that virtue must be shown "to the imagination in as lively representation as possible, by ornament of words":

> For the method of the Stoics, who thought to thrust virtue
> upon men by concise and sharp maxims and conclusions, which
> have little sympathy with the imagination and will of man,
> has been justly ridiculed by Cicero.[26]

In 1623, then, Bacon condemns the method of the Stoics in moral
counsel expressly because aphorisms have little imaginative appeal;
then, having detected another vanity in the Senecan style, he agrees
with Cicero in ridiculing the Stoic method in moral essays. That this
objection was not so sharply defined for Bacon in 1605 or even in
1612 seems the plain inference from the change in his essay style,
since that change really does not appear until the 1625 edition. The
difference between the parallel essays of 1597 and 1612 is chiefly one
of slight revision or addition; it is not so striking as the difference between the parallel essays of 1612 and 1625, for the latter can truly be
said to be revised and even rewritten from the point of view of Methods.[27] Only in 1625 does the aphoristic character of the *Essays* appear

seriously modified, if not forsaken. Aphorisms, Bacon seems to have concluded, are appropriate to philosophy or science because they "invite men to enquire farther"; they are permissible to "dispersed meditations" (his early essays) because they give "dispersed directions"; but Methods are more appropriate to moral essays because "methods are more fit to win consent or belief."

If the *Advancement of Learning* contained the seed of disapproval of Senecan style, the *De Augmentis Scientiarum* brought the full-grown plant. After his condemnation of the Ciceronian style, Bacon now adds this criticism:

> Litle better is that kind of stile (yet neither is that altogether exempt from vanity) which neer about the same time succeeded this *Copy* and *superfluity of speech.* The labour here is altogether, *That words may be aculeate, sentences concise, and the whole contexture of the speech and discourse, rather rounding into it selfe, than spread and dilated:* So that it comes to passe by this Artifice, that every passage seemes more witty and waighty than indeed it is. Such a stile as this we finde more excessively in *Seneca;* more moderately in *Tacitus* and *Plinius Secundus;* and of late it hath bin very pleasing unto the eares of our time. And this kind of expression hath found such acceptance with meaner capacities, as to be a dignity and ornament to Learning; neverthelesse, by the more exact judgements, it hath bin deservedly dispised, and may be set down *as a distemper of Learning,* seeing it is nothing else but a hunting after words, and fine placing of them.[28]

One of "the more exact judgements," as we have seen, was Sir Henry Savile; the "meaner capacities" with whom this kind of expression had found such favor were, as we know, actually the Senecan essayists and character-writers for whom Bacon had set the example. Perhaps Bacon only perceived the dangers of his own style when it fell into the hands of meaner talents; at any rate, he could not be charged with the "vanity" of it, which is what he really condemns after all. Since he prized above all "weight of matter," it is not surprising that he should condemn his own style when it merely disguised the lack of weight. But to be weighty in his day it was necessary to be Senecan, and Bacon moderated rather than deserted his own Senecanism.

III

The greatest vanity of Senecan style, however, appeared in the sermons of Bacon's friend, Bishop Lancelot Andrewes. As we have already observed, Bacon suggested (perhaps unintentionally) the propriety of Senecan style to the scholastic mind: "as was said of Seneca, *Verborum minutiis rerum frangit pondera;* so a man may truly say of the schoolmen, *Quaestionum minutiis scientiarum frangunt soliditatem.*" Bacon fell upon the schoolmen's "digladiation about subtilities," since all their thirst for truth proved only "fierce with dark keeping"; "in the inquiry of the divine truth their pride inclined to leave the oracle of God's word and to vanish in the mixture of their own inventions."[29] The same charges were brought against preachers like Andrewes. Bacon also remarked that in contrast to the Ciceronian the scholastic "writings were altogether in a differing style and form; taking liberty to coin and frame new terms of art to express their own sense and to avoid circuit of speech, without regard to the pureness, pleasantness, and (as I may call it) lawfulness of the phrase or word."[30] In short, the schoolmen were guilty of Senecan faults when compared with the Ciceronians. Bacon's remarks on the schoolmen contain suggestions of two charges later brought against Andrewes's sermon style; both charges have a curious relevance to Quintilian's criticism that Seneca broke the weight of his matter by cultivating *sententiae.* One of these charges relates to Andrewes's practice of "division," of "crumbling" his text; and the other to his "wit" or levity in serious matters.[31] These two aspects of *"rerum pondera minutissimis sententiis fregit"* are implied in Quintilian on Seneca;[32] they suggest the propriety of the Senecan style to the scholastic mind.

Both Andrewes and Donne were not only scholastic but also Senecan in their traits of style; they were both greatly influenced by the church fathers who had a Senecan bent, such as Tertullian.[33] The most striking trait of "metaphysical" style, which has a close affinity to the Senecan, is the teasing out of ideas and figures so as to reveal their ambiguous, antithetic, or paradoxical aspects. This is present in Andrewes when he crumbles a text to pieces; it finds a place in the criticism which Dr. Johnson directed against the "metaphysical poets"; and it is not absent from the work of the character-writers. Senecan brevity, abruptness, and point characterize the sentences of Andrewes, and affect those of Donne, though less obviously. The stylistic aims once expressed by Donne are clearly Senecan:

. . . with such succinctness and brevity, as may consist with
clearness, and perspicuity, in such manner, and method, as may
best enlighten your understandings, and least encumber your
memories, I shall open unto you [the meaning of the text].[34]

In 1710 Steele remembers Donne in connection with such aims. Having remarked that Boccalini sentences a laconic writer, for using three
words where two would have served, to read all the works of Guicciardini, Steel comments:

This Guicciardini is so very prolix and circumstantial in his
writings, that I remember our countryman, doctor Donne,
speaking of that majestic and concise manner in which Moses
has described the creation of the world, adds, 'that if such an
author as Guicciardini were to have written on such a subject,
the world itself would not have been able to have contained the
books that gave the history of its creation.'[35]

The "majestic and concise manner" is as brief a formulation of Jacobean ideals as one could find; only the wit is wanting.
  But before the death of George Herbert the "wit" and "division" of
Andrewes, which have their analogues in Seneca, had begun to pro-
voke criticism. For his "country parson" Herbert prescribes another
style and method:

The parson's method in handling of a text, consists of two
parts: first, a plain and evident declaration of the meaning of
the text; and secondly, some choice observations drawn out of
the whole text, as it lies entire, and unbroken in the Scripture
itself. This he thinks natural, and sweet, and grave. Whereas
the other way of crumbling a text into small parts, as, the person speaking, or spoken to, the subject, and object, and the like,
hath neither in it sweetness, nor gravity, nor variety, since the
words apart are not Scripture, but a Dictionary, and may be
considered alike in all the Scripture.[36]

Thus Herbert anticipates the method of Tillotson and condemns that
of Andrewes, in which Donne was a lesser offender. Herbert begins
his criticism of "witty" preaching in these significant words:

By these and other means the parson procures attention; but the character of his sermon is holiness; he is not witty, or learned, or eloquent, but holy. A character, that *Hermogenes* never dreamed of, and therefore he could give no precept thereof.[37]

But while Herbert deplores the wit he reveals the profit to be derived from Senecan brevity. Of course Senecan wit was not "metaphysical" wit, but Seneca provided the chief classical model of a witty prose style.

By the time of Robert South there was something like a general disapproval of the witty preaching represented by Andrewes. At the same time that South cultivates the Senecan qualities which pass into Restoration style, he succumbs to some of the wit that he condemns in Andrewes or disparages by association with Seneca. In *The Scribe Instructed,* preached in 1660, South administers severe reproof to two kinds of preaching: that which sponsors "a puerile and indecent sort of levity," and that which follows a "mean, heavy, careless, and insipid way of handling things sacred," or the manner of the school of Andrewes and that of the Puritans. Of the former he declares:

> What Quintilian most discreetly says of Seneca's handling philosophy, that he did *rerum pondera minutissimis sententiis frangere,* break, and, as it were, emasculate the weight of his subject by little affected sentences, the same may with much more reason be applied to the practice of those, who detract from the excellency of things sacred by a comical lightness of expression: as when their prayers shall be set out in such dress, as if they did not supplicate, but compliment Almighty God; and their sermons so garnished with quibbles and trifles, as if they played with truth and immortality; and neither believed these things themselves, nor were willing that others should.[38]

Quintilian speaks to South even more pertinently about the wit of Andrewes than about that of Seneca, and South finds Quintilian relevant to the practice of "division":

> Such are wholly mistaken in the nature of wit: for true wit is a severe and manly thing. Wit in divinity is nothing else, but sacred truths suitably expressed. It is not shreds of Latin or

Greek, nor a *Deus dixit,* and a *Deus benedixit,* nor those little
quirks, or divisions into the ὅτι, the διότι, and the καθότι, or
the *egress, regress,* and *progress,* and other such stuff, (much
like the style of a lease,) that can properly be called wit. For
that is not wit which consists not with wisdom.[39]

South is here purging the Senecan or "differing" sermon style of its
"levity"—in both of the senses in which Quintilian suggested that it
was an enemy to *gravitas.* The standards by which South reproves this
wit are obviously Restoration.

But it would be a mistake to conclude that South was not Senecan
in style, or that his ideals of style were not definitely Senecan, in the
better sense of brevity and plainness rather than "point." No one can
overlook his clearly Senecan requirements for style in *A Discourse
against Long and Extempore Prayers.*[40] His thoroughly Baconian
view and an epitome of Jacobean stylistic ambitions find expression
in one short paragraph:

In fine, brevity and succinctness of speech is that, which, in
philosophy or speculation, we call *maxim,* and first principle;
in the counsels and resolves of practical wisdom, and the deep
mysteries of religion, *oracle;* and lastly, in matters of wit, and
the finenesses of imagination, *epigram.* All of them, severally
and in their kinds, the greatest and the noblest things that the
mind of man can shew the force and dexterity of its faculties
in.[41]

Here we are reminded of the advantage of "aphorisms" over "methods," and we should not forget that "oracle" and "epigram" led into
"strong lines." It is significant that in condemning the "vanity" of the
school of Andrewes, South confuses the "metaphysical" and "Senecan"
aspects of their levity; it is not less significant that he himself remains
stoutly Senecan in the plainer fashion of Bishop Hall.

Before we return to the secular prose, we should recall that clearness or perspicuity is not a trustworthy guide to the ideals or affinities
of styles, since perspicuity is the constant of language as a vehicle of
communication. It is rather the variants, or the qualities associated
with perspicuity, that give styles their peculiar character. Thus when
John Hughes tells us, in his essay *Of Style,* that the qualifications of
a good style are propriety, perspicuity, elegance, and cadence, it is the

propriety, elegance, and cadence that are significant. When Ben Jonson likewise names perspicuity, but in connection with other qualities, it is the other qualities that differentiate the ideals of Jonson from those of Hughes; the difference will tell us much of the evolution of style between Jonson and Hughes. Of course an emphasis upon brevity endangers perspicuity, and obscurity flies in the face of this constant of language; otherwise, the presence or absence of that constant is not in itself very significant. With this reminder, we may return to the seventeenth-century awareness of Senecan style in secular prose.

IV

Both Seneca and Tacitus were great favorites of the first half of the seventeenth century. Seneca appealed as a moralist who could put even the Christian to shame, and Tacitus rivaled Machiavelli for shrewd political wisdom. As Jonson's "New Cry" puts it, Tacitus appealed to "ripe statesmen, ripe!":

> They carry in their pockets Tacitus,
> And the Gazetti, or Gallo-Belgicus.

One of the first essayists, Robert Johnson, finds Tacitus the perfect historian and remarks his "iudiciall, but strangelie briefe sentences."[42] Seneca and Tacitus, as we have already observed, were the Jacobean models for such sentences.

But Seneca was also a model of another sort—the kind that Burton found in him. When Burton explains his own style in "Democritus to the Reader," he comments on the difference of tastes in style: "He respects matter, thou art wholly for words, he loves a loose and free style, thou art all for neat composition, strong lines, hyperboles, allegories . . ."[43] To Burton the alternatives are the "loose" style, which respects matter, and the "neat" style; which employs strong lines; for both of which Seneca provided a model. Respecting matter rather than words, Burton calls upon Seneca to support his "extemporean style":

> Besides, it was the observation of the wise *Seneca, when you*
> *see a fellow careful about his words, and neat in his speech,*

> *know this for a certainty, that man's mind is busied about toys,*
> *there's no solidity in him. Non est ornamentum virile concin-*
> *nitas.*[44]

The seventeenth century did not forget this other side of Seneca, but
his "curt" style attracted more attention. Somewhat later a more
elaborate Latin mould engaged the attention of Browne and Milton;
it cannot be called loose in quite the same sense that Burton is loose,
for it endeavored to suggest *concinnitas.*

In 1615 when Nicholas Breton, a belated Elizabethan, wrote *Char-*
acters upon Essaies, he dedicated his work to Bacon, but it was a
feeble imitation. Nevertheless, it received significant praise in the
eulogistic verse of I. B. *"In Laudem Operis":*

> I herein finde few words, great worth involve:
> A Lipsian stile, terse Phrase. . . .

But the praise was not significant enough for a modern editor,[45] who
explains "Lipsian" by the note "lip salve, flattering speech." A "Lipsian stile, terse Phrase," refers of course to the Senecan style of Justus
Lipsius. Less flattering is another reference to Lipsian style which
appears in John Earle's character of "A selfe-conceited Man" as set
forth in 1628:

> His tenent is always singular, and aloofe from the vulgar
> as hee can, from which you must not hope to wrest him. He
> ha's an excellent humor, for an Heretique, and in these dayes
> made the first Arminian. He prefers *Ramus* before *Aristotle,*
> & *Paracelsus* before *Galen,* and whosoever with most Paradox
> is commended & *Lipsius* his hopping stile, before either *Tully* or
> *Quintilian.*[46]

In later editions the Lipsian passage is deleted. Earle must have realized either that this style had become too common to be a paradox or
that his own style made the paradox invidious. At any rate, Earle
shows us that the abrupt or "hopping" style of Lipsius was the smart
fashion as opposed to the correct Ciceronian. These two references to
Lipsius give us the cardinal features of the Senecan style as it seemed
to the seventeenth century: it was terse in phrase and abrupt in movement.

Owen Feltham, who bears the clear imprint of Baconian imitiation, speaks of style in his essay "Of Preaching," which was added to his *Resolves* in 1628. His preferences in style are plainly Senecan:

> A man can never speak too well, where he speaks not too obscure. Long and distended clauses, are both tedious to the ear, and difficult for their retaining. A sentence well couched, takes both the sense and the understanding. I love not those *cart-rope* speeches, that are longer than the memory of man can fathom. . . . The weighty lines men find upon the stage, I am persuaded, have been the lures, to draw away the pulpit-followers.[47]

Sententious but not obscure, such is the good style; apparently the pulpit had not been Senecan enough. Feltham feels that besides the advantage of action, the stage has the benefit of a "more compassed language: the *dulcia sermonis,* moulded into curious phrase." Echoing the opinion that action is "the chiefest part of an Orator," Feltham adds:

> And this is *Seneca's* opinion: Fit words are better than fine ones. I like not those that are injudiciously made, but such as be expressively significant; that lead the mind to something, besides the naked term.[48]

But judgment is necessary for depth: as "Saint *Augustine* says, *Tully* was admired more for his tongue, than his mind." And yet studied language is not altogether vain, for "he that reads the Fathers, shall find them, as if written with a crisped pen." Fit words do not preclude study, but rather enjoin it. "He prodigals a mine of excellency," says Feltham, "that lavishes a terse oration to an aproned auditory"; but if the orator must have judgment, still a terse oration was a mine of excellency to Feltham.

If we have any doubt of Feltham's Senecanism, Thomas Randolph sets it at rest. His *Conceited Peddler* (1630), which W. C. Hazlitt calls "a shrewd satire on the follies and vices of the age," makes much of "points" and of "a sovereign box of cerebrum" produced by alchemy, "the fire being blown with the long-winded blast of a Ciceronian sentence, and the whole confection boiled from a pottle to a pint in the pipkin of Seneca."[49] Of course "points" were the favorite

form of Senecan wit, and the brevity of Seneca appeared by contrast
with Ciceronian length. Randolph shows that for his age the Senecan
and the Ciceronian were the two poles between which style turned.
His verses "To Master Feltham on his book of Resolves" place Feltham accordingly: "Nor doth the cinnamon-bark deserve less praise":

> I mean, the style being pure, and strong and round;
> Not long, but pithy; being short-breath'd, but sound,
> Such as the grave, acute, wise Seneca sings—
> That best of tutors to the worst of kings.
> Not long and empty; lofty, but not proud;
> Subtle, but sweet; high, but without a cloud.
> Well-settled, full of nerves—in brief 'tis such,
> That in a little hath comprised much.[50]

Little could be added to this character of Senecan style, for such it
appeared to that age; pithy, short-breathed, grave, acute, and nervous
—such was Seneca and such Feltham. "Round," here and elsewhere,
seems to acquire an Anti-Ciceronian significance if we recall Wats's
translation of Bacon on Senecan style: "The labour here is altogether,
That words may be aculeate, sentences concise, and the whole contexture of the speech and discourse, rather rounding into it selfe, than
spread and dilated." The Senecan style was concise and "round"
rather than "spread and dilated" like the Ciceronian; in Bacon's Latin,
"oratio denique potius versa quam fusa." Jonson, following Vives,
gives a similar significance to "round":

> The next thing to the stature, is the figure and feature in
> Language: that is, whether it be round, and streight, which
> consists of short and succinct *Periods,* numerous, and polished,
> or square and firme, which is to have equall and strong parts,
> everywhere answerable, and weighed.[51]

Here "round" goes with short and succinct periods, while "square"
goes with *concinnitas* or symmetry of structure.

Jonson pauses in his *Discoveries* (1641) to condemn all the essayists,[52] but a few pages later he eulogizes Bacon:

> Yet there hapn'd, in my time, one noble *Speaker,* who was
> full of gravity in his speaking. His language (where hee could
> spare, or pass by a jest) was nobly *censorious.* No man ever

spake more neatly, more pressly, more weightily, or suffer'd
lesse emptinesse, lesse idlenesse, in what hee utter'd. No member of his speech, but consisted of his owne graces. His hearers
could not cough, or looke aside from him, without losse.[53]

Of course, Jonson is speaking of Bacon as an orator, but it was for
speaking thus "prestly" that Cicero condemned the Stoics.[54] For Jonson, however, Bacon may "stand as the mark and acme of our language," and of the style which Jonson favored.

Much of his most personal stylistic doctrine Jonson draws from
Seneca's famous *Epistles* (114, 115) and from similar matter in
Vives's *De Ratione Dicendi*. Out of Vives comes his summary of the
varieties of succinct style:

> A strict and succinct style is that, where you can take away
> nothing without losse, and that losse to be manifest. The briefe
> style is that which expresseth much in little. The concise style,
> which expresseth not enough, but leaves somewhat to bee un-
> derstood. The abrupt style, which hath many breaches, and
> doth not seeme to end, but fall.[55]

Against this passage Jonson sets the names *Tacitus, The Laconic,
Suetonius, Seneca and Fabianus;* Vives refers to Seneca for the remark that Fabianus inclines to the abrupt style but Cicero ends everything. Jonson does not borrow intact one of Vives's most Senecan
comments: *"Venustissimae sunt periodi, quae fiunt vel ex antithetis,
vel acutè concluso argumento."* While Jonson echoes Bacon's words
on Ciceronian style, he removes their sting.[56] However, when Jonson
writes on epistolary style, his remarks are thoroughly Senecan. These
remarks present his most complete statement on style, and although
apparently drawn from John Hoskins's *Directions for Speech and
Style*,[57] are parallel to the requirements laid down in the *Epistolica
Institutio* of Justus Lipsius.

In the Lipsian scheme five qualities were necessary: *brevitas, per-
spicuitas, simplicitas, venustas,* and *decentia.* These are subsumed
under four heads by Hoskins, whose statement of the Lipsian doctrine is retailed by Jonson.[58] "The first is brevity":

> *Brevity* is attained in matter, by avoiding idle Complements,
> Prefaces, Protestations, Parentheses, superfluous circuit of fig-
> ures, and digressions: In the composition, by omitting Conjunc-

tions (*Not onely; But also; Both the one, and the other, whereby
it commeth to passe*) and such like idle Particles, that have no
great business in a serious Letter, but breaking of sentences; as
often times a short journey is made long, by unnecessary baits.[59]

Remembering that Jonson on epistolary style was merely the public
voice of Hoskins, we may say that Jonson particularizes the means
by which the disjunctive or disconnected Senecan style was
achieved.[60] But he remembers that Quintilian says "there is a brief-
nesse of the parts sometimes, that makes the whole long"; and comments thus: "This is the fault of some Latine Writers, within these
last hundred years, of my reading, and perhaps *Seneca* may be ap-
peacht of it; I accuse him not."

"The next property of *Epistolarie* style is *Perspicuity*," and with
this Jonson combines "Plainenesse," which is *simplicitas* in Lipsius.
Following Lipsius, who quotes Seneca's wish that his epistles might
be *"illaboratus et facilis,"* Jonson counsels informality or "a diligent
kind of negligence." The third quality is vigor or *"Life and Quick-
ness"*; Lipsius says, *"Venustatem appello; cum sermo totus alacer,
vivus, erectus est."* Here Lipsius names and Jonson suggests the *"ar-
gutae sententiae"* of Senecan style. The last quality, the *decentia* of
Lipsius, becomes *discretio*, "respect to discerne," or propriety in Jonson. In all these matters, however, Jonson was merely repeating Hoskins, who noted with some disapproval the new tendency toward a
"sententious" or Senecan style.

But this hierarchy of stylistic qualities, with brevity heading the
list, is Senecan; and perspicuity, being a constant in communication,
is less significant than vigor, which receives a Senecan definition.
Although Jonson is given to quoting Quintilian, his own practice
shows that Senecan doctrine was more persuasive in moulding his
style.[61]

The "English Seneca," Bishop Hall, was criticized by the eighteenth century because "he abounds rather too much with antitheses
and witty turns";[62] but his Senecanism had already been criticized
by Milton. In the Smectymnuan controversy Hall referred to his own
style in his *Answer to Smectymnuus's Vindication:* "In the sequel,
my words, which were never yet taxed for an offensive superfluity,
shall be very few; and such as, to your greater wonder, I shall be be-
holden for, to my kind adversaries." While defending the authors of

Smectymnuus in his *Apology*, Milton declares that Hall's design was "with quips and snapping adages to vapour them out," and that he could not endure that they "should thus lie at the mercy of a coy flirting style; to be girded with frumps and curtal gibes, by one who makes sentences by the statute, as if all above three inches long were confiscate."[63] Although his opponent was anonymous (Hall's son?), Milton was here answering Bishop Hall directly, and criticizing his style for its Senecan traits. Milton returns to the attack in a stronger vein when he declares that the Remonstrant

> sobs me out half-a-dozen phthisical mottoes, wherever he had them, hopping short in the measure of convulsion-fits; in which labour the agony of his wit having escaped narrowly, instead of well-sized periods, he greets us with a quantity of thumb-ring posies.[64]

Milton, who believed in well-sized periods, thus condemns "Lipsius his hopping style" and "this tormentor of semicolons."

Milton's own taste comes out more clearly in a later statement about the clerks of the university who are to be ministers:

> How few among them that know to write or speak in a pure style; much less to distinguish the ideas and various kinds of style in Latin barbarous, and oft not without solecisms, declaiming in rugged and miscellaneous gear blown together by the four winds, and in their choice preferring the gay rankness of Apuleius, Arnobius, or any modern fustianist, before the native Latinisms of Cicero.[65]

Here is clear disapproval of the "modern fustianist," who was commonly an Anti-Ciceronian. In 1622 Archbishop Abbot, in a letter to All Souls College, had found fault with the general deterioration of Latin style at Oxford: "The style of your letter is somewhat abrupt and harsh, and doth rather express an affected brevity than the old Ciceronian oratory. And I am sorry to hear that this new way of writing is not only become the fault of the College, but of the University itself."[66] Likewise, to Milton the humanist a pure style meant Cicero, and neither "the knotty Africanisms, the pampered metaphors, the intricate and involved sentences of the fathers,"[67] nor the Senecan style condemned by Abbot. As a humanist Milton scorned not only those who confused "the ideas and various kinds of style in Latin barbarous," but also those who introduced Senecan style into English prose.

The Latin mould of Milton's style is so obvious that we may pause to consider the contemporary awareness of such a mould in English. In "A Discourse of Languages" Richard Flecknoe attributes the variations of English style "to the severall Inclinations and Dispositions of *Princes* and of *Times*":

> That of our *Ancestors* having been plain and simple: That of Queen *Elizabeths* dayes, *flaunting* and *pufted* like her *Apparell*: That of King *Jame's, Regis ad exemplum,* inclining much to the *Learned* and *Erudite,* as (if you observe it) in the late Kings dayes, the *Queen* having a mayne *ascendancy* and *predominance* in the Court, the *French style* with the Courtyers was chiefly in *vogue* and Fashion.[68]

Flecknoe goes on to say that the inclination of the times has corrupted their metaphors with military terms; "much of the *Chican* having likewise entred for its part, even to the *Scripture* style amongst the common *Rabble,* who are our *Rabbies* now, and *Gypsies* cant it in the *Hebrew* phrase." The consequence of all this appears in another passage:

> For the differencing of *Stiles* (to go on with this matter, since we have begun) wee may divide them into the *Vulgar,* or that of the *Time,* and the *Learned* and *Erudite:* which he, who writes for *Fame* and *lasting,* should principally affect: It bearing Translation best, being cast in the *Latine mould,* which never varies: whilst that of the Time changes perpetually, according to the various humors of the *Time.*[69]

Those who would write for posterity must now write, not in Latin, but in the learned and erudite style which is cast in the Latin mould. Since the Jacobean style was of this persuasion, we might expect that a Jacobean writer would offer a suitable model; and in the refinement of English no name stood higher than that of Bacon at this time. In 1644 the writer of *Vindex Anglicus* tells us that "the renowned Lord Bacon taught us to speak the terms of art in our own language";[70] in

1650 Dr. Walter Charleton links Browne with Bacon in the "*Carmination* or refinement of English";[71] and in 1653 S. S. (probably Samuel Sheppard) praises Bacon for being "so succinct, elaborate, and sententious" that the best foreign wits think it the highest honor to translate him into their native languages.[72] If Bacon set a popular example in his *Essays*, he set a more learned example in his *Advancement of Learning;* for his terms of art carried from Jonson to Browne, and his period supplied an Anti-Ciceronian but Latin mould for more elaborate writing.

Sir Thomas Browne seems to have been of Flecknoe's mind when he explained why he wrote the *Pseudodoxia Epidemica* in English rather than Latin, and how the "paradoxology" of his subject sometimes carried him into "expressions beyond mere English apprehensions":

> And, indeed, if elegancy still proceedeth, and English pens maintain that stream we have of late observed to flow from many, we shall, within few years, be fain to learn Latin to understand English, and a work will prove of equal facility in either. Nor have we addressed our pen or style unto the people, (whom books do not redress, and [who] are this way incapable of reduction,) but unto the knowing and leading part of learning.[73]

Thus, in Milton's time, Browne suggests that there was an unusual effort to cast English into a Latin mould, or to bring Latin terms into English, at least when a writer was not addressing the vulgar. But where Browne went to extremes in the terms of art, Milton went to extremes in the Latin mould, setting his Latin constructions against the idiom of the "loose" period in English. This more elaborate Latin mould, which suggested *concinnitas,* was the result of an effort to stem the idiomatic current of the time.

In 1654 Richard Whitlock, in his preface to *Zootomia*, declared that Plutarch's discourses most invite imitation for the form, and are not behind any for matter, *"if mixt sometimes with those* Mucrones Sermonum, Enlivening Touches *of Seneca full of* smart Fancy, solid sense *and* accurate reason." The wit of Seneca was for Whitlock still a desirable addition to the essay; but "Exactness *of writing on any* Subject *in* Poetick heights *of* Fancy, *or* Rhetoricall Descants *of* Application," he left to others:

> *For my own part I may say, as* Lipsius *in his Epistle;* Ratio-
> nem meam scribendi scire vis? fundo, non scribo, nec id nisi in
> Calore & interno quodam Impetu, haud aliter quam Poetae.
> *Would you know (saith he) my manner of writing? it is a kind
> of voluntary* Tiding of, *not* Pumping for; Notions flowing,
> *not* forced; *like* Poets unconstrained Heats *and* Raptures: *such
> is* mine, *rather a* running Discourse *than a* Grave-paced Exact-
> nes. . . .[74]

Fundere, if we remember, was the aim of Seneca's "loose" style; and
Lipsius here echoes Seneca no less than when he subscribed to the
curt style in his *Quaestiones.* But Whitlock's subscription to this aim
suggests that the loose rather than the curt style was proving congenial to the essay as the product of "a mind thinking." Informality
is the effect of this style and the aim of the personal essay.

If Whitlock suggests that the loose style is to triumph in the Restoration, Thomas Blount's *Academie of Eloquence* shows that the
curt style still has some life before it. This rhetoric, which adopts
almost in full the *Directions* of Hoskins and borrows considerably
from Bacon, ran through five editions between 1654 and 1684; in
fact, no other rhetoric of that time seems to have been quite so popular. If we examine a passage in the *Academie* on *sententiae* (borrowed with some modernization from Hoskins), we shall discover
notwithstanding that the ideal form of the curt style is seriously
threatened:

> *Sententia,* if it be well used, is a Figure; if ill and too much,
> a Style, of which none that write humorously and factiously,
> can be clear in these days, when there are so many Schismes of
> Eloquence. We study now-a-days according to the predominancy
> of Criticall fancies. Whilst *Moral Philosophy* was in request,
> it was rudeness, not to be sententious; whilst *Mathematics* were
> of late in vogue, all similitudes came from *Lines, Circles* and
> *Angles;* But now that *Mars* is predominant, we must *recruit* our
> wits, and give our words a new *Quarter.*[75]

The *sententia,* which is still acceptable as a figure, is no longer quite
approved when used so much as to make a style, although it is still
popular in certain kinds of writing. Its association with moral philosophy, and so with the moral essay, is specified. But this wariness to-

ward the pure form of the curt style does not prevent Blount, any more than it prevented Hoskins, from retailing Senecan instructions for an epistolary style.

Blount, who repeats the instructions of Hoskins and Jonson, begins with their opening remark on the fashion of this style: "Now for Fashion, it consists in four qualities of your Style. The first is *Brevity*."[76] As a sample of Blount's borrowing, let me quote the passage which I have already cited from Jonson:

> Brevity is attain'd upon the matter, by avoiding idle complements, prefaces, protestations, long Parentheses, supplications, wanton circuits of Figures, and digressions, by composition, omitting conjunctions, *Not onely but also, the one and the other, whereby it comes to passe, etc.* and such like particles, that have no great business in a serious Letter; By breaking off sentences; as oftentimes a short journey is made long by many baits.[77]

"Omitting conjunctions" and "breaking off sentences" are precise phrases with which to describe the disconnected "curt period" that Professor Croll has analyzed. Blount, however, looks ahead when he adds a remark that is much more explicit than any similar idea in Jonson, not to mention Hoskins:

> Under this Notion somewhat may be said of Periods, which ought not to bee too long, nor yet too short, *QUO MAGIS VIRTUS, EO MAGIS MEDIETAS*. All vertue consists in a certain Geometrical mediocrity, equally distant from excess and default.

Again reflecting his time, Blount quotes Longinus in support of another requirement which suggests that the reign of abruptness is over: "There ought likewise to be a speciall regard had to the cadence of the words, that the whole contexture of the *Period* may yeeld a certain kind of harmony to the ear."[78]

But the next requirement carries Blount back to the text of Hoskins and Jonson: "The next property of Epistolary Style, is, *Perspicuity*, which is not seldom endangered by the former quality."[79] "Under this vertue," echoes Blount, "may come *Plainness*, which is, not to be too curious in the order," but to use "a diligent kind of negligence."[80] Blount likewise frowns upon "perfumed moding terms," but goes beyond Hoskins and Jonson by referring explicitly to Seneca:

> Besides, a vain curiosity of words hath so scandalized some Philosophers, that *Seneca* (in one of his epistles) says, Had it been possible to make himself understood by signes, he would rather serve himself of them, then of discourse, to the end he might the better avoid all manner of affectation.[81]

Blount's third and fourth qualities are identical with those of Hoskins and Jonson, the third being "Life" or "Vigor," and the fourth "Respect" or Propriety.[82] Thus Blount fulfills the promise of his Epistle Dedicatory "with some particular *Instructions* and Rules premised, for the better attaining to a Pen-perfection." As this Senecan scheme of style passed from Hoskins and Jonson to Blount it received important though slight alterations; and the *Academie of Eloquence,* perhaps because of this modification, renewed the life of Senecan ideals in the early days of the Royal Society—a fact which cannot be without significance.

V

In conclusion, we may attempt to place the curt Senecan style by comparing the stylistic aims expressed by Jonson, Blount, Glanvill, and Hughes. In these aims we shall find a simple graph or outline of the evolution of prose style during the century.

Jonson and Blount both advocate brevity, perspicuity (and plainness), vigor, and propriety; but Blount adds the requirements of cadence and medium length in the period. By placing brevity first, both testify to the reign of the terse Senecan style; but by advancing cadence and "mediocrity" in the period, Blount looks beyond that style. In the quality of plainness, which Jonson and Blount place under the head of perspicuity, we find the aim of style which becomes dominant after the reign of brevity.

Joseph Glanvill has as good a right as any to speak for the plain style, and his general theme is that "plainness is for ever the best eloquence." After such works as Sprat's *History of the Royal Society* (1667), Eachard's *Grounds and Occasions of the Contempt of the Clergy* (1670), and Arderne's *Directions concerning the Matter and Stile of Sermons* (1671), Glanvill gave vigorous expression to the doctrine of plainness in *An Essay concerning Preaching* and *A Sea-*

sonable Defence of Preaching: And the Plain Way of it," both published in 1678. Plainness is the watchword at this time, and Glanvill would have sermon style plain, natural, adequate, familiar but not mean; "obvious" rather than "Cryptick." Glanvill knew what the terse Senecan style was, for he had practiced it; hence the significance of his remarks on wit. While "some Sermons lose their efficacy and force by being too full, and close," he would not go so far as "what M. *Cowley* saith of Wit in Poetry,"

> *Rather than all be Wit, let none be there.*

Associating wit with "closeness," he concludes that the right course is to seek a mean between prolixity and brevity.[83] For Glanvill, who would not be dull, the "proper, grave, and manly wit" is still "sharp, and quick thoughts" set out in lively colours;[84] his wit still comes under the head of "vigor" or "life."

But Glanvill emphasizes Blount's new requirement of a mean between prolixity and brevity, and he elevates the rather subordinate plainness of Jonson and Blount to first place in the hierarchy of style. With Glanvill the reign of brevity has definitely given way to the reign of plainness; and plainness, "the best Character of Speech," is not "Bluntness," but rather a simplicity in which there are no "words without sence." Of the other qualities specified by Jonson and Blount, vigor outweighs propriety with Glanvill. If he believes that the wit which consists in "playing with words" is "vile and contemptible fooling," he points out that "there is a vice in Preaching quite opposite to this, and that is a certain road-dulness, and want of wit," which only philosophy will cure.[85]

In 1698 John Hughes is much more concerned that a man's learning be "polite"; the philosopher is now to be saved from the "Rust of the Academy" by "Polite Learning," which gives the mind a "free Air and genteel Motion." "In a Word," says Hughes, "it adds the Gentleman to the Scholar";[86] and Henry Felton soon found Dryden too much the scholar.[87] The qualifications of a good style are now these four: propriety, perspicuity, elegance, and cadence. "Propriety of Words, the first Qualification of a good Style," is to be learned from the "most correct Writers" and "People of Fashion."[88] As usual, perspicuity is necessary rather than significant: "Little need be said of the second Qualification, *viz. Perspicuity.* If your Thoughts be not clear, 'tis impossible your Words shou'd, and consequently you can't be understood."[89] For Hughes *"Elegance* of *Thought* is what we commonly call Wit," or "*Curiosa Felicitas*";[90] for Jonson it came under the head of "Life" or "Vigor." Cadence is "a sort of musical Delight" in the periods, but this had been anticipated by Blount. In Hughes the plainness of Glanvill gives way to propriety as the quality of prime importance. Elegance comes from the gentleman and may be called "ease"; it is the genteel and proper "Motion" of a polite mind.

The style which discovers a mean between brevity and prolixity was suggested in Blount, established in Glanvill, and maintained in Hughes; it developed out of the loose "unexpected" period of Seneca rather than out of the formal "expected" period of Cicero. To Henry Felton at the beginning of the eighteenth century a just style was threatened by obscurity from two directions: either by laboring to be concise, or by running into a "Prodigality of Words." Of course, Jonson had been aware of this, but he had, nevertheless, emphasized brevity. Studying to be concise produced "close contracted Periods," which were now outlawed; on the other hand, there could be no return to the copiousness that Bacon had condemned in the Ciceronians. Moreover, since the terse Senecan style often produced a tissue of epigrams, Shaftesbury could object that "every period, every sentence almost, is independent, and may be taken asunder, transposed, postponed, anticipated, or set in any new order, as you fancy." But the neo-classical impulse to order modified this "random way of miscellaneous writing" just as the neo-classical regard for "ease" rebuked what Hobbes had called "the ambitious obscurity of expressing more then is perfectly conceived, or perfect conception in fewer words then it requires."

NOTES

1. M. W. Croll's excellent studies of "Attic" or Senecan prose afford but a partial answer to this question; see *Studies in Philology*, vol. XVIII; *Schelling Anniversary Papers*, 1923; *PMLA*, vol. XXXIX; and *Studies in English Philology*, 1929. For the claim of science in the formation of seventeenth-century prose see the articles by R. F. Jones, *PMLA*, vol. XLV; *Journal of English and Germanic Philology*, vols. XXX and XXXI.

2. *Works* (London, 1913), III, 166-67. On the significance of Jacobean translation from Silver Latin see H. B. Lathrop, *Translations from the Classics into English from Caxton to Chapman*, 1477-1620 (Madison, 1933), chap. IV, especially pp. 235, 244, 252, 304.

3. See "The Rhetorical Pattern of Neo-Classical Wit," *Modern Philology*, XXXIII (1935), 60-67.

4. See "Strong Lines," *English Studies,* XVIII (1936), 152-59.
Two versions of the same Horatian warning describe the nature and the name of these lines. First in Jonson's translation of Horace's *Art of Poetry:*

> Myself for shortness labour, and I grow
> Obscure. This, striving to run smooth, and flow,
> Hath neither soul nor sinews.

Second in Soame's translation of Boileau's *Art of Poetry:*

> A verse was weak, you turn it much too strong,
> And grow obscure for fear you should be long.

5. *Characteristics,* ed. J. M. Robertson (London, 1900), II, 170.

6. *Ibid.,* p. 171. This "see-saw" suggests the antithetic wit of the Senecan essayists.

7. "Attic Prose: Lipsius, Montaigne, Bacon," *Schelling Anniversary Papers* (New York, 1923), p. 142.

8. J. W. Duff, *A Literary History of Rome in the Silver Age* (London, 1927), p. 198; cf. pp. 228-29 and 593 ff. See Montaigne's account of the "sharpe and witty fashion [d'une façon poinctue et subtile]" of Tacitus: "He draweth somewhat neare to *Senecas* writing. I deeme *Tacitus,* more sinnowy, *Seneca* more sharpe" (*Essayes* [Everyman ed.], III, 180). "Il ne retire pas mal à l'escrire de Seneque: il me semble plus charnu; Seneque plus aigu."

9. *Studies in English Philology,* ed. Malone and Ruud (Minneapolis, 1929), pp. 452-53. Croll describes four marks of the curt style: "first, studied brevity of members; second, the hovering, imaginative order; third, asymmetry; and fourth, the omission of the ordinary syntactic ligatures" (*ibid.,* p. 435); the loose style is differentiated by its relaxed syntactic ligatures, its "linked" or "trailing" period, and its "natural" order (*ibid.,* pp. 440-53).

10. "Muret and the History of 'Attic' Prose," *PMLA,* XXXIX (1924), 254-309.

11. *Notitia Historicorum Selectorum,* translated by W. D. (William Davenant), Oxford, 1678, pp. 217-18. Cf. Croll, *PMLA,* XXXIX, 300.

12. Quoted by Croll, *Schelling Anniversary Papers,* p. 122.

13. See *Epistles* 114, 59, 100. Cf. F. I. Merchant, "Seneca the Philosopher and his Theory of Style," *American Journal of Philology,* XXVI (1905), 57 ff.

14. See *Epistles* 75 and 115.

15. *The New-found Politicke,* translated by Florio, W. Vaughan, and Another (London, 1626), p. 15 (Part I, *Rag.* 86). J. G. Robertson (*The Genesis of Romantic Theory,* p. 246) seems to think the 1656 translation by Henry, Earl of Monmouth, the first in English; but Monmouth claims only to have made the first complete English version.

16. *Workes of Seneca* (London, 1620), sig. b1r.

17. *Ibid.*, sigs. b2r- b2v.

18. London, 1635, p. 285.

19. *Philosophical Works,* ed. J. M. Robertson (London, 1905), p. 54.

20. *Ibid.*, p. 55.

21. *Ibid.*, pp. 55-56. In the essay "Of Seeming Wise" Bacon attributes this quotation to A. Gellius and applies it to those who "are never without a difference, and commonly by amusing men with a subtilty blanch the matter."

22. *Ibid.*, p. 124.

23. *Ibid.*, p. 124.

24. *Ibid.*, p. 125.

25. *Ibid.*, p. 128.

26. *Ibid.*, p. 536.

27. See E. Arber's *Harmony of the Essays* (London, 1871) for parallel versions. Bacon's attitude toward rhetoric and Stoic method should be added to the explanation of his change of style in R. S. Crane's article on the *Essays, Schelling Anniversary Papers* (New York, 1923), pp. 98 ff.

28. *Advancement and Proficience of Learning,* translated by Gilbert Wats (Oxford, 1640), p. 29; cf. *Works,* ed. cit., p. 55 n.

29. *Works,* ed. cit., p. 56.

30. *Ibid.*, p. 54.

31. See W. F. Mitchell, *English Pulpit Oratory* (London, 1932), pp. 351-65, "The Attack on the 'Metaphysicals'."

32. Quintilian, *Institutiones Oratoriae,* X. 1.

33. On the Senecan cult in sermon style see W. F. Mitchell, *op. cit.,* items indexed under "Senecan" and "Tertullian."

34. *Works,* ed. Alford (1839), VI, 146; quoted by Mitchell, *op. cit.,* p. 191.

35. *Tatler,* No. 264, December 16, 1710. Cf. Donne, ed. Alford, IV, 491.

36. *Works* (London, 1836), I, 17-18. The *Priest to the Temple* was first printed in 1652. Herbert, it may be recalled, had acted as Latin scribe for Bacon.

37. *Ibid.*, pp. 15-16. The witty preacher used his "pyrotechnics" to procure attention.

38. *Sermons* (Oxford, 1842), II, 359.

39. *Ibid.*

40. *Ibid.*, I, 334-56.

41. *Ibid.*, p. 338. South, like Donne, praises the style of *Genesis* for its brevity; unlike Donne, he refers to Longinus in this connection.

42. *Essaies, or Rather Imperfect Offers* (London, 1601), "Of Histories."

43. *Anatomy of Melancholy* (Bohn ed.), I, 25.

44. *Ibid.*, pp. 30-31.
45. Ursula Kentish-Wright (ed.), *A Mad World My Masters and Other Prose Works* (London, 1929), I, 151.
46. *Micro-cosmographie* (London, 1628), "Character 12." Note that a love of paradox goes with a Senecan style.
47. *Resolves* (Temple Classics ed.), p. 62. "In the development of English style," says Joseph Jacobs, "the decisive and critical moment is the introduction of the easy short sentence" (Howell's *Familiar Letters* [London, 1892], I, lxi). But the curt style brought premeditated shortness rather than extemporary ease; cf. Howell's emphasis on brevity in his first letter.
48. *Ibid.*, p. 63.
49. *Works*, ed. W. C. Hazlitt (London, 1875), I, 40 and 44.
50. *Ibid.*, II, 575. This passage clearly suggests the pattern of Denham's apostrophe to the Thames; cf. "The Rhetorical Pattern of Neo-Classical Wit," *Modern Philology*, XXXIII (1935), 77.
51. *Discoveries*, ed. M. Castelain (Paris, 1906), pp. 105 and 106 n.
52. *Ibid.*, p. 39.
53. *Ibid.*, p. 47. Bacon, like Seneca, was nobly censorious "where he could spare, or pass by a jest."
54. Cf. *Brutus*, XXXI.
55. *Ibid.*, pp. 100-01. Quintilian (X. i. 106) says that "from Demosthenes nothing can be taken away, to Cicero nothing can be added."
56. *Ibid.*, pp. 108-109.
57. Edited from manuscript by Hoyt H. Hudson (Princeton, 1935). Although the *Directions* (1599?) was not printed under Hoskins's name, it was given to the public partially by Jonson and almost completely by Blount. The section "For Penning of Letters," which Hoskins adapted from Lipsius, is found almost verbatim in Jonson, and with some modification in Blount, whose version will be discussed later.
58. *Op. cit.*, pp. 112-16.
59. *Ibid.*, p. 113.
60. Suetonius records Caligula's contempt for Seneca's style as "sand minus mortar" (*Cal.*, LIII).
61. See Dryden's character of Jonson in the *Essay of Dramatic Poesy*: "If there was any fault in his language, 'twas that he weaved it too closely and laboriously, in his serious plays: perhaps too, he did a little too much Romanize our tongue, leaving the words which he translated almost as much Latin as he found them: wherein, though he learnedly followed the idiom of their language, he did not enough comply with the idiom of ours.
62. Cf. W. F. Mitchell, *op. cit.*, p. 367.
63. *Prose Works* (Bohn ed.), III, 99.

64. *Ibid.*, p. 135. This passage does not refer directly to Hall, but it repeats the charges already made against his style.

65. *Ibid.*, p. 155.

66. Quoted from the *Archives of All Souls* by Montagu Burrows in his edition of *The Register of the Visitors of the University of Oxford, 1647 to 1658* (Camden Society, 1881), p. xcvii.

67. *Prose Works*, II, 388. The effect of academic Latin composition upon English prose is often neglected in modern accounts of 17th century style. Both Lipsius and Muretus were read in the schools.

68. *Miscellania* (London, 1653), p. 77.

69. *Ibid.*, p. 78.

70. *Harleian Miscellany* (London, 1810), v, 431.

71. Epistle Dedicatory to Helmont's *Ternary of Paradoxes* (London, 1650), sig. clr.

72. *Paradoxes or Encomions* (London, 1653), p. 10.

73. *Works*, ed. S. Wilkin (Bohn ed.), I, 3.

74. *Zootomia* (London, 1654), sig. a5r.

75. *Academie of Eloquence* (London, 1654), p. 34. Cf. Hoskins, *op. cit.*, pp. 38-40. Although Hoskins retailed Senecan doctrine, he was critical of it; and Blount adapted this criticism to his own time. Jonson borrowed some of this dispraise, which is more discordant in him.

76. *Ibid.*, p. 142; cf. *Discoveries*, ed. cit., p. 112.

77. *Ibid.*, p. 143; cf. *Discoveries*, p. 113.

78. *Ibid.*, pp. 143-44.

79. *Ibid.*, p. 144; cf. *Discoveries*, p. 114.

80. *Ibid.*, p. 145; cf. *Discoveries*, p. 115.

81. *Ibid.*, pp. 145-46; cf. *Discoveries*, p. 116. John Wilkins's *Essay towards a Real Character and a Philosophical Language* (1668) was an effort in this direction.

82. *Ibid.*, p. 146; cf. *Discoveries*, p. 116.

83. *An Essay concerning Preaching* (London, 1678), p. 63. This is not, to be sure, his first word on the plain style, but it is one of the best statements of that style.

84. *Ibid.*, p. 72. Cowley had also said that wit is not "the dry chips of short lung'd *Seneca.*"

85. *Ibid.*, pp. 72-73.

86. "Of Style," *Critical Essays of the Eighteenth Century*, ed. W. H. Durham (New Haven, 1915), p. 79.

87. *A Dissertation on Reading the Classics and Forming a Just Style* (London, 1715), pp. 64-65. See pp. 92-93 for a condemnation of the close, contracted style of sententious writers.

88. Hughes, *op. cit.*, p. 80.

89. *Ibid.*, p. 81.

90. *Ibid.*, p. 82.

PERRY MILLER

🖎

The Plain Style

There is a story concerning the conversion of John Cotton that was well-known in the seventeenth century and was frequently retold in New England. Before his heart was humbled, when he was one of the great lights of learning at Cambridge, he preached to large audiences "after the *mode* of the *University* at that time, which was to stuffe and fill their Sermons with as much Quotation and citing of Authors as might possibly be," but once the sense of sin came upon him he went into the pulpit for a public lecture and spoke "after the plain & profitable way, by raysing of *Doctrines,* with propounding the *Reasons* and *Uses* of the same." The scholars, who "came generally with great expectation to heare a more then ordinary learned Sermon from him that was so famous throughout the *University*," were aghast, and perceiving his bent, "sate them downe in great discontent, pulling their hats over their eyes, thereby to expresse their dislike of the Sermon." Puritans were never troubled over the disapprobation of the critical, for those who thus rudely stopped their ears against the voice of a faithful preacher were sealing their own damnation, while those who listened were putting themselves in the path of a predestined election, as was proved in at least one instance at this very lecture, for John Preston, the future Master of Emmanuel,

From Perry Miller, *The New England Mind: The Seventeenth Century* (Cambridge, Mass.: Harvard University Press), pp. 331-361. Copyright 1939 by the President and Fellows of Harvard College. Reprinted by permission of the publishers.

was present and pulled his hat over his eyes with the other scholars, but in spite of himself he heard, and immediately "was so affected, that he was made to stand up againe, and change his posture, and attend to what was spoken, in another manner than he and the rest had done." In this fashion the sermon worked upon those for whom God had ordained it a means, and hence there was a fundamental tenet in Puritanism that the learned manner of speaking, the discourse stuffed with quotations and "gingling" with rhetoric, could never become such an instrument of vocation. Persuasion of men's intellects and awakening of their hearts could not be wrought through the cadences of a sermon in "the mode of the University," but only through the plain and profitable way.

Cotton's auditors came to his address expecting the sort of sermon we now call "metaphysical"; they were given instead the standard Puritan form, and they would have needed to listen but to the opening sentences to recognize the difference. There were many kinds of sermons delivered in English in the early seventeenth century, at least as the best modern authority, Mr. Fraser Mitchell, distinguishes them; there were Anglicans like Ussher who preached in a mode very similar to the Puritan, and there were moderate Puritans like Henry Smith or Thomas Adams whose works seem to us almost "metaphysical."[1] Disregarding for the moment all the intermediate shadings, we can recognize that before the 1640's, before the sectarians appeared on the scene, there were two opposed theories of the form, style, and function of the sermon which were identified with the two parties most radically opposed in theology and ecclesiastical doctrine. When Puritans speak of abuses and extravagances in sermon style they almost always have in mind sermons of the Laudian party, the discourses of Andrewes or Donne, the preaching that symbolized in manner as well as in content the preferences of the court, the Cavaliers, and those who loved the "beauty of holiness." Against this kind of oration Puritans opposed their own conception, the plain and profitable way of doctrine, reasons, and uses, which perfectly reflected in form and style as well as in substance the mentality and tastes of Puritans, Roundheads, and lovers of the Word of God.

Opposition between the metaphysical and the Puritan sermon was a matter both of form and style. There is no occasion in this work to describe in detail the method of the metaphysicals, which of recent years has been elaborately studied and its great charms revivified to a generation that recognizes in it an endeavor to resolve problems similar to its own. To compare a sermon of Andrewes or Donne with one of Cotton or of Hooker is to see at a glance the fundamental points of contrast; the difference of form is pronounced, for the Anglican sermon is much more an oration, much closer to classical and patristic eloquence, while the Puritan work is mechanically and rigidly divided into sections and subheads, and appears on the printed page more like a lawyer's brief than a work of art. The Anglican sermon is constructed on a symphonic scheme of progressively widening vision; it moves from point to point by verbal analysis, weaving larger and larger embroideries about the words of the text. The Puritan sermon quotes the text and "opens" it as briefly as possible, expounding circumstances and context, explaining its grammatical meanings, reducing its tropes and schemata to prose, and setting forth its logical implications; the sermon then proclaims in a flat, indicative sentence the "doctrine" contained in the text or logically deduced from it, and proceeds to the first reason or proof. Reason follows reason, with no other transition than a period and a number; after the last proof is stated there follow the uses or applications, also in numbered sequence, and the sermon ends when there is nothing more to be said. The Anglican sermon opens with a pianissimo exordium, gathers momentum through a rising and quickening tempo, comes generally to a rolling, organ-toned peroration; the Puritan begins with a reading of the text, states the reasons in an order determined by logic, and the uses in an enumeration determined by the kinds of persons in the throng who need to be exhorted or reproved, and it stops without flourish or resounding climax. Hence it was accurately described in contemporaneous terms as "plain," and the Puritan aesthetic led Puritans to the conclusion that because a sermon was plain it was also "profitable."

By the middle of the century the distinction between these two forms had become so sharply drawn, the types so exactly stereotyped, that ordinary laymen as well as Cambridge scholars would recognize the partisan sympathies of a minister by the form and technique of his pulpit utterance. Sermon style was not a matter of taste and preference, it was a party badge. Indeed, the various manners were so consciously formulated that in 1656, one Abraham Wright, an opponent of Dell and Webster, issued a book of *Five Sermons in Five Several Styles or Waies of Preaching,* in which he deliberately assumed the respective manners of "Bp. Andrewes His Way," of the Presbyterian way, and of the Independent way. These sermons are not outstanding literary examples, but because they were manufactured to order they purposely point up the typical features, and the contrast between Wright's performances in Andrewes' vein and in the Presbyterians' brings home the shock which John Cotton's auditors must have experienced as they comprehended his changed allegiance. The Andrewes-like sermon, Wright says, was actually delivered "before the late King"; it is upon the text, "And then shall they fast," which he also gives in Latin, "tunc jejunabunt." He weaves into his subject in characteristic metaphysical manner, taking up each word in the text, elaborating it adroitly with all the tropes and schemata of rhetoric, as for instance when he enlarges upon the word "fasting" by asking and answering the rhetorical questions, "cur sit?" "quid sit?" "an sit?" The sermon develops through an expanding suggestion of successive meanings, of denotations, connotations, and associations; the tapestry of elocution is assisted by a copious use of tags of Latin and Greek, by quotations from classical writers and church Fathers. But the Presbyterian sermon, which Wright delivered at St. Paul's after the Civil Wars had begun, hardly seems as though it could have been composed by the same man. It opens the text with a grammatical, rhetorical, and logical analysis, states the doctrine, gives the reasons and then the uses. There is hardly any quotation of authors, but Scripture references are affixed in the margin for every other sentence. In his Anglican sermon transitions are managed with skill, and he glides from discussion of the fast to the time of the fast with the aid of a polyglot antithesis: "And now we have got a fast for our time, let us see whether we can find a time for our fast, a *tunc* for our *jejunabunt*"; but in the Presbyterian way he pointedly makes no attempt at a rhetorical scheme, and bluntly asserts, "So much shall suffice for our first doctrinal position, rais'd from this first general part of the Text. The second observation that I shall draw from this general point of Charitie and Alms deeds, is. . . ." In the first oration he comes to a swelling peroration and a chord of rest, beginning, "let us therefore who professe our selves members of the Church be like affected . . . ," but in the second he ends when he has made the last application. The outline of numbered topics and sub-topics in the Presbyterian form stands out in clear relief, and nowhere more arrestingly than in passages that might in the Anglican form furnish occasions for purple patches; when he is speaking of the joys of heaven, he reduces even the rapture of resurrection to a numerical method. "Our bodies therefore shall be endued with most unspeakable perfections, and most perfectly clarified from all imperfections, but they shall not be disrobed of their natural properties: briefly they shal be spirituall in a three fold sense," and thereupon follow the three senses. When the reader turns to the rolling and sonorous accumulations of iterative phrases and modulated clauses with which Donne or Andrewes mount to an oratorical celebration of heaven, and compares it with the Puritan tabulation, he begins to perceive the meaning of the differences in style:

> A new earth, where all their waters are milk, and all their milk, honey; where all their grass is corn, and all their corn manna; where all their glebe, all their clods of earth are gold, and all their gold of innumerable carats; where all their minutes are ages, and all their ages, eternity; where every thing, is every minute, in the highest exaltation, as good as it can be, and yet super-exalted, and infinitely multiplied by every minute's addition; every minute, infinitely better, than ever it was before.[2]

The Puritan piety was no less intense, and the ecstasy of redemption was as deeply felt, but in Puritan sermons intensity of piety was balanced by the precision and restraint of a highly methodical form, a rigid dialectical structure, and the ecstasy was severely confined within the framework of doctrine, reasons, and uses.

Abraham Wright was performing a feat of virtuosity, and his Puritan sermon is no more than a *tour de force*; many New England divines preached sermons of infinitely greater literary value, but his incarnates the form and style in which all of them were deliberately cast. His volume is important because it demonstrates how completely realized, how thoroughly *a priori*, the pattern had become. A preacher spoke as his faction dictated, and he learned in advance the method in which he should express his faction's tenets. Consequently, just as students in the schools were taught to speak or write by formal rhetoric, so ministerial candidates were drilled out of manuals of preaching. It would be exceedingly naïve, as well as pedantic, for the historian to attribute the creations of Andrewes or Donne to the textbooks, or to assert that Puritans achieved their kind of speech for no other reason than that they were students of this or that teacher. The textbooks will not account for the literary genius of either John Donne or Thomas Hooker, but they do set forth explicitly the designs which these great preachers had in mind whenever they sat down to compose. Meanwhile, lesser lights in both camps turned out their orations according to the patterns in which they were educated, and their virtues or their defects are as apt to be those of their education as of their individual talents. This observation is especially true of the majority of New England productions in the seventeenth century; except for the most prominent of the first generation and one or two gifted speakers in the second and third, New England preachers were merely competent and fairly well-educated students, who practiced in their pulpits what they had been taught in their textbooks.

The teacher from whom, above all others, Puritans learned the lesson of sermon form was William Perkins, who gave the classic exposition in his *The Art of Prophecying*, available to most students of the century in the second volume of his collected works.[3] Whether all the maxims originated with him is difficult to say, for Puritans characteristically did not recognize that any of their precepts were derived from other men, but ascribed all of them, including this of preaching in doctrine, reasons, and uses, to the universal and eternal wisdom of God. At any rate, following chronologically after Perkins, a succession of Puritan manuals reaffirmed and developed his teaching; it was set forth by Abraham Scultetus in Germany, in his *Axiomata Concionandi Practica*, 1619, and in England most notably by Richard Bernard in *The Faithfull Shepherd*,[4] 1621, by Oliver Bowles in *De Pastore Evangelico Tractatus*, 1649, by William Chappell, known to fame as having been for a short and not too happy interval the tutor of John Milton, in *The Use of Holy Scripture Gravely and Methodically Discoursed*, 1653, and in *The Preacher, or the Art and Method of Preaching*, 1656, and by William Price, an English Puritan stationed at Amsterdam, in *Ars Concionandi*, 1657. Furthermore, Richardson and Ames wrote always upon the unquestioned assumption that this way was the only legitimate order of the sermon, and for three or four decades before the settlement of New England all the divines who influenced the thought of the colonies, most of the great Puritans of the early seventeenth century, John Preston, Richard Sibbes, and John Ball in particular, followed the plan unswervingly. Hence these doctrines of the organization of the sermon and of the plain style were prominent in the intellectual inheritance of New Englanders. By them was determined the form and technique of the sermon, of the one literary type in which the Puritan spirit was most completely expressed, and if these authors can be said to have had any critical conception of artistic achievement, it was that set forth in their manuals of preaching.

There were, of course, other manuals which contained instructions for the kinds of sermons of which Puritans disapproved. When a few of these are examined in comparison with Puritan works, they disclose at once their dependence upon the Aristotelian rhetorics, and therefore those which followed the lead of Perkins must derive from some other source. Many of the Aristotelian sermon manuals are no more than wholesale transcriptions from the Peripatetic rhetorics. In an early English work, *The Preacher, or Method of Preaching*, published in London in 1576, Nicholas Heminge avowed, "I doe not forge new precepts, but doe applie the common rules of Logitians and Rhetoritians, to a certain matter." Heminge exhibited as yet no awareness of the Ramist controversy; later Aristotelians applied the common rules of their logic and rhetoric to this certain matter with a more defiant exactness. In 1598, for instance, a Dutchman, Wilhelm Zepper, in his *Ars Habendi et audiendi conciones Sacras*, studiously reproduced the conventional outline of the rhetorics even though writing wholly about preaching; he divided his book into the usual five chapters of invention, disposition, memory, elocution, and pronunciation, and found the sermon partaking of the nature of all the three Aristotelian genres, deliberative, demonstrative, judicial. He carved the sermon, like any other oration, into the conventional parts, exordium, narration, proposition, confirmation, confutation, and epilogue. The first and last of these were to be entirely devoted "ad movendos & impellendos animos," and the others "ad rem docendam pertinent." He compared an exordium to the opening bars of a piece of music, making the audience docile and attentive; in a sermon, he said, narration should treat of the causes and circumstances of the text to parallel the ordinary setting forth of the occasion in a secular oration; proposition should be a statement of the doctrine or theological position, confirmation a demonstration of its truth to the intellect, confutation a rebuttal of objections and heresies, and epilogue should restate the proposition "cum affectu," so that the theme would be fixed in the memories of listeners and their last recollection be associated with its strongest emotional impact, just as the peroration of a political orator should be his rousing climax. Alsted's chapter on ecclesiastical rhetoric in the *Encyclopaedia* repeated essentially the same instruction, though probably the most influential Aristotelian treatise among English Protestants was Keckermann's *Rhetoricae Ecclesiasticae, sive Artis Formandi et Habendi Conciones Sacras,* always available to Harvard students in the second volume of his *Operum Omnium*. Keckermann's source is evidenced by inces-

sant citation of Aristotle, though he made some changes in the
schemes and terminologies in order to adjust them to the special requirements of Christian oratory. Instead of placing under invention
the general rules for finding "persuabilia," as he did in his *Systema
Rhetoricae,* he declared that when we come to ecclesiastical rhetoric
we find that invention is a very specialized art, being the extraction
of meanings from Biblical texts and not first of all a discovery of moving considerations, that it should therefore consist of five distinct
acts: "praecognitio textus quoad scopum," "partitio," "explicatio verborum," "amplificatio," and "applicatio." He reduced ecclesiastical
disposition from the secular five parts to three: "exordium," "tractatio
intermedia," and "peroratio," apparently feeling that narration and
proposition were sufficiently covered in invention, and that in sermons the middle sections should not be too mechanically divided
into confirmation and confutation, but instead should be devoted to
general amplification and exposition. However, Keckermann affirmed
that all these changes could be justified by the words of Aristotle,
even though Aristotle himself had never written precisely upon sermonizing, and that his own modifications did not alter the basically
Peripatetic character of the scheme.[5]

Mr. Fraser Mitchell suggests that the pattern of most "metaphysical" sermons, of John Donne's in particular, was taken from Keckermann,[6] and that such discourses are accordingly to be separated into
the sections of praecognitio, partitio, explicatio, amplificatio, and
applicatio, that they open with a formal exordium and come to a calculated peroration. Very often the artistry of a Donne completely
conceals the skeleton; it is more evident in the discourses of Andrewes and protrudes distinctly in Abraham Wright's imitation of
"Andrewes His Way." It is not surrpising that the metaphysical sermon, the expression of men who remained loyal to scholasticism not
merely in physics, as did the Puritans, but in logic and rhetoric as
well, to whom the reforms of Ramus were impious and ignorant assaults upon the historic splendor of these arts in the name of a crass
utilitarianism, should have had its theory couched in Aristotelian
terms. It was inevitable that men of the Renaissance should look
upon the sermon as a particular species in the genus of oratory, and
apply to the part the laws which governed the whole, that when
Aristotelians needed a treatise on preaching they should have devised
one out of the general treatises on speaking. Furthermore, there were
deep affinities between the Aristotelian way of thinking and religious

beliefs of the Anglican party, as can be seen in the methods and arguments of Richard Hooker; therefore, certain Anglicans were bound to perfect a way of preaching that would exemplify in its very structure the qualities exhibited by Aristotelian science. Consequently, the question then arises, if the metaphysical style is to be linked to the Aristotelian logic and rhetoric, if the theory of the metaphysical sermon is to be found in an adaptation of Aristotle to the needs of the preacher, does it follow that the opposing style, the Puritan form with its doctrine, reasons, and uses, was a consequence of the Puritan adherence to Ramus?

The answer to this question will be forthcoming only when more definite information can be discovered concerning the intellectual history of William Perkins, which at the moment is somewhat obscure. If we look on the continent for parallels to his *Art of Prophecying*, we discover that Ramist writers made several attempts to translate the rules of the *Dialecticae* and the *Rhetorica* into rules for preachers. Such efforts often emerged, as did Bisterveldus' *Ars Concionandi* in 1654, with nothing more than a regular Ramist textbook, combining the logic and the rhetoric, and teaching that the content of a sermon should be discovered by invention, its order arranged by disposition, its style regulated by elocution, and its delivery dictated by pronunciation. Perkins obviously did not go about formulating his scheme of the sermon in any such slavish spirit; if he was guided by Ramist principles, he at least worked with an original insight. Perhaps the nature of his inspiration is foreshadowed by an earlier work, the anonymous translation of the *Dialecticae* published in 1574, the preface to which pointed out the value of logic for divinity in terms that seem prophetic of Perkins' achievement:

> If thou be a deuine this method willethe thee that in place
> of the definition, thou sett forthe shortly the some of the text,
> which thou hast taken in hand to interprete: next to porte thy
> text into a fewe heads that the auditor may the better retaine
> thy sayings: Thirdly to intreate of euery heade in his owne
> place with the ten places of inuention, shewing them the
> causes, the effectes, the adiontes and circumstances: to bring
> in thy comparisons with the rest of artificiall places: and last to
> make thy matter playne and manifest with familiar examples
> & aucthorities out of the worde of God: to sett before the auditors (as euery heade shall geue the occasion) the horrible and

sharpe punyshing of disobedience, and the ioyfull promises ap-
partayning to the obedient and godlie.

This passage foretells so clearly the order which was ultimately fixed
in the Puritan form as to suggest that the order might easily have
been hit upon by any student of Ramus. Once the Ramist had been
freed from the domination of Aristotle, once he had realized that an
oration or sermon was not condemned inescapably to the five parts
and that it could be arranged in any sequence which the laws of
method might indicate, once he had learned that the invention of
arguments and their disposition were affairs of the reason and that
effective speaking was merely the delivery of disposed arguments
decked out "with familiar examples & aucthorities out of the worde
of God," what more natural than that he should throw aside the Aristotelian sermon and create a logical form *de novo* according to the
golden rules? In that case, the laws of invention applied to extracting
arguments from a Biblical text would teach him how to "open" it and
how to formulate the doctrine; Ramus' rules for memory would in-
struct him to "porte" his text into a few doctrines; the whole of the
Dialecticae would teach him how to prove them and how to dispose
doctrines and proofs in order. Ramus' constant insistence upon "use"
would show him the necessity for applying each doctrine to the auditors "as euery heade shall geue the occasion." For the embellishment with figures and tropes and for the methods of oral delivery,
Talon's rhetoric would teach him that these are secondary to the
analysis of arguments and the genesis of a method, that they are to
be added only after the theme and the demonstration are worked out.

Perkins' teaching seems so obviously to have resulted from some
such reasoning that we can hardly doubt he was a disciple of Ramus.
Further confirmation of this hypothesis is suggested by the fact that
he was at Cambridge University in the 1590's, as well as by the internal evidence of his book, by its vocabulary and its references. He
declares in what must be Ramist phrases that the art of prophesying
should be adorned "with variety and plenty of precepts," and that he
has ranged the precepts "in that method, which I have deemed most
commodious: that they might be better for use, and fitter for the
memory"; he uses dichotomy as a principle of classification, and when
he argues that doctrines must be collected from texts by logic he enumerates the "places" in a Ramist rather than in a Peripatetic order.
Finally he says that memory must be cultivated

> by the helpe of disposition either axiomaticall, or syllogisticall,
> or methodicall, the severall proofes and applications of the doc-
> trines, the illustrations of the applications, and the order of
> them all: in the meane time nothing carefull for the words,
> *Which* (as *Horace* speaketh) *will not unwillingly follow the*
> *matter that is premeditated.*

He expresses indebtednesses to Augustine, Erasmus, and Beza, and
does not mention either Ramus or Talon; yet the phrase "disposition
either axiomaticall, or syllogisticall, or methodicall" can hardly be
anything but a summary of the *Dialecticae,* and his assumption that
the speaker need not be too careful over words, because right words
will automatically follow right matter, is the essential meaning of
Talon. Certainly, if Perkins was not wholly guided by Ramus, he
must have been strongly influenced, and assuredly the best of the
later writers, Bernard, Chappell, and Price, were completely Ramists.
We have already seen how undeniably Richardson and Ames had
embraced the doctrines. Consequently this much seems clear: the
Puritan form of the sermon, which was first advanced by Perkins and
then expounded in Puritan manuals, was altogether congenial to
Ramist ways of thinking, and hence there is good cause to suppose
that Perkins arrived at it by pondering the question of form in the
light of Ramus' logic and rhetoric. If this is so, our account of the
genesis of the form would resolve itself into some such statement as
this: Puritan theologians were committed by their continued acceptance of the Peripatetic psychology to conceiving of the sermon
as a means that operates upon both the intellects and passions of
men; at the same time the Ramist dialectic supplied them with a concrete method for persuading the intellect and the Ramist rhetoric with
a method for moving the passions; the concurrence of all three factors, psychology, logic, and rhetoric, resulted in their conception of
the form, of the plain and profitable way of doctrine, reasons, and
uses. If this statement is still too hypothetical to be taken for a factual
account of origins, we cannot doubt that however the form was hit
upon, even though the concurrence of these three influences may not
fully account for its devising or explain all its characteristics, nevertheless Ramist theories of logic and of rhetoric, combined with Peripatetic theories of human psychology, furnished the justification or
the formal rationalization of the Puritan sermon.

The three-fold convergence of these doctrines upon the Puritan

sermon appears more dramatically as we examine what the preceptors
had to say upon each part and upon the style in general. Thus we
may note the influence of Ramus, and also a trait of the Puritan
mind, when we find the authors defending the order of doctrine, reasons, and uses because it is "natural." This method, says Chappell,
is "a discourse upon a Text of Scripture, disposing its parts according
to the order of nature, whereby, the accord of them, one with the
other may be judged of, and contained in memory." This definition
is essentially the Ramist contention that all formal art is a methodizing of some "puissance naturelle," but also it suggests the concept
of nature which underlies technologia, the belief that the visible
world embodies the archetypal ideas of God, that these are simple,
efficient, and systematic, and that all man-made works must emulate
the divine perfections. The Puritan aesthetic, in other words, begins
with the Ramist assumption of a natural order that has been summarized in the arts, includes the veneration for learning, demands
the assistance of supernatural grace, and results in an exaltation of
"method":

> Nature with her three daughters, Wit, Memory, and Vtterance,
> giue all attendance in him at Learnings doore. Learning, with
> her arts, wait as hand-mayds vpon Grace. Grace is the Lady
> and Mistresse, which onely can and will rightly command them
> all, seasonably imploy them, and will keepe them euermore do-
> ing. Method keepes all within due precincts, sets their bounds,
> ranketh euery thing orderly in the proper place, which Nature,
> Learning and Grace haue conceiued to write, or speak.

Ergo, Puritan writers condemned the exordium because it was first
of all unnecessary to true believers, who should be sufficiently re-
gardful of the preacher without any artificial capturing of their attention, and because, secondly, it offended their concept of nature.
Believers who are "well instructed, acknowledging their Pastor, prepared and excited by prayers, both publike and private, to the hearing of the Word of God," do not require that their "good-will, docility
and attention" be sought before they will pay heed to the doctrine;
furthermore,

> To seeke for Proverbs, Apothegmes, Sentences, or select His-
> tories to make Exo[r]diums of, by the accommodating of them,

doth not onely savour of something humane, unworthy the
Word of God, but hath a childish kind of affectation, which
is not approved in the more grave speeches of men.

If the sermon is to be a means it must impress the mind and arouse
the heart, but only by thoroughly legitimate means, by the plain and
profitable way; exordiums and perorations are merely occasions for an
exhibition of the speaker's eloquence and hence superfluous in faithful preaching.

By the same token, the one part of the sermon in which a preacher
has least need for eloquence, the one section from which he should
banish it entirely and depend wholly upon unvarnished statement of
fact, is the opening paragraph, the exposition of the text. Puritan in-
structors always demanded that this be brief. "Some speciall occasion
may make the large explication of the text, or handling of the Doctrine to be necessary; but regularly, and ordinarily the principall
worke of the Sermon . . . is in the use and application." The
preacher should analyze his text in order to collect "a few and profitable points of doctrine out of the naturall sense." Puritans assumed
that only one sense was natural to any passage of Scripture, that the
Word of God was plain and explicit and did not need to be enhanced
or enlarged by any words of men. Yet technologia, inspired by the
Ramist dialectic, taught that the Bible should be approached exactly
as should the natural world, as a welter of raw material out of which
the propositions of art were to be refined by the processes of invention
and disposition. The meaning of Scripture, therefore, was plain, but
not too plain; it had only one literal signification, and yet it was not
to be taken too literally. The divines were to collect from its random
histories, songs, and preachments the axioms of theology and to dispose them in systematic, creedal order. Every sermon was an effort
to abstract from a Biblical verse one or more such axioms, and the
procedure, as Ramus had shown, was to take it apart by the method
of analysis into its constituent elements and then by the method of
genesis to recombine the elements into a succinct proposition. The
first work of a preacher was always to translate the Bible into doctrines, to deliver the meaning of a parable, of the Song of Songs, of
the Psalms or a prophecy, "in proper, significant, perspicuous, plaine,
vsually knowne words and phrase of speech, apt, and fit to expresse
the thing spoken of to the vnderstanding of the hearers without ambiguity." Sermons were to reveal that the inner structure of the Bible

was the same platform of ideas outlined in the Westminster Confession of Faith, just as the arts were to show that the inner structure of the universe was the platform of ideas outlined in technologia.

Generally the analysis of a text required the help of the whole trivium, of grammar, logic, and rhetoric. "A doctrine must first be rightly found out, and then afterward hand[l]ed," said Ames; "The finding out is by Logick Analysis, unto which Rhetoricke also and Grammar serveth." With grammar the preacher expounded the meaning of the words, and therefore he had to know the original tongues as well as the vernacular. With logic he was able to decipher the intellectual meaning and extract from the verse its appropriate doctrine or doctrines. When verses were "Analogicall and plaine," the rules of invention and axiom were sufficient; when a verse was more involved—for in spite of the supposed clarity and the assertion of one literal meaning, some texts were found to be "Crypticall and darke"—then the rules of the syllogism had to be invoked and doubtful axioms tested either by simple or composite figures. The important caution to be observed was that no doctrine be "writhen" from a text, but Puritans were supremely confident that the logic of Ramus, because it was a method for discovering or unveiling arguments concealed in matter and not a way of devising them by mere human wit, was precisely suited to collecting only such doctrines as were truthfully contained in the text. If a passage were rightly analyzed into its arguments, and these were laid out in order and considered in relation to the "places" of dialectic, they would infallibly compose themselves into axioms. Deduction of doctrines therefore was achieved "by the Logicall affection of Arguments; as from a generall to a speciall, from the whole to the parts; from the proper adiunct to the subiect; so from the cause, effect, subiect, adiunct, notation, contrary, comparat, definition, distribution." The opening of a text, said Perkins in Ramist imagery, is an action "whereby the place propounded is as a Weavers web, resolved (or untwisted and unloosed) into sundrie doctrines." Bernard illustrated again the Ramist character of these instructions by saying that once the arguments were discovered, the doctrine should be established by noting the "method" of the text, whether it be axiom, syllogism, or disposition.

Among the arguments isolated and defined by logic would be the time, place, circumstances, and context of the passage, but a different sort of analysis would be required when the passage happened to be a piece of Biblical imagery, some figure of speech, some metaphor or hyperbole. At this point the minister would turn to the rhetoric of Talon. "If by the influx of latter arts (namely Grammar, Rhetorick, &c.) into the Text, Logick cannot be immediately examined," said Chappell—that is, if the Holy Spirit spoke this or that truth in a simile or a synecdoche and therefore the logical axiom was not at once visible—"then the words are first to be stript of those arts by some general explication, and the sense to be made plain, and so the way made ready for the Logical Analysis and assignation of the axiomes that they may appear therein." Talon's rhetoric was ideally suited to just this "stripping" of figures from the logical sense, for it made tropes and schemes the secondary and subsequent wrappings of a plain speech, accidentals that could be separated from substantials, not integral parts of the thinking.[7] By this linguistic machinery Biblical syntax could be unraveled, as by dialectical invention all arguments were sifted out of concrete things. Samuel Willard, for instance, could begin with a word meaning "to bind" and argue that it signifies *Metaphorically to chasten,* and then *Metonimically, to reform or reclaim,*" and finally state his doctrine as a proposition concerning reformation. Rhetoric was a tool with which Puritans could plane off the colors of speech from Scriptural utterances, leaving the smooth white surface of "that one entire and naturall sense." The intention of the parables, for instance, was "to explicate and clear up a Truth to the understanding by the help of the senses," to appeal to the sensible faculties by means "of sensible things, such as are obvious to our eyes, ears, &c. and so lead us to a conception of spiritual things," but the minister's task when preaching upon them amounted to what might be called unscrambling them, to give "the Reddition or Interpretation of them," thereby to bring "more light to mens understandings." Talon's rhetoric, in other words, was a godsend to men who professed to believe in a literal interpretation of the Bible, who were not gifted with poetic insight, and who were somewhat deficient in humor: "Must wee actually sell all, taking up a Gibbet daily, lend freely, looking for nothing againe, turne the other cheeke to him which smiteth one, plucke out our eyes, cut off right hands, &c.?" Fortunately we need not, for rhetoric makes us understand that these expressions are figurative, conveying an abstract truth that is much less incommodious. The groundwork of Scripture is logical, though in style it seems poetic. God chooses this way of speaking because He is adapting Himself "to the way and manner that men express themselves in, one to another"; consequently,

> The *Rhetorick* is such as men make use of, to speak in Meta-
> phors, Metonymies, Allegories, and Similitudes, & are to be so
> interpreted; the *Logick* of them is such as man's Reason is want
> to make use of, whether Axiomatical or Syllogistical; and hence
> are to be so taken, hence the word is called *Logical milk*.

When the minister had provided himself with such works as Smith's
Mysterie of Rhetorick Unveil'd, or Hall's *Centuria Sacra,* which provided a handy "Synopsis or Compendium of all the most materiall
Tropes and Figures contained in the Scriptures," he could use them
as a kind of dictionary, looking up the figure or metaphor of his text
and finding the meaning of it in straight-forward prose, exactly as
though he were looking up words in a Hebrew lexicon to find English equivalents.[8]

Many Biblical texts contain facts or rules which touch upon other
arts than logic or rhetoric; some of them exemplify principles of
physics or astronomy, others of medicine or mathematics. Consequently, in order to make proper expositions, a Puritan divine needed
some acquaintance with all the disciplines.

> For there is occasion offered of the vse of variety of learning,
> as of Grammar, Rhetorick, Logicke, Physicks, Mathematicks,
> Metaphysicks, Ethicks, Politicks, Oeconomicks, History, and
> Military Discipline. The knowledge whereof are as so many
> lights to see into a Text by, both to find out and to lay open
> such variety of matter, as lye couched in the words.

But the purpose served by all knowledge of the arts was to facilitate
the rewording of texts into doctrinal statements. The preacher was to
use no rhetoric in phrasing any doctrine, he was to employ no art but
grammar in stating the propositions of his sermons, because his first
task was to sink the abstract doctrine into the minds of listeners.
Viewed in the light of the theory of means, the "opening" of a text
was the initial step in preaching because it was the first means of
reaching the understanding. Everyone agreed that the arts "in themselves considered are not able to convert a soule," yet as Thomas Hall
explained to Webster, "being spiritualliz'd and improved to the right
opening and expounding of the Scripture, they may be a meanes the
better to convince our judgements, and work upon our affections, and
so help forward our conversion." William Perkins declared that "right

cutting, or the right dividing" of a text was the means "whereby the word is made fit to edifie the people of God." Since the first stage in any human response to phantasms was intellectual comprehension, and the actions of will and affection were to follow and not precede the actions of mind, then the first endeavor of the minister should properly be "to edifie." "To fall to application before the truth be explained, and proved, is to make confusion"; so first the minister must teach the doctrine, which consists "in laying open the Truth, so as the understanding may apprehend it, and be made to give its assent to it; we must have a conception and a conviction of it, and this must go before application, being to prepare for it." Thus the Puritan interpretation of psychology as well as of logic and rhetoric determined that the initial part of a sermon be the opening of a text and the rephrasing of it in an assertion, that because the preacher's first task was to inform the intellect, his first work was to "fall into a common place; which is to handle a thing by the definition, distribution, cause, effect, by the agreeablenes with, or disagreeing from other things: all which are to be proued by Scripture, reason, and testimonies." As both Ramus and Richardson had declared, "there is nothing true or false, unlesse it be an Axiome," and therefore as soon as the arguments are isolated and defined, they must be enunciated in their "Logical directrix."

> And an Axiome being a disposal of an argument with an argu-
> ment, and a Syllogism of two in question with a third, and as
> the arguments are affected one with the other, so they actually
> exhibit their force in both places, it will be of much concern-
> ment here, to know well and weigh the affections of the Argu-
> ment.

Here also was a reason for the Puritans' strenuous objection to the metaphysical manner of handling the text, their hostility to what they called the "Topical way of preaching," which they described as preaching "according to the series of the words, where each arguments, or Topical places, are proposed as Doctrines, or foundations of the discourse, especially when each one carryeth some kind of em-
phasis with it." Donne's famous sermon on the text, "The last Ene-
mie that shall be destroyed, is Death," weaves its subtle texture by permutations upon the words "enemy," "last," "death," and finally upon "destroyed," but Chappell, whom some of his contemporaries

called "a rich magazine of rational learning," declared that on Ramist grounds, Donne's method was a logical absurdity. It was taking individual "arguments," in the Ramist sense of the word, by themselves, whereas discrete and unconnected arguments are meaningless, merely serving the preacher as occasions for sensual eloquence. "For because the Argument, considered in it self, is only affected to argue, and that there is no act of judgement but where the argument is disposed with an argument, it is impossible to bring any proof, or inferre any use, of a bare argument." What Donne should have attemped, after analyzing his text into the discrete arguments of enemy, last, death, and destroyed, was to make out of them some such axioms as "At the resurrection God will abolish death," or "Death is the worst enemy of mankind," and then he should have proved and applied the axiom. The remedy for the evils of the "Topical way" was "to select, and constitute in the first place that axiome . . . which by nature is first, and contains in it self the compleat, and independent sense: and then joyn unto it that argument which may make that axiome that by order of nature is next." So Puritans saw no charms in the intricate web of the metaphysical sermon; they swept it aside as a violation of logic and a hindrance to the working of the means. Instead they would have had all preachers unraval a text by a grammatical, logical, and rhetorical analysis and then put the ravelings together into as many doctrines as could be composed out of them. If this seemed a strange procedure, Chappell replied that "none will aske me a reason of it, have he but any touch, and be never so little versed in the Dialecticks, whose judgement and memory . . . will desire an order. . . . I will rather advise you to reserve to each axiome, that which is Homogeneal to it, that the treaty may agree with the order of the axiomes."[9] It was, obviously, impossible to be a Ramist and still preach like John Donne; to English Puritans it seemed impossible, once they had become Ramists, to preach otherwise than in doctrines, reasons, and uses.

The reasons or proofs which followed the statement of doctrine in enumerated sequence were declared by the manuals to reinforce the intellectual acceptance of the doctrine and to commence the emotional reception. They were to be drawn first from confirming passages of Scripture or from some principle in systematic divinity; secondly, they could come from any principle in nature, from one of the "universall rules" of technologia; and thirdly, "from common experience and sense," because this "is euery mans certaine knowledge of

the vse, nature, and quality of a thing to bee euer one and the same.
. . . This experience uniuersal hath these degree[s], sense, obserua-
tion, induction, and so infallibility of the thing." The reasons were
not to add to the Word of God, which of course was final and complete in itself, but for men the adducing of rational proof served at
least two valuable ends: it helped the people to receive the doctrine,
as the principles of psychology would explain—"This giuing of reasons is to compleate the vnderstanding of the hearers in the Doctrine,
and to assure their perswasion of the equity thereof, and so make
them more ready to receiue it, and more stable in beleeuing it"—and,
as the principles of technologia would make clear, it helped to establish the unity of all knowledge, the continuity of theology with the
arts, by showing that theological revelation could at least be substantiated by human reason.

> Though no weights of reason can adde any thing to the firm-
> nesse of that which is grounded upon divine testimony, never-
> thelesse Scripture being, though above, yet not against good
> reason, and doth not take away, but perfect it, it will not be
> much from the purpose sometimes to make use of reasons, and
> other things, as drawn from the art of Nature, if they shall be
> judged fitting, easie and profitable for the hearers.

Inevitably the greater part of the reasons was supplied by logic, for it
was logic that demonstrated the unity of the arts in the body of technologia, and by logic alone could be maintained the harmony of revelation and reason. The other arts were used for illustrations and analogies, but next to explicit warrants from Scripture, the best reasons
were always those drawn "our selues from the Doctrine Logically";
in order so to draw them,

> wee must consider of the subject and predicate of it, or the
> Antecedent or consequent, and marke what relation one hath
> to another, whether *consentanea* or *dissentanea*, whether cause
> and effect, subiect adiunct, or any other topick place, and so
> thereafter make the reason, which reason must bee the medius
> terminus, in a Categoricall Syllogisme.

A doctrine must be stated in accordance with the laws of dialectic—
"as that Arguments agreeing bee affirmed; that contraries bee denyed

. . . that things to bee conioyned bee not seuered, and so contrarily"
—and its proofs must then be framed by the same laws. Over the
first two parts of the New England sermon presided the *Dialecticae*
of Petrus Ramus.

The uses, however, were primarily regulated by rhetoric, for in
them the preacher's intention was predominantly to move the emotions, to drive down the channel of the nerves to the heart, to the
will and passions, those phantasms he had imprinted through the
doctrine and the reasons upon the understanding. Proof "is for the
vnderstanding, the other is for the will." The Puritan minister was to
eschew rhetoric in opening his text, in stating his doctrine, and to
employ it sparingly in the reasons, but in the applications he was free
to call upon all the tropes and figures he knew, to modulate his voice
and quicken his gestures, for here he was attempting what rhetoric
was designed by God to abet, to become the means of calling men to
right conduct, of arousing them to a sense of sin and an abhorrence
of evil. To make applications, said Bernard, a minister "must make
vse of the figures of Rhetorick . . . which haue an incredible power
of attraction, & pulling to them the affections of hearers, if they bee
well managed, still from the grace of the heart, and by good judgement brought in aptly in their due places." Eight flowers of speech,
he thought, were particularly efficacious: exclamation, interrogation,
compellation, obsecration, aptation, prosopopeia, apostrophe, sermo-
cination, and dialogue, and these are the devices which most frequently appear in the applications of New England doctrines. Still
more occasion for the use of vigorous or arresting speech was furnished when the uses were addressed specifically to the various kinds
and conditions of men. Perkins distinguished seven degrees of uses
for the seven degrees of spiritual conditions, from believers to the
fallen, with the intermediate gradations of those humbled, those having knowledge yet not humbled, those teachable but ignorant, and
those both ignorant and unteachable; in order to set forth the fine
distinctions among these states all the arsenal of tropes and schemes
stored in Talon's *Rhetorica* were mobilized and set to work. Furthermore, the doctrine of the means gave an added incentive for using
rhetorical embellishments in the applications, for in spite of its teaching that emotions should not be appealed to before the mind was persuaded, it held that the preacher might, after informing the mind
through the doctrine and reasons, legitimately attack it a second time
through the emotions. "Because the heart or will hath a great influx

into the mind . . . therefore it is lawful (though it is possible and customary to falter exceedingly in this thing) . . . to insinuate something either hiddenly or openly, whereby we may possesse the hearers affections, and by them, as by setting scaling ladders invade the fort of the mind." All the more reason, therefore, why the preacher should be expert in the devices of rhetoric, particularly in the eight most telling figures!

However, if the Puritan minister was free in the uses to let himself go rhetorically, he had still to observe the limits prescribed by Ramist theory. He could not devise applications first and foremost as "per-suabilia" but only as logical deductions from his doctrine. The content of his oration, here as in the earlier sections, was supplied by dialectic; rhetoric was used more copiously at this point merely to ornament and decorate the doctrine. Because the uses were addressed to the heart, said Chappell, they "doe vindicate to themselves all manner of Rhetorical preparation," but this did not mean that they were "to be undertaken without the salt of wisdom and gravity, as is befitting a sacred person and businesse." Richardson declared, "We have among us a distinction of doctrine and use," but doctrine, he explained, "is properly the first rule of Art, and use is the application thereof, or the special deducts gathered from the first."[10] The understanding of an auditor is to be exercised not only for discerning the truth, said Samuel Willard, but "also to be improved in judging of the goodness of the Truth so exhibited"; accordingly the minister must draw his uses as "practical inferences from the general truth, which are for our *Instruction*." Thus even in the portion of his discourse where eloquence was most permissible, the Puritan minister could not indulge in the rhetoric of the metaphysical preachers, the wit and verbal play of Thomas Adams or Thomas Fuller, nor in the unrestrained emotional exhortations of Ranters and Antinomians. In order to move the heart in the one way considered proper by Puritan theorists, the preacher had not only to be learned in rhetoric, but to "have his senses well exercised in Scriptures, and be well skilled both in the art of reasoning, the nature of the humane soul, and the divers means of Gods operating." He needed always to be a theologian, a logician, and a psychologist, as well as an orator.

For this reason applications of doctrines never became full-dress oratorical perorations, for their delivery was restrained by the laws of dialectic and the method of enumeration. The authors of manuals made out a regular scheme of uses—uses for confutation, instruction,

reprehension, dehortation, exhortation, consolation—and the uses in
New England sermons often appear in printed texts so labeled, thus
testifying to the essential supremacy of logic in Puritan thinking,
even at the one point where the ministers were most intensely concentrating upon emotion. The "use of confutation," for instance,
made it unnecessary that Puritan writers assign a separate section of
ecclesiastical rhetoric to rebuttal; confutation could be achieved in
the reasons by proposing and answering a possible "objection,"
though the more usual custom was to assign the first use to a declaration that the reasons have shown by inference the error of Arminians,
Antinomians, or Quakers. Experienced preachers gave the novice a
valuable piece of advice concerning such uses: "what error soever he
brings upon the stage, let him doe it nervously, solidly, and manifestly; lest the refutation vanish away, and the error stick fast." Naturally, the phrasing of confutations was determined as much by logic
or by psychological theory as by rhetoric; it was adjusted to the circumstances, in accordance with Ames's instruction that in delivering
confutations "zeale and truth must be tempered with such mildnesse
and moderation as becomes the cause, and as may distinguish such
as erre out of simplicitie, from such as blaspheame impiously." The
other uses, though not involved with polemic, required as much help
from the various sciences, and in order to apply his doctrines to the
people a preacher needed to "bee well studied in the cases of conscience, to be able to giue satisfaction to the weake and tender-
hearted." He needed knowledge more than art, and he had to take
more heed that he find applications of all types, of dehortation as
well as of exhortation, that he bring the uses to bear upon specific
problems of his community and his congregation, than that he phrase
them with artificial eloquence.

As for style, the manuals all begin with a simple assertion that it
was to be kept wholly subordinate to the Bible, to be nothing but a
transparent glass through which the light of revelation might shine,
to have no character of its own, to be unrelievedly plain. But even
the manuals were not able to dismiss it without further discussions;
the religious controversies of the period continually forced writers to
more explicit statements, until at last, even though Puritans would
have preferred to hold that style presented no problems, that it was
merely an affair of speaking truth directly and simply, they were
compelled to give much attention to it. The instructions and formal
professions were all of one tenor: preachers were to make a "plaine

delivery of the Word without the painted eloquence of mens wis-
dome, high & stately phrases of speech"; God "would have Christ
Crucified to be preached in a Crucified phrase." William Ames offered no apologies for "the drinesse of the style, and harshnesse of
some words," for he was ready "to exercise my selfe in that heresie,
that when it is my purpose to Teach, I thinke I should not say that
in two words which may be said in one"; the efficacy of the Holy
Spirit, he said, "doth more cleerely appeare in a naked simplicity of
words, then in elegancy and neatnesse," and "So much affectation as
appeares, so much efficacy and authority is lost." An admixture of human words not only violates the purity and perfection of the Word
of God, but "withall there is a scandall given to the hearers, who
being accustomed to such humane flourishes, oftentimes, contracting
itching eares, doe begin to lothe, the simplicity of the Gospell." The
greatest of New England preachers, Thomas Hooker, foresaw that
many would criticize his *Survey* for being "too Logicall, or Scholas-
ticall," but he answered that in his compositions he sought only
"plainesse and perspicuity, both for matter and manner of expression," because writings should come abroad "not to dazle, but direct
the apprehension of the meanest," and that the highest achievement
of any writer was "to make a hard point easy and familiar in explication." His profession is the essence of the Puritan stylistic ideal:

> As it is beyond my skill, so I professe it is beyond my care to
> please the nicenesse of mens palates, with any quaintnesse of
> language. They who covet more sauce than meat, they must
> provide cooks to their minde.

John Preston had taught the New Englanders that a minister must
know all the arts and sciences in writing his sermons, "yet not to
bring forth Eloquence, but to make us more able to Preach the pure
Word"; to cover apparel with gold seemed by Puritan standards to
spoil it, and so with the Bible, "though the Word may seeme to be
gilded with Eloquence or Philosophy, yet it were better that it were
alone, for so much of it as is covered with these, so much of the ex-
cellencie of the Word is hid." Accordingly the first classes at Harvard
were ready to maintain in disputation that it is more excellent to
speak aptly than ornately, and that copiousness of words should yield
to ornament, and ornament give way to perspicacity.

Following upon these general principles, Puritan discussions found that the virtues of style consisted primarily in the concreteness of phrase used in applications, in the speaking of truths so that the most simple and unlearned of auditors would comprehend them, and in concealing the learning and art by which the composition had been assisted. Christ did not give men "a kind of intimation, afar off what he would," but told them "their own in English as we say. . . . He lets fly poynt blanck." The "greatest plainesse imaginable," even down-right bluntness should be cultivated when ministers "speak home to the Consciences of men."[11] The editor of Perkins' voluminous works praised him "for the manner of his deliuering the same, he condescendeth to the capacitie of the meanest of Gods children"; "my care and study," repeatedly say the New England divines, "was to accommodate it to the meanest hearer." "Let men if they please," boasted Increase Mather, "look on me as One that is . . . *Of a low Style*, which indeed is what I affect"; he thanked his creator that he was not as Cardinal Bembo, "who thought nothing but what is Ciceronian, worth Reading," and who advised authors against studying the Epistles of Paul lest these "should prove some prejudice to their Style in Writings." Any one with education, Mather once declared, would have no trouble in discoursing upon such mysterious subjects as the double nature of Christ "after such a Metaphysical strain as none but Scholars should have understood any thing," but it was more difficult, in addition to being more creditable, to stoop lower:

> Let the *learnedest* of us all try when ever we please, we shall find, that to lay this ground work right, that is, *to apply our selves to the capacity of the common Auditory,* and to make an *ignorant* man understand these *Mysteries* in some good measure, will put us to the tryal of our skill, & trouble us a great deal more, then if we were to discuss a *Controversy* or handle a subtile point of Learning in the Schools.

Throughout the century all Puritan manuals advised against quoting "humane testimonies" in the sermon, whether of philosophers or church Fathers, and they roundly condemned the citation of Latin, Greek, or Hebrew sentences, even though immediately translated. All the arts which a minister might use "whilest he is in framing his sermon," he "ought in publike to conceale all these from the people, and not make the least ostentation." As the current Puritan maxim

had it, "So much Latine is so much flesh in a Sermon."[12] Quoting in
a strange tongue "hinders the conceit of most hearers . . . it is a
hiding from them what wee professe." The first requirement of Puritan writing was that it exhibit what Puritans professed, and so they
felt that there was no necessity for saying more about style than that
it should make the profession clear.

However, during the course of the seventeenth century, Puritans
themselves learned some inklings of what is now clear to us, that a
great deal depends on just what is meant by "plainness" and "naked
simplicity" and "perspicacity." The fact that these are relative concepts began to dawn upon Puritan theorists with the beginning of
the Civil Wars, when the hot gospellers and the Antinomians, when
Tobias Crisp and James Saltmarsh, commenced to preach and their
sermons to appear in widely sold volumes. It then became apparent
that there were greater fidelities to Scriptural language than the orthodox Puritans had dreamed of, resulting in a florid and lurid compound of Biblical imagery that was wholly distasteful to judicious
theologians; it was then revealed that while Puritans had despised
those who preferred the sauce to the meat, they had always wanted
at least some sauce on even the best meat, and they were far from
happy at the prospect of going without it. They perceived that there
were extremes in the applying of theological doctrines concretely and
factually to ordinary life which they had no desire to emulate, that
the sectarian preachers could practice with a vengeance all their admonitions against citing Latin and Hebrew, since these divines were
totally ignorant of the languages; and as for making some things
clear to the meanest, when How the cobbler had dared to climb a
pulpit, he could give the learned a thousand pointers. In the light of
these disclosures, it became obvious then, and it is still more obvious
today, that the Puritan literary style was plain only in relation to the
less plain styles of contemporaneous metaphysical preachers, of
"witty" preachers like Adams and Fuller, of Senecan orators like Hall
and Sanderson. It may have been less rhetorical than these modes,
but it was still rhetorical; it may have been more popular, but it was
still scholarly. It was still a cultivated achievement of the learned that
emphasized the distinction between themselves and the "meaner
sort." Why should an orator speak "after the vulgar manner, and deliver his mind as a cobler would doe?" asked Wigglesworth in his
college oration; "His hearers might then have some ground to say
they knew as much as their oratour could teach them." The Puritans

subordinated finish to zeal, and they put the maintenance of orthodoxy ahead of the creation of works of art, but their ideal did demand
discipline and much care for formal qualities. The manuals called
for simplicity, but did not believe that a minister should "come into
the place rawly and rudely, without very serious meditation and
preparation"; they declared that the "sudden conceits of the minde,
not digested, must needs be rawly deliuered, and often little to the
purpose." The plain style did not preclude that a man's words "be
apt and significant to expresse the matter whereof he speaketh"; since
Scripture uses "a godly eloquence," men must endeavor to imitate it,
"and it is a grace to speake well, and which may be attained vnto."
John Eliot was conspicuous even among the pious of his generation
for the simplicity of his spirit, yet "he lik'd no Preaching, but what
had been *well studied* for," and he would invoke the Lord to help
the ministry "always by good Study to beat our Oyl, that there may
be no knots in our Sermons left undissolved." As Cotton Mather said
proudly of John Cotton, his "Composures all *Smelt of the* Lamp,"
and so also, by deliberate intention, did those of every New England
preacher in the seventeenth century.

This fact goes far to account for the additional fact that although
Puritan authors gave a comprehensive allegiance to the principles of
the plain style and methodical structure, there were yet some striking
variations among their practices. Everything depended, in short, on
how much rhetoric was thought compatible with "naked simplicity."
Obviously Bishop Andrewes or Thomas Adams used too much, but
nevertheless some degree of it, some embellishment with tropes and
figures, some use of similes and word-patterns, at least a few devices
of formal eloquence, were not inconsistent with "painful" preaching.
There were also the considerations of time and place. Whether Nathaniel Ward preached in the style of the Simple Cobler is unknown; probably he did not, but when writing a secular book addressed to his warring countrymen, there was no reason in the
Puritan tradition why he should not go the limit, as he did, in pa-
rading the turns of rhetoric, coining words, quoting Latin, and devising intricate schemata. Joshua Moody, preaching in 1674 before
the Ancient and Honourable Artillery Company, professed that "had
I been to handle the same *Head of Divinity* on another occasion and
before another Auditory, I could and should have sought out other
words," but since it was incumbent upon any orator to "take Measure
of his Theam to cut out his Language by, and make it up something

according to the mode of his Auditory," he gave the Company a highly rhetorical discourse that is possibly the most ornate and colored of all early New England writings, full of sustained metaphors and complicated schemata. The historian Edward Johnson had not been to the university, but had given himself some kind of education, in which he would inevitably have included a study of rhetoric, and therefore attempted in *The Wonder-Working Providence of Sions Saviour in New England* to write with a copious use of rhetorical flowers, though hardly with what we can call artistic success. Even among preachers of the immigrant generation, there were great differences; John Cotton adhered fairly strictly to the ideals of plain speech, whereas in Shepard or Hooker appear more freely all the tropes listed in Talon and many of the schemata. Of the later generations, Urian Oakes, for instance, followed the examples of Shepard and Hooker, and won the praise of his contemporaries for being a "Master of the true, pure, *Ciceronian* Latin & Language," which Ciceronianism he would exemplify in English in a "copious and florid Oration," whereas Increase Mather won equal esteem for keeping continually in view "plainness, perspicuity, gravity in delivering the Truth," abandoning "all Additional Ornaments whatever, betaking himself alone unto the Exercise of a sound Judgment and Spiritual Wisdom, in giving Evidence and Authority unto the Truth." Even though Puritan manuals frowned upon Latin quotations or the instancing of "humane authorities," learned New Englanders could not resist occasional exhibitions of their erudition, and the people did not seem to object. This bent toward rhetorical ornament and plentiful citation was most indulged among New England writers by Cotton Mather, who had to defend his *Magnalia* against the charge of being "Embellished with too much of *Ornament,* by the multiplied References to other and former Concerns, closely couch'd, for the Observation of the *Attentive,* in almost every Paragraph." Samuel Mather rather lamely apologized for him: "It is next to impossible, that a Man should keep from *writing learnedly,* and as if he were acquainted with Author's and their Sentiments, when his Mind is stored with their *various Ideas* and Images, and he is a compleat *Owner* of them." Other divines often yielded to the like temptation, for they also were acquainted with authors, though fortunately their range was generally more circumscribed and their taste more highly sensitive, so that they did not commit the absurdities which fill the pages of Cotton Mather. Of course, by his time the old rhetoric was waning and the earlier standards becoming less precise, so that he is not to be taken altogether as a product of genuine Puritan instruction, yet even for his day he went to extremes. His biographer acknowledged that "his Treatises were *stuck with Jewels,*" but attempted to deny they were "*burthen'd* with them"; "No, There were just eno' to render a strong and easy *Splendor.*" However, Judge Samuel Sewall, who better remembered what the first generations had held, found himself "somewhat disgusted" by Cotton's filling a sermon with such expressions "as, sweet sented hands of Christ, Lord High Treasurer of Æthopia, Ribband of Humility," and was all the more sorry for them "because of the excellency and seasonableness of the subject, and otherwise well handled."

The moral would thus appear to be that even within the limits of Puritan theory considerable freedom was possible in practice. Even the division into doctrine, reasons, and uses was not absolutely obligatory; if Cotton Mather's account is to be trusted, John Wilson, the colleague of Cotton at Boston, used to preach in his younger years in the methodical way, "and was therefore admired above many, by no less auditors than Dr. Goodwin, Mr. Burroughs, and Mr. Bridge, when they travelled from Cambridge into Essex, on purpose to observe the ministers in that county," but after becoming a New Englander he left the methodical way to his more methodical colleague, "and gave himself a liberty to *preach* more after the primitive manner, without any distinct propositions, but chiefly in exhortations and admonitions, and good wholesome councils, tending to excite good motions in the minds of his hearers." If there were many Puritans preachers like Wilson, then there were more sermons delivered than survive in print like the exhortatory utterances of the sectarians, for the hall-mark of these was generally their omission of "distinct propositions," but it should be noted that Wilson's evangelical excitations were made only "upon some texts that were doctrinally handled by his colleague instantly before." In brief, whatever the differences among Puritan writers, from the rhetoric of Nathaniel Ward and Cotton Mather to the simplicity of William Bradford, whatever the divergence in their sermon styles, from the rigor of John Cotton to the impassioned eloquence of Thomas Hooker, the guiding principle was the assurance that content was more important than form, that the essence of any composition was the doctrinal handling of the text, and that style was a secondary concern, a dress or an ornament, that could be varied to suit times and places, that

could be furnished with more or less rhetoric, that could be ornamented with many or with few tropes, the only universal requirement being that the eloquence must not interfere with the major
purpose of impressing a Gospel theorem upon the minds of listeners
and readers, that it serve as a legitimate means for exciting good affections, and never become an artistic end in itself. Even if he had
been able to answer any man's desire in daintiness of speech, said
Hooker, he would not so have injured his matter; "The substance
and solidity of the frame is that, which pleaseth the builder, its the
painters work to provide varnish." Literary style in the Puritan aesthetic was "varnish"; it was useful, even commendable, and a good
workman should know how to apply it, but his first consideration always was to secure the substance and solidity of the frame.[13]

It will be seen at once that this was exactly the conclusion of
Ramist doctrine, the aesthetic moral implied by Ramus' detaching
the laws of invention, disposition, and memory from the art of rhetoric and leaving as an adequate body of instruction for teaching the
"ars bene dicendi" merely the precepts of elocution and pronunciation. It would, again, be attributing too much weight to an academic
influence even in an age when the intellectual life centered upon
universities, to argue that Puritan style resulted from the teachings of
Talon. But the Puritan temperament and Talon's doctrine obviously
fitted together; Puritan taste would determine that the Puritans
choose his rhetoric instead of the Aristotelians', and then, once it became their textbook, it would accentuate their taste and confirm their
natural inclination. When John Norton translated from Latin into
English the letter he and other New England parsons had written
to John Dury, he apologized because in the vernacular "much of the
Elegancy" of the words was taken away; his conception of elegance
then revealed itself when he said that books like bodies "are nothing
so comely when arrayed with a strangers, as with their own proper
clothing and habit," but nevertheless, he had so contrived it that
"wherever appeared a necessity of changing the phrase, the sense is
preserved whole and entire." Preserving the whole sense was all-important; afterwards the dress could be arranged. John Saffin sang the
praises of Samuel Lee because although his style was "florid," yet it
was also

> full of Sence,
> So fraught with Rhetorick, and with Eloquence
> With all Accomplishments of every sort.[14]

Saffin found similar virtues in William Hubbard's "most exact History of New-England Troubles":

> Such is thy modest Stile enrich'd with Sence,
> Invention fine, faced with Eloquence:
> Thy *florid Language* quaintly doth express
> The *Truth* of matter in a comely Dress;
> Couching the Sence in such a pleasing Strain
> As makes the *Readers* Heart to leap again.

Reading the Bible according to this conception of rhetoric, Puritans found the Song of Songs its most eloquent book, "with more store of more sweet and precious, exquisite and amiable Resemblances, taken from the richest Jewels, the sweetest Spices, Gardens, Orchards, Vineyards, Winecellars, and the chiefest beauties of all the workes of God and Man," but they read it primarily for its "truth of matter," which was a series of propositions concerning the great love of Christ for the way of the churches in New England, and looked upon all its amiable resemblances as eloquent facing, as a comely dress, making the heart leap. When John Cotton preached upon Canticles, he analyzed its verses by the laws of invention and disposition, and he rigorously compressed its metaphors into theological prose.

Talon's *Rhetorica* aided this sort of analysis and pointed to the kind of eloquence which Puritans cultivated. Yet they had to place certain curbs even upon it. Ramus and Talon had divided elocution into tropes and figures; the metaphysical and the witty sermons depended more for their effects upon figures than upon tropes; they were built upon the schemata of balance, antithesis, parallelism, and assonance in the sentence more than upon similes and metaphors in the words. Puritan orators found a few of these schemata, like exclamation or dialogue, very effective in their applications, but they perceived that too large a dependence upon schemata always became a tendency to forget the "Sence" in the fascination of the eloquence. Therefore the Puritan doctrine demanded extreme caution in the use of figures and advised in general that preachers speak in simple indicative sentences; but tropes, being more obviously facings, more clearly supernumerary additions to the content, separable raiment merely decorating the propositions, were considered more admirable. "Trope is to the learned the sweetest part of elocution, figure to the unlearned," declared a Harvard thesis in 1678, reflecting a passage in the *Medulla* where Ames had acknowledged that the Prophets and Apostles had employed both tropes and figures, but insisted that "Figures of words, which consists in likenesse of sounds, measures, and repetions," were the less frequent. The reasons, he said, were clear, and he enumerated them in Puritan fashion: first, "the harmony of elocution is the lighter part of Rhetoricke, which more agreeth to light persons and things, then to grave, sacred and divine"; second, they serve "only for naturall delight, not for spirituall edification"; and third, they hinder demonstrations of the spirit, so that those "doe foolishly therefore which in their Sermons, affect sounds ending alike, but specially they which propound such rimes in unknowne Latine or Greeke words." The most useful tropes, in the Puritan view, were those which could be worked into the text after the abstract proposition had been posed: similes, metaphors, illustrations, and examples. By facing their doctrines with comparisons, by announcing flatly that this truth is comparable to this fact or to such and such an experience, they could achieve the ends of rhetoric, appeal to the sensible soul by a sensory image, and yet the doctrine would not be submerged in the rhetoric.

> Amongst these three wayes of teaching: Authority, Reason, & Example: the last is peculiarly accommodated to the capacitie & nature of man, as that which both inlightens & affects. Examples make difficult things plain, and doubtfull things certain . . . upon the reception whereof, all experience attests unto a perswasive & operative influence, concomitant in rational subjects.

Examples and comparisons were the best means for sugaring the pill; "it will goe downe the better," says Hooker in a metaphor. "When we read only of Doctrines, these may reach the understanding, but when we read or hear of Examples, humane affection doth as it were represent to us the case as our own." Thus if Puritan sermons are read in comparison with the sermons of other English factions, the most marked technical feature of their style appears to be the similes and examples, whereas the others exhibit a wider range of sentence figures. One or two passages taken at random will show us in the shortest possible compass the essential qualities of the Puritan style in its contemporaneous setting. The rhetoric of John Donne reveals itself in this quotation as primarily a manipulation of schemata:

Let the head be gold, and the armes silver, and the belly brasse,
if the feete be clay, Men that may slip, and molder away, all is
but an Image, all is but a dreame of an Image; for forraine helps
are rather crutches then legs. There must be bodies, Men, and
able bodies, able men; Men that eate the good things of the
land, their owne figges and olives; Men not macerated with ex-
tortions: They are glorified bodies that make up the kingdome
of Heaven; bodies that partake of the good of the State, that
make up the State.[15]

The same dependence upon "likenesse of sounds, measures, and repetions" is manifested in the style of Thomas Adams as he portrays the
hypocrite:

Hee hath a flushing in his face, as if he had eaten fire; zeale
burnes in his tongue, but come neere this gloe-worme, and he
is cold, darke, squallid. Summer sweates in his face, winter
freeseth in his conscience: March, many forwards in his words,
December in his actions; pepper is not more hot in the tongues
end, nor more cold at heart; and (to borrow the words of our
worthy Diuine and best Character) wee think him a Saint, hee
thinks himselfe an Angell, flatterers make him a God, GOD
knowes him a Deuill.[16]

And then, to take a characteristic Puritan passage, the plain-speaking
John Cotton, making the distinction between a true saint and a
hypocrite, illustrates it thus:

Observe when those ends part, which will be at one time or
other. When two men walk together, a dog follows them, you
know not whose it is, but let them part, then the dog will follow his Master.

The more eloquent Hooker shines best in his comparisons, but he
shows the ultimate limit of Puritan ornamentation in typical similes;
this one, for instance, in his more homely vein, is on the resurrected
body:

It is in the nature of many things to increase, when as nothing
is added unto them: As may be observed in an Onyon, take a
great Onyon, and hang it up in the house, and it will grow

bigger and bigger: what is the cause of it? not because any thing
is added, but because it spreads itself further; so then there shall
be no new body, but the same substance enlarged and increased.

In his happier moments his images are more moving, as when he
thus explains how the reprobate are responsible for their own fate:

> Looke as it is with a childe that travels to a Faire with his fa-
> ther, or goeth into a crowd, his eye is always upon his father:
> he bids him doe not gaze about and lose mee, the childe is care-
> full to keepe his father within sight and view, and then if hee
> bee weake and weary, his father can take him by the hand, and
> lead him, or take him into his armes and carry him; or if there
> be any thing hee wants, or would have, his father can buy it
> for him, bestow it upon him; but if the childe bee carelesse and
> gazeth about this thing and that thing, and never lookes after
> his father; hee is gone one way, and his father another, he can-
> not tell where to finde him: whose fault is it now? it is not be-
> cause his father would not be within his sight, or because hee
> could not keepe within the view of him, but because hee out of
> carelessnesse lost the sight of his father.

The contrast of these passages tells in summary the whole story of
Puritan style and of the Puritan mind. Donne's balance of head,
arms, and belly, with gold, silver, and brass, Adams' antithesis of
March in the words and December in the actions, and then the
Puritan's homely illustrations: the resurrected body is like an onion,
the reprobate is like a careless child, and the appended moral in unmistakable prose—to this difference in technique the Puritan conception of logic and rhetoric, the Puritan reading of "the capacitie &
nature of man," and the Puritan piety led the Puritan orator.
    The supreme criterion of the style was, inescapably, the doctrine
of means. Metaphors were more prized than antitheses, similes more
admired than assonances, because they were better instruments for
convincing the mind and moving the passions. Scripture itself used
"earthly Similitudes," comparisons and parables, to convey truth "to
us under sensible things, things that wee can feele, because that we
are lead with senses in this life." The choice of words was subordinated to the selection of matter, because men are humbled by matter
rather than manner. In preface after preface New England authors

explained that their sermons were stylistically "unfit . . . for the vein of this curious carping Age," but that they always intended "to edifie more then to please, any further than pleasing is a means to edification."[17] Increase Mather "was very careful to be *understood,* and *concealed* every other *Art,* that he might Pursue and Practise that one *Art of Being Inteligible,*" and proudly affirmed that his "*Simple Discourses,* which they that account themselves the Wits of the World, look upon as *Babling,* will either be blessed by Christ for the Conversion and Edification of Souls, or turn for a Testimony to the Speaker." The danger that artistic cultivation might become an impediment to intelligibility lay behind the Puritan rejection of all other prose styles of the day. Richard Baxter expressed the aesthetic standard when he declared "painted obscure sermons" to be "like the Painted Glass in the Windows that keep out the Light."[18] The iconoclasm of the New Model Army was not vandalism, it was artistic criticism; neither Cromwell's soldiers nor the New England ministers could perceive anything beautiful in the sermons of John Donne or the stained glass which they tossed upon rubbish heaps: both alike "kept out the Light." Excess ornamentation in the sermon was impious in Perkins' eyes because it required "absurd, insolent and prodigious cogitations, and those especially, which set an edge upon and kindle the most corrupt affections of the flesh." It was sinful in the eyes of Bernard because it glorified man rather than God, for metaphysical preachers "weigh euery word they intend to vtter in the balance of mans corrupt imagination, marking how tuneable to the eare, how farre from offending, how expressing wit and conceits and all for an applaudite for their owne praise, not caring at all how little they shall profit their hearers, or how well before God they discharge their duties." It was damnable in Ames's judgment because it prevented understanding:

> When the speech is carried on like a swift stream, although it catch many things of all sorts, yet you can hold fast but a little, you can catch but a little, you cannot find where you may constantly rest: but when certaine rules are delivered, the Reader hath, always, as it were at every pace, the place marked where he may set his foot.

And when we come to the bottom of these criticisms, we shall find always that there is a social implication which, in historical terms, may perhaps be the basic explanation for the differences in style. John Donne declared that it was good art both "to deliver deep points in a holy plainness, and plain points in a holy delightfulness," because without the first the unlearned part of our auditory will not understand us, but without the second, "another part understands us before we begin, and so they are weary."[19] Certainly one large factor in inspiring metaphysical and courtly preachers to deliver plain points with holy delightfulness was their consciousness that a large part of their audience would be bored unless regaled with rhetorical brilliance, but the Puritan asserted that the preacher should be as plain as possible so "that he may be understood by the lowest Capacities," and at the same time "so Solid and Rational as that he may be admired by the greatest Divines." The uneducated in both a Puritan congregation and in John Donne's would need deep points delivered to them with holy plainness, but in a Puritan assembly the educated would not grow weary when plain points were not made delightful; educated Puritans did not find life that dull, and they were awakened not by elocution but by solidity and rationality.

We have spoken thus far of style only in the sermon. There were, of course, other types of expression in New England of the seventeenth century, the histories, diaries, narratives of travel and of special providences, biographies, and above all the poetry. There is no occasion in this study for a review of Puritan literature; it is enough to point out that the authors of that literature, who in most cases were divines, did not conceive of themselves as writing in literary genres. They had practically no sense of what we might call belles-lettres, and all their writings were simply other ways of achieving the same ends they were seeking in their sermons; histories, poems, or tracts were treatises on the will of God as revealed in nature, experience, history, or individual lives, and the style was determined by precisely the same considerations and the same rhetorical doctrines as governed the sermons. Daniel Gookin was not a parson, but he declared that he had, "through the grace of Christ," transmitted his *Historical Collections of the Indians in New England* to the reader, "not clothed in elegancy of words and accurate sentences; but rather I have endeavoured all plainness that I can, that the most vulgar capacity might understand, and be thereby excited to praise and glorify God. . . ." Histories, in other words, were first of all means, and the plain style, with its qualities determined by the requirements of a means, was as fitting for them as for orations.

It is a desireable thing, that all the loving kindnesses of God,
and his singular favours to this poor and despised out cast might
be Chronicled and communicated (in the History of them) to
succeeding Ages; that the memory of them may not dy and be
extinct, with the present Generation.

To chronicle the providence of God in the settlement of New England was the entire purpose of the New England historians, of Bradford, Johnson, Hubbard, Gookin, Winthrop, and the Mathers; consequently, for them subject-matter was primary, and a style which
was basically designed for conveying the subject-matter of theology
served perfectly for their narratives. Even the Puritan letter was
written in the style of a pulpit discourse, and Margaret Winthrop
said of one epistle from her loving husband—she was paying it the
most extravagant of compliments—that it had served her in the place
of a sermon.

The poetry of early New Englanders has been variously exhumed
and studied in recent scholarship, and probably more attention has
been devoted to it than either the intrinsic or historical value of the
verse will justify. However, I do not believe that hitherto it has been
connected with the background of rhetorical theory, and some tenets
in the Ramist doctrine help as much as those in the religious creed to
account for the Puritan attitude toward poetry. To a Ramist rhetorician, verse was simply a heightened form of eloquence, it was speech
more plenteously ornamented with tropes and figures than prose,
but still speech; like the oration, its function was to carry inartificial
arguments from man to man. Poetry as well as prose, according to
Richardson, was bestowed by God as a part of rhetoric, not because
it was necessary in respect of things, but in respect of men, so that
men might understand things more easily. Therefore "Rhetorick
serves to deliver the matter more soberly and gravely; and Poetry yet
makes it more fine where all things must be done by measure and
sweet sounds." Before the fall, Richardson suggests, Adam must have
spoken naturally in poetry, but now "we know some men are not delighted at all with Poetry; which if it be from their nature that they
despise it, it argueth a distemperature of it, otherwise 'tis wisdom in
others." This theory incorporated verse into the scheme of God's creation, among the arts arranged in technologia, but only at the cost of
putting upon it the same restrictions placed upon prose style. Poetry
existed primarily for its utility, it was foredoomed to didacticism, and
because it was the most highly ornate of the arts, it was always in

grave danger of overstepping proper limits and becoming pleasing
for its own sake. "Poetry," said Richardson, "may . . . be compared
to a fine Frenchman of the French fashion, or to a Courtier: Oratory
to a grave Alderman." Puritans were not usually very hospitable to
either fine Frenchman or courtiers; they were at home with grave
aldermen. Hence the New England parsons who put the Psalms into
what they were pleased to call meter did not worry about their poetic
shortcomings: "Wee have . . . attended Conscience rather then Elegance, fidelity rather then poetry. . . . Gods Altar needs not our
pollishings." Wigglesworth wrote verses when he was too ill to
preach, proposing therein "the Edification of such Readers, as are for
Truth's dressed up in a *Plain Meeter*," and Jonathan Mitchell pref-
aced the versified *Day of Doom* with a religious rationalization which
he borrowed from the Anglican Herbert: "A Verse may find him who
a Sermon flies." Poetry in Puritan eyes, therefore, was a species of
rhetoric, a dress for great truths, a sugar for the pill. Only some two
persons in seventeenth-century New England have left any evidence
that they were deeply imbued with a true poetic insight; the greater
of these, the Reverend Edward Taylor of the frontier village of West-
field, set forth the poetical theory of Puritanism all the more arrestingly for our purposes since he phrased it in the language of psychology. The elegance, the dress and fine embellishment of poetry he
conceived as the creations of fancy. A poet discoursing upon wordly
topics may be permitted, even by Puritan standards, to "invent" exotic conceits and startling figures to enhance his subject or to win
belief for his inartificial arguments, but when he comes to the solid
truths of religion he will find the products of human ingenuity, the
spawn of a finite imagination, inadequate and irrelevant. Taylor's
verse combines into one motif the themes of the limitation of human
faculties and of the theological necessity for a plain style even in
poetry:

> I fain would have a rich, fine Phansy ripe
>   That Curious pollishings elaborate
> Should lay, Lord, on thy glorious Body bright
>   The more my lumpish heart to animate.
>   But searching o're the Workhouse of my minde,
>   I but one there; and dul and meger finde.

> Hence, Lord, my Search hand thou from this dark Shop
>   (Its foule, and wanteth Sweeping) vp vnto

> Thy Glorious Body whose bright beames let drop
> Vpon my heart: and Chant it with the Show,
> Because the Shine that from thy body flows,
> More glorious it then is the brightest Rose.[20]

The other of the true New England poets, Anne Bradstreet, expressed the gist of the matter more succinctly: "I haue not studyed in this yov read to show my skill, but to declare the Truth—not to sett forth myself, but the Glory of God."

Upon reviewing the results of our study, we might reflect that any criticism which endeavors to discuss Puritan writings as part of literary history, which seeks to estimate them from any "aesthetic" point of view, is approaching the materials in a spirit they were never intended to accommodate, and is in danger of concluding with pronouncements which are wholly irrelevant to the designs and motives of the writers. Up to the point at which their rhetorical theory permitted a care for form, the form may be criticized, but hardly beyond that. We shall do nothing but misread the literature if we do not always remember how their great teacher, William Ames, had told the Puritans, "That key is to be chosen which doth open best, although it be of wood, if there be not a golden key of the same efficacy." The undoubtedly excessive number of quotations in which I have indulged this work offer enough samples of Puritan expression to enable the reader to form his own impressions of Puritan literary competence. However, if our study of stylistic theory does not lead to definite critical estimation, it does point up once more certain elements in the historical situation and the consequent effects upon the Puritan mind. In their concept of style as in their theories of nature, Puritans mingled attitudes of Christian piety with ideas inherited from secular accretions. Augustine and Ramus coöperated to produce the doctrine of the plain style; social pressure coincided with ideology to create the profitable method of organizing a sermon in doctrine, reasons, and uses. The manner incarnated the thought, it reflected the spirit of the thinkers; the technique as well as the content of the writings exhibited the combination of deep religious passion and severe intellectual discipline which is the supreme characteristic of Puritanism. The style was adapted to the dual purpose of preaching a truth revealed arbitrarily from on high, but also manifested naturally in the order of things and in the laws of reason, of showing how men were tangled in the insanity of depravity and yet could remain fundamentally logical. Aided by formal logic and rhetoric, the Puritans constructed their doctrine of style upon their assumption that beauty is the efficient order of things, and saw nothing incongruous in making the manner of their expression serve simultaneously to advance the glory of God and to cement the social or ecclesiastical order. As William Perkins said in the first of the Puritan manuals, the speech must be both spiritual and graceful, "both simple and perspicuous, fit both for the peoples understanding, and to expresse the Majestie of the Spirit." Occasional passages may even now manage to express for us something of the majesty of the spirit; granted a Puritan community, probably many that are dull to us then succeeded in being majestic, but there can be no doubt that every word uttered from New England pulpits was eminently fitted for the people's understanding.

NOTES

1. W. Fraser Mitchell, *English Pulpit Oratory from Andrewes to Tillotson* (London, 1932), p. 365.

2. John Donne, *Works* (ed. Henry Alford, London, 1839), VI, 266.

3. The works of William Perkins are found in practically every book list in early New England; cf. in addition to *The Art of Prophecying*, his treatise on pastoral care, *Of the Calling of the Ministrie*.

4. Copies of Bernard existed in early New England: Charles F. and Robin Robinson, "Three Early Massachusetts Libraries," *Publications of the Colonial Society of Massachusetts*, XXVIII (1935), 126, 155.

5. The Aristotelian method of sermonizing can also be studied in Gulielmus Bucanus, *Ecclesiastes* (1604), and Nicholaus Caussinus, *De Eloquentia Sacra et Humana* (3 ed. Paris, 1630).

6. W. Fraser Mitchell, *English Pulpit Oratory*, pp. 94-98.

7. Compare Perkins' definition of the interpretation of a text: *"Opening* of the words and sentences of the Scripture, that one entire and naturall sense may appeare," "Art of Prophecying," in *Workes* (London, 1626-31), II, 651.

8. W. Fraser Mitchell, *English Pulpit Oratory*, pp. 91-92; cf. Perkins, "Art of Prophecying," in *Workes*, II, 656-659.

9. William Chappell, *The Preacher* (London, 1656), p. 26; the pronounced Ramist character of Chappell's method can be seen clearly in his classifications of the kinds of axioms in which a doctrine is to be stated, which follow word for word the classifications of Ramus; furthermore, he exhibits the characteristic Ramist preference for positive axiomatic statement as against the syllogism; if a text can be

adequately analyzed, he says, "according to the axiomatical judgement . . .and that the full sense of the place may be had by it; it will not be necessary to resolve the Text into a Syllogistical consideration, every time as we shall have power so to doe." *The Preacher*, pp. 116ff.

10. Alexander Richardson, *The Logicians School-Master* (London, 1657), p. 275. From the point of view of the Ramist logicians the "use" of a sermon was an inevitable consequence of the doctrine itself, exactly as the praxis of any art followed inescapably from its propositions; cf. Chappell, *The Preacher*, p. 133: "As the Arguments or places of invention, representing unto us the various affections of things amongst themselves doe yeeld foundations of deductions, so the force of affections the firmnesse and necessity of the same."

11. From a MS. sermon of William Brattle, 1696 (Massachusetts Historical Society); cf. Thomas Cobbett, *A Fruitfull and Usefull Discourse* (London, 1656), p. A3 recto: "Who knoweth not, that mans dull and deceitfull heart, will not oftimes be moved with generals, and common heads of holy doctrine, or practice, lightly touched upon, but when drawn out into particulars, and these being distinctly handled, wisely applyed, and strongly urged and pressed upon the conscience, the strong holds of sin and Satan, in man, come to be thrown down. . . ."

12. W. Fraser Mitchell, *English Pulpit Oratory*, p. 116.

13. *Ibid.*, pp. 78-79.

14. *John Saffin, His Book* (ed. Caroline Hazard, New York, 1928), p. 47; Saffin could find authority in Bacon as well as in Ramist rhetoric for the Puritan stylist ideal, e.g., his entry, pp. 60-61, under the heading "Sundry Reading Epitomiz'd": "It was well said of Themistocles to the king of Persia that Speech was Like Cloth of Arras opened and put abroad; whereby the Imagery doth appear in figure whereas in Thoughts they Lye out as in packs out of view."

15. Donne, *LXXX Sermons* (London, 1640), p. 145.

16. Thomas Adams, *The White Devill* (London, 1621), p. 34.

17. Cf. James Allen, *Serious Advice to delivered Ones from Sickness* (1679), and *New Englands choicest Blessing* (1679), "To the Reader."

18. W. Fraser Mitchell, *English Pulpit Oratory*, p. 104.

19. Donne, *Works* (ed. Henry Alford, London, 1839), I, 216.

20. From the Taylor MS.

A. C. HOWELL

Res et Verba: Words and Things

Sometimes a phrase appeals to men and becomes a commonplace because it seems to meet a need they have experienced. The pair of terms under consideration, *words* and *things,* had an interesting history during the seventeenth century because it served as a corrective comment on the heavily ornamented style of writing then in vogue. It is the purpose of this paper to trace briefly through the seventeenth century the use of this combination of words and the idea represented by it. Although the passages quoted do not by any means exhaust the possibilities of its use, they very probably represent a cross-section and tend to demonstrate a changing conception of style and a rising interest in the technical study of words in terms of meaning. As will appear, the term *res,* meaning *subject-matter,* seems to become confused with *res* meaning *things,* and the tendency to assume that *things* should be expressible in *words,* or conversely, *words* should represent *things,* not metaphysical and abstract concepts, may be discerned. The controversy has some current interest because of the present concern with semantics and the problem of meaning discussed by Alfred Korzybski, C. K. Ogden, I. A. Richards, S. I. Hayakawa, Stuart Chase, and others.

The origin of the use of this pair of words is, of course, classical; and it was from their study of classical rhetoric that seventeenth cen-

From *English Literary History,* vol. 13, no. 2 (1946), pp. 131-142. Copyright by The Johns Hopkins Press. Reprinted by permission.

tury critics learned of it. An early expression of the idea, with the two words in close juxtaposition, is the statement attributed to Cato the Elder: "Rem tene, verba sequentur,"[1] which may be translated, "take hold of things and words will naturally follow, or will take care of themselves." In the rhetorical writings of Cicero the pair of words appears frequently, usually in expressions concerning the relation of style to subject-matter, for which *res* was the normal rhetorical term. In such sentences as this: "Ergo utimur verbis aut eis quae propria sunt at certa quasi vocabula rerum paene una nata cum rebus ipsis; aut eis quae transferuntur. . . ."[2]—translated in the Loeb Classical Library edition, "The words we employ then are either the proper and definite designations of things, which were almost born at the same time as the things themselves; or terms used metaphorically . . ." etc.—in such sentences Cicero seems to recognize the distinction between *words* as representing *things* and words used metaphorically, a distinction which will be noted later. Again, commenting on the five ornaments of oratory, he names as one of them the quality of brevity and goes on, "Brevitas autem conficitur simplicibus verbis semel una quaque re dicenda, nulli rei nisi ut dilucide dicas serviendo."[3] Here again *res* and *verba* are paired, and the meaning seems to be that brevity is attained by using simple words, saying each thing once, and observing nothing except that you speak with lucidity. Cicero does not suggest that *words* should represent *things* merely; he was more interested in ornamentation than in the plain style. When he used the term *res,* he was normally referring to subject-matter. However that may be, readers of Cicero often meet with the pair of words under discussion.

But the phrasing with which Quintilian expressed the relationship of *words* and *things* seems to have made the strongest impression on seventeenth century readers and may have been the basis for their use of the pair of words in relation to style. In the *Institutes* Quintilian advised the writers: "Curam ergo verborum rerum volo esse sollicitudinem. Nam plurumque optima rebus cohaeret et cernuntur suo lumine,"[4] which Professor C. S. Baldwin translates as follows: "Let care in words be solicitude for things. For generally the best words are inseparable from their things and are discovered by their light."[5] It is possible here to translate the term *rerum* as *subject-matter,* as does the Loeb Classical Library translator; yet it remains a fact that *res* and *verba* appear together in the Latin, which every seventeenth century reader would have used, and consciously or unconsciously he would have recalled the simple meaning of the two terms, *things* and *words*.

But the rhetoric of Cicero prevailed during the Renaissance, to the general neglect of Quintilian's admonition, with only a rare voice raised in opposition. Thus, when Donne began to preach, he was only following the prevailing style when he chose words for sound and for their ornamental value as well as for their meaning. It was Francis Bacon who began the condemnation of Ciceronianism, and perhaps first used *res* and *verba* in a contemporary discussion of style. But his condemnation did not begin to take effect until the Restoration, as will be noted. The point to note here is the use of the terms. Discussing the first distemper of learning in *The Advancement of Learning*, Bacon first mentions the causes of Ciceronianism, then goes on:

> . . . these four causes concurring, the admiration of the ancient authors, the hate of the schoolmen, the exact study of the languages, and the efficacy of preaching, did bring in an affectionate study of eloquence and copy of speech. . . . This grew speedily to an excess; for men began to hunt more after words than matter.[6]

When Bacon turned *The Advancement of Learning* into Latin under the title *De Augmentis Scientarum*, he translated the last phrase quoted above as ". . . atque hinc factum est, ut paulo postea major apud plurimos coeperit haberi verborum cura quam rerum."[7]—using the exact phrase of Quintilian, "Curam ergo verborum rerum." In the next section of the *Advancement* Bacon again uses the terms and goes on to point out a distinction of which Hobbes was to make vigorous use. "Here then is the first distemper of learning," said Bacon, "when men study words and not matter . . . for words are but the images of matter. . . ."[8] In the Latin this becomes "Hic itaque cernere est primam literarium intemperiem, cum (ut diximus) verbis studetur non rebus . . . quid enim aliud sunt verba quam imagines rerum. . . ."[9] Thus, for Bacon the pair of words, *res* and *verba, matter,* or *things,* and *words* was clearly associated with a way of writing which did not approve of words used as ornament, "full of sound and fury, signifying nothing."

His voice was raised in protest even at the moment when the preaching of Donne and Andrewes was popular, and the pursuit of *words,* rather than *things* was considered the proper ornament of style. In 1629, however, another voice was raised in protest, using the same pair of words to plead for a simpler style. Sir John Beaumont sounded the warning, echoing Quintilian, in a poem which anticipates a number of the conceptions of style which were to be in vogue in the Restoration. In his poem "To His Late Majesty, Concerning the True Forme of English Poetry," he advised the poet to seek:

> . . . pure phrase, fit epithets, a sober care
> Of metaphors . . .   (lines 51-52)
> Strong figures drawn from deepe invention's springs
> Consisting less in *words* and more in *things*
> A language not affecting ancient times
> Nor Latin shreds, by which the pedant climbs. . . .[10]
>   (lines 55-58; italics mine)

Although Ben Jonson has much to say about style in his *Timber,* he seems not to have used the pair of words under discussion. Perhaps he comes closest to it in such statements as, "In all speech, words and sense are as the body and the soule."[11] and "Pure and neat language I love, yet plain and customary."[12] The quotations are cited from the section entitled "De Stylo, et Optimo Scribendi Genere," which, according to Springarn, is almost literally translated from Quintilian's *Institutes.*[13] That he knew the passage may be gathered from other evidence. He cites a statement attributed to Julius Caesar, "Verborum delectus origo est eloquentia,"[14] and in the margin refers the reader to "Quintil. L. 8." He also told William Drummond of Hawthornden in the "Conversations" that "Quintilian's 6, 7, 8 books were not only to be read but altogether digested."[15] Certainly he would have agreed with Beaumont that good style should consist "less in *words* and more in *things.*"

No reader of early seventeenth century prose needs illustrations of the extravagant over-use of words, the evident love of words for themselves, which marks the sermons and essays of the period. The authors were hunting more after words than matter, to use Bacon's phrase, and paid small attention to Beaumont's suggestion. The trick of the redoubled phrase, common in Donne and Browne, the piling up of alliterative synonyms of which Taylor and Donne were often guilty, the choice of strange, unusual terms often without meaning to their auditors—all these can be abundantly illustrated in the prose published between 1620 and 1660. Four sentences may therefore, serve as examples of the usages against which Quintilian's admonition, "let care of words be solicitude for things," was directed.

(John Donne) . . . we have no such rule or art to ground a presagition of spiritual death, and damnation . . . for the mercies of God work momentanely, in minutes. . . . [Sermon 158][16]

(Sir Thomas Browne) . . . But who were the proprietaries of these bones, or what bodies these ashes made up, were a question above antiquarism; not to be resolved by man, nor easily perhaps by spirits, except we consult the provincial guardians, or tutelary observators. . . .[17]

[From *Hydrotaphia*, or *Urn-Burial*, Chapter 5]

(Jeremy Taylor, telling the story of three false witnesses who swore oaths) . . . the first wishing that, if he said false, God would destroy him with fire; the second, that he might die of the King's evil; the third, that he might be blind: and so it came to pass; the first, being surprised with fire in his own roof, amazed and intricated, confounded and despairing, paid the price of his slander with the pains of most fearful flames; and the second perished by pieces, and chirurgeons and torment; which when the third saw, he repented his fault . . . but wept so bitterly, that he found at the same time the reward of his calumny, and the acceptance of his repentance. . . .[18]

[Sermon 24, from *Twenty-five Sermons preached at The Golden Grove*]

(John Gauden) . . . darkness and disputes, division, distractions, dissatisfactions, and confusions must needs follow . . . [any opposition to Apostolic Succession][19]

[*Funeral Sermon for Dr. Brownrig*, London, 1660]

With Hobbes the distinction between "words," Bacon's "images of things (or matter)," and the "things" themselves becomes clearer as he champions the cause of the simple, plain style in his *Leviathan* (1651). His keen interest in clarity and definition led him to deplore the use of words which had vague referents, to use the term of modern writers on semantics. He attacks vagueness and absurdity in language and drives home his point by singling out for particular sarcasm the writers on divinity, and by implication the preachers. Thus in Chapter 3 of the *Leviathan* he takes up the problem of classification of nouns, concluding that words are only "wise men's counters," having no value if not related to verifiable facts. Discussing absurdities in language, he remarks that the cause of the seventh absurdity is the use of "names that signify nothing; but are taken up and learned by rote from the schools, as 'hypostatical,' 'transubstantiate,' 'consubstantiate,' 'eternal-now,' and the like canting of schoolmen."[20] Again, he concludes: "the light of human minds is perspicuous words, but by exact definitions first snuffed, and purged from ambiguity . . . and on the contrary, metaphors, and senseless and ambiguous words are like *ignes fatui*. . . ."[21] Later, he remarks on "another fault in the discourses of some men; which may be numbered amongst the sorts of madness; namely the abuse of words . . . and that is, when men speak such words, as put together, have in them no signification at all. . . ." That his readers may "be assured their words are without anything correspondent in the mind . . ." he proceeds to give examples of such combinations of words which have no referents in the minds of readers, from "the schoolmen," such as the title of a chapter in Suarez's book, "The first cause does not necessarily inflow anything into the second, by force of the essential subordination of the second cause. . . ." And, concludes Hobbes, not without a slight dig at theologians in general, "When men write whole volumes of such stuff, are they not mad?"[22] And mad, or at least "enthusiastick," to use a term then coming into vogue,[23] these writers were beginning to be considered by the rising generation which produced the Royal Society.

Hobbes, then, approved of a style "consisting less in words and more in things," and his powerful influence sounded the deathknell of the ornate style, especially in preaching. Jeremy Taylor, writing "Rules and Advices to the Clergy," which appeared after his elevation to the Bishopric of Down and Connor in 1660, had by this time seen the need for a less ornate style; and hence cautions the preacher as follows: "In your sermons . . . use primitive, known, and accustomed words, and affect not the new fantastical, or schismatical terms."[24] Coming from Taylor, the most ornate preacher of the period, this advice surely marks the advent of a new style in preaching, where words are no longer to be fantastical or unknown to the auditory.

Other essays on preaching contained the same advice in more detail, advocating the doctrine that *words* should move nearer to *things* and that vague, abstract terms should be avoided. John Eachard, writing in 1670, condemns the high-flown style popular in the universities; saying, ". . . for the most part, an ordinary cheesmonger or plum-seller, that scarce ever heard of a university, shall write much better sense and more to the purpose than these young philosophers, who, injudiciously hunting for great words, make themselves learnedly ridiculous. . . ."[25] Continuing the theme, Eachard attacks ornate preaching:

> Among the first things that seem to be useless, may be reckoned *the high tossing and swaggering preaching*. . . . For there be a sort of Divines, who, if they happen of an unlucky hard word all the week, they think themselves not careful of their flock, if they lay it not up till Sunday, and bestow it amongst them in the next preachment. . . .
>
> Those that are inclinable to make these useless speeches . . . do it, for the most part, upon one of these two considerations. Either out of simple phantastic glory. . . . Or else, they do this to gain a respect and reverence from their people. . . . For if the Minister's *words* be such as the constable uses: his *matter* plain and practical, such as comes to the common market: he may pass possibly for an honest and well-meaning man, but by no means for a scholar! Whereas if he springs forth, now and then, in high raptures towards the uppermost heavens; dashing, here and there, an all-confounding word! . . . if he soars aloft in unintelligible huffs! preaches points deep and mystical and delivers them as darkly and phantastically! "this, is the way," say they, "of being accounted a most able and learned Instructor."[26]

The obvious irony needs no comment, but the use of the terms *words* and *matter* brings in a strong echo of the commonplace which the century could not forget.[27]

It was the poet Abraham Cowley, however, who was next after Beaumont to use the actual pair of words under discussion. Familiar as he was with the idea of Bacon and Hobbes and the dear friend of Bishop Thomas Sprat, historian of the Royal Society, Cowley was much concerned with the problem of language. It was natural, therefore, for him to consider *words* and *things* when he wrote his "Ode to the Royal Society." Stanza 4 of the Ode begins:

> From Words, which are but Pictures of the Thought,
> (Though we our Thoughts from them perversely drew)
> To Things, the Mind's right Object, he it brought. . . .[28]

The "he" refers to Philosophy, a fact which the poet is at some pains to establish in a previous stanza. As will appear shortly, the use of *words* and *things* may have occurred to Cowley as the result of the deliberations on style in the Royal Society, for Bishop Sprat was to make the pair famous in his *History*. The lines also recall Bacon's statement that "words are but images of matter," and Hobbes's insistence on a distinction between words and objects of reality.

Another member of the Royal Society caught the phrase—perhaps not unaware that he was echoing Quintilian, Beaumont, and Cowley —when he wrote in his "tagged" version of Milton's *Paradise Lost,* which He made into a sort of drama and entitled "The State of Innocence," the following lines:

> From words and things, ill sorted and misjoined
> The anarchy of thought and chaos of the mind.[29]

John Dryden did not find his phrase about *words* and *things* in John Milton's poem, but he may have heard it discussed at the meetings of the Royal Society, where he was one of those particularly concerned with the problem of language and style.

For in the deliberations of that important body is found the clearest expression of a growing desire to make *words* represent *things.* This interpretation may not have been what Quintilian meant when he used the phrase "Let care in words be solicitude for things"; but the statement phrased by Sprat and embodying the pair of words under consideration did mean that *words should* stand for *things* and has become almost a classic definition of the plain style advocated by Hobbes and other Restoration critics.

As Bacon had traced in the *Advancement of Learning* the rise of Ciceronianism, Sprat in the History of the Royal Society traces the rise of the ornate style. He notes that after the days of Henry VIII the language "received many fantastic terms, which were introduced by our Religious Sects; and many outlandish phrases, which several

Writers, and *Translators,* in that great hurry, brought in, and made free as they pleased. . . ."[30] As a result of this confusion in the use of terms, the Royal Society, he remarks, 'did not regard the credit of *Names,* but *Things*: rejecting or approving nothing because of the title which it bears. . . ."[31] When he comes to discuss "Their Manner of Discourse"[32] he notes that they have been "most sollicitous [sic]" in regard to it, because:

> . . . unless they had been very watchful to keep in due temper, the whole spirit and vigour of their design, had been soon eaten out, by the luxury and redundance of *speech.* The ill effects of this superfluity of talking, have already overwhelmed most other *Arts* and *Professions.* . . . Nothing may be sooner obtain'd than this vicious abundance of *Phrase,* this trick of *Metaphors,* this volubility of *Tongue,* which makes so great a noise in the World. . . .[33]

But they have agreed upon a style which corrects these evils, he says:

> They have, therefore been most rigorous in putting in execution, the only *Remedy,* that can be found for this *extravagance*: and that has been, a constant Resolution, to reject all the amplifications, digressions, and swellings of style: to return back to primitive purity, and shortness, when men deliver'd so many *things,* almost in an equal number of *words.* . . .[34]

To illustrate that the Royal Society meant what it said when it demanded "so many *things* almost in an equal number of *words,*" Bishop Sprat explains how the reports of the Society, called "Histories" are collected "by the plainest Method and from the plainest *Information* . . . from . . . *experienc'd Men* of the most unaffect'd, and most unartificial kinds of life." By "experienc'd" the Bishop meant, of course, practical men. He then proceeds to give a number of samples of such "Histories," from which are taken the following sentences illustrating the style of reporting:

> In the Month of *May* the *Oysters* cast their Spaun (which the Dredgers call their Spat;) it is like a drop of candle, and about the bigness of a half-penny. The Spat cleaves to Stones, old Oyster-shells, pieces of Wood, and such like things, at the bottom of the Sea, which they call Cultch. . . .[35]

The use of *words* which may be identified with *things,* in full accordance with the Society's instructions, is here plainly evident.

But attention to *things* to the exclusion of *words,* which the Royal Society both preached and praticed, "soon grew to an excess" as Bacon remarked of the opposite tendency a century earlier. Consequently it, too, was condemned—and by no less a person than the satirist Swift. Readers will recall the passage in *Gulliver's Travels,* Book 3, the Voyage to Laputa, where Gulliver visits the Grand Academy, a generally recognized satire on the Royal Society. Section four of the fifth chapter entitled "Gulliver's visit to the Laboratories of the Grand Academy of Lagado," gives an account of a device for framing a universal language.

> The other project was a scheme for entirely abolishing all words whatsoever; and this was urged as a great advantage in point of health as well as brevity. . . . An expedient was therefore offered, that since words are only names for things, it would be more convenient for all men to carry about them such things as were necessary to express the particular business they are to discourse on . . . many of the most learned and wise adhere to the new scheme of expressing themselves by things.[36]

Here Swift, satirizing the style of the Royal Society, picks up for special attention Bishop Sprat's phrase "so many things almost in an equal number of words," and produces one of the most delightful passages in his book. Noticeable also are the side glance at Bacon's "words are only images of matter" and Hobbes's emphasis on concrete words in Swift's phrase, "words are only names for things."

Thus a simple pair of words, used technically by classical writers on rhetoric, was picked up in the seventeenth century, expanded into a commentary on style, made a rallying cry for the new plain style, adopted by the Royal Society, and was finally laid low by the trenchant pen of Swift. Or was it? Perhaps it was only scotched; for the semantic writers have resurrected the spirit of the phrase when they point out the dangers of "high order abstractions" and agree with Hobbes that the use of words which have no communicable meaning leads to absurdity and madness. They praise "pointer-words," that is, *words* which stand for *things,* as did the Royal Society. And once more the poet comments—a modern Beaumont this time, writing another essay on the true form of English poetry. So

Karl Shapiro brings the wheel full circle when in his *Essay on Rime* he writes:[37]

> The question is one of language. No conception
> Too far removed from literal position
> Can keep its body. Ideas are no more words
> Than phoenixes are birds. The metaphysician
> Deals with ideas as words, the poet with things,
> For in the poet's mind the phoenix sings.

Thus perhaps in spite of Swift's strictures, the words of Quintilian are still in point, "Curam ergo verborum rerum volo esse sollicitudinem."

NOTES

1. Found in C. Julius Victor, *Ars Rhetorica,* Chap. 1.
2. Cicero, *De Oratore,* 3, 149. The translation is that of E. W. Sutton, in the Loeb Classical Library (Cambridge: Harvard Univ. Press, 1942), 2. 118-119.
3. Cicero, *De Partitione Oratoria,* 19. (*Op. cit.* 2. 326). Other illustrations of the use are in *Orator,* 40. 9; and *De Oratore,* 3. 19.
4. Quintilian, *Institutes of Oratory,* Lib. 8, Proem, 20, 21.
5. C. S. Baldwin, *Ancient Rhetoric and Poetic* (New York, 1924), p. 78.
6. Francis Bacon, *The Advancement of Learning,* edited by William Wright (Oxford, 1920), p. 29.
7. Bacon, *Works.* Edited by James Spedding, Robert L. Ellis, and D. D. Heath (London, 1858), 1. 451.
8. Bacon, *Advancement of Learning, Ed. cit.,* p. 30.
9. Bacon, *Works, Loc. cit.*
10. "The Poems of Sir John Beaumont," in *English Poets,* Edited by Alexander Chalmers (London, 1810), 6. 30-31.
11. Joel E. Spingarn, *Critical Essays of the Seventeenth Century* (Oxford, 1908-1909), 1. 36.
12. *Loc. cit.*
13. Spingarn, *Op. cit.,* 1. 224.
14. *Ibid.,* 1. 37.
15. *Ibid.,* 1. 218.
16. John Donne, *Works,* edited by Henry Alford (London, 1839), 6. 289.
17. Sir Thomas Browne, *Works,* edited by Simon Wilkin (London, 1900), 3. 42.

18. Jeremy Taylor, *Works* (London, 1880), 1. 748.
19. Cited by Caroline F. Richardson, *English Preachers and Preaching,*
    1640-1670 (New York: Macmillan. 1928), p. 85.
20. Thomas Hobbes, *Leviathan*. Edited by Henry Morley (London,
    1889), p. 14.
21. *Ibid.,* p. 30.
22. *Ibid.,* p. 42.
23. George Williamson, "The Restoration Revolt against Enthusiasm."
    SP, 30 (1933), 571-603.
24. Jeremy Taylor, *op. cit.*, 3. 712.
25. John Eachard, *The Grounds and Occasions of the Contempt of the*
    Clergy and Religion (London, 1670). Reprinted in *Critical Essays*
    and Literary Fragments (English Garner), edited by John Churton
    Collins (New York, n. d.), p. 259-260.
26. *Ibid.,* p. 264.
27. Joseph Glanvil published two essays in 1678 which also favored the
    new style and advised the use of plain words. The titles are: "A Sea-
    sonable Defence of Preaching and the Plain Way of it," and "An
    Essay on Preaching." In this latter he has a division entitled "The
    Preacher should use Plain Words:", in which he advocated "a manly
    unaffectedness and simplicity of speech . . ." (Reprinted in Spin-
    garn, *op. cit.*, 2. 273.)
28. *The Works of Abraham Cowley*. The Tenth Edition. (London,
    1707), 2. 603.
29. The speech is a part of Lucifer's soliloquy in Act 3, Sc. 1. Looking
    on Adam and Eve sleeping, Lucifer remarks:
    >   Their reason sleeps, but mimic fancy wakes
    >   Supplies her part, and wild ideas takes,
    >   From words and things ill sorted . . . etc.
    >   (lines 140-144)

    (*Works of John Dryden,* edited by Scott and Saintsbury [Edinburgh,
    1883] 5, 147) The soliloquy is, of course modelled on *Paradise Lost*
    4, lines 803-808, which runs as follows:
    >   Him . . . they found assaying [to] forge
    >   Illusions as he list, phantasms and dreams
    >   Or if, inspiring venom, he might taint
    >   The animal spirits, that from pure blood arise
    >   Like gentle breaths from rivers pure, then raise
    >   At least distempered, discontented thoughts
    >   Vain hopes, vain aims, inordinate desires. . . .
30. Thomas Sprat. *The History of the Royal Society* (London, 1667),
    p. 42.
31. *Ibid.,* p. 105.
32. Part 2, Section 20.

33. *Ibid.*, pp. 111-112.
34. *Ibid.*, p. 113.
35. From "The History of the Generation and Ordering of Greenoysters, commonly called Colchester-Oysters." *Ibid.*, p. 307.
36. Jonathan Swift, *Gulliver's Travels* (Edited by G. Ravenscroft Dennis). In *Prose Works of Jonathan Swift* (London, 1899), 8. 192, 193.
37. Karl Shapiro, *Essay on Rime* (New York: Reynal & Hitchcock, 1945), p. 1.

JACKSON I. COPE

✍

Seventeenth-Century Quaker Style

The early Quakers, who liked to call themselves the First Publishers
of Truth, swept from the north of England across the nations
roughly between 1650 and 1675.[1] And during this same quarter century what we have dubiously labelled "plain" style manifestly supplanted the highly-ornate, rhetorical tradition of English prose which
had burgeoned in extravagances of Arcadian rhetoric and Euphuism
to flower in the earlier seventeenth century's "Senecan amble."
Clearly, rhetorical analysis can tell us much about the skeletal structure of prose style even in the later years of the century,[2] but it can
no longer lay open the center of energy-informing expression, as it
can in much earlier prose. The aim of this essay will be to discover
those bedrock aspects of expression which are demonstrably homol-
ogous with the profoundest conception of life shared by the first
Quakers, the most feared and fastest-growing sect of the later seventeenth century, as well as the religious body most neglected by modern students of prose form.[3] The rise of the new "plain" prose has
been attributed to the heightened philosophic interest in scepticism,
with its pragmatic theories of action; to the intensified interest in empirical science which centered in the Royal Society; and to the rise
of a semi-educated bourgeoisie. But these decades in England's story
were characterized most widely by continuous theological debate and

From *PMLA*, LXXI (1956), pp. 725-754. Reprinted by permission of the
Modern Language Association of America.

exhortation. So it would seem probable, granting the convergence of several streams of cause, that the peak swell on which the new prose tradition rode to dominance can most intelligibly be traced to an ultimately theological tide. The literature of early Quakerism is of unparalleled value in testing and illustrating this hypothesis because— with the incalculable human distance between George Fox and William Penn—this evangelistic group cut across all social and educational distinctions, even dimmed the dualism in the rôles of the sexes. Yet when the Quakers pour forth their heart's belief and hope, they do so again and again in the same modes of expression, modes only approximately and infrequently appearing in the sermons and tracts of non-Quaker contemporaries like Everard and Saltmarsh. These characteristics, explained by and explaining the earliest Quaker faith, I should like to call seventeenth-century Quaker style.

I

"For the Lord showed me that though the people of the world have mouths full of deceit . . . my words should be few and savoury, seasoned with grace; and that I might not eat and drink to make myself wanton but for health. . . ."[4] The confidence of George Fox in this passage from the beginning of the *Journal* is characteristic; the imagery is not. With their inner ear hearing David's injunction, "O taste and see that the Lord is good" (Ps. 34:8), many a Puritan enthusiast expressed his realization of a better world as a taste of manna.[5] However, for Fox, although the universe of spirit might smell of heavenly flowers, or might glisten with holy light, spiritual food was no staple of his religious imagery.[6] Invited to look carefully at this passage, then, because of its unexpectedness, one sees that Fox, in "seasoning" his "savoury" speech with grace when his actual practice of eating and drinking is in the front of his mind, is evidencing a tendency to break down the boundary between literalness and metaphor, between conceptions and things. It is, in a way, what William Penn was doing in his homonymic reference to "the principle and principal, Christ Jesus."[7] And it is an illustration in little not only of the most embracing literary characteristic of Fox's *Journal,* but of the relationship of language to experience in the early Quaker mind.

In the *Journal* one finds the distinction between metaphoric and literal expression wholly obliterated on occasion, as in Fox's description of his first sight of the rugged, thistled Scottish glens and downs: "when first I set my horse's feet a-top of the Scottish ground I felt the Seed of God to sparkle about me like innumerable sparks of fire, though there is abundance of thick, cloddy earth of hypocrisy and falseness that is a-top, and a briary, brambly nature which is to be burnt up with God's word" (p. 331). Again, Fox wrote that all who have "gone from the image of God" are "in the nature of beasts, and serpents, and tall cedars, and oaks, and bulls, and heifers, . . . in the nature of dogs and swine, biting and rending, and the nature of briars, thistles and thorns, and like the owls and dragons in the night, and like the wild asses and horses, snuffing up, and like the mountains and rocks, and crooked and rough ways." At first glance this appears only a hodgepodge of vaguely-expressive metaphors and similes drawn out of Scriptural contexts. But as Fox concludes, "So all these names were spoken to man and woman since they fell from the image of God; and as they do come to be renewed up again into the image of God, they come out of the nature and so out of the name" (pp. 121-122), one finds that metaphor has transcended its normal function, and instead of merely indicating a point of resemblance between two differentiable entities, it has totally merged them.

And this habit of sliding literalness and metaphor into one another informs the total structure of Fox's *Journal* as well as such individual passages. Let us listen for a moment to Bunyan describing a crucial event in his spiritual development: "one day, as I was betwixt *Elstow* and *Bedford* the temptation was hot upon me, to try if I had Faith, by doing some Miracle; which Miracle, at that time, was this; I must say to the *Puddles* that were in the Horse-pads, *Be dry*; and to the dry places, Be you the puddles. . . ."[8] The passage is typical of Calvinistic spiritual biographies in its immediacy of detail. There is a scene—a few strokes and one can see it all: the country road patchworked from the horses' hooves, muddy yet with innumerable miniature lakes in the little craters, and the lone, God-absorbed man in its center. Bunyan thus dresses to the life a hundred times. Fox, on the other hand, *records* much history, but he *depicts* less the life of a traveller for truth threading England from its dungeons to Cromwell's palace, than an immense, recurring dream in which only now and again one of the murky counters emerges clearly from the blinding lights and shadows.[9] For as his vocation was to draw men forth from the Dark Night of Apostasy into the Day of the Lord, so his

Journal has for a setting which transcends the monotonous catalogue of places and persecutions the ever vivid passage from night into day, from day the lapse into night.

Before he had understood his own mission, Fox travelled to London and "saw all was dark and under the chain of darkness." This is metaphor. But we are in another dimension when he relates that "after some time I went into my own country again, and was there about a year, in great sorrows and troubles, and walked many nights by myself" (*Journal*, pp. 4-5). Here the "nights" are literal enough, and yet one feels the spiritual darkness merging into them—darkening a world in which their spiritual symbolism seems always to absorb material states. In 1647 young Fox, now aware of his aim, and yet often faltering, cried out under his cross: "when it was day I wished for night, and when it was night I wished for day"; going into Derbyshire, Leicestershire, Nottinghamshire at this time, he tells nothing particular but the place names. The physical scene is not England, but the image of his spiritual struggle: "I fasted much, and walked abroad in solitary places many days, and often took my Bible and went and sat in hollow trees and lonesome places till night came on; and frequently in the night walked mournfully about by myself" (p. 9). At Patrington he was turned away from an inn, and followed by threatening ruffians, "and it grew dark" before he reached the end of town. Passing on, he arrived at another house, but was again turned away, "and then it grew so dark that I could not see the highway" (p. 91). Continuing this same walk through the countryside, he "at night came to another town." The town is nameless, the townspeople, recalcitrant to his requests for lodging as to his spiritual warnings, have no names, no shapes, no dialogue—they are vague denizens of the night. Passing through this place, Fox concludes, "And when it grew dark I spied a haystack and sat under it all night till morning" (p. 94). He arrived at Wensleydale on a "market day" in 1652. Here he was locked up for mad, but his "Truth" convinced his captors, "and they let me forth and would have had me to have stayed all night, but I was not to stay but admonished them and turned them to the light of Christ by which they might come to see their salvation, and so passed away and wandered in the night" (p. 105).[10] Again, it is not that the night is lacking in reality, it is that reality for long stretches of the narrative seems to consist only in Fox, and in the sweep of day and darkness; and that the day and darkness of the journey seem so irresistibly to mirror the spiritual state of Fox,

that they become charged with spiritual content even as they alternate over an interminable history. Perhaps this peculiar merging of
realism and spiritual symbolism, with the timeless dimension which
it creates, are most succinctly conveyed by a single brief passage:
"from Major Bousfield's I came to Richard Robinson's; and as I was
passing along the way I asked a man, which was Richard Robinson's;
he asked me from whence I came and I told him, 'From the Lord'"
(p. 106). And perhaps Fox was not entirely unaware of the peculiar
effect, for he had said that in the Lord's day "all things are seen, visible and invisible, by the divine light of Christ" (p. 29). But it was
not only Fox's effect, it was the essential quality of seventeenth-century Quaker expression, manifesting itself in several guises. Before
looking at these stylistic habits, however, it will be profitable to examine the idea which was even more important to Quaker theology than
the Light Within, the conception of the "Name."

II

Isaac Penington saw that "the end of words is to bring men to a
knowledge of things beyond what words can utter."[11] It was an ideal
to which Fox attained at least once, an experience he described apoc-
alyptically: "I saw into that which was without end, and things
which cannot be uttered, and of the greatness and infiniteness of the
love of God, which cannot be expressed by words" (*Journal*, p 21).[12]
But a few months after his insight into the inexpressible nature of
God, Fox saw the obverse of the coin: the perfect expression of God's
nature in the universe. Again it is related in terms of language:
"being renewed up into the image of God by Christ Jesus, . . . I
was come up to the state of Adam which he was in before he fell.
The creation was opened to me, and it was showed me how all things
had their names given them according to their nature and virtue"
(p. 27).[13]

For the Quakers, the root of this conception of language as a key
to the essence of proper reality lay in the Johannine Gospel. "In the
beginning was the Word, and the Word was with God, and the
Word was God. . . . All things were made by him. . . . In him
was life; and the life was the light of men. . . . *That* was the true
light, which lighteth every man that cometh into the world . . . to
them gave he power to become the sons of God, *even* to them that
believe on his name" (John 1:1-12). No amount of repetition seemed

able to dry the spiritual marrow out of these verses for the early Quakers, who adapt them to every circumstance: they serve as exultant cries of thanksgiving as readily as the materials for Jeremiads; and Penn's *Primitive Christianity Revived* (1696) utilized them in one of the most closely-reasoned and clearest expositions of the Inner Light.

With this prologue to John's Gospel in mind, then, let us turn to an arresting passage from one of Fox's early epistles:

> And so you that are gathered in the Name of Jesus, who have bowed to the Name of Jesus, whose Name is called the Power of God, and the Word, Light, Life and Truth; and for bowing to his Name, for his Name sake have you suffered all along by many powers; but the Name is a strong Tower: so who is bowed to the Name, and gathered in the Name of the Lord, ye are in the strong Tower, in which is safety and peace; for being gathered in the Name of Christ Jesus, whose Name is above every Name, for all things that was made, was made by Christ, whose Name is above every Name, into his Name are you gathered; so above all other names and gatherings are you gathered, who are gathered in the Name of Jesus Christ, by whom all things were made and created; and being gathered in the Name of Jesus Christ by which salvation is brought, by the Name of Christ, and not by any other Name under Heaven, but by the Name of Jesus Christ is salvation brought, by whom all things were made; for you being gathered in this Name by which salvation is given, here you come to be heirs of salvation, and then to inherit salvation, which is Christ; *and by this you come to fathom all other names under the whole Heaven,* and to see them, that there is no salvation in them; and so likewise all other gatherings in all other names, no salvation in them; therefore cry people, There is no assurance of salvation upon earth, who are gathered in other names, but not in the Name of Christ, by whom all things were made; and this is the standing gathering in the Name, in the strong Tower, where is the safety, where is the salvation, given and brought. Rejoice ye all that are brought into this gathering, and have bowed to the Name of Jesus.[14]

The passage clearly shows the important implications of the Johannine prologue for Quaker thought. The "power of the Lord" is perhaps the most insistent single phrase in Fox's *Journal,* but here, in company with the "Light," it is subsumed under the concept of the "Name"—that name which was in the beginning the Word. As Fox proceeds, he brings his rejection of dependence upon Scripture into the net of subordinations to the "Name" by warning that there is no nourishment for protestants in "the Tongues, which makes their Divines, the beginning of which was *Babel.*" Rather than master the ancient Scriptures with such care, he pleads, "feed upon the Milk of the Word, that was before *tongues;* and when you are redeemed from Tongues, and see the ceasing of Tongues, and the beginning of Tongues, *Babel,* . . . thou must go before *Babel* and *Babylon* was . . . up into the Word Christ, whose Name is called the Word of God" (pp. 11-12).

It was not only Fox, but early Quakers in general who were fascinated by the "Name," and by the problem of the relation between language and being. Luke Howard could sum up the first chapter of John in a great circle: "for the Word of God is the life of God, and the life of God is the light of men, and the light of men is Jesus, the Saviour of all which believe in him, and his Name is called the Word of God, the entrance whereof giveth life."[15] William Smith could orient Scripture around the "Name" with even greater economy: "And here *Moses* and *John* meet in unity, and their Testimony agrees in one, and all the Dispensations and Administrations did hold forth this excellent Glory which unto *John* was revealed in the Spirit; and from the beginning to the end of all that is declared and written in so many Words it is but a Testimony of him *whose Name is called the Word of God,* Rev. 19 (Mark), the Word is his Name, and it was in the beginning, . . . all the Holy Men of God received it, . . . and they testified that there was not another Name given whereby any could be saved."[16] John Crook, fearing lip-service literalism, explains: "we do not believe that the outward letters & syllables are that Name, that are to be bowed to by the outward knee, . . . but that Name which saves, is the Power and Arm of God, that brings Salvation from Sin, and makes every soul that names it, to depart from Iniquity . . . the Power of God that then saves, is that Grace that comes from the fulness of Christ the Saviour. And without this vertue, *Christ* and *Jesus* are but empty names. . . ."[17] In sound alone there is no salvation; and yet the process of salvation involves the naming of the Name. When the First Publishers were dying, Robert Barclay could say of the name of Jesus, "Salvation lieth

not in the literal, but in the experimental Knowledge,"[18] and the
early followers of Fox would agree with him. But they would have
long hesitated over his corollary that the name need not be known
and spoken outwardly. Barclay and Penn moved Quakerism into a
world made by triumphant Anglican anti-enthusiasts, by the cautious
spokesmen of the Royal Society, a world spoken for by Tillotson and
Dryden, not by Milton and Bunyan. That time was dead now when
language's holy destiny was to ignite the fire of divine enthusiasm in
the newest prophets of the old faith.[19] Fox's fellow warrior Stephen
Crisp saw the change coming even in 1666. In *An Epistle to Friends
Concerning the Present and Succeeding Times,* he chides a new and
restless liberty. Quakers do not live so carefully as once they had
done, and this is an evil; but the really corrosive decline began in language, not morality: "Actions [are] sometimes blameworthy, the
Words and Speech again corrupted, and run into the old Channel
of the World, like them again, and the pure Language, learned in
the Light, in the time of their Poverty and Simplicity, almost lost
and forgotten, and so the work of God which he wrought, in a
manner laid waste."[20]

III

With this palmary emphasis upon the "Name" in hand, let us turn
back to Fox's passage on the subject and look at its form. In an era
when Puritan and Anglican preachers, when Christian virtuosi and
secular essayists, were proudly boasting that their imaginative heat
had been enough stifled to allow them to write a "plain" prose, the
Quakers were yet known as the people of plain speech—Fox, indeed,
described the whole spirit of Quakerism as being "plain and low as
a meadow." Yet his exhortation to salvation in the "Name," with its
long alternately periodic and additive, repetitive structure, its Scriptural, somewhat exotic vocabulary, does not strike us as "plain" prose
in the immediate way that Dryden, Tillotson, or Bunyan, different
as they are, appear to write a "plain" style. Still, the passage from
Fox is typical of early Quaker style. That it seemed "plain" to Friends
is implied in a defense of Quaker language by Thomas Lawson, one
of the most learned of the Early Publishers of Truth, when he
writes: "[Quaker language] is the only and heavenly Eloquence and
Rhetorick . . . though Plain, Simple, and [though it] be accounted
Rude, Clownish and Babbling by the VVordly VVise."[21] "Babbling"

is the adjective which an unfriendly critic might apply to Fox's treatment of the "Name"; indeed, Anglican Joseph Glanvill came close
when he disgustedly called enthusiastic talk of *"closing with Christ,
getting into Christ, rolling upon Christ, relying upon Christ"* mere
"Gibberish."[22]

But remembering the Quaker attention to the "Name," one is prepared to give this aspect of Quaker style a less pejorative and more
adequately descriptive term. A critic once made the pregnant suggestion that "Both the corporate and the individual message of Friends
has, perhaps, been characterised less by variety than by reiteration."[23]
This quality is epitomized in what I should like to call the Quakers'
"incantatory" style. Its central characteristic, so clearly displayed in
the quotation from Fox, is an incredible repetition, a combining and
recombining of a cluster of words and phrases drawn from Scripture.
In itself, this repetition is highly reminiscent of the "witty" Anglican
sermons made popular by Bishop Andrewes in the age of the first
James, and revived self-consciously in some Establishment pulpits
after the Restoration.[24] But a brief look at a typical "repetitive" pattern from one of Andrewes' sermons dealing with a topic dear to the
Quakers, Christ as the Word made flesh (John 1:14), will make
manifest important differences:

> It will not be amisse to pause a little on the three termes,
> *Verbum caro,* and *factum est. The Word.* I. There be, that take
> this name to be given Him, as who should say: *Hee,* of whom
> so many excellent *words* are spoken, all along this Booke; so
> many *words of promise,* and *prophesie,* and all of *Him:* So, the
> word *Objectivè.* 2. Others: for that he discloseth to us all Gods
> counsell, even as the *word* openeth the minde of man; by
> whom as his *Word,* wee know whatsoever we know of the
> *Fathers* minde. So the *word Effectivè.* 3. A third; for that he
> commeth, not onely as *Iesus,* to *save* us; but, as the *Word,* to
> *teach* us: We, as to honour *Him;* so learne His *Word,* as the
> way to our *Salvation.* So the word, *Praeceptive.*
>
> These are all well, and true all: but, all short. We may have
> use of them; but there is a further matter, than all these. . . .
> As the *Sonne* is, to the *Father;* so is the *Word* to the *Minde.*
> The *Son, Proles Parentis;* the *Word, Proles mentis:* They *pro-
> ceed,* both: the *Sonne,* from the *Father;* the *Word,* from the
> *minde:* and so note out unto us, a *Party proceeding,* a *second*

person, from the first: from Him that begetteth, the *Sonne;* from Him that speaketh, the *Word.*[25]

The effect seems almost antithetical to that of Fox's passage on the "Name." Andrewes has a carefully controlled divisioning and logically-developed examination of the terms he is treating of; it is the method of the philologist turned rhetorician: he anatomizes his terms until he can relate the nerves giving each life, then proceeds to relate them with a variety of modes of rhetorical balance, assonance and other sound patterning. In Fox's passage, on the other hand, there is no varying of stance, no moving about the object to exhaust all of its facets of meaning; the idea is logically static throughout all of its repetitions.

Further, and this is not unusual in such passages, as Fox breasts forward on the sound waves of his exhortation, he loses sight of the grammatical structure which usually offers even the most strenuously turgid seventeenth-century author assurance of being comprehended. "And so you that are gathered in the Name," he begins, but caught in the effect of his own repetition of the old *logoi* of the Scriptures, he is drawn away from his intention into the vortex of this divine mystery, until through the words themselves he seems to see the light at their center. The "you" of his address does not receive the predication of action implied in the opening; instead, Fox discovers through their epithet, "gathered in the Name," not only the divinity which was in the beginning, but his audience's participation in a time-conquering *stasis* of Christian perfection. What had begun as warning, instruction, or exhortation becomes, through the hypnotic utterance of the divine names, a vision of human beatification for the Children of the Light. The incantation of the "Name" has undercut the progression implicit in grammar because it has revealed the heart of a world above time.

It has been common to attribute such passages in Fox's writings to his social and educational deficiencies, a view fathered by William Penn, who apologizes that though Fox's expression of ideas "might sound uncouth and unfashionable to nice ears," and that "abruptly and brokenly as sometimes his sentences would fall from him about divine things, it is well known that they were often as texts to many fairer declarations."[26] But to rebut this inference that Fox's "incantatory" passages merely reflect his social status, we need only turn to other early Quakers who joined the Children of Light from a more

sophisticated world. Margaret Fell, eventually to be Fox's wife, was
in 1660 the mistress of Swarthmore Hall, the educated daughter of a
gentleman, and the wife of a former Parliament member and Assize
Judge. Listen to her discourse on faith with Pauline phrases in a
pamphlet issued in that year:

> For none are justified by the works of the Law, but by the
> Faith of Jesus Christ, and by faith you stand, for God hath put
> no difference betwixt the Jews and the Gentiles, if their hearts
> be purified by faith, whose eyes are opened, and who are
> turned from the darkness to the light, from the power of Satan
> unto God, that they may receive the forgiveness of sin, and an
> inheritance among them that are sanctified by faith in Christ,
> even the Righteousnesse of God which is by faith of Jesus
> Christ unto all, and upon all them that believe; For there is no
> difference, for all have sinned and come short of the glory of
> God; For if the first fruit be holy, the lump is holy also, and if
> the Root be holy so are the branches, and if some of the
> branches be broken off, it is because of unbelief, and thou
> standest by faith, be not high-minded but fear.[27]

As with Fox, there is no logical progression, but working the word
"faith" into a texture of Scripture phrases, Margaret Fell's grammatical structure progressively disintegrates into shorter and shorter
sentence members linked by tenuous, sound-dictated conjunctions,
until her final fragmentary quotation turns St. Paul's logic (Rom.
12:16-20) into mere ejaculation. So could a Quaker "motion" of
heart reveal a patrician speaker weaving herself into the web of her
own incantation. The result is not ungrammatical, but agrammatical:
the intense concentration upon individual words wholly removes the
process of expression from a grammatical frame of reference, as the
mind is driven on too rapidly to formalize the restraining relationships between sentence elements. But the essential aspect of this
mode of Quaker expression is not aggrammaticism, nor the typical
Quaker vocabulary. John Swinton was a converted Scottish Calvinist
lawyer who, say contemporaries, "had received as good an education
as any man in Scotland," and was "the man of all Scotland most
trusted and employed by Cromwell" as a Counselor of State. Converted to Quakerism in 1657, he concluded an early testimony with
this "lamentation":

A Lamentation, a lamentation, a lamentation, in the Life, over the Seed, the oppressed Seed.

Oh! oh! how shall *Jacob* arise, for he is small? Oh! how shall *Jacob* arise, for he is small, and the Mountains and Hills are high and weighty, and the Rubbish, the rubbish, the rubbish is great. Put on, put on thy strength O Arm of the Lord, that the Mountains may flow at thy presence, and the little Hills may flock together, and thy Mountain may arise, stand over, shew itself over al; Verily, verily, verily, it shall do so, the Mouth of the Lord of Hosts hath spoken it. I have heard it once, often and again, the whole, the whole, the whole earth shall not hinder it; verily, the whole earth shall not hinder it; if anything could, though it may for a season let, it should be the devisions of *Reuben,* but nothing shall hinder; the time, the set time is come, the rubbish, the rubbish shall be removed; the Glory shall arise, flow down, shew it self over all, and that which will not bow, shall be broken with an everlasting breach; the mouth of the Lord of Hosts hath spoken it, and will perform it in due time.[28]

Swinton does not abandon grammar, and he uses simple language interspersed with Biblical phrases which are not commonplace in Quaker tracts. He is a man absorbing the Scripture for himself, with a personal eye; but he is learning it in that logically unprogressive, repetitive concentration upon the "word," which is the central mode of knowing the high moments of spiritual experience for the Quaker. Untypical as are his phrases and form among Quaker tracts in externals, they reflect as clearly as Fox's writings the epistemology of verbal incantation.

This "incantatory" style is ubiquitous in early Quakerdom. Fox employs it throughout his lifetime in exhortations and warnings to the faithful.[29] It permeates most of the work of Edward Burrough, that notably pious boy whose eagerness to travel for truth would not allow him to pause for education, and is especially notable in *A Warning from the Lord to the Inhabitants of Underbarrow* (1654), the spiritual biography which tells of his passage from an Anglican upbringing through Presbyterianism and Independency to a conversion by Fox. We find the style employed in *A Few Plain Words of Instruction* (1658) by the quondam shoemaker Luke Howard, as well as by Alexander Parker, a well-educated London merchant who was Fox's

most constant travelling companion for several years, when he rose to
a moment of ecstasy as he wove together "light" and "darkness" until
he seemed to be at the ultimate center of these spiritual conceptions.[30] William Smith, a University man turned Independent
preacher turned Quaker attempted to redeem through dinning repetition of Scriptural warnings to the "inhabitants of Babylon" the
promise of his title page: *The Morning-Watch: Or, A Spiritual
Glass Opened, Wherein a Clear Discovery is made of That which
lies in Darknesse* (1660); a few years later he chanted an incantation
of the "coming of the Deliverer" to those who wait in *Joyfull Tidings
to the Begotten of God in All* (1664). William Bayly, a Baptist ship-
master who had sought truth in Boehme's books until he was convinced by George Fox, passed from mere turgidness to ejaculatory
Scriptural outcries in the group of "motions" which he collected
under the title, *The Life of Enoch Again Revived, . . . and The
Cry of the Sins of Sodom is Great this Day before the Lord* (1662).
William Dewsbury, Yorkshire shepherd and cloth-weaver, heaped
flocks, and lights, and dragons in wild stacks as he defended the truth
against the "hat" apostasy of John Perrot,[31] and his transmission of
The Word of the Lord to His Church and Holy Assembly (1666) is
carried out wholly through the incantatory repetition of a few Scriptural images.[32]

But perhaps the occasions of its absence speak almost more clearly
for the import of "incantatory" style than those of its employment.
For the seventeenth-century Quaker, as observant of decorum in
styles as were his contemporaries, reserves this mode of perception
through repetition for those times at which he is exhorting and en-
couraging fellow saints toward eternity. But he lived in this world,
too, and no one sought a place in it more energetically. So that when
Peter Hardcastle addresses the secular authorities for toleration and
liberty from court oaths, he writes in series of sorites, without an
image in the whole;[33] when John Crook addresses the county magis-
trates to the same end, he embroiders his carefully-divisioned arguments with law terminology, quotations from Juvenal, balanced antitheses, and Latin punning,[34] William Smith, whose Jeremiads are
ecstatic jumbles of imagery, addresses his Nottingham jailers and the
King on liberty of conscience with quiet logic.[35] This difference in
style is present whenever the early Quakers address themselves outside the Friends' community on matters concerning social action:
Margaret Fell, whose "incantatory" style we have sampled, defends

women preaching in short paragraphs of short, limpid sentences without resort to metaphor,[36] and the usually enthusiastic Richard Farn-
worth rebuts the principles of the Clarendon Code in a closely-reasoned argument free even of the usual "light" imagery when plead-
ing with parish constables and law officers.[37] The "incantatory" style
is an epistemological tool: it appears when Christ is speaking within
the Quaker, and showing forth the Word which is Alpha and
Omega, beginning and end of understanding the runes of eternity.

But we are not the first to identify the habit of incantation. It
seemed the very essence of Quaker style to the subtle and elegant
English-born Franciscan apologist John Vincent Canes, who described it without comprehending it in 1661

> The *Quaker* . . . books [are] spiritual enough to one of our
> vulgar readers, unto whose judgement they be well propor-
> tioned; for good words are put together there to promote solid
> and sincere honesty, . . . But these words are so strangely
> jumbled together, that every line has good sens in it, but all to-
> gether none . . . I have never seen any thing that for the stile
> and context of the speech doth more nearly resemble *Ma-
> homets* Alcoran than a good *Quakers* book, for in both be hand-
> som words, som dreaming conceits interlarded with undeniable
> truths, . . . endless tautologies, and no connexion. . . .[38]

IV

Henry More, the Cambridge Platonist, implied in his *Divine Dialogues* that while the Quakers were descended from the Familists,[39]
they had escaped the sadducism of that sect through the impact of
Jakob Boehme's insistence upon inward spirituality, saying that
Boehme was the refiner of "the Modern *Nicolaitans,* with their more
visible Off-spring the *Quakers.*"[40] And an analysis of "honest Jacob's"
"strain of Melancholy" by two of his creatures in the *Dialogues* indicates that he found and objected to a theory of language in Boehme
closely parallel to that which we have found in early Quakerism:

> *Bathynous.* Do not you think, O *Sophron,* that it is a super-
> lative strain of Melancholy, for a Man to conceit that he has
> the knowledge of the *Language of Nature* communicated to
> him?

> *Sophron:* I suppose the Skill of the Signatures of Plants, and
> the Presages of Meteors, and other such like *Phænomena* of
> Nature.
> *Bathynous.* No, to tell you *syllabátim* in the Words of any Lan-
> guage what they naturally signifie. As suppose he would take
> the Word *Tetragrammaton* to task, he would tell you what all
> the Syllables signifie from *Te* to *Ton.*[41]

More had in mind the esoteric commentary on Genesis furnished by
the *Mysterium Magnum,* in which Boehme says that the "Word and
power of God . . . is hidden to the visible sensible elements: and
yet dwelleth through and in the elements; and worketh through the
sensible life and essence"; and "Thus man hath now received ability
from the invisible Word of God to the re-expression: that he again
expresseth the hidden Word of the divine science into formation and
severation: . . . as we plainly see, that the understanding of man
expresseth all powers in their property, and giveth names unto all
things, according to each thing's property, by which the hidden wisdom is known and understood in its power: and the hidden God is
made manifest with the visible things. . . ."[42] In spite of their numerous agitated denials to those, like Lodowick Muggleton, who insisted that "Jacob Behmont's Books were the chief Books that the
Quakers bought, for there is the Principle or Foundation of their Religion," it is beyond dispute that some important early Quakers read
the works of Boehme with some sympathy.[43] And it seems probable
that Henry More was on the right track in implying a connection between Boehme's conception of "natural language" and that of the
Quakers. Yet the theory, although it explains the "incantatory" style,
would not necessarily imply that style as a corollary. Boehme, with
a theory of language practically identical, lived in a different world
from that of Fox and the First Publishers. His insistence upon the
essential language of nature leads him to explicate Genesis by moving
ever farther away from the Scripture itself, moving out through psychological allegorization into the systematic re-imaging of even that
in terms of Paracelsian alchemy. His constant effort is to conceptu-
alize the literal into system. The Quaker understanding of how one
reaches the spiritual truths locked in the magic of words, on the other
hand, demands an ever closer attention to the words "syllabatim"
until one is drawn physically into the special literalness in which
alone words can give up their secrets. So it seems improbable that

Boehme's theory of the relation between language and being played any part in developing the form of Quaker "incantatory" style, although it contributed to the motivating conception of essential "names."

The form itself was likely based to some degree on sheer imitation. The Johannine writings, the *Gospel,* the *Revelation* and the *Epistles* alike, were the very heart of the Scriptures for the seventeenth-century Quaker. It was most frequently by applying to themselves the opening verse of John's First Epistle, "That which was from the beginning, which we have heard, which we have seen with our eyes, which we have looked upon, and our hands have handled, of the Word of life," that the Quakers set their "experimental" knowledge of God and Christ against the merely notional knowledge of the high professors in the "steeplehouses." And this favored book gave the Quakers a model for their "incantatory" repetition. I John is a litany of love which moves to an emotional crescendo when it centers down into the idea through just that mode of repetition which we have found so typical of Quaker style: "Beloved, let us love one another: for love is of God; and every one that loveth is born of God, and knoweth God. He that loveth not, knoweth not God; for God is love. . . . Beloved, if God so loved us, we ought also to love one another. No man hath seen God at any time. If we love one another, God dwelleth in us, and his love is perfected in us. . . ." (I John 4:7-12; cf. the whole of chapter four).[44] But if John's epistle was an important source, imitation alone does not account for the omnipresence of the style in early Quaker writings. To understand not only where it originated, but why it was in such constant prominence, we must turn to the wider Puritan context of "spiritual perception" which will explain how a theory influenced by Boehme and a style out of the *New Testament* came to interact.

The conservative Presbyterian hierarchists who created the New England theocracy, taking their lead from the great Elizabethans William Perkins and William Ames, declared that regeneration came through the dual causation of divine influence and a sensible phantasm, "the grace of God must always invade a soul through the vehicle of a sense impression." The chief practical result of this theory was the glorification of the sermon. "The one means above all others which was perfectly adapted to working upon all faculties, that simultaneously could carry phantasms to both reason and affection, that would impress the species of Gospel theorems upon the understand-

ing and at the same time plunge them deep into the heart, was clearly
the spoken word."[45] In such a theory the word is assuming to itself
an independent, arational spiritual importance unrelated to any rhetorical or logical theory of language function. And if this was true in
the world of conservative Presbyterianism, sensible "phantasms" like
the word advanced to yet profounder spiritual importance in the
world of Independency and enthusiastic sectarianism. Geoffrey Nuttall has demonstrated that "The radical Puritans, in particular, . . .
sought to associate the Holy Spirit less with reason or conscience and
more with spiritual perception analogous to the physical perception
of the senses and given in 'experience' as a whole. It was possible to
avoid the charge of dependence upon something irrational by pointing out that reason has an intuitive aspect as well as a discursive."
For instance, citing a frequently-used Scripture text, Peter Sterry,
the Puritan Platonist, said, "I can no more convey a sense of the difference (between Reason and Spirit) into any soule, that hath not
seen these two Lights shining in it self: than I can convey the difference between Salt and Sugar; to him, who hath never tasted sweet or
sharp. These things are discerned only by exercise of senses. *Heb.*
5.14." Even more to the point is the Puritan divine Richard Sibbes'
query, "How do you know the word to be the word? It carrieth proof
and evidence in itself. It is an evidence that the fire is hot to him that
feeleth it, and that the sun shineth to him that looks on it; how much
more doth the word . . . I am sure I felt it, it warmed my heart, and
converted me."[46]

This Puritan insistence upon the perception of spiritual truths
being analogous to and intimately dependent upon physical perception is the tradition which ultimately forms the framework for the
Quaker theory of the function of words and their utilization in passages of "incantatory" repetition. Since a word, properly grasped, reveals the essential quality of a datum *sub specie aeternitatis*, an idea
remains static throughout its repetitions, as we have noticed. It cannot be explained by man, but only understood. The Quaker is constantly exhorted to "wait" for the call to the inner man which will
enlighten the understanding and allow it to acquiesce in the spiritual
conception presented to it for consideration by the Light from the
Day of the Lord. This was, of course, the rationale of the "silent"
worship for which Quakers were so notorious. One did not speak out
with the voice of human piety, as did the Puritan preacher, but
waited until some Friend became the instrument of the Lord, and

felt the Light of Christ Within answer to the Light of the Lord's Day without. When the answer came, it came as an immediate grasp of spiritual reality; and when it was spoken out to the meeting, it was the voice of God which sounded the deeps of divine significance in the words. In the Presbyterian theory the Word of God could become immediate and "saving" only through the words of man. The Quaker theory pressed to the apotheosis: the Word of God spoke its unveiled mysteries immediately to the ears of the saints. But the very fact of the demand for silence until the Spirit moved one implied clearly enough that even the saints who knew the Lord's Day to be upon them could sometimes be cold and unreceptive. What better stimulus to the whole understanding of mind and heart, then, while it waits upon its awakening to an immediate, God-spoken conception, than an incantation by which the word, the name, which *is* that conception, permeates the mind and the senses through the echoing and re-echoing voice of God?

V

The aim of Christianity, an aim paradoxically intensified for the Augustinian cast of mind with its emphasis upon Will and the individual religious experience, has always been to pass beyond the parable of the flesh to the reality of the divine. The Puritans, with their Augustinian heritage, wrote and wrote again the *Confessiones* in the seventeenth century, climaxing the tradition with Bunyan's *Grace Abounding*. Alert to catch the call to their election, and to discipline all of their psychic powers to renewed efforts in response to this call, they searched every detail of their daily life for reflections of their spiritual standing, and recorded much of it in laboriously conscientious diaries, lest any premonitory sign should pass without giving sufficient warning. The spiritual autobiographies, the collections of preachers' lives, tell of the unceasing self-analysis which was the Puritan way of insuring passage from the Old Man to the New. "The devout Puritan turned his back on stage plays and romances, but only in order to look in his own heart and write what happened there."[47] The result was a ubiquitous sense of *person* dominating, and giving its peculiar character to, Puritan religious writing. The image through which they can manipulate experience is that of an individual in mortal daily conflict with a world his fallen fathers made; if this is

most obviously to be remarked in the spiritual autobiographies, we
have but to recall the "characters" embedded in Puritan sermons, to
recall not only *Grace Abounding* but *Pilgrim's Progress, Mr. Bad-
man,* and *The Heavenly Footman* to realize that it is a central mode
of Puritan thought.

But there were men of another mind in the seventeenth century,
men like John Everard, who could say, "all that thou callest I, all
that selfness, all that propriety that thou hast taken to thyself, whatsoever creates in us Iness and selfness, must be brought to nothing."[48]
And it was among these saints that the Quakers moved at ease. For
what was the individual in oneself but an accident and a tool, a thing
to be used only for its own annihilation in that glorious moment
when the Inner Light of Christ broke forth the same in every man,
to blend with the blazing truth of the Day of the Lord? And when
the Light Within gleamed unto salvation, it was not because man
was crossing to join Christ in the Celestial City, but because Christ
had risen again in man. Therefore, when the Quaker records his long
travel from Babylon to Bethel he exhibits none of the Calvinistic
Puritan's minutely-detailed psychological percipience, none of his circumstantial narrative framework of names and dates and scenes, none
of his careful recording of Scripture verse and chapter for each meditation. Instrumentalities are as nothing to him. Recalling the Puritan
reportorial insistence upon physical fact, as when Bunyan records,
"about ten or eleven a-clock on that day, as I was walking under an
hedge (full of sorrow and guilt God knows) . . . this word took
hold upon me, *The blood of Jesus Christ his Son, cleanseth us from
all sin,* I Joh. I. 7,"[49] let us listen to that "Ancient Servant of Christ"
Stephen Crisp:

> Then went I again down into the *North* of *England,* my heart
> being abundantly drawn out towards the noble Seed of God
> in those parts, and my Love and Tenderness of Heart towards
> them, made all Travel and Labour, and Perils easie; because
> I still saw the tender Plants of my Heavenly Father in a thriv-
> ing or growing way or condition, and I felt the vertue of Life
> daily springing in me, which was given me to Water the Herit-
> age and Garden of God with; and so soon as I was clear, I re-
> turned, having more and more still the care of the Church of
> God coming upon me, which constrained me to Diligence, and
> to be as swift as I might be, that so I might be as serviceable

as possible in my Generation, and might keep myself clear of the Blood of all Men, which I found to be no easie or Slight Work.[50]

What first strikes one is that Crisp conveys almost nothing personal or even concrete in trying to tell his own history—a history which, as the mention of perils and travels and spiritual struggle suggest, must have been stirring. There is only the vaguest localization in the "*North* of *England*." The personality of the spiritual adventurer is suppressed under the consistent passivity: he was "drawn out" to make his journey, "the Vertue of Life" *sprang up* within him. And other personalities are made even more thoroughly passive ornaments of the Lord as "tender Plants of my Heavenly Father," as the "Garden of God." By insisting upon the spiritual experience, Crisp almost denies existence to the physical experience, reducing it to the one clause, "and my Love and Tenderness of Heart towards them, made all Travel and Labour, and Perils easie," which acknowledges the activities of the traveller only that they can be simultaneously subordinated to the activities of the spirit working within him. But perhaps most suggestive of all, we cannot judge even roughly how long the experience took, because it does not exist in a framework of time. The only temporality in the passage lies in the few suggestions of continuity. Crisp sees his whole life (for this is a typical section of the "Journal") as the reflection in continuously-repeated events of the eternal life of the invisible "Church of God."[51]

The effect is antithetical to that of the Puritan spiritual records because in these latter the experience is specific, details are supplied, and the inevitable illuminating Scripture phrase itself, often as an auditory hallucination, becomes one of the details of a total physical experience which has had spiritual significance for the subject. In the Quaker records, on the other hand, personal histories are made so vague that they seem almost to lose reality.[52] This does not always mean that they are not vivid, as evidenced when quondam constable Richard Sale of Hoole writes to Fox of his activities at Chester in 1655:

In thy dread and fear I was exceedingly kept, and my countenance was as fierce as a lion, which was dreadful unto the wicked. And when the lion roared through the streets, the beasts of the field began to tremble, and many faces gathered

> paleness before me, and the strong was made weak, and many
> was brought into tenderness. For my mouth was opened in
> much power, and my mourning habit was exceeding dreadful,
> so that those which were clothed in hoods, veils and rings and
> changeable suits of apparel did hide themselves and were
> ashamed, and those that did come by me were made to blush,
> and their glory became their shame.[53]

Fox's *Journal* was earlier characterized as a vast symbol of his spiritual mission, in which the figures of people and the sight of places
are lost and merged. And yet, since Fox's intention was largely to
preserve the actual history of Quaker origins, it is true also that the
Journal embraces a considerably greater amount of historical detail
than is usual in Quaker accounts. A typical passage, I believe, can
reconcile the two descriptions:

> And as I travelled through markets, fairs, and diverse places,
> I saw death and darkness in all people, where the power of the
> Lord God had not shaken them. And as I was passing on in
> Leicestershire I came to Twycross, where there were excise-
> men, and I was moved of the Lord to go to them and warn
> them to take heed of oppressing the poor, and people were
> much afflicted with it. Now there was in that town a great
> man, that had long lain sick and was given over by the physi-
> cians; and some Friends in the town desired me to go to see
> him. And I went up to him and was moved to pray by him;
> spoke to him in his bed, and the power of the Lord entered
> him that he was loving and tender. (p. 49)

Even when we have the place and events, Fox presents only the results of an experience rather than a visualization of the experience
itself. Twycross is as little a place as the shadowy "markets, fairs, and
divers places" which flit past; one cannot guess where Fox met the
excise-men, nor how he warned them; we do not know the great
man's identity, his illness, his circumstances. We only know—and this
is the point—that Fox has focused the whole passage on an experience which brings before the reader Jesus' healings. Let us look now
at the continuation of the letter Richard Sale wrote to Fox. If the
lion's roaring was metaphoric, what follows is all too literal: "But
those that did stand afar off me, I was made to hold up my left hand

over the multitude, and to show them their figure. For I was made by thy command to take a leathern girdle, and to bind the sackcloth to my loins, and to take some sweet flowers in my left hand, and ashes strowed upon my head, bare footed and bare legged, which did astonish all that were out of the life." Even the literally reported is—as in Fox's implied healing of the "great man"—*scriptura rediviva*.[54] And this should bring to mind the characteristic "incantatory" style which attains the essence of a spiritual experience through sheer repetition of that Scripture word which contains the key to such an essence; the passage to the Word of God through the words of God. For what occurs in the de-personalizing of Quaker autobiography is that the Scripture phraseology which is inevitably borrowed or adapted for the telling becomes more important than any temporal events it might obscure,[55] as when James Nayler says, "the light of his Covenant led me in the spirit of *Elias* turning my heart towards him, that he might not smite the earth with a curse at his coming. . . ."[56] This is Nayler talking about some event that happened to him. But he sees it *only* as another instance of the spiritual experience embodied in Elias. Contemporary Quaker experiences seem to have no import to their subjects but as a framework upon which to string the language wherein the Scriptures tell the spiritual history of patriarchs and apostles alike.

Like "incantatory" repetition, this is a characteristic of Quaker style which weaves into homogeneity all levels of the Quaker community. It is a marked feature of Fox's *Journal*, especially in the earlier years,[57] as well as of his early pamphlets, such as *Old Simon the Sorcerer* (1663), which finds a ministry paid by tithes to be in the nature of Simon Magus. And it was taken up in numerous tracts and journals, ranging from shepherd William Dewsbury's *First Birth* (1655), in which his whole life is annotated by Scripture parallels, or London goldsmith John Bolton's *Testimony in that which Separates between the Pretious and the Vile* (1673), to *A Brief Account of My Souls Travel Towards the Holy Land* by the cultivated Lord Mayor's son, Isaac Penington, or *An Epistle for Vanity, to Prevent the Wiles of the Enemy* (1661) by John Crook, the wealthy Justice of the Peace who on another occasion, as we have noticed, could quote Juvenal and exhibit his Latinity in punning.

Cotton Mather, no friend, put his finger upon the point in a singularly incisive comment: "There is in every man a certain excusing and condemning *principle;* which indeed is nothing but some *re-*

mainder of the *divine image,* left by the compassion of God upon the *conscience* of man after his *fall;* and this *principle* the *Quakers* called, *a measure of the Man Christ, the light,* the *seed,* the *word.* The whole history of the *gospel* they therefore beheld as acted over again every day as *literally* as ever it was in Palestine."[58] The emphasis upon Christ Within misled Mather into limiting the Quakers to the "gospel." But this aside, he had seen deep into the Quaker mind, for it was just this conception of the Scripture histories being constantly lived over which gave their peculiarly atemporal cast to almost all Quaker attempts to talk about their own spiritual life before the age of Ellwood's maturity. Biblical imagery, of course, was a marked characteristic of all spiritual autobiography of the seventeenth century, most notably the call from bondage in Egypt and the journey to the promised land. But, as one reader has observed, it is merely "used extensively to explain and clarify the writers' experiences."[59] A much more organic function for such imagery is implied in Isaac Penington's comment that, "truly, there is as real deliverances witnessed inwardly, by those that wait upon the Lord and are faithful to the leadings of his Holy Spirit, as ever there was by the *Jews* outwardly, in their faithful following *Moses* and *Joshua:* and Christ is as truly an Healer of his People, in this Ministration of Life to them by his holy Spirit, as ever he was an Healer of Persons outwardly in the days of the Flesh. That (with the other Miracles which he wrought then) was but a shadow of what he would work and perform inwardly in the day of his Spirit and holy Power."[60] Remembering the conception that the essential nature of spiritual truths could be grasped through their outward names, we can see in Penington's remarks a justification of Mather. If the words embodying them give access to the vital essence of inward spiritual experiences, then we realize that it is just in terms of their Scriptural outward "shadows" that inward experiences can best be expressed. Such a theory clearly lies behind Fox's mode of statement when he unites all the elements—Scriptural expression, contemporaneity, and the integration of inward and outward faces—in a discovery of evil: "And I went back into Nottinghamshire, and there the Lord shewed me that the natures of those things which were hurtful without were within, in the hearts and minds of wicked men. The natures of dogs, swine, vipers, of Sodom and Egypt, Pharaoh, Cain, Ishmael, Esau, etc. The natures of these I saw within, though people had been looking without."[61] If the immediate realization is in the present, the mode of that realization is in the past. Yet this is to say it too simply. For if the same spirit informed the prophets of old, the apostles of Christ, and the modern saints—as the Quakers taught that it did, if the same light shines forth in all who come to see the Day of the Lord, then all true spiritual realization is alike at its heart. Indeed, all man's spiritual experience can only be a continuous reiteration of what has gone before, and before from the temporal point of view.[62] So when Fox says of a "false accuser," "I called him Judas, . . . told him again that he was Judas and that it was the word of the Lord and of Christ to him, and Judas's end should be his . . . [and] this Judas went away and hanged himself shortly after,"[63] it is not that there are certain analogies to be observed between the accuser and the Scriptural betrayer, but that the man's experience *is* Judas' experience, just as the Christ Within makes Fox able to say so bluntly of his own prophecy, "it was the word of the Lord and of Christ to him." It was as though the Quakers had found the great book of all mankind's spiritual history, too, written in a style of "incantatory" repetition which was the key to its own meaning.

VI

As Quakerdom passed on into the third quarter of the seventeenth century, this mode of viewing life as *scriptura rediviva,* like the "incantatory" style, withered and disappeared. Penn approaches the old perspective when he cries out, "Have you faith? Doth it overcome the world? . . . Turn out Ishmael? Offer up Isaac? . . . have a care lest you partake of the plagues that God hath prepared for Babylon. . . ."[64] But this is only an exhortation, and does not carry the clear impress of personal empathy which marks the style at its peak. And even so, one is hard-pressed to find such passages in Penn's works. Much commoner in all later-century Quaker writing, is a self-conscious analogizing through Scripture imagery which sounds only a faint echo of the immediacy of the same phrases on the tongues of the early Publishers of Truth. Robert Barclay is typical when he writes in the *Apology*: "For in our Day, God hath raised up Witnesses for himself, as he did Fisher-men of old; many, yea, most of whom, are Labouring and Mechanick Men; who altogether without that Learning, have, by the Power and Spirit of God, struck at the very Root and Ground of *Babylon*" (pp. 316-317). And Barclay's theory of the usefulness of Scriptural history corresponds to his diluted imagery: "herein we should, as in a Looking-Glass, see the Conditions and Experiences of the Saints of old; that finding our Experience *answer to* theirs, we might therein be the more confirmed and comforted and our Hope strengthened of obtaining the same end" (p. 84). The eternal epic of mankind, spoken by God and re-enacted by his saints forever, had dwindled to a *speculum mentis* for fallen man.

The cause of this decline in spiritual ardency and expressive vigor lay in the theological and social history of the Society. The evangelizing energy of the First Publishers had put them rapidly in "the vanguard of the enthusiastic movement"[65] which was climbing mercurially to its peak in the Commonwealth England of the forties and fifties. They "still regarded themselves as a spiritual Israel within the nation rather than as a separated sect."[66] Having built to a membership of forty thousand within a dozen years of their beginnings,[67] they were offered a great opportunity to make all England spiritual Sion in 1659. Sir Henry Vane and other Army partisans in that year of confusion petitioned the Quakers to submit lists of dependable local commissioners, justices, and other officers, and even to themselves participate in government directly (one symptom being the offer of a colonelcy to Fox).[68] Fox, to whom the Quaker meetings naturally turned for decision, wrestled in his soul for ten weeks, then rejected the proposals. The opportunity was past. And the aggressive, surging evangelism rising from the same sense of an immediate inward millennium that fostered the stylistic traits of early Quakerism had laid its own boundaries.

In 1657 John Camm died, marking the first passing among the twenty-odd itinerant evangelists who formed the first ring of strength around Fox and his dream. But within a dozen years more than half of those who had seen with the eyes of their own souls the first brilliance of the new Day of the Lord were gone. And the new generation of leaders had been born into a world immeasurably different from that of the dying First Publishers. It was the Restoration world of Penn, a world of "reasonable" temper whose aim was clarity and polish, whose hobby was natural science, and whose chief fear and detestation was that enthusiasm which had been the badge of prophecy to the early Quakers. From this later viewpoint it was as the Anglican critic Charles Leslie said: "the Ingenious Mr: *Penn* has of late refin'd some of their gross Notions, . . . has made them speak

Sense and *English,* of both which *George Fox* (their First and Great Apostle) was totally Ignorant. . . ."[69] But few of the First Publishers would have agreed. It is little wonder that in an epoch naturally so inimical to the original ideals the stylistic manifestations of the early theology were tempered,[70] but they could not have disappeared completely had the theology itself survived. That it did not and could not is a fact so intimately twisted into the accidents of milieu that it is fruitless to ask which was cause, which effect. The only certainty is that the theology and style of the First Publishers died together.

Although he was unable to decide which had bred the other, Stephen Crisp warned in 1684 that a cooling of spiritual zeal and a new concern with abstruse theological speculation were gnawing at the vitals of the Society.[71] He was one of the first who saw what had by that time already become fact. Fox was no Calvinist. Optimistic in his conception of man, he assumed the human will to be free to choose or to reject God, and he envisaged the possibility of salvation for every man. And yet, as has been recently demonstrated, there was an undercurrent of Calvinism even in Fox. It appears in his constant emphasis upon the "Dark Night of Apostacy" in which the world had long struggled, and in which "the interrelation of the self-wills of men forms an evil reality whose existence seems to be something more than the sum of the specific evils that constitute it . . . it has made the whole world a dark world of sin and death from which man must be led by a divine light." It appears in his frequent insistence upon God "crashing violently into a man's life both at conversion and afterward," so that Fox half retains "the Calvinistic idea of the manipulation of man by God." And it appears also in his view (although it was one he did not hold consistently) that man enters a new and secure state when he is regenerated.[72] This undercurrent obviously contains the germ of an attitude which could temper the evangelical optimism that drove Fox and his followers tirelessly over England, across America, to Turkey, into Rome itself. That germ began to grow with the appearance of Penn's *Christian Quaker* in 1674. Penn had studied with that original theologian Moses Amyraldus in his youth, and in the treatment of the Light Within in *The Christian Quaker* he adapted Amyraldus' "hypothetical universalism" to this central conception of Quaker theology.[73] Amyraldus—dissatisfied with Calvinist orthodoxy's claim that Christ died only for the elect—insisted that he had died for all, making the benefits of his death to be *intended* for all men, although in practice they were only *appropriated* by the elect. Penn, through a historical survey of the ancient philosophers, shows that the "Light which is Christ" has been known to men in every age of the world. And he further argues that the goodness of God cannot be supposed unless this has been a "sufficient" means to salvation for all men. But some men allow themselves to be blinded by the temptations of the world, and so fall into darkness by their refusal to accept the Light. "In short, all have light to reprove, unless they have quite put out their eyes; but only such have it beneficially, as their teacher and director, who receive it in the love of it."[74] In such a theology the universal Day of the Lord could be retained to shine in sterile theory, without disturbing the practical development of a deep-seated pessimism that would undermine the crusader hopeful of regaining paradise in this world. But it remained for Robert Barclay, raised in Scottish Calvinism and educated in French Catholicism, to make this Puritan strain dominate the Quaker theology. From its appearance in 1676 his *Apology for the True Christian Divinity* became, through the sheer thoroughness of its scholastically-organized *theses theologicae,* the authoritative voice of the Soceity's beliefs, and it spoke Calvinism. It began by asserting boldly man's evil: "We cannot suppose, that Men, who are come of *Adam* naturally, can have any good thing in their Nature, as belonging to it; which he, from whom they derive their Nature, had not himself to communicate unto them" (p. 97). Good comes of a Light or Seed implanted in man by God, a *vehiculum Dei* by which God can operate from a distance upon a soul alien to spirituality in its own right. This Seed can fall on stony ground, and be rejected by man, with his natural evil, "Therefore it is not by our works wrought in our will, nor yet by good works, considered as of themselves, but by Christ, who is both the Gift and the Giver, and the Cause producing the Effects in us [that our Justification is obtained]."[75] The rationale for "election" or the "gift" is as inscrutable as in Calvinistic orthodoxy. And like later Calvinism, Barclay sought assurance of election in tangible works: good works "are rather an Effect of *Justification,* than the Cause of it: But . . . good works as naturally proceed [from it], as Fruit from a fruitful Tree."[76] With the *Apology,* the last gleam of the millennium from within died away, and Quakerism was a sect and a morality.[77]

The anti-evangelical force of this rising Calvinism within the Society, merging with the natural anti-enthusiasm of men like Penn, was the ideational cause for the disappearance of the vivid stylistic

traits we have seen in the earlier prose of Quakerism. But the new
ideas and ideals culminated in a single act which greatly hastened
the total change in character which distinguishes Quaker writing of
the middle from that at the end of the century. This was the establishment of the Second-Day's Morning Meeting in 1673.

At the beginning, Friends had frequently consulted Fox or other
leaders when they intended printing tracts, but the practice was soon
made unfeasible by the numerous long imprisonments of the leading
First Publishers. But with a growing interest and the temporary success in securing toleration and civil rights for the Society, climaxed
by George Whitehead's interview with Charles II in 1672 which
resulted in a long list of pardons for imprisoned Quakers, the need
for curbing extravagancies seemed pressing.[78] Under these conditions,
Fox established the Second-Day's Morning Meeting in London. This
group's most important function was to pass upon Quaker manuscripts offered for publication. It was soon apparent that the leaders
were determined to stamp out everything which smacked of "enthusiasm": there are numerous records of their rejections and wholesale
alterations of manuscripts. Ellwood's version of Fox's *Journal*—an
editorial task assigned by the Morning Meeting—bears faint resemblance to the manuscript version made at Fox's dictation, and Fox's
whole corpus was minutely smoothed out, theologically and stylistically, for republishing.[79] Even Robert Barclay suffered posthumously, the Meeting deciding not to publish in his collected folio anything he had written after 1676 because he had given to "strange,
intricate and unlearned questions" "some nice and disputable answers and replications tending to bring new and unusual controversies into the world."[80] And this censorship not only altered the course
of later Quaker style, but was made retroactive in the total omission
from early Friends' "collected works" of some enthusiastic tracts,[81]
and the toning down of others. The Meeting particularly repressed
Jeremiads (in which the "incantatory" style had been so prominent),[82] apocalyptic papers, and anything chaotic in expression (as
certainly the "incantatory" style must have seemed to a later generation). The age of plainness had come, and Quaker style henceforth
was to be distinguished only by a few pathetic anachronisms of diction. And when the Morning Meeting listened to the ancient voices
of the First Publishers of Truth, they heard only an "abrupt and
broken" uncouthness where once God had spoken, and strong hearts
had quaked in the glory of the sound.

NOTES

1. This study was made possible during 1954 by a Folger Library Fellowship, a grant from the Graduate School of the Ohio State University, and a Gustav Bissing Fellowship at The Johns Hopkins University.
2. As has been so amply demonstrated in George Williamson's *The Senecan Amble* (London and Chicago, 1951).
3. The only literary study worthy of mention is the ground-breaking survey by Luella M. Wright, *The Literary Life of the Early Friends, 1650-1725* (New York, 1932).
4. *The Journal of George Fox,* ed. John L. Nickalls (Cambridge, 1952), p. 2. This is a composite text (see pp. vii-xii) which incorporates the *Cambridge Journal,* the *Short Journal,* Ellwood's edition, and the American diaries. Modernized spelling, checked against the *Cambridge Journal,* has been adopted in this study.
5. Geoffrey F. Nuttall, *The Holy Spirit in Puritan Faith and Experience* (Oxford, 1947), pp. 39-40.
6. Rachel Knight—*The Founder of Quakerism: A Psychological Study of the Mysticism of George Fox* (London, 1922)—although she insists upon Fox's keen senses, can adduce no passage but the one I have quoted to illustrate his gustatory sensitivity (pp. 62-63).
7. *Rise and Progress of the Quakers* in *The Peace of Europe and Other Writings by William Penn* (Everyman's Library, London, n.d.), p. 209.
8. *Grace Abounding,* ed. John Brown (Cambridge, 1907), p. 20.
9. One major reservation must be made. In the several vividly-detailed scenes of mob punishment and prison conditions Fox—like George Bishop in *New England Judged* or William Sewell in *The History of the Quakers*—is acting as a deliberate Quaker propagandist, not as a spiritual diarist. On this Quaker concern for creating an *acta martyrorum* from Friends' lives see Wright, *Literary Life of Early Friends,* pp. 87-96.
10. Other interesting occurrences of the sort appear on pp. 21, 235, 242, 349, 375, 542 and 544.
11. Quoted by M. Whitcomb Hess, "A Quaker Plotinus," *Hibbert Jour.,* xxix (1931), 483.
12. Cf. 2 Cor. xii:4.
13. This was no passing flight of imagination for Fox. Ten years later he met a group of "mountebanks" whom he asked "whether any knew the virtue of all the creatures in the creation, whose virtue and nature was according to its first name, except they were in the wisdom of God by which they were made and created" (*Journal,* p. 287).

14. *A General Epistle to be Read in all the Christian Meetings in the World* (n.p., 1662), pp. 1-2. My italics indicate a passage showing that Fox believed all who come to perceive Christ Within will share his own experience of being "showed how all things had their names given them according to their nature and virtue."

15. *A Few Plain Words of Instruction given forth as Moved of the Lord* (London, 1658), p. 18.

16. *The Morning-Watch: Or, A Spiritual Glass Opened* (London, 1660), pp. 11-12.

17. *Truth's Principles* (London, 1662), pp. 8-9.

18. *Apology for the True Christian Divinity*, 6th ed. (London, 1736), p. 184.

19. Cf. Kate W. Tibbals, "The Speech of Plain Friends," *Amer. Speech*, 1 (1926), 200: "Every word in the specific Quaker vocabulary is a Bible word to which a still more mystical connotation has been given. The whole intent of Friends was to direct attention away from the *creature*, their expression for the material side of phenomena, the *created* things, live or not, to the spirit, the *indwelling principle* that formed the essence of their specific variation of primitive Christianity."

20. In *A Memorable Account of the Christian Experiences of Stephen Crisp* (London, 1694), pp. 122-123. Besides those cited in the text, the following are some important statements of the primary place of the "Name" in Quaker thought during the early years: Fox, *Journal*, pp. 2, 122, 125, 603, 604; James Nayler, *Love to the Lost* (London, 1665 [1656]), sig. B2^r, pp. 1-7, 10-11; Edward Burrough, *A Standard Lifted Up* [1657] in *Memorable Works of a Son of Thunder and Consolation* ([London], 1672), pp. 249-250; William Smith, *The Morning-Watch* (London, 1660), pp. 1-3, 13; Robert Barclay, *Apology*, Prop. II, sect. v; Prop. XII, sect. viii; Margaret Fell, *A Brief Collection of Remarkable Passages and Occurrences* (London, 1710), p. 194, and *An Evident Demonstration to Gods Elect* (London, 1660), p. 3; William Penn, *Primitive Christianity Revived in the Faith and Practice of the People Called Quakers* [1696], Everyman ed., pp. 236-237.

21. *A Mite into the Treasury, Being a Word to Artists, Especially to Heptatechnists, the Professors of the Seven Liberal Arts, So Called* (London, 1680), p. 17.

22. "Anti-fanatical Religion and Free Philosophy," *Essays on Several Important Subjects* (London, 1676), pp. 31-32.

23. Anna Cox Brinton, "The Function of Quaker Literature," *Friends' Quarterly Examiner*, LXVI (1932), 367.

24. On the vogue and revival of the "witty" sermon see W. Fraser Mitchell, *English Pulpit Oratory from Andrewes to Tillotson* (London, 1932), pp. 148-194, 308-309, 352-357.

25. Lancelot Andrewes, *XCVI Sermons* (London, 1635), p. 45.
26. *Rise and Progress of Quakers*, Everyman ed., p. 208.
27. *An Evident Demonstration to Gods Elect* (London, 1660), pp. 5-6.
28. *A Testimony for the Lord, by John Swinton* (n.p., n.d. [London, 1663?]), pp. 6-7.
29. Cf. esp. *A Warning to all Teachers which are Called School-Masters and School-Mistresses* (London, 1657); *A General Epistle* (n.p., 1662) already cited; *The Line of Righteousness and Justice Stretched forth over All Merchants* (London, 1661); *An Epistle to be Read in all the Assemblies of the Righteous* (n.p., 1666); *Journal*, pp. 13, 59-60, 228, 575-576. Extended "incantatory" passages in the *Journal* occur (with a single exception) in "epistles" interpolated into the narrative.
30. *A Manifestation of Divine Love* (London, 1660), pp. 13-14.
31. *To All the Faithful in Christ Who Have Stood in his Council the Light* (n.p., 1663).
32. Circumstances which we shall later examine converged to cool the evangelistic optimism which the First Publishers brought to the founding of Quakerism and, as a corollary, to curb the "incantatory" outbursts of the earlier prose. Yet the old mode held on sometimes when writers of the second generation were "moved" to intense exhortation, and one finds occasional vestiges even in such an unlikely author as the courtly William Penn. A passage in his *Advice to His Children* (Everyman ed., pp. 96-97) is the most interesting, because Penn is there writing within a conscious rhetorical structure. Having explained the Light and Spirit logically, he launches into an "incantatory" passage of exhortation, then drops back into an explanation of Grace, after which he again adapts the "incantatory" style to an exhortation to "love the grace." It is a late example (publ. posthumously 1726, composition date indeterminate) of the style which shows its adaption to a larger rhetorical pattern. Penn, apparently unaware of the aim of such passages in earlier Quaker literature and meetings (as his remarks on Fox's "broken" style indicate), simply utilizes it as a sort of imagination-stirring purple passage which is common in his religious tradition.
33. *The Quakers Plea, Answering All Objections, and they proved to be no way dangerous, but Friends to the King* . . . (London, 1661).
34. *An Apology for the Quakers: Wherein is shewed, How they Answer the Chief Principles of the Law, and Main ends of Government* (London, 1662).
35. *Liberty of Conscience Pleaded by Several Weighty Reasons on the Behalf of the People of God Called Quakers* (London, 1663).
36. *Womens Speaking Justified, Proved and Allowed of by the Scriptures* (London, 1666).

37. *A Tolleration Sent down from Heaven to Preach* (n. p., 1665).
38. *Fiat Lux* ([Douay?], 1662), pp. 171-172. Canes's attitude was more generous than that of most critics of "Foxonian" Quakerism. Charles Leslie thought Fox and his fellows ignorant of *"Sense and English"* (*The Snake in the Grass* [London, 1696], p. 5; cf. p. 58), and Cotton Mather found Fox a "proud fool who could scarce write his name," and hence an appropriate leader for the Quakers (*Magnalia Christi Americana*, [1702; Hartford, 1820], II, 455). Henry More was suggestive. Having discussed Quakers, he passed to David George with whom—through Familism and mistakenly—he associated the sect. Of George he says: "For a man illiterate, as he was, but of good parts, by constant reading of the Bible will naturally contract a more winning and commanding Rhetorick then those that are learned; the intermixture of Tongues and of artificiall Phrases debasing their style, and making it sound more after the manner of men, though ordinarily there may be more of God in it then in that of the *Enthusiast*" (*Enthusiasmus Triumphatus* [1656] in *A Collection of Several Philosophical Writings*, London, 1662, p. 24).
39. It was a common 17th-century view that the 16th-century Family of Love, founded by the German, Henrik Niklaes, and extant in England from about 1560 into the 18th century, was the origin of Quakerism. Cf. Allen C. Thomas, *The Family of Love, or the Familists*, Haverford Coll. Studies, XII (Haverford, 1893), pp. 25-26, 34-37; Rufus M. Jones, *Studies in Mystical Religion* (London, 1909), pp. 428-448; and Marjorie Nicolson, *Conway Letters* (New Haven, 1930), pp. 378-383. The latter book treats More's relations to Quakerism, pp. 378-451. Cf. also Nicolson's "George Keith and the Cambridge Platonists," *Philos. Rev.*, XXXIX (1930), 36-55.
40. *Divine Dialogues* [1668] (London, 1713), pp. 456-470.
41. Ibid., p. 461. Closely relevant, because of the analysis of interaction between sensible outwardness and inward essence, is More's warning *a propos* of Boehme's pretension to having discovered the internal Kingdoms of the "Light World" and the "Dark Fire World": "He that will averr he has discovered those *internal Worlds* by Sense, must first assure himself that he is not imposed upon by his Imagination. . . . But if they did believe there were such an *internal* World, and did vehemently desire to converse there, how exceedingly credible is it that these People would take their inward Phantasms for external Objects in that *inward* World!" (ibid., p. 466).
42. Trans. John Sparrow [1654] (London, 1924), I, ix-x.
43. All of Boehme's books were in English by 1662. Cf. Robert Barclay, *Inner Life of the Religious Societies of the Commonwealth* (London, 1876), pp. 213-215; Margaret L. Bailey, *Milton and Jakob Boehme* (New York, 1914), pp. 96-104; Rufus M. Jones, *Spiritual Reform-*

ers of the 16th and 17th Centuries (London, 1914), pp. 221-227;
Henry J. Cadbury, "Early Quakerism and Uncanonical Lore," *Harvard Theol. Rev.*, XL (1947), 203-204; Nils Thune, *The Behmenists and the Philadelphians* (Uppsala, 1948), pp. 62-67, all of which support an influence of Boehme upon the Quakers. Nuttall, *Holy Spirit*, pp. 16-18, rejects the influence of Boehme more sweepingly than his evidence would seem to justify.

44. Harold C. Dodd, *The Johannine Epistles,* Moffatt New Testament Commentary (London, 1946), p. xxi, uses terms to describe the style of the First Epistle which might be applied to the Quaker characteristic under discussion. He finds "little direct progression" as "the author 'thinks around' a subject," and he echoes a previous description of the style as "spiral."

45. Perry Miller, *The New England Mind: The 17th Century* (New York, 1939), p. 295. Pages 280-299 expound the system and its relations to the sermon.

46. *Holy Spirit,* pp. 38, 39. Cf. pp. 38-41, 135, 139, 142. The *Gospel according to St. John:* 6:26-63 and 17:9-26, shows a diffused version of the style, but scarcely seems capable of arousing the same effect.

47. William Haller, *The Rise of Puritanism* (New York, 1938), p. 96. Cf. pp. 94-117.

48. *Some Gospel Treasures opened* (London, 1653), p. 230.

49. *Grace Abounding,* p. 44.

50. "A Journal of the Life of Stephen Crisp," in *A Memorable Account,* pp. 27-28.

51. It is pertinent to notice Fox's claim that "we were redeemed out of days by Christ Jesus and brought into his day" (*Journal,* p. 669).

52. For general discussions of Quaker spiritual lives see Wright, *Literary Life of Early Friends,* pp. 155-198; Howard H. Brinton, "Stages in Spiritual Development as Recorded in Quaker Journals," in *Children of Light,* ed. Brinton (New York, 1938), pp. 381-406; Owen Watkins, "Quaker Spiritual Biographies," *JFHS,* XLV (1953). Both Wright (p. 158) and Brinton (p. 384) insist upon the "dual characteristic of the writers' motives, merging with those of the group" (Wright).

53. Quoted from Swarthmore MSS. 4.211, in Geoffrey Nuttall, *Studies in Christian Enthusiasm* (Wallingford, Pa., 1948), pp. 34-35. Cf. William C. Braithwaite, *The Beginnings of Quakerism* (London, 1912), pp. 126-127, on Sale and this letter.

54. Sale here demonstrates one of the most notorious Quaker practices by which Scripture was made to live anew in a naïve sense. Going in sackcloth and ashes, carrying candles at midday, walking naked in the streets were common behavior among Quakers who wished to give "signs" of warning to the "world's" people. It embraced both

sexes and all classes—even Robert Barclay once felt called upon so to humiliate himself. See Braithwaite, *Beginnings of Quakerism*, pp. 126-127, 148-151, 252-258; Nuttall, *Holy Spirit*, p. 26; Nuttall, *Christian Enthusiasm*, pp. 33-34.

55. It is interesting to see that a student of Quaker terminology says of "experiences": "this word is never used of outward events, mere *creaturely* happenings" (Tibbals, p. 200).

56. *What the Possession of the Living Faith Is* . . . (London, 1659), p. 12. This whole first-person narrative of Nayler's passage through successive spiritual states is an excellent example of the stylistic phenomenon under discussion.

57. See *Journal*, pp. 15, 19, 21, 31, 57, 96, 98, 106, 108, 133, 142, 192, 358, 367-368, 407, 416, 424, 663 for the most interesting occurrences. Occasionally Fox speaks only of the similarity of his own and Scriptural experiences, but in these few cases he is anxious to show detailed coincidences of event as well as of spiritual state. Nuttall suggests that Fox spoke inaccurately of the First Publishers as "a matter of 70 ministers" because he had in mind the seventy sent out by Jesus (*Christian Enthusiasm*, p. 18). A subsidiary cause for this stylistic trait is suggested in an exhaustive analysis of Fox's "craving for the unchanging, and the deep impression that the transitoriness of events made upon him" (Rachel H. King, *George Fox and the Light Within: 1650-1660*, Philadelphia, 1940, pp. 113-116, 166).

58. *Magnalia Christi Americana*, II, 452. John Whiting, in the definitive Quaker answer to Mather's attack, flatly denied the charge, of course: "this is false, and I dare him to prove who ever said so" (*Truth and Innocency Defended* . . . *In Answer to Cotton Mather* [1702] printed with George Bishop, *New England Judged*, Philadelphia, 1885, p. 442). The point was that no one said so, but that the fact was implicit in the whole structure of the Quakers' expression of spiritual experience and insight.

59. See Owen Watkins, "Early Quaker Biographies," *JFHS*, XLV (1953), 69.

60. *Concerning the Sum or Substance of Our Religion Who Are Called Quakers* [1666] *in Works of the Long-Mournful and Sorely-Distressed Isaac Penington* (London, 1681), I, 459-460.

61. *Journal*, p. 19. Cf. p. 31.

62. With what caution and yet sublime confidence the First Publishers must have chosen the Scriptural terms for describing their experiences can be partially inferred from their general demur from psalm singing because persons in a wicked state, or those who felt no genuine "motion," would thus take the holy words of David into their own mouths (Barclay, *Inner Life of the Religious Societies*, pp. 456-458; Braithwaite, *Beginnings of Quakerism*, p. 237).

63. *Journal*, p. 96. Cf. Fox's statement about a man who saved him from stoning: "and he was Lot, I told him" (p. 98), or his accusation to Cromwell that "he was Pilate, though he would wash his hands" (p. 192).

64. *A Call to Christendom* [written 1677], Everyman ed., p. 155.

65. Nuttall, *Christian Enthusiasm*, p. 23.

66. Braithwaite, *Beginnings of Quakerism*, p. 508.

67. Ibid., p. 512.

68. See J. F. Maclear, "Quakerism and the End of the Interregnum: A Chapter in the Domestication of Radical Puritanism," *Church Hist.*, XIX (1950), 240-270. Questionnaires had actually been tabulated by some Quaker county groups.

69. *Snake in the Grass*, p. 5.

70. Cf. Luella M. Wright, *Literature and Education in Early Quakerism*, Univ. of Iowa Stud., Humanistic Stud., v, ii (Iowa City, 1933), p. 26, on the infrequency of "distinct 'openings' or of mystic voices" in the writings of the later generations.

71. *A Faithful Warning and Exhortation to Friends to Beware of Seducing Spirits and to Keep on the Armour of Light . . .* in *A Memorable Account*, pp. 478-497.

72. I have condensed and quoted from the analysis by King, *Fox and the Light Within*, pp. 39-47.

73. The influence of Amyraldus is analyzed in Herbert G. Wood, "William Penn's *The Christian Quaker*," in *Children of Light*, pp. 1-23. It is ironic that the most learned and persistent Quaker-baiter among contemporary Puritans was Richard Baxter, whose own theology owed a considerable debt to Amyraldus' "hypothetical universalism" (see F. J. Powicke, *The Reverend Richard Baxter Under the Cross, 1662-1691*, London, 1927, pp. 236-238).

74. *The Christian Quaker* in *Select Works of William Penn* (London, 1782), I, 279. Cf. pp. 277-282 for the argument as I have summed it up.

75. *Apology*, p. 9. Cf. Leif Eeg-Olofsson, *The Conception of the Inner Light in Robert Barclay's Theology* (Lund, 1954), pp. 71-82.

76. *Apology*, p. 205. Cf. p. 305, where Barclay is willing to grant a special degree of Grace to ministers in whom the Seed has brought forth extraordinary morality. Cf. Eeg-Olofsson, *Inner Light*, pp. 56-60, 120.

77. Rufus M. Jones, in his introduction to William C. Braithwaite's *Second Period of Quakerism* (London, 1919), pp. xxx-xlv, first traced the Quietistic decline in vigor of 18th-century Quakerism to Barclay's Calvinism.

78. Braithwaite, *Second Period*, pp. 82-87.

79. See Norman Penney, "George Fox's Writings and the Morning

Meeting," *Friends' Quarterly Examiner*, XXXVI (1902), 63-72. The fullest account of the Morning Meeting's censorship activities is in Wright, *Literary Life of Early Friends*, pp. 97-109.

80. Arnold Lloyd, *Quaker Social History, 1669-1730* (London, 1950), pp. 150-151, 156.

81. Nuttall, *Christian Enthusiasm*, p. 40. So far as I know, Leslie was the first publicly to notice this Quaker practice. He pounced with delight upon the fact that *"in the Reprinting the Works of their Prophets since 1660, they leave out these* NOW *unsavory passages. Their* Infallibility *needs an* Index Expurgatorius *as well as that of Rome,"* then went on to give chapter and verse from the collection of Burrough's works (*Snake in the Grass*, pp. xcvii-civ).

82. Wright, *Literary Life of Early Friends*, pp. 128-129.

Individual Styles

WALTER R. DAVIS

✍

The Imagery of Bacon's Late Work

In a recent article suggesting, among other things, that Bacon's program for the advancement of learning might have "the status of a
work of the imagination" or wit, Arnold Stein draws attention to an
interesting passage on images in *De Sapientia Veterum*:

> When the inventions and conclusions of human reason . . .
> were as yet new and strange, the world was full of all kinds
> of fables, and enigmas, and parables, and similitudes: and
> these were used not as a device for shadowing and concealing
> the meaning, but as a method of making it understood. . . .
> For as hieroglyphics came before letters, so parables came be-
> fore arguments. *And even now if any one wish to let new
> light on any subject into men's minds . . . he must still go
> the same way and call in the aid of similitudes.*[1]

At the beginnings of philosophy—and afterwards in any very new
philosophy such as Bacon's certainly was—images and similitudes prepare the mind for the arguments that follow. If Bacon followed this
precept in his actual practice, then his images should perform a
hitherto unsuspected function in his works in spite of their subordination to argument; they should deepen statements or even produce

From the *Modern Language Quarterly*, XXVII (1966), pp. 162-173. Reprinted by their permission.

suggestions going beyond statement in readying the reader's consciousness for what is new.

I think that we see this very function evident in Bacon's mature works, and I shall try to illustrate it by examining the tight imagery of a single late essay, "Of Truth," and the dispersed images of his great work, the *Novum Organum*. "Of Truth," added to the *Essays* in 1625 (five years after the publication of *Novum Organum*), indicates, as some of the other late essays do, a shift from the dry aphoristic style which cut off "discourses of illustration" and "recitals of examples" to a more highly embellished hortatory style—and an imagistic one.[2] In "Of Truth" Bacon accomplishes his usual shift from a pragmatic, often Machiavellian, view of his topic to a deeper ethical view of it, not only by the sudden introduction of Augustine's moral judgment of the lie (which Bacon had treated so coolly before), but by images as well. The first half of the essay had been dominated by images of light and artifice:

> But I cannot tell: this same truth is a naked and open day-light, that doth not shew the masks and mummeries and triumphs of the world, half so stately and daintily as candle-lights. Truth may perhaps come to the price of a pearl, that sheweth best by day; but it will not rise to the price of a diamond or carbuncle, that sheweth best in varied lights. (XII, 82)[3]

But now at the turning point, the image of light takes on a new meaning: it is not man's physical light but God's Light, the effluence of Wisdom and creative power; and the style, in response to this new view of things, becomes tightly controlled by curt tripartite (or Trinitarian) series:

> The first creature of God, in the works of the days, was the light of the sense; the last was the light of reason; and his sabbath work ever since, is the illumination of his Spirit. First he breathed light upon the face of the matter or chaos; then he breathed light into the face of man; and still he breatheth and inspireth light into the face of his chosen.

The subsidiary images have changed, too, from man's shimmering artifacts to God's brilliant Creation, and so this portion of the essay ends with an image of the mind of the just man as God's microcosm: "Certainly, it is heaven upon earth, to have a man's mind move in charity, rest in providence, and turn upon the poles of truth." Bacon has transferred his reader from the realm of man's depraved judgments of truth to that of its real nature *sub specie aeternitatis* by means of images. And he backs them up by his wide allusions to providential history; starting in the midst of postlapsarian life with Pilate's supreme denial of truth and Truth and with all men's "natural though corrupt love of the lie itself," he then takes us back to Creation, then through corruption, to end with the Last Day when man's view and God's view of this topic must coalesce:

> For these winding and crooked courses are the goings of the serpent; which goeth basely upon the belly and not upon the feet. There is no vice that doth so cover a man with shame as to be found false and perfidious. . . . For a lie faces God, and shrinks from man. Surely the wickedness of falsehood and breach of faith cannot possibly be so highly expressed, as in that it shall be the last peal to call the judgments of God upon the generations of men; it being foretold, that when Christ cometh, *he shall not find faith upon the earth*. (XII, 83-84)

One might describe the intellectual action effected by this essay as a large shift in point of view—engineered by images and supported by allusions—producing a change in tone, from the dry wit of the opening to the earnest contemplation of the Second Coming at the end.

"Of Truth" has special relevance to the *Instauratio Magna*: its subject is that of the great work, it treats the "masks and mummeries" of human pomp in terms reminiscent of the Idols of the Theater, and its list of the "vain opinions, flattering hopes, false valuations, imaginations as one would, and the like" fostered by love of the lie recapitulates the Idols of the Tribe treated in Aphorisms XLV-XLVII of the *Novum Organum,* Book I. Moreover, its structure resembles that of the *Novum Organum* in little, Book I of that work being a consideration of human lies, Book II attempting to find truths dissociated from human distortion, or facts "in relation to the universe, not simply in relation to man" (VIII, 217). And Bacon uses images in a similarly suasive manner in *Novum Organum,* though of course he scatters them throughout his discourse.

Elizabeth Sewell considers the task of *Novum Organum* as the in-

vention of "new models and methods to understand new things" or
as "an attempt to discover a new myth for thought" which must now
be seen as the reproduction of Nature in the human mind instead
of the mind proliferating itself outward.[4] Therefore, *Novum Organum* attempts to bring men from their self-created cosmos of mixed
truth and lie to a purer state where they can see their universe, not
with inhuman eyes, but with human eyes nearly as clear as Adam's.
The analysis of the Idols in Book I constitutes an extended critique
of the mind focused in on itself, the basic "rage for order" of the
Tribe producing the espousal of single criteria for truth in the Cave,
the conveniently ambiguous terms that seem to give some unity to
totally diverse phenomena in the Marketplace, and the full-blown
pleasing systems of the philosophical Theater. Book II, on the other
hand, is dedicated to constructing tools for getting those two very
different systems, the mind and Nature, together without distortion.

Bacon's images tend to support the negative and the positive parts
of his campaign. On the one hand, Bacon is concerned to devaluate
images expressing the neat and self-contained, images that correspond to the mind of man and his imaginations about reality. On the
other, he exalts images expressing at the same time distinction and
connection, images that correspond to the kind of meeting between
the mind and Nature which, for him, alone constitutes human reality. A classic instance is his contrast between the three types of
philosophers:

> The men of experiment are like the ant; they only collect and
> use: the reasoners resemble spiders, who make cobwebs out of
> their own substance. But the bee takes a middle course; it
> gathers its material from the flowers of the garden and of the
> field, but transforms and digests it by a power of its own. Not
> unlike this is the true business of philosophy. (VIII, 131)

The true philosopher does not spin consistent systems out of himself
(nor, for that matter, does he merely pile up observations); rather,
he takes the diverse and combines them—or, as he had said earlier in
another image, binds up the faggots in the band (VI, 123).

One of the principal images for containment in Bacon is the circle;
his treatment of it is boldly iconoclastic. Marjorie Nicolson has explored thoroughly the traditional associations of this image: the old
symbol of immortality and eternity, the visual sign of a limited and

fulfilled universe, and hence an emblem of beauty as proportion.[5] It was the breaking of this circle that symbolized for John Donne the death of the world:

> We thinke the heavens enjoy their Sphericall,
> Their round proportion embracing all.
> But yet their various and perplexed course,
> Observ'd in divers ages, doth enforce
> Men to finde out so many Eccentrique parts,
> Such divers downe-right lines, such overthwarts,
> As disproportion that pure forme. . . .[6]

Bacon's use of the circle image, as this passage shows, is new and different in its associations:

> It is idle to expect any great advancement in science from the superinducing and engrafting of new things upon old. We must begin anew from the very foundations, unless we would revolve for ever in a circle with mean and contemptible progress. (VIII, 74)

The circle is not an image of perfection or beauty, only one of stagnation; and Bacon tends to apply it to all of the old systems which he strives to replace by sound methods—to the old empiricists, for instance, who "fetch a wide circuit and meet with many matters, but make little progress" (VIII, 100). In fact, the circle seems to be associated not with proportion or order but with any giddy motion which turns in upon itself: "in what is now done in the matter of science there is only a whirling round about, and perpetual agitation, ending where it began" (VIII, 18). Contemporary logic, therefore, is not only stagnant but giddy, being "carried round in a whirl of arguments" (VIII, 30).

The image of the circle as stagnant chaos seems to have been with Bacon ever since *The Advancement of Learning* of 1605, where he used it in connection with many different aspects of the old systems. "Every obtaining a desire hath a shew of advancement, as motion though in a circle hath a shew of progression" (VI, 322), he wrote, and then went on to apply it to the methods: "Methods are more fit to win consent or belief, but less fit to point to action; for they carry a kind of demonstration in orb or circle, one part illuminating another, and therefore satisfy" (VI, 291-92). The image characterized not only the systems which were to become Idols of the Theater, but also their parts, such as the old logic by "congruity, which is that which Aristotle calleth *demonstration in orb or circle,* and not *a notioribus*" (VI, 280), and even the periodic style of the Ciceronian methodists with their "round and clean composition of the sentence" and their unfailingly artful "circuit of speech" (VI, 118-19).

Another important image of containment for Bacon is architecture. If we remember that the image of the universe as the frame of order had dominated men's minds since the Middle Ages and that Hooker, for instance, conceived of his *Ecclesiastical Polity* as a work of architecture in imitation of the great world,[7] then the unorthodoxy of a statement like the following from *De Augmentis* will be apparent:

> If that great workmaster had acted as an aedile, he would have cast the stars into some pleasant and beautiful order, like the frets in the roofs of palaces; whereas one can scarce find a posture in square or triangle or straight line amongst such an infinite number. So differing a harmony is there between the spirit of man and the spirit of nature. (IX, 100)

And Bacon proceeds to apply this image of the pleasing fiction of containment and beauty to the old philosophies, as he had the circle image: "the entire fabric of human reason which we employ in the inquisition of nature, is badly put together and built up, and like some magnificent structure without any foundation" (VIII, 18). The final effect of this closed structure is to present to its students the image of a dark labyrinth rather than an exquisite whole:

> Let men therefore cease to wonder that the course of science is not yet wholly run, seeing that they have gone altogether astray; either leaving and abandoning experience entirely, or losing their way in it and wandering round and round as in a labyrinth. (VIII, 115)

To the mind of man in this state of affairs, the universe "is framed like a labyrinth . . . while those who offer themselves for guides are (as was said) themselves also puzzled, and increase the number of errors and wanderers" (VIII, 32).

Bacon's counterimages all suggest at the same time qualities distinct and separate and qualities firmly related, usually by interdependence instead of by merging; the mind, they imply, is both separate from Nature and dependent on it. One such pervasive image is the mirror, which shows the mind to be a faculty facing outward to catch the image of Nature and bring it into itself, instead of a circle or sphere focusing inward. Like the circle, this image had been with Bacon since *The Advancement of Learning*. There he had drawn from Ecclesiastes 3:11 the image of the mirror for the mind as God had created it:

> God hath framed the mind of man as a mirror or glass capable of the image of the universal world, and joyful to receive the impression thereof, as the eye joyeth to receive light; and not only delighted in beholding the variety of things and vicissitude of times, but raised also to find out and discern the ordinances and decrees which throughout all those changes are infallibly observed. (VI, 93)

But the Fall darkened the mirror; and only the images of the Adversary now play on it:

> For the mind of man is far from the nature of a clear and equal glass, wherein the beams of things should reflect according to their true incidence; nay, it is rather like an enchanted glass, full of superstition and imposture, if it be not delivered and reduced. (VI, 276)

Novum Organum has as its task this deliverance; Bacon takes as his starting point the bent and discolored mirror that the mind of man now is:

> For it is a false assertion that the sense of man is the measure of things. On the contrary, all perceptions as well of the sense as of the mind are according to the measure of the individual and not according to the measure of the universe. And the human understanding is like a false mirror, which, receiving rays irregularly, distorts and discolours the nature of things by mingling its own nature with it. (VIII, 77)

So, too, each man's Cave "refracts and discolors the light of nature," and each man's mirror is filled with idols or phantoms instead of true images. The task of *Novum Organum* is metaphorically conceived as straightening the steel glass and polishing its surface: "But since the minds of men are strangely possessed and beset, so that there is no true and even surface left to reflect the genuine rays of things, it is necessary to seek a remedy for this also" (VIII, 45). The next step after the polishing will be the illumination of Nature by natural history so that the images on the mirror will become brilliant and distinct: "For it is in vain that you polish the mirror if there are no images to be reflected; and it is as necessary that the intellect should be supplied with fit matter to work upon, as with safeguards to guide its working" (VIII, 47). Therefore, the cluster around the image of the mirror includes not only the idols and phantoms which Bacon has detected on its surface, but also the images of darkness and light, illumination and obscurity, with which *Novum Organum* is suffused.

A second major image expressing the commerce that should exist between the separate fields of the mind of man and the nature of the universe is that of the model. Bacon says, "I am building in the human understanding a true model of the world" (VIII, 156); he does this by the Forms, which, in his interpretation, are the reproductions in the human mind of the laws of universal action, and hence link the mind and Nature firmly. In *The Ladder of the Intellect,* therefore, he will reveal "actual types and models, by which the entire process of the mind and the whole fabric and order of invention from the beginning to the end, in certain subjects . . . should be set as it were before the eyes" (VIII, 51).

The image of the model in the mind differs from the architectural images, to which it runs counter, in that it expresses relation to something else as original rather than independent containment; it is, in fact, related to the mirror-image, for the end of true reflection is to establish a total image of the universe in the mind. Bacon's own observations in the *Instauratio Magna* are "copied from a very ancient model; even the world itself and the nature of things" (VIII, 23). "God forbid," he writes, "that we should give out a dream of our own imagination for a pattern of the world; rather may he graciously grant to us to write an apocalypse or true vision of the footsteps of the Creator imprinted on his creatures" (VIII, 53); a prefabricated model must not be projected upon the world, but rather "the divine

wisdom and order must be our pattern" (VIII, 101). The final vision
of the mind stored with true images so fully as to become a complete
model of the external universe is reserved for the House of Solomon
in *The New Atlantis*. With its upper and lower regions in imitation
of the universe and its complete re-creation of natural phenomena by
artifice, this house represents the true architecture which takes the
external world into itself instead of acting as a buffer against it. The
House of Solomon, like Spenser's House of Alma, is a spatial image
of the mind of the wise man.

Toward this image of the model gravitate the many metaphors of
the natural philosopher as creator—creator, of course, of this model of
the world in the mind much in the manner of Coleridge's primary
Imagination, "the living Power and prime Agent of all human Perception . . . a repetition in the finite mind of the eternal act of creation in the infinite I AM."[8] The House of Solomon, we may remember, was also styled "the College of the Six Days Works," for "God
had created the world and all that therein is within six days; and
therefore he [the founder] instituting that House for the finding out
of the true nature of all things . . . did give it also that second
name" (V, 383). The natural philosopher, then, acts as God's vice-
regent recreating in the mind of man a little world modeled after
God's great world:

> But the true method of experience . . . first lights the candle,
> and then by means of the candle shows the way; commencing
> as it does with experience duly ordered and digested . . . and
> from it educing axioms, and from established axioms again
> new experiments; even as it was not without order and method
> that the divine word operated on the created mass. (VIII, 115)

By this means, the scientist will create an orderly microcosm instead
of "wandering round and round as in a labyrinth"—for, as the mirror counteracts the circle and the model the house, so the appearance
of an ordered world in the mind counteracts the image of a labyrinth
or web which sophistical philosophy has constructed for itself. As the
preceding passage implies, the philosopher not only strives to imitate God's Creation, but also by analogy works with Him:

> Now God on the first day of creation created light only, giving
> to that work an entire day, in which no material substance was

created. So must we likewise from experience of every kind
first endeavour to discover true causes and axioms; and seek for
experiments of Light, not for experiments of Fruit. (VIII, 101)

This passage gives new dimensions to the images of the scientist as
light-giver; it is not a Promethean image but a Christian one, for the
light-giver is not stealing light from heaven but trying, like that first
Maker, to make a world in the mind by " 'Experimenta lucifera,' experiments of *light,* to distinguish them from those which I call '*fruc-
tifera,*' experiments of *fruit*" (VIII, 135). Therefore, Bacon can end
his Preface to *Instauratio Magna* with a prayer to that first light-giver
to "guard and protect this work, which coming from thy goodness
returneth to thy glory" (VIII, 53).

   This prayer suggests a third great metaphor for the joining of the
distinct, for Bacon frequently conceives of himself as a priest performing a definite office. In his experimental method, he writes, "I
perform the office of a true priest of the sense . . . while others only
profess to uphold and cultivate the sense, I do so in fact" (VIII, 44);
his office is that of the priest joining two parties in holy matrimony,
two parties at present distinct but soon to become one body:

   And by these means I suppose that I have established for ever
   a true and lawful marriage between the empirical and the rational faculty, the unkind and ill-starred divorce and separation
   of which has thrown into confusion all the affairs of the human family. (VIII, 34)

The marriage of the mind and the senses is only part of the full and
eventual marriage he has in mind, the marriage of the human mind
and the external world: "I therefore, well knowing and nowise forgetting how great a work I am about (viz. that of rendering the human understanding a match for things and nature), do not rest satisfied with the precepts I have laid down" (VIII, 209).[9] Therefore, he
considers the *Novum Organum* as the preparation for the wedding
day:

   The explanation of which things, and of the true relation between the nature of things and the nature of the mind, is as
   the strewing and decoration of the bridal chamber of the Mind
   and the Universe, the Divine Goodness assisting; out of which

> marriage let us hope (and be this the prayer of the bridal
> song) there may spring helps to man, and a line and race of
> inventions that may in some degree subdue and overcome the
> necessities and miseries of humanity. This is the second part of
> the work. (VIII, 46)

And so, near the end of Book I of that work, he can say that he has
"purged and swept and levelled the floor of the mind" and can now
place it "in a favourable aspect towards what I have to lay before it,"
the coming of the bride (VIII, 146-47).

The metaphor of marriage brings us close to the grand myth that
underlies most of Bacon's images in the *Instauratio Magna*. It is a
myth of Fall and Regeneration, the intellectual counterpart of the
pastoral myth of innocence restored which we find in *The Winter's
Tale* and *The Tempest*. Man's Fall caused a fatal divorce between
the mind and Nature. Left to itself, the mirror of the mind became
clouded and bent, full of phantom errors; it turned back on itself
circuitously, with the result that all of its fine constructions became
as dark labyrinths. The *Instauratio Magna* proposes a restoration of
what was lost. Bacon will rectify the senses by the aids of the experimental method; then he will remarry the purged senses to the mind.
He will rectify the mind by the inductive method whose insistence
on negative instances will prevent it from embracing a perilously easy
consistency; then he will marry the mind to Nature once again, repair the divorce.

> All trial should be made, whether that commerce between the
> mind of man and the nature of things, which is more precious
> than anything on earth, or at least than anything that is of the
> earth, might by any means be restored to its perfect and orig-
> inal condition, or if that may not be, yet reduced to a better
> condition than that in which it now is. (VIII, 17)

If the harmony between the mind and Nature lost in the Fall can be
to any degree re-established, then man will be in Eden again; he will
no longer see things with a clouded mind (or with an inhuman
mind), but with the clear sight of Adam. And his life will be joyful
and innocent when the divine nature again will "admit the human
spirit for his playfellow" (VIII, 36), the way back into Eden, "the
entrance into the kingdom of man, founded on the sciences, being

not much other than the entrance into the kingdom of heaven, where-into none may enter except as a little child" (VIII, 99).

The vision Bacon's great work points to is a unitive vision of man in commerce with Nature under the aegis of God. Since the scope of this vision is usually not stated but rather suggested by image and metaphor, the reader is meant to respond to it unitively, with his senses and emotions as well as with his intellect. The received (or at least uncontested) opinion of Bacon's style is that it suffers from the fatal divorce between statement and image; that is the opinion best conveyed by L. C. Knights in "Bacon and the Seventeenth-Century Dissociation of Sensibility," an article whose title shows the importance of this matter for intellectual history as well as for stylistic study.[10] But our examination of Bacon's mature style shows how fully that received opinion—and perhaps the concept of the "dissociation of sensibility" beneath it—needs to be modified.

NOTES

1. *Works,* ed. James Spedding, Robert Leslie Ellis, and Douglas Denon Heath, 15 vols. (Boston, 1860-72), XIII, 80 (italics mine); quoted by Arnold Stein, "On Elizabethan Wit," *Studies in English Literature,* I, No. 1 (Winter, 1961), 89.
2. See R. S. Crane, "The Relation of Bacon's *Essays* to His Program for the Advancement of Learning," in *Schelling Anniversary Papers* (New York, 1923), pp. 97-103.
3. Parenthetical references are to volume and page of the Boston edition of Spedding, Ellis, and Heath.
4. *The Orphic Voice: Poetry and Natural History* (New Haven, 1960), pp. 57 and 143.
5. *The Breaking of the Circle: Studies in the Effect of the "New Science" upon Seventeenth-Century Poetry* (New York, 1960).
6. "An Anatomie of the World," lines 251-57, in *Poems of John Donne,* ed. Herbert J. C. Grierson, Vol. I (Oxford, 1912).
7. See *Of the Laws of Ecclesiastical Polity,* ed. Christopher Morris (London, 1964), I. 157 and 149, respectively.
8. *Biographia Literaria,* ed. J. Shawcross (Oxford, 1907), I, 202.
9. The Latin is *ut faciamus intellectum humanum rebus et naturae parem* (I, 389). Thus the passage does not suggest an actual betrothal, but rather the raising of one member of the marriage to be a fit partner of the other—as in the Lamentations of Jeremiah.
10. *Explorations* (London, 1946), pp. 92-111; see especially pages 99, 101, and 108.

STANLEY E. FISH

✍

Georgics of the Mind: The Experience of Bacon's Essays

> "And surely if the purpose be in good earnest not to write at leisure that which men may read at leisure, but really to instruct and suborn action and active life, these Georgics of the mind, concerning the husbandry and tillage thereof, are no less worthy than the heroical descriptions of Virtue, Duty, and Felicity."
>
> *The Advancement of Learning*

I

There has been a general recognition in the twentieth century of the close relationship between Bacon's *Essays* and his scientific program. In 1871 Edward Arber could still write that the essays are "no essential part" of Bacon's real work, "the proficiency and advancement of knowledge";[1] but in 1923 R. S. Crane pointed out that these "Counsels Civill and Morall" speak directly to a need first articulated in *The Advancement of Learning* and five years later Jacob Zeitlin was referring to this same body of materials as "a science of pure selfishness."[2] This view of the *Essays* opened the way for a consideration of their successive revisions which were seen to correspond to the successive stages of scientific method. Thus, in the 1597 version, Bacon is

From Chapter II of the author's forthcoming book, *Self-Consuming Artifacts*.

"content to offer us the *disjecta membra*" without the ordering super-structure of a "methodical scheme"[3] while in the 1625 *Essays* these discrete observations are related to one another and to the abstraction they collectively illuminate by "a clear and explicit organization."[4] This description of the essays and of their progress is now standard: Bacon, Douglas Bush tells us in his volume of the *Oxford History of English Literature,* "wished to fill a gap in practical psychology and ethics, to contribute to . . . knowledge of the genus *homo*" (196). Paoli Rossi takes his text from Bush and treats the essays as "another contribution to that science of man to which Bacon dedicated for many years the best part of his inexhaustible energies."[5] And for Brian Vickers, the most recent of the commentators, the connection between these "literary productions" and Bacon's scientific labors, is not a point of issue; he assumes it, and goes on to draw illuminating parallels between the style of the *Essays* and the methodology of the *Novum Organum* and other works.[6]

Yet, for all this unanimity, the casual judgments these critics make on the *Essays* suggest that they do not really understand what is "scientific" about them. For the most part they take their cue from Bacon's praise of Machiavelli:

> . . . we are much beholden to Machiavel and others, that write what men do and not what they ought to do. For it is not possible to join serpentine wisdom with the columbine in-nocency, except men know exactly all the conditions of the serpent.
>
> (III, 430-31)[7]

To know exactly what men do. This seems to be a call for "objectivity," for accurate and disinterested observation of particulars; and objectivity is the quality most commonly attributed to the *Essays.*

> Bacon's essays are for the most part as impersonal, as objective, as the essays of Macauley.
> . . . his method was that of the detached, impersonal observer, his presentation was concise, dogmatic, formal.
>
> (Zeitlin, 518, 519)

> In the *Essays* his attitude is conditioned by the whole rationale of the work towards dispassionate objective observation and analysis.
>
> (Vickers, 133)

> . . . Bacon's cool objectivity . . . represents also the attitude
> of the scientific analyst who does not gossip and ramble, whose
> mind is a dry light.
>
> (Bush, 195)
>
> It [the style of the *Essays*] thus represents a clear parallel to
> the scientific style of report.[8]

But if the *Essays* are objective in fact, analytic in method, impersonal
in tone, and practically instructive in purpose, they are not, according
to these same critics, without their problems. Zeitlin is uncomfortable
with the "baldly analytic or coldly intellectual consideration" of the
topics Bacon treats and he sees the essays as a battle between the "two
spirits" that fight for the author's soul, the spirit of the scientist and
the spirit of the moralist (512, 510). Bush speaks of the "utilitarian
motives" that "keep Bacon's *Essays* in the category of admired books
rather than among the well-thumbed and beloved" (197); and he
notes the simultaneous presence of "some wholly admirable counsels
of moral wisdom and public and private virtue" and "an atmosphere
of 'business,' of cold-blooded expediency, and sometimes of unscrupu-
lous self-interest" (196). And while Vickers seems to dismiss the notion of any such tension existing in the *Essays,* he at least acknowledges it in passing: "I think that an unbiased analysis would show a
constant and non-ambivalent dependence on traditional ethics" (92).

In short the characterization of the *Essays* as objective, dispassion-
ate, and concisely analytic is hardly borne out by the collective response of those who so characterize them. An impersonal report does
not leave its readers wondering about the inner life of the author; nor
does it encourage speculation as to whether its own focus is "traditional," "utilitarian," "moral," or blurred. A student of Bacon criticism
may be excused if he asks, only half in jest, will the real Bacon's
Essays please stand up?

The difficulty, I think, lies in the assumed equation of "scientific"
and "objective"; for this involves the further assumption that Bacon's
concern as a scientist is wholly with the form of his presentation. I
would suggest however that his primary concern is with the *experience* that form provides, and further, that this experience, rather than
the materials of which it is composed, is what is scientific about the
Essays. I believe such a hypothesis to be consistent with the psychological emphasis of Bacon's theoretical writings and with his repeated
classification of styles according to their effect on readers and hearers;

but for now I prefer to rest my case on the primary evidence and proceed inductively, in good Baconian fashion, to the discovery of general principles.

Let us begin by examining a section of the 1625 essay, "Of Love":

> You may observe, that amongst all the great and worthy per-
> sons (whereof the memory remaineth, either ancient or recent)
> there is not one that hath been transported to the mad degree
> of love: which shews that great spirits and great business do
> keep out this weak passion. You must except nevertheless
> Marcus Antonius, the half partner of the empire of Rome, and
> Appius Claudius, the decemvir and lawgiver; whereof the
> former was indeed a voluptuous man, and inordinate; but the
> latter was an austere and wise man: therefore it seems (though
> rarely) that love can find entrance not only into an open heart,
> but also into a heart well fortified, if watch be not well kept.
>   (VI, 397)

Everything about the first sentence serves to inspire confidence in its
contents. Before a reader reaches the main statement, he has been
assured (by the parenthesis) that it is based on exhaustive research.
Both the rhythmic and argumentative stresses fall on the phrase "there
is not one," and nothing that follows qualifies this absoluteness. The
formal conclusion of the "which" clause is hardly necessary—it is
clearly implied—but it does add to the impression of completeness and
finality, especially since the opposition of "great" and "weak," "business" and "passion," is so strongly pointed. The form of the whole is
almost syllogistic, moving from the primary proposition—"there are
great and worthy persons"—to the secondary proposition—"not one of
them hath"—to the inevitable therefore—"which shows that." In short,
the reader is encouraged in every way possible to confer the status of
"truism" or "axiom" on the assertion this sentence makes. Of course,
there are potential ambiguities. As we read it for the first time, "You
may observe" is simply a rhetorical formula which allows us to anticipate something unexceptionable; but, strictly speaking, that formula
includes the possibility of *not* taking the action referred to: You may
observe, or, on the other hand, you may not observe. The material in
the parenthesis contains a similar "logical out," since it acknowledges
indirectly the possibility of their being a whole body of great and
worthy persons whereof *no* memory remains, persons whose existence

more trustworthy" (21). It will be the business of his presentation to
"arouse" men rather than to "force or ensnare" their judgments (12).

This concern with a method of communication which neutralizes
the errors the understanding is prone to is on display everywhere in
Bacon's writings. There is now, he complains in *The Advancement of
Learning,* "a kind of contract of error between the deliverer and the
receiver: he that delivereth knowledge desireth to deliver it in such
form as may be best believed; and he that receiveth knowledge desireth rather present satisfaction than expectant inquiry." Such a
form of delivery—Bacon terms it "Magistral"—is proper for the transmission of settled truths, but tends to discourage further inquiry. Far
more fruitful is the way of "Probation" whereby knowledge is "delivered and intimated . . . in the same method wherein it was invented" (404).[10] The opposition of "Magistral" and "Probative" is
transferred in the same work to another pair of terms, "Methods" and
"Aphorisms," and the advantages claimed for Aphorisms are exactly
those claimed for the new induction:

> . . . the writing in Aphorisms hath many excellent virtues,
> whereto the writing in Method doth not approach.
>   For first, it trieth the writer, whether he be superficial or
> solid: for Aphorisms, except that they should be ridiculous,
> cannot be made but of the pith and heart of sciences; for dis-
> course of illustration is cut off; recitals of examples are cut off;
> discourse of connexion and order is cut off; descriptions of prac-
> tice are cut off; so there remaineth nothing to fill the Apho-
> risms but some good quantity of observation: and therefore no
> man can suffice, nor in reason will attempt, to write Apho-
> risms, but he that is sound and grounded. But in Methods
> . . . a man shall make a great shew of art, which if it were
> disjointed would come to little. Secondly, Methods are more fit
> to win consent or belief, but less fit to point to action; for they
> carry a kind of demonstration in orb or circle, one part illumi-
> nating another, and therefore satisfy; but particulars, being dis-
> persed, do not agree with dispersed directions. And lastly,
> Aphorisms, representing a knowledge broken, do invite men to
> enquire farther; whereas Methods, carrying the shew of a total,
> do secure men, as if they were at furthest.

(405)

Again, the distinction and the evaluation are made on the basis of psychological effect rather than literal accuracy. The content of aphorisms is not necessarily more true than the content of methodical writing; but one form has a more salutary effect than the other because it minimizes the possibility that the mind, in its susceptibility, will take the internal coherence of an artful discourse for the larger coherence of objective truth. Like induction and the way of Probation, writing in aphorisms sacrifices present satisfaction to the hope of a fuller knowledge in the future.

Later in *The Advancement of Learning*, Bacon turns to a consideration of the "wisdom touching Negotiation or Business," and here too the emphasis is on the dangers of a procedure which facilitates the mind's tendency to rest in the notions it already possesses:

> The form of writing which of all others is fittest for this variable argument of negotiation and occasions is that which Machiavel chose wisely and aptly for government; *discourse upon histories or examples*. For knowledge drawn freshly and in our view out of particulars, knowest the way best to particulars again. And it hath much greater life for practice when the discourse attendeth upon the discourse. For this is no point of order, as it seemeth at first, but of substance. For when the example is the ground . . . it is set down with all circumstances, which may sometimes control the discourse thereupon made and sometimes supply it, as a very pattern for action; whereas the examples alleged for the discourse sake are cited succinctly and without particularity, and carry a service aspect toward the discourse which they are brought in to make good.
>
> (453)

If you are committed to a proposition, you will find evidence to support it; but if a proposition is drawn from the evidence you *disinterestedly* find, your commitment is to truth. In this formulation "examples" stand to "discourse" as "particulars" stand to artificially filled out systems (including syllogisms) and Aphorisms to Methods. When a discourse is controlled by examples, its form is discovered rather than imposed and its general conclusions are independent of the author's preconceptions which, indeed, may be altered in the process of discovery; but when the examples carry a "servile" aspect to the discourse—that is when they are brought in to make it good or left out because they do not make it good or distorted so that the "axiom now in use" can be "rescued and preserved"—those preconceptions are allowed to limit what can be discovered. As A. N. Whitehead has put it, in an aphorism Bacon would have admired, "Our problem is . . . to fit the world to our perceptions, and not our perceptions to the world."[11]

III

We are now in a position to define more precisely the relationship between Bacon's *Essays* and his method of scientific inquiry. The point of contact, of course, is the *experience* the *Essays* give. If we return to my analysis of the passage from "Of Love," and keep in mind the vocabulary of the *Novum Organum* and *The Advancement of Learning,* the correspondence between what happens in that essay and what should happen in a responsible scientific investigation is immediately apparent. First the reader is presented with an axiom-like statement enclosed in "such form as may be best believed, and not as may be best examined." The sentence is "rounded"; the progression of its thought is apparently logical; its parts "carry a kind of demonstration in orb or circle, one . . . illuminating another, and therefore satisfy." In short the mind's desire "to have something fixed and immovable, upon which in its wanderings and disquisitions it may securely rest" has been gratified. (One should note in this connection that the sentence flatters the reader, since it allows him to include himself among "all the great and worthy persons.")

But, unexpectedly, the examples that follow do not "attend upon the discourse" but begin instead to "control and supply" it. The reader is "aroused" from his complacency and becomes involved in a refining operation in which the commonly received notion is subjected to the test of "proper rejections and exclusions." Qualification follows upon qualification with the double result that the original axiom is discredited—it is not sufficiently "wide" (*N.O.,* I, cvi) to include "new particulars"—and the possibility of formulating another is called into question.

What then is the value of this experience? Obviously, it has not yielded the promised clarification of the nature of love, but in Bacon's scale of values it has yielded much more:

1. a felt knowledge of the attraction generalities have for the mind

and therefore a "caution" against a too easy acceptance of them in the future.

2. an awareness of the *unresolved* complexity of the matter under discussion.

3. an open and inquiring mind, one that is dissatisfied with the state of knowledge at the present time.

In short, the demands of the prose have left the reader in a state of "healthy perplexity," neither content with the notion he had been inclined to accept at the beginning of the experience, nor quite ready to put forward a more accurate notion of his own. This is of course the mental set of the scientist, observant, methodical, cautious, skeptical, and yet, in long range terms, optimistic. (The question of just how Bacon's style contains and communicates this optimism will be dealt with later.)

My description of the essay, or, more precisely, of its effects, is noteworthy for an omission; it says nothing at all about the nominal subject, love; but as I have suggested earlier, the real subject of the essay is what men think about love, or, perhaps, *how* men think about love; and I would suggest further that the same formula should be applied to the other essays which are about how men think about friendship and fortune and dissimulation and studies and so on. This of course would tend to make all of the essays one large essay in the root sense of the word—one continuing *attempt* to make sense of things, with the emphasis on the "making sense of" rather than on the "things." The alternative (and more usual) view is well represented by Anne Righter:

> . . . the 1625 edition is not a tidy knitting together of various ideas which interested Bacon; it is an accumulation of disparate pieces as difficult to generalize about, or to connect internally, as Donne's *Songs and Sonets,* and it is to be read in a not dissimilar fashion.[12]

This statement has been endorsed recently by Vickers who adds that the *Essays* were "not . . . composed from a consistent impelling attitude or plan" (132). Miss Righter and Vickers are no doubt correct if one looks for a consistency of content or attitude (remember the "two" Bacons who trouble Zeitlin and Bush); but there is, I think, another kind of consistency to the essays, a consistency of experience, which in turn is a reflection of what might be called an "impelling plan." The *Essays* are to be read not as a series of encapsulations or expressions, but as a process, a refining process which is itself being enacted by the reader; and to some extent, the question, in any one essay, of exactly what abstraction is being refined, is secondary.

Thus, in the 1625 essay "Of Love," for example, the title merely specifies the particular area of inquiry within which and in terms of which the reader becomes involved in a characteristic kind of activity, the questioning and testing of a commonly received notion. The excerpt analyzed above is followed in the 1625 text by a sentence which begins: "It is a poor saying. . . ." The "poor saying" in question turns out to be one of Epicurus', but the phrase might well apply (as it seems to for a moment) to the generalization that has dominated the essay to this point, "amongst all the great and worthy persons . . . there is not one. . . ." Indeed the true focus of the essay is the many "poor sayings" that have accumulated about this one abstraction; and the purpose of the essay is to initiate a search for "better sayings," sayings more in accordance with the observable facts.

This same pattern—the casual proffering of one or more familiar and "reverenced" witticisms followed by the introduction of data that calls their validity into question—is found everywhere in Bacon's *Essays*. A particularly good example is the late essay "Of Usury" which moves immediately to the point other essays make only indirectly:

> Many have made witty invectives against Usury. They say that it is a pity the devil should have God's part, which is the tithe. That the usurer is the greatest sabbath-breaker, because his plough goeth every Sunday. That the usurer is the drone that Virgil speaketh of;
>
> *Ignavum fucos pecus a praesepibus arcent.* That the usurer breaketh the first law that was made for mankind after the fall, which was, *in sudore vultus tui comedes panem tuum;* not, *in sudore vultus alieni;* [in the sweat of thy face shalt thou eat bread—not in the sweat of another's face] That usurers should have orange-tawny bonnets, because they do judaize. That it is against nature for money to beget money; and the like.

(*Sp.,* VI, 473-74)

No practiced reader of Bacon's *Essays* will be likely to miss the sneer in "and the like"; and its effect is retroactive, extending back to the governing verb phrase, "They say." In other essays, "They say" will appear in slightly changed form as "men say" or "as has been thought," while "and the like" will be shortened to "and such"; but the implication is always the same: what men say and think about things may be far from the truth about them. In this case, the current sayings are "poor" because they have not been formulated with a view to the facts of the human condition:

> I say this only, that usury is a *concessum propter duritiem cordis;* [a thing allowed by reason of the hardness of men's hearts:] for since there must be borrowing and lending, and men are so hard of heart as they will not lend freely, usury must be permitted. Some others have made suspicions and cunning propositions of banks, discovery of men's estates, and other inventions. But few have spoken of usury usefully. It is good to set before us the incommodities and commodities of usury, that the good may be either weighed out or culled out; and warily to provide, that while we make forth to that which is better, we meet not with that which is worse.

In the *Novum Organum,* Bacon uses the phrase "sciences as one would" to refer to internally coherent, but objectively inaccurate, systematizations of knowledge: "For what a man had rather were true he more readily believes" (xlix). Here, in "Of Usury," the object of the philosopher's contempt is "morality as one would," a morality of wishful thinking based on "what men ought to do" rather than on "what men do." Such a morality, he implies, may well be immoral (useless), for it leaves a man ignorant of and defenseless against the real complexity of the situations which will confront him. It is a mistake to term the essays a "science of pure selfishness," if by that one means that they advocate selfishness: the essays advocate nothing (except perhaps a certain openness and alertness of mind), they are descriptive, and a description is ethically neutral, although if it is accurate, it may contribute to the development of a true, that is, responsible, ethics. The distinction is made beautifully by the last sentence in this first paragraph. The "good" of "it is good to set before us" is a purely procedural good; the "good" of "that the good may be," on the other hand, seems to have some ethical content, but more in the direction of "beneficial" than "right"; and, finally, the "better" of "make forth to that which is better" is unambiguously moral. Sig-

nificantly, this "better" is placed in the future, while the emphasis is
on the "making forth." Indeed the temporal movement of the entire
sentence prefigures the successive stages of a truly scientific inquiry:
first the collecting of observations, then the tentative drawing out
("culling") of axioms, and finally, but only after a wary and rigorous
process of "exclusions and rejections," the specification of what is
"better" and what is not. At this point, what emerges as unequivocally
"good" is the methodical disposition of the facts about usury, or any
other "thing" and it is this task that Bacon sets his readers in the
essays. The making of "witty invectives" or of unrealistic rules is, as
Bacon says in the second paragraph, "idle." Talk of the "abolishing
of usury," for instance, "must be sent to Utopia" (475). Bacon is even
more vehement in "Of Suspicion," another late essay: "What would
men have? Do they think those they employ and deal with are
saints?" (454). In "Of Riches," the reader is warned, "have no abstract nor friarly contempt of them" (460): (Bacon's attitude toward
religious "sayings" will be discussed later). And the tone of the essays
in this connection is established at the very beginning, in "Of Truth":

> Doth any man doubt, that if there were taken out of men's
> minds vain opinions, flattering hopes, false valuations, *imagina-
> tions as one would, and the like,* but it would leave the minds
> of a number of men poor shrunken things, full of melancholy
> and indisposition, and unpleasing to themselves?
>
> (377-78)

Taking out of the reader's mind all vain opinions, flattering hopes,
false valuations, imaginations as one would, and the like, is the business of these essays. There is no room in Bacon's program for illusions, and especially not for the illusions projected naturally by the
order-loving, simplicity imposing, human understanding.

"Of Usury," however, is not typical of the essays because so much
of the work is done *for* the reader. In the more characteristic essay,
the "vain opinions" and "false valuations" are exposed gradually, and
then only after the reader has been given an opportunity to accept
them or to let them go by unchallenged. This results in a more self-
conscious scrutiny of one's mental furniture and helps to foster the
curious blend of investigative eagerness and wary skepticism which
according to Bacon distinguishes the truly scientific cast of mind. "Of
Adversity" is such an essay, and for our purposes it has the advantage
of being brief enough to be quoted in full:

It was a high speech of Seneca (after the manner of the Stoics), *that the good things which belong to prosperity are to be wished; but the good things that belong to adversity are to be admired. Bona rerum secundarum optabilia; adversarum mirabilia.* Certainly if miracles be the command over nature, they appear most in adversity. It is yet a higher speech of his than the other (much too high for a heathen), *It is true greatness to have in one the frailty of a man, and the security of a God. Vere magnum habere fragilitatem hominis, securitatem Dei.* This would have done better in poesy, where transcendences are more allowed. And the poets indeed have been busy with it; for it is in effect the thing which is figured in that strange fiction of the ancient poets, which seemeth not to be without mystery; nay, and to have some approach to the state of a Christian; that *Hercules, when he went to unbind Prometheus* (by whom human nature is represented), *sailed the length of the great ocean in an earthen pot or pitcher;* lively describing Christian resolution, that saileth in the frail bark of the flesh thorough the waves of the world. But to speak in a mean. The virtue of Prosperity is temperance, the virtue of Adversity is fortitude; which in morals is the more heroical virtue. Prosperity is the blessing of the Old Testament; Adversity is the blessing of the New; which carrieth the greater benediction, and the clearer revelation of God's favour. Yet even in the Old Testament, if you listen to David's harp, you shall hear as many hearse-like airs as carols; and the pencil of the Holy Ghost hath laboured more in describing the afflictions of Job than the felicities of Salomon. Prosperity is not without many fears and distastes; and Adversity is not without comforts and hopes. We see in needle-works and embroideries, it is more pleasing to have a lively work upon a sad and solemn ground, than to have a dark and melancholy work upon a lightsome ground: judge therefore of the pleasure of the heart by the pleasure of the eye. Certainly virtue is like precious odours, most fragrant when they are incensed or crushed: for Prosperity doth best discover vice, but Adversity doth best discover virtue.

(*Sp.*, VI, 386)

In one of the more recent editions of the essays, "high" is glossed as "presumptuous," but this is hardly the meaning that will occur to the casual reader as he first moves into the essay. More likely he will assume, too easily, perhaps, but naturally, that by "high" Bacon intends "elevated" or "exalted" or "lofty," even "noble"; and in the same way, the parenthetical "after the manner of the Stoics" will seem at first to be a point of identification rather than a criticism. Only after the last word is read is the meaning of "high" clarified, and even then "presumptuous," while it is more accurate than "noble," does less than justice to the felt experience of the word's complexity. An understanding of that complexity is the chief product of the essay which is finally more about "high speeches" (for which read "poor sayings" or "abstract" or "friarly") and their relationship to what is than it is about "adversity."

This first "high speech" exhibits many of the characteristics Bacon associates with the delivery of knowledge "in such form as may be best believed and not as may be best examined." This is the form Bacon condemns in the *De Augmentis* because it "seemes more witty and waighty than indeed it is":

> The labour here is altogether, *That words may be aculeate, sentences concise, and the whole contexture of the speech and discourse, rather rounding into it selfe, than spread and dilated.* . . . Such a stile as this we finde more excessively in *Seneca* . . . it is nothing else but a hunting after words, and fine placing of them.[13]

The "fine placing" of the words results in a pointed and schematic prose in which the argument is carried more by the clinking harmony of like endings than by the "matter." In short, one assents to the form, which is designed to satisfy the physiological needs of the receiving consciousness, rather than to the content; and this makes the Senecan style, at its most mannered, as debilitating as the "sweet falling . . . clauses" of an extreme Ciceronianism; for both persuade by alluring and short-circuit the rational processes.

Williamson has noted how carefully Bacon's translation preserves the Senecan mannerisms, and even perfects them: "Bacon duplicates Seneca's balance, suggests his transverse like-endings, but adds alliteration to the parallelism of the second member." And he adds, "If this form be considered accidental, it may be argued that the similarities could have been, but are not, avoided."[14] The similarities are not avoided because Bacon wishes to secure, at least momentarily, the extreme Senecan effect, the unthinking acceptance of this "high speech." The reader is allowed to anticipate a comfortable and untaxing journey through the essay, and this expectation is strengthened by the first word of the next sentence, "Certainly." But the second word of the sentence is "if" and suddenly the hitherto sharp outlines of the discussion are blurred. "Certainly, if" is a particularly concise instance of a pattern that appears everywhere in the essays: words like "surely," "doubtless," "truly," and phrases like "in truth," "it is doubtless true," "certainly it is true" suggest strongly that what follows is to be accepted without qualification; but within a word or a phrase or, a most, a sentence, Bacon drops in one of another group of words and phrases—"but," "except," "although," "nevertheless," "and yet," and the most devastating of all, "it is *also* true." The result is a change in the quality of the reader's attention, from complacency to a kind of uneasiness, an uneasiness which takes the (perhaps subconscious) form of a silently asked question: "What, exactly, is the truth about——?" At that moment the reader is transformed from a passive recipient of popular truth into a searcher after objective truth, and this transformation follows upon the transformation of the essay from a vehicle whose form is designed to secure belief into an instrument of inquiry and examintion.

This is, perhaps, too great a burden to place on the phrase "Certainly, if" in "Of Adversity." Its effect is less dramatic; it simply introduces doubt where there had been none before and that doubt, while it is unfocused, nevertheless extends to the word "adversity" which does appear in a prominent position. (Incidentally this is the only function of the sentence, to foster doubt and uncertainty; that is, its purpose is not communicative or expressive, but rhetorical; Bacon is not really interested in whether or not miracles can be defined as "the command over nature.") The reader's active involvement in the essay begins with the next sentence, which returns to the concept of "highness." However straightforwardly the first "high" had been accepted, there is something uncomfortable and awkward about the comparative "higher," and of course with the parenthesis ("much too high for a heathen") the word can no longer be taken as honorific. It is here that the meaning "presumptuous" comes into play and with it an implied hierarchy of authorities—heathen vs. Christian. This second "high speech," then, will be viewed with more suspicion than the first, and that suspicion will be confirmed and given body by its association in the following sentence with "poesy" and "transcendences." A third meaning of "high" now emerges—"unreal" or "remote from the world of facts"—a meaning reinforced by the phrase "strange fiction." Together with "heathen," "poesy," and "transcendences," "strange fiction" forms a system of related terms which begin to displace "adversity" as the subject of the essay. In this system, "mystery" occupies an ambiguous position: on one hand it shares with poetry "and the like" the taint of "fantasy"; and on the other it looks ahead to the more respectable category of "Christian." But that word too, coming as it does at the end of the series, can not escape the pejorative associations that have been clustering around "high" and its equivalences. The opposition of "heathen" to "Christian" now seems less firm and controlling than it did a few moments ago and the reader is further away than ever from knowing the "truth" about adversity, largely because the authorities contending for his attention have been overtly or implicitly discredited.

In short, the effect of the first half of the essay is to disabuse the reader of whatever confidence he may have had in the sayings of heathen philosophers, poets, traffickers in mysteries, or even Christians. At this point Bacon introduces another of his "code phrases"—"But to speak in a mean"—which will be read by the initiated as, "Now that we've taken note of the opinions men commonly hold on the subject, let us look to the truth of the matter." In "Of Usury" the phrase is "to speak usefully" and in "Of Cunning," "To say truth," while in "Of Truth" the distinction implied by all these is made more fully:

> To pass from theological and philosophical truth, to the truth
> of civil business.
>
> (*Sp.*, III, 378)

In terms of the methodology of scientific inquiry, "theological truth" is no more to be honored than any other body of commonly received notions. One of the most remarkable statements in the *Novum Organum* is this variation on the biblical commonplace, "Render therefore unto Caesar the things which be Caesar's" (*Luke*, 20:25):

> . . . some of the moderns have with extreme levity indulged
> so far as to attempt to found a system of natural philosophy on

the first chapter of Genesis . . . from this unwholesome mixture of things human and divine there arises not only a fantastic philosophy but also an heretical religion. Very meet it is
therefore that we be sober-minded, and give to faith that only
which is faith's.

(lxv)

Being "sober-minded" means speaking "usefully" or "in a mean," de-
scending from the aery heights where adversity is characterized by
the image of the frail bark of flesh sailing through the waves of the
world (this is almost comical) to the level plain of empirical observation and a plainer style: "The virtue of Prosperity is temperance,
the virtue of Adversity is fortitude. . . . Prosperity is the blessing of
the Old Testament; Adversity is the blessing of the New." But these
speeches, while they are less "lively" and metaphorical than the
others, are still "high" in the all important sense of being above the
facts; and moreover the parallel members and the pointed schemes
operate to secure the kind of facile assent Bacon is always warning
against. Once again knowledge is being delivered "In such form as
may best be believed" and once again Bacon breaks the spell of his
cadenced rhythms with a characteristic qualification: "Yet, even. . . ."
But the qualifying statement has a rhythm of its own in addition to a
network of patterned oppositions—"David's harp"-"pencil of the Holy
Ghost," "hearse-like airs"-"afflictions of Job," "carols"-"felicities of
Salomon"—and for the third time the reader is encouraged to relax
while his powers of judgment are taken over by the movement of
the prose. The transverse patterning continues—"Prosperity"-"fears
and distastes," "Adversity"-"comforts and hopes"—as the distinction
between the two abstractions becomes increasingly blurred. The argument, which is, of course, rhetorical rather than logical, is helped
along by the unheralded reintroduction of "lively" language. Amidst
talk of "embroideries" and "lightsome grounds," the emotional and
physical realities of adversity fade, and when Bacon concludes "Judge
therefore of the pleasure of the heart by the pleasure of the eye" he is
in fact urging something his style has already effected. As the final
sentence unfolds, the reader is once more in the position he occupied
at the beginning of the essay, the passive receiver of "high speeches,"
assured by an introductory "certainly" that nothing will be required
of him but a nod of the head. The sentence itself is the "highest"
speech imaginable, complete with an elaborate and fanciful simile

and ending with a perfect and pointed *isocolon*. But the effect is spoiled, intentionally of course, by a single superfluous phrase—"or crushed"—which not only upsets the symmetry of the parallel members, but serves, for the last time, to arouse the reader from the intellectual lethargy he has fallen into. Supposedly offered as a synonym for "incensed," "crushed" is instead a comment on it and on "precious odours" and "fragrant" too, revealing what "incensed" and all incense-like "high speech" is designed to hide, the hard, and ultimately saving, truth. Without it the last pair of neat antitheses—"Prosperity doth best discover vice, but Adversity doth best discover virtue"—would have been received with the reverence we usually accord a comforting *sententiae,* but with its near onomatopoeic sound ringing in our ears, the response is more likely to be, "that's all very nice, but. . . ." The essay ends, then, as it began, with a "high speech," but in between the two the deficiencies of any speech that flies above the facts have again and again been exposed along with the attraction such speeches hold for the mind of the reader. The question of what exactly "adversity" is is no more settled here than the question of what "love" is is settled in that essay. In fact, the experience of the essay is *un*settling, and therefore it meets Bacon's criteria for "useful" and "fruitful" discourse, discourse, which, because it does not pretend to completeness, invites men "to enquire farther."

IV

The movement characteristic of this essay, the uneasy and unsettling juxtaposition of sententiae and observations from the "real world," has not gone unnoticed by the critics who for the most part regard it as an accidental by-product of Bacon's revisions:

> . . . compositions which were originally pervaded by an atmosphere of clear moral stimulation were overlaid with considerations of immediate practical utility, till their primary inspiration became altogether obscured.
>
> (Zeitlin, 514)
>
> In the later editions . . . although the ligatures are good, unlike elements are joined and chronology is ignored.
>
> (A. W. Green, *Sir Francis Bacon,* 84)

The assumption is that the presence in a single work of "unlike elements" is regrettable, and in some sense, unintentional—Bacon either

lost control of his form in the successive editions or unwittingly allowed the essays to become a battleground for the warring elements
of his personality. But "Of Adversity" is a late essay, as are others in
which the same pattern can be seen. The "accidents-of-revision" theory
will just not hold water, no more than will Vickers' assertion that
Bacon is without a plan: "Bacon . . . added new material at any
moderately suitable point, without much thought to the overall development" (132). These statements are further evidence of a general failure to see that the coherence of the *Essays*—singly and as a
whole—inheres in the experience they provide. A study of the revisions, with a view to the changes effected in the reader's response,
will, I think, reveal a determined effort to make the *Essays* the kind of
experience I have been describing.

Let us turn once again to the essay "Of Love," but this time in its
1612 guise, a perfectly straightforward piece of conventional moralism:

> Love is the argument alwaies of *Comedies,* and many times of
> *Tragedies.* Which sheweth well, that it is a passion generally
> light, and sometimes extreme. Extreame it may well bee, since
> the speaking in a perpetuall *Hyperbole,* is comely in nothing,
> but *Loue.* Neither is it meerely in the phrase. For whereas it
> hath beene well said, that the *Arch-flatterer* with whom al the
> petty-flatterers haue intelligence, is a Mans selfe, certainely
> the louer is more. For there was neuer proud Man thought so
> absurdly well of himselfe, as the louer doth of the person
> loued: and therefore it was well said, that it is impossible to
> loue, and to bee wise. Neither doth this weakenes appeare to
> others only, and not to the party loued, but to the loued most
> of all, except the loue bee reciproque. For it is a true rule, that
> loue is euer rewarded either with the reciproque, or with an
> inward and secret contempt. By how much the more, men
> ought to beware of this passion, which loseth not onely other
> things, but it selfe. As for the other losses, the Poets relation
> doth wel figure them: That hee that preferred *Helena,* quitted
> the gifts of *Iuno* and *Pallas.* For whosoeuer esteemeth too
> much of amorous affection, quitteth both riches and wisdome.
> This passion hath his flouds in the verie times of weakenesse;
> which are great prosperity, and great aduersitie. (though this
> latter hath beene lesse obserued) Both which times kindle loue
> and make it more feruent, and therefore shew it to be the

childe of folly. They doe best that make this affection keepe quarter, and seuer it wholly from their serious affaires and actions of their life. For if it checke once with businesse, it troubleth Mens fortunes, and maketh Men, that they can no waies be true to their own endes.

(*Sp.*, VI, 557-58)

This admirably structured paragraph answers to the idea most people (who have not read them) have of Bacon's *Essays*. The argument moves smoothly from one point to the next; the prose is "pithy" and aphoristic; the moral vision clear and unambiguous. The first two sentences seem almost to generate what follows: Comedy and Tragedy are used to specify the two chief characteristics of love, its excessiveness and its triviality ("lightness"). This "division" is then expanded into an indictment of love as an unworthy passion which interferes with the "serious affaires and actions of . . . life." The example of Paris is brought in to "prove" Bacon's thesis and the essay ends with a predictable and unexceptionable exhortation: avoid love, especially when it threatens to make you forsake your "own endes."

Much of this is retained in 1625, but the additional materials work a profound change in the tone of the essay and completely transform the phrases and sentences that have been carried over from the earlier version. The nature of this change can be seen by a comparison of the two openings:

Love is the argument alwaies of *Comedies,* and many times of *Tragedies.* Which sheweth well, that it is a passion generally light, and sometimes extreme.

(*Sp.*, VI, 557)

The stage is more beholding to Love, than the life of man. For as to the stage, love is ever matter of comedies, and now and then of tragedies; but in life it doth much mischief; sometimes like a syren, sometimes like a fury.

(*Sp.*, VI, 397)

In place of the easy correspondence between life and the stage, we now have a clear separation of the two, and a suggestion that the view of love projected on the stage is an oversimplification. This implied criticism extends to the whole of the earlier essay which, like other presentations whose coherence is merely formal, excludes more of the truth than it contains. Bacon's additions operate to break that coherence, and to substitute for the almost physical satisfaction of a "closed" experience the greater satisfaction of a fuller understanding. Specifically, the emphasis is shifted from the prescriptive moral—avoid love—to the difficulty, if not impossibility, of doing so. This is clearly the effect of the passage analyzed at the beginning of this paper. The first sentence holds out the promise of an easy and formulaic distinction between wise men and mad lovers; but as exceptions to it are admitted, that formula becomes less and less reliable, until the phrase "if watch be not well kept" discards it altogether by transferring the responsibility from the labels to the individual. Wise man or fool, austere man or voluptuary; it doesn't seem to matter; love can always find entrance into a heart that is not constantly on guard against it. Later, when the two versions of the essay coalesce, sentiments that had seemed unexceptionable in the tightly controlled framework of 1612 now ring somewhat hollowly in the looser, but more inclusive, framework of 1625. This is particularly true of that most familiar of proverbs, "it is impossible to love and be wise." In the earlier essay that old saw is accepted without qualification or reservation as the inevitable conclusion to the arguments preceding it; but in 1625, with the examples of Marcus Antonius and Appius Claudius fresh in our memories, the response to that same sententia is made up of equal parts of skepticism and wonder. It may indeed be "well said" that "it is impossible to love and be wise," but is it *true*? After all, Bacon's original assertion, that "amongst all the great and worthy persons . . . there is not one that hath been transported to the mad degree of love" was also "well said," as was, presumably, the "poor saying" of Epicurus. Not that the reader will flatly reject this "saying"; the conflicting evidence is itself too inconclusive for anything so drastic. The effect of Bacon's revisions is never to cancel out what had been asserted previously, but to qualify it: something assumed to be true on the basis of what now appears to be inadequate evidence is not declared false (necessarily); rather, something else is declared to be true *also*. And if the fact of the two "true things" poses difficulties for the logically oriented consciousness, well, that's life. And that is also the experience of a Bacon essay.

In addition to inserting new material and (as a consequence) repositioning the old, Bacon achieves his complicating effects by slightly altering the phrasing of individual sentences. In 1612, the reader is advised that "they doe best that make this affection keep quarter, and

sever it wholly from their serious affaires." In 1625 a single clause
is added, but it makes all the difference in the world:

> They do best who, *if they cannot but admit love,* yet make it
> keep quarter and sever it wholly from their serious affaires.

In the light of the revised essay's emphasis on the difficulty of keeping
love out, the parenthetical qualification is more than a gesture. The
sentence, in its expanded form, reflects the delicate and shifting relationship between the absoluteness of a moral imperative ("morality
as one would") and the realities of a difficult world, and serves as a
further reminder to the reader that there are no easy answers.

   As is often the case, the later essay is given a new conclusion, one
which reveals more baldly than anything else the transformation that
has been wrought in the vehicle:

> I know not how, but martial men are given to love: I think it
> is but as they are given to wine; for perils commonly ask to be
> paid in pleasures. There is in man's nature a secret inclination
> and motion towards love of others, which if it be not spent
> upon some one or a few, doth naturally spread itself toward
> many, and maketh men become humane and charitable as is
> seen sometime in friars. Nuptial love maketh mankind;
> friendly love perfecteth it; but wanton love corrupteth and
> embaseth it.
>
> (398)

A statement like "I know not how" would have been unthinkable at
the beginning of the essay. The posture usually assumed by the
moral essayist does not allow for an admission of ignorance. But by
this time, a more assertive stance would be out of place. Both the
speaker and the reader have long since given up the illusion that love
could be easily defined or contained; all we can do for the present is
note the operation of this strange passion. It is a fact that martial men
are given to love, but aside from a hardly serious reference to an old
wives tale, there is no explanation for the fact. Bacon must resort to
the evasion of positing a "secret inclination" whose visible effects are
the actions we group under the rubric "love." In this penultimate
sentence love becomes a kind of disease spreading of its own volition
into every corner of our varied lives. So powerful is this force that it
literally overwhelms the qualitative distinctions we usually make be-

tween its manifestations. "Humane" and "charitable" love lose their positive associations and become just two more instances of this "spreading"; the religious life is less a noble and chosen calling than it is an involuntary response to an irresistible urge. An essay that began by identifying a "mad degree" of love and implying the existence of other, more manageable degrees, concludes by suggesting that all love is uncontrollable and, perhaps, mad. In the end, Bacon does return to the pointed prose and neat schematizations of the opening paragraph, but the familiar and comforting labels—"nuptials," "friendly," "wanton"—are here nothing but the skeletal remains of a simpler vision that is no longer ours.

V

I do not mean to suggest that the effect of a Bacon essay is wholly negative. The exposing of the inadequacy of our received notions has as an important by-product a heightened awareness of the need for better notions. While we may reject the easy formulations of this final sentence, we still feel the pull of the methodizing impulse it represents. The desire for definitions and schematizations is basic to the human mind and Bacon nourishes it at the same time that he exposes definitions and schematizations that have been accepted without sufficient validation. He does this in part by refusing to abandon the rhetorical and syntactical forms of systematization even when a particular system is found wanting. Indeed a noteworthy feature of the later essays is the persistence and prominence of a methodical structure even though the materials placed inside that structure are constantly threatening to burst its confines. One might say, for example, that in its 1625 version "Of Love" is an essay with two focuses and two structures. On one hand there is the 1612 structure, a smoothly flowing succession of aphorisms and counsels uncomplicated by any moral ambiguity; and within the same physical space a number of awkwardly placed observations from the real world. Moreover, the two structures ignore each other; the essay concludes as if nothing at all had occurred to disturb its tranquility since the patterned cadences of the opening sentences. It has been argued that when Bacon revises an essay whatever remains of the original functions as an "ornamental framework";[15] but "envelope" would seem to be a better word, at least in this case, since the old essay surrounds and holds in (with some difficulty) the new material. This relationship between the two versions is another indication of the essential unity of Bacons' scientific and literary programs. I have made much of Bacon's insistence that the form of a presentation not suggest more finality than the state of knowledge presently warrants; but there is another side to Bacon's strictures. Excesses in systems, he explains in the *Novum Organum,* are of two kinds: "the first being manifest in those who are ready in deciding, and render sciences dogmatic and magisterial; the other in those who deny that we can know anything, and so introduce a wandering kind of inquiry that leads to nothing" (lxvii). One school begins with general laws to which all particulars are referred for judgment; the other believes the discovery of general laws to be beyond the powers of man and so proceeds haphazardly from isolated particular to isolated particular. One school "is so busied with the particles that it hardly attends to the structure [of both the world and the inquiry]; while the others are so lost in admiration of the structure that they do not penetrate to the simplicity of nature" [i.e. they ride roughshod over distinctions that do not sort well with their preconceptions] (lvii). The twin dangers, then, are complacency and despair, the facile assumption that everything is known and the equally facile (and debilitating) assumption that nothing is (or can be) known: and by refusing either to sacrifice the observable facts to his structure or to wholly abandon that structure when some of the observable facts will not be accommodated within it, Bacon avoids both, fostering hope and a healthy skepticism at the same time. This is a large assertion and it will require more time and space than are available to me here to substantiate it; but as an indication of the direction such a substantiation will take I offer the following analysis of two versions of a single sentence from "Of Marriage and Single Life":

Certainly, Wife and Children are a kinde of Discipline of humanity; and single men	Certainly, wife and children are a kind of discipline of humanity; and single men, though they be many times more charitable, because their means are less exhaust; yet, on the other side, they are more cruel and hardhearted
are more cruell and hard hearted good to make severe Inquisitors.	(good to make severe inquisitors) because their tenderness is not so oft called upon.[16]

In 1612, the expectations aroused by "Certainly" are more than fulfilled: everything in the sentence is tied to the central opposition of
married and single men; the balanced rhythms of the two members
lead the reader's eye to places of obvious point and contrast—those with
wife and children: single men; humanity: cruell and hard hearted—
and the "extra" clause—"good to make severe Inquisitors"—serves as a
restful and cadenced close to an assertion that is not in any way qualified. In 1625 nothing is deleted, and despite the addition of more
than half again as much material, the outlines of the original structure remain clearly visible. But that structure and the argument it
processes no longer have the reader's undivided attention because
they no longer constitute the whole of his experience. That is, while
the rhythmic pattern of the sentence is retained, and along with it
the central opposition of married to single men, the reader's experience of that pattern, and therefore of that opposition, is interrupted
as he makes his way through the qualifying clauses which now follow
"and single men." As a result, the distinction on which the sentence
ultimately rests loses much of its firmness: for a moment single men
seem *more* humane than those with wife and children; but then that
humanity is revealed to be the accidental by-product of an economic
difference ("there means are less exhaust") and the pendulum swings
back in the direction of married men. At this point, the phrase "yet,
on the other side," is more confusing than directing. What exactly is
the other side? what side are we turning from? As in 1612, there are
only two sides, but in the course of explaining them, Bacon has
brought them closer together, so that at this late date in the sentence
the reader is less sure of his ground than he might like to be. Of
course the confusion is only momentary, and the larger outlines of
the argument soon come into focus again; but the damage has been
done, and however firmly the sentence concludes, those few moments
when the reader is side-tracked in a *cul de sac* have occurred and they
do contribute to the total effect.

    As a matter of fact, the sentence does not conclude firmly at all,
but tails off into still another qualification of the main point: "because their tenderness is not so oft called upon." This implies that if
single men were called on to be tender, they would respond in such
a way as to weaken further the basis for distinguishing between them
and men with wives and children. In 1612 the fitness of single men
to be Inquisitors provided a witty conclusion to a univocal argument;
now however that observation is relegated to parenthetical status and

the emphasis of the sentence finally falls on the reserves of tenderness such men probably have within them.

What we have then are two discursive structures in a single space, and to the extent they pull against each other or point in different directions, the reader's experience of them is strenuous and, what is more important, inconclusive. Not that one cancels the other out; rather, neither finally carries the day, with the result that the reader remains suspended between the conclusions each of them is separately urging and ends by asking a question instead of assenting to an argument. In 1612 the distinction between married and single men is absolute and unchallenged; in 1625, that distinction is blurred; but, because the structure which carried it is retained (although it is no longer controlling), the possibility of arriving at such a distinction remains a part of the sentence's assertion. That is, the presence in the new sentence of the old structure, including the introductory "Certainly," asserts the continuing relevance of Bacon's goal—the specifying of the relationship between married and single men—while the material which strains against that structure and resists its organizing pressure tells us that the task is not yet complete. Bacon's style, then, looks both *outward* (in its movement toward logical form) to the object reality he would ultimately describe, and *inward* (as a kind of caution) to the mind which is attempting the description; thus the sense of incompleteness and unresolved complication *within* a logical and discursive scaffolding, and the resulting avoidance of either complacency or despair. In other words, the form of the *Essays* (of which this sentence is a mirror example) is a reflection of (1) Bacon's fidelity to his goal and (2) his awareness of the individual mind's limitations and of the provisionality of all stages preliminary to the final one. Writing the *Essays* and reading them involves a continuing and *scientific* acknowledgment of Aristotle's insight concerning the "defects of our hearers."

NOTES

1. *A Harmony of Bacon's Essays* (London, 1871), p. xxvii.
2. "The Relation of Bacon's *Essays* to his Programme for the Advancement of Learning," in *Schelling Anniversary Papers* (New York, 1923), pp. 87-105.
   "The Development of Bacon's *Essays* and Montaigne," *JEGP*, XXVII (1928), p. 503.

3. Zeitlin, p. 507.
4. Crane, p. 97.
5. *Francis Bacon: From Magic to Science* (London, 1968), p. 187.
6. *Francis Bacon and Renaissance Prose* (Cambridge, 1968), p. 53.
7. References are to the *Works* edited by James Spedding, R. L. Ellis, and D. D. Heath (London, 14 volumes, 1857-74), hereafter referred to as *Sp.*, followed by the appropriate volume number.
8. H. Fisch, *Jerusalem and Albion* (London, 1964), p. 29.
9. References to the *Novum Organum* and the *Preface* to *The Great Instauration* are to *The English Philosophers from Bacon to Mill*, ed. E. A. Burtt (New York, 1939).
10. *Sp.*, vol. III.
11. *The Limits of Language*, ed. Walker Gibson, p. 14.
12. "Francis Bacon," in *The English Mind*, ed. H. S. Davies and G. Watson (Cambridge, 1964), p. 26.
13. *De Aug.*, trans. Gilbert Wats (Oxford, 1640), p. 29.
14. *The Senecan Amble* (London, 1951), p. 117.
15. The phrase is Zeitlin's.
16. The arrangement is taken from Arber, pp. 268-69.

EDWARD I. BERRY

✒

History and Rhetoric in Bacon's *Henry VII*

In a perceptive critique of Bacon as a historian, F. Smith Fussner observes that "the gap between theory and practice, so evident in his scientific writing, was also evident in his historical thought."[1] Fussner's criticism centers on Bacon's failure to realize in the *History of the Reign of Henry VII* the revolutionary potential of his historical theory. Whereas the inductive method implies factual accuracy, painstaking original research, and a critical methodology, the *History* itself betrays many of the familiar weaknesses of the humanistic tradition—among them carelessness in matters of fact, the use of invented speeches, and an uncritical reliance on the work of previous historians. Because of this disjunction between theory and practice, Fussner concludes that *Henry VII* is "a tribute to the humanism which Bacon supposedly despised."[2]

That Bacon's historical theory is inimical to humanism is beyond dispute. The essence of the humanistic approach, captured in a phrase by Degory Wheare, is that "History is nothing but Moral Philosophy, cloathed in Examples."[3] Diametrically opposed to this is Bacon's definition of history as a discipline "properly concerned with individuals, which are circumscribed by place and time."[4] For Bacon history is not

This essay is based on Chapter II of the author's unpublished doctoral dissertation, "Francis Bacon's *History of Henry VII*," submitted at the University of California, Berkeley, December 1969.

moral philosophy but the *basis* for a "scientific" philosophy, the "primary matter" or "particulars" from which philosophic axioms can be eventually induced (IV, 298). Bacon's approach to history is thus exploratory and "scientific," the humanist's didactic and moralistic. What Fussner fails to consider in his criticism of *Henry VII*, however, are the literary implications of this "scientific" approach. Although Bacon's hostility toward the humanistic tradition may not be manifested in the methodology of his *History*, it is clearly apparent in its rhetoric. The *History of Henry VII*, I would suggest, is both an imaginative projection of the "scientific" impulses underlying Bacon's historical theory and a revolutionary attempt at a new rhetoric of history.

Bacon actually begins the *History* from a distinctly humanistic perspective. Departing from the annalistic methods of his chief source, Hall's *Chronicle*, he devotes his first few pages not primarily to Henry himself but to his predecessor, Richard III. Richard's sixteenth-century reputation is familiar to readers of Shakespeare; Bacon's readers needed no introduction. From the time of More, Richard had served poets, dramatists, chroniclers, preachers, and pamphleteers as an archetypal tyrant, a man whose very name was synonymous with political villainy.[5] One would expect Bacon to reject what had become by his day a stereotype. But instead he uses it; his description of Richard epitomizes both the conventional view of the man and the mode of historical analysis which had created and fostered it. The technique is as arresting and provocative as the openings of the *Essays*.

The first sentence of *Henry VII* introduces Richard III as having met the fate reserved for all tyrants in a providentially directed universe: he has been not merely "overthrown" but "overthrown and slain" by the "Divine Revenge" (27). Throughout the description Richard's character is morally defined, divided into vices and virtues rigidly separated by means of an antithetical syntax: "cruelties and parricides" are thus juxtaposed with "virtues and merits"; "feigned and affected things to serve his ambition" with "true qualities ingenerate in his judgment or nature." His personality is conceived of as almost allegorical in its simplicity and rigidity. Change, development, complexity of any kind are rigorously excluded by an interpretative method which traces every action to the "deep root of ambition" and dismisses contradictory qualities as mere hypocrisy. Richard's "cruelties" and "parricides" not only outweigh his "virtues and merits"; in the opinion of "wise men" the latter are not virtues at all, but "rather feigned and affected things to serve his ambition." His "politic and wholesome laws" are likewise "but the brocage of an usurper." The interpretation is magisterial in tone and factually unsubstantiated; evidence is brought to bear only in the form of "the opinion of wise men" or "men of great understanding," and even the list of Richard's crimes includes those which are only "vehemently suspected." The sentence which concludes the portrait is typical:

> And as for the politic and wholesome laws which were enacted in his time, they were interpreted to be but the brocage of an usurper, thereby to woo and win the hearts of the people, as being conscious to himself that the true obligations of sovereignty in him failed and were wanting.
>
> (28-29)

The antithetical balance of the first two members, the alliteration of "woo" and "win," the length of the period, the cadenced ending produced by the repetition of nearly synonymous verbs—all serve to heighten the impact of Richard's villainy. The portrait as a whole is typically humanistic, its style and effect distinctly reminiscent of More's.[6]

Immediately following this sentence, however, occurs an abrupt and startling shift in perspective:

> But King Henry, in the very entrance of his reign and the instant of time when the kingdom was cast into his arms, met with a point of great difficulty and knotty to solve, able to trouble and confound the wisest King in the newness of his estate; and so much the more, because it could not endure a deliberation, but must be at once deliberated and determined.
>
> (29)

The coordinating conjunction with which the sentence begins implies a contrast between Richard and Henry, a distinction which in context can only be that between a king who lacked the "true obligations of sovereignty" and one who possessed them. The praise which the context demands, however, is not forthcoming; instead Bacon plunges the reader immediately into a detailed analysis of the political dilemma which confronts Henry upon his victory on the battlefield. Henry's problem lies in establishing a claim to the throne, and its difficulty is matched by the complexity of his response. Bacon analyzes the various options in a manner which suggests an internalized debate, a method which dramatizes the difficulty of choice. None of them is a satisfactory solution. And when the decision is made, we find (to quote only part of a sentence which will be examined later) that it springs from motives which are as complicated and obscure as Richard's were simple: an "affection to his own line and blood," a desire for that title "which made him independent," a "nature and constitution of mind not very apprehensive or forecasting of future events afar off . . ." (30-31). Character is here psychologically not morally defined, and is analyzed in a sentence which in its looseness and asymmetry comes close to reproducing the mental state it describes.

This juxtaposition of realistic political and psychological analysis with the highly conventional providential and moralistic portrait of Richard III results in a disconcerting interference with the reader's expectations. The effect achieved reminds one of the *Essays*, where the clash between commonplace and original observation is often unsettling. After the portrait of Richard we anticipate what Hall's *Chronicle*, Bacon's source, actually provides—a description of the triumphal entry into London, the rejoicing throng, the wise and magnanimous monarch ordained to set England at peace.[7] By introducing a convention only to break it, Bacon indirectly calls into question the view of historical reality from which it derives. The remainder of the *History*, in fact, constitutes an implicit criticism of that view and an alternative approach to historical experience.

The "Divine Revenge" with which the narrative begins disappears after the portrait of Richard III. Aside from a few conventional references to the "secret providence of God," designed apparently to flatter James I, His purposes remain throughout the work unknown and uninvestigated.[8] When Providence is taken seriously as a determinant of human affairs, the context is always ironic, as in the case of the wily French ambassador who attributes Charles VIII's great "affection" for Henry to God, who had put it "into the heart of our master, no doubt for the good of Christendom, and for purposes yet unknown to us all . . ." (105); or in that of the maudlin Perkin Warbeck, who in his address to James IV attributes his salvation to "Almighty God, that stopped the mouth of the lions, and saved little Joas from the tyranny of Athaliah . . . and did save Isaac when the hand was stretched forth to sacrifice him . . ." (164). In humanistic histories, as in

More's *Richard III,* the will of God is a reality; in *Henry VII* it is rhetoric.[9]

When one considers the practice of historians such as Machiavelli or Guicciardini, both of whom Bacon admired, his reticence concerning God's will loses some of its novelty. Yet even these authors tend not to abandon the Providential view of the humanists entirely but to translate it into more secular terms. As John R. Hale points out, even the most "secular-minded" Renaissance historians are prone to "eke out their grasp of causation" by invoking a deity—Providence's pagan counterpart, the goddess Fortuna.[10] In Book XXV of *The Prince,* for example, Machiavelli makes a desperate attempt to dethrone this capricious *femme fatale,* while in Guicciardini's *History* she reigns undeniably supreme. As Felix Gilbert observes, "the strongest, most permanent impression which the *History of Italy* imparts—and was meant to impart—is that of the helplessness and impotence of man in the face of fate."[11] In Bacon's *History,* as in the essay "Of Fortune," the "mould of a man's fortune" remains chiefly "in his own hands" (VI, 472).

The extent to which Bacon's "scientific" rationalism supplants the traditional role of Fortune or Providence is revealed in his treatment of the Queen Dowager's sudden "fall," an event which in Hall's *Chronicle* is considered so mysterious and irrational that it provokes an apostrophe on mutability: "Suche are all worldly chaunces, nowe in prosperyte and aboundaunce, mutable and chaungeable and full of inconstancy. . . ."[12] Bacon himself includes the Queen Dowager "amongst the examples of great variety of fortune" and, in self-conscious imitation of the set-pieces on Fortune's powers so familiar to readers of More, Hall, or Holinshed, calls attention to the vicissitudes of her career: her rise in Edward's reign from distressed widow to queen; her subsequent eclipse in Richard's reign—her two sons deposed, bastarded, and murdered; her new-found glory ("upon the rise of the wheel") as mother-in-law to the king; and finally her banishment into a nunnery (50-51). Bacon, however, unlike any of his predecessors, provides a hypothetical reconstruction of the Queen Dowager's complicity in the Simnell plot and thus deprives her fall of its mystery: her own conniving and Henry's shrewdness in discovering it, not some capricious and irrational element in the nature of things, are responsible for her downfall. By alluding to Fortune only to rationalize her out of existence, Bacon commits himself and his reader to a completely secular approach to historical causation.

Throughout *Henry VII* similar historical conventions are either undermined or invested with new meaning.

In *The Idea of History* R. G. Collingwood calls attention to Bacon's rejection of Providential history and attributes it to an exclusive concern with "the facts themselves" rather than their underlying causes.[13] In emphasizing fact at the expense of causation, Collingwood seems to have been misled by an inconsistency in Bacon's theory. When schematizing the varieties of learning, Bacon does consider history to be a function of memory, and the historian a mere compiler, cataloguing facts. Facts are important for Bacon, of course; they stand at the basis of his inductive pyramid. But by far his most important preoccupation is with causation: "Above all things (for this is the ornament and life of Civil History), I wish events to be coupled with their causes" (IV, 300-301). As George R. Nadel observes, only if causes are known can axioms be induced from the "particulars" of history; Bacon's insistence upon the historian's duty to couple events with their causes is "no mere professional injunction but a philosophically meaningful requirement."[14] The true historian is for Bacon one who seeks out causes, who pierces "the bottoms of pretences and the secrets of governments," tasks which require "great labour and judgment" (IV, 302).

The necessity to look behind men and events, to probe their inner meaning, is apparent in Bacon's most characteristic metaphors for political action. The imagery of *Henry VII* points consistently to a divorce between what Collingwood calls the "outside" of an event, the action itself, and its "inside," the thought of its agent.[15] What makes the discovery of the "inside" of an event so difficult in *Henry VII* is that the "outside" obscures rather than suggests it. Actions are never what they seem; appearances are invariably deceptive. Charles VIII, for example, attempts to "veil over his ambition" for acquiring Brittany (69). The Lady Margaret, hoping to "draw at one time or another some birds to strike upon it," casts as a "lure" the rumors that Richard Duke of York is still alive (132). Perkin Warbeck, who is described as a "finer counterfeit stone than Lambert Symnell" (132), sends his proclamation before him as a "perfume" when he prepares to invade England (166-67).

Imagery of plays and acting, most of which clusters around Perkin Warbeck, suggests throughout the *History* the illusory quality of political actions. As preparation for the "part he was to play," Perkin is instructed by Margaret in "princely behaviour and gesture" (135).

He is shown "acting the part of a prince handsomely" during the Scottish invasion (172), and responding to his eventual dismissal by James with "stage-like greatness" (187). His impersonation, Bacon informs us at its end, was "one of the longest plays of that kind that hath been in memory" (203). If the metaphor of stagecraft points thus to a discrepancy between appearance and reality, it conveys as well a subtler notion, that appearances tend to merge with rather than merely cloak the reality they serve to disguise. Perkin, for example, while acting his role, comes almost to believe it: "Nay himself with long and continual counterfeiting and with often telling a lie, was turned (by habit) almost into the thing he seemed to be, and from a liar to a believer" (139). His acting, moreover, leads paradoxically from self-deception to self-recognition, for once he is captured and brought "upon the stage in his new person of a sycophant or juggler, instead of his former person of a Prince," he is able to "tell better what himself was" (194-95). Henry himself, all along the audience of Perkin's drama, becomes at its conclusion the director of a pageant of his own, leading Perkin through the streets in a kind of "may-game" for the "solace" of the city (195). Truth and deception thus wear the same guise.

A related group of metaphors involves magic, superstition, and idolatry. Simnell is variously an "idol," an "image of wax," a "phantasm"; his plot is an "enchantment" (46, 59, 48). Perkin is a "sprite" raised up to "haunt" Henry by Margaret's "magic and curious arts" (132). As befits his incorporeal state, he is "smoked away" by Charles VIII— "upon the first grain of incense that was sacrificed upon the altar of peace at Bulloigne" (138). Like Simnell, he has a "bewitching fashion both to move pity and to induce belief" and arouses in his audience a "kind of fascination and inchantment" (133). As Bacon writes in the *Advancement,* the mind of man is "like an enchanted glass, full of superstition and imposture, if it be not delivered and reduced" (III, 394-95).

The illusions inherent in political action extend as well to speech. Each of Bacon's invented addresses, in fact, proves to be deceptive in intent, thus perverting what the *Advancement* holds up as the true end of rhetoric—"to second reason, and not to oppress it" (III, 410). Morton's address to Parliament on the war between France and Brittany is perhaps the most brilliant. The speech is structured by means of *partitio,* or division, a technique which Brian Vickers demonstrates is in the majority of Bacon's writings the basic method of organization and a source of their clarity and precision.[16] After a brief introduction, Morton announces the problem to be treated—whether to "enter into an auxiliary and defensive war for the Britons against France"—and divides it into three topics, indicating to his audience at the same time his purpose:

> And the better to open your understandings in this affair, the King hath commanded me to say somewhat to you from him of the persons that do intervene in this business; and somewhat of the consequence thereof, as it hath relation to this kingdom; and somewhat of the example of it in general; making nevertheless no conclusion or judgment of any point, until his Grace hath received your faithful and politic advices.   (77)

According to Vickers, the chief legitimate and traditional purpose of division is, in the words of Cicero, to render "the whole speech clear and perspicuous."[17] Morton's speech uses *partitio* to subvert this end. As Bacon informs us, the king had commanded Morton "to carry it so as to affect the Parliament towards the business; but without engaging the King in any express declaration" (79). The elaborate *partitio,* with its reassuring clarity and symmetry, its ostensible impartiality, is for Morton a subtle means of persuasion. By ostentatiously clarifying the issues he is able the more effectively to obscure them. Through insinuation, through emotionally compelling imagery, through subtly fallacious reasoning, the entire speech becomes not an impartial analysis but an argument in favor of war with France. Words in *Henry VII* are thus themselves like "idols" or "plays"; if accepted at face value they blind one to the realities which underlie them.

The discrepancy between appearance and reality conveyed throughout *Henry VII* by means of imagery and political rhetoric points beyond the merely political level at which deception is an adjunct to policy to a more philosophical one at which it becomes a fact of life. Deception in *Henry VII* is not, as it is in the histories of More or Tacitus, for example, an index of moral stature, a means of distinguishing a virtuous man like Edward IV or Germanicus from a Richard III or a Tiberius; or merely a symptom of tyranny conceived of in opposition to a natural order of relative justice—under an Edward IV or an Augustus. Nor is there in *Henry VII* the kind of amoral imperative to be found in Machiavelli's *Prince* or *History of Florence,* where deceit and intrigue become the necessary and therefore desirable attributes of a ruler. In *Henry VII* deception of one kind or another is merely the *sine qua non* of political behavior, and although the episodes of Henry's reign, particularly the impersonations, are conducive to such a portrayal, there is nothing in the *History* to suggest that such a state of affairs is in any way unnatural, restricted to a particular historical period, praise- or blameworthy.

In view of the importance of "idols" in *Henry VII*, it is probably not coincidental that Bacon's first use of the word to represent the mind's "fallacies and false appearances" occurs in the work undertaken immediately after the *History*, the *De Augmentis*. In his discussion of the "idols of the market-place," Bacon proposes a means of coping with these delusions which seems applicable to *Henry VII*: "it must be confessed that it is not possible to divorce ourselves from these fallacies and false appearances, because they are inseparable from our nature and condition of life; so yet nevertheless the caution of them . . . doth extremely import the true conduct of human judgment" (III, 397). The prerequisite for political as well as scientific success, then, is accurate perception. One must clear away "idols" in order to see the realities which they obscure. Hence the extraordinary number of references to sight in *Henry VII*—to "keeping one's eye on," to "keeping watch," to "looking," "seeing," "foreseeing"; the constant emphasis on Henry's characteristic lack of foresight; and the brilliance of the metaphor with which Bacon concludes the Perkin Warbeck episode: "This was the end of this little cockatrice of a King, that was able to destroy those that did not espy him first" (203).

At the level of perception the duties of Bacon's kings, historians, and scientists converge; all are engaged in distinguishing the true from the apparent amidst a welter of perplexities and ambiguities. Henry VII must "espy" cockatrices, penetrate to the "roots and causes" of internal dissension (60), send out "pioners" to uncover the truth of Perkin's story and undermine his support (143), get to the "bottom" of his danger in the case of Lambert Simnell (47). The historian, as Bacon explains with regard to the Simnell affair, must, in spite of "relations" which are "so naked" that they leave the episode "scarce credible," make his "judgment upon the things themselves, as they give light to one another, and (as we can) dig truth out of the mine" (44). The scientist must enter a "labyrinth," or make his way through "the wood of experience and particulars" by means of "the uncertain light of sense" (IV, 18). According to Paolo Rossi, in fact, "Bacon's doctrine of scientific knowledge is entirely conditioned by his conception of the universe as a labyrinth and forest filled with 'so many ambiguities of way,' 'deceitful resemblances of objects and signs,' 'natures irregular in their lines and so knotted and entangled.' "[18]

The thread of Bacon's labyrinth, whether scientific or political, is a knowledge of causes, from which true axioms can be ultimately derived by philosophy. In *Henry VII* the search for the causes of events, the political realities which both imagery and rhetoric compel us to uncover, centers on human nature. It is the human mind which is responsible for the atmosphere of deception and delusion which pervades the narrative. Behind the Simnell plot lie the priest Simon's ambition and the Queen Dowager's resentment at the ill treatment of her daughter. Holding the prompt book for Perkin's long "play" is Margaret, giving full vent to her hatred of Lancastrians in general and Henry in particular. Beneath the consistently devious political rhetoric lie schemes such as Charles' annexation of Brittany or Henry's heaping up of treasure.

The extent to which Bacon funnels all of our concern for causation into questions of character—at the expense of the social and economic causes preferred by the modern historian—is revealed in his treatment of Henry, who as monarch is conceived of as the chief cause of the events of his reign. Whether in the Perkin Warbeck episode, in his dealings with successive Parliaments, or in his negotiations with the French, both the successes and failures of Henry's policies are almost invariably traced to a source in his own mind. Political problems resolve themselves into psychological ones. A striking instance of this process is the Simnell plot, which affords Henry the first crucial test of his reign. The "roots and causes" of the Simnell revolt are to be found, according to Bacon, in Henry's "depressing of the house of York," a grievance which he eventually sets right "(at least in ceremony)" by holding the coronation of his queen (60). But the resentment of the Yorkists stemmed originally from Henry's inadequate response to the initial dilemma of his reign—the choice of a title. It was Henry's decision to assume the title "without mention of the Lady Elizabeth at all," as Bacon informs us, which afterward "did spin him a thread of many seditions and troubles" (31). The basis of that decision is set out in the sentence alluded to earlier:

> But the King, out of the greatness of his own mind, presently
> cast the die; and the inconveniences appearing unto him on all

parts, and knowing there could not be any interreign or suspension of title, and preferring his affection to his own line
and blood, and liking that title best which made him independent, and being in his nature and constitution of mind not
very apprehensive or forecasting of future events afar off, but
an entertainer of fortune by the day, resolved to rest upon the
title of Lancaster as the main, and to use the other two, that of
marriage and that of battle, but as supporters, the one to ap-
pease secret discontents, and the other to beat down open mur-
mur and dispute; not forgetting that the same title of Lancaster
had formerly maintained a possession of three descents in the
crown; and might have proved a perpetuity, had it not ended
in the weakness and inability of the last prince.   (30-31)

If we wish to discover the ultimate origins of the Simnell revolt—its
real "roots and causes"—they are to be found in the state of mind
which this sentence through its tortuous syntax not only describes but
imitates. The slight suggestion of irrationality implicit in the introductory metaphor—"cast the die"—is progressively reinforced as the
parallel participial constructions cut deeper and deeper into Henry's
motives: from his knowledge of the "inconveniences" attendant upon
each course of action, and the impossibility of an interreign, to his
preferences and likes, and finally to his "nature and constitution of
mind." The progression from "knowledge" to "nature," however, does
not simplify or clarify, for the syntax, instead of subordinating certain
motives, merely coordinates them, creating thereby an impression of
a mind at once multidimensional and somewhat obscure. The verb
"resolved," which introduces the relative simplicity of action and a
reassuringly symmetrical statement of Henry's plan, offers only a
temporary respite from the complexities of thought; for the semicolon,
preventing as it does the anticipated full stop, gives way to a further
reflection on the title, which spawns in turn yet another thought on
the Lancastrian claim. Symmetry, then, is built only to be collapsed
by an after-thought—reproducing, in effect, the turmoil in Henry's
mind and indicating the multiplicity of factors which contribute to
his decision. The sentence as a whole seems to mirror the perplexities
of actual experience rather than order them, to plunge the mind, in
fact, into what Bacon calls elsewhere a "very Tartarus of turmoil and
confusion" (IV, 110).

The compulsion to trace events to their psychological origins, to analyze the complex motives from which actions spring, is responsible for the "split between straightforward factual material and knottier analysis" which Robert Adolph identifies as one of the characteristics which distinguishes Bacon's historical style from that of Tacitus.[19] Bacon's most famous blunder as a historian, in fact, his elaboration of John Speed's misreading of *latenter* [secretly] for *laetanter* [joyfully], provides an illuminating example of this "split." Observe the progression from André, the original source, to Bacon:

> André: *Rex ipse Richemundiae comes Saturni luce, quo etiam die de hostibus triumpharat, urbem Londinum magna procerum comitante caterva laetanter ingressus est.*[20]

> Speed: Henry staied not in Ceremonious greetings and popular acclamations, which (it seemes) hee did purposely eschue, for that (*Andreas* saith) hee entered covertly, meaning belike, in an Horse-litter or close chariot.[21]

> Bacon: . . . he entered the City; himself not being on horseback, or in any open chair or throne, but in a close chariot; as one that having been sometimes an enemy to the whole state, and a proscribed person, chose rather to keep state and strike a reverence into the people than to fawn upon them.   (32)

Through the intermediary of Speed's error, the triumphant procession described by André becomes in Bacon's version the basis for a subtle analysis of political motivation. What in André is conceived of primarily as event, is in Bacon conceived of as thought.

This emphasis upon mental action is constant throughout the narrative and results in a distinctive syntactical pattern:

> And therefore being now too wise to disdain perils any longer, and willing to give some contentment in that kind (at least in ceremony), he resolved at last to proceed to the coronation of his Queen.   (60)

> The King, ever willing to put himself into the consort or quire of all religious actions, and naturally affecting much the King of Spain (as far as one King can affect another), partly for his virtue and partly for a counterpoise to France; upon the receipt

> of these letters sent all his nobles and prelates that were about the court, together with the mayor and aldermen of London, in great solemnity to the Church of Paul's; there to hear a declaration from the Lord Chancellor, now Cardinal.   (126)

> The King also being fast-handed and loth to part with a second dowry, but chiefly being affectionate both by his nature and out of politic considerations to continue the alliance with Spain, prevailed with the Prince (though not without some reluctation, such as could be in those years, for he was not twelve years of age) to be contracted with the Princess Katherine: the secret providence of God ordaining that marriage to be the occasion of great events and changes.   (215-16)

The salient characteristic of these sentences syntactically is of course the separation of subject from verb. Between the king and the "action" of each sentence intrudes a host of qualifiers—participial phrases, parenthetical interjections and the like—which seem to breed among themselves even subtler qualifications, distinctions, and explanations. The "action" itself, in fact, tends to become anti-climactic, an interlude of repose after a spate of mental gymnastics.

Needless to say, the mind under analysis is as knotty as the prose which describes it. Consider, for example, the psychological implications of the middle sentence, above. The event narrated is simple enough: Henry's officials go to St. Paul's to celebrate the Spanish victory at Granada. What prompts the king, however, to hold this celebration? The fact that he is "ever willing" to associate himself with "religious actions" suggests political shrewdness, but the phrase is ambiguous enough to recall the inborn respect for religious observance which is equally characteristic of Henry throughout the work.[22] "Naturally" means "in his nature" and seems to imply as well "what one might expect"—the two kings have much in common, after all—but the parenthesis deflects any incipient sentimentality with a telling reminder of the tenuousness of kingly affection. The stated reasons for Henry's affection—a combination of moral respect and political expediency—are similarly complex, suggesting by their parallelism a mind in which morality and Machiavellism are simultaneously present and of equal importance. The equivalence is essential to Bacon's conception of Henry; in spite of his "policy," he is never reduced to the simplicity of a machiavel.

The complexity of Henry's character is insisted upon throughout the narrative. Despite the obvious emphasis on Henry's avarice, Bacon's portrayal is of a man not a moral quality. The concluding portrait of Henry, in fact, draws together and synthesizes the complicated and varied traits of character revealed singly as the narrative develops. Piety, avarice, distrust, courage, political shrewdness, seriousness, closeness, lack of foresight—all contribute to a detailed rendering of a whole mind. Unlike humanistic historians, whose tendency is to simplify character, to chisel away all but the essentials, Bacon tends to complicate, to add a variety of important and sometimes relatively trivial psychological traits.

The humanistic tendency to reduce character to an essential quality derives at least in part from an aim that is moral rather than "scientific." If history is moral philosophy, if its end is the understanding and evaluation of moral qualities, then ambiguities and complexities of character are a hindrance; they obscure the outlines of virtue and vice which it is the business of the historian to clarify. Bacon's tendency to complicate rather than simplify, on the other hand, results from his commitment to history as a "science," and to personality as the chief cause in history. When character is taken "scientifically" as a cause, and when the progression of knowledge rather than the perfection of morality is taken to be the main purpose of the historian, accurate and detailed observation become essential. Psychology then replaces morality as a mode of analysis; understanding of personality becomes of more importance than moral judgment. The historian's allegiance shifts from Truth to truth: "what men do, and not what they ought to do" becomes the proper subject of history (III, 430). Bacon's prefatory assertion of objectivity toward Henry VII—"I have not flattered him, but took him to life as well as I could" (25)—is thus not the commonplace it seems at first glance.

The ultimate end of historical knowledge, in fact, as George R. Nadel so ably demonstrates, is for Bacon a new science of man, a science intended to replace the traditional moral philosophy which humanistic historians "clothe in examples."[23] In two lengthy and important passages in the De Augmentis, Bacon calls attention to the "wiser sort of historians" as the best sources for studies dealing with "the different characters of natures and dispositions" and the "affections and perturbations." The former of these is especially significant because it appears only in the De Augmentis and was thus composed immediately after Henry VII.

> But far the best provision and material for this treatise is to be
> gained from the wiser sort of historians, not only from the com-
> memorations which they commonly add on recording the
> deaths of illustrious persons, but much more from the entire
> body of history as often as such a person enters upon the stage;
> for a character so worked into the narrative gives a better idea
> of the man, than any formal criticism and review can. . . .
>
> (V, 21)

Out of these materials, Bacon continues, a "full and careful treatise"
is to be constructed, in order that "we may have a scientific and accurate dissection of minds and characters, and the secret dispositions
of particular men may be revealed; and that from the knowledge
thereof better rules may be framed for the treatment of the mind"
(V, 21-22). Moral and political reform, then, are to be achieved in
Bacon's system not through praise or blame but through "scientific"
observation—an "accurate dissection of minds and characters."

Bacon's "scientific" approach to personality leads to an achievement
in historical characterization which today we are too apt to take for
granted—the portrayal of change and development. In the humanistic
histories of his predecessors and contemporaries, character is essentially static. This is because the true subjects of humanistic histories
are not men but unchanging moral qualities: ambition in More's
Richard III, "unkyndnes" in Ascham's *Report of Germany,* "politic
governaunce" in the portion of Hall's *Chronicle* devoted to Henry
VII. Bacon's Henry VII, on the other hand, is conceived of as a developing organism, subject both to external pressures and to its own
inner laws of growth. The course of Henry's development, though it
can only be sketched here, is subtle and paradoxical: on the one hand,
he moves toward an increasing maturity and wisdom in political affairs, crowned with the power and prestige they bring; on the other,
toward an increasingly irrational desire for money, which ultimately
threatens to destroy him. The narrative as a whole is structured on
this contrapuntal progression.[24]

The Lambert Simnell plot, the first of many threats to his power,
finds Henry politically somewhat immature—"green in his estate"
(44)—and suffering the consequences of his mistaken decision to exclude his queen from all participation in the title. He continues to
make errors during the first phase of the Brittany affair—because of
"an ill-measuring of the forces of the other party" (73)—but the epi-

sode concludes with a brilliant vindication of his policies: a pledge of tribute from France so profitable that "it was paid both to the King and to his son Henry the Eighth, longer than it could continue upon any computation of charges" (130). By the middle of the Perkin War-beck episode the king's "reputation for cunning and policy" has become so great that "every accident and event that went well was laid and imputed to his foresight, as if he had set it before" (156); and by the end of the Warbeck affair he occupies a position of preeminence among his rival monarchs. The marriage of his daughter Mary to Charles Prince of Castile, the "last act of state that concluded this King's temporal felicity," provokes Henry to assert that "he had built a wall of brass about his kingdom, when he had for his sons-in-law a King of Scotland and a Prince of Castile and Burgundy" (236-37). Henry ends his reign "at the top of all worldly bliss" (237).

Henry's avarice keeps pace with his developing political wisdom and seems, in fact, an inseparable part of it. Although present in his nature from the first, the trait does not become obsessive until the end of his reign. His early restoration of Edward Stafford "not only to his dignities, but to his fortunes and possessions" is evidence that the virtues of "nobleness and bounty . . . at that time had their turns in his nature" (40); and his motives in the Brittany affair, though chiefly economic, include as well a desire for "honour, friends, and peace" (74). Shortly after the traitor Stanley's execution, however, the arrest of Sir William Capel marks a new stage in the development of Henry's avarice: "About this time began to be discovered in the King that disposition, which afterwards nourished and whet on by bad counsellors and ministers proved the blot of his times: which was the course he took to crush treasure out of his subjects' purses, by forfeitures upon penal laws" (155). At the end of his reign, at the height of his prosperity, his avarice finally dominates his character and threatens to undermine his authority. Dudley and Empson, his "horse-leeches and shearers," fill their own and Henry's coffers while turning "law and justice into wormwood and rapine" (217), and Henry himself becomes fit subject for caricature: extorting money from his host, the Earl of Oxford (219); signing a memorandum for a debt of a mere five marks—"Otherwise satisfied" (220).

Bacon's method of structuring and defining this twofold development is subtle and indirect; explicit statement yields constantly to metaphor. The most pervasive of the images associated with Henry's political and psychological development are those of turbulent weather—storms, clouds, rough seas. At the beginning of his reign Henry's "confidence and assurance" are dismissed as premature: "But the King, in his account of peace and calms, did much over-cast his fortunes; which proved for many years together full of broken seas, tides, and tempests" (42). The subsidy which provokes the Yorkshire revolt "was inned at last into the King's barn; but it was after a storm" (88). Henry welcomes the French treaty at Boulogne because he "foresaw at that time a storm of inward troubles coming upon him, which presently after brake forth" (131). The constant threat of invasion during the Perkin Warbeck affair makes Henry cast "a careful eye where this wandering cloud would break" (161). The Cornish in revolt are likened to tides, their leaders to "stirring winds" which "make them more rough" (176). Bacon signals the beginning of Henry's prosperity, appropriately enough, through the same metaphor: "At this time the King's estate was very prosperous . . . all noise of war (like a thunder afar off) going upon Italy." At this very moment in which the king's outward state is calm and secure, however, Bacon shifts the application of the metaphor to his newly troubled mind: "Wherefore nature," he continues, "which many times is happily contained and restrained by some bands of fortune, began to take place in the King; carrying as with a strong tide his affections and thoughts unto the gathering and heaping up of treasure" (217). The "broken seas, tides, and tempests" which previously troubled Henry's reign have now become internalized. Bacon's final use of the metaphor, in a reference to Henry's great riches, captures brilliantly the ironic reversal of his fortunes: "So that it was a strange thing to see what golden showers poured down upon the King's treasury at once" (225). Henry's "storms" become finally Jove's "golden showers."

The portrayal of the divisive forces in Henry's nature culminates in a final assessment of Henry's position immediately before his death. In a single sentence Bacon draws together the themes which have formed the bulk of the narrative and suggests the central dilemma of Henry's mind and reign. Having built his "wall of brass" around the kingdom, Henry finally feels himself secure:

> So as now there was nothing to be added to this great King's felicity, being at the top of all worldly bliss, in regard of the high marriages of his children, his great renown throughout Europe, and his scarce credible riches, and the perpetual constancy of his prosperous successes, but an opportune death, to

> withdraw him from any future blow of fortune: which cer-
> tainly (in regard of the great hatred of his people, and the
> title of his son, being then come to eighteen years of age, and
> being a bold Prince and liberal, and that gained upon the
> people by his very aspect and presence) had not been impos-
> sible to have comen upon him.   (237)

As the references to "fortune" and "worldly bliss" make clear, the
convention underlying this sentence is that of the apostrophe to Fortune mentioned earlier in the case of Hall's *Chronicle*. The structure
of the sentence is in fact contrived to heighten the feeling of mysterious and threatening power occasioned by the sudden reversals of
Fortune. The beginning, assuring us as it does that "there was nothing to be added to this great King's felicity," lulls the reader into a
comfortable acceptance of Henry's security "at the top of all worldly
bliss," an acceptance which the apparently interminable enumeration
of successes reinforces. The repetition of the coordinating conjunction,
"and," coupled with the *isocolon* and alliteration in the final item—
"the perpetual constancy of his prosperous successes"—leads us to expect the completion of the period. Instead, however, we are jolted by
the recognition that there *is* one further felicity the king needs—an
"opportune death." And, lest we falter in accepting death as a "felicity," the final portion of the sentence, in a sweeping circular movement which brings the period to a symmetrical but unexpected conclusion, informs us of the reality of the dangers which lie in wait for
him. It is Bacon's manipulation of the Fortuna convention which gives
this sentence its power. Nevertheless, the feeling of wonder, the
heightened sense of the precariousness of the human situation which
it evokes derive not from a mysterious deity external to humanity but
from human nature itself: the "great hatred of his people," the origin
of which, as is well substantiated throughout the work, is in Henry's
own mind. Bacon replaces the mysteriousness of Fortune with the
mysteriousness of human nature.

His uncompromising rationalism, then, seems to lead Bacon to a
vision of history in its own way as potentially deterministic as those
which trace events to a first cause in God's will or the whims of Fortune. By concentrating exclusively on the psychological origins of historical events, and at the same time eschewing the humanistic emphasis on moral reform, he seems to present a view of history in which
man is trapped by his own infirmities, perpetually torn between a

capacity for rational control and irrational desires. The *History of Henry VII* provides no answer to this dilemma, but the portrait of Henry which concludes the work points the way to one—a new understanding of man. The mystery of character, which compels the providential historian and secular humanist to seek ultimate answers in religion and moral philosophy, leads in *Henry VII* to further historical and "scientific" exploration.

Bacon introduces his *descriptio* of Henry with an observation of great importance: "This King (to speak of him in terms equal to his deserving) was one of the best sort of wonders; a wonder for wise men. He had parts (both in his virtues and his fortune) not so fit for a common-place as for observation" (237-38). The purpose of this brief preface is not merely complimentary; its terms are crucial ones in Bacon's philosophy. "Wonder," the feeling evoked, as we have seen, by the immediately preceding allusion to Fortune's powers, is in Bacon's view the ultimate origin of knowledge itself. As defined in the *Advancement,* "wonder" is "broken knowledge." As such, however, it is not an admission of perpetual ignorance, but a prelude to further inquiry: "wonder" is in fact the *seed* of knowledge" (III, 266; my italics). The second part of the preface is equally significant. A "common-place," of course, represents the use, or over-use of knowledge for didactic ends, not the progression of knowledge. The conventional portrait of Richard III, for example, is "fit for a common-place" and was used as such *ad nauseam* in sermons and political tracts of the period.[25] Henry is fit for "observation," and in that concept, as is well known, lies the germ of Bacon's new science: "MAN," he announces in Aphorism I of the *Novum Organum,* "being the servant and interpreter of Nature, can do and understand so much and so much only as he has observed in fact or in thought of the course of nature: beyond this he neither knows anything nor can do anything" (IV, 47).

The distinction between "common-place" and "observation," between the use and progression of knowledge, characterizes accurately the shift in historical perspective which occurs in *Henry VII* and which underlies the contrasting portraits which frame it. Stylistically the descriptions of Richard and Henry are examples of what Bacon calls the "magistral" and "initiative" methods, the one suasive and utilitarian in effect, the other suggestive and exploratory. The different purposes of the two styles correspond exactly to the difference between "commonplace" and "observation":

> The magistral method teaches; the initiative intimates. The
> magistral requires that what is told should be believed; the ini-
> tiative that it should be examined. The one transmits knowl-
> edge to the crowd of learners; the other to the sons, as it were,
> of science. The end of the one is the use of knowledges, as
> they now are; of the other the continuation and further pro-
> gression of them.   (IV, 449)

We have already observed the "magistral" quality of the description
of Richard III and the stylistic devices which accentuate it—the structural balance achieved through figures such as alliteration and *isocolon,* the lengthy and generally symmetrical periods, the authoritative
and moralistic tone. The portrait of Henry, in contrast, is "initiative."
Its style consists of a blend of the closely related categories which
Morris W. Croll labels "curt" and "loose": the periods are terse, tending toward the aphoristic, asymmetrical, bound by loose syntactical
ligatures or none at all. Its effect is to reproduce the exploratory motions of the natural flow of thought.[26]

The style of the concluding *descriptio* is particularly difficult to
illustrate because it depends for its effect not so much on the individual sentence as on the organic development of the whole. Hence a
rather lengthy extract (although itself scarcely one-third of a paragraph) is necessary:

> He did much maintain and countenance his laws; which
> (nevertheless) was no impediment to him to work his will.
> For it was so handled that neither prerogative nor profit went
> to diminution. And yet as he would sometimes strain up his
> laws to his prerogative, so would he also let down his preroga-
> tive to his Parliament. For mint and wars and martial disci-
> pline (things of absolute power) he would nevertheless bring
> to Parliament. *Justice was well administered in his time, save
> where the King was party; save also that the counsel-table inter-
> meddled too much with meum and tuum. For it was a very
> court of justice during his time; especially in the beginning.
> But in that part both of justice and policy which is the durable
> part, and cut as it were in brass or marble, which is the making
> of good laws, he did excel.* And with his justice he was also
> a merciful prince: as in whose time there were but three of the
> nobility that suffered; the Earl of Warwick; the Lord Chamber-

lain; and the Lord Audley: though the first two were instead of numbers in the dislike and obloquy of the people. But there were never so great rebellions expiated with so little blood drawn by the hand of justice, as the two rebellions of Black-heath and Exeter. As for the severity used upon those which were taken in Kent, it was but upon a scum of people. His pardons went ever both before and after his sword. But then he had withal a strange kind of interchanging of large and in-expected pardons with severe executions: which (his wisdom considered) could not be imputed to any inconstancy or in-equality; but either to some reason which we do not now know, or to a principle he had set unto himself, that he would vary, and try both ways in turn. But the less blood he drew the more he took of treasure: and as some construed it, he was the more sparing in the one that he might be the more pressing in the other; for both would have been intolerable. Of nature assuredly he coveted to accumulate treasure; and was a little poor in admiring riches. (239; my italics)

The periods in this passage, unlike some of those analyzed previously, are characterized by brevity and asymmetry. Although members are sometimes of equal or similar length (as in the third sentence), this use of *isocolon* is virtually the sole gesture toward syntactical symmetry. The more elaborate "Ciceronian" figures—verb suspension, *parison, antimetabole, paramoion, anaphora, epistrophe*—which Brian Vickers discovers throughout the *Advancement,* and which, significantly, are appropriate to that work's persuasive aim, are omitted from the portrait of Henry VII.[27] The connectives, moreover, as in Croll's "loose" style, are generally coordinating conjunctions which contribute to the "linked" or "trailing" movement of associative thought.[28] The characteristic progression of thought, as illustrated by the italicized sentences, is cumulative, proceeding from a simple, definitive assertion through qualifications and contradictions to an imaginative synthesis of the whole. Out of the idea that "Justice was well administered in his time" springs the immediate qualification, "save where the King was party," which gives birth in turn to a further qualification, "save also that the counsel-table intermeddled too much with *meum* and *tuum.*" The mention of the counsel-table provokes an explanation of its role—"For it was a very court of justice during his time"—which leads to yet another qualification, "especially in the beginning." The thought then jumps back to the original point, the sound administration of justice, re-asserting its validity by a reference to Henry's greatest achievement, "the making of good laws." The impression created is of the paradoxical nature of Henry's mind and the consequent impossibility of reducing it to manageable simplicity.

This impression is strengthened by the rapid, usually abrupt shifts from one general trait to the next. The movement from the laws to justice, from justice to mercy, from mercy to avarice is determined not by an external structure but by the natural order of associative thought. The moral qualities at issue, instead of being drawn with the hard, clear outlines characteristic of Bacon's assessment of Richard III, become diffuse because of the incessant qualification. Good and evil qualities, moreover, merge with one another. The discussion of Henry's mercy, for example, develops almost imperceptively into that of his avarice: "But the less blood he drew the more he took of treasure. . . ." The moral clarity necessary for praise or blame, the traditional function of such commemorations, is blurred throughout by this juxtaposition of qualities which are virtually contradictory—justice and injustice, mercy and avarice, respect for and willful manipulation of the laws. Character is presented as an organic whole, in which vices and virtues are inextricably intertwined, not separated into neat categories for praise or blame.

Morris W. Croll contends that such a style is directly imitative of Tacitus.[29] Compare, then, part of a *descriptio* from the *Annals*, that of Augustus, whose portrait, although critical, is much more balanced than that of Tiberius and thus resembles Henry VII more closely:

> Nor did criticism spare his private life. He had stolen Nero's wife, then insulted the pontiffs by asking them whether it was in order to marry her when she was pregnant. There had been the gross extravagance of Vedius Pollio. Finally, Livia had been a national disaster as a mother, a calamity to the house of Caesar as a stepmother. There was no scope for the worship of the gods, when Augustus wished to foster his own cult through temples, divine effigies, and the service of flamens and priests. Even the selection of Tiberius as his successor had not been prompted by affection or regard for the state. Once Augustus had grasped his arrogance and cruelty, he sought glory for himself by the worst of possible comparisons. And indeed, a few years earlier, when Augustus had asked the Senate to renew

Tiberius' powers as tribune, he had made certain references to his dress, deportment, and habits. Outwardly these were excuses; in reality, they were criticisms.

Augustus' funeral was duly held, and he was endowed by decree with a temple and divine worship.[30]

In certain respects the style does resemble that of Bacon. The periods are terse, bound to one another only by their common relationship to the initial sentence, asymmetrical. The penultimate sentence has an aphoristic brevity comparable to the final one in our example from *Henry VII*.[31] But the effect is entirely different. Tacitus' method is not exploratory but condemnatory, not psychological but moralistic. The clipped and asymmetrical periods serve to heighten the impact of Augustus' moral blemishes; the matter-of-fact tone exaggerates by means of understatement the immorality of his deeds. The ironic and satirical thrust of the entire passage is epitomized in the final sentence. Ostensibly a mere statement of fact, its position converts it into a cry of moral indignation: this man "was endowed by decree with a temple and divine worship."

The fact that this example forms part of the negative half of Augustus' portrait merely serves to emphasize Tacitus' relationship to the humanistic tradition; praise and blame are for him distinct categories, and he divides his *descriptio* accordingly. His treatment of Augustus, moreover, is consonant with his avowed moral purpose: "The proper function of history, as I conceive it, is to insure that merits are not passed over, and that base words and deeds will have occasion to fear the judgment of posterity."[32] It is no wonder, then, that More's *Richard III* so often echoes the *Annals,* or that his portrait of Richard is so clearly indebted to that of Tiberius.[33] As Robert Adolph maintains, "The greatest difference between Tacitus and Bacon, and the one decisive for style, is in Bacon's amoral conception of history."[34] The most accurate labels for Bacon's historical style, then, are those which describe its effect—"initiative," "probative" are Bacon's own terms—not merely its structure, whether "Ciceronian" or "Tacitean."

In Bacon's theory the initiative manner of delivery is the stylistic counterpart of the inductive method. His description of the process lying behind the initiative style is applicable to the portrait of Henry VII and illustrates its inductive basis: "a man may revisit and descend unto the foundations of his knowledge and consent; and so transplant it into another as it grew in his own mind" (III, 404). The organic metaphor, of course, emphasizes the role of such a process in the "continuation and progression" as opposed to the "use" of knowledge. The complexity of character which emerges from the portrait of Henry is in large part a result of Bacon revisiting the foundations of his knowledge—both arriving at and testing generalizations about Henry's character through particular details, either presented in the portrait itself or embedded in the history as a whole. One of the most obvious differences between the portrait of Henry VII and those of the humanistic tradition, in fact, is its extraordinary particularity, as an early writer for *The Guardian* acutely if unappreciatively recognized:

> The character of *Henry* the Seventh, at the end, is rather an Abstract of his History than a Character. It is tedious, and diversified with so many Particularities as confound the Resemblance, and make it almost impossible for the Reader to form any distinct idea of the Person. It is not thus the Ancients drew their Characters; but in a few just and bold Stroaks gave you the distinguishing Features of the Mind . . . in so distinct a manner, and in so strong a Light, that you grew intimate with your Man immediately, and knew him from an hundred.[35]

That the concluding portrait is an "Abstract of his History" is, of course, exactly the point. The history of the reign has been in essence the history of Henry's mind; the narrative itself, beginning as it does with a character unknown and unintroduced to the reader, has proceeded gradually and "inductively" toward a multidimensional view of him.[36] The final *descriptio* caps the inductive process, abstracts from the diverse particulars of the narrative the fundamental qualities of Henry's nature. It does so, moreover, without abandoning the details upon which it is based. For particulars, although they complicate and obscure, are nevertheless the only test of truth; "knowledge drawn freshly and in our view out of particulars knows best the way back to particulars again . . ." (V, 56). Upon such a foundation Bacon hoped to build a new science of man.

The particularity of Henry's portrait is of course characteristic of Bacon's method throughout the narrative. Henry is not a model but a man—complicated and individualized to an extent which renders him entirely unsuitable as a humanistic "pattern" for imitation. Not only in his treatment of character does Bacon avoid the generalizing tendencies of the humanists; he avoids as well their overt didacticism. The precepts and general truths invariably embedded in humanistic narrative are noticeable by their absence in *Henry VII*—a fact which is especially significant in view of Bacon's reputation as an aphorist.[37] Political precepts are implicit in his analysis, of course, as he says they are in any "wise" history, but the reader himself must "play the midwife"—at his own risk (IV, 311). Bacon's account of Henry and his career serves as a model for future imitation only in the sense that it exemplifies a new approach to history. The method is capable of universal application; the man and his reign, unique.[38]

The *History of Henry VII* thus has its roots in the same soil which nourishes the Baconian philosophy. This is not to say that it fulfills all of the requirements of Bacon's formal theory of history; as F. Smith Fussner quite rightly points out, the essence of his theory consists in factual accuracy, and for that Bacon had neither enough critical tools nor the patience to use those he had.[39] From a modern point of view, the real revolution in historical writing was a methodological one, for which we must turn to humbler, less vociferous revolutionaries than Bacon—a Selden, Camden, or Stow. Yet the discrepancy between Bacon's scientific theory and practice is by now a commonplace of intellectual history. We should not be surprised, therefore, to find a similar disjunction in his historical thought. Bacon's excellence derives not from scientific achievements but from his imaginative grasp of a new approach to reality. The *History of Henry VII*, in its uncompromising secularity, its vivid rendering of the deceptions and illusions of political experience, and its unremitting search for the causes behind events, the mainsprings of human psychology, reflects this new approach and, in style and structure, gives it form. On an imaginative level, at least, Bacon's theory and practice are one.

NOTES

1. F. Smith Fussner, *The Historical Revolution: English Historical Writing and Thought, 1580-1640* (London, 1962), p. 254.
2. Fussner, *op. cit.*, p. 264.
3. Degory Wheare, *The Method and Order of Reading Both Civil and Ecclesiastical Histories,* trans. Edmund Bohun (London, 1685), p. 298. The locus classicus of humanistic theory is Amyot's Preface to *Plutarch's Lives,* as translated by North. The chief features of this view are discussed in the introductory chapters of Lily B. Campbell, *Shakespeare's 'Histories,'* San Marino, Calif., 1963; in Felix Gilbert,

Machiavelli and Guicciardini: Politics and History in Sixteenth-Century Florence (Princeton, 1965), pp. 203-35; and in F. J. Levy, *Tudor Historical Thought* (San Marino, Calif., 1967), pp. 33-78. For Bacon's theory of history see Fussner, *op. cit.,* pp. 253-64; Leonard F. Dean, "Sir Francis Bacon's Theory of Civil History-Writing," *ELH,* VIII (1941), 161-83; and George H. Nadel, "History as Psychology in Francis Bacon's Theory of History," *History and Theory,* V, 3 (1966), 275-87. I am particularly indebted to the latter article.

4. *The Works of Francis Bacon,* ed. James Spedding, R. L. Ellis and D. D. Heath. 14 vols. (London, 1857-74), IV, 292. Henceforth citations to this edition will be included parenthetically within the text: by page alone in the case of *Henry VII* (vol. VI); by volume and page in the case of other works.

5. The literary and historical treatment of Richard's character is amply documented in G. B. Churchill, *Richard the Third up to Shakespeare* (Palaestra, X), Berlin, 1900; see also Campbell, *op. cit.,* pp. 32-34.

6. See More's description of Richard in *The History of King Richard III,* ed. Richard S. Sylvester (New Haven, 1963), pp. 7-9. In referring to a humanistic rhetoric of history, I am of course generalizing about an extraordinarily diverse body of literature. I shall allude to More's history throughout this essay as by far the most influential and most interesting case in point, but my observations can be applied as well, I believe, to a substantial number of historical narratives written in England in the sixteenth century; particularly persuasive examples, in addition to *Richard III,* are Polydore Vergil's *Anglia Historia,* Hall's *Chronicle,* which was Bacon's main source, and Roger Ascham's *Report of the Affaires and State of Germany.* The term "humanistic," although it may occasionally seem pejorative, is not intended as such, especially in the case of More's *Richard III,* which lack of space forces me to oversimplify.

7. *Hall's Chronicle,* ed. Henry Ellis (London, 1809), pp. 422-23.

8. See, for example, pp. 198-99 and 215-16.

9. See More, *op. cit.,* pp. 86-87, where Richard's "wretched end" is held up as an example of God's retributive justice.

10. See Hale's Introduction to *Guicciardini: History of Italy and History of Florence,* trans. Cecil Grayson (New York, 1964), p. xxxv.

11. Gilbert, *op. cit.,* p. 288.

12. Hall, *op. cit.,* p. 431.

13. R. G. Collingwood, *The Idea of History* (Oxford, 1946), p. 58.

14. Nadel, *op. cit.,* p. 279.

15. Collingwood, *op. cit.,* p. 213.

16. Brian Vickers, *Francis Bacon and Renaissance Prose* (Cambridge,

1968), pp. 30-59; see especially p. 49, where Morton's use of *partitio* is mentioned.

17. Vickers, *op. cit.*, p. 36.

18. Paolo Rossi, *Francis Bacon: From Magic to Science,* trans. Sacha Rabinovitch (Chicago, 1968), p. 206.

19. Robert Adolph, *The Rise of Modern Prose Style* (Cambridge, Mass., 1968), p. 36.

20. Bernard André, *De Vita atque Gestis Henrici Septimi Historia,* in *Memorials of King Henry the Seventh,* ed. James Gairdner (London, 1858), pp. 34-35.

21. John Speed, *History of Great Britaine* (London, 1611), sig. 5S1.

22. On p. 27, for example, Henry is characterized as "in his nature a great observer of religious forms"; on. p. 32 his second *Te Deum* is attributed merely to a political motive—that the people should not "forget too soon that he came in by battle." A similar balance is maintained in the concluding portrait of Henry, p, 238.

23. Nadel, *op. cit.*, pp. 283-87.

24. Also contributing to the work's structural unity, as F. Smith Fussner observes, is its division into four general "topics," each of which is treated chronologically: the problems of Henry's succession; foreign affairs; attempted usurpation; the consolidation of power. These narrative units, however, are less important and less clearly defined than Fussner implies (*op. cit.*, pp. 273-74).

25. See Campbell, *op. cit.*, pp. 32-34.

26. *Style, Rhetoric, and Rhythm: Essays of Morris W. Croll,* ed. J. Max Patrick and Robert O. Evans (Princeton, 1966), pp. 224-30.

27. Vickers, *op. cit.*, pp. 116-40.

28. Croll, *op. cit.*, p. 224.

29. Croll, *op. cit.*, pp. 188-95.

30. *The Annals of Tacitus,* trans. D. R. Dudley (New York, 1966), pp. 25-26. The original, as in the Loeb edition, vol. II (London, 1931, I, x, is as follows:

> *Nec domesticis abstinebatur: abducta Neroni uxor et consulti per ludibrium pontifices an concepto necdum edito partu rite nuberet; Vedii Pollionis luxus; postremo Livia gravis in rem publicam mater, gravis domui Caesarum noverca. Nihil deorum honoribus relictum, cum se templis et effigie numinum per flamines et sacerdotes coli vellet. Ne Tiberium quidem caritate aut rei publicae cura successorem adscitum, sed, quoniam adrogantiam saevitiamque eius introspexerit, comparatione deterrima sibi gloriam quaesivisse. Etenim Augustus, paucis ante annis, cum Tiberio tribuniciam potestatem a patribus rursum postularet,*

*quamquam honora oratione, quaedam de habitu cultuque
et institutis eius iecerat, quae velut excusando exprobraret.
Ceterum sepultura more perfecta, templum et caelestes re-
ligiones decernuntur.*

31. Dudley actually splits the original into two sentences here but only
in order to approximate the aphoristic thrust of Tacitus' concluding
phrase—*quae velut excusando exprobraret.* John Jackson's translation in the Loeb edition captures the "Baconian" qualities of this
conclusion—"which were offered as an apology and designed for
reproaches."

32. *Annals,* trans. Dudley, p. 134.

33. See Richard S. Sylvester's excellent Introduction to *Richard III,* pp.
xcii-xcviii.

34. Adolph, *op. cit.,* p. 37.

35. *The Guardian,* no. 25 (9 April 1713).

36. That Bacon does not begin the narrative with an evaluation of
Henry's character is again indicative of his departure from standard
humanistic practice; More, Ascham and Speed all introduce their
main characters before describing their actions. Speed, in fact, prefaces his acount of the events of Henry VII's reign with a remark
which highlights the rhetorical effect of this technique: "Let us now
behold his vertues as they are shiningly *deduced* into action" (*op.
cit.,* sig. 5S1; my italics).

37. There are, in fact, four true aphorisms in over two hundred pages
of text, and even they have not the overtly didactic intent of humanistic precepts; see pp. 74, 140, 153, 234.

38. Bacon's avoidance of generalization and his emphasis upon psychology rather than political principles serve to differentiate *Henry VII*
from the "politic" histories with which F. J. Levy associates it. "Politic" historians, Levy maintains, wrote "to teach men political wisdom" and avoided psychological analysis because "if carried too far"
it would emphasize "the particular actor rather than . . . the universal situation" (*op. cit.,* p. 237). Levy interprets *Henry VII* as a
remarkably simple-minded attempt on Bacon's part to show James I
that "his political advice was still worth seeking." To achieve this
end, according to Levy, Bacon intended a "parallel" between the
characters and situations of Henry and James, although in execution it was "far from perfect." The parallel issues in "advice" such
as the following: "If Henry VII had been greedy and amassed treasure, James might find that example useful—he was given more to
spending" (p. 257). Other "didactic" interpretations of *Henry VII*
have proved similarly reductive.

39. Fussner, *op. cit.,* pp. 267-69.

JONAS A. BARISH

Prose as Prose

The writers whom Croll calls "baroque"—a term that will be adopted here for its convenience without any insistence on its exactness[1]—shared a distrust of the Ciceronian mode of sentence formation. This is not to say that they despised Cicero, the Vitruvius of Renaissance prose, or were uninfluenced by him, but only that they reacted against his oratorical manner. Jonson's admiration of Cicero is writ large (too large) in *Catiline*, and elsewhere, but Jonson was one of the least Ciceronian of writers. Ciceronian style was marked above all by the periodic sentence . . . where the syntax remains incomplete up to some well-defined turning point, with phrases and clauses tending to mass themselves in parallel formation on both sides of the turning point. The characteristic effects of this style were achieved by advance planning: one knew from the outset of a period where it was going and how it was going to get there. When it reached its destination, it afforded the gratification of a design finally complete, every piece falling into its place in the whole. Baroque style, on the other hand, aimed to give the impression, at least, of spontaneity, and hence its first concern was to break the stranglehold of the suspended sentence, to keep its syntax unencumbered and uncommitted, so as to be free to improvise in any way at any moment. . . .

From *Ben Jonson and the Language of Prose Comedy* (Cambridge, Mass.: Harvard University Press), pp. 48-77. Copyright 1960 by the President and Fellows of Harvard College. Reprinted by permission of the publishers.

In any event, baroque writers regarded Ciceronianism as an invitation to glibness and insincerity, and their first aim was to replace its logical schemes with various nonlogical maneuvers of their own, which Croll has grouped into the two categories of the "curt style" and the "loose style."

The curt style . . . owes its name, and its other names of *stile coupé* and *stile serré*, to its abruptness and choppiness in contrast to Ciceronian "roundness"; its characteristic device is the so-called "exploded" period, formed of independent members not linked by conjunctions but set apart by a vocal pattern of stress, pitch, and juncture rendered typographically by a colon or a semicolon, sometimes a comma. The members of the exploded period tend to brevity, also to inequality of length, variation in form, and unpredictability of order; hence they are likely to suggest the effect of live thinking rather than of logical premeditation. The "mere fact" or main idea of the period is apt to be exhausted in the first member; subsequent members explore the same idea imaginatively, through metaphor or aphorism or example, but not through ordered analysis.

> *Natures* that are hardned to *evill*, you shall sooner breake, then make straight; they are like poles that are crooked, and dry: there is no attempting them.[2]   (*Disc.* 36-38)

> They are, what they are on the sudden; they shew presently, like *Graine*, that, scatter'd on the top of the ground, shoots up, but takes no root; has a yellow blade, but the eare empty.
>   (*Disc.* 685-688)

> *The great* theeves of a State are lightly the officers of the Crowne; they hang the lesse still; play the Pikes in the Pond; eate whom they list.   (*Disc.* 1306-08)

In each of these instances, the initial member encompasses the central idea at a single stroke; the members that follow illuminate or particularize with metaphor. In the last example, Jonson exchanges one metaphor for another: the officers of the crown start as thieves of the state and end as great pikes in a pond. And if one were to quote the period that follows, one would discover the same officers turning into fowlers who spread nets for harmless birds but allow the hawks and buzzards to escape. The progress of such a period, then, is typically not a logical sequence but "a series of imaginative moments occurring in a logical

pause or suspension,"[3] in which ideas develop out of each other asso-
ciatively rather than according to any predetermined scheme. That the
curt style cannot dispense with logic altogether is perhaps too obvious
to need saying. What it can do is to excise logical ligatures, to play
haphazardly and capriciously with its elements so as to minimize the
sense of logical straitness.

Because of the freedom of its internal elements, the curt period
lends itself to the expression of quick shifts in feeling, afterthoughts,
self-corrections, unexpected interpolations or dislocations of attention,
and since in so doing it simulates so convincingly the processes of live
thought, it becomes an ideal instrument for certain kinds of theatrical
prose.[4] Jonson uses it in a variety of ways. One characteristic way is
to turn it into a vehicle for wit, allowing each successive clause, as it
springs from its predecessor, to exploit the latent potentialities of a
metaphor:

> Ne're trust me, *Cvpid,* but you are turn'd a most acute gallant
> of late, the edge of my wit is cleere taken off with the fine and
> subtile stroke of your thin-ground tongue, you fight with too
> poinant a phrase, for me to deale with.   (*CR* I.i.77-81)

Here the epithet "acute" used by Mercury in the first clause prompts
its own figurative extension into the "thin-ground tongue" of the second, after which the pointed tongue becomes the sword with which
Cupid "fights" his combats of wit. A related instance of the curt style
used for purposes of wit proves to be an "exploded" period in more
senses than one. Each clause ignites a verbal fuse that goes off as a
pun in the next clause, after the manner of a chain of firecrackers.

> He walkes most commonly with a cloue, or pick-tooth in his
> mouth, hee is the very mint of complement, all his behauiours
> are printed, his face is another volume of *essayes;* and his
> beard an *Aristarchus.*   (*CR* II.iii.87-91)

The puns kindle each other by association. "Cloue" suggests a pun on
"mint," which leads to an equivocation on "printed," which generates
a quibbling metaphor on "volume" and "*essayes.*"

In such cases, the language focuses sharply on its satiric object. The
tone may be biting or not, but its primary purpose is to demolish its

object, not to define its speaker. Used more complexly, the curt period does both at once: it sheds light on the creature being described, and it reveals the creature who is speaking.

> . . . a leane mungrell, he lookes as if he were chap-falne, with barking at other mens good fortunes: 'ware how you offend him, he carries oile and fire in his pen, will scald where it drops: his spirit's like powder, quick, violent: hee'le blow a man vp with a jest: I feare him worse then a rotten wall do's the cannon, shake an houre after, at the report.
>
> (*EMO* I.ii.212-218)

Carlo Buffone, whose spiteful disposition is revealed chiefly in his penchant for coining scurrilous similitudes, leaps here from the figure of the starved dog to that of scalding oil and fire to that of gunpowder to describe Macilente, and then to a variation of the gunpowder figure in which he imagines himself as a rotten wall blasted by the cannon of Macilente's wit: a good illustration of the spiraling or rotating movement of the curt period, and of how its sputtering rhythms may be made to define an excitable temperament like Carlo's. The unstable tension of the curt period serves similarly to characterize another high-strung individual, Pantilius Tucca, whose invectives against Horace flicker back and forth between metaphoric and literal abuse, and whose speech rhythms tend even more than Carlo's to stumble and trip in nervous jabs of clauses.

> Hang him fustie *satyre,* he smells all goate; hee carries a ram, vnder his arme-holes, the slaue: I am the worse when I see him.   (*Poet.* III.iv. 367-369)
>
> A sharpe thornie-tooth'd *satyricall* rascall, flie him; hee carries hey in his horne: he wil sooner lose his best friend, then his least iest.   (*Poet.* IV.iii.109-111)

As these extracts suggest, the curt period serves especially well to characterize angry or indignant, impatient or volatile, or merely dis-two irate clauses, and follow these with two more of stinging censure tracted or simple-minded people. Quarlous can dismiss Edgeworth in on his way of life.

> But goe your wayes, talke not to me, the hangman is onely fit
> to discourse with you; the hand of Beadle is too mercifull a
> punishment for your Trade of life.   (*BF* IV.vi.26-28)

Or the curt period can portray the spluttering, almost incoherent indignation of a Wasp, who states a proposition ("I am no Clearke")
and particularizes it in a series of nonlogical convulsions.

> That's well, nay, neuer open, or read it to me, it's labour in
> vaine, you know. I am no Clearke, I scorne to be sau'd by my
> booke, i'faith I'll hang first; fold it vp o' your word and gi' it
> mee; what must you ha' for't?   (*BF* I.iv.6-9)

Or it can reproduce the idiotic flapping about of a half-witted mind,
swayed aimlessly in opposite directions by the gusts of childish ap-
petite.

> I ha' paid for my peares, a rot on 'hem, I'le keepe 'hem no
> longer; you were choake-peares to mee; I had bin better ha'
> gone to mum chance for you, I wusse.   (*BF* IV.ii.73-75)

> S'lid, this is an Asse, I ha' found him, poxe vpon mee, what
> doe I talking to such a dull foole; farewell, you are a very Cox-
> comb, doe you heare?   (*BF* IV.ii.105-107)

It may implement the language of abuse, as we have already seen, or
it may serve to convey the disordered prattle of semisenility, as in the
speeches of Venus in *Christmas his Masque.*

> Yes forsooth, I can sit any where, so I may see [my] *Cupid* act;
> hee is a pretty Child, though I say it that perhaps should not,
> you will say: I had him by my first Husband, he was a Smith
> forsooth, we dwelt in Doe-little lane then, he came a moneth
> before his time, and that may make him somewhat imperfect:
> But I was a Fishmongers daughter.   (123-129)

The scatterbrained effect is secured by the multiplicity of brief
clauses, most of them syntactically unconnected; each starts off afresh
with its own new subject, so that the result is a pepper pot of random
remarks, loosely governed by chronology but otherwise innocent of

logic. The "But" that introduces the final statement not only lacks logical force: it is disruptive of logic, and so crowns the effect of incoherence.

It should perhaps be emphasized that the speeches of such characters as Wasp, Tucca, and Carlo Buffone do not represent a mere tic of punctuation on the one hand or a mere slavish transcription of heard language on the other, but a distinct style; their barking phrases translate into stage idiom the staccato effects of *stile coupé*. It is true enough that people often speak so, and it is also true that one may find patches of similar language in the popular comedy of the 1590's. But what in earlier writers is a mere incidental twitch Jonson transmutes into a structural principle. He takes the sprawling, ramshackle popular language and disengages from it the strain congenial to his own rhetorical bent, thus effecting a kind of merger between colloquial speech and his own Stoic models. The result is a stage prose that combines the vitality of live language with the authority and expressive potency of a formed rhetoric.

The highly impressionable Shakespeare was not likely to be immune to influence from this rhetorical current, and it may be suggested that along with the primary voice discussed in the first chapter, Shakespeare has a subsidiary voice that sounds much like a modified version of the curt style. One might, however, prefer to call the Shakespearean variant something like "plain statement," since it tends to consist of a procession of simple declarative or imperative clauses with little of the "explosiveness" peculiar to curt style:

> I haue dogg'd him like his murtherer. He does obey euery point of the Letter that I dropt, to betray him: He does smile his face into more lynes, then is in the new Mappe, with the augmentation of the Indies: you haue not seene such a thing as tis: I can hardly forbeare hurling things at him, I know my Ladie will strike him: if shee doe, hee'l smile, and take't for a great fauour.   (L.284; *TN* III.ii.81-89)

> I would the Duke we talke of were return'd againe: this vn-genitur'd Agent will vn-poeple the Prouince with Continencie. Sparrowes must not build in his house-eeues, because they are lecherous: The Duke yet would haue darke deeds darkelie answered, hee would neuer bring them to light: would hee were return'd.   (L.92; *MM* III.ii.183-190)

Looke, th'vnfolding Starre calles vp the Shepheard; put not
your selfe into amazement, how these things should be; all difficulties are but easie vvhen they are knowne. Call your execu-
tioner, and off with *Barnardines* head: I will giue him a present shrift, and aduise him for a better place.

(L.95; *MM* IV.ii.219-227)

When I bestryde him, I soare, I am a Hawke: he trots the
ayre: the Earth sings, when he touches it: the basest horne of
his hoofe, is more Musicall then the Pipe of *Hermes.*

(L.435; *HV* III.vii.16-19)

Leaue him to my displeasure. *Edmond,* keepe you our Sister
company: the reuenges wee are bound to take vppon your
Traitorous Father, are not fit for your beholding. Aduice the
Duke where you are going, to a most festi[n]ate preparation:
we are bound to the like. Our Postes shall be swift, and intelligent betwixt vs.   (L.807; *Lear* III.vii.6-13)

Alas, the storme is come againe: my best way is to creepe
vnder his Gaberdine: there is no other shelter hereabout:
Misery acquaints a man with strange bedfellowes: I will here
shrowd till the dregges of the storme be past.

(L.27; *Temp.* I.ii.37-43)

Such speeches show certain traits of the *stile coupé*: its discontinuous-
ness, its avoidance of logical particles, its shifts in grammatical form,
perhaps above all its apparent innocence of rhetorical cunning. They
differ from their Jonsonian counterparts in that the members tend to
be more equal in length, and also longer, so that the rhythm is slower
and gentler. Characteristically Shakespeare will insert into the middle
of an otherwise highly wrought discourse one or two such clauses,
which have the effect of tranquilizing the rhythm, of affording a moment's breathing-space for the actor and a pause in the forward march
of the argument.

What the Shakespearean passages do not have is the bristling asymmetry of the Jonsonian speeches. George Williamson has objected to
Croll's emphasis on this trait, and suggested that Croll, having committed himself to the analogy with baroque, was led to discover asymmetry in places where, in fact, symmetry predominates.[5] Williamson,
by way of rejoinder, illustrates from Bacon, and with this correction,

insofar as it applies to Bacon, one can only gladly agree: asymmetry, where it occurs in Bacon, remains tangential. But Jonson is another matter. "Asymmetrical" seems to define the shape of Jonson's prose so exactly that one is tempted to use it to describe the topography of his mind. Jonson delights in bending the logical axis of syntax a few degrees one way or another in order to interrupt a symmetrical pattern, to sprawl suddenly or compress unexpectedly in a way that pulls the reader up short. One may get at the difference between Bacon's style and Jonson's by comparing a passage from *The Advancement of Learning* with Jonson's adaptation of it in the *Discoveries*.

> This grew speedily to an excess; for men began to hunt more after words than matter; more after the choiceness of the phrase, and the round and clean composition of the sentence, and the sweet falling of the clauses, and the varying and illustration of their works with tropes and figures, than after the weight of matter, worth of subject, soundness of argument, life of invention or depth of judgment.[6]

The thing that impresses itself on one immediately here is the careful regularity of the sentence. The exact antithesis "more after words than matter" undergoes artful expansion in the member that follows, first into four aspects of the hunt after words:

> the choiceness of the phrase,
> the round and clean composition of the sentence,
> the sweet falling of the clauses,
> the varying and illustration of their works with tropes and
>   figures.

The four phrases fall neatly into two sets of two each. In each set the second phrase is longer than the first, and each of the phrases of the second set is longer than its counterpart in the first. One result of this strict geometrical plotting is to produce an effect of climax, to bring us to a rhythmic plateau on the phrase "with tropes and figures," after which the second half of the antithesis elaborates itself serenely into a series of five component phrases that observe exact correspondence of parts. If one were to continue quoting at this point, one would discover Bacon launching into a new sequence of parallel statements extending through five sentences: "Then grew the flowing and watery

vein of Osorius the Portuguese bishop, to be in price. Then did
Sturmius. . . . Then did Car of Cambridge. . . . Then did Erasmus. . . . Then grew. . . . In sum. . . ." As for the sentence preceding the quoted extract, it leads up to the antithesis between words
and matter by enumerating four reasons why "eloquence and variety
of discourse" came to be preferred to solidity of thought. The extract
from Bacon, then, not only displays a high degree of formal clarity in
itself: it forms part of a sequence that is highly articulated logically,
that unfolds in parallel and antithetic statements, and that preserves
parisonic correspondence in many of its inner parts in order to emphasize its logical divisions.

When we turn to Jonson's paraphrase, the first thing we notice is
that the period in question is no longer a complete grammatical unit.
It is fused to what precedes it, by virtue of the fact that its first verb,
"make," simply forms the last in a series of subordinate verbs dependent on "Wee must" in the prior sentence. The prior sentence itself
issues a plea for patience in the study of style that flickers restlessly
back and forth between positive and negative counsel. The plea concludes, then, with the paraphrase from Bacon:

> Then make exact animadversion where style hath degenerated,
> where flourish'd, and thriv'd in choisenesse of Phrase, round
> and cleane composition of sentence, sweet falling of the clause,
> varying an illustration by tropes and figures, weight of Matter,
> worth of Subject, soundnesse of Argument, life of Invention,
> and depth of Judgement. This is *Monte potiri*, to get the hill.
> For no perfect Discovery can bee made upon a flat or a levell.
>   (*Disc.* 2116-24)

Jonson has eliminated Bacon's dichotomy between rhetorical curiosity
and solidity of thought, and lumped together the phrases from both
sides of Bacon's antithesis in a single top-heavy series. Further, he has
cut away most of the articles and all the connectives, so that the period
now produces an unexpected effect of abruptness. Finally, he has embedded the passage in what is itself, so to speak, an asymmetrical context, commencing with the freely zigzagging period that precedes the
quoted excerpt, and ending with the two brusque periods that close
the section like two hammer blows. He ends, hence, with a gnarled
and knotted texture only remotely akin to the clearspun weave of the
Baconian original.

One does find occasional stretches of exact or nearly exact symmetry in Jonson, but these tend to have a sledge-hammer brevity that transmits first of all a sense of power, and only secondarily the feeling of balance: "Some wits are swelling, and high; others low and still: Some hot and fiery; others cold and dull: One must have a bridle, the other a spurre" (*Disc.* 678-680). And when Jonson uses exact symmetry in his plays, he is almost always ridiculing it as an affectation on the part of the speaker. But in fact symmetrical repetition in Jonson infrequently extends—as it does here—beyond the bounds of a single clause. For the most part it is phrasal rather than clausal symmetry, which means that it appears in unpredictable clumps; and so instead of shaping the outlines of the syntax as a whole, and providing clear signposts from one unit of utterance to the next, it merely intensifies the prevailing irregularity.

> There shall the Spectator see some, insulting with Joy; others, fretting with Melancholy; raging with Anger; mad with Love; boiling with Avarice; undone with Riot; tortur'd with expectation; consum'd with feare: no perturbation in common life, but the Orator findes an example of it in the Scene.
>
> (*Disc.* 2537-43)

The violent verbal adjectives, the absence of linking terms, the heavy pointing, place a greater and greater weight on each member of the series, especially since nothing signals to us when the series will end. The series erupts, flings itself at us with steadily increasing pressure, and then gathers and collapses into the summary that follows the colon. The sentence travels through fields of force rather than through preordained paths of logic.

The fact is that although Bacon pioneered in anti-Ciceronianism, his own style remains conservative in another way. As George Williamson has shown, Baconian prose has close affinities with Euphuism,[7] and Euphuism imposes constraints of its own. If the suspensions of a Ciceronian period demand grammatical resolution, the symmetrical configurations of Euphuistic prose demand psychological resolution—the more so the more the logicality of the design becomes evident, the more the reader comes to expect for each turn a counterturn. In a context of precise antitheses, the first half of an antithesis, no matter how self-contained grammatically, cries out for its matching other half. "The unicorn is white; the hippogriff is black. The unicorn

is graceful; the hippogriff is clumsy. The unicorn is caught by maid-
ens; . . ." One might speak of such a suspension as paratactic, occurring after a grammatically closed unit, in the manner of a coordinate clause, in contrast to the hypotactic suspension of Ciceronian
style, where the grammar remains "open" until the suspension is resolved. But whatever term one applies to it, one must recognize that
such a technique sets up expectations as exigent as those of the more
familiar Ciceronian variety. Bacon's style, on the whole, commits itself
to satisfying such expectations. The baroque writers properly speaking are those who eschew both sorts of suspension, the hypotactic and
the paratactic, or—even more important—who initiate periodic or symmetrical motions only to frustrate them.

   This is precisely Jonson's procedure. Where he arouses expectations
of symmetry, it is usually for the purpose of violating it. When an
implicitly symmetrical pattern is perpetually being disturbed and
thwarted by small changes in form, we have the phenomenon of
symmetry clashing with asymmetry that is at the heart of baroque
stylistic practice.[8] The following passage, encompassing several periods, adheres as closely as Jonson ordinarily ever does to a strict oratorical pattern:

> And an intelligent woman, if shee know by her selfe the least
> defect, will bee most curious, to hide it: and it becomes her.
> If shee be short, let her sit much, lest when shee stands, shee
> be thought to sit. If shee haue an ill foot, let her weare her
> gowne the longer, and her shoo the thinner. If a fat hand, and
> scald nailes, let her carue the lesse, and act in gloues. If a sowre
> breath, let her neuer discourse fasting: and alwaies talke at her
> distance. If shee haue black and rugged teeth, let her offer the
> lesse at laughter, especially if shee laugh wide, and open.
>   (SW IV:i.37-46)

The anaphoral "If shee" and "let her" establish a repeated figure on
which Jonson plays constant and surprising variations. The short first
member of each period undergoes its own vicissitudes: "If shee *be*
short," "If shee *haue* an *ill foot*," "If a fat hand, and scald nailes" (the
verb vanishes, and its object unexpectedly doubles), "If a sowre
breath" (the object becomes single again), "If shee haue black and
rugged teeth" (the verb re-enters with a new configuration of one
noun and two modifiers as object). The parallel apodoses shift form

even more fluidly, maintaining an air of exact symmetry and yet escaping from it at every moment. The result is not symmetry but asymmetry, perpetual displacements and dislocations of detail within a rhythmically symmetrical framework. This, moreover, from the play of Jonson's which more than any other simulates effects of balance in its dialogue.

The loose style, Croll's other subcategory of the baroque, differs from the curt style in that it prefers to multiply connectives rather than to suppress them. It tends also to longer members and longer periods, but its character is determined by its habit of heaping up conjunctions and by the kind of conjunctions it chooses: simple coordinates such as "and" and "or," which involve the least possible syntactic commitment to what has gone before, and, even more typically, the stricter relative and subordinating conjunctions used as though they were mere coordinates. And all this, as Croll urges, in order to free the period from formal restraints, to enable it to move with the utmost license from point to point, to follow nothing but the involutions of the thinking mind. For the enchaining suspensions of the Ciceronian period the loose style substitutes its own devices, the parenthesis and the absolute construction. The usefulness of the latter especially to a writer working in a resolved style is, as Croll has explained, that of all constructions it is "the one that commits itself least and lends itself best to the solution of difficulties that arise in the course of a spontaneous and unpremeditated progress."[9] It gives a writer carte blanche, enabling him to interrupt himself at will so as to travel in any cross-direction he pleases without dictating any alteration of the original syntax. It may be thrust in almost anywhere, and by its very nature—absolute, independent—forces most of the burden of logical connection upon the reader. Both the parenthesis and the absolute construction are favorites with Jonson, and sometimes he uses the two together in the same sentence:

> . . . and presently goe, and redeeme him; for, being her brother, and his credit so amply engag'd as now it is, when she shal heare (as hee cannot him selfe, but hee must out of extremitie report it) that you came, and offered your selfe so kindly, and with that respect of his reputation, why, the benefit cannot but make her dote, and grow madde of your affections.   (EMO V.viii.14-20)

Jonson has here made the absolute construction elliptical, by with-
holding the subject, "he," while the parenthesis intrudes with the
utmost casualness and tenuousness of reference into the middle of a
subordinate clause.

The most massive instance of Jonson's use of the absolute construction may be quoted as a curiosity of the loose style:

> Mary, your friends doe wonder, sir, the *Thames* being so
> neere, wherein you may drowne so handsomely; or *London*-
> bridge, at a low fall, with a fine leape, to hurry you downe the
> streame; or, such a delicate steeple, i' the towne, as *Bow,* to
> vault from; or, a brauer height, as *Pauls;* or, if you affected to
> doe it neerer home, and a shorter way, an excellent garret win-
> dore, into the street; or, a beame, in the said garret, with this
> halter; which they haue sent, and desire, that you would
> sooner commit your graue head to this knot, then to the wed-
> lock nooze; or, take a little sublimate, and goe out of the world,
> like a rat; or a flie (as one said) with a straw i' your arse: any
> way, rather, then to follow this goblin *matrimony*.
>
> (*SW* II.ii.20-32)

In this quintessentially Jonsonian loose period, we are confronted immediately either with a drastic ellipsis, which must be filled in with
some phrase ("Mary, your friends doe wonder, sir, *why do you not
make away with yourself at once*") in order to complete the sense, or
else with a huge series of absolute constructions that seems to behave
as a suspension and yet never leads to a resolution. Seems to behave
so, at least, to a reader. A reader is likely to demand the completion of
syntactic patterns much more stringently than a listener, who is accustomed, in talk, to hearing such patterns form, dissolve, and drift off
into others without ever fulfilling themselves. The reader awaits with
a certain tension the decisive return that will close the orbit; a listener
may be perfectly content to let the syntax turn into a wandering fire.
And since Jonson was in this case writing for the stage, he may simply
have pushed to an extreme the tendency of the baroque period to deal
brusquely with its own syntactic commitments.

The absolute constructions here, it may be noticed, are in themselves, after the first, somewhat elliptical, requiring the reinstatement
of the verbal phrase "being so neere" in each case. Then the extreme
iregularity of the parallel members should be observed; each has its

own unique configuration of subordinate clauses or modifying phrases or epithets, so that gradually the sense of parallel form all but evaporates, and we are left with a series of defiantly dissimilar constructions hooked together with "or's" and "and's," spinning freely in grammatical space and almost uncontrolled by any center of gravity. The effect of climax proceeds partly from the simple agglomeration of details and partly from the rhythmic speedup toward the end that leads into the recapitulary formula, "any way, rather, then to follow this goblin *matrimony*."

A further trait of loose style illustrated in this passage is what Croll has called the "linked" or "trailing" period, occurring "when a member depends, not upon the general idea, or the main word, of the preceding member, but upon its final word or phrase alone."[10] The effect of such tactics is, as usual, to reduce to its mimimum the interdependence of the successive members, to give the period, at any moment, a thrust forward into new areas. Truewit enumerates several of the high places from which Morose may fling himself before leading up to the mention and then to the proffering of a noose. At this point a shift to the relative "which," dependent as it is solely on the word "halter," deflects the absolute constructions from their course and leaves them stranded, at the same time catapulting the period into new grammatical territory. The period now follows a trajectory determined by the verb "desire," and lands finally a great distance from its starting point. This technique of pushing a period forward into fresh syntactic domain with scarcely a backward glance at the ground already traveled is one way in which anti-Ciceronian writers avoided the oratorical or "circular" Ciceronian period with its necessary return to some initial syntactic postulate. And it was this disregard of what he considered self-evident principles of grammatical law and order that led Coleridge to describe Senecan style as a series of thoughts "strung together like beads, without any causation or progression,"[11] and caused Saintsbury to complain of the abuse of conjunctions among seventeenth-century writers, who tended "apparently out of mere wantonness, to prefer a single sentence jointed and rejointed, parenthesised and postscripted, till it does the duty of a paragraph, to a succession of orderly sentences each containing the expression of a simple or moderately complex thought"[12]—a stricture from which he unaccountably exempted Jonson.

But the writers in question intended to be wanton as the mind is wanton, to transcribe the process of thought onto the page instead of stifling it, as they thought, within prescribed logical schemes. "Je ne peints pas l'estre. Je peints le passage: non un passage d'aage en autre, ou, comme dict le peuple, de sept en sept ans, mais de jour en jour, de minute en minute."[13] Whether in fact a process of thought has any verifiable reality apart from the words that incarnate it, and whether, if so, the irregular modes of syntax preferred by most of the anti-Ciceronians are necessarily any truer to thought, any more "natural," than the suspensions of the Ciceronians or the perfected antitheses of Euphuism, are questions that Renaissance authors did not raise. They assumed that regularity was artful, irregularity natural and spontaneous, and they wrote accordingly. In the case of Jonson, a mild paradox emerges: despite his fervent belief in the hard labor of composition, for which he was both admired and ridiculed by his contemporaries, he adopted a rhetorical mode associated with improvisation. Probably —despite his own protestations to the contrary (*Disc.* 695-700)—he worked as hard to roughen and irregularize his prose as others did to polish and regularize. As George Williamson has demonstrated, imitation of Seneca could lead to something very close to Euphuism.[14] In Jonson's case it did not. He copied in Seneca only the vein of curtness and asymmetry for which he had a temperamental affinity, and in so doing produced a style more Senecan than Seneca's, insofar as Senecanism implied rebellion against rhetorical constraint.

The spontaneity implied in the loose style triumphs most decisively, as Croll points out, just when it seems most in danger of succumbing to orthodox periodicity. It falls into complex syntactic movements and then extricates itself in hairbreadth fashion by improving fresh members or absolute constructions. Jonson finds himself entangled characteristically in his own habit of multiplying relative pronouns; he escapes from his own snares not by unraveling the constructions he has initiated, but by effectively cutting the Gordian knot of the constructions and then proceeding undisturbed. He will, for example, substitute a new subject that shunts the old one onto a siding and allows the thought to advance unimpeded on a new track. In the following excerpt Crites has been exclaiming against the use of perfume by men:

> Yet, I doe like better the prodigalitie of jewels, and clothes, whereof one passeth to a mans heires; the other, at least weares out time: This presently expires, and without continuall riot in reparation is lost: which who so striues to keep, it is one

speciall argument to me, that (affecting to smell better then
other men) he doth indeed smell farre worse.

                                    (CR V.iv.334-340)

Parenthetically one may notice here a signal feature of the loose style
in the fact that the member that elaborates the second half of the
antithesis grows and grows until it outweighs everything that has
preceded it, almost engulfing the period, and inhibiting all possibility
of exact balance. More germane to our present purpose is the way it
grows: the linking relative *which*, referring back to *this* (which in
turn refers back to the perfume previously mentioned), becomes the
object of a complex syntactic motion vice-governed by "who," but this
motion is instantly sidetracked by the introduction of a new indefinite-
pronoun subject, "it." The member commencing with "it" is elliptical,
since we do not know except by implication what "it" is a special
argument *of*, and it starts syntactically from scratch, so that the clause
"which who so striues to keep," perilously close to the "nonchalant"
anacoluthon of which Croll speaks,[15] dangles in mid-air even after
the fresh start has come to its rescue and completed the period.

One may add that it is probably as much as anything else Jonson's
practice with relative conjunctions that has led his editors and critics
to speak of his style as "packed" and "weighty." On the one hand
he will employ relative connectives that cross-refer and intertwine
densely with one another, and that may, while still incomplete, sprout
further subsidiary relative clauses, as in the passage just cited. But he
may, on the other hand, at any moment that it pleases him, throw
them overboard for new constructions and leave them shipwrecked.
Some fairly drastic instances of this kind of procedure appear in *The
Entertainment at Highgate*.

> . . . vouchsafe your eare, and forgiue his behauiour, which
> (euen to me, that am his parent) will no doubt be rude
> ynough, though otherwise full of salt, which, except my pres-
> ence did temper, might turne to be gall, and bitternesse; but
> that shall charme him.   (199-203)

In this jungle of relatives and ellipses, the phrase "though otherwise
full of salt" refers back to "which," itself dependent on "behauiour."
A second "which," dependent solely on "salt" immediately preceding
it, now makes its entry, introducing a trailing semiperiod half again
as long as the member from which it springs, and subverting the ini-

tial construction entirely. The final demonstrative "that" refers back over a considerable distance to "my presence." The "packed" and "weighty" texture, then, seems to spring from the conflict of two opposing tendencies: the centrifugal force of the loose style struggling against the centripetal impulse of the Latinate conjunctions. A tightly integrated syntax is implied by the connectives and then carefully left unrealized.

If the curt style is peculiarly suited to expressions of quick wit, excitement, distraction, and the like, the loose style, by virtue of its greater floridity, lends itself well to purposes of formal declamation. It can be and is used by Jonson in a variety of ways: straightforwardly, as in Crites' censure of perfume, or with self-conscious exaggeration and heightening, as in Truewit's tirade against matrimony—or it may become the vehicle for the affected eloquence of fops like Amorphus and Fastidious Brisk eager to show off their aureate vocabularies. But whereas the dramatic versions of the curt style derive in part at least from prose as it was used in the popular drama of the 1590's, Jonson's theatrical adaptations of the loose style are his own original creation. Nothing in the comic prose of the preceding decade, whether in plays, novels, or pamphlets, really prepares us for such a baroque virtuoso piece as Fastidious Brisk's rhapsody on the court:

> A man liues there, in that diuine rapture, that hee will thinke himselfe i' the ninth heauen for the time, and lose all sense of mortalitie whatsoeuer; when he shall behold such glorious (and almost immortall) beauties, heare such angelicall and harmonious voyces, discourse with such flowing and *ambrosian* spirits, whose wits are as suddaine as lightning, and humorous as *nectar;* Oh: it makes a man al *quintessence,* and *flame,* & lifts him vp (in a moment) to the verie christall crowne of the skie, where (houering in the strength of his imagination) he shall behold all the delights of the HESPERIDES, the *Insulae Fortunatae,* ADONIS gardens, *Tempe* or what else (confin'd within the amplest verge of *poesie*) to bee meere *vmbrae,* and imperfect figures, conferr'd with the most essentiall felicitie of your court. (*EMO* IV.viii.18-32)

Having glanced at the major landmarks on Croll's baroque landscape, and having tried to show their relevance to Jonson's practice, we may carry the discussion into more particularly Jonsonian country

by mentioning a few traits of style that, though not always exclusive
with Jonson, are habitual enough with him to be regarded as idiosyncratic. These will in every case exemplify further the baroque syntax
already outlined.

One of Jonson's customary techniques is to disturb, by one means
or another, what we would ordinarily regard as logical word order.
The frequent result of such tactics is to promote oddness of emphasis,
to undermine expectations of "normal" arrangement; words will fail
to appear in looked-for places and then emerge bizarrely where we
least expect them. Jonson's simplest transposition of this sort is to add
some element—subject, object, or modifier—postgrammatically, and
thus to isolate it. In the statement "Men are decay'd, and *studies*"
(*Disc.* 127), "Men are decay'd" forms a self-contained grammatical
unit onto which Jonson has tacked an extra subject. The delayed
subject comes as a kind of afterthought, and lends an improvisatory
flourish to the remark. At the same time, paradoxically, it completes a
rhythmic curve. If we put it back into its "normal" place in the sentence ("Men and studies are decay'd"), we make a more orderly
period, and a flatter one. The same detail that roughens the syntax in
one way, by separating elements that grammatically go together,
smooths it out in another way by producing a cadence. And so with
most instances of this device. One might, then, tentatively add to
Croll's types of baroque effect the kind of tension that arises when
the syntax is doing one thing grammatically and another rhythmically.
And this could be classified as a further species of asymmetry, since
the grammatical logic and the rhythm are out of phase with each
other, instead of synchronized as in Euphuistic or Ciceronian prose.
The effect of irregularity in such cases depends on the distance between the postscripted element and its natural grammatical mate.

A Trumpet should fright him terribly, or the Hau'-boyes?
                                                (*SW* I.i.160-161)

. . . when some groome of his has got him an heire, or this
barber. . . .   (*SW* I.ii.54-55)

Some Diuine must resolue you in that, sir, or canon-Lawyer.
                                                (*SW* IV.iv.148-149)

I'll tell you, MOROSE, you must talke diuinitie to him altogether, or morall philosophie.   (*SW* IV.iv.81-82)

> If there bee neuer a *Seruant-monster* i'the *Fayre;* who can
> helpe it? he sayes; nor a nest of *Antiques?* (*BF* Ind. 127-128)

The fact that this pattern occurs so much oftener in the plays than
in the *Discoveries* suggests that Jonson was seeking to vitalize his
language rhythmically for the stage in ways that would have been
needless for the library.

Another way of driving a wedge between two words grammatically
related is to separate a relative pronoun from its antecedent by interposing a word or phrase between them:

> Come forward, you should be some dull tradesman by your
> pig-headed Sconce now, that thinke there's nothing good any
> where; but what's to be sold.   (*NNW* 12-14)

> Nor is that worthy speech of *Zeno* the Philosopher to be past
> over, without the note of ignorance: who being invited to a
> feast in *Athens*. . . .   (*Disc.* 370-372)

Jonson, one observes, does not assume that a relative or subordinate
clause must tread like a porpoise on the tail of its antecedent. He
constantly, and sometimes perplexingly, delays the pronoun while he
interpolates other matter.[16] This habit probably stems in part from
Latin, a language in which, since inflected endings carry the burden
of grammatical connection, the word order tends to be abstract—capable of manipulation for purposes of emphasis and design. At the same
time, the cavalier distribution of elements recalls colloquial speech,
which rarely pauses to pickle over the logicality of its word order. So
that with this detail as with others, Jonson's "Romanizing" tendency
and his fascination with living speech unexpectedly reinforce each
other; the same device that on the page can suggest pressure of
thought and evoke memories of classical prose, can in the theater serve
to create a sense of conversational *désinvolture*.

Sometimes Jonson deliberately suppresses some grammatical element in order to avert an impending symmetry, to sabotage in advance
what threatens to evolve into too fussy a balance: "But now be pleased
to expect a more noble discovery worthie of your eare, as the object
will be [of] your eye" (*NNW* 301-303). Here the ellipsis of an introductory *as* ("a more noble discovery, *as* worthie of your eare, *as*")
leaves the reader unprepared for the exact antithesis that follows and

hence unable to feel its full impact. Since symmetry depends to a large extent on preparation, and unfolding according to plan, it may be upset by a refusal to usher it in with recognizable anticipatory formulas. Conversely, a severely antithetic scaffolding may be erected in one clause only to be knocked to pieces in the next: "A woman, the more curious she is about her face, is commonly the more carelesse about her house" (Disc. 192-193); "His modesty, like a riding Coat, the more it is worne, is the lesse car'd for" (Disc. 1328-29). No reader of Euphuistic prose could have failed to expect perfect matching between the two halves of the antithesis ("the more it is worne, the lesse it is car'd for"), but Jonson wrenches askew the second member so as to produce a lopsided rather than a balanced antithesis. Or, again, the effect of balance may be undone by the interpolation of a qualifying phrase between symmetrical elements: "If I doe not, let me play the mounte-bank for my meate while I liue, and the bawd for my drinke" (SW IV.i.151-152).

If we leaf through Jonson for the symmetrical formulas so abundant in Shakespeare, we find that where Jonson uses them he commonly manages to derange their stability in one way or another. The "as . . . so" parallelism, in Jonson, is likely to come out like this: "In short, as Vinegar is not accounted good, untill the wine be corrupted: so jests that are true and naturall, seldome raise laughter, with the beast, the multitude" (Disc. 2657-59), where the second half invents an entirely unforeseen syntactic combination for itself, abandoning in particular the notion of change from sweetness to corruption and embarking on explicit mention of those who are judging and condemning. The "though . . . yet" antithesis is liable to emerge in a form like this: "For though the Prince himselfe be of most prompt inclination to all vertue: Yet the best Pilots have need of Mariners, beside Sayles, Anchor, and other Tackle" (Disc. 1246-49), where the antithetic "yet" clause takes a sudden leap into metaphor, and elaborates that metaphor almost to the point of obscurity. In all of these instances, Jonson contrives to balk the kind of satisfaction that arises from a regular design fully articulated. Instead of a sense of fulfillment, he seeks effects of tension, instead of the feeling of repose as the pattern rounds itself out, a feeling of energy from the breaking of the pattern.

The asymmetry peculiar to baroque prose appears in Jonson in still another stylistic mannerism: the coupling in parallel relation of two elements that are either grammatically non-congruent or, if congruent on one level, so aggressively non-parisonic as to produce a feeling of incongruity, creating that slight sense of *offness* that baroque writers, their ears surfeited by Lylian parison or Ciceronian periodicity, evidently delighted in.

> . . . they find nothing new, or to seeke.   (*Disc.* 1677)

> But, beware of presuming, or how you offer comparison with persons so neere Deities.   (*Pan* 154-155)

> . . . to doe this with diligence, and often.   (*Disc.* 1704-05)

> . . . to taste all by degrees, and with change. (*Disc.* 1654-55)

> . . . has a yellow blade, but the eare empty. (*Disc.* 687-688)

> . . . with a Funnell, and by degrees, you shall fill many of them . . .   (*Disc.* 1794)

The parallel elements of a series may of course be set at odds with each other in the same way. In the following example, the third member rebelliously refuses to conform to the pattern of infinitives established by the first two: "*For* a man to write well, there are required three Necessaries. To read the best Authors, observe the best Speakers: and much exercise of his owne style" (*Disc.* 1697-99). In the next, Jonson charges headlong from a past participle, "*banish't*," to the nouns "want" and "disease": "As to wish a friend *banish't*, that they might accompany him in *exile*: or some great want, that they might relieve him: or a disease, that they might sit by him" (*Disc.* 440-443).

But irregularity need not restrict itself to a habit of interfering with symmetry, nor need it be confined within the compass of one period. Jonson's prose is marked by an almost dizzying variety of mutations of form. There are passages in which the subject changes from clause to clause, or from sentence to sentence:

> His language, (where hee could spare, or passe by a jest) was nobly *censorious*. No man ever spake more neatly, more presly, more weightily, or suffer'd lesse emptinesse, less idlenesse, in what hee utter'd. No member of his speech, but consisted of the owne graces: His hearers could not cough, or looke aside from him, without losse. Hee commanded where hee spoke;

and had his Judges angry, and pleased at his devotion. No
man had their affections more in his power. The feare of every
man that heard him, was, lest hee should make an end.

(*Disc.* 888-898)

Despite a certain regularity here—from the steady march of subject,
predicate, subject, predicate, subject, predicate—the effect of irregularity predominates because of the nervous mobility of the subject, in
which respect Jonson outdoes the passage from Seneca that serves as
his model. One result is to emphasize the independence and, so to
speak, defiant integrity of each clause, to brace it sharply against its
neighbors and force the reader to readjust his perspective at every
pause. Jonson demands similar reaccommodations when he causes a
subject to materialize out of thin air: "Then men were had in price
for learning: now, letters onely make men vile. Hee is upbraydingly
call'd a *Poet*, as if it were a most contemptible *Nick-name*" (*Disc.*
279-282).

He is no less in revolt against regularity in his handling of verbs.
Sometimes he pitches abruptly from the declarative mood into the
imperative:

In Picture, light is requir'd no lesse then shadow: so in stile,
height, as well as humblenesse. But beware they be not too
humble; as *Pliny* pronounc'd of *Regulus* writings: You would
thinke them written, not on a child, but by a child.

(*Disc.* 1541-45)

The change of pace here jolts the reader even more sharply because
at the same time there erupts from nowhere the pronoun "they,"
for which the reader must scramble to invent an antecedent. At other
times Jonson will suddenly shift gears into neutral, so to speak, by
switching into the infinitive:

A strict and succinct style is that, where you can take away
nothing without losse, and that losse to be manifest[17]

(*Disc.* 1970-72)

Have not I seen the pompe of a whole Kingdome, and what a
forraigne King could bring hither. Also to make himselfe gaz'd,
and wonder'd at, laid forth as it were to the shew, and vanish
all away in a day?   (*Disc.* 1404-07)

And sometimes he will without warning shift a plural verb (with its plural subject) into the singular: ". . . what Iustice or Religion is to be expected? Which are the only two Attributes make *Kings* a kinne to *Gods;* and is the *Delphick* sword, both to kill Sacrifices, and to chastise offenders" (*Disc.* 1288-91). Or he will coolly switch tenses within the space of a single period. "But the fees of the one, or the *salary* of the other, never answer the *value* of what we received; but serv'd to gratifie their labours"[18] (*Disc.* 476-478). This happens especially when he is recounting the scenic effect of a masque, as if he were aiming to convey a vivid sense of immediacy together with the precision of objective reporting:[19]

> In his hand he bore a golden censor with perfume, and censing about the altar (hauing first kindled his fire on the toppe) is interrupted by the *Genius.* (*King's Ent.* 551-553)

> When the Spectators had enough fed their eyes, with the delights of the *Scene,* in a part of the ayre, a bright cloud begins to breake forth. (*Chlor.* 28-30)

And finally there is the kind of irregularity that occurs when members of a sequence not only vary internally one from another, but from the start are launched in diverse directions by differing conjunctions:

> *Metaphors* farfet hinder to be understood, and affected, lose their grace. Or when the person fetcheth his translations from a wrong place. As if a Privie-Counsellor should at the Table take his *Metaphore* from a Dicing-House. . . .
> (*Disc.* 1905-09)

It scarcely matters, in short, what sort of regularity or continuity one presupposes in prose style: Jonson manages to avoid them all. Discontinuity, change of pace, interruption of design, are the materials with which he works. Despite a certain amount of incidental symmetry, Jonson's prose is irregular on principle, and the irregularity transmits itself from the largest phenomena of style down to the smallest, from the formation of the most massive block of loose periods down to the parallel coupling of discongruent adverbs. Saintsbury's dictum that Jonson "preserves—his kind cannot but preserve—the balance of Ascham and Lyly as his chief rhetorical instrument"[20] must

then be severely emended, if indeed it is to stand at all. If Jonson preserves balance, he does so only to upset balance. If he deploys symmetrical patterns, he does so only to violate their symmetry. Everywhere he is restlessly interfering with the expected structure of a
phrase or clause. The asymmetrical tactics that pervade his writing
form a rhetoric distinct from, and as distinct as, any of the more orthodox rhetorics, an antirhetorical rhetoric that seeks to disguise itself
almost as a nonrhetoric. The necessarily stricter attentiveness of the
reader to such a style, since he cannot let his mind coast in the suspensions of a periodic sentence or in the exact correspondences of the
aculeate style, perhaps suggests why the laborious Jonson adopts a
manner apparently most congenial to effects of improvisation. In the
hands of writers like Burton, baroque prose ambles or scampers with
skittish whimsicality. Jonson, by his reluctance to fulfill expectation,
his defiance of stock responses to syntax, creates an impression of
granitic strength: the participation of the reader or listener becomes
an exercise in rock-climbing over the jagged, twisted, craggy terrain
of the syntax.

NOTES

1. The struggles to convert this concept from art history into a mean-
   ful term for literary history have not been entirely happy. The further attempt to differentiate, as the art historians do, between
   "baroque" and "mannerist" in literature has only compounded confusion and darkened counsel. René Wellek's caveat against the
   promiscuous use of "baroque" ("The Concept of Baroque in Literary
   Scholarship," pp. 77-109) has not prevented the appearance of more
   speculation concerning the baroque *Zeitgeist,* more freewheeling analogies between the arts, more attempts to define "baroque" in
   narrowly stylistic terms, as well as a generous quota of rebukes from
   the cautious. The present study will use the term "baroque" because
   Croll used it, because there is no satisfactory substitute, and because
   —for all its uncertainties—it still seems a useful way of suggesting
   stylistic procedures that may, in the last analysis, transcend the
   bounds of a single art and relate to a whole cultural conformation.
2. Citations from Jonson throughout are to the edition of C. H. Herford and Percy and Evelyn Simpson, 11 vols. (Oxford, 1925-1952).
   The following abbreviations are used in the present chapter:
   Disc.: Timber, or Discoveries
   CR: Cynthia's Revels
   EMO: Every Man out of his Humour

> Poet.: Poetaster
> SW: Epicene, or The Silent Woman
> BF: Bartholomew Fair
> NNW: News from the New World Discovered in the Moon
> Pan: Pan's Anniversary
> King's Ent.: The King's Entertainment in Passing to His
>   Coronation
> Chlor.: Chloridia

3. Croll, "Baroque Style," p. 433.
4. The transference of language from the printed page to the speaking voices of actors in a theater involves, necessarily, many accommodations. Most of these, however, occur on the level of phonology, and hence are properly analyzable only by microlinguistic techniques, including scrutiny of phonetic sequences, stresses, pitch, juncture, and the like. Even for a contemporary text, it is doubtful whether such an analysis would produce very satisfactory results. George L. Trager and Henry Lee Smith, Jr. (An Outline of English Structure, Studies in Linguistics, Occasional Papers 3 [Norman, Oklahoma, 1951], pp. 50-51) list at least eight different ways of saying "How do they study?" where the variations are confined entirely to pitch, stress, internal juncture and terminal juncture, and even so are not exhaustive. When we deal with such far more complex utterances as Jonson's sentences, when we take into account the problems of declamation in a theater whose declamatory techniques are at best only half understood, in a language three hundred years old whose phonology has been only fragmentarily reconstructed, we are facing a set of variables so formidable as to make any meaningful phonological appraisal a will-o'-the-wisp. One must, then, renounce formal discussion of this problem and confine oneself to repeating truisms, such as the fact that a good playwright somehow contrives to make his dialogue speakable, that—as actors know—an intricate sentence of Congreve's can be pronounced more trippingly on the tongue than a simpler one from William Archer's translation of Ibsen, because the former was written by a master of theatrical speech and the latter was not.

In Jonson's case, one can of course point to certain details of phonetic realism—his growing tendency to substitute the "-s" ending of third person singular verbs for the more literary "-eth" inflection, his use of clipped forms (as he would have thought them) such as "'hem" for "them"—and to his employment, on a massive scale, of modish phrases and cant terms that he would have scorned to use in his own person. But in sentence structure, if it can be separated from the rest, significant differences between the stage prose and the nondramatic prose are few, partly because of the very nature of the baroque rhetoric to which Jonson was committed. What Jonson does, in fact, as this chapter is trying to show, is to take syntactic strategies normal in his critical prose and use them in the theater for specifically theatrical purposes, for characterization and effects of realism and satire.

I should like here to thank my former colleague James Sledd for turning the gimlet eye of a trained linguist on an earlier version of this chapter. In so doing, he rescued it from many errors. What errors it now contains have been perpetrated since he read it.

5. *The Senecan Amble,* p. 145, p. 156, n. 1.
6. *The Advancement of Learning,* Everyman ed., p. 24.
7. *The Senecan Amble,* pp. 89, 115, 118, 120, 184, and *passim.*
8. Croll, "Baroque Style," p. 437.
9. "Baroque Style," p. 443.
10. "Baroque Style," p. 447.
11. *Miscellaneous Criticism,* ed. Thomas Middleton Raysor (Cambridge, Mass., 1936), p. 217.
12. "English Prose Style," in *Miscellaneous Essays* (London, 1892), p. 7.
13. Montaigne, "Du repentir," *Essais,* ed. Albert Thibaudet, Bibliothèque de la Pléiade (Paris, 1958), p. 899.
14. See note 7 above.
15. "Baroque Style," p. 452.
16. For the "possessive as antecedent of a relative pronoun," a peculiarity of Elizabethan syntax in general, see A. C. Partridge, *Studies in the Syntax of Ben Jonson's Plays* (Cambridge, 1953), pp. 46-47, and for the (baroque) use of "a common relative with different case functions," p. 70. Jonson's own *English Grammar* (Herford and Simpson, VIII, 453-553), it might be added, is, disappointingly, of little help. The section on syntax (pp. 528ff.) devotes itself mainly to combinations required by idiom (agreement of noun and verb, position of article and noun, etc.) and a few minor variations. It deals only hastily and perfunctorily with connectives, and it ignores (as do other grammars, for that matter) the whole area of the "probable" and "possible" in syntax, of acutest interest to stylistic study.
17. The fact that these lines form part of a long excerpt borrowed almost intact from John Hoskins does not invalidate them as evidence of Jonsonian style. It is, in fact, remarkable how smoothly the extract from Hoskins (itself an adaptation of Lipsius) fits into Jonson's own prose. On Hoskins, and the borrowings in the *Discoveries,* see the *Directions for Speech and Style,* ed. Hoyt H. Hudson (Princeton, 1935).
18. Here, as in the quotation above from *Disc.* 1404-07, I have restored

the Folio reading. Herford and Simpson correct "hither. Also" to "hither also," and "serv'd" to "serve." The original reading in both cases strikes me as thoroughly Jonsonian. While certainty in such matters is impossible—Jonson *may* have intended "serve"—I trust that the evidence of this chapter as a whole will suffice to leave the benefit of the doubt with the text as it actually stands. It seems as rash to force Jonson's grammar to conform to modern practice as it was for earlier editors of Shakespeare to correct Shakespeare when he followed a plural subject with a singular verb or took other liberties later regarded as unorthodox. For tense shift as a characteristic of baroque poetry see Lowry Nelson, Jr., "Góngora and Milton: Toward a Definition of the Baroque," *Comparative Literature,* VI (1954), 53-63.

19. The fact that other writers do the same thing in similar circumstances leads one to suspect a special convention at work. See, for example, Dekker, *The Magnificent Entertainment, lines* 67-76, 175-179, 309-312, 456-465, 497-500, 831-845, in *The Dramatic Works,* ed. Fredson Bowers, 3 vols. (Cambridge, 1953-1959), II, 253-303; Middleton, *The Triumphs of Truth* and *Civitatis Amor* in *Works,* ed. A. H. Bullen, 8 vols. (Boston, 1886), VII, 239, 284-285, etc.; and Carew, *Coelum Britannicum,* in *Poems,* ed. Rhodes Dunlap (Oxford, 1949), pp. 154, 168, 176.

20. *A History of English Prose Rhythm* (London, 1912), p. 205.

JOAN WEBBER

☙

Celebration of Word and World in Lancelot Andrewes' Style

There is still a popular and even respectable notion that the seven-teenth-century Royal Society was absolutely right in its effort to purify the English language of both the excesses and the essence of "meta-physical" prose; and that the Puritans were right in their claim that "Truth loves the Light, and is most Beautiful when most naked. . . . And therefore painted obscure sermons (like the Painted Glass in the Windows that keep out the Light) are two [sic] oft the Marks of painted Hypocrites."[1] James Sutherland, approving what he sees as a progressive development of prose from age to age, writes, "It is good prose when it allows the writer's meaning to come through with the least possible loss of significance and nuance, as a landscape is seen through a clear window."[2] In his view, the better the prose, the less one is aware of it. Critics primarily concerned with religious prose are almost unanimously hostile to the metaphysical style. W. Frazer Mitchell, summarizing the objections, writes that "the components of 'metaphysical' preaching were not such as were in themselves intrinsi-cally valuable," that "the use to which they were put by the 'witty' preachers was not consonant with the great ends of Christian oratory,"

From the *Journal of English and Germanic Philology*, LXIV, (April 1965), pp. 255-269. Reprinted by permission of the University of Illinois Press.

and that "both the material and methods employed rendered impossible the cultivation of a prose style suited either to delivery in the
pulpit or to give to religious discourses in their printed form the dignity of literature."[3] Given such attitudes in those most familiar with
metaphysical prose, and given our twentieth-century indifference to
sermons as art or as instruction, it is not surprising that Lancelot Andrewes, the greatest of all the metaphysical preachers, is now little
known and less approved.

But since Andrewes cannot go to school to us, and would not if he
could, and since it is clear that his prose was once popular because it
expressed at least some central aspects of his age, we might well obey
T. S. Eliot's well-known request that we attend to Andrewes.[4] Reading him, we learn that expository prose can gratify and persuade us
in unexpected ways. His insistence upon stylistic brevity, upon "the
day of small things," reflects both the artistic interest of his age in the
manipulation of space, and his own pastoral concern with the little
world of man. His creative use of words both as signs and as things is
an artistic and religious eulogy of creation and transformation in God's
Word and world. His mingling of fancy and plain rhythms and rhetoric, while making his prose both beautiful and durable, reflects the
indecorous mingling of styles in Christ's birth, ministry, crucifixion,
and resurrection.

His God and Donne's made form its own content in a manner theo-
retically independent of mortal aesthetics. Although the Anglicans
were touchy about letting anyone think they would pay undue attention to language, it is certainly true that the concept of God as Word,
and of Biblical language as an incarnation of the Word, required
them to respect language, and to consider the preached word too as
sharing in an incarnation.[5] George Herbert, in a poem called "The
Windows," that accepts and approves the Puritans' stained-glass metaphor, calls the preacher a window in whom God anneals His story,
making His light shine within. The glass and the story annealed in it
are not distinguishable from one another, nor does one give place to
the other, as the clear window does to the landscape. So the Anglican
preacher would consider his sermon—a vehicle which through God's
grace incarnates God, annealing His story in language.

Exegetical tradition encouraged this view of language, by enforcing
a very close attention, in reading the Bible, to the meaning of all
grammatical or rhetorical forms. The function of the preacher commenting on a given text was to notice the process by which God

brings words to life, incarnates them, makes them things. But since the sermon itself is an extension of the Bible text, some preachers, like Andrewes, developed a style that observes upon its meaning even as it is being formed. For Andrewes, this intense concentration upon language leads to a peculiarly sensitive, conscious, and multileveled rhetoric, in which words play many different parts. They are meaning, and guides to meaning; and sometimes, made things and nearly detached from meaning, they become abstract musical shapes, to be used almost like building blocks in the construction of a sentence with expressive form.

Besides exegetical tradition, church history, and church Latin, Andrewes, like all English writers, inherited and used to his own purposes a basic English sentence. This sentence is straightforward and simple, beginning with a noun, which is followed by a verb and a direct object. Articles, adjectives, and adverbs precede the words that they modify. Each clause connects with other clauses by means of coordinating conjunctions; subordinate clauses are added as necessary, although they may sometimes be placed before a main clause. This basic sentence is a free, open form, proceeding as if unpremeditated, and its irregular iambic rhythm has characterized English prose from the *Ancrene Riwle* to *The Sun Also Rises*.

Both Anglican rhetoricians, inheritors of the same traditions in language and Biblical exegesis, and in belief, John Donne and Lancelot Andrewes yet found room to express in their writing very different temperaments and habits of thought. What Andrewes does to the loose sprawling English period is to compress it, eliminate its circumlocutions, and discipline it with his own peculiar elegance. His signal characteristic is economy. As a seventeenth-century artist, he differs from Donne in the same way in which the Baroque architect Borromini differs from Bernini: the one impresses by means of his compactness, his denial of space, his talent for concentrated intensity; while the other strives for spaciousness, eloquent redundancy, and freedom from confinement. Time and again, Andrewes defends his insistence upon the minutiae of existence: "And heare you, you are to begin with *datum, Not to despise the day of small things*: It is the Prophets Counsaile; to learne to see *God* in them, *Caesars Image,* not onely in his *coine of gold,* but even upon the *poore penny.* See GOD in *small,* or you shall never see Him in *great;* in *good,* or never in *perfect.*"[6]

The small thing may also be the richest: "The words are few, and the sentence short; no one in Scripture so short. But it fareth with *Sentences* as with *Coines:* In coines, they that in smallest compasse containe greatest value, are best esteemed: and, in sentences, those that in fewest words comprise most matter, are most praised" (p. 299). The reasons Andrewes gives for preferring short, rich sentences are that they are economical, and that they are more easily remembered. One of the best traits of ordinary vernacular English prose, already impressive in Malory, and raised to a high pitch in Shakespeare, is the short sentence intensified by its lean accuracy, used as a simple and final comment to summarize an essay or a view of life. "Thus can GOD worke," says Andrewes, concluding a passage on the wonders of Providence. And, speaking of the universal power of death, "None hath scaped the jawes of it."

Andrewes' sermons, while they impress the reader as being much shorter, are as long as Donne's; his economy is not structural, nor devised for the relief of the congregation. It is aesthetic and moral in intention, and is exercised primarily in devices that operate within or among the short sentences. For example, both Andrewes and Donne experiment with ellipses of various kinds, as a way of achieving syntactical freedom. But Donne's ellipses are often submerged in the great emotional sweep of his long periods, whereas Andrewes' are paraded before us, enforced upon us as a notable and urgent revision of the basic form:

> This, is a griefe: would, this alone. (p. 289)

> None so high: None on earth, not His *Saints*. (p. 962)

> All our excellencie, our highest and most perfect estate, is but
> to be, as they: therefore, they above us farre. (p. 3)

The omissions never obscure the sense, although they do require great concentration of attention, since a whole series of clauses may share a common subject or verb. And this close binding together of the brief spare paragraphs adds impetus and inevitability to the forward movement of the argument.

Andrewes employs an unusually large number of monosyllables in his prose; often whole sentences contain no longer word. Despite his habit of quoting extensively in Latin and Greek, his English vocabulary is more Anglo-Saxon than that of many of his contemporaries, and the Saxon words are generally shorter and harder than Latin ones.

Hence, the rhythm of his prose is intensely English. One convenient test of it is provided by Morris Croll's distinction between the Latin *cursus*, and English prose rhythms, both of which are found at emphatic or concluding parts of clauses and sentences.[7] Where the Latin meters tend to be long and complex, with unstressed endings, English ones are brief and simple, with accents on the final syllables: "pérfĕct ĕstáte," "to bé, ăs théy," "abóve ŭs fárre."

Andrewes proliferates the kind of details that can dominate short sentences. Almost as marked a technique as ellipsis is inversion, which contributes to the rapidity of the rhythm, and provides a functional emphasis on significant words. Placed at the beginning of clause or sentence, the focal words take a strong beat and enforce lighter accents upon what follows:

> Nothing we were; We, and all His *works.* (p. 963)

> *Exalt* us He could not, being in that plight: for love or pitie therefore, *purge* us He would. (p. 58)

In the following example, where Andrewes speaks of the impact of Christianity in time, his subject itself is echoed in the tempo created by the inversions, as his adverbs acquire verbal power:

> For, as weake in appearance as it [the Holy Ghost] is, by it were great things brought to passe. By this *puffe* of *breath,* was the *World blowne round* about. About came the *Philosophers,* the *Orators,* the *Emperors.* Away went the *mists* of *errour,* downe went the *Idols,* and their *Temples* before it. (p. 690)

The English prose rhythms dominate Andrewes' sentences much more than they could those of another writer, because when clause and period are short, these rhythms, proper only to conclusions, can span more of the whole sentence. And since the inversions at the sentence openings provide a focus of emphasis and music there as well, all of Andrewes' prose is very melodious.

While these stylistic techniques do contribute to the music of the prose and tighten the sinews of the argument, they are not *simply* agreeable. Inversion, in particular, evokes an understandable antagonism in some readers: it is so obvious a device, there is so little apparent reason for it, and it is so patently opposed to the "natural" current of English prose that, with its quick, heavy, unexpected accent, it is almost like a blow. As for ellipsis, while it tightens the argument, it also removes the possibility of relaxation. There seem to be no soft places in the prose; and its demanding angularity distinguishes it readily from some other elaborate prose—that of Lyly, for example, to whom Andrewes is similar in some respects. There is no such easily predictable pattern here.

The music of repetition, in Andrewes as in Donne, serves both a didactic and an affective purpose. It helps the reader to remember, and it provides the sermon with melodic refrains. But Donne and Andrewes are not usually repetitive in the same way. Donne translates his Latin and his metaphors, poses the same phrase in different ways; his style is very expansive, and the repetitions contribute to the expansiveness. Andrewes' repetitions suit an economical style: combined with his ellipses and his monosyllables, instead of implying luxury of words, they create a sense of confinement—of a design created within a very small space, and with the fewest possible materials:

> Běíng thén, ăt thís věrÿ tíme, thús spókěn, ănd dóne: Spókěn,
> hére nów; dóne, thrée yéares áftěr: Běíng (Ĭ sáy) spókěn, ănd
> dŏne, ănd ăt thís tíme spókěn ănd dóne; Něvěr sŏ fít ăs nów.
> (p. 482)

The tune, or melody, consists of the words "being at this time spoken and done"; the other words provide the necessary economical variations upon it. The dominant prose meter is the English 4–1 rhythm ("spókěn ănd dóne"); it is varied by a 3–1 cadence ("fít ăs nów") and by single strong accents. Heavy caesuras signal pauses that separate the words into rhythmic groups. The similarity to poetry is obvious. Andrewes makes prose poetic by a combination of techniques very like that which Donne uses to make poetry conversational—prose meters and the suggestion (rather than actual presence, as in Donne) of a more regular cadence, and verse structure.

There is considerable evidence, in his use of all these devices, of his conscious interest in and experimentation with language as an expressive instrument. One technique that he shares with Donne is to make words act in prose like the thing being discussed. Here, for example, the word "through" is made to stab *through* the words of the sentence, as the spear transfixed Christ on the cross:

> Therefore *trans,* is here a *transcendent;* through and through:
> through skinne and flesh; through hands and feet; through side
> and heart and all: the deadliest and deepest wound, and of
> highest gradation. (p. 336)

Simultaneously, the word is used as a thing, and the speaker explains
that it ought to be so used. Yet the fusion is so smooth that we are not
made very much aware of Andrewes' presence, as we sometimes are of
Donne's: the emphasis is upon the incarnation of thing in word, or
upon the imitation by language of Christ's story.

The next step after this involves a technique of turning words into
each other: transformation is an artistic theme and device of the
period. Interest in what a given medium can do (stone can look like
blowing draperies; a ceiling can look like airy heaven) is in Andrewes
an interest in what a given word can do: it can become another word.
His sermons are full of such mutations: *"Non,* none, one"; "see, seek,
sicut"; "Sign, signify, *signum,* signature." The elusive music of this
parsimonious technique sometimes practically frees itself of meaning,
in making a word a mutable thing, rather than just the sign of a
thing. In the following passage, where he plays with transmutations
of "own" to "none," "only," "onely," and "alone," the "onely" and
"only" of the concluding sentences are more a final variation and
summation of sound than they are needful to the meaning:

> Not so, He: It could not be so, in His. He, and *He alone:* He,
> and none but He: Vpon *His owne shoulders,* and none but
> His owne, bare He all. *He trod the wine-presse,* and bare the
> burthen *Solus, alone; Et vir de Gentibus,* and, *of all the Na
> tions, there was not a man with* Him. Vpon *His onely shoul-
> ders* did the burthen only rest. (p. 14)

"Owne" becomes "onely" in the last sentence for the sake of sound
and balance, and transformation.

Andrewes likes to build his clauses in such a way that they look and
feel the same at beginning and end—another means of paying attention to words as something more than signs of things. This patterning
is most evident, of course, in the flashiest and best-known types of
antitheses and balanced phrases:

> This a natural man would answer: The soule is to be regarded
> of the body, for it maketh the body to be regarded. (p. 329)

> If not, here is your doome: where you have had your *counsell*,
> there seeke your *comfort*: he that hath beene your *counsellour*,
> all the time of your life, let him be your *comforter*, at the houre
> of your death. (p. 636)

Economy of language is an obvious aspect of the figures, as is the careful physical ordering of the sounds on paper. The balancing of a
limited number of sounds was probably as important to Andrewes as
the wittiness of the phrases.

His prose brims with the word-plays and word-chimes that medieval
ecclesiatics enjoyed in Latin, and that may never have been so well
Englished as they are in his sermons:

> No *tenendum* to our *habendum*, to *hold it when we have it*.
> (p. 236)

> That, if wee waste it in *needlesse* expences, wee shall not have
> enough for necessairie charges: If wee lavish out in *wasting*,
> wee shall leave but little for *well doing*. (p. 287)

> Out of which their *destruction, Asaph* frameth an *instruction*
> for us. (p. 174)

He delights in heavy-handed alliteration ("Shall wee heare no more
of him, as soone as he sees us so set?"), and never avoids an easy
rhyme ("Of that *history*, this the Mystery").

One must constantly realize, however, that Andrewes' style is not
precious, because he took care not to allow it to be. I have already
shown that he likes Anglo-Saxon monosyllables, with strong English
rhythms. For although Andrewes is so often "explained" by his affection for such Latin Church Fathers as Tertullian, he must also be read
in terms of his own English heritage. Like many less well-educated
preachers, he enjoys colloquialisms, and uses them constantly: "ever a
whit," "cold comfort," "gone through with it," "bear with it," "hot
pursuit," "other such like," "whist," "tush." These are as constant a
character of his style as are the elaborate rhetorical figures, and have
as much to do with its whole effect. Like the ellipses and inversions,
they prevent inattentiveness, and help to keep the music unique
rather than pretty.

In analyzing a text, he anticipates his congregation in putting the
practical, obvious questions and comments that would occur to any

seventeenth-century man of sense when confronted with some Biblical extravagance. His colloquialisms, chosen as they are to dramatize a problem, make a vivid scene of it—one which economically presents both the expected and the actual circumstances:

> Now, there was reason to aske this question, for none would ever thinke it to be CHRIST. There is great odds; it cannot be He. 1. Not He: Hee was put to *death*, and put into His *grave*, and a *great stone* upon Him, not three daies since. This Party is alive and alives like. His *Ghost* it cannot be: He *glides* not (as Ghosts, they say, doe) but *paces the ground very strongly*. (p. 570)

Again combining the expected with the actual, he explores the reasons for Christ's having forbidden Mary Magdalene to touch Him after the Resurrection; He said to her, *Noli me tangere*:

> *Me:* not *Me*, not CHRIST. Why not *Him?* CHRIST was not wont to be so dainty of it. Diverse times, and in diverse places, He suffered the rude *multitude* to *throng* and to thrust Him. What speake we of that? when, not three daies since, He suffered other manner of *touches* and *twitches* both. Then, *Noli me tangere* would have come in good time; would have done well on *Good-friday*, Why suffered He them then? why suffered He not her, now? (p. 545)

The fact that Andrewes is not dainty of his text, or about his text, the fact that he understands how Christ could be both intimate and remote with Mary Magdalene—these things help to explain his style. As Erich Auerbach pointed out in *Mimesis*, Christ's Incarnation and Passion combine the grand style with the humble; one thing that always keeps Christ's disciples off-balance is that they never know how to take Him.[8] And Christian rhetoricians brought up on the classics had difficulty for centuries in accepting the style of the Bible. By the time of Andrewes, a Christian rhetoric which combined the lofty with the mean had grown acceptable. His intermixture of a colloquial tone with untranslated Latin; of the pithy wisdom of the short, sturdy sentence, with rhythmic sound patterns; of an English vocabulary and meter with Latinate chimes—all this indecorous blending of court and country is typical of Andrewes, and its evident ease is possible only because he stands where he does in his several traditions.

His is not a highly metaphoric style. Occasionally he will, like Donne, develop a symbol through the course of a whole sermon; or use a vivid figure to illustrate a point. But his figurative language is in general quieter than Donne's, and the metaphor can run submerged through most of a sermon before it becomes noticeable. He does have a particularly good supply of homely figures: how do we know Christ rose from the dead? Because we are told so by the twelve disciples, "which is a full Iury, able to finde any matter of fact, and to give up a *verdict* in it" (p. 385). More typically, the vivid brief figure merges with ironic conversation, an imitation of an attitude:

> For, when this was written, the whole world stopt their eares at this report; would not endure to heare them; stood out mainly against them. The *Resurrection!* why, it was with the *Grecians,* at *Athens,* χλεμαδμα, a very *skorne.* The *Resurrection!* why, it was, with *Festus* the great Roman, μανια, a sicknesse of the braine, a plaine phrensie. (p. 385)

As these three last passages show, Andrewes enjoys finding the paradoxes in Christianity. But he never uses the paradox as grounds for exotic analogy (as Donne and Crashaw sometimes do), nor does he simply rejoice in the wonder of the unknowable (as Thomas Browne does). It is the blend of homeliness with majesty which interests him, and so affects his style: the closest poetic parallel, I believe, is Herbert.

The liveliness of Andrewes' sermons almost always comes from his colloquial ability to make a scene or attitude familiar by bringing it close. Why then does he distance it by inserting the unnecessary Greek words, pedantic intrusions which for us are one of the greatest difficulties in his style? He was preaching, of course, for a learned (and pedantic) audience—King James I and his court, at a time when Latin was the ordinary language of learned conversation, and Greek familiar to many. His audience liked sermons, and Greek in their sermons. We are in these respects at such a disadvantage that in order even to appreciate the effect of the Latin and Greek words, we must work through an analogy. In our time, novels and stories set in the past or in a foreign country frequently employ, for the sake of local color, phrases ranging from a *"Oui, Madame,"* to the Italian puns of

Thomas Mann's "Mario and the Magician." To his contemporaries, Andrewes' classical phrases would have seemed just as natural. They provide the local color of the Bible in the traditions which brought it to the seventeenth century, and which made Latin and Greek more familiar and natural than either Hebrew or English.

There are other reasons too, easier for us to understand. At this time, the Latin Bible was as well known as the English one, and Andrewes presented his texts in both languages. For peasant and scholar alike the use of Latin asserted the continuity of a tradition upon which the Anglican church was glad to rest. The reiteration, throughout the sermon, of the words of the text in Latin as well as English, emphasizes the text itself, and provides a kind of refrain, both memorable and pleasing.

I should like to return now to the generalizations made at the beginning of this essay, in order to try to establish the significance of Andrewes' style to the extent that it is a combination of these dominant characteristics. I have already shown some of the ways in which a content, a meaning, is "annealed" in this odd economical prose. For the most part, it is affective meaning, describing his involvement with his age and its traditions. The style says, in its humility and in its flashiness, "Glory be to the Word, celebrated in Anglo-Catholic tradition, and in the Bible, and in man's seventeenth-century world and word." It does not say "Glory be to Lancelot Andrewes." Like most preachers, though quite unlike his theatrical colleague John Donne, Andrewes avoids use of the first person, obliterating himself as a personality in his upraising of word and Word. T. S. Eliot's mention of Andrewes' relevant intensity, and contemplative rather than personal emotion, recognizes this habitual stance.[9]

The analogy made earlier between Borromini and Andrewes, as workers in miniature, as opposed to Bernini and Donne, whose art constantly expands, is not one that can be taken very far. But it suggests the different ways in which one preoccupation of the period was expressed in different media. It is an age as conscious of space as ours. The great Baroque churches with their *trompe-l'oeil* ceilings are intended to include infinity: and this new awareness of space also produced buildings where space is shrunken and compressed, as in Borromini's churches, whose walls seem to close in instead of opening out. Odette de Mourgues has pointed out analogous developments in seventeenth-century French poetry, in the infinite universe of d'Aubigné and the microscopic one of Saint-Amant: here vocabulary and imagery provide the patterns.[10] In prose, the interest in space becomes a problem of syntax, although it can involve imagery as well. Donne piles clause on clause, keeping as vague as possible the boundaries between one sentence and another. Andrewes, in contrast, shrinks his already brief sentences, by means of ellipses, and by the heavily accented openings and closings that seem to collapse the middle sections. His repetitions emphasize the rich brevity of his material.

The fact that Andrewes concentrates on the small, compact sentence rather than on the long and oceanic one illuminates basic differences between him and Donne. Donne's nature is to try to embrace the universe, infinity, and eternity, whereas Andrewes is more concerned with the world of human time and space. It is significant that they develop their sermon texts in quite different ways. Donne begins with something actually or imaginatively before him—a couple whom he is about to marry, or a symbol of his own making. But whatever he begins with, he spirals outward and upward until from the couple before him he has arrived at the marriage of Christ and the church, or until from the present moment he has arrived at a celebration of eternity. His method is expansive, and he ends upon an *O altitudo*. With Andrewes, there is no such emotional, temporal, or spatial progression: his scenes remain earthly and immediate, often becoming more and more intimate as the sermon progresses. He is more likely to choose a Bible scene than to invent or use a symbol. He is less likely than Donne to relate explicitly his theme to local occurrences. His theme is a Bible text; his development is an analysis of it, as when discussing *"Noli me tangere"* he probes the details of Christ's encounter with Mary Magdalene, and their significance. He keeps himself within a small compass, and when he refers to things outside of it, the reference seems rather to have the effect of pulling them in, than of expanding it out.

In a recent doctoral dissertation,[11] Elizabeth McCutcheon shows that while Donne considers time mainly as a way of getting into eternity, which chiefly interests him, Andrewes more often focuses his attention upon the temporal process of redemption through time. Where with Donne the present moment can be made to expand into eternity, with Andrewes one follows a series of rationally ordered steps through present and future to arrive at eternity. This I think explains why Donne's method is symbolic—the present moment or the present object becomes a means of egress out of time. And it explains not only Andrewes' short sentences and concentration of manner, as descriptive of what is brief and temporal, but enriched by God's mercy; but also his much more logical way of ordering these short sentences. As they are held together more firmly by the ellipses, so they are also united by a logical coherence which the more poetical and intuitive Donne seldom attempted.

I should like now to survey one particular sermon, following its progress from beginning to end, in order to show in a fuller and more coherent way how all these different elements vary and blend in Andrewes' prose. This is a sermon on the Resurrection, preached before the King at Durham, on 20 April 1617. The text is Matthew 12:39:

> But He answered and said unto them; An evill and adulterous generation seeketh a signe, but no signe shall be given unto it, save the signe of the Prophet Ionas. For, as Jonas was three dayes and three nights in the Whales belly; so shall the Sonne of man be, three dayes and three nights, in the heart of the earth. (p. 505)

The twenty-three paragraphs of the first section, whose average length is about forty words, are particularly short because he is dividing his text: the opening previews the sermon, and, with its many Roman and Arabic numerals marking the divisions, could best be described as a table of contents, were it not for the music of Andrewes' prose, which sounds at once in the first paragraph:

> The *Signe of the Prophet Ionas,* is the *signe* of the *Resurrection:* And, this is the *Feast* of the *Resurrection.* Being then the *Signe* of this *Feast,* at this *Feast* to be set up: *Signum temporis, in tempore signi,* The *signe* of the *time,* at the *time* of the *signe,* most properly, ever. (p. 505)

The long rhythmic first line tapers at the end of the paragraph to the single word, "ever." The only verbs are those of the first two clauses. Throughout the passage, the rhythm follows the word "sign," as it occurs in various combinations: "sign of the prophet," "sign of the Resurrection," "feast of the Resurrection," "sign of this feast, at this feast," "*signum temporis, in tempore signi*"—here the word gains increasing impetus—"the sign of the time, at the time of the sign, most properly, ever."

Physically and musically separable as the paragraphs are, they are nevertheless carefully interwoven with one another in music and meaning. In fact, one reason why Andrewes' sermons are less well known than Donne's is that they are so obviously seamless. He has no purple passages or really distinct scenes; one cannot appreciate him without reading a whole sermon, and this is true both because he does not indulge in momentary flashes of brilliance, and because what F. P. Wilson calls the "steady march of logic and passion"[12] is unbroken. In one paragraph of this section, he says that although the Pharisees deserved no sign, Christ gave them one. Meaning and music of "give them one" then open the next paragraph:

> Gives them one: and one, that is worth the giving. Put *Non* and *Nisi* together, it is a *Non nisi*. If you speake of a *Signe*, None to it: a *Signe, instar omnium*. (p. 506)

The music can be isolated from the sense. The transmutations of "one," "*non*," "none"; the two Latin words pushed together; the repetitions of the same words at beginning and end of the first two sentences; the centering of the two "ones" in the first sentence—all these things make their own impression. But without the preceding paragraphs, there is no subject for the first word (the verb), no antecedents for the second and third words (the pronouns). For the sense of any given sentence, the whole context is required.

The sermon then opens again, so to speak, with fuller analyses of each point touched upon in the introduction. In paragraphs now averaging about a hundred words each, Andrewes explicates the text, considering, first, the motives of Christ and the Pharisees; second, the likenesses between Christ and Jonah. The compressed music of the introduction, which still dominates transitional and summary paragraphs, gives way in the body of the sermon to easy commentary:

> *Evill*. There be marks of evill minded men, even in their very suit. They *would see a Signe*: If they had never seene any before, it had not beene evill: but, they came now, from a *Signe;* they had scarce wiped their eyes, since they saw one (the *Signe* of the *blind* and *dumbe man*, made to see and speake) immediately before: It was *Spirans adhuc*, yet warme, as they say. That, they saw; and saw they not a Signe? (p. 507)

Colloquialisms and dramatic sentence devices bring the sermon to the kind of oral vividness at which Andrewes excels. This first part of the sermon is a series of questions and answers. Why was it wrong to seek a sign? What kind of men were they who sought it? Why did they seek it? After the labor of such urgent inquiry, the second part of the sermon presents the adventures of Jonah as a story, within an extended comparison of Christ's crucifixion and burial, with the swallowing of Jonah by the whale. Here is Jonah in the whale's belly:

> There hee was; but tooke no hurt there. 1. As *safe,* nay more *safe* there, than in the best ship of *Tharsis:* no flaw of weather, no foule sea could trouble him there. 2. As safe, and as safely carried to land: The ship could have done no more. So that upon the matter, he did but change his *vehiculum;* shifted but from one vessell to another; went on his way still. 3. On hee went, as well, nay better than the ship would have carried him; went into the ship, the ship carried him wrong, out of his way cleane, to *Tharsis*-ward: Went into the *Whale,* and the *Whale* carried him right, landed him on the next shore to *Nineve;* whither (in truth) hee was bound, and where his errand lay. 4. And all the while, at good ease, as in a cell or studie; For, there, hee indited a *Psalme,* expressing in it, his certaine hope of getting forth againe. So as, in effect, where hee seemed to be in most danger, hee was in greatest safetie. Thus can God worke. *And the evening and the morning,* were *Jona's second day.* (p. 513)

The Herbertian sense of familiar wonder informs both these last passages, in Andrewes' description of the "still warm" sign, and of the whale's belly, as calm and safe as a monastic cell. Here also is the suggestion of present alternatives—reasonable and unreasonable skepticism; expected or unexpected transportation. But despite the availability of more than one line or level of thought, the absence of digression in Andrewes' style is notable. What he says elsewhere of St. Gregory's taking hold of a subject and "following it hard" (p. 398) is true of him as well. It is one more thing that distinguishes his from the loose, highly parenthetical style of Donne, and in fact from almost all the other Anglican writing of his time; and it is one more thing that helps to give the boundaries of his sentences the effect of being held in rather than pushed out.

His eye is always on the text, and on the argument. He keeps himself out of the way, and he keeps agitation out of the way too. He does not probe consciences, nor does he bully his congregation emotionally. He leads them through an argument, and when the hard discipline of that is finished, he tells them an absorbing story. Here the colloquial flavor is predominant, but the music is always near the surface. The English rhythms sound throughout; he employs verbal repetition, as in the use of "there" at the beginning; antithesis, in the contrast between whale and ship; alliteration, as in "safe—safe—there—ship—Tharsis—flaw—foul—sea—trouble—there" (in fact, in this prose, almost every word alliterates with something); and the final sentence is a refrain used to mark off one day from another, and maintain the analogy with Christ as the story progresses.

The last part of the sermon is the application of the text to the congregation. Here, by retaining the figures of the first parts, he gives the conclusion a sturdy homely flavor: sin is a land-whale, a red dragon; Jonah's deliverance is a Cape of Good Hope; sin is the whale's belly, and Satan's sieve. Step by urgent step, the temporal story of Jonah, with its Christian implications, brings Andrewes to the subject of repentance, and from there to resurrection, and the sermon's end.

It has often been suggested that the relationship between these posthumously published sermons and those actually preached is uncertain, but I think that only a willful misreading of Laud and Buckeridge's dedication of the seventeenth-century text can create such uncertainty: "There came to our hands a world of Sermon-notes, but these came perfect. Had they not come perfect, we should not have ventured to adde any limme unto them, lest mixing a pen farre inferiour, we should have disfigured such compleat bodies." "As the *Sermons* were preached, so are they *published*" (sig. A2). Compared to these, much of Andrewes' controversial prose is quite conventional. We know from contemporary evidence how much care he lavished upon the sermons:[13] his is a studied and intentional style. Noted linguist in an age of distinguished linguists, master of his own English, Andrewes was a pioneer in prose, and deserves the homage that T. S. Eliot asked for him.

NOTES

1. Richard Baxter, *Gildas Salvianus: The Reformed Pastor,* in *The Practical Works of . . . Richard Baxter* (London, 1707), IV, 358.
2. James Sutherland, *On English Prose* (Toronto, 1957), p. 77.
3. W. Fraser Mitchell, *English Pulpit Oratory from Andrewes to Tillotson* (London, 1932), p. 194.
4. T. S. Eliot, "Lancelot Andrewes," in *Selected Essays, 1917-1932* (New York, 1932), pp. 289-300.
5. See, for example, *The Sermons of John Donne,* ed. Evelyn Simpson and George Potter (Berkeley, 1953-62), V, 56.
5. Lancelot Andrewes, *XCVI Sermons,* 2nd ed. (London, 1632), p. 749. All subsequent references are to this edition, and will be given in the text.
7. Morris Croll, "The Cadence of English Oratorical Prose," *SP,* XVI (1919), 1-55.
8. Erich Auerbach, *Mimesis* (New York: Doubleday Anchor Books, n.d.), p. 36.
9. Eliot, p. 292.
10. Odette de Mourgues, *Metaphysical, Baroque, and Précieux Poetry* (Oxford, 1953).
11. Elizabeth McCutcheon, "Lancelot Andrewes and the Theme of Time in the Early Seventeenth Century" (unpub. diss., University of Wisconsin, 1961). See also my *Contrary Music: The Prose Style of John Donne* (Madison, 1963), esp. Ch. VI.
12. F. P. Wilson, *Seventeenth Century Prose* (Cambridge, 1960), p. 99.
13. See John Buckeridge, *A Sermon Preached at the Funeral of the Right Honorable and Reverend Father in God Lancelot Late Lord Bishop of Winchester* (London, 1629), p. 21.

DENNIS QUINN

᪣

Donne's Christian Eloquence

The Christian orator is, according to St. Augustine, "divinarum Scrip-
turarum tractator et doctor," the commentator and teacher of the
Sacred Scriptures. John Donne, as preacher, answers this description,
but as Augustine intended it, not as the *moderni* of the 17th and 20th
centuries understand it. Donne's sermons embody the traditional
Augustine conception of Christian eloquence and its connection to
the Bible.[1]

I

St. Augustine created the theory of Christian eloquence in Book IV
of *De Doctrina Christiana*.[2] The guiding principle is that the Christian orator wins souls by expressing the truth as it is embodied in the
Scriptures. The first three books concern *inventio*, the discovery of
the truth of Scriptures; and Book IV concerns *elocutio*, the expression
of that truth.

The chief weapons of pagan oratory were argument and the emotional appeals of language. Aristotle had insisted that probable reasoning (as opposed to scientific reasoning) is the only proper device of
rhetoric, but the emphasis of his *Rhetoric* falls upon those sub-logical

From *English Literary History*, vol. 27, no. 4 (1960), pp. 276-297. Copyright
by The Johns Hopkins Press and reprinted with their permission.

appeals which the orator must employ in order to win over an ignorant auditory. Augustine, reacting against the elaborate dialectic and verbal display of Roman decadence, sought to found Christian oratory on more solid ground—on things rather than words, on truth rather than probabilities; hence the material of the sermon is the truth of God as expressed in the Bible. Augustine encouraged use of all the instruments of human science (including pagan rhetoric) in interpreting and conveying the truth of the Scriptures, but it is the truth which saves souls, not human argument or devices of language. The central burden of Book IV of *De Doctrina* is the eloquence of truth, the coincidence of eloquence and wisdom in the Bible. All Christian oratory, therefore, must imitate the eloquence of the Bible and especially of St. Paul, who achieves the perfect harmony of wisdom and eloquence, "for, not by human effort were these words devised; they have been poured forth from the Mind of God both wisely and eloquently, so that wisdom was not bent upon eloquence, nor did eloquence separate itself from wisdom" (IV, 7, 187).

Since it is God's Word, not the preacher's, which saves souls, Augustine's conception of the use and nature of the Scriptures is inseparable from his conception of Christian eloquence. Love of God and neighbor is Augustine's criterion for a true interpretation of the Biblical text: ". . . we are to realize that the plentitude and the end of the law and of all Sacred Scriptures is the love of a thing which is to be enjoyed and the love of another thing which can enjoy that first thing with us . . ." (I, 35, 39). Hence an interpretation which does not contribute to the development of the two-fold love is not understanding at all. Augustine knew perfectly well that the true meaning of Scripture is the meaning intended by its author (I, 36, 40); but this meaning always contributes toward charity as does everything in the temporal dispensation.

The Bible, then, is for the preacher a book of love. Augustine speaks also in *De Doctrina* of keeping interpretations consistent with the doctrines held by faith, for certainly the Bible teaches understanding of God as well as love, but for the purposes of preaching his emphasis is on love, not doctrine (I, 40, 60). Hence Augustine's own sermons are moral in emphasis, his greatest commentary, *Enarrationes in Psalmos* being a vast series of sermons which focus the saving words upon the souls of the hearers.[3]

For present purposes it is sufficient to say that Augustine's theory of Christian eloquence together with his conception of the Bible was definitive until the time of the Renaissance.[4] St. Bernard represents the highest point of development of Christian eloquence in the Middle Ages. His masterpiece, *Sermons on the Canticle of Canticles,* is a study of the operation of love between the soul and God, who is love, especially in the person of the divine Word. The whole Bible is an instrument of love, the expression of love, since it is given to man as a consolation for Adam's loss of direct communication.[5] Scriptures serve love: ". . . charitas cui scripturas servire oportet."[6] In his exegetical devotions Bernard follows this injunction in the most positive sense. Every syllable of Scriptures contributes immediately to the building up of charity. Thus it is not a book containing certain facts and truths which one may extract for use—not like a painting from which we may draw facts and morals, but like the paint and the brush out of which the painting is made, an infinitely adaptable spiritual tool. In his conception of eloquence, too, Bernard follows Augustine. His own rich style imitates that of the Song of Songs, and his language is a tissue of phrases, words, and images borrowed from Scriptures.[7]

In the Renaissance a complex of forces gradually transformed the patristically inspired conception of the sermon. Briefly, these forces were a new approach to the Bible, a new conception of rhetoric, and a new idea of the function of sermons.

The last force is apparent in both theory and practice. That Reformation preaching, after its initial evangelical surge, rapidly degenerated into hectic theologizing and polemics is a notorious fact.[8] Even when neither hectic nor doctrinaire, Reformation sermons are theological in emphasis. Luther himself apparently did not distinguish lecture from sermon.[9] Even when dealing with the Psalms, which traditionally had been a book of spiritual and moral aid, Luther is building his own theological edifice. Hence "the reading of this psalm [51, a Penitential Psalm!] will be especially useful in teaching us to understand these points of our doctrine properly and in providing us with a learned and serious refutation of our opponents. . . ."[10] The very survival of Protestantism depended upon the formulation, promulgation, and defense of sound doctrine; and the pulpit was the best means of reaching the people. In reaction, the Catholic pulpit too, especially under Jesuit leadership, rang with dogma and angry countercharge.

The Protestant *Artes Predicandi* do not encourage polemics or neglect the reforming of morals, but their emphasis is on doctrine. In his very popular and influential treatise, Hyperius admits that he will "bestow somewhat the most diligence" on the "didascalic" mode.[11] Similarly, William Perkins makes the collecting of "points of doctrine" the primary task of the preacher, while the application of the doctrine (N. B., not of the Bible itself) to "life and manners of men" is secondary and is urged on the preacher only "if he have the gift."[12] Clearly Augustine's *doctrina* has been narrowed; in the face of a militant Reformation, love has retreated to the private devotion.

Closely related to this change (partly as effect, partly as cause) was the change in the rhetoric of the Renaissance sermon. Theologizing and apologetics called for and got appeals to logic and affections. The medieval preachers were not innocent of classical rhetoric (as Augustine was steeped in Cicero), as the *Artes Predicandi* show; but always there was a clear distinction made between secular and divine oratory[13] based on Augustine's synthesis. Whatever the incursions of scholastic method, the medieval preacher continued to aim at "animarum aedificatio."[14]

In the 16th century, however, Christian eloquence was absorbed by classical rhetoric. Reuchlin in his little treatise, *Liber congestorum de arte praedicandi* (1504), Melancthon in *De officiis concionatoris* (1535), and Erasmus in *Ecclesiastes* (1536) establish the aims, rules, and types of classical oratory as the bases of Christian oratory. Erasmus attempted to distinguish divine from secular oratory, as do both Hyperius and Keckermann later; but they fail to go beyond insistence on Christian subject matter, aims, and categories of argument and feeling. They achieve merely a *modus vivendi,* not a new theory to replace the Augustinian synthesis. In the last analysis they can see the sermon only as an argument or an appeal to religious feeling. The preacher clarifies the text, extracts its true doctrinal and ethical content, and then attempts to persuade his audience to believe and put into practice this content. The Augustinian or Bernardine imitation or re-creation or spiritual translation of the text is no longer acceptable. In any case, the rationalist emphasis of Richard Bernard and the English Puritans is nearest the spirit of the typical late 16th- and 17th-century sermon: "For by Logicke we see the method of the Spirit, we behold the arguments, the coherence and the scope; by it we collect doctrines, confirme them, enlarge the proofes, gather thence consequently apt uses, and urge them by reason upon the hearers."[15] The upshot, at its best, is to be the rational sermon of Tillotson.

Most significant of all and underlying these doctrinal and rhetorical changes was the new conception of the Bible. The philological studies of Reuchlin, Valla, and Erasmus made the Bible a historical document rather than a spiritual instrument. The manipulation of texts to save souls became to Luther and Calvin an abomination; they discovered in the Scriptures, instead, a body of doctrine and guide for morality— especially the former. For Protestant and Catholic alike the Bible became an arsenal of proof-texts which could be extricated by the science of philology. Tremellius himself complains in the preface to his Latin translation, one of the triumphs of the new philology, that past exegetes have selected their interpretations for purposes of present edification without sufficient attention to solidity of doctrine.

When exegetes and preachers of the time did turn their attention to moralizing, moreover, it is a moralizing very different from that of Bernard and Augustine. At least one theorizer of the time distinguished "ethical" from "spiritual" interpretations of Scriptures.[16] Tropology ("chopology" Tyndale calls it) became to the humanists a perversion rather than the spiritual essence that it was for Bernard. As he and Augustine handled it, the moral sense was typological, identifying especially Old Testament events and figures with those of the New Testament and with eternal abstractions or institutions. Hence, Job was a type of Christ, of man's soul, and of the Church. The general disenchantment with typology made moralizing of the Old Testament one dimensional. Compare St. Gregory's *Moralia* with Calvin's *Popular Sermons on Job*. In the Reformer's hands Job has become, instead of a symbol, a man and little more; he is an exemplum, a lesson, a wise man, a "saint," sometimes a seer, almost a prophet—yet, after all, a great historical personage who teaches us virtue. It is undeniably religious virtue, but it is Christian virtue in no immediate way, for the historical author of Job was no Christian. Calvin's few mentions of Christ in these sermons are mainly digressions. Donne (to anticipate) has a very different view in his sermons. He has read Calvin's sermons and he respects them. His sermon on Job 4:18 is based on Calvin's reading, and the sermon (untypically) divides the text by questions rather than by words. There is no typology—but it is an Easter sermon! The sermon on Job 19:26 is more characteristic. Where Calvin draws his moral from a strictly literal interpretation, Donne's morals emerge from a manipulation of many possible interpretations (some of which he admits are non-literal), and they are morals which unite by typology present man with Job and both with the Resurrected Christ.

The traditional conception of Christian eloquence was not, of course, totally extinguished. Fray Diego de Estella (d. 1578), the celebrated Franciscan preacher, for example, continued to distinguish Christian and secular oratory along traditional lines.[17] Gradually and generally, however, as the Bible became subject to natural laws and the tools of scientific investigation, so preaching became a naturally persuasive art rather than an imitative application of the supernatural truth of Scriptures to the salvation of souls. John Donne's fundamental allegiance, however, is to the Augustinian principles. That allegiance reveals itself both in his statements about preaching and in his use of Scriptures in preaching.

II

"Eloquence is not our net . . . only the Gospel is."[18] This is Donne's consistent view: ". . . the matter, that is, the doctrine that we preach, is the form, that is, the soul, the essence; the language and the words we preach in, is but the body, but the existence" (Alford, V, 129). Donne is "far from forbidding secular ornament in divine exercises," but only, "as St. Augustine says, *ad ancillationem,* to convey, and usher the true word of life into your understandings, and affections . . ." (Alford, IV, 414-415). This orientation is the basis for the exegetical character of all Donne's sermons: that is, they "open" or "explicate" or "apply" the divine words of the text.

The preaching of God's Word, Donne often says, is an ordinary means of "manifesting Christ" (e.g., II, 253-254). This manifestation is a kind of incarnation—"*caro in verbo,* he that is made flesh comes in the word, that is, Christ comes in the preaching thereof" (II, 251). Just as the Son was made flesh in Christ, and just as He was incorporated in the Bible, so He is once more incarnated in preaching the words of the Bible. Christian eloquence, like Biblical eloquence, has more than natural power.

Unlike classical oratory, Donne's sermons are not addressed primarily to the reason.[19] Rational argument, though not excluded from the sermon, is more appropriate for a lecture, which concerns "*matters of Doctrine,* and points of Divinity"; a sermon "intends *Exhortation* principally and *Edification,* and a holy stirring of religious affections" (VIII, 95). Donne has his lectures, and he can be argumentative, but he knew as well as did Augustine (or Socrates) that one does not win souls by rational conviction. It is the memory which Donne most often addresses in his sermons. Donne's conception of memory as a faculty of great spiritual significance derives directly from the Augustinian tradition, which makes memory the instrument of self-knowledge, which is in turn the key to the knowledge of God.[20] And once again Donne feels that he is imitating the Scriptural ideal, for memory is the province of the divine Author, the Holy Ghost (IX, 84).

The psychology of preaching in general is, for Donne, the same as the psychology of the Bible, which works directly upon the soul and only indirectly upon men's reason. This is why the Holy Ghost is such a "Metaphoricall, and Figurative expresser of himselfe." Figurative language appeals directly to man's conscience but indirectly to the understanding, which works with abstractions and universals rather than particulars (IX, 328). Thus the preacher, like the Holy Ghost, assaults the soul through human affections (VIII, 82-83; 43-44). Donne's rhetoric, however, is no more simply natural than is the Holy Ghost's. It is "in Christ" that the Holy Ghost "speakes in such formes, and such phrases, as may most work upon them to whom he speaks" (II, 304). Biblical rhetoric springs from the double nature of Christ. Christ was a sensible image of God and He instituted "those sensible, and visible means, . . . Christ Jesus speaking in his Church, and applying his blood unto us in the Sacraments . . ." (II, 319-320). The preacher cooperates in the sacramental application of Christ's merits to men's souls by imitating the divine process visible in Scriptures. Platonic epistemology as Christianized by Augustine is here the immediate background of Donne's thought; but the book of nature is almost wholly supplanted by the Bible. The Scriptures are conceived of as a "comment" or "illustration" of the book of the creatures, a clearer and more direct vision of God (III, 264).

Donne frequently praises the eloquence of Scriptures, but it is an eloquence unlike that of other books.

> St. Paul, who would not allow legal figures, not typical figures, not sacramental figures, not circumcision itself, after the body, Christ Jesus, was once exhibited, does not certainly allow rhetorical figures, nor poetical figures, in the preaching, or hearing of Christ preached, so, as that that should be the principal leader of hearer, or speaker. But this St. Paul authorizeth in his own practice, and the Holy Ghost in him, that in elegant language, he incorporates, and invests sound and important doctrine . . . (Alford, V, 129-130).

Using a favorite metaphor, Donne says that the Gospel is honey, for God's truth is sweet (III, 238-239; VIII, 271-273). Similarly, David is the *"sweet Psalmist"* who "had an harmonious, a melodious, a charming, a powerfull way of entring into the soule, and working upon the affections of men"; but he was more, he was *"the sweet Psalmist of Israel"* who spoke "the Spirit of the Lord"—not the spirit of rhetoric or poetry or demonstration, but the spirit of fundamental doctrines of faith (IX, 252-253). In short, Christian rhetoric is grounded in the truth of faith; the devices of rhetoric are natural concomitants of supernatural gifts. Or, as Augustine says in *De Doctrina*, those zealous students to whom the meaning of Scriptures becomes clear "feast upon truth itself with delight" (IV, 11, 192). Donne himself cites a classic text, *"Si adsit palatum fidei, cui sapiat mel Dei*, saies S. *Augustine*, To him who hath a spirituall taste, no hony is so sweet, as the word of God preached according to his Ordinance" (V, 38-39). The punning "sapiat" expresses the point perfectly: God's wisdom is indeed sweet.

Donne's very terminology here and his frequent description of Biblical eloquence in terms of flavor is in itself evidence of his connection to the Augustinian tradition (IX, 266; II, 130). Surely Donne was conscious of using Bernard's favorite metaphor for the beauty of the Bible and for the means by which men receive its benefits—a spiritual sense of taste.[21] God's word as honey, an image of which Donne was fond, also has a rich tradition and is associated with the Bernardine psychology of love—"Mel in cera, devotio in littera est."[22] The beautiful language of Scriptures appeals to man's senses, of course, but as with Bernard, the appeal is simultaneously natural and supernatural—in the image of the Incarnate God. Scripture is the apparel of God's will, and as David says, *"All thy garments smell of Myrrhe"*; they "breathe the balme of the East, the savour of life, more discernibly unto us" (V, 248). The pattern of the Incarnation is just beneath the surface here: the beauty of the Spouse is reflected in the beauty of the Scriptures.

Donne has another way of expressing the relationship between the style of the Bible and its message. The purpose and intent of the Holy Ghost is the matter of the text while the declaring, proving, illustrating, heightening, and applying of that purpose is the form of the text (Alford, IV, 47-48). The matter itself is pure and powerful but the form is sweet and eloquent thus stimulating love in the hearer. The Word of God is the honey, the form is the honeycomb, which consists

in the "outward ordinance of God, and in the labour of the minister"
—in the distributing and sealing of the Word to the conscience of the
hearers (VIII, 271-273). The eloquence of the Holy Ghost actualized
the Word of God, and the preacher reactualizes the text by applying
it to the immediate needs of the hearers. The meaning of the Holy
Ghost is, thus, made flesh in the Bible and in preaching. In the words
of the preacher, one hears,

> the Word, that Word which is the soule of all that is said, and
> is the true Physick of all their soules that heare. *The Word was
> made flesh;* that is, assumed flesh; but yet the Godhead was
> not that flesh. The Word of God is made a Sermon, that is, a
> Text is dilated, diffused into a Sermon; but that whole Sermon
> is not the word of God. But yet all the Sermon is the Ordi-
> nance of God. *Delight thy self in the Lord, and he will give thee
> thy hearts desire:* Take a delight in Gods Ordinance, in mans
> preaching, and thou wilt finde Gods Words in that. To end
> all in that Metaphor. . . . As the word of God is as honey,
> so sayes *Solomon, Pleasant words are as the hony combe:* And
> when the pleasant words of Gods servants have conveyed the
> saving word of God himselfe into thy soule, then maiest thou
> say with Christ to the Spouse, *I have eaten my hony combe
> with my hony,* mine understanding is enlightned with the
> words of the Preacher, and my faith is strengthned with the
> word of God . . . (V, 56).

Because of the sacramental nature of the words of the Bible Donne's
emphasis falls upon the form, the manner, the style of Scriptures,
rather than the matter. To restrict oneself to the matter alone, to the
words only, would be to restrict sermons to grammar, logic, rhetoric,
and ethics—to reduce sermons to lectures. Donne's preference, then is
not for mysteries, but for so much of the mysteries as is apprehensible
in the incarnate forms of Scriptures. These forms create love, the first
act of the will, as Donne was fond of reminding us (IX, 251); truth,
not rhetoric or logic, is the tool of the Holy Ghost. Nevertheless the
form is only an instrument, for no matter who or what the honeycomb, the honey is the same—the "Word of God itself" (VIII, 271-
273). In this sense Donne valued the end of Scriptures, salvation, the
vision of God, above the Scriptures themselves.

As has appeared, Donne felt that the eloquence of preachers should

be modeled on Scriptural eloquence. Donne notes especially the skill
of the Fathers and Paul in applying the eloquence of Scriptures: in
reading the sermons of Ambrose, Chrysostom, or Chrysologus, he is
often "more affected, with the very citation, and Application of some
sentence of Scripture . . . then with any witty, or forcible passage
of their own"; and in Paul one can see "how artificially, how dexter-
ously, how cunningly, and how discreetly he makes his uses of those
places which he cites out of the Old Testament." Indeed, Paul sometimes even transforms some of the rustic and plain words of the
prophets into "flashes of lightening [which] possess, and melt, affect
and dissolve every soul they touch." And this is why, Donne concludes, he so often commends the Bible: it possesses both "purity and
elegancy, . . . force and *power*, . . . largeness and *extention* . . .
(VIII, 273).

In his conception of Biblical eloquence, then, and in his habitual
paralleling of pulpit and Biblical eloquence, Donne follows the tradition of Augustine. We have also seen suggestions that Donne saw the
Bible as a spiritual instrument, a net for saving souls. The point will
emerge more clearly in my analysis of Donne's preaching. For the
present it is enough to note Donne's explicit espousal of Augustine's
rules for "a right exposition of Scripture"—viz., that it contribute to
"the glory of God, the analogie of faith, the exaltation of devotion,
the extension of charity" (IX, 94-95; cf. *De Doctrina*, Bk. I). Further,
we find the familiar Augustinian view that "all knowledge is ignorance, except it conduce to the knowledge of the Scriptures, and all
the Scriptures lead us to Christ" (IV, 124). Donne even assents to
St. Basil's view that "there is a *restorative nature* in every word of the
Scriptures, and in every word, the soule findes a rise, and help for her
devotion . . ." (V, 171).

An examination of some sermons reveals the most significant implications of the theory of Christian eloquence and further demonstrates
Donne's allegiance to the Augustinian tradition.

III

In the first of a series of sermons on Psalm 38, Donne devotes nearly
all his time to the moral sense or the application of his text. David is
treated, however, not as an exemplum but as a type of fallen humanity; he is explicitly linked to Adam, Christ, and all men. It is not
merely that the words and acts of David convey and illustrate morality;

David *is* moral instruction in his symbolic reflection of Adam and Christ. At the beginning of this sermon Donne mentions his personal preference for the Psalms because of their poetic form, "such a form as is both curious, and requires diligence in the making, and when it is made, can have nothing, no syllable taken from it, nor added to it" (II, 50). It is precisely as a poem that Donne takes up the text; he strives to explicate and recreate the full meaning and effect of the verse. With the most scholarly of contemporary exegetes—Wolfgang Musculus,[23] for example—he considers how the metaphor "arrows" affectively conveys the qualities of temptation and tribulation. But the poems are still divine for Donne, and a sermon based on Musculus would add only accuracy while it would lack a full dimension which we find in Donne, Bernard, and Augustine; for those arrows did not, for Musculus, wound Adam, David, and Christ alike.

Similarly, the arrows did not wound the auditory of the fully modern Renaissance preacher in the same way that they did in Donne's sermon. The Biblical image is like the Platonic, not the poetic image; it is a physical shadow of a spiritual reality. It is these images which are at the center of Donne's sermons; hence the fear or solace which the sermons create is meant to be a symbolic reflection of the spiritual reality behind the text. This is Augustine's Christian oratory, which saves souls by truth rather than argument or rhetoric. In the present case Donne says that his intent is to make visible to the soul *"Cicatrices suas,* those scars which those fiery darts have left in her . . . and *contritiones suas,* the attenuating and wearing out . . . by a continuall succession of more, and more wounds upon the same place" (II, 56). Donne accomplishes his end by using the Biblical metaphor as an image of the mechanics of temptation. Thus the Bible is a tool for obtaining self-knowledge. This is not, of course, "spiritualizing" the Bible; the Bible makes the spiritual apprehensible and the preacher aids in the process by demonstrating the relationship between image and reality.

In this demonstration Donne is exceedingly detailed. The subtlest psychological activities are translated into the terms of the Biblical metaphor:

They stick, and they *stick fast: altè infixae;* every syllable aggravates our misery. Now for the most part, experimentally, we know not whether they stick fast or no, for we never goe about to pull them out: these arrows, these tentations, come,

and welcome: we are so far from offering to pull them out, that
we fix them faster and faster in us; we assist our tentations:
yea, we take preparatives and fomentations, we supple our
selves by *provocations,* lest our flesh should be of proof against
these arrows, that death may enter the surer, and the deeper
into us by them. And he that does in some measure, soberly
and religiously, goe about to draw out these arrows, yet never
consummates, never perfects his own work; He pulls back the
arrow a little way, and he sees *blood,* and he feels *spirit* to goe
out with it, and lets it alone: He forbears his sinfull companions, a little while, and he feels a *melancholy* take hold of him,
the spirit and life of his life decays, and he falls to those companions again. Perchance he rushes out the arrow with a sudden, and a resolved vehemence, and he leaves the head in his
body: He forces a divorce from that sinne, he removes himself out of distance of that tentation; and yet he surfets upon
cold meat, upon the sinfull remembrance, of former sins, which
is a dangerous rumination, and an unwholesome chawing of
the cud; It is not an ill derivation of repentance, that *poenitere*
is *poenam tenere;* that's true repentance, when we continue in
those means, which may advance our repentance (II, 63-64).

And this is but one third of his elaboration of the point. This is
Donne's familiar precision, conceitedness, ingenuity, elaborateness;
but the effect goes deeper. The exhaustiveness of Donne's parallels
suggests not comparability but identity in the two terms of the metaphor. Donne is not satisfied that an image should be like the subject
in one or two or three respects; he discovers so many and such surprising parallels that one receives the impression that the two terms are
in every respect alike: the arrows become temptations and the temptations arrows. This is not, however, a mere rhetorical device nor one of
Donne's mental quirks. The things of the Bible had been images of
reality to the whole Augustinian tradition, and the discovery of elaborate and ingenious parallels had become the hallmark of its Biblical
exegesis.

The second sermon of those extant on Psalm 38 concerns the faculty of memory, an idea based on the title, *Psalmus ad Recordationem.*
For his conception of memory Donne turns to St. Bernard. Man's soul
is created in the image of the Trinity, being composed of understanding, will, and memory. It is this last faculty of the soul, rather than

the perverse intellect or will, through which the Holy Ghost most readily operates. "The art of salvation, is but the art of memory." *"Plato* plac'd *all learning* in the memory; wee may place *all Religion* in the memory too. . . . All instruction, which he can give you to day, is but a remembring you of the mercies of God . . ." (II, 73-74). But there is yet one further step, the most significant of all:

> There may be enough in *remembring our selves* . . . Being lock'd up in a close prison, of multiplied calamities, this turns the key, this opens the door, this restores him to liberty, if he can *remember. Non est sanitas, there is not soundnesse, no health in my flesh;* Doest thou wonder at *that?* Remember thy selfe, and thou wilt see, that thy case is worse then so; *That there is no rest in thy bones.* That's true too; But doest thou wonder at *that?* Remember thy selfe, and thou wilt see the cause of all that, *The Lord is angry with thee;* Find'st thou *that* true, and wondrest why the Lord should be angry with thee? Remember thy selfe well, and thou wilt see, it is *because of thy sins.* . . . So I have let you in, into the whole Psalm, by this key, by awaking your memory, that it is a *Psalm for Remembrance* . . . (II, 74-75).

The psalm reflects the soul in the act of seeing itself and hence seeing its origin; the preacher's task is to make these visions available to the congregation. This theory is clearly at work in all the sermons on Psalm 38. In the first sermon his division provides reminders of David, Adam as Man, and Christ. About six-tenths of the sermon, however, are given to the second, moral sense, while the other two interpretations are given less than two-tenths of the whole. It is the remembrance of one's self which is the action of the sermon; the reminders of David and of Christ are only prologue and epilogue.

The body of the sermon asks that the listeners apply the text to themselves, that they remember their condition of affliction ("no soundnesse . . . no rest . . .") and its causes ("thine anger . . . my sin . . ."). Donne is not content, notice, simply to digress on the Fall, its causes and consequences; this would not be exegetical, would not stick to the text itself. Such an approach would reduce the verse to its simplest moral meaning and would in the process eliminate all sense of the particular situation, the particular words of the text. The imaginative advantage of Donne's word by word application of the text to the human condition is enormous. Every word becomes a metaphor; the whole text becomes an image. Memory and imagination are very closely related in Augustine's medieval heirs, the Franciscan philosophers. In Bonaventure, for example, imagination stores sensible species while the memory actively calls them forth to our consciousness.[24] Donne wishes the words and deeds of this verse of Psalm 38 to *remind* the hearer of Adam and his full significance; so Donne imitates the function of memory by making the text an image of Adam, type of all men.

Hence *non sanitas* recalls the passibility which accompanied the Fall—disease, natural needs, all fleshly frailties which lead to death (II, 80-82). *Non in carne* suggests the corruption of all flesh "by the sinne of Adam" and more particularly the substantial corruption of human flesh. Here Donne characteristically emphasizes the physical image relentlessly:

> Behold God hath walled us with mud walls, and wet mud walls, that waste away faster, then God meant at first, they should. And by sinnes, this flesh, that is but the loame and plaster of thy Tabernacle, thy body *that, all* that, that in the intire substance is corrupted. Those Gummes, and spices, which should embalme thy flesh, when thou art dead, are spent upon that diseased body whilest thou art alive: Thou seemest, in the eye of the world, to walk in *silks,* and thou doest but walke in *searcloth;* Thou hast a desire to please some *eyes,* when thou hast much to do, not to displease every *Nose;* and thou wilt solicite an adulterous entrance into their beds, who, if they should but see thee goe into thine own bed, would need no other mortification, nor answer to thy solicitation. Thou pursuest the works of the flesh, and hast none, for thy flesh is but dust held together by plaisters; Dissolution and putrefaction is gone over thee alive; Thou has over liv'd thine own death, and art become thine own ghost, and thine own hell (II, 83).

Is he saying that the words of the text really signify this? Or is he trying to frighten his auditory into holiness? Neither, exactly. Donne is trying to reveal the *affective* meaning, the fully realized meaning of the text. David's suffering, any suffering, to a Christian "means" the corruption of the flesh. Or, better still, it *reminds* him of that corruption. The quoted passage aims at the imagination in the Franciscan sense. Donne strives to awaken images of experiences dormant in the imagination, thus activating the memory.

Biblical images (i.e., the things, not the metaphors), are analogical for Donne, and his own images operate in the same way. They are not primarily illustrative, argumentative, or rhetorical. Men are saved by vision, not by persuasion, and Donne develops Biblical images to show how man is *like*, in the image of, Adam. The next phrase of the psalm, *Non pax in ossibus*, illustrates the point clearly. The sick man has no peace, no rest because of well- and ill-wishing visitors and because of the torments of his illness. And, finally, he is restless in his bones, i.e., his spiritual faculties, because of the fear which leads him to doubt his salvation and the instruments thereof. The phrase of the text is presented as an image of the sick man's torments. The text is seen not as a verbal or rhetorical communication but as a likeness: it does not *mean* what Donne says; it *resembles* what he says. And so the text is to Donne's image as that image is to the experience of the auditory.

Finding no image in *because of your anger*, Donne supplies one in the "anger of the Dove" (II, 85) and goes on to remind the congregation that all misfortune comes from God's anger. But there is an image in the Hebrew text preserved in the Vulgate as a *facie irae*, which had been reduced by most scholarly translators to *propter*. Donne seizes upon the old phrase and its patristic interpretation as a way of revealing the relation between man's calamities and God's wrath. Donne goes the Fathers one better, indeed, by seizing the very, very letter, "*Mippenei, a faciebus*, the faces, the divers manifestations of Gods anger" (II, 86). That is, God's present punishments serve as warnings, manifestations, of eternal punishment. "The fires of hell, in their place, in hell, have no light; But any degrees of the fires of Hell, than can break out in this life, have in Gods own purpose, so much light, as that through the darkest smother of obduration, or desperation, God would have us see him" (II, 92). Calamities in this life are in the *image* of the calamity of hell.

Donne concludes the central movement of the sermon with an analysis of *because of my sin*, a final revelation of the human condition in its fallen state. Here Donne's technique of anatomizing the text is especially in evidence. It strikes us at first as highly artificial, awkward, even obscure. He considers individually the words *sin* and *my*, the singularity of *sin*, and the phrase *in facie*. It is awkward enough. Donne summarizes his thought: ". . . [we] have made him

[man] see the cause of this anger, as it is *sinne,* so to be *his sinne,* sinne made *his* by an *habituall love* thereof, which, though it may be but *one,* yet is become an *outfacing* sinne, a sinne in *Contempt* and *confidence* . . ." (II, 91). To put into intelligible order four distinct points on four particles of a set phrase is a puzzle, we might say, which strains the ingenuity of even this wittiest of poets. Why does he not just give us a connected discourse on the sense of the whole phrase? The fault lies in our expectation. Donne is not explaining sin, he is revealing it. The Biblical phrase is only a vehicle, not the subject; sin is the subject. The text provides Donne four opportunities to thrust sin before his auditory. But he does not wish us to forget the vehicle, the text; he wishes us to be conscious of the words as *things.* Where there is no image Donne will work with the word itself as an image, not merely as a conventional sign. This stretching of thought to cover the text as an object creates that tension between idea and image which is so peculiar to Donne's poetic imagery. Donne keeps us always conscious of the effort, imaginative, intellectual and spiritual, which is required to see the connections between letter and spirit, image and thing imaged.

Having laid man low, as Donne concludes, in this central moral interpretation of the text, the sermon must now, at the end, offer consolation. Donne never rests in the purely moral realm though he habitually spends most of his time there. At last only a sacramental step can heal man. With a deluge of Old and New Testament texts Donne recalls the afflictions of Christ which come from the anger of sin, concluding,

> How exact and curious was the holy Ghost, in *David,* in choice of words? He does not say, *Non sanitas mihi, sed non in carne;* not that there is no health for me, but none *in me; non in carne mea, not in my flesh,* but *in carne ejus,* in the flesh and bloud of my Saviour, there is health, and salvation. *In ossibus ejus, in his bones,* in the strength of *his merits,* there is rest, and peace, *a facie peccati,* what face soever my sins have had, in my former *presumptions,* or what face soever they put on now, in my declination to *desperation* (II, 93).

This is not rhetorical play but witty exegesis in the tradition of Augustine. The universal applicability of Christ's merits (as against the

Puritan emphasis on special election here alluded to) was of great importance to Donne, and it is this sacramental application which the preacher tries to implement by means of the text. He himself makes the point at the end of his peroration on Christ's merits, thus returning to the central idea of the introduction to the present sermon: "We have done; *Est ars sanandorum morborum medicina, non rhetorica;* Our physick is not eloquence, not directed upon your *affections,* but upon your consciences."

The three sermons devoted to the fourth verse of Psalm 38, "For mine iniquities are gone over my head, as a heavy burden, they are too heavy for me," are rooted in the "two elegancies of the Holy Ghost," *supergressae* and *gravatae,* the two metaphors of the text. In the second sermon, for example, Donne works out the spiritual analogies for "burden"; this procedure he justifies by noting that "there is an infinite sweetenesse, and infinite latitude in every Metaphor, in every elegancy of the Scripture . . ." (II, 130). The infinite source of the Bible makes its eloquence infinitely appliable for salvation.

The two elegancies of the text, however, suggest to Donne a third and greater metaphor, but one which also has a more than rhetorical significance—the Fall. The image of fallen man subtly dominates and unifies these sermons. They begin with the reminder that all men are Adams, "terrestres, and lutosi, earth, and dirty earth"; sin drowns all our higher faculties; as a roof it prevents us from rising to God, as a cry it ascends to accuse us, as a flood it stupifies us, as a tyrant it rules over us: "Wee are all sold under hand, fraudulently sold, and sold under foot, cheaply sold by Adam." In the second sermon the image is even more consistent and obvious. Seen in this light the last sermon emerges as the full embodiment of the central theme, habitual sin. There he shows that sin is misdirection of love toward creature rather than creator—a descent; sin is idolatry—a bowing down before creatures until we are made crooked with our burden and our souls become chronically deformed. In his pursuit of the creature the fallen man wearies himself, and should he rise, he is slowed by his susceptibility to sin; should he progress, he is in danger of relapse. By means of the Biblical metaphors Donne is trying to make "the *sinner* to see himselfe" (II, 119), to remember himself, to become aware of the burden of sin, which is precisely what the habitual sinner must do. These sermons are conceived not as exhortation but as action; text and sermon image man's spiritual plight by analogy or by typology: the hearer remembers himself in Adam by suffering with David.

The text has still another dimension, however, beyond the purely moral plane. The real solution, beyond human awareness of the burden of sin, lies with Christ. He must assume the burden at last. Consequently the last half of the third sermon demonstrates Christ's imitation of man. Each word of the text reflects Christ's redemptive act—from *Peccatum* (He was made sin itself) to *Onus* (He was precipitated to his death before the thieves). Thus Christ enacts man's tragedy with absolute perfection. Donne follows the action from its metaphysical nature down to its full realization in the *Consummatum est*. In Christ the spiritual reality of sin reaches its transcendent maximum; the miraculous union of man and God, death and life, sin and goodness finally unburdens the sinner. The strictness, the literalness of the imitation in Donne enforces the miraculous literalness with which Christ redeemed man. The very wit, the very strain in the ingenuity, with the surprise it creates, drives home the awareness of analogy which might cause the sinner to realize that Christ died for *him*, for *his* sins. Thus there remains still one further step, for man incurred another burden in Christ—a burden of debt: *Et cum exonerat nos onerat*, as Bernard says. The sinner owes Christ an agony; he must suffer for his sin through repentance: "that sin which was forgotten with pleasure, must now be remembered with *Contrition*" (II, 137-142). Then at last man can escape in Christ, for He is the Head and through His sufferings man's sins were expiated and Christ's merit became man's.

The series of five sermons which Donne preached on Psalm 6 (probably in 1623) illustrate magnificently Donne's habit of using his text as an instrument of salvation. These sermons, following the text phrase by phrase, trace the soul's ascent to God according to St. Bernard's *De quatuor modis orandi*. The first sermon, on "O Lord, rebuke me not in thine anger, neither chasten me in thy hot displeasure," dwells on the fear which afflicts David when he becomes aware of God's anger. This corresponds to Bernard's *obsecratio*. In the next verse, Donne shows how the soul next asks for the lowest degree of God's help, mercy. Then the sinner pleads his own weakness and humility, which prepares for his petition asking strength because even his best acts ("bones") and powers ("soul") have been weakened. And finally in the broken-off "How long?" the soul reaches the final stage of silence or patience under affliction. Donne's sermons, then, re-enact the spiritual dialectic which the verses in their very structure embody. The congregation is expected to experience the psalm spiritually rather than to understand it or grasp its moral.

These sermons can be used to illustrate a further effect of Donne's allegiance to Augustine's theory of Christian eloquence. The first sermon in the series differs markedly from the others in the series. It has an intellectual, academic tone; in style it is generally less highly figured and magniloquent than the others. The audience and occasion for the sermon cannot be the cause of this difference since audience and occasion were the same for all this series. I think Donne is here imitating the style of his text, which is not metaphoric, or at least not clearly so, especially as interpreted by the best scholars of Donne's day. Secondly, the sermon on the first verse treats (though not exclusively) the letter, the human problem in its most human manifestation of affliction in this life.

The second sermon on Psalm 6 is richer in its rhetoric and more exalted in its spiritual power because it treats a more metaphoric and more spiritual text, "Have mercy on me, O Lord, for I am weake; O Lord, heale me, for my bones are vexed: My soule is also sore vexed; But thou, O Lord, how long?"

Despite the relatively low-pitched tone of the sermon on Psalm 6:1, Donne is not giving a lecture. What lifts the sermon to the level of true Christian oratory is an image which, while it does not appear in the text itself, is solidly founded upon patristic tradition. St. Augustine had said of the verse: "Quam damnationem metuens, orat Ecclesia in hoc psalmo, dicens; Domine, ne in ira tua arguas me." The eschatalogical element entered with the idea that the title, "For the eighth," refers to the day after the seven days of man's earthly life—Judgment Day. St. Gregory developed the moral implication of this idea.[25] Donne rejects the notion that the punishment and anger of the verse refer to the pains of hell, but he retains the legal, prisoner-at-the-bar image which St. Gregory developed. It is this image which not only ties together an otherwise loose and digressive sermon, but which also can bring Donne's auditory, in imitation of David, to acknowledgment and fear of God's justice in their afflictions.

As it happens, the sermon on Psalm 6:6, 7, which is not a part of this series since it is dated 1628, is a lecture rather than a sermon. It consists, therefore, almost entirely of theological discussion of the doctrines of repentence. Appropriately it is elaborately dialectical in style and structure, and it instructs rather than edifies. Here, moreover, there is practically no exegesis at all; the text is just a jumping-off place for the arguments. The success of the "sermon," hence, depends entirely upon the force of the argument. It is to discourses such as this that the standards of secular rhetoric are relevant.

Clearly then many of Donne's habits of sermonizing are governed by the Augustinian theory of Christian eloquence. His use of Biblical metaphors as the imagery of his sermons derives from the conviction that Scriptural rather than human eloquence saves souls; indeed Donne's own style varies to some extent according to the style of his text. This accords with the traditional effort to imitate Scriptural eloquence. In their very structure the sermons re-enact the truth which Donne sees in the texts, with the result that the sermons are actions imitative of or analogous to the Biblical action. Finally, the sermons are aimed primarily at the soul through memory rather than through rational intellect; in this they follow the Augustinian conception of memory as a great spiritual faculty.

Study and understanding of Donne's sermons must begin where the great Dean himself began—with the Biblical text. His eloquence —style, structure, images, psychology, wit—proceeds from that great source.

NOTES

1. I differ fundamentally with Fraser Mitchell, who sees metaphysical preaching as a contemporary fad, traditional only in certain features of style. Beyond this vogue and beyond certain personal eccentricities, Donne used rhetoric as it was taught in school (i.e., as a means of persuasion). In any case, metaphysical preaching was "not consonant with the great ends of Christian rhetoric"—*English Pulpit Oratory from Andrewes to Tillotson* (London, 1932), pp. 179-194. See also Robert L. Hickey, "Donne's Art of Preaching," *Tennessee Studies in Literature*, I (1956), 65-74.

2. References hereafter incorporated into the text are from *Christian Instruction*, trans. John J. Gavigan, in *The Fathers of the Church*, Vol. II (New York, 1950). I am as aware of Augustine's debts to Cicero and Quintillian as I am of Donne's to contemporary rhetorical fashions. Augustine converted Cicero just as he did Plato. See Henri-Irénée Marrou, *Saint Augustin et la fin de la culture antique* (Paris, 1938), especially Ch. VI on Christian eloquence; and Maurice Testard's definitive *Saint Augustine et Cicéron,* 2 Vols. (Paris, 1958), I, 287-291, 333-352. My account of Augustine's rhetoric is in fundamental accord with the account in Ruth Wallerstein, *Seventeenth-Century Poetic* (Madison, 1950), pp. 27-30. Marie Comeau, *La Rhétorique de Saint Augustin d'après les Tractatus in Ioannem*

(Paris, 1930), sees Augustine's contribution as less clear cut, but I am indebted to his excellent account of the features of Augustine's rhetoric—see especially pp. 71-98.

3. For a more detailed account of Augustine's approach to the Bible, see Maurice Pontet, *L'Exégèse de S. Augustin prédicateur* (Paris, 1946).

4. E. Gilson defines the essential medieval conception in "Michel Menot et la technique du sermon médiéval," *Les idées et les lettres* (Paris, 1932), p. 101.

5. P. Dumontier, *Saint Bernard et la Bible* (Paris, 1955), pp. 66-67.

6. Bernard, *In Cant.*, Serm. 51, *Patrologia Latina,* ed. Migne, Vol. 183, col. 1027A. (All references to Migne's editions will be reduced to PL followed by vol. and col. numbers.)

7. For a detailed exposition of this point, see Dumontier, *S. Bernard,* Ch.VI, "Le style biblique."

8. E. C. Dargan, *A History of Preaching,* 2 Vols. (New York, 1912), II, 8-185. Both the Council of Trent and James VI attempted to stem the flood of controversy. For similar conditions in Biblical exegesis, see F. W. Farrar, *History of Interpretation* (London, 1866), Lecture VII.

9. Jaroslav Pelikan, ed., *Selected Psalms,* I, in *Luther's Works* (St. Louis, 1955), 12, vii. Note also Calvin's *Lectures or Daily Sermons* (London, 1578), where the translator seems in doubt as to the exact genre.

10. Luther, *Selected Psalms, ed. cit.,* I, 304; cf. pp. 183-194.

11. Andreas Gerardus, *The Practice of Preaching,* trans. John Ludham (London, 1577), p. 54.

12. William Perkins, *The Arte of Prophecying . . .,* trans. Thomas Tuke (London, 1607), p. 148.

13. As Harry Caplan has shown—"Classical Rhetoric and the Mediaeval Theory of Preaching," *Classical Philology,* XXVII (April, 1933), 73-96.

14. Gilson, "Michel Menot," pp. 143-144.

15. Richard Bernard, *The Faithfull Shepheard . . .* (London, 1607), p. 25. On the general significance of logic and the sermon, see Perry Miller, *The New England Mind, the Seventeenth Century* (Cambridge, Mass., 1954), pp. 111-206.

16. Luis de León, *Un tratado inédito y desconocido de Fr. Luis de León sobre los sentidos de la Sagrada Escritura,* ed. O. G. de la Fuente (El Escorial, 1958), pp. 323-324.

17. Fray Diego de Estella, *Modo de predicar y Modus concionandi,* ed. and trans. Pio Sagüés Azcona, 2 Vols. (Barcelona, 1951), I, Chs. II and IV.

18. *The Sermons of John Donne,* ed. E. Simpson and G. Potter (Berkeley, 1955), II 307. References to this edition are hereafter incorporated

into the text and are reduced to vol. and page numbers. References to Alford's edition (used where the new edition is not available), *Works of John Donne,* 6 Vols. (London, 1839), are also incorporated into the text.

19. As R. L. Hickey shows in "Donne's Art of Memory," *Tennessee Studies in Literature,* III (1958), 30-31.

20. The superiority of memory as a spiritual faculty is implied in Book X of *Confessions.* Cf. the account in Hickey with that of E. Gilson, *Introduction à l'étude de Saint Augustin* (Paris, 1931), pp. 130-136. See also the account in the introduction to J. M. Colleran's translation of Augustine's *The Teacher,* in *Ancient Christian Writers* (Westminster, Md., 1950), IX, 123-124. In the Middle Ages memory was given a vital role in the process of self-knowledge by Wm. of St. Thierry: Gilson, *La théologie mystique de Saint Bernard* (Paris, 1947), pp. 220-222. St. Bonaventure also rates the memory high as a means of attaining knowledge of the soul and hence the vision of God: *Itinerarium mentis in Deum* in *Opera Omnia* (Quaracchi, 1891), V, 303-304.

21. See Dumontier, S. *Bernard,* Ch. III. Cf. Richard of St. Victor, *Adn. Myst. in Ps.,* PL 196, 351B; and Augustine *En. in Ps.,* PL 36, 315. Edgar de Bruyne traces the sense of spiritual taste throughout the Middle Ages in *Etudes d'esthétique médiéval,* 3 Vols. (Bruges, 1946): see index references under "gout."

22. Bernard, *In Cant.,* PL 183, 809B; cf. Richard of St. Victor, *Adn. in Ps.,* PL 196, 351-352.

23. In his commentary, *In sacrosanctum Davidis Psalterium commentaria* (Basel, 1551).

24. E. Gilson, *La philosophie de Saint Bonaventure* (Paris, 1953), p. 290; cf. St. Thomas, ST I. 78. 4, who makes both faculties passive.

25. Augustine, *En. in Ps.,* PL 36, 91; Gregory, *In septem Psalm. Poenit.,* PL 79, 552-553.

WILLIAM J. J. ROONEY

∕≪

John Donne's "Second Prebend Sermon"— A Stylistic Analysis

At the beginning of his "Second Prebend Sermon" John Donne proposes for his hearers an outline of what he is to say (*divisio*).[1] In developing the sermon, as each new phase of it opens, he recalls this logical division to his hearers' attention (52, 320-330, 490-508, and *passim*). Thus, a summary of the sermon, together with a description of the speaker's purpose in preaching it and the method he is to use, can be gathered in the author's own words. The expansion and development of this logical outline proceeds, however, in a fashion not at all logical, and the method of expansion is nowhere adverted to as such. The plan offered to the readers and the details by which the plan is expanded, while clearly related, are not correlated. The details would seem more accurately described not so much as the development of the outline as a development within it, or around it. The resulting design, which extends into every facet of the sermon—even into grammatical arrangements within sentences—is not only an interesting phenomenon in itself, but seems to be, in part at least, a key to much of what Donne does most effectively, not only in his prose, but in his poetry as well.

The opening sentence exemplifies the sermon's quality: "The

From *Texas Studies in Literature and Language,* IV (1962), pp. 24-34. Reprinted by permission of the University of Texas Press.

376 WILLIAM J. J. ROONEY

Psalmes are the Manna of the Church. As Manna tasted to every man
like that that he liked best, so doe the Psalmes minister Instruction,
and satisfaction, to every man, in every emergency and occasion." The
speaker starts by likening the psalms to manna. He then analyzes the
implications of the analogy in a way that would seem to be inevitably
close and precise. Since the aspect of the manna which he emphasizes
is that it suited the special taste of each man who ate it, it might be
expected that what he would say about the psalms is that they have
this special quality of manna, and are able to give to every man "that
that he liked best." And the speaker does say something like that, but
not precisely that. "So doe the Psalmes minister instruction, and satisfaction to every man, in every emergency and occasion." Where
manna is something passive (*tasted*), the psalms are active (*minister
to*). And to say that something gives instruction and satisfaction in
every emergency and occasion is not the same as saying that in its own
order it corresponds in taste to what a man likes best.

Lest this seem like a quibble, let us look at the fourth sentence in
this same paragraph:

> And as the whole book of Psalmes is *Oleum effusum,* (as the
> Spouse speaks of the name of Christ) an Oyntment powred out
> upon all sorts of sores, a Searcloth that souples all bruises, A
> Balme that searches all wounds; so are there some certaine
> Psalmes, that are Imperiall Psalmes, that command over all af-
> fections, and spread themselves over all occasions, Catholique,
> universall Psalmes, that apply themselves to all necessities.
> (6-13)

The relationship between percepts and concepts in this sentence is far
from precise. The whole book of the psalms is likened to oil poured
out. The comparison is then interrupted with a parenthetical entry
that is almost random in its introduction of the association of Christ
with the oil of salvation. Then *Oyntment* continues the perceptual
reference of oil, as do *searcloth* and *balme;* but with the introduction
of the specific psalms under consideration, we find that they are "Im-
periall Psalmes, that command over all affections, and spread themselves over all occasions, Catholic, universall Psalmes, that apply
themselves to all necessities." The percept of oil and medicinal balm
gives way here to the perceptual-conceptual reference of royalty and
the commands of royalty. *Spread themselves* continues the perceptual

development of Oleum, but it has lost its power by introduction of the image and idea of imperial royalty. The image of medicinal balm can be resurrected by positive effort from the predicate *apply;* but after royalty's commands, the further introduction of the concepts of *Catholique* and *universall* and *necessities* serves to dissipate whatever perceptual value the word may have had in relation to the principal image. The only point I make here is that the relationships in the sentence of perceptual and conceptual references are not precise. The structural image of the psalms as medicinal oil disintegrates under the pressure of other concepts and percepts which are introduced into the sentence but which cannot be related to the image which is central to the meaning developed in the sentence.

Lines 73-104 are a further and an especially good example of this kind of disparity:

> In the way of this Comparison, falls first the Consideration of the universality of afflictions in generall, and the inevitablenesse thereof. It is a blessed Metaphore, that the Holy Ghost hath put into the mouth of the Apostle, *Pondus Gloriae,* That our afflictions are but *light,* because there is an *exceeding,* and an *eternall waight of glory* attending them. It it were not for that exceeding waight of glory, no other waight in this world could turne the scale, or waigh downe those infinite waights of afflictions that oppresse us here. There is not onely *Pestis valde gravis* (*the pestilence Grows heavy upon the Land*), but There is *Musca Valde gravis,* God calls in but the fly, to vexe Egypt, and even the fly is a heavy burden unto them. It is not onely *Iob* that complains, *That he was a burden to himselfe,* but even Absaloms haire was a burden to him, till it was polled. It is not onely *Ieremy* that complains. *Aggravavit compedes,* That God had made their fetters and their chains heavy to them, but the workmen in harvest complaine, That God had made a faire day heavy unto them, (*We have borne the heat, and the burden of the day.*) *Sand is heavy,* sayes *Solomon;* And how many suffer so? under a sand-hill of crosses, daily, hourely afflictions, that are heavy by their number, if not by their single waight? And *a stone is heavy;* (sayes he in the same place) And how many suffer so? How many, without any former preparatory crosse, or comminatory, or commonitory crosse, even in the midst of prosperity, and security, fall under some

one stone, some grind-stone, some mil-stone, some one insup-
portable crosse that ruines them? But then, (sayes Solomon
there) *A Fooles anger is heavier than both;* And how many
children, and servants, and wives suffer under the anger, and
morosity, and peevishnesse, and jealousie of foolish Masters,
and Parents, and Husbands, though they must not say so? *David* and *Solomon* have cryed out, That all this world is vanity,
and levity; And (God knowes) all is waight, and burden, and
heavinesse and oppression; And if there were not a waight of
future glory to counterpoyse it, we should all sinke into nothing. (73-104)

The controlling principle of meaning in the paragraph is the metaphor of a scale. On one side are the afflictions of mankind and on the
other the only thing that balances them, *the eternall waight of glory.*
"If it were not for that exceeding waight of glory, no other waight in
this world could turn the scale, or waight down those infinite waights
of afflictions that oppresse us here." The development of the paragraph now proceeds out of this final subordinate clause, and is concerned not with the balancing of the scale but with oppression, until
the final sentence of the paragraph, where it returns to the notion of
one weight counterpoising the other.

This structural disparity is very important to note, for what it reveals is that there is no structural functioning of the percepts in the
paragraph, no concretely perceived relation between one image and
the other. The references to the Bible, which are all concretely realized,
have in them no suggestion of weight thrown into a scale, but only of
weight that grinds and oppresses. On the other hand the *waight of
glory,* which is the counterpoise of affliction, is nowhere concretized,
but remains an abstraction. Perceptually, therefore, the scale is never
balanced. The balance of the *waight of glory* against the *universality
and inevitablenesse of afflictions* (upon which in fact the whole sermon depends) is never achieved except as an undeveloped abstraction. The weight of glory never reaches the hearer's imagination,
whereas the weight of afflictions bears heavily upon it.

If we resort for a moment to metaphor and liken the speech to a
flow of meaning, then most of the meaning in the paragraph we have
quoted must be described as an eddy, and a considerable eddy, in the
flow. An elaborated *subordinate* clause becomes the dominant meaning of the paragraph. There is direction to this speech but not a to-

tally unified direction. Variety of function has not been completely subordinated in it to a principal end. Its effectiveness depends upon no measured fitness of detail but upon other factors like intensity. Even where the repetition of details takes on a kind of symmetry, as in "There is not only *Pestis Valde gravis* . . . but there is *Musca valde gravis. . . ,*" it is not symmetrical balance that is developed. Contrast is not explored. Affliction is not deepened by its opposition to glory; and glory does not develop concreteness from an opposed pain. All the massing is on one side. The result is not balance but emphasis.

This relation between affliction and glory continues through Part One of the sermon. On every page words recur like *sore, bruises, wounds, barrennesse, drought, thirst, pressures, distresses, burden, chains, fetters, sand-hill, crosse, grindstone, mil-stone, groane, squeasing, pant, suffer, fire, tempest loathesome, disease, ground to powder, blow, darknesse, hailestones, plague, scorched, spittle, sharpe, foul, infamous, wantonnesse, loathsomenesse, caterpillar, mildew, deject, impoverish, evacuate, shake, enfeeble, enervate, destroy, demolish, damps, vapours, diffidence, desperation, calumnies, misinformation, corrupt, evil, fever, malice, irresistible, inexorable, enemy, irreparably, irrevocably, irremediably, fearful, depth, banished, driven, warre, sicknesse, calamities, shut out, persecution.* This heavy massing of meanings, denoting or connoting misery and woebegoneness, is offset by an occasional sentence such as "But then there is *Pondus Gloriae,* an exceeding waight of eternall glory, and that turns the scale; for as it makes all worldly prosperity as dung; so it makes all worldly adversity as feathers" (142-144). *Dung* and *feathers* are concrete enough, but against the overwhelming weight of percepts accumulated around adversity, they do little to de-conceptualize the notion of heavenly glory and thus restore it to a position of balance in the meaning of the passage.

In Part Three (the middle portion [320-489] functions transitionally, working out in an abstract manner the idea of God's mercy as a key to the confidence and joy to be proposed in Part Three) the speaker develops and moves out from the ideas that David's prospect is not immunity from suffering or revenge but a *refreshing* under the shadow of God's wings and that this amounts to a joy. On the strength of God's power and in the face of affliction, especially in these days which are "complicated . . . with an extraordinary sadnesse, a predominant melancholy, a faintnesse of heart, a chearless-

nesse, a joylessnesse of spirit," the preacher would dilate their hearts
"with a holy Joy, Joy in the Holy Ghost, for *under* the shadow of his
wings, you may, you should, rejoyce."

In this third part there is a feeling almost of physical effort on
Donne's part to lift up his hearers' hearts. In the insistent repetition
of his argument he gives the impression of one physically anxious to
push them on and up into the joy of the blessed. Yet joy remains
little more than an abstraction, whereas the echoes in the passage of
the anguish of dissolution seem quite real. The pattern is very like
that in Part One, with this modification, however, that joy operates
more fully here than the *pondus-gloriae* did there; largely because the
sense of affliction, still the most real meaning in Part Three, is not
developed in this section so completely as it was in Part One. What
is common to both parts is a pattern of contrasts (affliction and
pondus gloriae, suffering and joy) in which the side of the relationship whose development the theme of the sermon and the intention
of the speaker would seem to demand is only lightly and schemat-
ically augmented, while the opposing part of the contrast strongly and
vividly evolves.

A related kind of contrast can be seen if we compare the dynamic
and static qualities of meaning to be found in this section. Let us take
the figure of the Holy Ghost as an example: "The Holy Ghost, who
is a Dove, shadowed the whole world under his wings; *Incubate
aquis,* he hovered over the waters, he sate upon the waters, and he
hatched all that was produced, and all that was produced so, was
good" (703). If this image is compared with the same image in Milton, it will be seen that Milton's image functions much more
dynamically:

> . . . with mighty wings outspread
> Dove-like satest brooding on the vast abyss,
> And madest it pregnant. (*PL.* I, 20-23)

In these lines the systematic structure of the sentence points up and,
in fact, synthesizes the effect of *outspread, brooding,* and *pregnant,*
and so develops and draws out the dynamic quality in the meaning.
In the passage from Donne's sermon on the other hand, the disconnected seriality of the image renders the meaning static and builds
up not a sense of lightness, refreshment, and release but one of pres-

sure. This is reflected in the emphasis which falls upon the preposi-tions *under, over,* and *upon.*

The passage from which this image is taken (703-749) is un-equivocally committed to joy; yet it is remarkable how pervasive in it is the suggestion of passive endurance. Despite the direct address, which tends to have a lightening effect and the dynamism of the image of the river and the ascent "through ayre, and fire, and moone, and sun, and planets, and Firmament," the hearer is left with a sense of being pressed down and acted upon. This quality of passsive en-durance is present in the sermon from the very beginning. It is re-flected in the multitude of references to weight and affliction which we have already cited from Part One. It is reflected also in the con-ception of the relation of God to man that prevails. God is conceived throughout in terms of an action upon man, and in most cases a quite violent action, as in lines 664-694, where the soul is described as "dissected and anatomized to God." Even in passages where the idea of affliction is not paramount, as in 360-388, passivity is found in another guise: "If he aske me an Idea of my Religion, and my opinions, shall I not be able to say, It is that which thy word and thy Catholique Church has *imprinted in me?*" (Italics mine) Examples like these can be multiplied from every page. It seems that the speaker exemplifies in himself and advocates both explicitly and implicitly an almost will-less passivity. There is one notable exception to this in the sermon and it stands out by reason of its singularity: "Be it known unto Thee, O Satan, how long soever God deferre my deliverance, I *will* not seeke false comforts, the miserable comforts of this world. I will not, for I need not: for I can subsist under this shadow of these Wings, though I have no more." Even here, however, the final clause has the effect of reducing the positive, active quality of the statement.

It must be noted, however, that while this meaning of "passive en-durance" pervades more than any other the whole sermon, there are variations in the intensity with which it appears. These variations approximate a pattern, which may be described as follows: Lines 1-141 open plainly in the tone of instruction. The sentences are short and matter-of-fact, with a tendency to be elliptical. This continues until line 45, when quite abruptly, a more affective note is struck. "Fixe upon God anywhere, and you shall finde him a Circle; He is with you now, when you fix upon him; He was with you before, for he brought you to this fixation; and he will be with you hereafter, for He is yesterday, and today, and the same forever." From this line the passage moves progressively towards a point of fairly high emotional intensity. The progression is not in a perfectly straight line but in a series of swirls that begin to reach a point of marked concentration about line 90; there are still, however, a scattering of sentences which are instructive and explanatory in nature (68-75 v.g.). By line 113, however, the speech has developed an intensity which is sustained to line 141.

Analysis of the line of meaning in this passage (113-141) reveals a pattern very significant for the effect achieved. The personal note is maintained throughout; but there is a shift from colloquy to declamation to soliloquy in the passage that tends to dissipate the meaning by creating in the matter of address a heterogeneous effect. The passage opens as a colloquy (line 113): "All our life. . . ; yet we must not groane." This conveys a sense of the audience's presence and their participation in the affliction being described. At line 119 the speaker shifts to the first person singular and to a more declamatory manner: "As soone as I heare . . . I finde. . . . As soone as I heare . . . I see. . . . And often I heare . . . I finde." The passage, then, closes without direct reference either to speaker or audience but in a kind of soliloquy, a universal complaint being voiced: "as though the greatest weakness in this world were man, and the greatest fault in man were to be good, man is more miserable than other creatures, and good men more miserable than other men." The fact of principal importance here is that this change from colloquy to declamation to soliloquy (a regularly recurring phenomenon through the whole sermon) is not the result of influence by the audience; nor is it caused by the nature of what is referred to. The cause lies in the kind of pressure brought by the speaker on the speech. The passage begins in sympathy, moves into a kind of declamatory detachment, and subsides into subjective soliloquy, the constant being a feeling of intensity. Nowhere, however, is this feeling brought into absolutely precise focus, so that what really emerges as the fundamental reference of the passage is a very generalized feeling of intense emotional pressure on the part of the speaker.

From line 142 and continuing to line 181 there is a subsidence from the intensity of the passage just looked at, but the speech does not return completely to the matter-of-fact tone of instruction with which it opened. Most of the sentences in this part are objective, many of them impersonal narrative. But the intensity reappears in phrases like "the last blow of God's hand upon the heart of men";

and it increases somewhat as we move toward the lines which follow
and which are not only the climactic passage of this portion of the
sermon, but the highest point of intensity reached in the entire work.
In an abrupt transition, both of voice and address, the speaker leaps
into passionate soliloquy:

Let me wither and weare out mine age in a discomfortable,
in an unwholesome, in a penurious prison, and so pay my
debts with my bones, and recompence the wastefulnesse of my
youth, with the beggery of mine age; Let me wither in a spittle
under sharpe, and foule, and infamous diseases, and so recompence the wantonnesse of my youth, with that loathsomenesse
in mine age; yet if God with-draw not his spiritual blessings,
his Grace, his Patience, If I can call my suffering his Doing,
my passion his Action, All this that is temporall, is but a cater-
piller got into one corner of my garden, but a mill-dew fallen
upon one acre of my Corne; The body of all, the substance of
all is safe, as long as the soule is safe. But when I shall trust
to that, which wee call a good spirit, and God shall deject, and
empoverish, and evacuate that spirit, when I shall rely upon a
moral constancy, and God shall shake, and enfeeble, and enervate, destroy and demolish that constancy; when I shall think
to refresh my selfe in the serenity and sweet ayre of a good
conscience, and God shall call up the damps and vapours of
hell itselfe, and spread a cloud of diffidence, and an impenetrable crust of desperation upon my conscience; when health
shall flie from me, and I shall lay hold upon riches to succour
me, and comfort me in my sicknesse, and riches shall flie from
me, and I shall snatch after favour, and good opinion, to comfort me in my poverty; when even this good opinion shall leave
me and calumnies and misinformations shall prevaile against
me; when I shall need peace, because there is none but thou,
O Lord, that should stand for me, and then shall finde, that all
the wounds that I have come from thy hand, all the arrowes
that stick in me, from thy quiver; when I shall see, that because I have given myselfe to my corrupt nature, thou has
changed thine; and because I am all evill toward thee, therefore thou has given over being good towards me; When it
comes to this height, that the fever is not in the humors but

in the spirits, that mine enemy is not an imaginary enemy, fortune, nor a transitory enemy, malice in great persons, but a
reall, and an irresistible, and an inexorable, and an everlasting
enemy, The Lord of Hosts himselfe, the Almighty God himselfe, the Almighty himselfe onely knowes the waight of this
affliction, and except hee put in that *pondus gloriae,* that exceeding waight of an eternall glory, With his owne hand, into
the other scale, we are waighed downe, we are swallowed up,
irreparably, irrevocably, irrecoverably, irremediably. (182-219)

This is first of all the most sustained use of the first person singular in
the entire sermon. Even more interesting however is that, except for
the shift to "we" in the last sentence, no direct contact with the audience is established. The address is not to the hearers of the sermon;
for they can have no control over the matter of the speaker's exhortation—his own diseases, for example. It is not God who is the ad-
dressee, for, except at lines 205-210, God is referred to in the third
person. The direction of address in the passage seems clearly to be to
no one. How, then, does it function? It can hardly be described as an
"outlet" for the speaker's emotions. This kind of break in continuity
would be suggested by nothing else in the speech. The very deliberateness of the construction argues against that, too. The alternative is
that such a passage functions as an illustration of what is really the
sermon's central meaning. If the subjective pressure which flows
through the whole sermon is to be in any sense made explicit, there
is no way for the speaker to make it so in the present context except by
the instrumentality of impassioned soliloquy. The sermon is profess-
edly an effort to arouse a feeling of confidence in God. It is to that end
the argument logically schematized by the speaker leads. But the logical argument, even though its schema is strictly adhered to by the
speaker, in actual fact recedes in importance before an argument peculiarly combining the appeals of both the "ethical" and the "pathetic"
arguments of classical rhetoric—an illustrative projection of the
speaker himself as afflicted humanity.

   The danger, of course, with such an argument is that it may become melodramatic. And certainly violence and the sensational incident necessary for melodrama are here in ready solution. Their
precipitation is avoided, however, because personal affliction and passive endurance, while emerging as the real theme of the sermon, are
in intention only a countertheme. That we are not led to an appre-

ciation of the *pondus gloriae* as more than an unreal abstraction and that we do not arrive at a sense of confidence and heavenly joy is irrelevant. Although joy and heavenly glory are left abstract and attenuated as compared to the countertheme of affliction and suffering, they are never relinquished as the proposed theme. This explicitly held primacy of the proposed theme functions to allow the execution of the countertheme a freedom to develop without burden of overt demonstration to an audience; it permits it to arrange itself in whatever density it will at any point of reference in the logical structure, like grapes on a vine, or to continue our original figure, vortices in a stream.

This tightening and relaxing of intensity (or this movement from vortex to vortex), which we have now described for lines 1-219 continues through the rest of the speech. In lines 220-312 the intensity subsides into a relatively objective, discursive passage. Lines 313-388 begin to develop a greater intensity again, with some increase of subjective reference and devices of repetition. Lines 389-457 represent a relative smoothing out of the speech without returning to anything like the discursiveness of the very early part. Here and there are eddies of intensity, as at lines 429-430. Lines 458-614 rise and fall in intensity with no great currents of passion, however. Lines 615-749 represent a series of small whirlpools that swirl into a final vortex (654-749) which is second only to the passage (142-181) quoted and discussed above, in the intensity of emotional pressure developed.

At these vortices of meaning certain constants in the speech converge with remarkable density. If we look back at the passage quoted immediately above (182-219) we can see these characteristics of the speech operating: First of all there is an effort to concretize abstract meaning by accumulation of vivid detail (*and God shall shake, and enfeeble and enervate, destroy and demolish that constancy . . . a cloud of diffidence. . . . an impenetrable crust of desperation*). The references are not so much to the sense of sight or hearing as to the tactile sense or sense of pressure. The movement in the passage is less linear than circular—a kind of secondary motion, disturbed and tumultuous, best described perhaps as agitation. The details spiral around the central reference to affliction in life. The manipulation of the meaning by devices of repetition serves only to intensify this turning of the meaning on itself. There is a piling up of references to examples and a multiplication and repetition of words which underline the affective quality of the meaning rather than their clarity or development as proof.

From this analysis of kinds of meaning found in the sermon it is clear that there is in it a special relation of emotional meaning to rational structure. If one wished to pursue this analysis further, support could be drawn from Donne's grammar, especially the structure of the sentences, which while basically simple, have an appearance of complexity that is derived from the accumulation of terse members paratactically behind loose connectives, the result being not an arrangement within a system, but a seriality of coordinate elements loosely aggregated. Something similar is true, also, of the paragraphs which are related coordinately, the tendency being for the larger blocks of meaning not to interact but to assemble by accretion. There is unity in this speech. It is not, however, a unity of systematic design.

The structural disparity which we have seen to be characteristic of the speech from its opening sentence is a clue to the kind of unity achieved in the sermon. Percept and concept, concretion and abstraction, dynamic meaning and static framework are not interrelated in terms of a centralizing notion; but neither do they threaten to fly apart. As we have seen in abundance, there is an explicit distinction between the static framework of the sermon and the dynamic meanings which explode the logical symmetry by their startling emphases. One kind of meaning, however, does not polarize against the other. The alogical meaning does not proceed precisely, nor in detail by way of the logical, but neither does it contradict it, nor does it exist independently of it. The factor controlling this speech is intensity rather than anything like measured fitness of the details. It is intensity in multiplicity that holds it together, or perhaps better, carries it along.

I do not think it inaccurate to compare what we have found here in the grammatical and rhetorical structure of this sermon to that quality in other arts which is often referred to as "baroque." An analogy might be made with a painting by El Greco—St. *Andrew and St. Francis,* for example, where the divisions in the canvas (even the subdivisions) are made quite clear, only to have symmetry exploded by startlingly excessive emphases. Or perhaps better, because there is such a similarity of theme, the sermon might be compared to the ceiling of the Church of Sant' Ignazio in Rome, in which the dense weight of detail seems to hang so fragilely within the vertical movement. The intensity of Donne's conviction that thought does lead somewhere is what makes him cling so firmly and return so insistently to his logical schemata; there is not perfect correlation between thought and feeling, but there is rational design; it is the design itself which is being exploded by the emphases.

NOTE

1. Lines 7-71. Throughout, the numbers refer to lines of the text, *The Sermons of John Donne,* edited by Evelyn M. Simpson and George R. Potter (Berkeley, 1954), VII, 55-71.

ROSALIE COLIE

🖎

Burton's *Anatomy of Melancholy* and the Structure of Paradox

Who can but pity the mercifull intention of those
hands that doe destroy themselves?
                                   Browne, *Religio Medici*, 1. 53

Jonathan Swift is the culprit responsible for the vulgar error that Burton's *Anatomy* is an amorphous literary creation, an infinite digression upon an infinity of subjects. Actually, the paradox can be defended, not only that the book is composed of very carefully constructed parts, but also that the parts are disposed in the decorum suitable to Burton's material. To begin with the most obvious element of all, Burton's material was by medical and philosophical tradition contradictory—"The Author's Abstract of Melancholy" asserts in its stilted measure that

> All my griefs to this are jolly,
> Naught so sad as melancholy;

and that

> All other joys to this are folly,
> None so sweet as melancholy—[1]

From *Paradoxia Epidemica: The Renaissance Tradition of Paradox,* pp. 430-460. Copyright 1966 by Princeton University Press and reprinted with their permission.

to remind us of the conflicting traditions, symptoms, causes, and results of the disease called Melancholy.[2] Again and again, as Burton
points out, cases of melancholy display contradiction: the same thing
may, in different cases, be cause and symptom, cause and cure; or, the
cure of one case may be the cause of another.[3] For a subject such as
melancholy, in which cause, symptom, and cure are so confused and
so confusing, decorum demands the mixture of mode and of genre.
When one looks at the separate parts of the book, one sees remarkable
examples of different literary genres.

Most obviously, Burton's book is an "anatomy," an analysis of a
state of mind which, when examined closely, turns into many states
of mind. His title of course derives from Vesalius' contribution to the
new medicine in *De corporis humani fabrica,* a technical book whose
subject provided a metaphor for all sorts of examinations, of "discoveries," uncovering of areas of the globe or of knowledge analogous to
the anatomical uncovering of the systems of the human body. Anat-
omies of Renaissance subjects abounded—of wit, of abuses, of popery,
of antimony, of immortality, of the world, to name only a few. Vesalius' method proceeds inward, to strip the perfect human creature of
layer upon layer, until all that remains of him is an inarticulate heap
of bones. It is not the bones, though, that are the *object* of the investigation: the investigation is its own object; the investigation itself is
the voyage of discovery, the total process of acquiring knowledge.
Though there is much in Burton's book that is encyclopedic, he does
not attempt the classical circumscription of all knowledge; instead of
beating the bounds of the parish of human understanding, he begins
like Vesalius from the outside and proceeds on an inward voyage of
discovery which, as I hope to show, is in both the literal and the spiritual sense a revelation.

On the face of it, the *Anatomy of Melancholy* is a medical book,
like Timothy Bright's *Treatise of Melancholy,* like the many books of
the medical writers Burton cites, Du Laurens, Fernel, and Vesalius
himself. Compared with modern medical books, however, Renaissance
books of medicine were themselves much more than mere compendia
of symptoms and remedies or directions for treatment. Of English
books, for instance, Timothy Bright, Helkiah Crooke, and Thomas
Cogan all dealt with questions of both body and soul, recognizing the
psychosomatic elements of disease, elements which necessitated moral
and spiritual attention as well as physical care. Because medical books
dealt with physical regimen and control, they habitually commented
upon public and private morality, lectured on ethics, politics, eco-

nomics, and society in general,[4] as Burton's *Anatomy* so conspicuously does.

In obvious ways, Burton's casebook simply exploits the material of other books in general medicine, though, as he was careful to indicate early in the *Anatomy,* melancholy was by its nature not the professional consideration of medical men alone (1. 34-35). Since it was a disease of the soul, melancholy belonged quite literally in Burton's professional purlieu, since by his ordination he was charged precisely with the cure of souls. Furthermore, as he pointed out solemnly, contribution to medicine by divines was common enough to form a legitimate tradition of its own: he cited as authorities for this aspect of his enterprise Ficino, Linacre, Braunus, Hemingius, Lessius the Jesuit, Beroaldus, St. Luke, and, finally, Hercules and Aesculapius as types of Christ Himself (1.34-37; 111. 375).

As a practical and theoretical textbook in both physic and divinity, Burton's *Anatomy* joined the casuist traditions stemming from both professions. His *Anatomy* is a tremendous display of casuistry, with cases drawn not from the practice and experience of its author only, but from the whole range of western—for Burton, human—history. He was engaged in the taxonomy of melancholy, and his cases can be classified—the man who thought he was glass, the man who thought he was butter; the predicaments of maids, nuns, and widows are all assigned to classes of causes, symptoms, and cure; but each case is, as Burton continually stressed, unique, requiring particular variations in treatment, a fact which the skilled practitioner must realize. Burton's book, literally, is about cases of conscience, in both senses of that word, both understanding, and moral sensibility: it provides the intellectual historian, moreover, with a useful demonstration of the close connection between the casuistic method and the empiricisms of the Renaissance. In law canon, civil, and merchant; in medicine and (gradually) in the mathematical branches of natural philosophy; in religion, each *casus,* each case, could claim the right to particular scrutiny.[5] For the divine, charged with the cure of souls, *casus* has a double significance, since it is the word for "fall," and the divine's business is to deal with the particular, unique tumble by which each man recapitulates the general Fall in Eden.

Burton's scene was set in Eden:

> [Man's] disobedience, pride, ambition, intemperance, incredulity, curiosity; from whence proceeded original sin and that general corruption of mankind, as from a fountain flowed all

> bad inclinations and actual transgressions, which cause our sev-
> eral calamities inflicted upon us for our sins.   (1. 131)

Since, in Burton's world, the most general of all diseases was melancholy, with its manifold forms physical and spiritual, he was able to
trace without ado all cases of melancholy back to the first Fall:

> . . . from these melancholy dispositions, no man living is free,
> no Stoic, none so wise, none so happy, none so patient, so gen-
> erous, so godly, so divine, that can vindicate himself; so well
> composed, but more or less, some time or other, he feels the
> smart of it. Melancholy in this sense is the character of mor-
> tality.   (1. 143-44)

Melancholy is the mark of living: all mortal men, by the Judaeo-
Christian dispensation, are marked for life by original sin, which in
Burton's language is translated into melancholy.

But Christian book that it is, the *Anatomy* is also the book of a
humanist, whose roots go deep into antiquity. With his striking independence in the use of sources, Burton demonstrates the typical humanist disregard of the contextual demands of those sources, pillaging
for his own purposes, to suit himself, to buttress his argument or to
illustrate his point, however he chose to do so. As a gallimaufry of
humanist wisdom and opinion, the *Anatomy* is matched only by the
self-help learning of Erasmus' *Adagia* and the idiosyncratic constructions of the *Essays* of Montaigne. Like Montaigne himself, whom
Burton cites as authority for his own style of writing,

> This roving humor. . . I have ever had, and like a ranging
> spaniel, that barks at every bird he sees, leaving his game, I
> have followed all, saving that which I should, and may justly
> complain, and truly, *qui ubique est, nusquam est* . . . that I
> have read many books, but to little purpose, for want of good
> method; I have confusedly tumbled over divers authors in our
> libraries, and with small profit for want of art, order, memory,
> judgment.   (1. 17-18)

Montaigne's view—or his fiction—of himself was that he too had no
memory, no learning, and little judgment; that his essays, in their sequence and their philosophy, were simply the records of his undisci-

plined considerations; that they were, insofar as possible, the informal and direct recapitulation of a man, of himself. The master of irony and of tone, naturally Montaigne did not present "himself," though in a formal time and out of formal literary traditions, he came remarkably close, in illusion at least, to presenting himself as he "really was." Burton's book belongs in the genre to which Montaigne gave the name, the essay; like Montaigne, Burton was busy weighing, assaying, in his case the scruples of melancholy men as well as the physic by which they could be cured.

But he assayed grosser weights, too—the values of his culture, the worth of ancient and popular wisdom, of ancient and popular learning, of ancient and vulgar errors. He weighed, again and again, himself, not just in the successive editions of his book, but also as a total man, a man in sum. Montaigne's book took the weights of the various, mutable man its author was; its tones followed the needs of his moods and his subjects. Like Montaigne's book, the *Anatomy* is various by design, since it too must match the vagaries of both its author and its subject, according to Burton's whimsical application of the principle of decorum:

> . . . 'tis not my study or intent to compose neatly, which an orator requires, but to express myself and readily and plainly as it happens. So that as a river runs sometimes precipitate and swift, then dull and slow; now direct, then *per ambages;* now deep, then shallow; now muddy, then clear; now broad, then narrow; doth my style flow: now serious, then light; now comical, then satirical; now more elaborate, then remiss, as the present subject required, or as at that time I was affected. And if thou vouchsafe to read this treatise, it shall seem no otherwise to thee than the way to an ordinary traveller, sometimes fair, sometimes foul; here champaign, there enclosed; barren in one place, better soil in another: by woods, groves, hills, dales, plains, etc. I shall lead thee *per ardua montium, et lubrica vallium, et roscida cespitum, et glebosa camporum,* through variety of objects, that which thou shalt like and surely dislike.   (I. 32)

That passage was written, as the book was, by a self-conscious disciple of Montaigne, but though the *Anatomy* is a long and constant weighing, it is not quite a collection of essays. Burton was bound by his material and his method to a more complicated effort, to articulate, as anatomy does, the disparate parts into a fitting whole.[6]

The passage just cited tells us a great deal—not to expect consistency, for example; to adjust to many different tones, different styles, and different genres. Following Burton's own leads, his appeals to various sorts of authority and tradition, I want to explore some of the range of his use of genre and of traditional tone.

To begin with an obvious example, the synopses with which each Partition begins demonstrate Burton's training in the schools: even if we are not particularly reminded of scholastic division in Burton's additive accounts, the construction of the book as a whole follows the conventional patterns of scholastic demonstation and argument, particularly as applied to books of instruction.[7] To pass from this to a more concealed genre, the book as a whole bears the message, if not the shape, of something quite different. The entire book is a *consolatio philosophiae*,[8] the promise of the limited comfort learning can give to men under the pressure of their painful daily lives. Under singular stress, Socrates remembered to award the consolation of philosophy to his friends anticipating their bereavement; Cicero's recapitulation of philosophical strength after the death of his daughter Tullia and Boethius' remarkable testament in prison have become the classics of a reflective and didactic genre. As Burton said of himself, "I writ of melancholy, by being busy to avoid melancholy" (1.20): he shakes himself out of his disease by attacking it foursquare, and he consoles his miseries by that activity. "Cardan professeth he wrote his book *de Consolatione* after his son's death, to comfort himself; so did Tully write of the same subject with like intent after his daughter's departure. . . ." (1.21)

The whole book is located within the genre, and there are two quite different integral consolations of philosophy within it. One, in the Second Partition, warns against undue mourning at the death of friends and relations, and provides a discourse against the fear of one's own death. In this essay, almost all the references are classical: the comfort given is moral rather than spiritual, and of the whole Bible, only the Stoical Ecclesiastes is cited. Though in general, the tone is elevated and Stoical, at the end, the permissive, understanding doctor has his say. If the patient cannot meet the austere demands of Stoic self-control, then he should indulge in remedial diversions such as men in other countries do—

The Italians most part sleep away care and grief, if it un-
seasonably seize upon them; Danes, Dutchmen, Polanders,
and Bohemians drink it down; our countrymen go to plays. Do
something, something or other, let it not transpose thee. . . .

> (II. 185)

In addition to this classical *consolatio*, Burton provided a Christian consolation, in the form of a sermon, his "Consolatory Digression," where he once more enjoins his patients to "merriment" and to
holy joy:

Go then merrily to heaven. If the way be troublesome, and
you in misery, in many grievances, on the other side you have
many pleasant sports, objects, sweet smells, delightsome tastes,
music, meats, herbs, flowers, etc. to recreate your senses. Or
put case that thou art now forsaken of the world, dejected,
contemned, yet comfort thyself; as it was said to Hagar in the
wilderness, "God sees thee, he takes notice of thee": there is
a God above that can vindicate thy cause, that can relieve
thee. . . . For thy part then rest satisfied, "cast all thy care
on him, thy burden on him, rely on him, trust on him, and
he shall nourish thee, care for thee, give thee thine heart's desire"; say with David, "God is our hope and strength, in
troubles ready to be found" (Ps. xlvi, i). "For they that trust
in the Lord shall be as Mount Zion, which cannot be removed.
As the mountains are about Jerusalem, so is the Lord about his
people, from henceforth and forever" (Ps. cxxv, 1, 2).

> (II. 132-133)

One might expect at this point a pendant to the *consolatio*, the
contemptus mundi, such as that provided in Donne's Anniversary
Poems;[9] but Burton gives us no such thing. He was certainly under
no illusions about the pains of this world—the book, after all, deline-
ates them in often tedious detail: but the solitary scholar, the spectator of other men's activities, whose Egeria was melancholy herself,
nonetheless never gladly renounced the world into which he was
born, never for one moment underestimated the values conferred by
the painful, beautiful, various world. "Solitariness," the great cause and
symptom of melancholy, is always suspect: hermits are to be reinte-
grated into human society, and private men brought forth into com-

munity again. The world itself Burton could regard as a great box of simples from which to select the remedy proper to one's own kind of melancholy.

Burton followed Aristotle and Ficino in believing that melancholy is an heroic disease; that its principal sufferers were endowed with perceptions far more intense, more poignant, often more obsessive and more painful than those of ordinary men, but perceptions at the same time more authoritative and significant than those granted to the healthy or to sufferers from melancholy to a lesser degree. Melancholy was the malady of creative people: a bad case heightened the melancholiac's perceptions overwhelmingly, so that he might be reduced to folding his arms and pulling his hatbrim over his face, or she to sitting with her head on her hand, her elbow on her knee, staring into space, paralyzed by the grandeur of her inward vision of the outward world.[10] The melancholiac is in very interesting symbiosis with the world. His perceptions of its multiplicity may overwhelm him with fear of his own meaninglessness; but his perceptions of the world are precisely what make him heroic, and he appreciates his perceptive power even when in the grip of his pains. The world is the melancholiac's dear enemy, and as such cannot be disposed of by *contemptu mundi*. Burton never attempted rejection of the world: his whole book is informed by respect for its vigor and variety, not by a sense of its decay.

This is not to say that Burton wrote a paean to the world's wonders like that of Pico della Mirandola, for the world was not, in Burton's vision, a friendly place or a haven for the sufferer. Burton's own attitudes toward the world varied, as he himself said. Though he attempted, like Democritus, to see it as comedy, all too often he was forced, like Heraclitus, to see it as tragedy:

> *Fleat Heraclitus, an rideat Democritus?* in attempting to speak of these symptoms, shall I laugh with Democritus, or weep with Heraclitus? they are so ridiculus and absurd on the one side, so lamentable and tragic on the other: a mixed scene offers itself, so full of errors and a promiscuous variety of objects, that I know not in what strain to represent it.
>
> (III. 346)

In his Heraclitan mood, Burton was capable of jeremiad. His humanist discourse on the horrors of war is an example of this, the horrors particularly of the recent wars fought, he felt, on religious

pretexts rather than religious grounds (1.56; 111.346-53). More specifically, Burton wept for the victims of melancholy; his sensitivity to
cases of suffering is, at this long distance, very touching:

> . . . [S]o by little and little, by that shoeing-horn of idleness,
> and voluntary solitariness, melancholy, this feral fiend, is drawn
> on . . . it was not so delicious at first, as now it is bitter and
> harsh; a cankered soul macerated with cares and discontents,
> *tedium vitae,* impatience, agony, inconstancy, irresolution, pre-
> cipitate them into unspeakable miseries.   (1. 406-07)

Of men driven by sleeplessness upon despair, he wrote,

> They can take no rest in the night, nor sleep, or if they do
> slumber, fearful dreams astonish them. In the day-time they
> are affrighted still by some terrible object, and torn in pieces
> with suspicion, fear, sorrow, discontents, cares, shame, anguish,
> etc., as so many wild horses, that they cannot be quiet an
> hour, a minute of time, but even against their wills they are
> intent, and still thinking of it, they cannot forget it, it grinds
> their souls day and night, they are perpetually tormented, a
> burden to themselves, as Job was, they can neither eat, drink,
> nor sleep.   (1. 431-32)

Naturally enough, in someone who chose to call himself "Democritus junior," Burton attempted to maintain a tone of ironic criticism
for the better part of his work, to laugh at foolish foibles rather than
to denounce human depravity. The figure of Democritus played a
part in the mixed play of the Renaissance satirist;[11] Burton's choice
of the laughing philosopher of antiquity as his *persona* gained him
entrance into another legitimately mixed genre, that of satire. He certainly wrote more satirical passages than jeremiads: it is difficult,
however, to maintain a tone of humorous detachment for the melancholy man, predisposed to weep like Heraclitus; and difficult for
Burton, too, with his extraordinary sympathy for the almost infinitely
varied excruciations inevitable to the condition he described. All the
same, for Burton as for Juvenal, *difficile est satiram non scribere:*[12]

> If Democritus were alive now, he should see strange altera-
> tions, a new company of counterfeit vizards, whifflers, Cuman

asses, maskers, mummers, painted puppets, outsides, fantastic
shadows, gulls, monsters, giddy-heads, butterflies.   (1. 52)

If Democritus were alive now, and should but see the superstition of our age, our religious madness. . . , so many professed Christians, yet so few imitators of Christ; so much talk
of religion, so much science, so little conscience; so much
knowledge, so many preachers, so little practice; such variety
of sects, such absurd and ridiculous traditions and ceremonies;
if he should meet a Capuchin, a Franciscan, a pharisaical Jesuit,
a man-serpent, a shave-crowned monk in his robes, a begging
friar, or see their three-crowned Sovereign Lord the Pope,
poor Peter's successor, *servus servorum Dei,* to depose kings
with his foot, to tread on emperors' necks, make them stand
bare-foot and bare-legged at his gates, hold his bridle and
stirrup, etc. (O that Peter and Paul were alive to see this!);
if he should observe a prince creep so devoutly to kiss his toe,
and those red-cap cardinals, poor parish priests of old, now
princes' companions, what would he say?   (1. 54)

Had he seen, on the adverse side, some of our nice and curious
schismatics in another extreme abhor all ceremonies, and rather
lose their lives and livings than do or admit anything papists
have formerly used, though in things indifferent (they alone
are the true Church . . .); formalists, out of fear and base
flattery, like so many weather-cocks turn round, a rout of
temporizers, ready to embrace and maintain all that is or shall
be proposed in the hope of preferment; another Epicurean
company, lying at lurch as so many vultures, watching for a
prey of Church goods, and ready to rise by the downfall of
any: as Lucian said in like case, what dost thou think Democritus would have done, had he been spectator to all these
things?   (1. 55)

Certainly Burton's material lent itself to satire, and satire had its
uses, both in the general essay and in specific moral essays. In the
long introduction to his work, Burton's description of his society—the
falseness of rulers, of laws and lawyers, the fragility of family ties and
all other bonds of trust, the dubious relations between the sexes—recalls its major source, Raphael Hythlodaye's picture of England in

the first book of More's *Utopia*.[13] As in that book, in which satire and utopian prescription were mutual requirements, Burton provides us with a utopian remedy for Stuart abuses:

> I will yet, to satisfy and please myself, make an Utopia of mine own, a New Atlantis, a political commonwealth of mine own, in which I will freely domineer, build cities, make laws, statutes, as I list myself. And why may I not? *Pictoribus atque poetis,* etc.—you know what liberty poets ever had, and besides, my predecessor Democritus was a politician, a recorder of Abdera, a law maker, as some say; and why may I not presume so much as he did?   (I. 97-98)

Like More's, Burton's utopia both was and was not a "witty fiction" merely; like Plato's, Andreae's, Campanella's, and Bacon's, it dealt with the realities of social and political organization, and provided generously for health, education, and welfare in England; like More's, his commonwealth was a humanist prescription rather than a scientific or political fantasy.[14] Burton's vision is in itself interesting: his observations can be matched again and again in the grievances laid before king and parliament; his eye was in for the good of England. Like More and unlike parliament, though, Burton was far from radical in his plans for reform. More's pastoralism and communism have their roots in an early Christian spiritual arcadia, and Burton shared the spiritual if not the communal ideals of his predecessor. Both men were conservative, therefore: neither realized the beneficent implications in the spectacular industrial revolution going on about them. In certain respects, however, Burton was more modern in his social outlook than More; for example, his utopians were not protectionists, as More's had been, but mercantilists organized for trade free of the monopolies of which all England, except the monopolists, complained. Economically Burton was modern, but socially he was not: "I will have several orders, degrees of nobility, and those hereditary," said Burton. "My form of government shall be monarchical" (I. 101).

One might think that Burton wrote his utopia merely to gratify a whim or to demonstrate his stylistic facility and imaginative ingenuity. There is, though, a contextual justification for this odd section, embedded so deeply in the preface to the book that many readers have not recognized what they were reading. As Democritus had license to write of public matters as a law-maker in Abdèra, so had Burton as a physician license to write of the ills of the commonwealth as well as the ills of the people in it. In the ancient metaphor, the body politic is likened to the human body: society is seen as diseased or disordered, its diseases and disorders are diagnosed, remedies are prescribed.[15] By extension of this metaphor, political analysis is part of the physician's correspondent task.

Burton's political commentary is closely linked to his commentary on religious institutions. The Church is, as the state is, a body, with habits and traditions, As a divine, Burton wrote much of *The Anatomy of Melancholy* within the generic traditions appropriate to his Church and about the ecclesiastical problems, public and private, of his time. Sometimes his satire turns to jeremiad, as in his strictures on Roman Catholic "superstition":

> When I see a priest say mass, with all those apish gestures, murmurings, etc., read the customs of the Jews' synagogue, or Mahometan meskites, I must needs laugh at their folly: *Risum teneatis amici?;* but when I see them make matters of conscience of such toys and trifles, to adore the devil, to endanger their souls, to offer their children to their idols, etc., I must needs condole their misery . . . when I see grave learned men rail and scold like butterwomen, methinks 'tis pretty sport, and fit for Calphurnius and Democritus to laugh at. But when I see so much blood spilt, so many murders and massacres, so many cruel battles fought, etc., 'tis a fitter subject for Heraclitus to lament.   (III. 346)

Like most Anglican priests, Burton was aware of the debt of his Church to the Roman one. He saw the Anglican Reformation as the restorer of the true religion, the English Church as the true balance between the superstitions of an overinstitutionalized Rome and the individual eccentricities of sectarians (III. 324, 423). Withal, Democritus laughed and Heraclitus wept over the state of divinity in early Stuart England, in language matched by many a Presbyterian and Independent divine:

> This is that base and starveling class, needy, vagabond, slaves of their bellies, worthy to be sent back to the plough-tail, fitter for the pigsty than the altar, which has basely prostituted the study of divinity. These it is who fill the pulpits and creep into

> noblemen's houses. Having no other means of livelihood, and
> being incapable both mentally and physically of filling any
> other post, they find here an anchorage, and clutch at the
> priesthood, not from religious motives, but, as Paul says,
> "huckstering the word of God."   (1. 328)

A divine himself, Burton had chosen not to take the conventional
track to preferment:

> . . . had I been as forward and ambitious as some others, I
> might have haply printed a sermon at Paul's Cross, a sermon
> in St. Mary's Oxon, a sermon in Christ Church, or a sermon
> before the right honourable, right reverend, a sermon before
> the right worshipful, a sermon in Latin, in English, a sermon
> with a name, a sermon without, a sermon, a sermon, etc.
> But I have ever been as desirous to suppress my labours in this
> kind, as others have been to press and publish theirs.   (1. 35)

Like all Oxford divines, Burton was obliged to deliver sermons, both
for his college chapel (the cathedral of the diocese), and in the
Church of St. Mary the Virgin that served the university community.
He was able to make up a fine sermon, too, as the consolatory digres-
sion demonstrates, as well as the first section in the book, "On Man's
Excellency, fall, Miseries, and Infirmities."

Burton certainly excelled in hortatory rhetoric. Viewed another
way, the parts of the *Anatomy of Melancholy* dissolve into a treatise
on education, *de regimine hominis*, a mirror of man. Once more, the
genre itself, of which Erasmus' *Enchiridion* and Machiavelli's *Prince*
are the most notable Renaissance examples, was closely related both
to the medical treatise and to the dissertation in political theory. The
most trivial Renaissance behavior book derives from the highest ancient tradition of moral discourse, in which it is assumed that the
commonweal depends upon the health, physical and spiritual, of
each participant.

The descriptive, prescriptive, and remedial sections of the *Anatomy*
naturally refer to the moral tradition of which they are a part;
Burton's book was a "macaronicon," as he said, but a macaronic not
of genres territorially divided, but of genres mutually serviceable. So
his remarkable chapters on the origin and etiology of melancholy,
"Parents, a Cause" (1. 211), and nurses as a cause (1. 330ff.), "Edu-

cation a Cause of Melancholy" (1. 333), favorite chapters of twentieth-century readers, may be seen as genre recapitulations of the *de
regimine principis* (itself, incidentally, a paradoxical title, the ruler
ruled), drawing upon ethical, educational, political, and medical traditions all at once, but laying stress on the negative rather than the
positive formation of human beings. Burton's long, careful chapters
on the "rectifications" of melancholy, by diet, air, exercise, and moderation of the passions make up a behavior book for every fallen man
and woman. What distinguishes his book from most of those in the
tradition is his assumption that all educations, all growings-up, must
take place against a background and often in the foreground, of
spiritual or nervous malady.

Burton's Third Partition, the section on love and religious melancholy, falls into a particular subtype of Renaissance behavior book,
the love dialogue, or love treatise, of which Landino, Ficino, Bembo,
Castiglione, and Leone Ebreo are only the most famous composers.
Because the better part of Burton's discourse on love deals with the
afflictions of the condition it is easy to overlook the fact that Burton
the solitary scholar, celibate by reason of his post, also wrote a praise
of love the more moving because he was so manifestly acquainted
with love's complicated pains. He knew the power and the extent of
the passion of love, so strong that the mightiest have dutifully gone
down before it; he knew the self-hatred that unworthy love induces
in the lover; he knew the equivocations of jealousy—all that his anatomy lays bare. Like Rabelais in his *Tiers Livre,* Burton presents the
humanist defense of women and marriage, but not without the coun-
terevidence for Chaunticler's position. Like Pantagruel, Burton (or
Democritus junior) is detached during the marriage debate; the case
is far from a clear ruling, however: though marriage can bring the
greatest of earthly joys, for the most part it seems not to do so. Pan-
urge seems to have hesitated indefinitely between the joys and the
frustrations anticipated in marriage, but the fact that love went attended by pain was not, for Burton, a sufficient argument to reject
either love or marriage. Venus, as he thoroughly explained, was a
cause of much melancholy; but she is also its cure, as maids, nuns,
and widows conspicuously know.

Like Plato, Ficino, Leone Ebreo, and the rest, Burton passes up
the scale from Aphrodite Pandemos, Venus Vulgaris, to Aphrodite
Ouranos, Venus Coelestis, or from physical to spiritual, human to divine love. His dissertation is, however, radically different from the

conventional love treatise, in which increased contentment is promised to the lover progressing from stage to stage on the ladder of love.
Burton's treatise is a Renaissance love dialogue turned inside out: the
Anatomy describes the dark side of the Platonic scale, with all the
sufferings involved in every step up it.[16] The most heroic form of
melancholy, and therefore the most serious case of the malady, is the
melancholy suffered in loving God Himself.[17] Not only does passage
up Burton's ladder of love give no assurance of general happiness, but
it also carries with it the greatest threat of all, the despair lurking in
every case of religious melancholy.

One form of religious melancholy proceeded directly from the cure
of love melancholy. Appreciation of God's extraordinary beauty was
the most reliable cure for sufferers from love of an earthly object; but
contemplation of God's perfection characteristically reinforced awareness of human imperfection. Since God Himself was not always accurately presented to His worshippers, His distorted figure might induce or increase the fear or the madness of religious despair: the
crime of misleading Christians in the worship of God Burton attributed particularly to the priests of the Roman Church (III. 331-36).

Albeit in some ways a moderate one, Burton was a product of the
Protestant Reformation: the Augustine he selected as authority for
his views is the Augustine of *Contra Pelagianos,* quite a different Augustine, for example, from the one Milton selected as his authority.
For Burton men were less powerful than passions. Though medical
and humanist tradition both required that every possible remedy be
devised to help men in their unequal fight against themselves, only
God's grace could really bring men through, and even God's grace
was no warranty for earthly happiness:

> So that affliction is a school or academy, wherein the best
> scholars are prepared to the commencements of the Deity. And
> though it be most troublesome and grievous for the time, yet
> know this, it comes by God's permission and providence; He
> is a spectator of thy groans and tears, still present with thee;
> the very hairs of thy head are numbered, not one of them can
> fall to the ground without the express will of God.
>
> (III. 425-26)

Religious fear could also come and go in the mind of man without
effectively contaminating it: not even the most timorous need be

damned by their terrors. When Christ Himself knew something very like religious despair in the garden, common men might take some comfort in their affliction:

> 'Tis no new thing this, God's best servants and dearest children
> have been so visited and tried. Christ in the garden cried out,
> "My God, my God, why hast Thou forsaken me?" His son
> by nature, as thou art by adoption and grace.   (III. 426)

By theological definition, grace is beyond understanding, though not beyond recognition. All divinity is above reason; faced with the paradoxes of divinity, one is supposed to lose one's self in "O altitudo!" Divinity is, practically speaking, unknowable and therefore unknown. For the medical man, accustomed to the vagaries of disease, for a divine trained on cases of conscience, for a literary man brought up on Montaigne, *unknowing* is a familiar condition. Recognition rather than knowledge is the most such men can hope for. For the Christian, recognition is just that: the *most* one can hope for. Discovery brings revelation; the revelation it brings is of irresistible grace.

No amount of human knowledge has the slightest effect upon God's grace, of course: but human knowledge can help to identify and to recognize conditions. Burton's book is a paradoxical exercise in many ways, but chiefly because it is about paradoxical subjects, about divinity, about epistemology, about medical problems at the frontiers of research, and therefore at the limits of discourse. Further, as one is increasingly aware in reading the medico-spiritual matter of *The Anatomy of Melancholy,* the material is itself full of contradiction. God is the first cause of melancholy and its only sure cure; love is cause and cure; idleness, solitude, sorrow, and fear are cause and symptom; melancholy itself is both the disease and its own cure. Elsewhere I hope to discuss some of the significance of these duplicities and multiplicities: here I want merely to stress the composed, contradictory, paradoxical nature of the disease itself.[18]

The practitioner treating melancholy, finding himself faced by, say, a patient exhibiting sorrow, must somehow determine the relation of this sorrow to the total disease, must sort out the contradictions of this case from others, must discover each paradox of the disease. To find out, for example, whether sorrow is the cause or the symptom in any particular case, the physician must undo the disease, determining the disorders of each layer, just as Vesalius uncovered the layered sub-systems of the human body. Each case becomes a separate investigation, a separate discovery; the whole enterprise, made up of all the cases, is a voyage of intellectual discovery.

Any voyage of discovery involves the interdependent enterprises of map-making and taxonomy, as Burton recognized in his attempts both to organize melancholy as a whole and to classify its subdivisions. The metaphor of the voyage attracted him, as the preface early notes—

> I never travelled but in map or card, in which my unconfined thoughts have freely expatiated, as having ever been especially delighted with the study of cosmography.   (1.18)

The book is chock-a-block with the rich comparative material brought home to Europe by the voyagers into the geographical new world.[19]

Not only the real but the imaginary voyage also has its tradition,[20] from Lucian's Icaromenippus to space fiction, often related to or overlapping with the utopian tradition and the satiric one. In the "Digression of the Air," Burton sets out on his imaginary journey:

> As a long-winged hawk, when he is first whistled off the fist, mounts aloft, and for his pleasure fetcheth many a circuit in the air, still soaring higher and higher till he be come to his full pitch, and in the end when the game is sprung, comes down amain, and stoops upon a sudden: so will I, having now come at last into these ample fields of air, wherein I may freely expatiate and exercise myself for my recreation, awhile rove, wander round about the world, mount aloft to those ethereal orbs and celestial spheres, and so descend to my former elements again.   (II. 34-35)

This time, the trip is around the world and through the conjectural cosmos. Burton's voyage is particularly interesting, because it is not the usual fantasy of the planetary voyage, like Lucian's or Cyrano's; it is an imaginary voyage about the real world. In other words, it is not what it seems: it is a paradox. More than this, it is a double paradox, since it is also and equally a real voyage about the imaginary world, or the world of the imagination. To put it another way, the book belongs to still another genre of discovery, of venturing into the unknown, namely, the picaresque. Instead of a fictional hero, Democritus and his reader go hand in hand through the hills and valleys, the deserts, the seas, and the airy spaces of this book. He takes us in picaresque disorder from one consideration, one intellectual incident to the next, evidently at random, though with a randomness corresponding to real experience and consequently, in the *Bildungsroman* tradition, a randomness at once significant and constructive.

The picaresque is the generic privilege of every man. Every man is, before God, a rogue: every man makes his way at hazard through the journey of his life—and only some men are, like Odysseus, lucky enough to find their way home. Burton's technique, like that of Cervantes in *Don Quixote,* is to assimilate landscape—in Burton's case, the landscape of the entire universe—to mood, to inward need. The actual voyage of discovery is only apparently through the sensible world. Actually the voyage is inward, through the fantastic worlds the imagination creates, a world like that of Bruegel's "Mad Meg," where an entire landscape is made up by the action of one picaresque, errant, wandering mind.

The climate of Burton's book is of opposites and oppositions, contradictions and paradoxes: we become so acclimated to these anomalies that we tend to overlook their meanings in the large. Burton never presents his readers with a choice between one explanation for melancholy and another different or contradictory explanation. He does not present us with either the Galenical or the homeopathic remedy for any symptom. He does not present us with the choice between being and not being melancholy. His is a pluralist world, accommodating all the alternatives, even some which in conventional logic close one another out. Since Bacon, kicking stones *can* refute Berkeley: experience can make logical and metaphysical systems seem irrelevant. Burton is not dialectic, for all the rigidly imposed organization of his matter; he is like the philosopher whose name he took, ready to assume the existence of mutual contradictions, and to assume that they are the material of which the world is made up. As one perceives this, one perceives as well the fundamental way in which Burton's whole book is a medical paradox, introducing a new psychology. Ostensibly within the frame of the old faculty and humoral psychology, Burton argues against the old narrow concepts of melancholy and of human nature, providing a new way of regarding both those things.

Necessarily, in so various a world as Burton's, paradox becomes domesticated, becomes a homely mode of perception. Because we come to regard Burton's paradoxes as normal, the *Anatomy* has been over-

looked, I think, as a major document in the genre of paradox. In the
very simplest sense, it is a rhetorical paradox, since it is designed to
cheat the reader's expectation. We are led to expect a straightforward
medical treatise, like Bright's, and we get a great many utterly different things thrown in—a spiritual treatise, an atlas, a book of me-
teorology, a behavior book, and so forth, and so forth. As the paradoxist is supposed to, furthermore, Burton misleads his readers exactly: speaking of Democritus, he warns us not to expect

> a pasquil, a satire, some ridiculous treatise. . . , some pro-
> digious tenent, or paradox of the earth's motion, of infinite
> worlds, *in infinito vacuo, ex fortuita atomorum collisione,* in
> an infinite waste, so caused by an accidental collision of motes
> in the sun, all which Democritus held, Epicurus and their
> master Leucippus of old maintained, and are lately revived by
> Copernicus, Brunus, and some others.   (1. 15)

Each of these things, from pasquil to the notions of Bruno, is of
course displayed in the treatise, and each of them more than once.
Burton sets out to contradict himself; he has produced by calculation
a series of rhetorical paradoxes within the limits of his book as a
whole. The rhetorical paradox furthermore is the form most suited to
Burton's material, which is, quite literally, anything and everything:
the paradox, even more than the permissive satirical form, allows for
anything, encourages *genera mixta* and the breaching of all limits established by any convention. Under paradox's protection, pasquil,
satire, jeremiad, eulogy, sermon, utopia, behavior book, and so on and
so on, may be—even should be—juxtaposed.

There is more to Burton's paradoxology than this. It has seemed
possible, for example, to collect Burton's comments on himself and to
subject them to psychiatric scrutiny.[21] Burton's self-references, then,
provide genuine autobiographical data. This might seem to be direct,
empirical self-reference on the model of Montaigne, had not Burton
specifically said that he "would not be known" (1.15). Not to have
recognized him, however, would have been impossible in the limited
world of the seventeenth-century English gentry, since he registered
his father's and mother's names, the place of his birth, the name of
his brother's only book and the only such book then in print, as well
as his own present occupation and habitation.[22] Rather more like
Erasmus' figure of Folly than like Montaigne, Burton refers to him-

self sometimes sharply and frankly, sometimes implicitly or by denial, within the fiction he sets up. "I have laid myself open (I know it)," he says, "in this treatise, turn'd mine inside outward. . . ." (1.27) Reflection in mirrors is the infinite regression in the language of things, the "real" correlative of the intellectual construct of self-reference. Burton's self-references are in a dark glass, but they reflect him right enough, his face shadowed by the disease which he served.

On closer scrutiny, Burton's service to the disease turns out to be more unconventional than at first sight it appears. The title of the book, the vocabulary in which the descriptions were cast, are those of the humoral psychology. But Burton's extraordinary fragmenting of the categories of phenomena, together with the extensive generalization he makes of the melancholy phenomena he describes, his identification of cause, symptom, and cure, the very universalization of the disease into the whole condition of humanity: all this pulverizes the structural schemes of the psychology of humors, removes the medical and spiritual problems of melancholy into a far wider area of consideration and reference. In other words, the book turns out to be paradoxical about its very material: ostensibly a treatise well within the traditional psychology and medicine, it breaks through the boundaries of that tradition to universalize for common understanding and insight what had been a technical and restricted medical problem. In the simplest sense, the achievement of the book is paradoxical, the presentation of a proposition contrary to popular opinion. In a deeper sense, the fact of that commonplace paradox is in turn paradoxical in practice: the melancholiac's anatomy of melancholy determines melancholy to be other than it appeared. In Burton's dark mirror, melancholy saw herself as she really was, as quite different from what she had been thought, perhaps even quite different from what she had thought herself before her long scrutiny.

Erasmus' Folly refers not only to Erasmus, her creator, but always to herself: *The Praise of Folly* is a huge self-reference, Folly's shameless praise of herself, as she tells us, an exercise in *philautia,* or self-love. In moral theology, *philautia* is usually translated as pride, the root sin of all the rest. True to his custom, Burton supplied several words to translate the shades of meaning involved in the concept of *philautia:* "Philautia, or Self-love, Vainglory, Praise, Honour, Immoderate Applause, Pride, overmuch Joy, etc." (1. 292). Immediately following this section is Burton's longest digression, in many ways his most touching and personal essay, the "Digression of the Miseries of

Scholars" (1. 300ff.). By the end of the digression, Burton has slid into
using the first-person plural, identifying himself with all miserable,
all naturally and properly melancholy scholars. Even then, though,
he contradicts the implications in that use of "we," ultimately agreeing with his invoked impartial observer that the clergy, of whom he
is a member, make up "a rotten crowd, beggarly, uncouth, filthy, melancholy, miserable, despicable, and contemptible" (1. 330).

To degrade one's class is of course to degrade one's self, to deny
one's importance and significance. The paradox, a linguistic self-
denial or self-contradiction, may well ask for this kind of fictional
attitude toward one's self—as, for example, Folly herself so classically
demonstrates. The extreme acting-out of such self-denial in life is the
act of suicide, the all-too-common close to cases of melancholy. Burton
provides us with his brief *biathanatos*, or debate upon the lawfulness
of suicide (1. 435-39). As a divine and a physician, we might expect
him to condemn suicide outright and without equivocation; but once
more, he cheats our expectation by the sympathy, and even the hope
of divine pardon, which he extends to men led by desperation to risk
their salvation as well as their bodily health.

Actually, Burton's toleration of suicides is but another mark of his
general comprehension of melancholy and of all spiritual ills. He
never underestimated melancholy's miseries and tortures: but also, he
never underestimated the benefits melancholy may grant to her victims. Creation is deeply involved in melancholy—the muses are melancholy, as he wrote in his digression on scholarly miseries (1. 300).
The proposition is reversible: melancholy is the muses, too. Intensity
of human perception, creativity in all fields are in the gift of melancholy: or, melancholy favors the gifted. Melancholy distinguishes
men, one from another, and most of all those particularly qualified as
men. Melancholy, as "Albertus Durer" had depicted her, was an
angel fixed upon the point of her own contemplation, arrested by the
intensity and depth of her understanding.

Burton's book is, first and last, a paradox of the fundamental kind,
a praise of folly.[23] The melancholy man knows how to praise melancholy because of the perceptions his melancholy gives him, because it
is melancholy that drives a man to seek solitude and to contemplate
truth. Burton's vision was as arresting and complete as that of Dürer's
intellectual giantess: for him, melancholy itself became the organizing principle of the world. Primarily his book belongs in the tradition
of Nicholas of Cusa, who praised *docta ignorantia;* of Montaigne,

who provided a learned proof of universal ignorance and uncertainty; of Henry Cornelius Agrippa, who learnedly proved the inadequacies of all branches of learning; of Erasmus, who praised at once folly and, by indirection and darkly, a wisdom beyond that of men; of Sebastian Brandt, for whom the world was a ship full of fools. All these works were, in varying degrees, didactic essays aimed at human error and pride, at human *philautia;* all were paradoxical encomia, praising what most men were accustomed to think vile. Taking their texts from Ecclesiastes and Paul, all, even Brandt, reinterpreted ignorance, uncertainty, folly, and melancholy as the true wisdom and means to grace. The paradoxist denies dialectic, forbids a choice between one absolute and another; he insists upon *et,* upon the simultaneity of double and plural truth.

Like Montaigne, who calls doubt upon the method of his "Apologie" just as he is about to lunge home, like Folly who questions her whole oration, Burton is critical of his own discourse. Again and again he refers to Erasmus and his *Encomion;*[24] like Folly, Democritus junior warns the reader of his own unreliability:

> I have overshot myself, I have spoken foolishly, rashly, unadvisedly, absurdly, I have anatomized mine own folly. And now methinks upon a sudden I am awaked as it were out of a dream; I have had a raving fit, a phantastical fit, ranged up and down, in and out, I have insulted over most kind of men, abused some, offended others, wronged myself; and now being recovered, and perceiving mine error, cry with Orlando, *Solvite me,* pardon, *O boni,* that which is past, and I will make you amends in that which is to come; I promise you a more sober discourse in my following treatise.   (I. 122)

The following treatise may be more sober, but Democritus promises no more than sobriety. That treatise too may give offense, and if it does, it does:

> I hope there will no such cause of offense be given; if there be, *Nemo aliquid recognoscat, nos mentimur omnia.* I'll deny all (my last refuge), recant all, renounce all I have said, if any man except, and with as much facility excuse as he can accuse; but I presume of thy good favour, and gracious acceptance (gentle reader). Out of an assured hope and confidence thereof, I will begin.   (I. 123)

So begins the book proper, calling doubt on its own matter; but the books ends quoting Augustine, who turns doubt itself into opportunity for salvation:

> Do you wish to be freed from doubt? do you desire to escape uncertainty? Be penitent while of sound mind: by so doing I assert that you are safe, because you have devoted that time to penitence in which you might have been guilty of sin.
>
> (III. 432)

Those are the book's last words, in the tradition of paradox, an anticlimax: one is not sure that the end has been reached, one is tempted to turn the page for the climax proper to such a book. But this end is a proper ending, all the same, for the paradox does not conclude, does not close off for good. The book does not quite end, and yet it does end, realistically speaking, as any intimate discourse ends, in the expectation of continued life and continued discourse. Spiritually speaking, too, the book has come to its end, which is the assertion of belief in the life to come, in both the rest of mortal life and in a life in heaven; it ends in an assertion of trust, amidst a dangerous and mutable world, in the flexible, tolerant, comprehensive grace of God. Melancholy is simply the condition of mortality, or of living; like life itself, it is the only medium in which anyone can become a man or hope for a life after death. As in Cusanus', Montaigne's, and Erasmus' books, out of acknowledged folly grace has grown; melancholy proves to be a heavenly as well as an earthly muse.

NOTES

1. Robert Burton, *The Anatomy of Melancholy* (3 vols., London, Everyman's Library, 1948), 1. 11. All quotations from the *Anatomy* are from this edition, henceforth referred to as *AM*, with volume and page numbers.
2. Erwin Panofsky and Fritz Saxl, *Dürers Melencolia I, Studien der Bibliothek Warburg* (Leipzig, 1923), the great study of the etiology and iconology of the disease, must be consulted; the work has recently been published in an enlarged English translation: Raymond Klibansky, Erwin Panofsky, and Fritz Saxl, *Saturn and Melancholy* (London and New York, 1964). Lawrence Babb's two books, *The Elizabethan Malady* (Michigan State University Press, 1951), and *Sanity in Bedlam* (Michigan State University Press,

1959), deal with literary melancholy in English, and with Burton specifically.

3. As for example: idleness and solitariness are both causes and symptoms of melancholy (I. 245); sorrow is a cause (I. 259) and a symptom (I. 389); love a cause and a cure (III. 256); melancholy a cure for melancholy (II. 206). In a further study of the *AM*, I hope to develop this notion of interchangeability of cause, symptom, and cure.

4. The best discussion of Burton's book against its medical background is that of Naomi Loeb Lipman, "Robert Burton's *Anatomy of Melancholy* and its Relation to the Medical Book Tradition of the English Renaissance," Columbia University, unpublished master's essay, 1952, which is full of valuable material on the range of subject matter in conventional medical writing.

5. A sensible, ranging study of the many Renaissance "empiricisms" in the professions, trades, and religions is badly needed. Burton's association with one such tradition, that of religious casuistry, has been commented on before: see William R. Mueller, *The Anatomy of Robert Burton's England* (University of California Press, 1952), p. 20.

6. See F. P. Wilson, *Elizabethan and Jacobean* (Clarendon Press, 1945), pp. 46-48; John L. Lievsay, "Robert Burton's *De Consolatione*," *South Atlantic Quarterly*, LV (1956), p. 329; Northrup Frye, *Fables of Identity* (Harbinger, 1963), pp. 155-63.

7. Lipman, "Robert Burton's *Anatomy*," pp. 40-41, especially n. 7.

8. Lievsay, "Robert Burton's *De Consolatione*," notes the principal classical consolation, but fails to show its connection either with its Christian counterpart in the book, or with the book as a whole.

9. For Donne's Anniversary Poems, see above, Chapter 13.

10. Panofsky and Saxl, *Dürers Melencolia I*, passim.

11. See Lila Hermann Freedman, "Satiric Personae. A Study of the Point of View in Formal Verse Satire in the English Renaissance from Wyatt to Marston," unpublished doctoral dissertation, University of Wisconsin, 1955, pp. 326-30; Northrup Frye, *Anatomy of Criticism* (Princeton University Press, 1957), pp. 311-12.

12. See William R. Mueller, "Robert Burton's 'Satyricall Preface,'" *MLQ*, XV (1954), 28-35.

13. For Burton's utopianism, see J. Max Patrick, "Robert Burton's Utopianism," *PQ*, XXVI (1948), 345-58. As hardly needs pointing out by now, More's title, "Utopia," or nowhere, designates his book as a paradox, an assertion in its own terms self-contradictory or self-denying.

14. J. H. Hexter, *More's Utopia: The Biography of an Idea*; see Mueller, *The Anatomy of Robert Burton's England*, passim.

15. See Lipman, "Robert Burton's *Anatomy*," passim; Mueller, *The Anatomy of Robert Burton's England*, p. 9.

16. Burton did not by any means invent the anti-love treatise, a form Italian in origin, with (so far as I know) Battista Fregoso's *Anteros* (Milan, 1486), translated into French and published in 1581 by Thomas Sébillet, *Contramours. L'Antéros, oux contramour de Messire Baptiste Fulgose, iadis Duc de Gennes* (Paris, Martin le Jeune, 1581); the translation is dedicated to Pontus de Tyard.

17. *AM*, III. 311-24; though a discussion of Bruno's *Gli heroici furori* has not been included in this chapter, it properly should have been. Bruno's work is important for heroic suffering and heroic madness, and therefore belongs in a consideration of melancholy; furthermore, the metaphysical love of God prescribed in that treatise may have provided Burton with some of his ideas in the last section of the *Anatomy*.

18. See Panofsky and Saxl, passim.

19. See especially, *AM*, I. 80-81; II. 35, 48, 171, 173-75.

20. Marjorie Hope Nicolson, "Cosmic Voyages," *ELH*, VII (1940), 83-107; and *Voyages to the Moon* (New York, 1948), especially p. 225. For Burton's cosmology, see Robert L. Brown, "Robert Burton and the New Cosmology," *MLQ*, XIII (1952), 131-48.

21. Bergen Evans and George Mohr, M.D., *The Psychiatry of Robert Burton* (New York, 1944).

22. *AM*, I. 36; his birthplace: II. 68, 250; his school: II. 63; Oxford, Christ Church, and the Bodleian: I. 17, 417; II. 66, 91, 97, 214; his brothers: I. 36; II. 68; his mother: II. 251; his living at Segrave: II. 63-64; his patroness, II. 68.

23. Irene Samuel, "The Brood of Folly," *N&Q*, CCIII (1958), 430-31; Walter J. Kaiser, *Praisers of Folly*.

24. *AM*, I. 27, 28, 29, 39, 52, 59, 247, 310, 325, 343; II. 92, 126; III. 3.

AUSTIN WARREN

The Styles of Sir Thomas Browne

We should distinguish between *Style* and *a style*. Speaking norma-
tively and evaluatively, we praise the presence of Style; speaking de-
scriptively, we hold that every author has a style, and turn our attention to analyzing its specific character in this author or that. Yet the
two concepts are not completely alternative; for, if all authors have
a style, some of them—a minority—participate in Style.

Browne is one of those thus doubly endowed. He both has a style,
a markedly characteristic one, and he merits, according to almost
universal consent for at least a century and a half, high position
among English writers who have Style.

Those who are said to have Style—whom hereafter we may call
'stylists'—have, at least up till now, always been representatives of the
'grand style' (Johnson, Burke, and Gibbon) or of poetic prose (De
Quincey and Ruskin), or writers like Jeremy Taylor, Newman, and
the later Henry James, who, though perhaps inexactly called either
'grand' or 'poetic,' yet have an elegance and opulence in excess of
purely expressive needs. All of these, it would appear, belong to the
tradition devoted to the phonetic figures called by the ancients
schemes, to euphony and cadence—to ornament, to what the Renaissance called *copia* (richness, not in the sense of compactness but in
the sense of inexhaustible abundance), to development not by selec-

From *Connections,* pp. 11-23. Copyright by the University of Michigan Press
and reprinted with their permission.

tion but by expansion. Masters of the 'plain style,' like Swift, Cobbett, and Franklin, have never, it seems, been given the honorific title of *stylist*—nor, commonly, have such masters of the 'middle style' as Addison and Jane Austen.

This restriction suggests the concept of style which Croce, with much justification, rejected as one of applied ornament and which certainly suffers from the rigidity of its caste distinctions. We should, I think, abandon such use of the term 'style,' unrestricted by generic epithets like *grand* or *poetic,* as inacceptably normative.

Style is not something external to 'meaning'—even when the style is 'grand.' Rhetoric need not be 'mere' rhetoric. And it is patently old-fashioned and 'pseudo-classical' to identify style with the 'grand style.' But I think it possible to conceive and name modernly the shared character of the famous Stylists. They are those authors whose linguistic form is most expressive, most closely integrated; whose writing seems most spiritually signed and identifiable. Their distinction as writers is closely bound up with their vocabulary and syntax and rhythm; the 'meaning' of their works is, like the 'meaning' of poems, correspondingly difficult to translate or to summarize. Style, as W. K. Wimsatt finely defines it, is "the last and most detailed elaboration of meaning." Though this definition is applicable to any author, the 'stylist' is he who, at this stage or level, achieves his distinction: whose originality lies not in his big ideas (his major concepts, often philosophically derivative and 'eclectic') but in his discriminations and nuances, in his intellectual sensibility.

In speaking thus much of Style, I have said much which is relevant to style: the difference between the two may be ultimately quantitative—the degree of expressiveness.

Modern stylistics is a brave effort to produce an objective literary analysis. It defines style as the "expressive system of a work, of an author, or of a period," and then seeks to infer or induce from the linguistic traits of an author the spiritual (the psychological or philosophical) character which they 'express'—as some critics have sought to reconstruct the Baroque *Geist* from its tropes of catachresis, oxymoron, and paradox.

But has a writer only one style? Shall we not speak rather of the *styles* of Shakespeare, or even of Milton? It would be easier to characterize, clearly and sharply, the style of *Love's Labour's Lost* and the style of *The Tempest* than to characterize Shakespeare's style; yet it would seem to be an article of faith in the metaphysics of literature that there must be a perceptible and describable integrity to the life work of a great writer, perceptible in the continuity and development of his style.

A writer develops, or at any rate, changes, from style to style. His style may mature, then decay—perhaps into an exaggeration or even parody of itself.

Again, a writer may adjust his style to his audience, his theme, his occasion—in short, to the proprieties of his genre. There is the aesthetic principle of decorum, or *keeping*.

Classical antiquity and the Renaissance postulate a hierarchy of styles. Thus 'grand' style is for persons of grandeur to use for grand purposes on grand occasions; otherwise it becomes absurd, pathetic, or disgusting, becomes bombast and irrelevance.

There are, to be sure, persons who, on grounds of convenience, inflexibility, or principle adopt an invariable garb—the clerical black of the priest, the leather suit of George Fox, the sober and plain habit of Shakers and Mennonites, the archaic mode retained by a gentleman of the 'last age,' or the anticipation of some future mode. The uniform is a witness to a simple conception of integrity: it is keeping one's hat on in the presence of kings, or one's crown on while traveling in the subway or visiting the zoo.

Natural, if finally inadequate, is the analogy of style and dress. Some writers appear to have but one style, used upon all occasions; the later Johnson and the later Henry James are judged to be such. Johnson was accused of 'talking *Ramblers*'; the anecdotes of James report his directions to chauffeurs and addresses to children as never less than ripely James. In such cases a man devises or creates a style suited to express and sustain his characteristic or dominant attitude and interests, but then the style, like the institution a man has founded, acquires an existence of its own, and, at last, may make a man say what *it* intends, the tune prescribing the words.

Johnson and James were awkward and embarrassed in the world of things and gadgets; their masterly ease was taken in a verbalized world of qualities and relations. Both were capable of parodying their own styles, and the parody is a kind of ironic recognition that the language capable of serving a man's needs in his own country cannot be expected to serve *in partibus infidelium*.

Curiously, and indeed bafflingly, Browne, who might seem to belong with Johnson and James, with Coleridge and Father Hopkins, does not. Dr. Browne's letters addressed to his sons, and concerned with facts and practical life, are composed in a style scarcely recognizable as that of the ornate Sir Thomas. He writes to his son Edward, physician in London:

> Pray present my service to Sir John Hinton when you see him; 'tis a long time ago since I had the honor to know him beyond sea. Mr. Norton married Sir Edmund Bacon's daughter, who was a very good lady and died last summer, and I think he was a member of the last parliament. Perform your business with the best ease you can, yet giving everyone sufficient content. I believe my Lady O'Bryon is by this time in better health and safety; though hypochondriac and splenetic persons are not long from complaining, yet they may be good patients, and may be borne withall, especially if they be good-natured.

A cherisher of Browne's literary mysticism may well be disturbed upon first discovering his letters. Browne ought, it seems, to have been incapable of such discourse. Then, recalling the familiar paradox of the mystics, that they are often practical and even successful organizers and administrators, one feels, at least temporarily, reassured that his integrity may yet be inviolate.

It is at any event clear that Browne is not the writer of a single style, rich but rigid. Though our persistent idea of Browne is likely to be of a compulsive writer, not readily conscious of what he is moved to do, we must revise it to that of a writer knowing of modes and textures. In an essay on Browne, John Addington Symonds shrewdly suggests, "There is a sustained paradox in his thought which does not seem to belong to the man so much as to the artist."

Impressive critical analyses have been made on the basis of a single work. Croll's examples, in "The Baroque Style," are all drawn from the *Religio;* Saintsbury's study of Browne's prose rhythm is restricted to the fifth chapter of *Hydriotaphia.* Hostile criticism has often taken as typical the style of *Christian Morals,* written at the end of his life and unpublished till 1756—a work showing signs of decadence in its exaggeration and stiffening of Brunonian traits. In diction it is the most insistently Latinic; in sentence structure the most Senecan and aphoristic. The wit has lost resourcefulness and gaiety; its devices have become—what they were not in Browne's earlier work—predictable.

Browne has at least three styles—a low, a middle, and a high—the low represented by *Vulgar Errors,* the high by the *Garden of Cyrus,* the medium by *Religio* and (in decadent form) by *Christian Morals*.

The basis for differentiation is primarily one of generic decorum. Without doubt, Browne designed *Vulgar Errors* as a contribution to "philosophy" and the advancement of learning, a fulfillment of one of Bacon's proposals, not as a piece of literature. He composed with his Commonplace Books before him, attempting to transfer his notes into his folio after the manner of an academic dissertation, and to write a sober, straightforward, technical style.

The *Religio* is his masterpiece in the middle style. In a brilliant essay on "Seventeenth Century Prose," Francis Thompson called attention to the Silver Latin antecedent of the *stile coupé*. In contrast to the "Ciceronian Hooker," Browne is found "steeped in classic models more compact and pregnant than Cicero. Like his French contemporaries, he was influenced by the great Latin rhetoricians— Lucan, and Seneca, whose rivalry it was to put an idea into the fewest possible words." Thompson is most struck by Browne's "serried" style (the *stile coupé*). Yet at least as frequent in the *Religio* is the "loose or libertine style," associated with Pyrrhonism and Montaigne, which expresses the movement of ordering the mind in the process of thinking. Syntactically, this is a style in which the sentences, beginning with the main clause, proceed by annexation and juxtaposition of relative and adverbial clauses, participial or prepositional phrases— rhetoric and logic triumphing over grammar. The serried style and the loose style, in sensitive intermixture and proportion, compose Browne's middle manner.

Urn Burial and the *Garden of Cyrus,* both written in Browne's fifties and published as a single volume, share a generic character, even though we have no term for it. They are artistic compositions, prose poems, meditations. *Religio* is an intellectual autobiography, a 'familiar essay'; *Vulgar Errors,* by its author's intention, is a work of instruction and enlightenment, soberly expository. But the two prose poems, though they may at first appear to be on or about topics, are but speciously so. As one needs no experience of fishing to follow, with delight, Walton's *Angler,* so one need have no extrinsic interest in Browne's scholarly materials. Out of facts, antiquarian or scientific, he makes poetico-philosophical meditations.

It is these two essays which raise the question of prose rhythm. Some theorists exclude the study of rhythm from stylistics on the assumption that stylistics deal with the expressive, and that rhythm, whether in verse or prose, is rhetorical or decorative—not integral to the meaning of a literary work. In my judgment, however, prose rhythm belongs to stylistics; has expressive as well as formal character. It has a formal character generically expressive.

In terms of the two rival traditions of prose style, the Ciceronian (or oratorical) and the Senecan (or philosophical), the tropes or thought-figures, like metaphor and paradox, belong to the latter; the schemes, or sound figures, under which the *cursus*—like rhyme and alliteration—was classified, belong to the oratorical, or ornate, tradition.

The distinguished historian of style, Morris Croll, who divided prose masters into the orators and the essayists, named Browne as (along with Seneca, the presumed master of essayists), "fond of the cadences of oratory." The collects of the Anglican Prayer Book, so familiar to Browne, offer identifiable versions of the Latin *cursus* or cadence; and there are easily audible specimens of the *cursus* in Browne. The first pattern of the *planus,* a dactyl followed by a trochee, gives, in Latin, *potentiam suam;* in the Prayer Book, "help and defend us"; in Browne, "Christian religion," "noble believers." The frequent use of the *Tardus,* ending with a trisyllable, contributes much to the Latinate grandiosity of Browne and Gibbon; from *Urn Burial* come these cadences: "There were a happiness," "life of Methusaleh," "our last necessity," "princes and counselors," "restless inquietude." Still more impressive is the second pattern of *Tardus,* with its stresses on the third and seventh syllables, counted from the end of the cadence: "antiquates antiquities," "balsam of our memories," "angles of contingency," "raptures of futurity."

Cadences are frequent and a marked feature of style in *Hydriotaphia,* comparatively rare in *Religio,* and almost absent from *Vulgar Errors.* That is to say: they are inappropriate to expository writing, but, as Browne's discourse becomes more general and more poetic, as it becomes *oraison funèbre,* it becomes also cadential. Surely, then, there is an expressive character to the use of the phonetic device. It marks, and partly makes, the shift of tone.

Browne's celebrated diction is as calculated as the other features of his writing. Corroboratory evidence is his short, ninth tract, "Of Language," which includes six specimens of "Saxon," composed by Browne, to show what pre-Conquest English, or West Saxon, was like, together with word for word paraphrases into a modern English admitting no word of Latin or Romance origin.

His specimen of modern English keeping to "Saxon" roots does not exaggerate the contrast between English monosyllables and polysyllabic Latin, but offers "unworthy," "almighty," "manifold," "unrighteousness," and copious disyllables. And he characterizes English as a language Saxon in its system of relationships, or syntax, into which substantives and modifiers of other origin can readily be fitted. These observations are consistent with what has been generally observed— that though Browne's diction is Latin his sentence structure, unlike Milton's, rarely is.

Why did Browne not write in Latin? The question is engaging; the answer not obvious. In the preface to *Vulgar Errors* he rules out any notion that his choice was motivated by the desire to dispel those errors from the "vulgar"—from readers limited to the vernacular. He avowedly addressed those English gentlemen whose modern equivalents retain enough of their college Latin to profit, in some degree, from the left-hand page of the Loeb Library: his first readers must have known some Latin to understand his English, for the technicality of the subject, as he says in the same preface, "will sometimes carry us into expressions beyond mere English apprehensions. And indeed, if elegancy still proceedeth, and English pens maintain that stream we have of late observed to flow from many, we shall within few years be fain to learn Latin to understand English, and a work will prove of equal facility in either." He raises the fancy of a literary Esperanto equidistant from English and Latin.

To such a general amphibian as Browne, one can plausibly attribute the preference of a 'macaroni' language over a straight, and a personally compounded over an inherited. One might suppose the scientist responsible for the Anglo-Saxonism, and the mystic and artist for the Latinic; but the hypothesis does not work: both the scientist and the Christian Platonist, or Gnostic, in Browne, are linguistically on the same side. His one violence of attitude, his one antipathy, is against the masses—whom he commonly calls the "vulgar"; and the errors against which he inveighs are allegedly "vulgar errors," not the heresies of intellectuals. Latinity—whether scientific, theological, or literary—is the mark of the intellectual, of the citizen of the world, the 'good European,' and the inheritor of Greco-Roman culture, of Mediterranean civilization. Browne is an intellectual snob: one of the most charming of the kind, indeed, yet a natural Gnostic and initiate of the Hermetic Way.

The Anglo-Saxon constitutent of his style is more difficult to relate to a corresponding element in his thought and nature. We can say,

of course, that Sir Thomas is a loyal Englishman and communicant
of the Anglican Church—as well as a Christian Platonist; and we can
call attention to his study of Old English and his clear assumption
that the syntax and the relational words of English would remain
"Saxon" while the substantives and adjectives might, with profit, have
large augmentation from the "everlasting languages," as he calls Latin
and Greek. Or we can say that the "Saxon" element corresponds to
that practical side shown in letters to his son—the matter of fact, com-
mon-sense side which was obviously not wanting.

Now, reversing our direction, let us start from attitude and tone,
while directing our aim at correlative patterns of syntax and diction.
One *persona* of Browne is speculative, casuistical, and skeptical: delights in accumulating *catenae* of intellectual difficulties, baffling
questions, scruples, distinctions, and qualifications. This Browne, like
the corresponding Newman, expresses itself in long sentences proceeding by annexations and parentheses. There is another Browne
who is a Stoic and a pragmatist, aphoristic of utterance: "The heart
of man is the place devils dwell in," "The man without a navel yet
lives in me." "If thou hast not mercy for others, yet be not cruel unto
thyself."

Yet it cannot be neatly concluded that Browne identified the aphoristic with the Saxon. He writes, "'Tis too late to be ambitious";
"There is nothing strictly immortal but immortality"; and the most
relentlessly aphoristic work of Browne's is also the most Latinate, the
Christian Morals: "Move circumspectly, not meticulously; and rather
carefully sollicitous than anxiously sollicitudinous." There is no need
that the aphoristic sentence be a saying of the folk.

Browne has a general consciousness of the two linguistic lines he
is uniting. In the *Religio,* there is a constant use of doublets, Latin
and English, the international word and the regional: "a stair, or
manifest scale, of creatures." The Angels are certainly the "magisterial
and master-pieces of creation." In these examples, there is a general
syllabic and rhythmic equivalence; but in others the Latin correlate
gives also a climactic prolongation or cadence: "the fire and scintilla-
tion of that noble essence," God; the "warm gale and gentle ventila-
tion of this Spirit," "that name and compellation of 'Little flock.' . . ."

The doublets, here Latin and Saxon, turn, in *Christian Morals,* to
the coupling of abstract and concrete: "To well manage our Affections and wild Horses of Plato"—"the Areopagy and dark Tribunal of
your hearts."

As metaphorist, Browne has no such originality as Donne, Herbert, or Cleveland. He is almost completely lacking in visual imagery or other overt thrust into the writing of the world unsubdued to language. Of martyrs he wrote, he who was tolerant but not courageous, who was a man of culture, not of passion or action, "They may sit in the orchestra and noblest seats of Heaven, who have held up shaking hands in the fire and humanly contended." But I cannot claim the wonderful epithet, "shaking," as characteristic.

His characteristic figures are, at one extreme, sound patterns, and, at the other, logical or etymological figures. In view of his amphibian nature, oxymoron is unexpectedly rare; his Pascalian "man is a noble animal," a special case. This trope, with its coupling of adjective and noun in opposition, is probably too showy or sensational for Browne. More proper are metaphysical puns, uniting sound with sense: "The last and lasting part"; "Time, which antiquates antiquities"; "To strenuous minds, there is an inquietude in over-quietness, and no laboriousness in labor.

There is an aspect of Browne's diction to consider which is to consider also his total meaning: his use of epistemological terms—words and phrases showing his constant sense of the realms of discourse, the context within which a statement is being made.

There is, first of all, his naming of the great traditional divisions of knowledge—Divinity, Metaphysics, Philosophy (by which, of course, Browne means natural science), Logic, and Rhetoric (under which Poetics is subsumed). Then there is his witty use of technical terms from Grammar, Rhetoric, and Logic. "That Rhetorical sentence and Antimetathesis of Augustine. . . ." In God, there is no distinction of tenses. "Who . . . can speak of Eternity without a solecism?"

The main use of these terms is structural. Though in a world of intellectual unity, the trivium and the quadrivium would be hierarchic but also mutually consistent, there is still a latent tension of claims between these modes of contemplative activity; of this, Browne is steadily aware, though not upset or disturbed by it. "In Philosophy, where truth seems double faced, there is no man more paradoxical than myself; but in Divinity. . . ."

There is the contrast between what the nineteenth century called science and religion; but the persistent opposition in Browne is, rather, between logic and rhetoric. Logic is the discipline of reason; rhetoric, an appeal to the imagination. Many things in the *Religio*, says Browne, are "delivered Rhetorically"; many expressions are "merely Tropical"; and "there are many things to be taken in a soft and flexible sense, and not to be called unto the rigid test of Reason."

More generally, one feels the constant presence in Browne's writing of the grammar, or logic, of belief—the levels or degrees of assent. Here one is again reminded of Newman and such distinctions of his as, "Ten thousand difficulties do not make a single doubt."

A kind of *catena* or litany can be drawn from the *Religio*: "to speak more narrowly," "to speak strictly," "to speak properly"; "I am, I confess, naturally inclined to . . . ;" a heresy "I did never positively maintain . . . but have often wished had been consonant to Truth. . . ." "These opinions I have never maintained with pertinacity. . . ." "If we shall literally understand it. . . ." "If we shall strictly examine. . . ." "I can neither prove nor absolutely deny that. . . ." "I do believe that," "I wonder how," "It is a riddle to me now," "I could easily believe that," "Now if you demand my opinion, I confess. . . ."

And here is another litany of the degrees of assent. The archetypal pattern of this, an eminently characteristic kind of Brunonian sentence, is an indefinite number of noun or adverbial clauses beginning *what* or *whether* and terminated by a brief main clause in the form of a cadence. "But whether the ancient Germans, who burned their dead, held any such fear to pollute their deity of Hertha, or the earth, we have no authentic conjecture. . . ." "Or whether . . . it cannot pass without some question"—"Whether . . . may favorably be doubted," "But whether . . . were a query too sad to insist on."

These extraordinary sentences, in which a catalogue of dubieties terminates in a cadence of melancholy—these "notes and queries" set to music, give the chief basis for the charge against Browne, first made in his lifetime and most effectively—almost convincingly—put by Ziegler's *In Divided and Distinguished Worlds*. If one is to reconstruct the spirit of Browne from these sentences, of one type eminently characteristic of him, one might plausibly conclude that, if not an atheist, he was a skeptic. But taken in conjunction with other characteristic types of sentences—notably the aphorism—I read them as the thought-form of an inquiring, even a speculative, mind which delights to entertain conjectures and to ask unanswerable questions for the sake of the vistas they open.

Encyclopedic in his interests, he is something of a laboratory scientist, something of a skeptic (but after the mode to be hyphenated, as also in Pascal, with *fideist*)—even something of a mystic. A believer in a pluralist epistemology, in the concomitance of three or four modes of knowledge, he was unable—and aware that he was unable—to harmonize them all into an impregnable system; yet he was tranquilly confident of their ultimate concord.

"Or whether . . . it cannot pass without some question" is countered by "Life is a pure flame, and we live by an invisible Sun within us." *The Garden of Cyrus,* almost at the end, still has space for questions, Biblical and biological—"Why Joseph designed five changes of raiment unto Benjamin, and David took just five pebbles out of the brook against the Pagan champion?" and "Why amongst sea-stars nature chiefly delighted in five points?" But we end with resolution, with faith that all these questions have an answer, though we may not know it. "All things began in order; so shall they end, and so shall they begin again, according to the Ordainer of order and mystical mathematics of the City of Heaven."

FRANK L. HUNTLEY

✑

Sir Thomas Browne: The Relationship of
Urn Burial and *The Garden of Cyrus*

The discoveries which have hitherto been made in the
sciences are such as lie close to vulgar notions, scarcely
beneath the surface. In order to penetrate into inner
and further recesses of nature, it is necessary that both
notions and axioms be derived from things by a more
sure and guarded way. . . . [Bacon, *Novum Organum*,
I, xviii.]

Why did Browne publish together in 1658 two essays as different in
subject matter as the recent unearthing in Norfolk of a few crema-
torial remains and the ancient method of planting trees by fives in the
shape of the quincunx? And why in that order? Dr. Johnson[1] treated
the two essays quite separately, and so did Wilkin.[2] In 1896 Greenhill's annotation was published after his death, unfortunately with
no critical introduction.[3] Sir Edmund Gosse explained the concatena-
tion of these two treatises by typographical utility: "The *Urn Burial*
was too short to be published by itself, and therefore there was added
to it a treatise on which Browne, apparently at the same time, had
been working."[4] By 1931 the French scholar Leroy has surrendered:
"Après un silence de douze ans, Browne publia deux opuscules arbi-
trairement réunis."[5] Although Professor Cline has explained the para-

From *Studies in Philology*, LIII (1956), pp. 204-219. Reprinted by permission of *Studies in Philology* and Professor Huntley.

dox of *Hydriotaphia*,[6] only three or four critics at the most have attempted to insist that *Urn Burial* is not complete without *The Garden of Cyrus*.[7]

That they stand together[8] by design rather than by accident is suggested in the fact that their author gave each five chapters. For the caption under the engraving of urns that preceded *Hydriotaphia*, moreover, Browne chose from Propertius' imagined funeral speech of Cornelia a quotation which, in its use of the number *five*, contains the merest hint of the quincunx of the second essay: En sum, quod digitis quinque legatur, onus.[9] Also, Browne wrote the two epistles dedicatory at the same time, "May 1, 1658," the *fifth* month. In the dedication of the second essay to Nicholas Bacon of Gillingham, he not only states their main relationship but challenges his readers to discover the concinnity of the whole: "That we conjoin these Parts of different Subjects your Judgment will admit without impute of Incongruity; since the delightful World comes after Death, and Paradise succeeds the Grave."

From this sentence it would appear that the second essay is the more important, though few modern readers would agree. One-third longer than *Urn Burial*, it grew out of Browne's first and last study: botany, and biology, and "God's other manuscript"—nature. The design of *The Garden* is primary, leading up to the very mind of the Infinite Geometrician. The number of its chapters, five, illustrates the quincunx they describe, whereas *Urn Burial* has five chapters more by "sympathy" than by organic necessity. Dr. Johnson, a kindred spirit in many ways, was impressed by the research in *The Garden of Cyrus*, but said of *Urn Burial*: "It is scarcely to be imagined, how many particulars he has amassed together, in a treatise which seems to have been occasionally written; and for which, therefore, no materials could have been previously collected."[10] The funeral urns broke in upon the more serious enquiry: "We were hinted by the occasion," Browne apologized in his dedication, "not catched the opportunity to write of old things, or intrude upon the Antiquary. We are coldly drawn unto discourses of Antiquities, who have scarce time before us to comprehend new things or make out learned Novelties."

In spite of the fact that many readers today see little to choose between the two essays in their antiquarianism, Browne's "learned novelties" form the heart of *The Garden of Cyrus*, its long third chapter.[11] The central of five chapters, this is Browne's true "decussation," its order made clear from the title page, from the running titles at the

top of the pages, and from the introductory transitions at the beginnings of its chapters. This order is a Platonic progression from "artificial" (i.e., imitations of the quincunx in man-made objects), to "natural" (i.e., imitations of the quincunx in nature), to "mystical" (i.e.,
the archetype of the design in the Creator's intelligence).[12]

   This key to the second essay is best given in Browne's own words.
Not only is the very first allusion in *The Garden* (I, par. 1) to
Plato's *Timaeus,* but Browne is pleased to find his central image in
that dialogue of Plato;[13] in the next to the last paragraph of Chapter
IV of *The Garden of Cyrus,* he writes:

> Of this Figure *Plato* made choice to illustrate the motion of
> the soul, both of the world and man; while he delivereth that
> God divided the whole conjunction length-wise, according to
> the figure of the Greek X, and then turning it about reflected
> it into a circle; By the circle implying the uniform motion of
> the first Orb, and by the right lines, the planetical and various
> motions within it. And this also with application unto the soul
> of man, which hath a double aspect, one right, whereby it be-
> holdeth the body and objects without; another circular and
> reciprocal, whereby it beholdeth itself. The circle declaring the
> motion of the indivisible soul, simple, according to the divinity
> of its nature, and returning unto itself; the right lines respect-
> ing the motion pertaining unto sense, and vegetation, and the
> central decussation, the wondrous connexion of the several
> faculties conjointly in one substance. And so conjoyned the
> unity and duality of the soul, and made out the three sub-
> stances so much considered by him; That is, the indivisible or
> divine, the divisible or corporal, and that third, which was the
> *Systasis* or harmony of those two in the mystical decussation.
>   And if that were clearly made out which *Justin Martyr* took
> for granted, this figure hath had the honour to characterize and
> notifie our blessed Saviour, as he delivereth in that borrowed
> expression from *Plato: Decussavit eum in universo, . . .*[14]

   The purpose of this article is to propose that the unity of Browne's
twin discourses is to be found in this emblem or hieroglyph. If we do
what Plato and Browne tell us to do, that is make two strips of paper
into two circles, then place one circle within the other so that each
bisects the other (as the equator bisects the prime meridian at zero

and 180 degrees), and turn our figure with the "equator" line horizontal—we can easily perceive the three adjuncts. The circle is God, perfection, immortality; the horizontal that crosses the circle represents the corporal, divisible, death; where the two lines meet we perceive the "mystical" decussation, the cross, or quincunxial figure, i.e., the systasis of the main opposition between "death" and "life." The single object before us (which as I suggest represents the world) gives us successively two emblems: that of the Greek Θ, or *thanatos*, death, and that of the cross, or quincunx, four points equidistant on a circle and the fifth point in the exact center.[15] Browne, deeply read in Egyptian lore, the Cabbala, and Hermetic corpus, loved to exploit such emblems as these. At the end of *Urn Burial*, he tells us: "Circles and right lines limit and close all bodies, and the mortall right-lined circle must conclude and shut up all. There is no antidote against the Opium of time, which temporally considereth all things" (Ch. V, p. 178). Again, at the beginning of *The Garden of Cyrus*, the Egyptians ". . . expressed the process and motion of the spirit of the world, and the diffusion thereof upon the Celestial and Elementall nature; implyed by a circle and right-lined intersection" (Ch. I, p. 196).[16]

As in a Platonic dichotomy, then, these twin essays are two parts of a single whole; the two parts are opposed, yet conjoined; and there is a "rising" from the lower, or elemental, part, which is *Urn Burial*, to the "higher" or celestial part, which is *The Garden of Cyrus*, the "numerical character" of reality. More particularly, the two discourses are related in at least three ways: (1) in their subject matters, as two parts of a whole, yet eternally opposed; (2) in their epistemologies, as they pass from ignorance to knowledge; and (3) in their images, which take us in circles from darkness to light to darkness again, from womb to urn to new birth, from the "sleep" of death to drowsiness when the "quincunx of heaven runs low" and "the huntsmen are up in America."

I

That Browne intended us to read the two essays in this manner and in the order he gave them is seen most obviously in the deliberateness of their opposition in subject matter. One concerns death, the other life; one the body, the other the soul; one passions, the other reason; one accident, the other design; one substance, the other form. Together and only together they become a subject "not impertinent unto

our profession, whose study is life and death" (Dedic. of *Urn Burial*).
The first essay treats of time; the second, space. And together these
two concepts delineate the mind of God, in that time is an image of
his Eternity, whereas number and geometrical figures in space (as in
the *Timaeus*) are a key to his Unity.

The main subject of *Urn Burial* is momentary and local. It is a few
bones and fragments of cinder, and even these will rejoin the dust
in time. After an introduction of "this way of burial" or "the Roman
practise of burning," Browne lays the subject before us at the beginning of Chapter II:

> In a Field of old *Walsingham,* not many moneths past, were
> digged up between fourty and fifty Urnes, deposited in a dry
> and sandy soil, not a yard deep, not farre from one another:
> Not all strictly of one figure [as the quincunx is most strictly
> of one figure], but most answering these described: some con-
> taining two pounds of bones, distinguishable in skulls, ribs,
> jawes, thigh-bones, and extraneous substances, like peeces of
> small boxes, or combes handsomely wrought, handles of small
> brasse instruments, brazen nippers, and in one some kinde of
> Opale [II, 144].

From this point on, Browne takes us into the most distant corners of
antiquity in order to bring our minds back to this occasion and to
these bones. He does not know when *"these* Urnes" were deposited
(II, 148), but *"these* Urnes may challenge above thirteen hundred
years" (II, 149). A discourse on Roman cremation sharpens the
abruptness with which he returns us to "the contents of *these* Urnes"
(II, 150). "The *present* Urnes" are of varying capacities. He has seen
many red urns, but *"these"* are black, though some of *"these* Urnes"
seem to have been silvered over (III, 154). He could not be sure of
the coverings "among *these* Urnes" (III, 155), in spite of his belief
that *"These* pieces" within the urns seemed to be wood, and "our
little Iron pins" held well together (III, 157), although *"these* Os-
suaries" were well burnt (III, 158). The skulls of *"these* Urnes" (III,
163) were no less burnt than the other bones despite the humidity of
the brain. It is useless to look for urns in the ruins of a temple: *"these"*
(III, 163) were found in a field. Severe contemplators of *"these* lasting reliques" (III, 166) may well think of a resurrection, and yet
"these" were not the bones of persons struck with fire from heaven

(IV, 171). After such concentration upon the demonstrative adjective, no one can be surprised that the final chapter begins: "Now since *these* dead bones. . . ." For that is what *Urn Burial* is about. Its subject is small, temporal, local, *sui generis*, mutable, pathetic, nameless. The subject of *The Garden of Cyrus*, however, is the diametric and complementary opposite: it is large, universal, immutable, everlasting, and as far from being unidentifiable as experimental botany and the propositions of Euclid can give exact names to things.

Urn Burial emphasizes dryness and even sandy soil, while *The Garden* flourishes amid rivers. *Urn Burial* is distraught with the passions of human beings who see those who were once perfect in form now a handful of ash. *The Garden,* however, takes us from "crude pubescency unto perfection" (III, 216) in plants, and in the whole treatise from man's imperfect imitation of the quincunx in beds and fishnets to the perfect figure of "the ordainer of order and mystical Mathematicks of the City of Heaven" (V, 252). In the first essay the large bulk of a man has shrunken into a small measure weighing some two pounds (III, 162).[17] In the second essay a minute seed expands into an immense frond (III, 217), not only botanically but in Browne's very composition.

The moral grows out of this kind of opposition. *Urn Burial* preaches vanity; *The Garden of Cyrus,* its opposite: humility. When the poor mortals in the first essay mistakenly attempt to "participate" in God's eternity, they fail. In the sequel, where human work imitates nature and nature imitates God, there can be nothing but triumph. The first is Ecclesiastes, the second the Song of Solomon.

II

This inescapable nexus through contrast in subject matter is maintained, just below the surface, in the epistemology of the two treatises: in the mode of their knowledge, the kinds of questions each can raise and answer. In the *Religio Medici* Browne had heightened his paradox by setting side by side expressions of rationalistic doubt and assertions of intuitive certitude. Both kinds of statements exist in these twin works. But, as though to give the impression that he was a professional botanist and only an amateur antiquarian, Browne made *The Garden of Cyrus* a volume of exact knowledge and the first four chapters of *Urn Burial* a tissue of doubt. In the second and longer discourse he knows particulars through universals, whereas the best knowledge any one can attain of "these dead bones" is that of particulars through other particulars. Truth is at stake here. And Browne's two essays argue (as does *Vulgar Errors*) that it is better to seek truth in nature than in the authority of the past.

Urn Burial, therefore, presents no more pattern and regularity of knowing than does the subject matter known. The very lack of uniformity in customs of disposing of the dead, in monuments raised to the dead, and especially in the poor fragments of evidence before him purposefully contrasts with the procedures of "regularity" and "rule" and "order" in *The Garden of Cyrus*. The first chapter of *Urn Burial* should lay before us as a universal norm which Browne can evaluate these urns by: he finds only a wide variety of methods of disposing of the dead. Of the two main ways, however, the Roman way of cremation too quickly reduces the body. Sepulture in the ground, on the other hand, "God himself, that buried but one, was pleased to make choice of" (I, 138). Again, "Christians abhorred" cremation and preferred "a depositure" to an "absumption," "properly submitting unto the sentence of God, to return not unto ashes but unto dust again, conformable unto the practice of the Patriachs, the interrment of our Saviour, of *Peter, Paul,* and the ancient Martyrs" (I, 142). Even under subjection to Rome they refused cremation, thereby bringing about the prophecy "concerning the body of Christ, that it should not see corruption, or a bone should not be broken" (I, 143). Here, in the customs of mankind, is a norm—God's and nature's way of gentle return to the elements of which the body is made. But "these Urnes" do not represent that way, and consequently there is a lack of anything certain. For though, quite apart from religion, there are disadvantages to sepulture, at least it allows one to *know* more about the dead: it leaves a bony *form* from which an anatomist can reconstruct the appearance of the flesh (*Urn,* III, 165; *Garden,* II, 208).

Hence the questions asked in *Urn Burial* are mostly impossible to answer, like "What song the Sirens sang, or what name Achilles assumed when he hid himself among women?" Who were these people? What did their friends say? Was this opal burnt on the finger of the dead person's hand, or was it cast into the fire as a gesture of affectionate grief? Suffice it to know here that "it will consist with either custome" (III, 156). The Platonic tradition decrees that confession of ignorance alone can lead to knowledge, and before we can assent in the fifth chapter to the proposition that "nothing is strictly immortal but immortality" Browne must first overwhelm us with the necessity of guesswork. "We have no Authentick conjecture" (I, 141) of this; only a "wavering conjecture" (I, 144) of that; and "no obscure conjecture" (II, 145) of something else. One historian says this, another that (II, 151). For the cessation of urn burial in England "we can discern no assured period" (II, 152). The fact that these fragments are black and dull-sounding "begat some doubt" (III, 154) as to whether they were actually burned or merely oven-baked. Such an admission would be shattering in an essay purporting only to exhaust the human methods of disposing of the dead that the cultural anthropology of the day can furnish. The point is that the final court of appeal which science can give—experimental observation and reason —is absent from the first of these twin treatises.

At this stage of his treatment of knowledge all that Browne is absolutely sure of is that these bones were calcined and were dug up in Norfolk. His ambling through the labyrinths of antiquity accentuates this bleak fact. And though Sir John Evans quite rightly pointed out[18] that a glance at Browne's engraving of the urns shows their origin to be not Roman but Saxon and much later than Browne supposed, does not Browne actually convey that, *as far as he can tell*, they are Roman? The Romans cremated their dead. The Romans came as far north as East Anglia. These urns were discovered near Brancaster, not far from the seven Burnham villages (II, 145)—etymological straws which in the absence of real evidence he must grasp at to answer his question. The fact is: "A great obscurity herein, because no medall or Emperours Coyne enclosed, which might denote the date of their interments . . . (II, 148; cf. IV, 12th par., p. 171). After inclining for pages toward the Roman theory—"no obscure conjecture" (II, 148)—he suddenly confesses:

> Some men considering the contents of these Urnes, lasting peeces and toyes included in them, and the custom of burning with many other Nations, might somewhat doubt whether all Urnes found among us were properly Romane Reliques, or some not belonging unto our *British, Saxon,* or *Danish* Fore-fathers [II, 150].

Then he gives a detailed account of non-Roman cremations. His qualified conclusion is that ". . . the most assured account will fall upon the Romans, or Brittains *Romanized*" (II, 153). But, though these bones were unmixed, there can be no exact knowledge when

The ashes of *Domitian* were mingled with those of *Julia,* of *Achilles* with those of *Patroclus:* All Urnes contained not single ashes; Without confused burnings they affectionately compounded their bones; passionately endeavouring to continue their living Unions [III, 158].

By no accidental alliance are we introduced to the contrasting epistemology of *The Garden of Cyrus.* Browne dedicated it to the kinsman of Sir Francis Bacon, warning him not to expect "mathematical Truths" and generalities in nature without exemption. And yet, as Cyrus himself "brought the treasures of the field into rule and circumscription" (I, 193), so Browne employs the possibilities of exactitude which an advancement of learning can furnish him. The process of knowing is sure, and even the adumbrations lead toward useful, rather than vain, knowledge.[19] Whereas in Chapter 12 of the fourth book of *Vulgar Errors* Browne had shown how deluded mankind had been in making anything mystical of the number seven, here his "augmenting glasses" disclose the quinary arrangement in plants which he brings forward into the art of man and takes back into the mystery of intelligent creation. Where there is ignorance in *The Garden of Cyrus,* almost invariably it comes with the assumption that some day man will know when better instruments can lead him to the discovery: "He that would exactly discern the shape of a Bees mouth," he writes, "needs observing eyes, and good augmenting glasses" (III, 221). Other impossibilities of knowing are due not to the inadequacy of the evidence or of the instruments but only of time and the occasion. For instance, had not the examination of the famous 1652 whale been so necessarily swift amid its stench, "we might have perhaps discovered some handsome order in those Net-like seases and sockets, made like honey combs, containing that medicall matter" (III, 225).

In *Urn Burial* knowledge is soon exhausted, and the favorite verb is "conjecture" rather than "discern" or "discover." But in *The Garden of Cyrus* knowledge keeps opening like an ever-budding flower for further and further investigation in directions which Browne can merely suggest to a universal forum of enquiry. "The elegancy of this order" will be "discerned" by any one who "more nearly considereth" (I, 197). "Studious Observators," again, "may discover more analogies in the orderly book of nature, and cannot escape the Elegancy of her hand in other correspondencies" (III, 226). Browne's knowing as well as his knowledge is that of "well-contrived order" (I, 197). It partakes of "the generality and antiquity of this order" (I, 198), and the scientist is like the wise Solomon, "that eminent Botanologer and orderly disposer" (I, 199). The process of knowing in *The Garden of Cyrus* is one of "regular ordination" (I, 194), as strict as the figure itself.

As a sign of this opposition in epistemology, Browne's main questions in *Cyrus* lead us to first causes in a Mind as far behind nature as nature lies behind the human artificer. Again and again in the second discourse, a series of *why's*, even though they are not always answered, serves to enlarge the enquiry: "why the form of the germe doth not answer the figure of the enclosing pulp," "why" we rarely see two nebs in a single seed, "why" in the infinite reaches of plenitude trees give forth so many times their own weight in fruit (III, 218)—these cannot be answered yet, but they are laboratory notes for future investigation. It is only lack of room and not of science that prevents him from answering whole paragraphs of typical *why*-questions in *The Garden of Cyrus* (IV, 235).

Something has been made[20] of the irony of Browne's "single contribution to science" appearing in the "quaint" pages of *Urn Burial*: his discovery of *adipocere,* the fatty substance like "Castle soap" that clings to certain cadavers (III, 165). And yet in the contrasting and complementary epistemologies of these two essays, this is altogether appropriate. It is a single, accidental, unimportant discovery, like much of the antiquarian knowledge in *Urn Burial*. But knowledge in *The Garden of Cyrus* is only brought to end when "the Quincunx of Heaven runs low" in this peroration for "acuter enquirers":

> A large field is yet left unto sharper discerners to enlarge upon this order, to search out the *quaternios* and figured draughts of this nature, and moderating the study of names, and meer nomenclature of plants, to erect generalities, disclose unobserved proprieties, not only in the vegetable shop, but the whole volume of nature; affording delightful Truths, confirmable by sense and ocular Observation, which seems to me the surest path, to trace the Labyrinth of Truth [V, 251].

He meant what he said long before in *Religio Medici:* "Now one reason I tender so little Devotion unto Reliques, is, I think, the slender and doubtful respect I have always held unto Antiquities. For that indeed which I admire, is far before Antiquity, that is, Eternity; and that is, God Himself. . . ."[21]

III

Finally, as in all good prose, the stylistic traits of these two essays are inseparable from the philosophy they convey. All the rhetorical devices at Browne's command are employed to underscore this relationship of opposition and conjunction between *Urn Burial* and *The Garden of Cyrus*. The first essay in languid sentences plays upon death and the endings of things; the second nervously speaks of life, conjugal numbers, and seminal activity. The famous "organ peal" in the final chapter of *Urn Burial* adumbrates the "rising" into the "mystical considerations" of *The Garden of Cyrus*. Space will permit us here to examine only one aspect of style: that is, two basic groups of images whose subtle contrivance opposes and unites Browne's twin treatises. The first of these is the *womb-generation-birth-death* cluster. The other, practically inseparable from it, is a series of evocations of *darkness-light-depth-surface*. Both of these image groups convey the Christian and Neoplatonic thought in the form of a metaphor in mathematical proportion: our mortal birth is to our mortal life what our mortal death is to a new life beyond the grave. The womb is the truest microcosm and God's infinitude the only macrocosm, which we enter by dying.

The very shape of the urns discovered at Walsingham reminded Browne of the womb: ". . . the common form with necks was a proper figure, making our last bed like our first; nor much unlike the Urnes of our Nativity, while we lay in the nether part of the Earth, and inward vault of our Microcosme" (*Urn*, III, 154). This made Browne wonder at urns being placed in the earth with their mouths downward (II, 153). Some people even buried their dead in crouched positions, not "unlike our pendulous posture, in the doubtful state of the womb" (IV, 170). Thus, the image of the two unborn infants discussing their imminent expulsion from their narrow world of experience, which so often has been taken out of context as one of Browne's *jeux d'esprits*, becomes part of the construction in the whole of Browne's thought in these twin essays: "A Dialogue between two Infants in the womb concerning the state of this world, might handsomely illustrate our ignorance of the next, whereof methinks we yet discourse in Platoes denne, and are but *Embryon* Philosophers" (*Urn*, IV, 173).[22] The reference to Plato's cave, with the overtones of Bacon's idols, anticipates the Christian teleology of the second essay dedicated

to Nicholas Bacon of Gillingham. In the following sentence, for example, the *Urn Burial* and *The Garden of Cyrus* are stylistically
linked:

> And since death must be the *Lucina* of life, and even Pagans
> could doubt, whether thus to live, were to dye. Since our
> longest sunne sets at right declensions, and makes but winter
> arches, and therefore it cannot be long before we lie down in
> darknesse, and have our light in ashes. Since the brother of
> death daily haunts us with dying *memento's* and time that
> grows old in it selfe, bids us hope no long duration: Diu-
> turnity is a dream and folly of expectation. Darkness and light
> divide the course of time, . . . [*Urn*, V, 180].

Already we are drawn into the second image-cluster, that of shadow
and light to express ignorance and knowledge. In *Hydriotaphia* the
bones that have been invisible in their womb-like urns for three con-
quests are suddenly and shockingly exposed to the prying eyes of day.
In *The Garden of Cyrus,* the visible effects of man's ingenuity and
nature's law receive their life from the invisible seeds in the mind of
God. Those things which are God's lie deep, but the urns were only
a yard underground. Hence the images of depth, surface, light, and
dark in the very first sentence of *Urn Burial* anticipate *The Garden
of Cyrus:*

> In the deep discovery of the Subterranean world, a shallow part
> would satisfie some enquirers; who, if two or three yards were
> open about the surface, would not care to rake the bowels of
> *Potosi,* and regions towards the Centre. Nature hath furnished
> one part of the Earth, and man another. The treasures of time
> lie high, in Urnes, Coynes, and Monuments, scarce below the
> roots of some Vegetables. Time hath endlesse rarities, and
> shows of all varieties; which reveals old things in heaven,
> makes new discoveries in earth, and even earth itself a dis-
> covery. That great Antiquity *America* lay buried for a thousand
> years; and a large part of the earth is still in the Urne unto us.

Then from the fitful light of *Urn Burial* we are taken into a deeper
darkness where growth is getting ready for a steadier kind of light:

> But seeds themselves do lie in perpetual shades, either under
> the leaf, or shut up in coverings; and such as lye barest, have

their husks, skins, and pulps about them, wherein the nebbes
and generative particle lyeth moist and secured from the injury
of ayre and Sunne. Darknesse and light hold interchangeable do-
minions, and alternately rule the seminal state of things. Light
unto Pluto is darkness unto *Jupiter*. Legions of seminall *Ideas*
lye in their second Chaos and *Orcus* of *Hipocrates;* till putting
on the habits of their forms, they shew themselves upon the
stage of the world, and open dominion of *Jove*. They that
held the Stars of heaven were but rayes and flashing glimpses
of the Empyreall light, through holes and perforations of the
upper heaven, took of the natural shadows of stars, while according to better discovery the poor inhabitants of the Moone
have but a polary life, and must passe half their dayes in the
shadow of that Luminary [*Cyrus,* IV, 241].

"Meanwhile [from *Urn Burial*] *Epicurus* lyes deep in Dante's hell,
wherein we meet with Tombs enclosing souls which denied their
immortalities" (IV, 174).

Images of light and shade divide Browne's two essays and at the
same time draw them together. The colors of *Urn Burial* are the
blackness of the cinders and the white pieces of bone. *The Garden
of Cyrus* has all the "colours of mediocrity" (IV, 239), that is, the
colors between those two extremes. Mostly the *Garden* is green, but
as the roots penetrate deep they maintain their original white (IV,
240). When the brazen fragments emerge from the dark urns into
"the piercing atomes of ayre," they begin to "spot and betray their
green entrals" (*Urn,* III, 157). In *Urn Burial* there is darkness—"the
dark habitations of the dead" mentioned in *The Garden of Cyrus*
(IV, 232)—occasionally brightened with great funeral pyres or sometimes dimly lit with sepulchral lamps (but "No lamps . . . attended
these rurall Urnes"—III, 155). Bright fires analyze that which has
been created, whereas the sun synthesizes (*Urn,* III, 163). Hence fire
reduces us to the formlessness of our precreation, to the chaos of black
night before the great First Command. Thus, "Life is a *pure* flame,
and we live by an invisible Sun within us" (*Urn,* V, 183). The light
in the generally dark *Urn Burial* is balanced with the darkness in
the generally light *Garden of Cyrus;* in that darkness the seeds begin
to sprout according to God's preconceived idea for them. And most
plants bend and incline towards the sun (*Cyrus,* IV, 232) until
they die.

This is why the fundamental figure is of night and day in both treatises. *Urn Burial* is night: "The night of time far surpasseth the day," and "we lie down in darkness, and have our light in ashes" (*Urn,* V, 180). This, the "uncomfortable night of nothing" (V, 181), is the time of poppies and opium and sleep, the simulacrum of death, when "the iniquity of oblivion blindely scattereth her poppy" (V, 179). *The Garden of Cyrus* opens with "shooting rayes" and "luminaries"; it closes with the famous passage on night and sleep to bring Browne's whole thought to complete circle: "But who can be drowsie at that hour which freed us from everlasting sleepe? or have slumbering thoughts at that time, when sleep itself must end, and as some conjecture all shall wake again?" The urns are chaos; the quincunx, design. And "Night which Pagan Theology could make the daughter of Chaos, affords no advantage to the description of order" (*Cyrus,* V, 252). The shadow of *Urn Burial* and the sunlight of *Cyrus* unite to form this paradox:

> The greatest mystery of religion is expressed by adumbration, and in the noblest part of Jewish Types, we find the Cherubims shadowing the Mercy-seat: Life itself is but the shadow of death, and souls departed but the shadows of the living: All things fall under this name. The Sunne itself is but the dark *simulachrum* and light but the shadow of God" [*Cyrus,* IV, 242].

Christ looks through the lattice-work,[23] "that is, partly seen and unseen, according to the visible and invisible sides of his nature" (*Cyrus,* II, 202), who as the seed of God passed from the womb of Mary into death in order to achieve immortal life.

These images of the womb and the urn, of darkness and light, of depth, surface, height, are only a few of those in Browne's prose that fortify the oppositions, conjunctions, and risings in the subject matters and the processes of apprehending truth in *Urn Burial* and *The Garden of Cyrus.* Like the *Timaeus* itself, according to Proclus' commentary on it, the whole that Browne has given us combines the modes of Socrates and Pythagoras. For the two essays are Socratic in their good manners, ease of demonstration and ethics. They are Pythagorean in elevation, in a definition of reality by number, a suspending of all things from intelligibles, and in their symbolic, anagogic language. Browne conceived them as one, for their double dialectic carries us upward from mutability to deiformity.

Readers will continue to prefer *Urn Burial,* as they do Dante's *Inferno.* Although it is quite possible that Browne fell short in the latter and main half of his design, the first essay can be grasped by all of us at home in the "flux." The eternal mind, however, requires a flight which only a few are willing to make.

To grant this basic design is not to rob the discourses of their perennial delight. Browne apologizes for "the extraneous things": we accompany him through the surprising turns of funereal custom, and cry out with Coleridge's surprise, "Quincunxes in everything!" If from Plato or from his followers Browne inherited a sense of opposition as being a law of life, then the opposition between seriousness and playfulness must also be present in these works, as it is in *Religio Medici.* To be able to play in the face of eternity marks that type of mind which we meet in the puns of metaphysical poetry, in Hamlet's wry jokes on sex, in the fantastic horseplay of the Zen Buddhist on the verge of *satori,* and in T. S. Eliot's mingling of Martinis and chitchat with the prince of redemption. In *Religio Medici* Browne defined God (apart from Hermes Trismegistus' "circle whose center is everywhere and whose circumference is nowhere") as Wisdom and Eternity (*R. M.,* I, x). A religious view that conceives God alone as neverending must unmask all human pretensions to immortality without Him (*Urn Burial*); and one that defines God as all-wise, must insist that man's final knowledge of reality is to be found only in the mind of God as it is reflected in nature (*The Garden of Cyrus*).

NOTES

1. "The Life of Sir Thomas Browne," *Christian Morals.* London, 1756.
2. "Memoirs of Sir Thomas Browne," *Works. London,* 1835-6. Wilkin even reversed the order of the two essays.
3. *Sir Thomas Browne's Hydriotaphia and the Garden of Cyrus,* ed. W. A. Greenhill. London, 1896.
4. *Sir Thomas Browne,* English Men of Letters Series (London, 1905), p. 121.
5. *Le Chevalier Thomas Browne* (Paris, 1931), p. 31.
6. James M. Cline, *Hydriotaphia, Univ. of Calif. Pubs. in English,* VIII (1940), 73-100.
7. Cf. *The Works of Sir Thomas Browne,* ed. G. L. Keynes, IV (London, 1929), vii, where they are called "twin stars in the firmament of literature"; cf. William P. Dunn, *Sir Thomas Browne: A Study in Religious Philosophy* (Minneapolis, 1950), p. 176; cf. especially Margaret A. Heideman, "*Hydriotaphia* and *The Garden of Cyrus:*

A Paradox and a Cosmic Vision," *Univ. of Toronto Quarterly,* XIX
(1950), 235-46.

8. Browne kept the two essays together in the four editions published
during his life: two in 1658, one in 1659, and one in 1669.

9. *Propertius,* IV, xi 14. At the end of her oration (as in Ch. V of
Urn Burial) Cornelia enters the gates of glory, but at the beginning she bids her husband Paulus not to weep: "what death takes
it holds fast; I am now a handful of ashes," she says, "a small
burden that can be lifted with the five fingers of one hand."

10. Johnson (1756), p. xxi.

11. Hence Dr. Henry Powers' correspondence with Browne about the
1658 publication entailed, not a polite appreciation of the organ
tones of the first essay and the fantastic quaintness of the second,
but rather a serious conversation between two scientists on the re-
productive principle in plants (*Letters of Sir Thomas Browne,
Works,* ed. G. L. Keynes, VI [London, 1931], 288-95).

12. The first two chapters are the "artificial"; the central chapter, the
"natural"; and the final two chapters, the "mystical" considerations
of the quincunx.

13. *Timaeus,* 34c-39a.

14. Fortunately these two essays offer few textual problems. The definitive text is that of Keynes, which I have consulted with Greenhill's.
But for the sake of my readers I quote from the most readily available text now, that of the American "Everyman Library" (New
York: E. P. Dutton, 1951). References to the two treatises, by chapter and page in the 1951 "Everyman" edition, will hereafter be
incorporated to save a needless multiplication of footnotes.

15. Cf. *The Garden,* III, 220: "Now the number of five is remarkable in every Circle. . . ."

16. Cf. *The Garden,* III, 227: "Right lines and circles make out the
bulk of plants. . . ."

17. Cf. *The Miscellaneous Writings of Sir Thomas Browne,* ed. G. L.
Keynes, *Works,* V (London, 1931), 202.

18. *Hydriotaphia* (London, 1893).

19. Dr. Johnson was struck by the epistemological "vanity of human
wishes" in the *Urn Burial:* "Of the uselessness of all these en-
quiries, Browne seems not to have been ignorant; . . ." (1756 ed.,
p. xxi).

20. Most recently by J. S. Finch, *Sir Thomas Browne,* The Life of Science Series (New York, 1951), p. 182.

21. *Religio Medici,* Part I, par. xxviii; this edition, p. 33.

22. Cf. Keynes, ed., *Works,* V, 236.

23. Cf. Songs of Solomon ii. 9: ". . . he looketh forth at the windows,
shewing himself through the lattice."

LEONARD NATHANSON

Urn Burial: The Ethics of Mortality

Before we could analyze *Religio Medici* certain questions about genre
and intention had to be raised and at least provisionally answered.
Urn Burial and *The Garden of Cyrus* pose such questions in an even
more acute form. The relationship of the *Religio* to the personal essay,
autobiography, and various forms of religious writing allowed us to
employ, as an initial step, methods appropriate to those types. No such
literary starting points are available for the companion pieces, even
though they are Browne's most purely literary efforts. Response to
them is certainly more for themselves as distinct from anything they
are about than is the case with the *Religio*, which Browne's speculations about philosophic, religious, and scientific issues invest with the
interest of a document in intellectual history. Yet the companion
pieces are learned treatises; each is definitely about something extrinsic to itself or to the personality of the author; the perspective of the
Religio, on the other hand, is, as we saw, always the first person, however wide-ranging its subject matter.

Analysis and interpretation of *Urn Burial* and *The Garden of Cyrus* have proceeded from considerations such as their simultaneous
publication in the volume of 1658, their dedicatory epistles, and the
division of each into five chapters—these being taken as clues to
Browne's formal literary intention. The question much recent criti-

From *The Strategy of Truth*, pp. 177-202. Copyright 1967 by the University
of Chicago Press and reprinted with their permission.

cism has started from is the reason for the simultaneous publication and the significance of the order of the two prose works. It is now customary to assume that a profitable approach to the companion pieces must provide single access to both. Accordingly, explanations like that of Sir Edmund Gosse have been dismissed, that *The Garden of Cyrus* was added to *Urn Burial* because the one work was too short to be published by itself.[1]

Two recent studies exemplify the tendency to read these treatises as companion pieces in a strict sense by tracing their parallels and contrasts in materials, themes, and symbols. The older view of two fortuitously joined works has been replaced by an assumption of complementary relation which calls to mind *L'Allegro* and *Il Penseroso* and would seem to require analysis such as has long been afforded to Milton's companion poems. Indeed, Margaret A. Heideman implies a thematic relationship similar to the one existing between *L'Allegro* and *Il Penseroso,* what may be called a co-ectype of the same pattern.[2] Miss Heideman finds that *Urn Burial's* "dominant and unifying symbol . . . is that mystery of similitude which Browne finds in the burial urn and the human womb."[3] In *The Garden of Cyrus* there is the reiteration "in a variety of aspects under one dominant conception" of the image of light, and the entire work "is as inspired with quiet joy as the *Hydriotaphia* with penetrating sadness."[4]

Frank L. Huntley provides the most cogent reading of the companion pieces as the two parts of an encompassing vision.[5] A summary cannot do justice to the reasoning and elaboration of his thesis, but no serious student can now read these "twin essays" without Huntley's study in mind. Showing how the number five operates geometrically, structurally, and symbolically, he goes on to examine the relation of subject matter, design, and epistemology in the two prose pieces. Professor Huntley points out—not with absolute originality, but certainly with a very original force of definition—that *Urn Burial* is concerned with death, the body, passions, accident, and substance, while *The Garden of Cyrus* is concerned with life, the soul, reason, design, and form. The chaotically irregular materials of one are fraught with the uncertainties of human ignorance, while the Platonic-mathematical uniformity of the quincunx witnesses the certainty of divine order.

It is now an accepted premise that each of the companion pieces gains in fullness and precision of interpretation when placed beside the other. But the relationship, I would insist, is not equal. For there

are issues and resolutions in *Urn Burial* more profound than any
schematic paralleling with its sequel can reveal. To establish the true
stature of *Urn Burial* it is necessary to examine it primarily as an
independent creation rather than as a mutually important foil for *The
Garden of Cyrus*.[6] I plan, therefore, to treat each work individually.
A significant relationship between the two can nonetheless be exhibited—one in essential agreement with Professor Huntley's conclusions—though arrived at through a different route, and providing,
along with an individual view, the perspective of the larger context
of Browne's thought.

I

The disparity between the prosaic archaeological occasion of *Urn
Burial*—the unearthing of forty or fifty sepulchral urns—and the extraordinary imaginative height to which this work rises has always
seemed a little preternatural. To the nineteenth century, the fifth
chapter showed how Browne, fired with the nobility to which his subject was allied, could abandon his modest scholarly purpose and a
pedestrian scholarly style to seize upon the poetic possibilities of
mortality, transforming what had started out as an antiquary's report
into a work of undeniable, if baffling, greatness. This view of Browne
as artist in spite of himself has been exorcised by modern criticism.
The evidence that he intended *Urn Burial* to be a literary composition and made conscious use of the resources of art now appears overwhelming. This in no way diminishes the wonder at Browne's power
to show mundane things in a magical light; indeed, the wonder increases as the deliberateness of his design unfolds.

Browne was not "carried away" from an original antiquarian purpose, but exploited the discovery of the burial urns "In a Field of old
Walsingham, not many moneths past" to fulfill an intention that was
literary from the outset. The dedicatory epistle addressed to Thomas
Le Gros, a Norfolk neighbor of Browne's, may be adduced first to
support this contention. Both its style and substance indicate that the
larger (what we might call the "liberal" as opposed to the "specialist")
aspects of "the fate of [men's] bones" provided the motive and the
emphasis for his treatment. "We were hinted by the occasion, not
catched the opportunity to write of old things, or intrude upon the
Antiquary" (*Works,* I, 132). He disavows any predisposition to "discourses of Antiquities"; the discovery of the urns forced the occasion

upon him. That Browne almost certainly wrote the dedication after the treatise itself was completed scarcely matters. His interest in the urns and his treatment were clearly not in the line of routine scholarly investigation; this is implicit in the cadenced periods and elevated tone (anticipatory of the final chapter) of the prefatory dedication.

> 'Tis opportune to look back upon old times, and contemplate our Forefathers. Great examples grow thin, and to be fetched from the passed world. Simplicity flies away, and iniquity comes at long strides upon us. We have enough to do to make up our selves from present and passed times, and the whole stage of things scarce serveth for our instruction. A compleat peece of vertue must be made up from the *Centos* of all ages, as all the beauties of *Greece* could make but one handsome *Venus*. (*Works,* I, 132)

The sense of a great heritage that outweighs any present or future possibilities and is in danger of being swept away; the transitoriness of human glory, decaying to nothingness unless transferred to the plane of memory and imagination which alone partakes of permanence— these haunting themes of the concluding chapter are emphatically foreshadowed in this dedication, and, it is reasonable to assume, Browne wished to establish their tone as the proper perspective for reading *Urn Burial.*

Browne's organization provides further evidence that the urns and specifically archaeological questions they might raise did not provide the real focus of his interest. Instead of beginning with the circumstances of the discovery or other first-hand data, he devotes the first chapter to an historical survey of burial customs. But it is a survey with a difference. It is not the mass of encyclopedic information and heterogeneous curiosities we might expect from the author of *Vulgar Errors.* Nor, significantly, is it composed in the low style suited to factual material, but in the middle, meditative style of individual intellectual exploration. The first chapter has, moreover, a firm thematic shape that anticipates the two final chapters.

The expectations of ordinary discursive strategy may well lead us to read Chapter I simply as background which introduces and places in larger context the particular discovery to be detailed in Chapters II and III. However, Browne structures this historical account of burial customs so as to direct our attention to certain other questions. The

opening paragraphs picture the secrets of nature and history that lie
buried within the earth. "Time hath endlesse rarities, and shows of
all varieties; which reveals old things in heaven, makes new discoveries in earth, and even earth it self a discovery" (I, 135). Things as yet
unknown, "the treasures of time," like these long-buried bones, are
"still in the Urne unto us." The urn becomes symbolic of all that man
does not know, of all that he may discover ("That great Antiquity
America lay buried for thousands of years . . ."), and of much more
that he will never know, the inevitable incompleteness of human
knowledge.

In the fourth paragraph Browne turns to the announced subject of
his discourse by making a broad generalization about burial customs.

> Many have taken voluminous pains to determine the state of
> the soul upon disunion; but men have been most phantasticall
> in the singular contrivances of their corporall dissolution;
> whilest the sobrest Nations have rested in two wayes, of simple
> inhumation and burning. (I. 136)

The major interest in death is the destiny of the soul, but the chief
practical activity has necessarily been the disposal of the body. The
subsequent paragraphs of Chapter I develop as a comparative examination of inhumation and burning, with Browne ransacking history
and literature for examples obvious or recherché of these alternative
methods.

He begins in the manner of a formal disputation with a comparison
of the relative antiquity of the two. "Carnall interment or burying,
was of the elder date," its origins associated with the Hebrew Biblical
world; "the practice of Burning was also of great Antiquity," as shown
in Homer and other sources of our knowledge of the pagan world.
The introductory maneuver is the traditional oratorical one of comparing two opponents in relation to certain *topoi*. When Milton, as
a Cambridge student, argued "Whether Day or Night is the More
Excellent," he arranged this academic exercise about a comparison of
the antiquity, origins, and associations of each—all topics that a textbook of rhetoric like Aphthonius' would prescribe. But, of course,
Browne, while borrowing from this habit of discourse, does not really
follow it, since he is not trying to persuade his audience of the greater
praiseworthiness of burning or burying. His aim, rather, is to discern
and evaluate the bases on which different civilizations or sects have

opted for one practice or the other. What is significant about these practices are the assumptions upon which they are built and, indeed, that they stem from attitudes having a broader base. Browne seeks to define the rationales underlying the welter of differing customs. "Now as all customes were founded upon some bottome of Reason, so there wanted not grounds for this; according to severall apprehensions of the most rationall dissolution" (I, 137). The variations in burial customs are to be understood, then, as the product of varying conceptions of material nature, of the make-up of the human body, of fire and water, and of the way these interact.

> . . . Some being of the opinion of *Thales,* that water was the originall of all things, thought it most equall to submit unto the principle of putrefaction, and conclude in a moist relentment. Others conceived it most natural to end in fire, as due unto the master principle in the composition, according to the doctrine of *Heraclitus.* And therefore heaped up large piles, more actively to waft them toward that Element, whereby they also declined a visible degeneration into worms, and left a lasting parcell of their composition. (I, 137)

The natural philosophy and views on the continued existence of the soul have determined for each civilization the outcome planned and hoped for in the dissolution and preservation of human remains. And while "Some apprehended a purifying virtue in fire," others found the rationale for burning not in the attempt to withstand the effects of nature or to cooperate with them, but in the practical expedient of foiling predatory human action. "Others pretending no natural grounds, politickly declined the malice of enemies upon their buried bodies. Which consideration led Sylla unto this practise; who having thus served the body of *Marius,* could not but fear a retaliation upon his own . . ." (I, 137). The Chaldeans, "the great Idolaters of fire," avoided cremation because of religious considerations: they "abhorred the burning of their carcasses, as a pollution of that Deity." On the other hand, "The Ægyptians were afraid of fire, not as a Deity, but a devouring Element, mercilesly consuming their bodies, and leaving too little of them; and therefore by precious Embalments, depositure in dry earths, or handsome inclosure in glasses, contrived the notablest wayes of integrall conservation" (I, 138). Browne does not claim any special scientific authority for the opposition of Christians to burning, but simply gives the rationale for their practice, as he does for others, in terms of their religious beliefs and tradition.

> Christians abhorred this way of obsequies, and though they stickt not to give their bodies to be burnt in their lives, detested that mode after death; affecting rather a depositure than absumption, and properly submitting unto the sentence of God, to return not unto ashes but unto dust againe, conformable unto the practice of the Patriarchs, the interrment of our Saviour, of *Peter, Paul* and the ancient Martyrs. (I, 138)

The rich mass of detail in Chapter I is, we can see, presented so as to explore the alternatives of burial and burning in terms of their underlying assumptions and motives. Browne, of course, settles on no answer; instead, he raises questions which must be settled at a different level altogether. The choice between interment and cremation turns upon certain larger issues—the decay or disturbance of physical remains, the life of the soul, and the preservation of men's names from oblivion—about which the chapter is organized. But the whole matter is pointedly and deliberately left in abeyance, as Browne moves into the account of the urns themselves. The final paragraph slides off the main track into a curious byway: conjecture as to whether "some examples of sepulture," which lawyers would restrict to the "Law of Nations," may legitimately be seen "in Elephants, Cranes, the Sepulchrall Cells of Pismires and practice of Bees; which civill society carrieth out their dead, and hath exequies, if not interrments" (I, 140). With a reversed Montaignesque comparison of man to the animals, Browne concludes by raising a curious epistemological question: Do man's burial practices, dictated by posited law or custom, find counterparts in the instinctive observances of animals and therefore confirmation in natural law?

Browne opens Chapter II with the announcement that "The Solemnities, Ceremonies, Rites of their Cremation or enterrment, so solemnly delivered by Authours," surveyed in the preceding chapter, "we shall not disparage our Readers to repeat." He will treat "Only the last and lasting part in their Urns," the actual materials of the discovery at Walsingham (II, 140). As he turns to this data there is an appropriate descent from the middle style of meditative exploration to the low style, with its short, unadorned sentences, pure information that is often as flat as raw notes being directly transcribed.

He examines the urns and their contents, weighs the evidence as to their being Roman or British, attempts to date them by means of coins discovered nearby, speculates that Britons may have imitated the Roman custom of burning. All conjectures are kept within the bounds of his scholarly investigation; apparently tangential bits of information such as the discovery of some urns definitely not Roman in Norway and Denmark are tightly related to the problem at hand. Browne shows no inclination here for anything more than patient examination of the evidence itself and a few cautious hypotheses. There is no hint of opening up the larger aspects of the subject. Yet even this mass of data is presented with an unmistakable thematic direction. For through the entire chapter runs a strong sense of uncertainty, an almost resigned awareness of the contradictoriness of much of the evidence, and an emphasis upon the difficulty of drawing conclusions from physical and historical materials, however carefully studied. This chapter, like the first, closes with some puzzling bits of information, characteristically in the form of a problem. And Browne's final words raise a suggestive enigma: "why the *Anglesea* Urnes are placed with their mouths downward, remains yet undiscovered" (II, 147).

Chapter III, the longest of the five, continues to describe the urns and their contents, but moves freely from physical to speculative observations. The perspective shifts, now widening from "many fragments of sculs in these Urnes," suggesting perhaps "a mixture of bones," to historically recorded instances of "the Ashes of . . . nearest friends and kindred" in the same urn (III, 151); now narrowing from "the Iron Reliques . . . found all rusty and crumbling into peeces. . . . In the Monument of King Childerick" to the good state of preservation noted in "our little Iron pins which fastened the Ivory works" (III, 150). The significance of the urns is deepened by the reverberating names of the distant past, and great personages of ancient civilizations are brought into intimate relation with these very urns.

The universal truths Browne extracts from this data are expressed in the aphoristic manner of the curt Senecan style, with its tendency to reduce immediate observation and experience or accumulated learning to terse and memorable form, and also to make such inductions extend the range of moral insight to other particulars only hinted at. The following paragraph is composed almost entirely of a series of aphorisms, rhythmically harsh, syntactically disjunctive, but tightly articulated to the central idea, stated now as an essence distilled from the data under consideration, now as general truths shaped to the function of ethical suasion and reaching out indefinitely in human application.

> He that lay in a golden Urne eminently above the Earth, was not likely to finde the quiet of these bones. Many of these Urnes were broke by a vulgar discoverer in hope of inclosed treasure. The ashes of *Marcellus* were lost above ground, upon the like account. Where profit hath prompted, no age hath wanted such miners. For which the most barbarous Expilators found the most civill Rhetorick. Gold once out of the earth is no more due unto it; What was reasonably committed to the ground is reasonably resumed from it: Let Monuments and rich Fabricks, not Riches adorn mens ashes. The commerce of the living is not to be transferred unto the dead: It is no injustice to take that which none complains to lose, and no man is wronged where no man is possessor. (III, 152-53)

The peculiar success of this paragraph—its ever-widening scope of forward movement—depends upon Browne's use of the two discursive tendencies of the aphoristic style to add a larger pattern of balanced alternation to the obvious and characteristic syntactical feature of strongly marked balance and antithesis within the individual member.

Style, then, as well as statement, contributes to the larger human context of the subject; called forth in Chapter I, this context is reestablished with renewed force in Chapter III. The note of uncertainty dominating Chapter II is now sounded with greater poignance. The sizes, shapes, and colors of the urns, the jewels and relics found within, the clues bones give as to the sex, race, and physiognomy of the dead, the effects of fire on different parts of the body—all have as their steady accompaniment an overwhelming uncertainty that any burial practices can achieve their desired ends. That man has employed both reason and what some would call superstition with such ingenuity and precise care in order to preserve his remains and his name—and to no purpose—destroys all assurance about any customs of burial. The most extravagant memorials have failed to preserve men's names to posterity. "The variety of Monuments hath often obscured true graves: and *Cenotaphs* confounded Sepulchres. For beside their reall Tombs, many have founded honorary and empty Sepulchres" (III, 152). The attitude of uncertainty is now invested with a sadness absent from Chapter II, where the scholarly investigator was frustrated in his search for firm conclusions. As the perspective changes to that of human involvement, the uncertainty is no longer abstract or limited to the quest for a clear view of things; it acutely touches the author, his audience, and all the living and therefore makes detachment impossible.

The history of how supposedly rational customs were defeated again and again by nature, which follows its own laws, and by chance, which follows none, points relentlessly to the same lesson. To pursue mundane remembrance and corporal preservation is to chase down a labyrinth in which wherever one turns in the maze of custom one must at last confront that twice-hideous Minotaur—Death and Oblivion. It is not necessary to consider in very great detail the material gathered into the embodiment of this argument, since there is general agreement that the information and speculation woven through the first three chapters all underscore this inescapable conclusion: the universal failure of man's efforts at self-perpetuation. While this enables Browne to insinuate a rather facile Christian irony against "Ulysses in Hecuba [who] cared not how meanly he lived, so he might finde a noble Tomb after death" (III, 147), the fate of the remains of the dead raises certain stubborn questions about the Resurrection. For, on the one hand, "that power which subdueth all things unto it self, that can resume the scattered Atomes . . . [makes] it superfluous to expect a resurrection out of Reliques." But, on the other hand, "if according to learned conjecture, the bodies of men shall rise where their greatest Reliques remain, many are not like to erre in the Topography of their Resurrection, though their bones or bodies be after translated by Angels into the field of *Ezechiels* vision, or as some will order it, into the Valley of Judgement, or *Jehosaphat*" (III, 157).

II

In the role of antiquary Browne exposes the frailty of human custom to his better self, Browne the scientific student of nature. The lengthy survey of burial customs demonstrates how they succeed only in tracing a bewildering maze of custom among the impregnable walls of nature. As Browne deepens his meditation on the paradoxes of death, the irony implicit in the earlier chapters becomes the dominant strain of Chapter IV. The irrefutable evidence that time and

nature reduce all human effort to nothingness prepares for the conclusion asserted by Browne's best self in Chapter V, that only Christian faith can surmount the destruction that must finally overtake all
things. Against the vanity of "hope for Immortality, or any patent
from oblivion, in preservations below the Moon" (V, 168), there is
the assurance that "in the Metaphysicks of true belief" lies the promise of "infallible perpetuity" (V, 171, 170).

The elements composing the theme of *Urn Burial* thus correspond
to the three levels of Browne's Platonic epistemology. However, the
theory of knowledge defined in this study and shown to impart thematic direction to *Religio Medici* functions quite differently in *Urn
Burial*. The central issue of the earlier work is, we saw, the deter-
mination of truth: what, Browne asks, is the relative weight of the
various authorities and methods—scientific, philosophic, and religious
—man invokes in his quest for truth? *Urn Burial* too implies an
epistemology, but the problem of knowledge focuses here upon the
realm of value and is resolved in terms of it. As he points out the
absurd lengths to which men have gone to preserve their remains and
memory, Browne works closer and closer toward the values on which
they can be clear. The meditation on death finally brings out what is
significant in life.

The unfolding of these values is not limited to the anticipated declaration of Christian truth at the end, but is intrinsic to the development of the entire work. In the *Religio,* custom, nature, and Idea,
functioning as epistemological norms underlying certain controversial
questions, produce what we called an intellectual action. In *Urn
Burial,* this same triple scheme is implicit to the historical process
whereby Christian faith is discovered as the only assurance of immortality, and, therefore, as the best guide to what is valuable in mortal
life. As with the *Religio,* this theme is not presented primarily
through explicit argument. We can and do reduce Browne's theme
to the conclusion of an argument or the solution of a problem when
we summarize in one or another of the schematic approaches unavoid-
able for criticism. But the actual process for discovering how the futility of human effort can be transcended operates as an action within
the work and is experienced as such by the reader.

The account of burial customs and the accompanying meditation
on their uncertainties is an excursion into history. There is first the
examination of the objects of history, the books, monuments, and
relics which preserve the record of civilization. Then there is the con-

templation of history as a confirmation of the revealed truth about
human destiny, history as Augustine conceived of it. One study is
conjecture and hope for preservation in its realm futile; only the other
study produces assurance. "Study" here means not a disinterested
intellectual activity but the whole direction of life as a commitment
to what the contemplation of history teaches is most enduring. The
value toward which Browne has been moving is also a norm upon
which he operates all along. We are guided throughout toward a
vantagepoint from which an increasingly insistent irony is cast upon
man's attempts to deal with death from the limited perspective of
natural knowledge. In the penultimate paragraph of Chapter V, the
Christian norm that has functioned obliquely is stated as the true
ethic of mortality.

> Pious spirits who passed their dayes in raptures of futurity,
> made little more of this world than the world that was before
> it, while they lay obscure in the Chaos of pre-ordination, and
> night of their forebeings. And if any have been so happy as
> truly to understand Christian annihilation, extasis, exolution,
> liquefaction, transformation, the kisse of the Spouse, gustation
> of God, and ingression into the divine shadow, they have al-
> ready had an handsome anticipation of heaven; the glory of
> the world is surely over, and the earth in ashes unto them. (V,
> 170)

To those rare individuals living in and for purely spiritual truth, the
fact of death poses none of the problems that so disturb ordinary men.
But Browne, it must be stressed, does not offer this image of mystical
otherworldliness as a prescriptive guide for actual living. Despite the
specifically Christian lesson toward which the meditation on death
leads, he never relinquishes his very human interest in the world and
in the merely human, of which burial practices themselves are one
manifestation. This representation of "pious spirits" reawakens, rather,
an awareness of life under its eternal aspect. Though incapable of
being sustained as man's usual attitude, it provides the sense of a final
perspective.

   In terms of its epistemology, then, the "action" of man's long quest
through history for the "patent against oblivion," culminating in the
anagnorisis of Christian faith, may be defined as follows. Man frames
customs according to the best lights of his reason to avoid the conse-

quences of death for his name, deeds, glory, and mortal remnants, but finds his devices unavailing before nature. Only when he learns to place his hope for immortality in faith does he free himself from the paths of custom and soar beyond the labyrinth of human ignorance and uncertainty to a plane secure from the destructive action of nature and time. Christian faith solves one part of the problem and dismisses the other, for in its context physical remains become "indifferencies" to the glory of salvation. There is no need, therefore, to concern oneself too precisely with the disposal of the body so long as it is done with decency.

> Christians have handsomely glossed the deformity of death, by careful consideration of the body, and civil rites which take off brutall terminations. And though they conceived all reparable by a resurrection, cast not off all care of enterrment. For since the ashes of Sacrifices burnt upon the Altar of God, were carefully carried out by the Priests, and deposed in a clean field; since they acknowledged their bodies to be the lodging of Christ, and temples of the holy Ghost, they devolved not all upon the sufficiency of soul existence; and therefore with long services and full solemnities concluded their last Exequies, wherein to all distinctions the Greek devotion seems most pathetically ceremonious. (IV, 157-58)

Because what is most valuable in man can neither be saved by material preservation nor destroyed by neglect of that preservation, human endeavors at immortality are doubly futile. Browne avoids, however, the smugness of conventional piety which heaps scorn on the blindness of those not privileged to possess Christian truth. He appreciates the significance of insights like that of Socrates (traditionally afforded a special place among the ancients because of his doctrine of the immortality of the soul and his martyrdom for belief in one God) who "was content that his friends should bury his body, so they would not think they buried *Socrates,* and regarding only his immortal part, was indifferent to be burnt or buried" (IV, 158). Chapter IV draws to a close on a note of the great good fortune of Christians as opposed to the uncertainty of even the noblest pagans.

> But all or most apprehensions rested in Opinions of some future being, which ignorantly or coldly beleeved, begat those

perverted conceptions, Ceremonies, Sayings, which Christians
pity or laught at. Happy are they, which live not in that disadvantage of time, when men could say little for futurity, but
from reason. Whereby the noblest mindes fell often upon
doubtfull deaths, and melancholly Dissolutions; With these
hopes *Socrates* warmed his doubtfull spirits against that cold
potion, and *Cato* before he durst give the fatall stroak spent
part of the night in reading the immortality of *Plato,* thereby
confirming his wavering hand unto the animosity of that attempt. (IV, 163)

At the same time that "Christian invention hath chiefly driven at
Rites, which speak hopes of another life, and hints of a Resurrection" (IV, 158), Christians do in fact attend to the form of their
burial and the preservation of their names through monuments. Likewise, the pagan's misguided quest to preserve his soul-like part
through allegedly rational burial customs evidences man's continuous
recognition of something uniquely valuable in himself. Browne's
perspective in *Urn Burial* is manifold. He reaches the crown of his
art in offering the Christian solution to the fact of death for at least
two reasons other than his acknowledged potency of style: first, his
presentation of the theme as an action of discovery contributes the
pleasure and force of originality to what was, after all, the most familiar verity of the age; second, Browne's conception of the issue
reaches beyond the ethical commonplaces and the predictable assertions of faith upon which it necessarily rests.

The entire history of burial customs may be read as a prelude in
shadowy and groping types to the knowledge of wherein immortality
truly consists: "if the ancient Gentiles held not the immortality of
their better part, and some subsistence after death; in severall rites,
customes, actions and expressions, they contradicted their own opinions . . ." (IV, 158). However fruitless the unillumined efforts of
pagans to protect the treasure within man, their sense of that treasure's existence was in itself a great thing. Splendor of burial rites
admittedly stands at a double remove from the real way to perpetuity
through salvation, but it satisfies impulses too deep to be denied. This
explains why in practice Christians "though they conceived all repa-
rable by a resurrection, cast not off all care of enterrment"—explains
it better than the reason Browne offers explicitly here, that the body
is the temple of the soul. There is after all another traditional, though

not quite orthodox, Christian attitude which makes the body the prison-house of the soul.

These equivocal reverberations of a mind profoundly moved by the absolutes of faith but also much given to a very humane (as distinct from fideistic) skepticism may recall, too, that in the *Religio* Browne holds human traditions to be indifferent to salvation, abhors persecution and schism resulting from them, yet shows himself keenly sensitive to and dependent upon ceremony in his own religious life. The underlying principles of opposition in *Urn Burial* and in *Religio Medici* are very similar, as are the terms of their resolution. In one work Browne shows that only Christian faith, by illuminating the true nature of the soul and its salvation, can free man from a parochial and superstitious adherence to burial customs, because it makes the body an indifferency to salvation. Carnal remains become irrelevant to immortality rightly understood, just as in the *Religio* Browne shows that rigid Laudian prescription of religious customs and zealous Presbyterian proscription of them are irrelevant to the essentials of salvation and to the fabric of a true church. Browne thus solves the problem of *Urn Burial,* as he did that of the *Religio,* in the framework of the Platonic hierarchy of custom, nature, and Idea, the epistemological scale at one with the Christian system of value it helped to formulate. In the *Religio,* where this triad of knowledge served as a norm in the exploration of various intellectual issues, no final solutions were offered. In *Urn Burial,* Browne's process of inquiry continuously intimates and finally reaches its conclusion. But this ostensibly clear-cut answer is not without its elusive shading, the product of peculiarly human tensions that resist any perfect solution.

III

I have attempted to read *Urn Burial* as a mimetic essay and have sought its excellence in an action which illuminates the structure of values and ideas upon which it rests. In doing so I have parted from earlier criticism which tended to look almost exclusively to the final chapter, and there primarily to stylistic merit, for the distinction of the work, and also from the attention more recently paid to the work as a totality by Professor Huntley, who interprets *Urn Burial* by setting it beside *The Garden of Cyrus.* The relation between the companion pieces will, as I promised, be considered after each has been examined individually. And in the interest of an integral approach the separate status usually conferred upon Chapter V has thus far been ignored. However, no discussion hoping to account with some degree of completeness for the success of *Urn Burial* can neglect the special achievement of Chapter V. It must indeed be recognized that without the extrordinary impact of the final chapter there would be much less critical motive for locating the causes of unity in this work. At the same time, seeing *Urn Burial* as a coherent whole can enhance our appreciation of Chapter V by enabling us to read it as more than a great coda. Crowning and resolving what has already been solidly built, its effect is heightened by what it stands upon. It will doubtless continue to be read by many as a detachable part for its purple phrases and compelling rhythms, much as the *Liebestod,* say, is for many what makes Wagner's *Tristan* worth listening to. But as the transcendent effect of Isolde's love-death is fully experienced only in relation to the long anguish of Tristan and to the other scenes of the opera, so the final chapter of *Urn Burial* best conveys its effect when experienced as the climax of an integral whole.

Chapter V penetrates the profoundest reaches of time and mortality; it opens, however, by carrying the reader back to the particular remnants.

> Now since these dead bones have already outlasted the living ones of *Methuselah,* and in a yard under ground, and thin walls of clay, out-worn all the strong and specious buildings above it; and quietly rested under the drums and tramplings of three conquests; What Prince can promise such diuturnity unto his Reliques, or might not gladly say,
>
> > *Sic ego componi versus in ossa velim.*
>
> Time which antiquates Antiquities, and hath an art to make dust of all things, hath yet spared these *minor* Monuments. . . . (V, 164)

The juxtaposition of "these dead bones . . . in a yard under ground, and thin walls of clay" to "all the strong and specious buildings" establishes a trenchant contrast, since these frail relics of nature have proved more enduring than many imposing and pretentious works of man. (One cannot help but recall how Donne gets at a similar point in "The Canonization": "As well a well wrought urne becomes/The greatest ashes as halfe-acre tombes," where public grandiloquence is slighted for private lyric expression.) Finally, of course, neither the "dead bones" nor the "strong buildings" really triumph, since both are pathetically weak in the face of time and mortality. This contrast serves instead to arouse emotion as well as awareness in support of the values toward which Browne is working.

The graves of obscure, private individuals may be spared, allowing them at least a nameless perpetuity, while the grandiose monuments of the illustrious have suffered complete obliteration and their remains destruction. Indeed, great tombs may defeat the very end for which they were designed. "In vain we hope to be known by open and visible conservatories, when to be unknown was the means of their continuation and obscurity their protection" (V, 164).

In Chapter V, Browne encompasses the vanity of human wishes for perpetuation in a still larger irony: the destruction of Time itself. "Pagan vain-glories which thought the world might last for ever, had encouragement for ambition, and finding no *Atropos* unto the immortality of their Names, were never dampt with the necessity of oblivion" (V, 166). The Christian's knowledge that the world will not continue forever but has its appointed surcease renders the "Vain ashes . . . Emblemes of mortall vanities" (V, 165) even more vulnerable.[7] Realization that the world has run well past the half-way mark of its career accounts for a pervasive nostalgia; more of life and time lie completed in the past than remains to the future, "one face of *Janus* holds no proportion unto the other" (V, 166). Knowledge that the universe itself is dying tells man that those in whose memory he strives to live on will themselves be reduced to ashes—to ashes, like those in the urns, which serve finally as "Antidotes against pride, vainglory, and madding vices" (V, 165). The insistent question must shift then from how best to dispose of the dead and insure their memory to how to conduct life "in this setting part of time," when "'tis too late to be ambitious"; for "the great mutations of the world are acted" (V, 166).

To this question there can be no clear-cut answer or positive course of action, other than the stance of Christian Stoicism. Therefore, again and again Browne sounds thematic variations on the irony of personal ambition, the nothingness of human glory.

> There is no antidote against the *Opium* of time, which temporally considereth all things; Our Fathers finde their graves in our short memories, and sadly tell us how we may be buried in our Survivors. (V,166)

Oblivion is not to be hired: The greater part must be content to be as though they had not been, to be found in the Register of God, not in the record of man. Twenty seven Names make up the first story, and the recorded names ever since contain not one living Century. The number of the dead long exceedeth all that shall live. The night of time far surpasseth the day, and who knows when was the Æquinox? Every houre addes unto that current Arithmetique, which scarce stands one moment. And since death must be the *Lucina* of life, and even Pagans could doubt whether thus to live, were to dye. Since our longest Sunne sets at right descensions, and makes but winter arches, and therefore it cannot be long before we lie down in darknesse, and have our light in ashes. Since the brother of death daily haunts us with dying *memento's,* and time that grows old it self, bids us hope no long duration: Diuturnity is a dream and folly of expectation. (V, 167-68)

. . . Others rather than be lost in the uncomfortable night of nothing, were content to recede into the common being, and make one particle of the publick soul of all things, which was no more than to return into their unknown and divine Originall again. Ægyptian ingenuity was more unsatisfied, continuing their bodies in sweet consistences, to attend the return of their souls. But all was vanity, feeding the winde, and folly. The Ægyptian Mummies, which *Cambyses* or time hath spared, avarice now consumeth. Mummie is become Merchandise, *Miszraim* cures wounds, and *Pharaoh* is sold for balsoms. (V, 168)

Despite the sad subject the tone is not despondent, as it often seems when Donne, for example, considers these themes. Browne's meditation on mortality is suffused by a witty gravity and weighty exuberance that communicate his own positive, almost cheerful, poise. The generation of energy and pleasure out of such melancholy matter stamps this writing as baroque art in the fullest sense. And the vast temporal perspective of these passages serves as a catalyst to fuse ideas in their universal aspect with detail drawn from the cultural tradition. Because Browne apprehends history almost as a personal experience, the thought that grows out of it—and the process of thought growing

out of history is palpably conveyed—is strengthened by the depth of
feeling latent in universal ideas.

The masterful achievement of the high style in Chapter V depends
upon the confluence of many specifically technical resources of style.[8]
While extended treatment of Browne's technique as such is outside
the scope of this study, certain features relevant to our interest in the
thematic substance of Chapter V may be described apart from any
underlying theory.

As we have noted, the phrases of Browne that live on in the ear
and the mind bear a similarity to the aphorisms of Bacon, but are
more witty, even consciously playful, and establish ampler patterns
of rhythm than do Bacon's pointed counsels and *aperçus*. Elaborate
schemes of sound, rejected by the proponents of Senecanism as an
abuse of the Ciceronian oratorical style, are nevertheless present in
Browne's ardent meditative prose. So far from abandoning "words"
for "things" Browne exploits the independent associations words *qua*
words can awaken both through their frame of cultural reference and
their intrinsic sound values. The opening paragraph of Chapter V,
for example, quoted and considered above, reinforces its ironic thematic contrast by projecting that contrast at the level of diction. The
long resounding words, chiefly Latin, embody what the curt monosyllables, chiefly native, must oppose and undercut; and yet, despite
the irony directed against them, their beauty enhances and confirms
their value, at least imaginatively. This balancing of feeling, and attitude through diction is common, of course, to all artistically effective
prose, but Browne handles this oblique and delicate device with a
degree of formal deliberation usually reserved to poetry. And the concentrated use of devices even more dependent upon the play of sound,
such as the vibrant continuants *m* and *n*, justifies in stricter terms
the label of prose-poet so frequently applied to the Browne of Chapter V of *Urn Burial*.

On the other hand, Browne's prose-poem lacks sensuously vivid
imagery and also the profusion of figures and tropes recommended for
the high style by classical rhetoric. The figures one does find tend to
be great archetypal symbols ("Life is a pure flame, and we live by an
invisible Sun within us" [V, 169].) and derive from the ingrained
habits of thought and expression in centuries of philosophy, theology,
and divine poetry rather than from any teeming power of fresh invention. The texture of Browne's high style might be better accounted
for, then, by reference to patristic rhetoric than in terms of the classi-

cal-humanist tradition. Professor Huntley has shown how certain clusters of images take on symbolic value in relation to the complementary themes of *Urn Burial* and *The Garden of Cyrus*; in my estimate, he correctly does not stress these images as primary to the structure or effect of the companion pieces. Such patterns of mentioning are less the cause of unity in *Urn Burial*, still less the locus of poetic pleasure, than they are artistically consistent projections at the level of language of a thematic direction determined elsewhere. They are symptoms and confirmations of a unified inspiration and purpose in *Urn Burial* rather than the source of unity. Finally, in so far as style may be talked about as a detachable element, the unique density and power legions of readers have found in Browne's prose texture (as distinct from his music) are created primarily by a cultural contextualism in which characters, places, and events in the Bible, history, and ancient literature are invested with an emblematically rich, yet controlled, suggestiveness. Because this learned imagination is essential to the fabric of Browne's prose, the merely verbal contextualism of the New Criticism does not offer an adequate method of analysis or basis for appreciation.

What is perhaps most remarkable about Browne's sustained flight in the high style is that it is also a continuous tissue of irony. Nowhere is Browne more caught up in the mood of Christian Stoicism; yet nowhere does he summon up more fully the moving eloquence of the grand style. So far from corroding its object, the irony embellishes what the whole tenor of *Urn Burial* is exposing and rejecting. Consider this sentence, the concluding one of the paragraph beginning "There is nothing strictly immortall, but immortality," in which Browne makes his explicit declaration that "the sufficiency of Christian Immortality frustrates all earthly glory, and the quality of either state after death makes a folly of posthumous memory":

> But man is a Noble Animal, splendid in ashes, and pompous in the grave, solemnizing Nativities and Deaths with equall lustre, nor omitting Ceremonies of bravery, in the infamy of his nature. (V, 169)

The superb effect of this derives from the simultaneous elevation and undercutting of the same object. Its relation to the argument of this paragraph reveals no unconscious division of mind; nor is the praise simply an outflow of emotion, the irony purely a function of intellect.

The admiration and the irony are each the response of a full play of sensibility. While Browne knows and feels *sub specie aeternitatis* the absurdity of what men have sought in burial customs, he can also see and appreciate the nobility of their motive.

Browne's irony is positive and creative and thus compatible with sublimity. It is no sharp instrument for rationalizing emotion, for confining it to the bounds of logic and casting away whatever will not fit within those limits. From the standpoint of Christian truth, "Ceremonies of bravery" are fit targets for ironic reduction. But they are also man's assertion of the value of his affective and imaginative life, an assertion that may, as *Urn Burial* demonstrates, find little support in hard fact, but which Browne instinctively and incurably respects and to which he therefore pays the tribute of the grand style. While his norm for judgment is the absolute of Christian truth, he can still maintain a stance, a sympathy, and a sense of commitment that are wholly human in a way that Donne, for example, rarely can in his funeral sermons. This is why *Urn Burial* avoids the crabbed accent and monotony of the medieval *contemptus mundi*, almost invariably associated with the theme of mortality and "vanity, vanity, all is vanity." The melancholy appropriate to Browne's theme never descends to despair, but maintains a healthy balance. This inviolable poise in the fact of searchingly examined contraries—custom and nature, reason and faith, the human and the divine, the relative and the absolute—is an important element of continuity between *Religio Medici* and *Urn Burial*. Each work explores the intellectual and emotional certainties and ambiguities existing between such opposites; each discovers through its subject matter, theme, and action the value as well as the limits of the peculiarly human. It is hardly surprising, therefore, that Browne's profoundest ironies do not express themselves as harshly mocking thrusts at human pride, ignorance, and error by a detached and all-knowing observer. Maintaining instead a balance of detachment and affective involvement, Browne encourages us to be happy participants in the human condition.

NOTES

1. *Sir Thomas Browne* (London, 1905), p. 121.
2. "*Hydriotaphia* and *the Garden of Cyrus*: A Paradox and a Cosmic Vision," *University of Toronto Quarterly*, 19 (1950): 235-46.
3. *Ibid.*, pp. 235–36.

4. *Ibid.*, pp. 245 and 241.

5. Huntley's study originally appeared as "Sir Thomas Browne: The Relationship of *Urn Burial* and *The Garden of Cyrus,*" *Studies in Philology*, 53 (1956): 204–19; this article was revised in his book on Browne (Ann Arbor, 1962), chap. 13.

6. J. M. Cline offered the first significant demonstration of the unity of *Urn Burial*: "*Hydriotaphia*," *University of California Publications in English*, 8 (1940): 73–100. George Williamson's analysis, aimed at defining the "rational structure of its eloquence," unfortunately appeared after my own study was substantially completed and has not been taken into real account: "The Purple of *Urn Burial*," *Modern Philology*, 62 (1964): 110–17.

7. It should here be noted, however, that Browne did not lend literal credence to the traditional calculation of 6,000 years as the "determinable" duration of the world. See *Religio Medici*, I, 45, 46; *Vulgar Errors*, Bk. 6, chap. 1 (*Works*, II, 389–410).

8. Discussions of Browne's prose style outnumber any other studies. In the tradition of impressionistic appreciation, the essays on Browne in the following retain interest: Walter Pater, *Appreciations* (London, 1889); Sir Leslie Stephen, *Hours in a Library*, 4 vols. (London, 1904, II, 1–41; George Saintsbury, *A History of English Prose Rhythm* (London, 1912); Lytton Strachey, *Books and Characters* (New York, 1922); Basil Anderton, *Sketches from a Library Window* (Cambridge, 1922). More technical studies include: Norton R. Tempest, "Rhythm in the Prose of Sir Thomas Browne," *Review of English Studies*, 3 (1927): 308–18; Edward L. Parker, "The Cursus in Sir Thomas Browne," *PMLA*, 53 (1938): 1037–53; Dietrich Bischoff, *Sir Thomas Browne (1605–1682) als Stilkünstler* (Heidelberg, 1943); Michael F. Moloney, "Metre and *Cursus* in Sir Thomas Browne's Prose," *Journal of English and Germanic Philology*, 58 (1959): 60–67; William Whallon, "Hebraic Synonymy in Sir Thomas Browne," *E L H*, 28 (1961): 335–52. Morris Croll's articles are, of course, relevant and "The Baroque Style in Prose," cited above, bears specifically on Browne's use of the loose Senecan style in *Religio Medici*; see also George Williamson, *The Senecan Amble* (Chicago, 1951). More comprehensive treatments of Browne's thought in relation to his style include: F. P. Wilson, *Seventeenth Century Prose* (Berkeley, 1960), chap. 4, on *Urn Burial* and *The Garden of Cyrus;* the superlative essay by Austin Warren, "The Style of Sir Thomas Browne," *Kenyon Review*, 13 (1951): 674–87, which analyzes the various levels of style in Browne's major works as related to their subject and discursive purpose; Frank L. Huntley, *Sir Thomas Browne*, pp. 117-34, 218–22.

KESTER SVENDSEN

✝

Science and Structure in Milton's
Doctrine of Divorce

The scientific and pseudo-scientific lore in Milton's prose, like that in his poetry, is impressive for its bulk and its conventionality. What may at first seem recondite information is anticipated repeatedly in such vernacular encyclopedias and common handbooks as Bartholo-mew's *De Proprietatibus Rerum* (c. 1230), Stephen Batman's *Batman vppon Bartholome* (1582), Peter de la Primaudaye's *The French Academie* (1618), and John Swan's *Speculum Mundi* (1643). The range is tremendous: astronomy, astrology, herbal, animal, and lapi-dary lore, physiology, medical lore—all are drawn upon in their cus-tomary associations for illustration, argument, invective, and the other devices of controversial prose.[1] Medical and anatomical allusions recur with great frequency. Anyone writing about the ills of the body poli-tic, as Milton did, will make the expected comparisons with human disease; but the emphasis in *Of Reformation* and *Eikonoklastes* on fevers, flesh and skin diseases, insanity, and other ailments goes be-yond the casual to the insistent and the directive. In *Eikonoklastes* and the *Defences,* for example, the stress falls upon disease and dis-tortion rather than remedy: distemper, palsy, abortion, false preg-nancy, and miscarriage. In these Milton is arguing more against an opponent than for an idea, and the morbid associations are part of his strategy.

From *PMLA,* LXVII (1952), pp. 435-445. Reprinted by permission of the Modern Language Association of America.

In this paper I propose to illustate some of the ways in which materials from natural science work as a feature of Milton's deliberate technique of prose argument, and to suggest a structural function of the imagery in one tract, *The Doctrine and Discipline of Divorce*. I am concerned with figurative language in a logical prose argument, with scientific lore as a basis for imagery both as tropes and as mentioned particulars. Theodore Banks's recent book, *Milton's Imagery*, catalogues many of the prose metaphors, similes, and formal constructions; but the author, regrettably pursuing Caroline Spurgeon's example, uses these merely to reveal, as he thinks, Milton's personality and character; he does not consider their rhetorical function in Milton's art. I am dealing with the substance and function of figurative language in general, and not only with formally constructed tropes; for much of what I cite is conventionally regarded in the twentieth century as but half-formed metaphor. I am interested in the things to which Milton refers in making his argument, and in the cumulative metaphorical effect of these allusions. The richly figurative elements in *The Doctrine and Discipline of Divorce* have more than a simple appropriateness to the argument; they express the argument, and in effect are the argument. And they are predominantly scientific in substance.[2]

What Milton does in poetry he does in prose—less often and less powerfully, to be sure, but as he tested many of his ideas first in the prose, we are not surprised to find poetic construction there. He was aware of the differences in genres and of the demands of decorum, no man more so. But the logical faculty, as Rosemond Tuve has shown, does not exclude the imaginative; and we are surprised only, I believe, to discover how much of the poet is here. *Areopagitica* is a case in point. Many of the arguments there have little or no significance for us today, but the poetry in it speaks to us. Milton describes getting "the power within me to a passion"; this power expresses itself, to take the most famous single example, in such a statement as "who kills a Man kills a reasonable Creature, Gods Image; but hee who destroyes a good Booke, kills reason it selfe, kills the Image of God, as it were in the eye."[3] This figure is more recognizable in our own time as the way of poetry, not prose; but it is found everywhere in good prose of any period and especially in Milton's. The same intensity emerges in *The Doctrine and Discipline of Divorce*. It is not so sustained, perhaps, as in *Areopagitica*; but Milton's method is in many ways what we would call the poetic method. Even constructions like the epic simile are frequent in this poet's prose: the myth of truth in *Areopagitica,* of the huge wen in *Of Reformation,* and here, in addition to that of Custom and Error, the allegory of Eros and Anteros.

Milton indicates at the outset that he intends an imaginative or poetic as well as a formally logical method in his pamphlet and that he will draw upon natural knowledge for his material. He calls the opening discourse of Custom and Error an allegory, and later says that he will use in his argument "allegorick precepts of beneficence fetcht out of the closet of nature." He interprets allegorically the myth of Eros and Anteros, which he defends as "no meer amatorious novel," for "to be wise and skilful in these matters, men heretofore of greatest name in vertue, have esteemd it one of the highest arks that human contemplation circling upward, can make from the glassy Sea wheron she stands."[4] This comparison would fit into the very fabric of *Paradise Lost.*

Milton deals here with four kinds of law: canon law, civil law, divine law, and natural law. His case rests upon the identity of the law of God and the law of nature as opposed to mere canon law, and upon the recommendation of this twofold law to Parliament, the makers of civil law. Milton must show, as he says, that it is against nature and therefore against God's will that the temperamentally incompatible remain yoked in an artificial and unnatural union. In his familiarity with Selden's *De Jure Naturali,* to which he refers, he is in agreement with the traditional opinion of natural law as proceeding from God.[5] In *Christian Doctrine* he defines the unwritten law of God as that law of nature originally given Adam. To Milton, Christian liberty, as Arthur Barker has shown, was "'the liberty we have in Christ' [which] frees the Christian from all external authority."[6] A most interesting feature of this line of reasoning, too involved to be discussed here, is the Christian Milton's pagan emphasis upon sins against nature rather than sins against grace.

Milton's fundamental comparison, carried all through the tract, amounts to this: canon law impediments to divorce have created diseases in human society which result in a distortion of nature; Milton's proposals are remedies drawn from nature and natural law. Canon law reasoning is described as indigestion, disorder of the humours, sores, blots, megrims, and the like. The law of nature is manifested in salves, medicines, and soothing treatments. There is a steady expressed or implied comparison between truth as health and error as disease, with canon law a pollution, an unhelpful remedy, a producer of still further disease by force exerted against the bent of nature. Something like an inner framework to the pamphlet is evident in the frequent imagery of nature as the creative power of the universe and as the created universe itself. The very words "nature," "natural," and "unnatural" recur in twenty-seven of the thirty-six chapters, some eighty-nine times in all. A measure of this recurrence might be expected, but if Empson were searching for the significant words here, he would find them to be "law" and "nature."[7] Milton refers, for example, to "blameles nature," the "unreducible *antipathies* of nature," the "radical and innocent affections of nature," and Christ's "fundamental and superior laws of nature and charity." "What is against nature," he concludes, 'is against Law, if soundest Philosophy abuse us not."[8] Astronomy, anatomy, and medical lore are combined into an explicit statement of the blindness of canon law and its adherents, the diseased condition of enforced marriage, and the cures and remedies consistent with the axiom expressed here and later[9] that God and nature bid the same.

The instability of categories based on vehicle or substance, such as medical or astronomical images, is well known and perhaps best demonstrated by Rosemond Tuve, who justly argues for the study of function.[10] But one will find a general agreement in content among the images discussed here: they all relate, both tropes and mentioned particulars, in some fashion to natural philosophy, to what was regarded by Milton as natural science. Since my intention is not to classify images but to show how natural science serves as a resource for imagery and to show how that imagery functions in the tract, the following groups are only a convenience for illustrating the scientific or pseudo-scientific origins. The astronomical and the medical-anatomical images are central; the others, through their function, partake of the content of these two. The interrelations of function are part of the point I am making. One group, roughly astronomical in content, with emphasis on the clear light of truth as opposed to the darkness of error and sin, relates in function to a group which concerns impediments to true sight: mists, blots, robes and clothing, obscurities. Taken together, they communicate the want of insight by the defenders of canon law. A third group, an imagery of flowing water or light and of their stoppage or the restraint of nature in any way, connects the previously mentioned groups with the last, the figures from anatomy and medicine, of disease and remedy, the dislocation or distortion of nature to which all these other images relate and refer. There are of course figures and particulars which do not fall into these groups or relate directly to natural science, but these are few in comparison. Most of the images function to amplify either the evil of the situation or the naturalness of the cure.

First astronomy. Milton may have been out of date in offering to devise "*Prutenick* tables" to mend the astronomy of the expositors who alleged "foule *Hypotheses* to save the *Phænomenon* of our Saviours answer to the Pharises" (p. 389); but the astronomical content of the allusion and its function are unmistakable.[11] So with his reference to the truth which is as impossible to soil by their touch as is a sunbeam (p. 370).[12] Marriage should not exist only "to remedy a sublunary and bestial burning" (416); and it is a violence against the "reverend secret of nature . . . to force a mixture of minds that cannot unite, and to sowe the furrow of mans nativity with seed of two incoherent and uncombining dispositions" (417). He refuses to attempt an astrological explanation of incompatibility: "But what might be the cause, whether each ones alotted *Genius* or proper Starre, or whether the supernall influence of Schemes and angular aspects or this elementall *Crasis* here below, whether all these jointly or singly meeting friendly, or unfriendly in either party, I dare not, with the men I am likest to clash, appear so much a Philosopher as to conjecture" (418). Eros, "soaring up into the high Towr of his *Apogæum,* above the shadow of the earth . . . darts out the direct rayes of his then most piercing eyesight," and later "repairs the almost faded ammunition of his Deity by the reflection of a coequal & *homogeneal* fire" (401). In arguing that sin and true law are *"diagonial contraries,* as much allowing one another, as day and night together in one hemiphere," Milton says, "if it be possible, that sin with his darknes may come to composition, it cannot be without a foul eclipse, and twylight to the law, whose brightnesse ought to surpasse the noon" (436).[13]

The blind side of Eros on earth and his piercing eyesight in his own sphere, "the clear light of nature in us, & of nations" (505), and the "Pharisaick mists rais'd between the law and the peoples eyes" (449) similarly exemplify the systematic metaphorizing of appearance and reality. The "thick-sighted" (468) cannot perceive the evils of enforced marriage because of a "blindnes in Religion" (372). The obstacles to true vision are "swoln visage" (367), "blots and obscurities" (368), veils (395), blurs, and stains (377), "impostures, and trim disguises" (401) as well as sottish blindness (449). A law which prohibits divorce and thus encourages sin is "no Law but sin muffl'd in the robe of Law, or Law disguis'd in the loose garment of sin" (389). The link of function between this sort of comparison and the medical-anatomical appears in Milton's mention of "the troubles and distempers which for want of this insight have bin so oft in Kingdomes, in States, and Families" (385).[14]

The free movement of light and truth and the dangers in blocking or stifling natural motions are expressed variously. Milton writes of the mind "from whence must flow the acts of peace and love" (393), of the tainted fountains of doctrine (505), of the "promiscuous draining of a carnall rage" (510), of the "issues of love and hatred distinctly flowing through the whole masse of created things" (418). Canon law, he says, places "more of mariage in the channell of concupiscence, then in the pure influence of peace and love, whereof the souls lawfull contentment is the onely fountain" (394).[15] In testifying that what is against the law of nature is against the law of God, and that lawful liberty ought not to be restrained, he draws this figure: "As by Physick we learn in menstruous bodies, where natures current hath been stopt, that the suffocation and upward forcing of some lower part, affects the head and inward sense with dotage and idle fancies" (426).[16] Canon lawyers argue "as if the womb of teeming Truth were to be clos'd up, if shee presume to bring forth ought, that sorts not with their unchew'd notions and suppositions" (368). Moses "commands us to force nothing against sympathy or naturall order" (419). The "adamantine chains" (425) which bind the unhappily married, which "clogge a rationall creature to his endlesse sorrow" (459), create not two souls in one flesh but "two carkasses chain'd unnaturally together . . . a living soule bound to a dead corps" (478).[17]

This restrictive force appears in references to the remora (410),[18] to fetters and bonds, and perhaps most vividly in a daring, epic-like, deliberately mixed figure near the end of the tract:

> To couple hatred therefore though wedlock try all her golden links, and borrow to her aid all the iron manacles and fetters of Law, it does but seek to twist a rope of sand, which was a task, they say, that pos'd the divell. And that sluggish feind in hell *Ocnus,* whom the Poems tell of, brought his idle cordage to as good effect, which never serv'd to bind with, but to feed the Asse that stood at his elbow. And that the restrictive Law against divorce, attains as little to bind any thing truly in a dis-

joynted mariage, or to keep it bound, but servs only to feed the ignorance, and definitive impertinence of a doltish Canon, were no absurd allusion.[19] (p. 500)

One more such image of restraint and stoppage will provide a transition to the disease-and-remedy clusters which dominate the tract. Near the end of his argument, Milton writes: "Let us not be thus over-curious to strain at *atoms,* and yet to stop every vent and cranny of permissive liberty; let nature wanting those needfull pores, and breathing places which God hath not debar'd our weaknesse, either suddenly break out into some wide rupture of open vice, and frantick heresie, or else inwardly fester with repining and blasphemous thoughts, under an unreasonable and fruitless rigor of unwarranted law" (509-510).

The imagery from anatomical and medical lore is the most extensive and most directly operative in the tract. Milton's deliberate recourse to this material is demonstrated in his declaration that "that which is true in Physick, wil be found as true in policie: that as of bad pulses those that beat most in order, are much worse then those that keep the most inordinat circuit, so of popular vices those that may be committed legally, will be more pernicious then those that are left to their own cours at perill" (472). References to disease, contagion, megrim, distempers, fevers, ulcers, and ruptures, like those to remedy, surgery, corrosives, salves, cures, and medicines, occur repeatedly. The remedies of nature and reason oppose the diseases of bad marriage and canon law. The pattern is set early when Milton says Custom's "sudden book of implicit knowledge . . . of bad nourishment in the concoction, as it was heedlesse in the devouring, puffs up unhealthily, a certaine big face of pretended learning, mistaken among credulous men, for the wholsome habit of soundnesse and good constitution; but is indeed no other, then that swoln visage of counterfeit knowledge and literature, which not onely in private marrs our education, but also in publick is the common climer into every chaire" (367-368). Medical metaphor enforces the point of a later question: "Did God for this come down and cover the Mount of *Sinai* with his glory . . . to patch up an ulcerous and rott'n commonwealth . . . [and] to wash the skin and garments for every unclean touch" (437)? The origin of truth is described as human birth: "Though this ill hap wait on her nativity, that shee never comes into the world, but like a Bastard, to the ignominy of him that brought her forth: till

Time the Midwife rather than the mother of Truth, have washt and salted the Infant, declar'd her legitimat, and Churcht the father of his young *Minerva,* from the needlesse causes of his purgation" (370).[20] The continuing equation of moral truth with a kind of natural-philosophical or scientific truth as found in medical lore emerges also in the passage on diseased thought: "And what though others out of a waterish and queasy conscience because ever crasy and never yet sound, will rail and fancy to themselves, that injury and licence is the best of this Book? Did not the distemper of their own stomacks affect them with a dizzy megrim, they would soon tie up their tongues . . . till they get a little cordiall sobriety to settle their qualming zeale" (370-371). He believes that his book "undertakes the cure of an inveterate disease crept into the best part of humane societie: and to doe this with no smarting corrosive, but with a smooth and pleasing lesson, which receiv'd hath the vertue to soften and dispell rooted and knotty sorrowes" (386).[21] And finally, in another of those mixed, prose-epic-similes noted earlier, Christ is distinguished from the canonists with their "unhelpful Surgery." He is

> like a wise Physician, administering one excesse against another to reduce us to a perfect mean . . . So heer he may be justly thought to have giv'n this rigid sentence against divorce, not to cut off all remedy from a good man who finds himself consuming away in a disconsolate and uninjoy'd matrimony, but to lay a bridle upon the bold abuses of those over-weening *Rabbies;* which he could not more effectually doe, then by a countersway of restraint curbing their wild exorbitance almost into the other extreme; as when we bow things the contrary way, to make them come to their naturall straitnesse.[22] (pp. 429-430)

Later the contraries are posed again: "this obdurat disease cannot bee conceiv'd how it was the more amended by this unclean remedy, is the most deadly and Scorpion like gift that the enemy of mankind could have given to any miserable sinner" (448).[23]

These many references to natural science constitute something like a dominant framework through which the prose argument is made effective. The logical emphasis on natural law against canon law is produced by a structure of scientific and semi-scientific metaphors and particulars, "allegorick precepts of beneficence fetcht out of the closet of nature." Milton the theocentric humanist was well aware of the

limitations of natural knowledge; but he was no less aware of its moral
implications than were compilers like Swan and La Primaudaye. His
use of such material in this tract is not by accident or for ornament,
but rhetorical, which is to say poetical. It appealed to him as a logician
and as a poet. By the time we reach the end of the pamphlet, Milton
has in effect created a symbolic statement of his case; for metaphor,
even submerged metaphor, repeated and extended, becomes symbol.[24]
Divorce actually and in a sense outrageously is represented by Milton
as a form of natural order to which "God and nature signifies and
lectures to us not onely by those recited decrees, but ev'n by the first
and last of all his visible works; when by his divorcing command the
world first rose out of Chaos, nor can be renewed again out of confusion but by the separating of unmeet consorts" (420).[25]

Structure in prose, like structure in verse, is not mere external arrangement; nor is the poetry of this tract a matter of occasional purple
passages. The Doctrine and Discipline of Divorce is in two books, in
thirty-six chapters, divided logically as to the branchings of subject.
The introduction and most of the content follow well-known rules of
rhetoric. But I have tried to show another kind of structure, something
like an inner form created by motifs in scientific imagery which make
the argument as well as support or embellish it. As to Milton's inten-
tions and his recognition of what he was doing, the preliminary allegory gives us our warrant for this sort of study if we need it. To the
encyclopedists, natural science had as one of its purposes the discovery
of nature's truth as the physical manifestation of moral truth; and
Milton's use of this material is consistent with their objectives.[26] Milton's systematic exploitation of scientific lore as a unifying and formative force in The Doctrine and Discipline of Divorce suggests that his
prose has a greater claim to attention than has been thought. Perhaps,
if this demonstration has been persuasive, one will wish to say, but
with an intent different from Eliot's in his belated and ungracious
palinode, that Milton's prose is really close to half-formed poetry.

NOTES

1. For studies of encyclopedic science in Milton's prose and poetry,
   see the writer's "Milton and the Encyclopedias of Science," SP,
   xxxix (1942), 303–327; "Cosmological Lore in Milton," ELH,
   ix (1942), 198–223; "Milton and Medical Lore," Bull. of the Hist.
   of Medicine, xiii (1943), 158–184, esp. p. 183. The 1535 print-

ing of Bartholomew and the Batman, La Primaudaye, and Swan as indicated above are quoted here as significant evidence of the scientific provenience of Milton's material.

2. The Renaissance cross-fertilization of rhetoric and logic and poetic has been richly documented in recent years, most notably by Rosemond Tuve, *Elizabethan and Metaphysical Imagery* (Chicago, 1947). A familiar example of Renaissance awareness of the fusion is in *Defence of Poesie,* where Sidney remarks that he should be "pounded for straying from poetry to oratory; but that both have such an affinity in this wordish consideration." See Allan Gilbert's note to the passage, *Literary Criticism, Plato to Dryden* (New York, 1940), p. 455.

3. Merritt Y. Hughes, ed. *John Milton: Prose Selections* (New York, 1947), pp. 206–207, cites passages from Daniel's *Musophilus* and Vaughan's *To his Books* as poetic expressions akin to Milton's famous definition.

4. *The Works of John Milton,* ed. Frank A. Patterson et al. (New York, 1931-38), III, ii. 368, 419, 402. See further allegorizing in the passage, p. 418, on the "twofold Seminary or stock in nature." Poetic implications of the Eros-Anteros myth have been traced from the *Phaedrus* forward by Robert V. Merrill, "Eros and Anteros," *Speculum,* XIX (1945), 265-284. See also Hughes, op. cit., p. 190. Evion Owen, "Milton and Selden on Divorce," *SP,* XLIII (1946), 237, remarks the myth in the lines contributed by Selden to William Browne's pastorals, but does not urge the parallel.

5. Cf. Thomas Hanley's statement, Pref. to his transl. of H. A. Rommen, *The Natural Law: A Study in Legal and Social History and Philosophy* (St. Louis, 1948), p. viii: "In fact, the church and its theologians have always viewed human nature, man's natural faculties and their objects, the natural law—in a word, the natural order—as indispensable sources for determining the proper lines of human conduct which, with the aid of divine grace and with supernatural equipment, man must follow in his quest of his supernatural goal." Owen (see n. 4), p. 356, shows that Milton's practical conclusions were similar to Selden's but that Milton did not use *De Jure Naturali* in this pamphlet because his views of Christian liberty and of marriage were different from Selden's.

6. "Christian Liberty in Milton's Divorce Pamphlets," *MLR,* XXXV (1940), 160.

7. William Empson, "Emotion in Words Again," *KR,* X (1948), 579-601, points out that the word "all," which occurs 612 times in *P. L.,* appears in nearly every scene of emotional pressure. Josephine Miles, *Major Adjectives in English Poetry from Wyatt to Auden,* Univ. of Calif. Pubs. in Eng., XII, iii (Berkeley, 1946), 317, finds

"heaven" the most frequently recurring important word in Milton's poetry (600 times). Her reliance upon the inadequate Bradshaw concordance and her special criteria and methods perhaps account for the discrepancy. She is less interested than Empson in analyzing the significant structural function of words in particular scenes and lines. But both these studies suggest a concern with recurrent words in total effect comparable to the concern of the present paper.

8. *Works*, III, 482, 496, 499, 476, 458. Cf.: "To forbid divorce compulsively, is not only against nature, but against law" (p. 501).

9. *P. L.* VI. 176.

10. Op. cit., pp. 251-280, and esp. Appendix R, pp. 422-423.

11. Cf. the poetic use of this astronomical commonplace about "saving appearances" in *P. L.* VIII. 82. Prutenic tables are the astronomical computations of 1551 based on the *De Revolutionibus Orbium* of Copernicus by Erasmus Reinhold and named for his patron Duke Albrecht of Prussia. See Allan Gilbert, "Milton and Galileo," *SP*, XIX (1922), 156, and Francis R. Johnson, *Astronomical Thought in Renaissance England* (Baltimore, 1937), pp. 111-112.

12. Batman, p. 139^V, in his chapter on light mentions that the sunbeam cannot be defiled. Bacon in *Novum Organon* and Peter Sterry also remark it; see V. de S. Pinto, *Peter Sterry, Platonist and Puritan* (London, 1934), p. 150.

13. The encyclopedias and other scientific treatises are of course full of this astronomical and astrological lore. Milton is using *crasis, apogæum,* and *homogeneal* in their technical senses. For other astronomical allusions, see in context "fals and dazling fires" (434); "Chaos . . . worlds diameter multiply'd" (442); "load-starre" (493); "firmament" (506).

14. For other allusions of this type, see in context "blind and Serpentine body" (368); "borrow'd garb," "blind side" (401); "polluted skirt" (446); "remorseles obscurity," "native lustre" (494).

15. Note that "influence" retains its Latin force and thus contributes to the sense of movement here.

16. La Primaudaye's discussion, p. 530, "Of the humours ioyned with the blood and of their vessels," reads like a gloss on this passage: "Now when these veines are stopt, dangerous diseases follow thereupon, chiefly when this happeneth to the first veine whereof I spake euen now. For when the liuer is not purged, his whole office is hindered, and it selfe decayeth by little and little, by retayning still the excrements thereof from whence the vapours ascending vp to the braine trouble it very much, and cause it to fall into very strange & foolish conceiptes."

17. For other allusions of this kind, see in context "[no]man should be shut up incurably under a worse evill" (392); "if it happens that

nature hath stopt or extinguisht the veins of sensuality" (393); "veille . . . body impenetrable" (395); "hazardous and accidentall doore of mariage to shut upon us like the gate of death" (461); "chains . . . curb . . . canon bit" (486); "ill-knotted mariage" (492); "Gordian difficulties" (494).

18. This famous fish appears also in *Eikonoklastes* (*Works*, V, 218). Descriptions of its power are to be found in dozens of Renaissance scientific books, among them Bartholomew, p. clxxv; Batman, p. 119ᵛ; John Maplet, *A Greene Forest* (London, 1567), p. 143; La Primaudaye, p. 783; Swan, pp. 375-376.

19. Milton combines here two common illustrations of futility, the rope of sand and the occupation of Ocnus, both of which he uses elsewhere. In *Tetrachordon* (*Works*, IV, 97) he says that compelling incompatibles into one flesh is as vain as trying "to weav a garment of drie sand." In the *Third Prolusion* (*Works*, XII, 169) "cunning quibblers," will have "this appropriate punishment inflicted: that they shall twist ropes in hell with the famous Ocnus." In *First Defence* (*Works*, VII, 475): "This man twists conclusions as Ocuns does ropes in Hell; which are but to be eaten by asses." The rope of sand was well known from legends about the tasks Michael Scot set his devil; see Herbert's "The Collar" and T. O. Mabbott's explanation, *Explicator*, III (1944), 12; F. T. Palgrave, ed. *The Poetical Works of Sir Walter Scott* (London, 1928), p. 499, n. 19; and J. Wood Brown, *The Life and Legend of Michael Scot* (Edinburgh, 1897), p. 218. Ocnus twisted ropes of straw; Renaissance writers knew the story from the 35th book of Pliny's *Natural History* or the 4th elegy of Propertius; see *Propertius*, ed. H. E. Butler (Cambridge, 1930), p. 283 and note, p. 357.

20. Hughes, p. 163, notes the bold use of the Minerva myth in *P. L.* II. 757-758. Bartholomew, p. lxxiiiiʳ, and Batman, p. 74ʳ, in their chapter "Of a mydwyfe," say that she "wassheth awaye the blode of the chyld, and baynyth hym with shalte and hony, to drye up the humours, and to comforte his lymmes and membres."

21. In their chapter "Of heed ache, and of the causes and sygnes thereof," Bartholomew, pp. lxxxvᵛ⁻ʳ, and Batman, pp. 86ᵛ-87ʳ, describe "an ache and an euyll, that phisycyens call Emigranea," which is one of those that come "of some cause, that is within . . . as of the stomak." Their chapter "Of gydines" (pp. lxxxviiᵛ-lxxxviiiʳ, 89ʳ,) assigns the cause to "to moche plentie of humours [which] . . . meue in the heed with ventosyte that comyth up fro the body, or fro the stomak to the brayne."

22. Several of the scientific figures are mixed. Some are uncomplicated by subtlety; e. g.: "when human frailty surcharg'd, is at such a losse, charity ought to venture much, and use bold physick, lest an over-tost

faith endanger to shipwrack" (p. 400). In others, the effect, as above, is clearly satiric; e.g.: "But how among the drove of Custom and Prejudice this will be relisht, by such whose capacity, since their youth run ahead into the easie creek of a system or a Medulla, sayls there at will under the blown physiogonomy of their unlabour'd rudiments, for them, what their tast will be, I have also surety sufficient, from the entire league that hath bin ever between formal ignorance and grave obstinacie" (377–378).

23. For other anatomical and medical allusions, see in context "joynt or sinew" (369); "peevish madnesse" (373); "lifegiving remedies of *Moses*" (385); "cure . . . complexion . . . melancholy" (391); "wast away . . . under a secret affliction" (392); "impetuous nerve" (394); "spirituall contagion" (407); "noysomnesse or disfigurement of body" (419); "weak pulse" (431); "rigorous knife" (450); "cordiall and exhilarating cup of solace" (461); "hand of Justice rot off" (474); "hard spleen . . . sanguifie" (484); *"bitter water . . . curse of rottenness and tympany"* (488); "misbegott'n infants" (505). Where gloss is necessary, these allusions can be explained from the medical sections of the encyclopedias. On the passage, "his will like a hard spleen draws faster then his understanding can well sanguifie," see Bartholomew, p. lvii^r; Batman, p. 58^r; La Primaudaye, pp. 358, 530, 422–425, 440–446.

24. See the discussion in René Wellek and Austin Warren, *Theory of Literature* (New York, 1949), pp. 190–218, for the best recent account of this progression.

25. The use of "signifies" and "lectures" in the singular, common enough as a grammatical construction, is none the less an explicit statement of the identity Milton makes between divine law and natural law. Compare Adam's conclusion, *P. L.* x.815–816: "both Death and I/Am found Eternal"; and the explication in "Adam's Soliloquy in Book x," *CE*, x (1949), 369.

26. La Primaudaye is particularly theological; Swan arranges his scientific information as an hexameron. See Louis B. Wright's chapter "The Strange World of Science," *Middle Class Culture in Elizabethan England* (Chapel Hill, 1935), pp. 549–602, esp. p. 555: "Compilers of encyclopedias always assured their readers that a study of the physical world and of man in his mental and physical aspects revealed profitable lessons of God's will."

THOMAS KRANIDAS

✴

"Decorum" and the Style of Milton's
Antiprelatical Tracts

Milton's antiprelatical tracts have been often viewed as embarrassing
mixtures of raptures and venom, rhetorically skilful but not finally
worthy of the poet of *Paradise Lost*. In an attempt to represent these
tracts more justly, the editors of volume one of the *Complete Prose
Works* provide us with an enormous and valuable apparatus for the
reconstruction of the context of this prose; and they include important
suggestions on the way the language operates as an imaginative instrument for polemic. Occasionally however, there are lapses into
apology for Milton's "masses of infamy, without discrimination,"[1] and
a kind of opposition is set up between the more or less temperate
tenor of Bishop Hall's prose and the harshness of Milton's. In a note
on that famous image of God vomiting over the bishops' deficiencies
Don M. Wolfe and William Alfred write

> This image . . . is a figure no one of Milton's Anglican oppo-
> nents would have dared to use, even against the Puritans. For
> such a harsh metaphor Milton has tried to prepare his readers
> in the apologetic passage on "vehement Expressions."[2]

From *Studies in Philology*, LXII (1965), pp. 176-187. Reprinted by permission of the University of North Carolina Press. The material of this article in
different form constitutes part of Chapter II of the author's book, *The Fierce
Equation* (Humanities Press, Inc., 1965).

What is directly involved is Milton's decorum and our understanding of it as it is expressed in his prose style.

I should like to argue that Milton's propriety is large enough and vital enough to comprehend and contain the passionate scurrility[3] which shocks us. I should like to argue, also, that Milton's propriety[4] is an ideal of unity as well as a habit of adjusting the intensities of language to the situation. Often Milton's vision of unity is to be deduced from its opposite. Thus, the harmonious vision is to be inferred from the pejorative image of the diseased and deformed which masquerades as the flashy "outside." Kester Svendsen has argued this[5] and Don M. Wolfe and William Alfred themselves direct the reader toward remarking how "the governing image of the pamphlet, that of the members of the true church as members of the mystical body of Christ" is related to the metaphors for Episcopacy "of nausea, disease, and deformity."[6] Anglican decency, its ceremonious wardrobe and language, is the object of Milton's furious attack. It becomes, too, a kind of inverse mirror which illuminates in a classic Miltonic procedure, "knowing good by evil," Milton's idea of radiant unity. I shall call this idea of unity, and the strategy of subordinating and relating local texture to that unity, *decorum*. I hope this will not seem merely arbitrary. Though Milton himself does not use the term in any but quite limited ways, there is warrant for a broader use of the term both in a traditional use like Puttenham's and in the vacuum created by Milton's destruction of Anglican concepts of decency.

I am not attempting a complete analysis of Milton's early prose, nor am I attempting to give a complete definition of the term "decorum." But I am trying to find factors in that prose which represent a central attempt on Milton's part to unify the materials of his discourse. That central attempt I should like to consider as a guidepost on the road toward defining Milton's decorum.

The propriety of Milton's prose is a fiery equilibrium of classic and neo-classic precepts, Christian traditions of language, and Miltonic aspirations, all tested in the religious controversies of the day. That propriety is no dead formula of received rhetorical precepts, nor is it something to be easily invoked for the testing of a given piece of discourse. The rules of the game are at least partly being written and revised as the game is played. I do not think this argues merely the fact of Milton's egoism, since that game is being played within a large and stable context which Milton never denies, his faith in God. So Milton's propriety of language is flexible and dynamic, but Milton's propriety is not finally relativistic. The ends of discourse are the glorification of God, to repair the ruin of our first parents, to offer a lively sacrifice to God. All language bends and stretches to that purpose even when one of the delights of craftsmanship is the delight of difficult conformity.

One of the most pervasive themes, or rather cluster of themes, in the antiprelatical tracts, is that of excess in language, frumpery, misused tradition, gaudiness. Milton again and again attacks the prelatical party for its excesses in language, clothing and ritual. Indeed a great deal of the vigor in these tracts is to be found in the violence, contempt, and rough humor in his images of excess. The attack on excess, and occasionally of defect, is basically an attack on disharmony and disproportion, on the disparity or misrelation of *inner* and *outer*, in the body, and the total man, and in the church and its rituals. Another way of expressing this is, quite simply, the separation of manner and matter, of letter and spirit.

Milton attacks the vestments of the church, sometimes the real garments of Episcopacy, sometimes the garments as a metaphor for the exterior life of the church. At the beginning of *Of Reformation,* Milton refers to "the Jewish beggery, of old cast rudiments . . . the new-vomited Paganisme of sensuall Idolatry" (Yale *Prose,* I, 520). He contrasts the "robes of pure innocency" with those "of pure Linnen, with other deformed and fantastick dresses in Palls, and Miters, gold, and guegaw's fetcht from *Arons* old wardrope, or the *Flamins vestry*" (p. 521).

This theme of garishness in clothing is related to the theme of excess in language.[7] Milton refuses to "run into a paroxysm of citations" (p. 566); he denounces the "knotty Africanisms, the pamper'd metafors; the intricat, and involv'd sentences of the Fathers; besides the fantastick and declamatory flashes; the crosse-jingling periods which cannot but disturb, and come thwart a setl'd devotion worse then the din of bells, and rattles" (p. 568). Milton attacks those who call for Antiquity because "they feare the plain field of the Scriptures, the chase is too hot; they seek the dark, the bushie, the tangled Forrest, they would imbosk."[8]

Milton himself is not unaware of the roughness of his prose style. In the *Of Reformation* he defends his use of vehement expressions (p. 535); and in the preface to *Animadversions* he writes:

And although in the serious uncasing of a grand imposture . . . there be mixt here and there such a grim laughter, as may appeare at the same time in an austere visage, it cannot be taxt of levity or insolence: for even this veine of laughing (as I could produce out of grave Authors) hath oft-times a strong and sinewy force in teaching and confuting. (pp. 663-664)

Here is a defence of the grim laughter in terms of the concept of decorum—appropriateness to place, time, person, and especially subject—but one which scrupulously avoids mention of the many classical antecedents. It is easy to see this as purely a matter of strategy—i.e. the refusal to use authority because the opponent falls back on it. But Milton has not tried to suppress the question of decorum; he has insisted on making it overt. In a real sense the question of decorum in the performance of religious duties becomes *the* theme. The definition of the proper harmony between inner and outer, form and content, appearance and reality, becomes the major consideration. Milton could have cited Aristotle, Horace, Demetrius, even Scaliger in defence of his roughness. But he does not cite these classical critics, as he does elsewhere; he cites instead Solomon and Christ. And this is in keeping with the pervasive imagery of the total harmony of the inner and the outer man, and the attack on disharmony, excess, imbalance of the inner and outer man.

In *Animadversions* the attack on affected language of all sorts continues: "they [the Smectymnuans] thought it best not to screw the English mouth to a harsh forreigne termination."[9] There is a long attack on the over-emphasis on Antiquity:

Why doe wee therefore stand worshipping, and admiring this unactive, and livelesse *Colossus,* that like a carved Gyant terribly menacing to children, and weaklings lifts up his club, but strikes not, and is subject to the muting of every Sparrow.[10]

Surely the large truth of Milton's traditionalism ought always to allow for this evidence of a ferocious opposition to the *merely* traditional, in language as in church government.

The last two antiprelatical tracts differ sharply in tone, the one is stately, the other sardonic. But both *The Reason of Church-Government Urg'd Against Prelaty* and *An Apology Against a Pamphlet* contain the same basic referents in imagery; his "contempt for learned grubbing" implies "his love for true learning";[11] his contempt for the externally garish and excessive implies his love for the harmonies of inner and outer. Against "libidinous and ignorant Poetasters" (p. 818) and the "Carnall textman" (p. 951) he sets up the "interpreter & relater of the best and sagest things" (p. 811). After Milton confides his plans for the future, he mentions with "what small willingnesse" he left his "pleasing solitarynes" to come into "the dim reflexion of hollow antiquities sold by the seeming bulk, and there be fain to club quotations with men whose learning and belief lies in marginal stuffings" (pp. 821-822).

The point about the abundance of the imagery of excess in language, dress, and "authority" is I think clear. And I have by no means exhausted the examples. The antiprelatical tracts are full of them. Often they are brilliantly fused with images of bodily illness. These images of illness are startling and have already received attention,[12] but I should like to re-examine them, to show they are related to the images discussed above, and to further push my suggestion that Milton has organized his tracts around the master image of excess and disharmony; only if we recognize this master image can we grasp the remarkable coherence, the true decorum of this prose.

First, Milton himself demonstrates how functionally right the illness image is in this clearly articulated metaphor of bodily excess with spiritual want:

> for in very deed, the superstitious man by his good will is an Atheist; but being scarr'd from thence by the pangs, and gripes of a boyling conscience, all in a pudder shuffles up to himselfe such a *God,* and such a *worship* as is most agreeable to remedy his feare, which feare of his, as also is his hope, fixt onely upon the *Flesh,* renders likewise the whole faculty of his apprehension, carnall, and all the inward acts of *worship* issuing from the native strength of the SOULE, run out lavishly to the upper skin, and there harden into a crust of Formallitie. (p. 522)

This example is characteristic, demonstrating as it does a literally fluid, dynamic relationship of the inner body (and by extension, soul) and the outer; unpleasantly, but consequently, Milton's most effective images of bodily disarrangement are done in terms of tumors and excrescences and regurgitation. The sick body implies the healthy body, and the healthy whole man makes possible the mention of the sick and fragmented man.

It is precisely the resonant harmony of inner and outer, the highest order, *decorum,* to which our study of the imagery of the antiprelatical tracts leads us. Over and over, in vivid, comprehensive and cohesive images, Milton will stress the relationships, the fit proportions, of inner and outer, spirit and word, appearance, and reality:

> The very essence of Truth is plainnesse, and brightnes; the darknes and crookednesse is our own. The *Wisdome* of *God* created *understanding,* fit and proportionable to Truth the object, and end of it, as the eye to the thing visible. (p. 566)

> Believe it, wondrous Doctors, all corporeal resemblances of inward holinesse & beauty are now past; he that will cloath the Gospel now, intimates plainly, that the Gospel is naked, uncomely, that I may not say reproachfull. Do not, ye Church-maskers . . . cover and hide his righteous verity with the polluted cloathing of your ceremonies to make it seem more decent in your own eyes. (p. 828)

> [the good Christian] will stirre him up to walk worthy the honourable and grave imployment wherewith God and the Church hath dignifi'd him: not fearing lest he should meet with some outward holy thing in religion which his lay touch or presence might profane, but lest something unholy from within his own heart should dishonour and profane in himselfe that Priestly unction and Clergy-right whereto Christ hath entitl'd him. (p. 844)

Anglican decency, the "beauty of holiness," becomes for Milton the emblem for a disproportionate emphasis on the externals of worship. What Bishop Hall and Archbishop Laud deemed proper and decent in worship, Milton deemed improper and indecent. The imagery of these early tracts, though violent, is channeled toward the destruction of the Anglican form of decency. The pressure behind the waves of excoriation and exaltation is the concept of decorum, the highest unity, the radiant harmony, the harmonious vision.[13] We can glimpse this unity in the "Nativity Ode," even in the *Prolusions* and we can see it in Milton's work through *Paradise Regained* and *Samson.* Now Milton only implies it in its highest sense. He consciously suppresses the narrower uses of the term *decorum* even where one might expect him to use it, in defence of his style. He could have used, among easily available sources, Calvin's discussion:

> We shall not call that *decorum*, therefore, which is merely a
> frivolous spectacle yielding an unprofitable gratification. . . .
> But we shall esteem that as *decorum*, which shall be so adapted
> to inspire a reverence of holy mysteries as to be calculated for
> an exercise of piety; or which at least shall contribute an orna-
> ment corresponding to the act; . . . Now, that ceremonies may
> be exercises of piety, it is necessary that they should lead us di-
> rectly to Christ.[14]

Milton takes the difficult way. He builds his propriety from the inside out, rather than applying it from the outside. Although he had
"authority" for his broad conception of decorum, many of Milton's
contemporaries did not accept or perhaps even grasp it. Thomas
Fuller, for example, accuses Milton of a violation of decorum in the
Of Reformation: "And one lately hath traduced them [the bishops]
with such language as neither beseemed his parts whosoever he was
that spake it, nor their piety of whom it was spoken."[15] For this kind
of decorum, Milton had little concern; but it is this kind of decorum
on which some editors and many critics have concentrated in considering the early prose and it is this "rhetorical" decorum which is emphasized in the first extended attack on Milton's work. *A Modest Confutation of a Slanderous and Scurrilous Libell, Entituled, Animadversions etc.* attacks Milton's style, learning and character. The anonymous author absolutely rejects or ignores Milton's defences of his
style in *Animadversions*. Concerning the precepts of Solomon and
Christ, the confuter cries: *"Horrid blasphemy! You that love Christ,
and know this miscreant wretch, stone him to death, lest yourselves
smart for his impunity."*[16] The attack has its effect. After a sustained
refusal to fight on certain conventional grounds, Milton comes down
to the rhetorical and limited grounds. Not completely, but for a good
part of the time, he is parrying the confuter's thrusts. And there are
signs of some weariness, of disappointment at the rejection or misun-
derstanding of his, Milton's, grounds:

> To beginne therefore an Apology for those animadversions
> which I writ against the Remonstrant in defence of *Smectym-
> nus*, since the Preface, which was purposely set before them,
> is not thought apologeticall anough. (p. 871)

There are some strictly technical literary comments related to decorum. One is a critique in terms of genre: "For a Satyr as it was

borne out of a *Tragedy,* so ought to resemble his parentage, to strike high, and adventure dangerously."[17] Milton had attacked the title of Hall's *Toothless Satires* in *Animadversions,* but there it was a casual part of the serious business of abuse. Here Milton is serious about genre. In another passage Milton uses the word *decorum,* its single use in the tracts and a use strictly limited to propriety of character:

> One thing I beg of ye Readers, as ye beare any zeale to learn-
> ing, to elegance, and that which is call'd *Decorum* in the writ-
> ing of praise, especially on such a noble argument, ye would not
> be offended, though I rate this cloister'd Lubber according to
> his deserts. Where didst thou learne to be so agueish, so pusil-
> lanimous, thou lozel Bachelour of Art, as against all custome
> and use of speech to terme the high and sovran Court of Parla-
> ment, a Convocation? (p. 920)

But Milton's chief claim to propriety of style is based on Scripture. The by-passing of classical authority is deliberate:

> If therefore the question were in oratory, whether a vehement
> vein throwing out indignation, or scorn upon an object that
> merits it, were among the aptest *Ideas* of speech to be allow'd,
> it were my work, and that an easie one to make it cleare both by
> the rules of best rhetoricians, and the famousest examples of the
> Greek and Roman Orations. But since the Religion of it is dis-
> puted, and not the art, I shall make use only of such reasons
> and autorities, as religion cannot except against. (p. 899)

We must note that though the antiprelatical tracts do not summon "the rules of the best rhetoricians," there is an implication that these rules have a parallel, as it were substantiating, life. Only rarely does Milton suggest that the religious view clashes with the classical rhetorical view. There is rather the assumption that Christian decorum contains classical, rhetorical decorum. So, Milton's defence of "the vehement vein" is not from Demetrius, but from Christ:

> Our Saviour . . . was Lord to expresse his indoctrinating
> power in what sort him best seem'd; sometimes by a milde and
> familiar converse, sometimes with plaine and impartiall home-
> speaking regardlesse of those whom the auditors might think he

should have had in more respect; otherwhiles with bitter and irefull rebukes if not teaching yet leaving excuselesse those his wilfull impugners. What was all in him, was divided among many others the teachers of his Church; some to be severe and ever of a sad gravity that they may win such, & check sometimes those who be of nature over-confident and jocond; others were sent more cheerfull, free, and still as it were at large, in the midst of an untrespassing honesty; that they who are so temper'd may have by whom they might be drawne to salvation, and they who are too scrupulous, and dejected of spirit might be often strengthn'd with wise consolations and revivings: no man being forc't wholly to dissolve that groundwork of nature which God created in him, the sanguine to empty out all his sociable livelinesse, the cholerick to expell quite the unsinning predominance of his anger; but that each radicall humour and passion wrought upon and corrected as it ought, might be made the proper mould and foundation of every mans peculiar guifts, and vertues. (pp. 899-900)

This is consistent with classical theory of discourse designed πρὸς τὸν ἀκροατήν; this "regard to the audience" is consistent with Colet's theory of accommodation; and it is consistent with Milton's own practice in the prose.[18]

In speaking of Christ's own freedom of language, Milton goes farther than the modest confuters of his time:

is it blasphemy, or any whit disagreeing from Christian meeknesse, when as Christ himselfe speaking of unsavory traditions, scruples not to name the Dunghill and the Jakes, for me to answer a slovenly wincer. (p. 895)

Doth not Christ himselfe teach the highest things by the similitude *of old bottles and patcht cloaths?* Doth he not illustrate best things by things most evill? (p. 898)

Turne then to the first of Kings where God himselfe uses the phrase; *I will cut off from Iereboam him that pisseth against the wall.* Which had it beene an unseemely speech in the heat of an earnest expression, then we must conclude that *Ionathan, or Onkelos the Targumists* were of cleaner language then he that made the tongue. . . . Whereas God who is the author both of purity and eloquence, chose this phrase as fittest in that vehement character wherein he spake. . . . Fools who would teach men to read more decently then God thought good to write. And thus I take it to be manifest, that indignation against men and their actions notoriously bad, hath leave and autority oft times to utter such words and phrases as in common talke were not so mannerly to use. (pp. 902-903)

This is as far as Milton will go toward a "literary" defense.

What emerges from this study of the antiprelatical tracts is a pervading concept of harmony, radiant unity, *decorum* which takes life from, and gives life to, the rhetoric of disharmony, illness, excess. There emerges, too, Milton's refusal to mention the rhetorical issues in other than their religious applications. There emerges an insistence on freedom of style based upon the propriety of it in terms of the subject, the goal of the inquiry. Milton does not simply reject the outside. What he rejects is the corruption of the outside, the disharmony of the outer with the inner. Milton uses the word *carnall* freely and pejoratively. But his description of the healthy body, or language, or garment is rarely crabbed or ascetic.

Throughout the tracts we have had visions of the healthy body, as individual, as state, as church. At the very opening of the first tract we have the Doctrine of the Gospel,

> refin'd to such a Spirituall height, and temper of purity, and knowledge of the Creator, that the body, with all the circumstances of time and place, were purifi'd by the affections of the regenerat Soule, and nothing left impure, but Sinne. (p. 519)

Very richly in the *Reason of Church-Government* we find a respect for the whole self:

> And if the love of God . . . be the first principle of all godly and vertuous actions in men, this pious and just honouring of our selves is the second, and may be thought as the radical moisture and fountain head, whence every laudable and worthy enterprize issues forth. (p. 841)

> But he that holds himself in reverence and due esteem, both for the dignity of Gods image upon him, and for the price of his

redemption . . . accounts himselfe both a fit person to do the noblest and godliest deeds, and much better worth then to deject and defile, with such a debasement and such a pollution as sin is, himselfe so highly ransom'd and enobl'd to a new friendship and filiall relation with God. Nor can he fear so much the offence and reproach of others, as he dreads and would blush at the reflection of his own severe and modest eye upon himselfe, if it should see him doing or imagining that which is sinfull though in the deepest secrecy. How shall a man know to do himselfe this right, how to performe this honourable duty of estimation and respect towards his own soul and body? which way will leade him best to this hill top of sanctity and goodnesse above which there is no higher ascent but to the love of God which from this self-pious regard cannot be assunder?[19]

The harmony of inner and outer man is not renunciation; it is proportion. Hence the rightness, not disparity, of his descriptions of the poems to come and the man who is to create them:

> Then amidst the *Hymns,* and *Halleluiahs* of *Saints* some one may perhaps bee heard offering at high *strains* in new and lofty *Measures* to sing and celebrate thy *divine Mercies,* and *marvelous Judgements* in this Land throughout all AGES; whereby this great and Warlike Nation instructed and inur'd to the fervent and continuall practice of *Truth* and *Righteousnesse,* and casting farre from her the *rags* of her old *vices* may presse on hard to that *high* and *happy* emulation to be found the *soberest, wisest,* and *most Christian People.* (p. 616)

This is the harmony we have insisted on. And though the word *sober* may bother some, there is nothing here of asceticism. There is richness, in the harmony, as resonance and complexity. The same effect is in the passage from *Animadversions:*

> And he that now for haste snatches up a plain ungarnish't present as a thanke-offering to thee, which could not bee deferr'd in regard of thy so many late deliverances wrought for us one upon another, may then perhaps take up a Harp, and sing thee an elaborate Song to Generations. (p. 706)

The imagery in these two passages operates in such a way that we tend to clothe *decorously* the singing figure in both cases. What we have then is the harmonious organic vision which gives meaning to, as it takes meaning from, a passage like this:

> And it is still *Episcopacie* that before all our eyes worsens and sluggs the most learned, and seeming religious of our *Ministers,* who no sooner advanc't to it, but like a seething pot set to coole, sensibly exhale and reake out the greatest part of that zeale, and those Gifts which were formerly in them, settling in a skinny congealment of ease and sloth at the top: and if they keep their Learning by some potent sway of Nature, 'tis a rare chance; but their *devotion* most commonly comes to that queazy temper of luke-warmnesse, that gives a Vomit to GOD himselfe. (pp. 536-537)

The unity of the human body and soul, its language, clothing and traditions, the idea of unity itself, is both a complex vehicle for Milton's polemical opinions and a superior theme in the antiprelatical tracts. Milton argues his position using the tools of this larger decorum of unity, and finally it is this higher unity he is arguing *for*. In the famous passage on his early reading, Milton gives us a climactic personal vision of the kind of harmony he means, the ultimate fusion of inner and outer:

> And long it was not after, when I was confirm'd in this opinion, that he who would not be frustrate of his hope to write well hereafter in laudable things, ought him selfe to bee a true Poem, that is, a composition, and patterne of the best and honourablest things; not presuming to sing high praises of heroick men, or famous Cities, unlesse he have in himselfe the experience and the practice of all that which is praise-worthy. (p. 890)

This is not some spectacular and interpolated naivete, but an intense working theme and program for the antiprelatical tracts.

NOTES

1. *Complete Prose Works of John Milton,* ed. by several hands (New Haven, 1953–), I, 536, note 72. Hereafter cited in footnotes as

Yale *Prose* with volume and page number; in the text of the essay I cite the page number in parentheses following the quotation.

2. Yale *Prose*, I, 537, note 73.

3. But I would like to remember W. R. Parker's admonition, "Scurrility is scurrility, even if it is conventional, even if it is seemingly justified." *Milton's Contemporary Reputation* (Columbus, 1940), p. iii.

4. Earlier studies of Milton's decorum restrict themselves to the rhetorical issues. See Ida Langdon, *Milton's Theory of Poetry and Fine Art* (New Haven, 1924), pp. 109–115, 232–235, and Kester Svendsen, "Epic Address and Reference and the Principle of Decorum in *Paradise Lost*," *PQ*, XXVIII (Jan. 1949), 185–206.

5. *Milton and Science* (Cambridge, 1956), pp. 186–187, 191–192. Professor Svendsen's treatment of the antiprelatical tracts and the *Doctrine and Discipline of Divorce* seems to me to be brilliantly aware of the claims of the prose as prose.

6. Yale *Prose*, I, 519.

7. This is a common theme in the *Prolusions* where it is not only related to Milton's hatred of Scholasticism, but has a life of its own and close connections with the problem of Milton's decorum, especially his rejection of "mere" rhetorical propriety. See especially *Prolusions* I, III, and VI, and VII and the following in Yale *Prose*, I, 220, 239, 245, 271, 276, 300.

8. *Ibid.*, I, 569. Again as in the *Prolusions* (Yale *Prose* I, 211–306, *passim*) Milton's disdain for excess in language is mingled with contempt for pedantry in general. In Book II of *Of Reformation,* he speaks of the "art of policie" as "slubber'd with aphorisming pedanty," (*ibid.*, I, 571), "Rotchet Apothegmes" and "Pedantick palmes." (*ibid.*, p. 587).

9. *Ibid.*, pp. 666–667. Cf. the attack on Hall's Senecanism, "your spruce fastidious oratory" (p. 670).

10. *Ibid.*, 699. There follows a description of the taking apart of this Colossus with "sledges . . . levers . . . and iron crows." The dismembering of this inert "entity" makes an interesting contrast with the dismembering of Truth in *Areopagitica* (Yale *Prose*, II, 549), where the reconstruction of that organism utilizes the very archetypes of regeneration. It is not too fanciful, perhaps, to see the "unactive, and livelesse Colossus" figure as corresponding to a rhetorical decorum without religious context; the body of Truth represents the pulsating unity of Milton's Christian decorum.

11. The phrases are those of Ralph A. Haug, editor of *The Reason of Church Government,* in Yale *Prose*, I, 737.

12. Svendsen, *Milton and Science,* pp. 174–210.

13. My use of this phrase without quotation marks should suggest the

pervasive influence of Don Cameron Allen's *The Harmonious Vision* (Baltimore, 1954).

14. John Calvin *Institutes of the Christian Religion* trans. by John Allen, 2 vols. (Philadelphia, n. d.), II, 478. We might remember, in passing, Milton's "as if we could be put off with *Calvins* name, unlesse we be convinc't with *Calvins* reason" (Yale *Prose,* I, 707).

15. Quoted in Will T. Hale's edition of *Of Reformation* (New Haven and London, 1916), p. xxxv. Cf. Yale *Prose,* I, 532 n.

16. Parker, *Milton's Contemporary Reputation,* p. iii.

17. Yale *Prose,* I, 916. See 914–915 for further discussion of this genre. And see p. 934 for Milton's comments on the kinds of style.

18. The backgrounds of Milton's decorum are traced in Chapter I of my book, *The Fierce Equation* (The Hague, 1965).

19. Yale *Prose,* I, 842–843. In the same passage Milton attacks the decency of the Prelates who have "driven holinesse out of living into livelesse things," and for having "proclaim'd the best of creatures, mankind, so unpurifi'd and contagious" (*ibid.,* pp. 844–845).

JOAN WEBBER

🖋

Donne and Bunyan: The Styles of Two Faiths

In late November or early December, 1623, John Donne, the famous Dean of Paul's, and a favorite preacher at the court of James I, fell ill of the relapsing fever,[1] and, in anticipation of his own demise, hastened the marriage of his daughter Constance to the retired actor Edward Alleyn. Edward LeComte's nomination of Alleyn as a father figure for Constance[2] sets off fascinating reverberations, since Donne himself was such a player of parts. At this time, he not only provided Constance with a dramatic replacement for himself; he provided the world with one, too, in his *Devotions Upon Emergent Occasions*. Then, somewhat anticlimactically, he recovered, and, outliving Edward Alleyn, saw his *Devotions* through three editions before his death.

Some thirty-seven years later, in 1660, John Bunyan, a Baptist preacher and former tinker, was arrested and charged with holding a conventicle. He was one of the first to suffer the repressive effects on dissenters of the Restoration settlement, but the results of his imprisonment were surely not what its Anglican administrators had in mind. His twelve-year confinement, while it worked immeasurable hardships upon his family,[3] was humane and at times even perfunctory. It gave him leisure to conceive and write books which, for many generations of readers, were to take second-place only to the Bible.

From Joan Webber, *The Eloquent I* (Madison: The University of Wisconsin Press), pp. 15-52. Copyright 1968 by the Regents of the University of Wisconsin.

Here *Pilgrim's Progress* may well have been begun. Here he wrote his spiritual autobiography, *Grace Abounding*.

Ideologically, personally, culturally, these two men are a world removed from one another. Their different uses of the "I" are very clearly distinguishable. And yet they do unexpectedly have much in common besides their Christian names. Their likenesses, especially as evidenced in the two works to be discussed here, make a comparison of their "I"s more possible, more relevant, and more exciting. Both books were written by preachers at a time when they were unable to preach, Donne because he languished in sickbed, and Bunyan because he languished in prison. These books, then, might be considered "second-choice"; they are not what their authors most wanted to be doing. Though both men were prolific writers, their principal business was the spoken word. Since both admired and imitated Saint Paul, considering themselves, like him, reformed sinners, they believed it proper to preach about themselves, as he did. In a period of crisis and isolation, deprived of books and auditors, they looked within, and wrote of what they saw.

The subjective pattern detailed by both men presents an alternation between joy and grief, hope and despair, which, as Henri Talon says of Bunyan, "constitutes the rhythm of our author's life and perhaps, in varying intensity, of every human life."[4] Both Donne and Bunyan, at least during the periods of their lives with which they are here concerned, were highly emotional, highly prone to extremes of feeling. Both were preoccupied with their souls' health. Both books end on a note of uncertainty; while Bunyan has resolved to stand fast and Donne's illness has abated, still Bunyan allows for the possibility of further pain, and in Donne's last meditation, the physicians warn of the possibility of a relapse.

The religious needs of the two men were somewhat similar. Both spend a good deal of time in their narratives voicing intellectual doubts, and both resolve their doubts in emotion rather than reason. Donne begs for God's thunder, and gets it in the organ voice of the prayers of the Anglican church. Bunyan, in a fine climactic passage, cries out, "I will leap off the Ladder even blindfold into Eternitie, sink or swim, come heaven, come hell; Lord Jesus, if thou wilt catch me, do; if not, I will venture for thy Name" (*G.A.*, p. 101). Bunyan was early attracted by Anglican ritual; Donne was by nature a passionate, rebellious man. Had circumstances been different, their roles might have been reversed.

Finally, directed by the fact that the sincerity of both men has been questioned,[5] we can find parallels in the effect of their self-consciousness upon their art. Mirrors and rulebooks guide the emergent self-awareness of the age, in the mannered confusion of life and art on the one hand, and the proliferation of how-to-do-it books (the art of living, loving, dying) on the other.[6] A seventeenth-century man who checks his progress in the mirror (like Donne), or is converted by the book (like Bunyan), may be different from his predecessors, but is probably no less sincere. And the art that he produces may exemplify a particularly valuable kind of originality just because one is constantly aware of the artist's awareness of his situation and his craft.

The question of sincerity confronts us head-on in the dedications of these two books, in the different arguments and styles in which the two men explain their reasons for publishing such personal writing. Donne's book is dedicated in a highly mannered and witty style to Prince Charles, soon to be Charles I:

MOST EXCELLENT PRINCE,

I Have had three *Births;* One, *Naturall,* when I came into the *World;* One *Supernatural,* when I entred into the *Ministery;* and now, a *preter-naturall* Birth, in returning to *Life,* from this *Sickness.* In my *second Birth,* your *Highnesse Royall Father* vouchsafed mee his Hand, not onely to sustaine mee *in it,* but to lead mee *to it.* In this *last Birth,* I my selfe am borne a *Father:* This *Child* of mine, this *Booke,* comes into the world, *from* mee, and *with* mee. And therefore, I presume (as I did the *Father* to the *Father*) to present the *Sonne* to the *Sonne;* This *Image* of my *Humiliation,* to the lively *Image* of his *Maiesty,* your *Highnesse.* It might bee enough, that *God* hath seene my *Devotions:* But *Examples* of *Good Kings* are *Commandements;* and *Ezechiah* writt the *Meditations* of his *Sicknesse,* after his *Sicknesse.* Besides, as I have liv'd to see, (not as a *Witnesse* onely, but as a *Partaker*) the happinesses of a part of your *Royal Fathers time,* so shall I live, (*in my way*) to see the happinesses of the times of your *Highnesse* too, if this *Child* of mine, inanimated by your gracious Acceptation, may so long preserve alive the *Memory* of

Your Highnesse
Humblest and
Devotedst
JOHN DONNE

For Donne, the king or prince is the significant audience, since all meaning is vested in him. The prince's power of patronage is just one aspect of this: whether Donne lives or dies, the dedication of the book to Charles guarantees the extension of *Donne* into Charles' reign. The book is born of his sickness, and so is he. It becomes both his child and his twin, and is also an "I" to live after him. He is not content to have it merely *an* other self; it is somehow a whole family of other selves.

The most interesting sentence in the dedication is this: "It might bee enough, that *God* hath seene my *Devotions:* But *Examples* of *Good Kings* are *Commandements;* And *Ezechiah* writt the *Meditations* of his *Sicknesse,* after his *Sicknesse.*" It is not clear whether he means that, since God saw him at prayer, it might be thought that he had no reason to write anything down at all, or that, since God read the manuscript, there might be no reason to publish it. Since the devotions are supposed to be taking place during his illness, and since he speaks of Hezekiah as writing his meditations after his illness, the more probable meaning is the former; the unwritten devotions might be thought sufficient. But there is ambiguity, and it is relevant, since the actual and written devotions, Donne praying and the written page, are being so closely identified with one another. Perhaps the devotion is the act of writing.

But why must there be an audience? If the sentence permits a backward reference, then one argument might be that since examples of good kings are commandments, and since King James presented his spiritual son John Donne to God, then Donne should present *his* spiritual child (the book) to the prince, soon to become God's representative. As Donne was brought to life by James, so the book will be "inanimated" by the prince. The immediate reference is more obvious, although also complicated. King Hezekiah, mortally ill, prayed to have his life extended, and God granted his wish. He then repeated a psalm reflecting upon his illness, praising God for his deliverance, and asserting that he would tell his children of God's goodness.[7] Thus, in reading of Donne's deliverance, we see Donne reading of Hezekiah's deliverance and citing what must have seemed to him a prototype of his own situation in order to prove his right to make his devotions public. If Hezekiah was simply repeating a psalm suited to the occasion, and written by someone else,[8] still another mirror image is added to the succession.

The sentence preceding this one, of course, has already provoked the life-art, reality-image confusion, when Donne says that as he presented himself (the book's father) to James (Charles' father), he will present the son to the son, "This *Image* of my *Humiliation* to the lively *Image* of his *Maiesty*." The first presumption is made to justify its re-enactment; the original will justify the copy. But meanwhile, art and life are equated in the comparison of Donne's book to Prince Charles, as the image is presented to the image, the son to the son.

This type of dedication is standard. But the kinds of ambiguity involved and the mirrors-within-mirrors images of conscious devotion are very Donnean. He had never published anything personal before. That he did it at this time, still confined to what everyone had feared was his deathbed, argues a unique strength and complexity of motivation that only partly emerges in this cryptic and mannered prose. Such motivation we find, I think, in the whole character of the book, but first of all in the unusually close connection between the life—and near death—of the author, and the book's creation.

R. C. Bald, in a brilliant final act of scholarship, left us this information about the *Devotions*:

> Constance Donne was married to Edward Alleyn on 3 December 1623, and we have Alleyn's word for it that the marriage occurred while Donne was ill: "Thus past it on till the beginning off your sickness and then you desire[d] our maryag showld bee performed with as much sped as might bee." If Donne had not passed, or had only just passed the crisis of his fever by 3 December, he must have fallen ill during the last few days of November. The *Devotions* were entered in the Stationers Register on 9 January, presumably after having been scanned by the licenser and, if Donne's correspondence is to be believed, after having been seen by more than one of his friends. . . . On 1 February Donne was able to send a presentation copy to the Queen of Bohemia enclosed in a dated letter to one of her ladies, who was to hand it to her. The book turned out to be larger than Donne anticipated, as it consists of 27 sheets, and thus would have taken about a month to pass through the press. If we assume that the book was in the printer's hands for the whole of January, we must then assume that the book was written during December. Yet this forces us to believe that the book was written in only a few weeks by a man who had very nearly died, whose body was weak and ex-

hausted by his illness, and who was in the early stages of a
long and slow convalescence. Even when the book was in the
press, he was barely able to sit up in a chair in his bedroom,
but had been unable as yet to leave it. For the circumstances
of its composition Donne's *Devotions* can have few, if any, parallels in the annals of literature.[9]

I have quoted Mr. Bald at length both to do justice to his account
and to emphasize its importance for us. A few years later, Donne was
to pose in his graveclothes for a picture that, according to Walton,
"became his hourly object"[10] as he lay dying. In 1624, he was still
able to be his own artist, and, in the face of death, to strive for
publication.

Besides the dedication, one literary device in particular, placed at
the entrance of the work, informs us of its extraordinary artfulness.
Disguised as a table of contents, a Latin poem in dactylic hexameters
describes the various stages of Donne's illness. The poem is called
"*Stationes,* sive *Periodi* in *Morbo,*" and the opening lines, halved by
the tiny pages of the 1624 edition, will serve to illustrate the verse,
which would be entirely unremarkable if it were not so entirely
unexpected:

> 1. *Insultus* Morbi primus;
> 2. Post, *Actio Laesa;*
> 3. *Decubitus* sequitur tandem;
> 4. *Medicusq,* vocatur;
> 5. *Solus* adest; 6 *Metuit;*
> 7. *Socios* sibi iungier instat.

Broken up according to their numbers, the pieces of the poem then
serve one by one, throughout the book, to introduce the twenty-three
"*stationes*" into which it is divided. Thus, the Latin poem is not just
mirrored by the devotions. It is explicated, and seen in this light, the
Devotions are an *explication de texte.* Donne is artist, art, and critic,
all three. And this is his sermon upon his own text, to and upon his
own soul.

From the midst of a consuming illness, in which one would imagine his whole impulse would have been to devote himself to God, he
made sure that in the posture of devotion he should be self-consciously immortalized as art. I believe it consistent with his dedica-

tion and table of contents, as well as with all his religious writings, to suggest that for him the perfect achievement of the art was essential to the perfect act of devotion, because for Donne to live was at least as much a literary as a physical endeavor. Mr. Bald's description of his convalescence bears dramatic witness to that.

The publication of the *Devotions* was partly a manifestation of real gratitude to King James, who gave Donne spiritual life (in the ministry) and physical health (in sending the royal physician to nurse him through his illness). Still, Donne's eyes question the public reaction: "But let me stop, *my God,* and consider; will not this look like a piece of art, & cunning, to convey into the world an opinion, that I were more particularly in his care, then other men? And that heerein, in a shew of *humilitie,* and *thankfulnesse,* I magnifie my selfe more then there is cause?" (*Dev.,* Expos. 8, pp. 186-87). Gratitude to James and to God do mingle with vanity and desire for immortality: that is already clear in the dedication. But publication may also have been partly occasioned by the unusual isolation that his sickness forced upon him. He had expressed his desire to die in the pulpit.[11] In the *Devotions,* his complaints about his solitude repeatedly suggest that he does not feel whole when he is alone: "But *Lord,* thou art *Lord of Hosts,* & lovest *Action; Why callest thou me from my calling? In the grave no man shall praise thee;* In the doore of the grave, this sicke bed, no Man shal heare mee praise thee: Thou hast not opned my lips, that my mouth might shew *thee* thy praise, but that my mouth might shew *foorth* thy praise" (*Dev.,* Expos. 3, pp. 53-54). If he can exercise his meditations only in private, then in some way he must manage to have them overheard. Yet, despite the necessary qualifications to Anglican individuality suggested in Chapter I, and exemplified by the fact that in the foregoing passage he speaks in Scriptural language, the devotions are personal; it is himself he exposes to view. The dilemma implied in the dedication is everywhere apparent in the body of the *Devotions.*

Bunyan in *Grace Abounding* avoids this dilemma from the outset. Thinking as common man toward common men, he dedicates his book to his congregation, his "children," in whom he finds life: "Your hungerings and thirstings also after further acquaintance with the Father, in his Son; your tenderness of Heart, your trembling at sin, your sober and holy deportment also, before both God and men, is great refreshment to me: *For you are my glory and joy,* (I Thes. 2.20)" (*G.A.,* p. 1). Instead of the heavy and repeated stress on the

"I," the emphasis is all on "you," or "your." If Donne is to find life in the "I" of his book, that is where his attention has to be centered. Bunyan is *using* his book as a way of continuing to find life in his "children." Hence, the book and the "I" of the book become instruments, means to an end.

Never in Donne's dedication or in the *Devotions* themselves is it suggested that his offering himself to the world as he does is simply to testify to God's goodness, or to provide inspiration to others. It would almost seem that the complexity of pose is a direct result of his refusal to stress this possibility: he could so easily have provided a supporting interpretation of Hezekiah's story. Bunyan does find it necessary to justify what he is doing, but for him the justification is easy:

> Moses (*Numb*. 33. 1, 2) writ of the Journeyings of the children of *Israel,* from *Egypt* to the Land of *Canaan;* and commanded also, that they did remember their forty years travel in the wilderness. *Thou shalt remember all the way which the Lord thy God led thee these forty years in the wilderness, to humble thee, and to prove thee, to know what was in thine heart, whether thou wouldst keep his commandments, or no,* Deut. 8. 2, 3. Wherefore this I have endeavored to do; and not onely so, but to publish it also; that, if God will, others may be put in remembrance of what he hath done for their Souls, by reading his work upon me (*G.A.,* p. 2).

In this passage the double intention of *Grace Abounding* becomes clear. It is, first of all, a personal exercise in remembrance; and then, secondly, when published, a tool to be used by others in their own memory exercises. How are they to use it? "By reading his work upon me." The phrase is very striking, first in its obvious subordination of Bunyan to God, and then in its use of the word "work." Although the word can slide back and forth between "book," and "action" or "effect," here it points toward the latter meanings, and focuses Bunyan's whole biography away from art, toward life. The contrast is total with the mirror-within-mirror literary self-consciousness that informs Donne's prose.

Bunyan says at the end of his preface that he could have written his book in a much higher style if he had thought it right to do so. He did allow himself this liberty in his dense employment of Biblical quotations and citations in the preface itself. This standard practice places his autobiography in the traditional context that gives it significance: "I now once again, as before from the top of *Shenir* and *Hermon,* so now from *the Lions Dens, and from the Mountains of the Leopards* (Song 4.8), do look yet after you all, greatly longing to see your safe arrival into THE desired haven" (*G.A.*, p. 1). On the one hand, evidence of salvation is to be found in plain, everyday experiences; reference must always be first to the individual daily life of the common man. On the other hand, reference to the Bible can explain and generalize that life, and make it more dramatic. In his preface, Bunyan goes very far toward making allegory of himself and his congregation. Then, consciously bringing himself down to earth, he makes allegory and realism touch briefly, before rejecting the former method for the present: "Have you never a Hill *Mizar* to remember? Have you forgot the Close, the Milk-house, the Stable, the Barn, and the like, where GOD did visit your Soul?" (*G.A.*, p. 3). And immediately after this he makes his comments about style. This book is to be confined to barn and milk-house, to the specific places and events which must be acknowledged before allegory can become meaningful. Like Donne's, Bunyan's is a chosen style. But its purpose is to reflect a consciousness less literary and more utilitarian, less inwardly than outwardly directed.

Bunyan's twelve years in prison gave him time to recall to himself the most significant episodes in his spiritual life. Remembering for him involved reliving; that is a difference between his autobiography and those of less memorable Puritans. Yet it is still a past, recollected and analyzed, and more or less summed up at the end of the volume: There I was; here I am now. This kind of perspective is conducive to successful story-telling, as the reception of the book makes clear. Unlicensed and poorly printed, Bunyan's book was used up like a commodity. Despite the very large printings, only three copies of the first edition remain: it was literally read to pieces.[12]

Already, then, in these few pages, distinct differences between Donne and Bunyan, and between the Anglican and Puritan sensibilities, have begun to emerge. Donne's prose is mannered, witty, and cryptic; his art, which for him is a higher form of life, centers itself on the showing forth of his symbolic "I." Bunyan uses his book to send a message or sermon to his "children," who constitute his life. He too lives in his work, but as a remembrance of God's work upon him, as example (or exemplum) more than as symbol.[13] Both God and the congregation so far have received more stress than he has. Bunyan chooses to keep his style relatively concrete and literal. From the type of prose so far visible, and the different presentations of the "I"s, we may expect Donne's to tend toward an associative, poetic style, and Bunyan's toward chronological narrative.

The differences suggested by the dedications make themselves felt on every page of the two works, beginning, of course, with the use of the first person. Particularly significant contrasts may be drawn between Donne's and Bunyan's presentation of the "I" with relation to the implied narrator and to spectators implied or present; the "I" as timeless (Donne) or temporal (Bunyan); the "I" as historical character (Bunyan) or generalized symbol (Donne); the "I" as cosmic (Donne) or localized (Bunyan). These patterns do overlap one another, being different aspects of the same subject rather than different subjects. In considering all of them, it may be useful to keep in mind as touchstones (never as causes) one pair of contrasting figures that can to some extent summarize the differences between the Anglican and Puritan ways of relating the self to the world. These figures are the microcosm and the wayfaring pilgrim.[14]

Dependent upon the old theory of correspondences, the idea of man as little world at once gives the Anglican an opportunity to see himself reflecting and reflected by a larger mirror-image, and in the process of such reflection to depart from absolute realism. In his symbolic identity with all things in time and space, he is familiar with the mysterious and remote. He can also fragment, or anatomize himself, into component symbols, each with its separate significance, arteries being rivers and so on. The Puritan figure of the pilgrim, on the other hand, implies men moving through history, achieving self-consciousness partly by intercourse with other men, achieving their meaning by finding vocations within the historical flow of time. The Bible explains where they have come from, where they are, where they are going, in terms quite specifically applicable to current events. The immediate and down-to-earth matters much more than the mysterious and remote: the theory of correspondences is simply irrelevant or untrue. The Anglican's favorite Old Testament character is Adam, who includes all men, while the Puritan prefers Biblical characters wholly immersed in history.

Donne's choice of subject is self-conscious in the mirror-gazing sense. Physical illness makes it necessary for him to be especially aware of himself—looking in the mirror for symptoms: "So that now, we doe not onely die, but die upon the Rack, die by the torment of sicknesse; nor that onely, but are preafflicted, super-afflicted with these jelousies and suspitions, and apprehensions of *Sicknes,* before we can cal it a sicknes; we are not sure we are ill; one hand askes the other by the pulse, and our eye askes our own urine, how we do" (*Dev.,* Med. 1, p. 4). He has chosen a particularly private subject. Physically, he is confined to bed and denied visitors. His solitude heightens his self-awareness and makes him more than usually inclined to anatomize himself. He is quick to descant upon reality; perhaps his proneness to hypochondria causes him to anticipate and magnify his symptoms.

Later, when first one doctor and then several become involved in the case, he watches them watching him:

> I observe the *Phisician,* with the same diligence, as hee the *disease;* I see hee *feares,* and I feare with him: I overtake him, I overrun him in his feare, and I go the faster, because he makes his pace slow; I feare the more, because he disguises his fear, and I see it with the more sharpnesse, because hee would not have me see it. He knowes that his *feare* shall not disorder the practise, and exercise of his *Art,* but he knows that my *fear* may disorder the effect, and working of his practise (*Dev.,* Med. 6, pp. 115-16).

This building of an audience into the work itself is characteristic of Donne. He often looks past himself in the mirror to see who is looking on, and then recognizes that his own poise is accordingly affected. But here, in this deathly illness, the price of self-consciousness is high. The tight, clipped rhythm of the prose reflects the fevered sense of time's quickening as Donne nearly condemns himself to death before his time.

Just as in the first passage Donne in a sense invented the disease, here he has invented the doctor, who does not speak, but is interpreted from the point of view of an "I" whose objectivity we have no reason to trust. This kind of eye-witness is usual in Donne. Recall "The Exstasie," where he hypothesizes first a Platonic lover, and later "some lover such as wee," to behold a private scene. He constantly imagines himself under observation, imagines a complexity of reaction on the part of the observer. And because Donne is never justified by "evidence," the chief reaction of the reader is to become more aware of the extreme self-consciousness of the "I." The lookers-on whom he invents are there to mirror for him some feeling of his own.

Bunyan, too, has chosen a subject that requires constant self-examination, but even though he deals directly with his spiritual condition —which one would assume to be more private than physical illness, his manner is considerably less private and subjective, less noticeably self-conscious. For one thing, instead of pretending that the reader does not exist, he talks to him, rather than (except as he quotes himself to the reader) to himself or to God:

> But one day (amongst all the Sermons our Parson made) his subject was, to treat of the Sabbath day, and of the evil of breaking that, either with labour, sports, or otherwise: (now I was, notwithstanding my Religion, one that took much delight in all manner of vice, and especially that was the Day that I did solace my self therewith.) Wherefore I fell in my conscience under his Sermon, thinking and believing that he made that Sermon on purpose to shew me my evil-doing; and at that time I felt what guilt was, though never before, that I can remember . . . (G.A., pp. 9-10).

Perhaps the most obvious characteristic of this prose in contrast with Donne's is that it lacks the atmosphere of solitude. We are never told that the "I" of this narrative is in prison. Bunyan does not provide himself with that very available excuse and setting for self-analysis, and thus he completely avoids that opportunity for examining himself in private. On the contrary, the "I" of his narrative is in constant contact with everyday, outdoor activity. Not only is he not in prison; he is also never at home. He is always to be found in public places, as, here, at a sermon, and his sense of what is happening within him must always compete with and/or be tested by what seems to be a reasonably objective version of reality.

Bunyan's inner thoughts never seem out of proportion with that reality. In the passage above, we are told that Bunyan was a Sabbath-breaker, that the preacher spoke against Sabbath-breaking, and that therefore Bunyan thought the sermon was aimed at him. It could be true, if the preacher knew his congregation. But Bunyan further saves himself from Donne's self-centering of reality by the use of three words, *"thinking and believing* that he made that Sermon on purpose." Here interpreter-Bunyan distances himself from his earlier "I," for the very purpose of correcting the earlier self's vision.[15]

Like Donne, Bunyan often has onlookers, to whom he is extremely responsive:

> But one day, as I was standing at a Neighbors Shop-window, and there cursing and swearing, and playing the Mad-man, after my wonted manner, there sate within the woman of the house, and heard me; who, though she was a very loose and ungodly Wretch, yet protested that I swore and cursed at that most fearful rate, that she was made to tremble to hear me; And told me further, *That I was the ungodliest Fellow for swearing that ever she heard in all her life; and that I,* by thus doing, was able to spoile all the Youth in a whole *Town, if they came but in my company.*
>
> At this reproof I was silenced, and put to secret shame; and that too, as I thought, before the God of Heaven . . . (*G.A.*, pp. 11-12).

Bunyan's observers are almost always located in time and space, and given their own parts to play in the action of the story. They are never there only to observe, and their objective importance is as clear to the reader as to Bunyan himself. The whole of the drama, then, is much more externalized. There is a great deal of speech in Bunyan's narrative, and, even when he phrases it as indirect discourse, it seems public and literal.

One particular kind of observer, constant in Puritan prose, makes an interesting exception to this pattern. We may call him the Slanderer. Although he sometimes has a local habitation and a name, often he has neither. His purpose is to undermine a man's public position by accusing him of a questionable private life, and especially of indiscretions with women. In this self-conscious age, slander had become a criminal offense, but was still only partially controllable; and of course different standards of tolerance were applied to pro- and anti-government slanderers.[16] Every Puritan has a standard Biblical response to such charges: "Now these slanders . . . I glory in, because but slanders, foolish, or knavish lies, and falsehoods cast upon me by the Devil and his Seed; and should I not be dealt with thus wickedly by the World, I should want one sign of a Saint, and Child of God. *Blessed are ye* (said the Lord Jesus) *when men shall revile you, and persecute you . . .*" (*G.A.*, p. 93). Yet neither Bunyan nor any other Puritan is able to bear meekly charges which cast doubt on the validity both of his conversion and of his calling, and strike, in him, at the faith he holds. In the effort to justify himself against the Slanderer's distortion of truth, Bunyan is moved to hyperbolical response:

> My Foes have mist their mark in this their shooting at me. I am not the man, I wish that they themselves be guiltless, if all the Fornicators and Adulterers in *England* were hang'd by the Neck till they be dead, *John Bunyan,* the object of their Envie, would still be alive and well. I know not whether there be such a thing as a woman breathing under the Copes of the whole Heaven but by their apparel, their children, or by common Fame, except my Wife (*G.A.,* p. 94).

Donne's self-consciousness leads him to imagine the thoughts of his doctors. Bunyan is made self-conscious partly at least by the accusations of his slanderers. One's sense of Bunyan's isolation is heightened by this portrayal of himself as the only just man in an unjust society. He moves *in* society in a way that Donne does not, but he is set off from it, because he is always being measured or measuring himself against its demands. With the Slanderer his rage is great, because he is so limited in his ability to strike back. The Slanderer is the under-voice of conservatism, blindly but powerfully attacking the unknown. We will hear of him again.

Where Donne actively invents the casts of his inner dramas, Bunyan suggests that he is continually being invented by other people. There is, of course, the conversion pattern that he must follow, and he is reminded of its importance by voices that come (or seem to come) from without. One's sense of his being acted upon is much increased by his habitually making himself the object of the sentence, or speaking of himself in the passive voice, another characteristic way in which the called Puritan describes the continuing experience of vocation:

> It would be too long for me here to stay, to tell you in particular how God did set me down in all the things of Christ, and how he did, that he might so do, lead me into his words, yea and also how he did open them unto me, make them shine before me, and cause them to dwell with me and comfort me over and over . . . (*G.A.,* p. 39).

> And now was that word fulfilled on me, and I was also re-
> freshed by it. . . . Thus was my Soul at this time, (and as I
> did then think for ever) set at liberty from being again af-
> flicted with my former guilt and amazement (*G.A.*, p. 61).

The passive expresses vocation as well as the related sense of being
predestined and thereby unable simply to choose one's own path.
God acts upon him.

The "I" is created or creates himself by means of (Puritan) or in
spite of (Anglican) human time. The chief obvious difference between *Grace Abounding* and the *Devotions* is that one is literally
autobiographical and the other is not. Autobiography in its literal,
chronological sense, and as practiced by really self-conscious men,
not just by diarists recounting external events, is a Puritan, not an
Anglican habit. The self-conscious Puritan hopes to be able to move
in time, in some sort of meaningful progression of events, from bad
to good, from heathen to Christian (or from unsaved to saved), from
tyranny to Utopia, from the City of Destruction of the New Jerusalem. The Anglican, committed to an older view, has no belief in
progress: his whole posture is likely to be contemplative rather than
active. In meditation, he seeks to learn the significance of what is.
Thus we see in Bunyan a chronological account of years that are
finished, of a struggle that exists in the past and in the memory; in
Donne, a picture of a mind presently in travail, which can know, almost simultaneously, states of pain and states of rest. The illness is
ended, and yet it still is wholly present.

Donne writes in the present tense, eclipsing time; he makes the experience happen to him on the printed page:

> In the same instant that I feele the first attempt of the disease,
> I feele the victory; In the twinckling of an eye, I can scarse see,
> instantly the tast is insipid, and fatuous; instantly the appetite
> is dull and desirelesse: instantly the knees are sinking and
> strengthlesse; and in an instant, sleepe, which is the picture,
> the copy of death, is taken away, that the *Originall, Death* it
> selfe may succeed, and that so I might have death to the life
> (*Dev.*, Med. 2, pp. 25-26).

There can be no transitions from one state of mind to another because there is no room in Donne's technique for commentary on the

experience; that is one reason for the separation of the *Devotions* into independently titled paragraphs, each concerning a separate mood or stage. Donne-the-author is absent; there is only Donne-the-work. Past and future cease to have meaning, and there is only an ever-changing present captured and created in art.

Bunyan recounts experiences that have happened to him in the past, and the page, the written narrative, is a seldom-adequate medium for describing these experiences:

> I cannot now express with what longings and breakings in my Soul, I cryed to Christ to call me. Thus I continued for a time all on a flame to be converted to Jesus Christ, and did also see at that day such glory in a converted state, that I could not be contented without a share therein. Gold! could it have been gotten for Gold, what could I have given for it! had I had a whole world, it had all gone ten thousand times over, for this, that my Soul might have been in a converted state (*G.A.*, p. 24).

He presents himself as *a* mortal man *in* time, the passage laced with changing tenses that call attention to the fact of time's movement, whereas Donne's identification of himself with the printed page seems to absolve him of mortality and time. It is entirely typical that Bunyan insists on his inability to recreate the experience (thus opposing art and life) while Donne's passage ends with the author's witty metamorphosis into art.

In *Grace Abounding*, we are shown Bunyan the "I"-in-process, and his feelings are clearly rendered through the interpreter-Bunyan of many years later. Thus we are immediately made aware of the passage of time in a completely different way from that in which we experience it in the *Devotions*. We watch Bunyan changing from year to year, and we also know that time exists and that Bunyan has changed, because interpreter-Bunyan is clearly an older man by whom these earlier experiences are being relived or recreated.

Stylistically we are informed of the difference between the two Bunyans in numerous ways. Interpreter-Bunyan signals his presence almost sentence-by-sentence, with such interjections as "I say," "you must know," "thought I," and "I thank God." As we have seen, he tells us sometimes that he cannot or will not report certain earlier feelings or events. Sometimes he explains an event that he could not understand at the time: "But so foolish was I, and ignorant, that I knew not the reason for this sound . . ." (*G.A.*, p. 30). Such passages as these are particularly apt ways of marking the difference between the experience and the recording of it, since they show clearly that the two Bunyans are different, existing in different periods of time.

Bunyan constantly mentions the time at which something happened, or the length of time during which he continued in a given state of mind or way of life. Even if these times are approximate and undated, they provide a sense of temporal significance: "But about ten or eleven a Clock one day, as I was walking under a Hedge, full of sorrow and guilt God knows, and bemoaning myself for this hard hap . . . suddenly this sentence bolted in upon me" (*G.A.*, p. 44); "That Scripture would lie all day long, all the week long; yea, all the year long in my mind, and hold me down" (*G.A.*, p. 44). One qualification of Bunyan's method needs to be made. The fact that in a very real sense he has brought his whole struggle to the present, making it palpable and vivid in his mind, is most obviously represented by his frequent use of the word "now," in a context charged with immediacy: "And *now* was I both a burthen and a terror to myself, nor did I ever so know, as *now*, what it was to be weary of my life, and yet afraid to die. Oh, how gladly now would I have been anybody but myself!" (*G.A.*, p. 45). He relives the experience with a vividness which gives his book much of its power and distinguishes it from more pedestrian and more typical Puritan autobiography. Still *was* vies with *now* in this passage, *then* with *now* in his vocabulary. It is always obvious that the time of the experience much precedes the time of writing; the narrator remains in the present while the actor visits the past. The chronological notation of time is definitive, and therefore even in the midst of pain, bad times can be endured:

So soon as this fresh assault had fastened on my Soul, that Scripture came into my heart, *This is for many days*, Dan. 10. 14. and indeed I found it was so: for I could not be delivered nor brought to peace again until well-nigh two years and an half were compleatly finished. Wherefore these words, though in themselves they tended to discouragement, yet to me, who feared this condition would be eternal, they were at some times as an help and refreshment to me.

> For, thought I, *many days* are not for ever . . . (*G.A.*,
> p. 62).

Donne too proceeds through a spiritual-physical crisis, but he indicates periods of time nowhere, and any forward movement is highly
qualified by several structural devices implied by his word *"stationes,"* or *"stations,"* which describes his alternative to chronological
time. I have already pointed out that this word first appears in the
title to his introductory Latin poem, which is then broken up into
headings for the twenty-three stations, or sections, of the book. Thus
before we being to read the story of Donne's illness, we have already
read it immortalized in timeless Latin. And yet both the poem and
the story through which it weaves are in the present tense, here used
perhaps like God's Hebrew, which (says Donne) has only one tense
because all times are one to Him.[17]

In the body of the book, each station is in turn divided into three
sections—Meditation, Expostulation, and Prayer—illustrating despair,
doubt, and peace, so that any forward movement is again qualified
by a constant recognition of a permanently self-divided state. Two
significant passages in the meditations illuminate his employment of
the word "stations":

> All things are done in *time* too; but if we consider *Tyme* to be
> but the *Measure of Motion,* and howsoever it may seeme to
> have three *stations, past, present,* and *future,* yet the *first* and
> *last* of these *are* not (one is not, now, & the other is not yet)
> and that which you call *present,* is not *now* the same that it
> was, when you began to call it so in this Line . . . (*Dev.,*
> Med. 14, pp. 333-34).[18]

> Though thou remove them [specific days, time, months] from
> being of the *Essence* of our *Salvation,* thou leavest them for
> *assistances,* and for the *Exaltation* of our *Devotion,* to fix our
> selves, at certaine *periodicall,* & *stationary times,* upon the con-
> sideration of those things, which thou hast done for us . . .
> (*Dev.,* Expos. 14, pp. 342-43).

What these passages seem to mean in relation to the *Devotions* is
this. On the one hand, time is meaningless: past, present, and future
alike are scarcely tangible. On the other hand, for the sake of devotions, we can fix ourselves upon certain symbolical times (or, to refer

to my earlier discussion of the table of contents, for the sake of better understanding, we can explicate a poem which cannot be paraphrased). Thus, the three sections of each station in the *Devotions* represent a psychological rendition of the constant flow of time in their portrait of a mind that is now dejected (in the meditations), now turbulent (in the expostulations), now exalted (in the prayers).[19] At the same time, the gathering together of the three as a station, each station representing a highly symbolized stage of Donne's illness, suggests that time can be redeemed and stilled through the creation of a symbolic pattern that gives the temporal phenomenon of the illness a permanent spiritual meaning.

Finally, the word "station," in another sense which Donne could hardly have escaped, refers to the Catholic service of the Stations of the Cross, in which a series of prayers is uttered before each of fourteen representations of Christ in his progress toward Calvary. At Donne's fourteenth station, in fact, the physicians recognize that he is at the critical stage of his illness. In the service of the Stations, the faithful follow in the path of Christ, imitating his progress, standing before the pictured or sculptured representations to make a tableau facing a tableau. Donne's use of the word "stations" thus underlines the public context in which he hoped to justify and immortalize his private experience.

Let me now briefly illustrate this theory in practice. At the twelfth station, the physicians apply pigeons to the soles of the feet in order "to draw the vapors from the Head."[20] Here Donne completes the three-part sequence in the prayer:

> And as thou hast caried this thy *creature* the *Dove,* through all thy wayes, through *Nature,* and made it naturally proper to conduce medicinally to our *bodily health,* Through the *law,* and made it a *sacrifice* for *sinne* there, and through the *Gospel,* and made it, & thy spirit in it, a witnes of thy *sonnes baptisme* there, so carry it, and the qualities of it home to my *soule,* and imprint there that *simplicity,* that *mildnesse,* that *harmelesnesse,* which thou hast imprinted by *Nature* in this *Creature.* That so all *vapours* of all disobedience to thee, being subdued under my feete, I may in the power, and triumphe of thy *sonne,* treade victoriously upon my *grave,* and trample upon the *Lyon,* and *Dragon,* that lye under it, to devoure me (*Dev.,* Prayer 12, pp. 308-9).

Donne need not wait until the end of some period of days or years
to be delivered, since this kind of salvation is available at any point in
the sequence. The rendering of the experience into symbolism enables the "I" to tread upon his own grave, in other words, to conquer
time. The "I" becomes art, making himself an emblem of his own
spiritual struggle.

The chronological and utopian aspects of Puritan thought explain
other characteristics of the stylistic difference between Bunyan and
Donne. Because Bunyan moves from one point to another in time and
meaning, the more effectively his prose can move the narrative forward, the better it can sustain his meaning. Hence, he is more likely
than Donne to discover the techniques of narrative, and to prefer pace
to decoration. His description of the several stages of his decision to
give up bell ringing as sinful takes 260 words, where Donne needs
5,000 words to ring all the possible changes upon the passing-bell as
symbol of man's unity. Having nowhere to go, he can move around
and around his symbolic subject, in meditative and associative, rather
than chronological, prose.

One of the commonest words in Bunyan's book, especially in the
earlier parts, is the verb "to walk." He had to walk, of course, in his
work, and in the course of his walking some of his most meaningful
experiences occurred. Walking brought him closer to heaven. Words
describing travel are, in fact, often used in contexts that blur the distinction between literal and metaphorical:

> Thus therefore for several dayes I was greatly assaulted and per-
> plexed, and was often, when I have been walking, ready to
> sink where I went with faintness in my mind . . . (G.A.,
> p. 21).

> Now I remember that one day as I was walking into the Coun-
> try, I was much in the thoughts of this, But how if the day of
> grace be past? and to aggravatate my trouble, the Tempter pre-
> sented to my mind those good people of *Bedford,* and sug-
> gested thus unto me, That these being converted already, they
> were all that God would save in those parts, and that I came
> too late, for these had got the blessing before I came (G.A.,
> p. 22).

> In the light and encouragement of this word, I went a pretty
> while . . . (G.A., p. 23).

In the second of these three quotations, the word "conversion" appears. To the Puritan, conversion or change is the painful day-to-day experience of learning to conform to the will of a mysterious God, and then attempting to find out whether grace has been granted. Whether or not it happens all at once, or over a long period of time, it does happen *in* time, although from that point forward the Puritan may sense himself as living on more than one level, as partaking somehow in allegory. Journey, walking, conversion bring the Christian to the New Jerusalem.

The words in the *Devotions* that correspond to Bunyan's travel words are "change," "translate," "transform," and "transmute." Man's changefulness is a condition of mortal life. Moreover, Donne is well acquainted with the paradoxes of Christianity, particularly those characterizing the main events of Christ's life and the Church's sacraments, as examples of double meaning that allow for transmutation. Considered symbolically, the bread and wine of the Eucharist are the flesh and blood of Christ. No forward movement is necessary; one must simply use the goods of this world as doorways to eternity. Change is instantaneous, and, again, chronological progress is without meaning. The symbolic character of the Anglican way of thought is here reinforced. For Donne, in the *Devotions,* all the external manifestations and trappings of his illness—physicians, fever spots, pigeons, bells, and so forth—have this sacramental nature. So another difference between Donne and Bunyan (and Anglican and Puritan) is the difference between a sacramental and a non-sacramental view of reality.

The way in which Donne uses, or ignores, time demonstrates that by gathering timeless human meanings into himself, he makes his individual "I" a symbol representing all men. Bunyan, on the other hand, in dissociating himself from the society of the Slanderer, and in submitting himself to the severing power of time, becomes more isolated as Donne becomes less so. This point becomes still clearer in the persona's third type of self-expression—as historical character (Bunyan) or generalized symbol (Donne). Where Bunyan confines himself to his own experience, Donne generalizes his predicament to—or from—that of all men. The Anglican's habits of thought are more closely allied to the deductive reasoning of old philosophies, while the Puritan gravitates toward the inductive reasoning of the new. No Anglican or Puritan is necessarily conscious of an issue; each naturally uses what is appropriate to the sustenance of his values and interests. To put it another way, it is the difference between symbol and exemplum. Donne is all men; Bunyan is an example of what a man can be. It is also beginning to be the difference between poetic and scientific (or evidential) truth.

Bunyan takes personally everything that happens to him; specific events of his life seem to him the best of all possible evidence of God's grace. In his opening sentence he tells his readers that he wants to begin by giving "a hint of my pedegree, and manner of bringing up; that thereby the goodness and bounty of God towards me, may be the more advanced and magnified before the sons of men" (*G.A.*, p. 5). Specific occurrences surrounding and comprising his conversion are clear and vivid. Physical events and dates are mingled in such a way that it would be impossible to mistake this autobiography for anyone else's: God saved him from drowning once in "a crick of the Sea," and again in Bedford River (*G.A.*, p. 7); he and his wife came together "without so much houshold-stuff as a Dish or Spoon," but she had with her *The Plain mans Pathway to Heaven,* and *The Practice of Piety,* which her father had left her (*G.A.*, p. 8); he ministered in Bedford; on the road between Elstow and Bedford he was tempted to try to work a miracle, making the dry places puddles, and the puddles dry (*G.A.*, pp. 18-19); he loved and worried about his blind child more than any of the others (*G.A.*, p. 98). He spares us the most mechanical phraseology of the standard autobiographies, and the vivid concreteness of particular temptations is no one's but his own.

In Donne's *Devotions* we are provided with almost none of this homely, immediate information. His book describes the course of an illness which afflicted him at the time of writing, and his illness is equated with spiritual disease. We know enough about his physical condition to diagnose it in modern terms. But we are told very little else about his circumstances, nothing of his family, dwelling place, position, or age, and almost nothing of his life preceding the illness. The opening lines of the *Devotions* cry out, "Variable, and therefore miserable condition of Man; this minute I was well, and am ill, this minute. I am surpriz'd with a sodaine change, & alteration to worse, and can impute it to no cause, nor call it by any name. We study *Health,* and we deliberate . . ." (*Dev.*, Med. 1, pp. 1-2). The alternation observable between the general and the particular, man and Donne, "we" and "I," does in itself definitively distinguish Donne's "I" from Bunyan's. Donne begins with a generalization about man's estate, in sickness and health assuming his lot to be that of fallen humanity. Significantly, he shares this very illness with many others, as one victim of an epidemic. While he may rebel against having to share man's common fate, he is not forced to quiver with uncertainty about the meaning of specific details of his life.

He can see very well that there is a difference between the general and the particular, between the tradition to which he belongs and his own individuality, but the existence of the distinction is strange to him—it both irritates and excites him, and he intensifies the problem by putting emphasis upon it. Hence, the alternation between "I" and "we"; the cosmic "I"; the generalizing parenthesis in an especially self-conscious figure: "Miserable and, (though common to all) in-human *posture,* where I must practise my lying in the *grave,* by lying still, and not practise my *Resurrection,* by rising any more" (*Dev.,* Med. 3, pp. 46-47). Between general and particular, a new tension exists. Donne cannot simply say "I" or "we."

While Donne's consciousness is coextensive with man's (he and mankind being involved and contained in one another), Bunyan questions whether he has any place among men at all. While he published his autobiography as a way of helping and consoling others who might be encountering similar experiences, and while he was certainly aware that his conversion followed a pattern, his moment-to-moment account of his successes or failures shows us a man standing alone:

> But the same day, as I was in the midst of a game at Cat, and having struck it one blow from the hole; just as I was about to strike it the second time, a voice did suddenly dart from Heaven into my Soul, which said, *Wilt thou leave thy sins, and go to Heaven? or have thy sins, and go to Hell?* At this I was put to an exceeding maze; wherefore, leaving my Cat upon the ground, I looked up to Heaven, and was as if I had with the eyes of my understanding, seen the Lord Jesus looking down upon me, as being very hotly displeased with me, and as if he did severely threaten me with some grievous punishment for these, and other my ungodly practices (*G.A.,* p. 10).

In an instant, Bunyan is cut off from all humanity. Other players in the game vanish. Only he, of all those playing at cat at such and such a place and such and such a time, was aware of a voice that unexpectedly required a choice between heaven and hell. No generalization protected him against its force or allowed him to consider the "thou" as plural. Having worked through to a belief in his own salvation, Bunyan could offer his own experience as an example for others, but he could not, as Donne could, symbolize his plight as it occurred. Nor, I think, could most Puritan writers. The preacher, finally, conversant with many particular cases, including his own, could build the moral allegory of *Pilgrims Progress,* which transmutes all particular men into General Man; but to do this, he had to put aside the self-conscious voice entirely, and, so to speak, objectify his findings.

We have seen some slight evidence of this beginning to happen in the preface to *Grace Abounding.* It also happens during the course of the narrative that the preacher comes momentarily to the fore in the person of interpreter-Bunyan, and then we get passages like this, where Bunyan is obviously generalizing:

> (And I am very confident, that this temptation of the Devil is more than usual amongst poor creatures then many are aware of, even to over-run their spirits with a scurvie and seared frame of heart, and benumming of conscience: which frame, he stilly and slyly supplyeth with such despair, that though not much guilt attendeth the Soul, yet they continually have a secret conclusion within them, that there is no hopes for them; *for they have loved sins, therefor after them they will go,* Jer. 2. 25 & 18. 12.) (*G.A.,* p. 11).

This sudden and extreme distancing of the subject, from "I" to "poor creatures" and "them," is dramatic. And Bunyan's inclusion of the paragraph within parentheses is interesting. He recognized that he was changing his style.

Disapproving or even unaware of much of Donne's whole system of correspondences, Bunyan separates general from particular completely, concentrating first on the particular, in autobiography, then on the general, in allegory. While diary and autobiography certainly have strong obvious tendencies toward allegory, still the two forms for the time being remain separate. Bunyan is not yet ready to talk about Common Man, because he is so preoccupied with the common man that he himself is. Like most Puritans, he spends his time com-

piling evidence. There has to be more diary than allegory, more item-
ization of detail than literary production.

By his use of external personal detail, and by his objective location
of himself in time and space, Bunyan persuades us to accept and trust
him as a person. Insofar as Bunyan-the-interpreter succeeds as narrator, we read the story from his point of view. With him, we fall into
sympathy with the life story of the younger Bunyan, accepting him as
a person "like ourselves." Still, interpreter-Bunyan, of whom we are
often unaware, is a person of enough sophistication to see all around
the younger Bunyan, and to guide our responses to him—a fact which
should be remembered when we judge the "I" of this work.

In Donne's book, there is only the one "I," with a widening vision,
unlocated in time and space. Superficially ignoring the reader, he
catches us up in other ways—by his inclusive symbolism, by his shifting between "I" and "we," and by the rhythms of his rhetoric. By his
use of these rhythms, he makes us take each moment of the sickness
as he takes it, accepting the cyclic psychological movement from despair to hope to confidence, and the cyclic esthetic movement from
flat realism to febrile questioning to symbolic art. To the extent that
we can share his rhythms and his language, we are brought with him
to the tense union of particular with general, "I" with "we," one
man with all men.

Elsewhere I have traced the particular sentence patterns which
comprise these rhythms,[21] and I do not want to reproduce the entire
argument here. The point is that the movement of this prose is meditative in a particularly purposive way—that the flat Senecan periods
of the meditations imitate the feeling of negation and despair that the
imagery and word choice encourage; that the turbulent periods of
the expostulations break up that sense of deadness, and replace it
with a feverish life; and that finally both give way to the stately Anglican cadence of the Book of Common Prayer, where man is wholly
reconciled to God. Donne's italics, as well as many other stylistic devices, help to point up these rhythms and enable the reader to hear
his voice.

There are other rhythms as well. From the significant repetition of
single words, to the choral refrain effect of a sentence given at the
beginning of a paragraph and then varied at the end (Meditation 1,
for example), repetitions account for much. Worth mentioning here,
again, is the broken-up poem whose Latin cadences so greatly affect
the tone of the whole work.

The rhythms of Bunyan's prose are those of common speech, the colloquial rhythms of a man speaking to men. His genius lies in his ability to reproduce and to heighten these rhythms, depending upon the occasion being described. For example, when he recounts his most crucial experiences, the language is intensified by means of repetition, italicization, direct quotation, and exclamation:

> So as I was a going home, these words came again into my thoughts, and I well remember as they came in, I said thus in my heart, What shall I get by thinking on these two words? this thought had no sooner passed thorow my heart, but the words began thus to kindle in my Spirit, *Thou art my Love, thou art my Love,* twenty times together; and still as they ran thus in my minde, they waxed stronger and warmer, and began to make me look up; but being as yet between hope and fear, I still replied in my heart, *But is it true too? but is it true?* at which, that sentence fell in upon me, *He wist not that it was true which was done unto him of the angel,* Act 12. 9 (G.A., p. 29).

Both men in different ways catch us up in an immediate sharing of experience through the compelling rhythms of their prose. Both also allow us different kinds of esthetic distance from personal experience, corresponding to the sacramental and homiletic approaches. Hoping to teach by example, Bunyan presents his story reportorially, in narrative form, making a distinction between the preacher and the story, Bunyan-now and Bunyan-then. Donne leads the reader, through shared experience, to see himself as a type of mankind. Rather than separating himself from his experience in any way, Donne makes it formal, public, and symbolic.

Finally, the two "I"s differ with regard to space. Where Bunyan limits his existence in space by use of concrete detail, Donne expands his in order to create a cosmic personality. Their common interest in bells will usefully illustrate the contrast. Discovering that bell-ringing was sinful, Bunyan learned to give it up a little at a time:

> I thought that such a practice was but vain, and therefore forced my self to leave it, yet my mind hanckered, wherefore I should go to the Steeple house, and look on: though I durst not ring. But I thought this did not become Religion neither,

yet I forced my self and would look on still; but quickly after, I began to think, How, if one of the Bells should fall: then I chose to stand under a main Beam that lay over thwart the Steeple from side to side, thinking there I might stand sure: But then I should think again, Should the Bell fall with a swing, it might first hit the Wall, and then rebounding upon me, might kill me for all this Beam; this made me stand in the Steeple door, and now thought I, I am safe enough, for if a Bell should then fall, I can slip out behind these thick Walls, and so be preserved notwithstanding.

So after this, I would yet go to see them ring, but would not go further than the Steeple door; but then it came into my head, how if the Steeple it self should fall, and this thought, (it may fall for ought I know) would when I stood and looked on, continually so shake my mind, that I durst not stand at the Steeple door any longer, but was forced to fly, for fear it should fall upon my head (*G.A.*, pp. 13-14).

Bunyan's imagination in this sequence operates tenaciously and personally, binding him closer and closer to the objects of his guilt and forcing him to take immediate literal action in regard to them. Realism is foremost both in the concreteness of details given—main beam, thick walls, the way the bell swings, and so forth, and in the concreteness of each of Bunyan's responsive actions. The story has to be told chronologically, with each movement in the sequence included. Committed to a literal rehearsal of the facts as he (at least) wishes us to suppose that he remembers them, Bunyan-narrator can allow Bunyan-actor to occupy no other part of space and time than those very limited places and times in which the event could actually have occurred.

As Donne lies ill in bed, he thinks about the passing bell in a personal way: it tolls for him. But already the facts are distorted, since it is not literally his funeral bell. In raising the bell to a symbol and himself to mankind's representative, he begins by reminding himself of other bells, and of writings about bells which enrich the meaning of this one at the same time that they cause its personal relevance to fade: "We have a *Convenient Author,* who writ a *Discourse of Bells* when hee was prisoner in *Turky.* How would hee have enlarged himselfe, if he had beene my *fellow Prisoner* in this *sicke bed,* so neere to that *steeple,* which never ceases, no more than the *harmony of the*

spheres, but is more heard" (*Dev.,* Med. 16, pp. 388-89). Like most
of Donne's puns, the play on the word "enlarged" is very fruitful.
The meditator gains freedom from personal bondage, and increased
freedom of language in the inspiration afforded by the bells; by these
means, he may himself become a larger person. Perhaps he is also to
be enlarged by becoming Donne's bedfellow. At any rate, Donne's
next step is to begin to suggest for himself the possibility of that kind
of human extension. He associates himself with another man by saying that his death is as likely, his sinfulness as certain as those of the
man for whom this bell now tolls. At this point, then, he is already
in his imagination both himself and the dead man. Elevation to universality follows, in the famous passage: "No man is an *Iland,* intire
of it selfe; every man is a peece of the *Continent,* a part of the *maine;*
if a *Clod* bee washed away by the *Sea, Europe* is the lesse, as well as
if a *Promontorie* were, as well as if a *Mannor* of thy *friends* or of
thine owne were; Any Mans *death* diminishes *me,* because I am involved in *Mankinde;* And therefore never send to know for whom
the *bell* tolls; It tolls for *thee*" (*Dev.,* Med. 17, pp. 415-16).

The more detail Bunyan supplies in the presentation of his story,
the clearer its boundaries become: it happens in a limited time and
space. The farther Donne elaborates his meditation, the more extensive he becomes. His limits are those of human consciousness, ultimately definable only in terms of the earth or the cosmos. Specifically,
here we notice first of all that as soon as he thinks, "they . . . may
have caused it to toll for me," he also thinks, "for *thee.*" It is a variation on his characteristic shifting between "I" and "we." Just as typical is the microcosm-macrocosm imagery which identifies mankind
with the earth. Donne's daring with his figures reflects his literary,
controlled use of his experience, whereas Bunyan's experience is
presented as if it were only accidentally literary, because he happened
to record it.

The contrast between the "artificial" and the "natural" record becomes even clearer if we compare passages where both writers involve
themselves at once in something other than literal reality. In the following passage, Bunyan describes what he calls "a kind of Vision," in
which he saw the people of Bedford on the sunny side of a mountain, and himself on the cold side, with a wall between:

> About this wall I thought myself to goe again and again, still
> prying as I went, to see if I could find some way or passage,

by which I might enter therein, but none could I find for some time: at the last I saw as it were, a narrow gap, like a little door-way in the wall, thorow which I attempted to pass: but the passage being very straight, and narrow, I made many offers to get in, but all in vain, even untill I was well nigh quite beat out by striving to get in: at last, with great striving, me thought I at first did get in my head, and after that, by a side-ling striving, my shoulders, and my whole body; then I was exceeding glad, and went and sat down in the midst of them, and so was comforted with the light and heat of their Sun.

Now, this Mountain and Wall, &c., was thus made out to me; the Mountain signified the Church of the living God; the Sun that shone thereon, the comfortable shining of his merci-full face on them that were therein: the wall I thought was the Word that did make separation between the Christians and the world: and the gap which was in this wall, I thought was Jesus Christ, who is the way to God the Father, *Job.* 14.6. *Mat.* 7.14. But for as much as the passage was wonderful nar-row, even so narrow, that I could not but with great difficulty, enter in thereat; it shewed me, that none could enter into life but those that were in down-right earnest, and unless they left this wicked world behind them; for here was only roome for Body and Soul, but not for Body and Soul, and Sin (*G.A.,* pp. 19-20).

The sense of spatial constriction strikes one very forcibly here. It is, of course, part of the character of this vision that such constric-tion has to exist, but it is also in the character of *Grace Abounding.* One has the same sense of spatial oppression in the episode with the bell tower, and in many other passages where Bunyan seems pinned to specific time and place, or forced from moment to moment to move from one limited space to another.

Bunyan is dealing with a dream or vision whose symbolism is in-trinsic to it; all he can do is try to find the "right" interpretation. And notice here the wording of the sentence that introduces the interpre-tation, "this Mountain and wall, &c. was thus made out to me," sug-gesting that Bunyan himself had nothing to do with it.[22] Just as in his reporting of events, he ascribes control of his experience and his understanding to an agent other than himself, here he suggests that both dream and its meaning were simply given him as scribe. The Biblical echoes, meanwhile, reveal the source of the vision.

Donne does not have visions, and the traditional character of his symbolism is obscured by its immense sophistication. At the thirteenth station of Donne's *Devotions*, "*the Sicknes declares the infection and malignity thereof by spots*" (*G.A.*, p. 312), and the symbolic meaning he ascribes to the spots is spelled out, if anything, too plainly:

> My *God, my God,* thou hast made this sick bed thine *Altar,* and I have no other *Sacrifice* to offer, but my self; and wilt thou accept *no spotted sacrifice?* Doeth thy *Son* dwel bodily in this flesh, that thou shouldst looke for an unspottednes here? Or is the *Holy Ghost,* the *soule* of this *body,* as he is of thy *Spouse,* who is therfore *all faire, and no spot in her?* or hath thy *Son* himself no *spots,* who hath al our stains, & deformities in him? Or hath thy *Spouse,* thy *Church,* no *spots,* when every particular limbe of that faire, & spotles body, every particular *soule* in that *Church* is full of staines and spots? Thou bidst us *hate the garment, that is spotted with the flesh.* The *flesh* it selfe is the *garment,* and it spotteth it selfe, with it self (*Dev.*, Expos. 13, pp. 320-21).

Very clear here is the way in which Donne becomes both subject and object of his meditations. He offers himself as sacrifice; the flesh sullies itself with itself. He is his own creation, an artificial and symbolic character, whereas Bunyan presents himself always as a human being made by God, upon whom God works his will. While Donne's fever spots presumably appeared unexpectedly, like Bunyan's vision, Donne is instantly prepared to employ them as the symbolic subject of a many-levelled exegesis. Eventually, they become his equivalent of Bunyan's narrow passageway to grace:

> Even my *spotts* belong to thy *Sonnes* body, and are part of that, which he came downe to this earth, to fetch, and challenge, and assume to himselfe. When I open my *spotts,* I doe but present him with that which is *His,* and till I do so, I detaine, & withhold *his right.* When therfore thou seest them upon me, as *His,* and seest them by this way of *Confession,* they shall not appear to me, as the *pinches of death,* to decline

> my feare to *Hell;* (for *thou hast not left thy holy one in Hell,*
> thy *Sonne* is not there) but these *spotts* upon my *Breast,* and
> upon my *Soule,* shal appeare to mee as the *Constellations* of
> the *Firmament,* to direct my contemplation to that place,
> where thy *Son* is, thy *right hand* (*Dev.,* Expos. 13, pp. 326-27).

Concentrating wholly upon himself, again he finds himself merging
with the universe. He is both contained and container, both the soul
seeking heaven, and the constellations that light the way. Bunyan in
his vision moves from one place to another. Donne simply expands,
becomes fragmented, eventually occupies the whole universe. The
very cause of his confinement, the spots of the fever, becomes the instrument of his "enlargement."

There is certainly a playfulness, too, about his extension of fever
spots into so complex a symbol. This playfulness is intrinsic to metaphysical wit, in its penchant for making farfetched analogies, in its
capacity to view the same object in several different lights, and in its
fascination with transformation. Donne uses all these devices here.
The exegetical character of this exercise gives the reader an opportunity to share the play. In a sense, he is led to believe that the whole
process is very logical, especially if he remembers, as Donne would
have, the connection between the words "spots" and "spotless" and
the Latinate "immaculate," with its religious connotations. It is amaz-
ing to see the least esthetic aspect of his illness become the starry firmament above his head, but our amazement is made respectful by the
knowledge that he has earned the right to work the transformation.

Like most Puritans, Bunyan is interested only in thought directly
translatable into action, especially a certain kind of action. Bunyan
hoped that he could find a place to stand where the bell would not
fall on him, and he hoped to be able to get to the sunny side of the
mountain. While the bell episode is meant partly to illustrate Bunyan's ignorance of God at the time, it is nevertheless a typically Puritan hope, whether expressed in such limited terms as these or in those
that filled the minds of men who wanted to build Utopia. The Puritans believed it possible to move physically, in space and time, from
a place that was not safe and perfect to one that was, and their whole
lives were given to this quest. It is united, of course, with their desire
for spiritual progress, but the fact that this too is commonly described
as physical movement is significant. Donne, in contrast, believes that
the bell summons all men to die, whoever and wherever they are, that

man's estate is miserable, and that the only hope is not in any kind of movement or progress, but in making time and space themselves open into eternity, just as the temporal fever spots, so limiting and limited in their "real" character, are made to become a vehicle of Donne's enlargement from the confines of time and space. Both Bunyan and Donne, in their different handlings of different material, bring the "I" to a point where he represents all men. But Donne's "I" has also become symbolic and non-representational, where Bunyan's functions as a representative human being in an allegorical situation.

A consideration of Donne's and Bunyan's conscious choices of language and of their comments on language can help us to understand the different theories of style according to which they proceed. I have already touched upon their contrasting types of imagery. Bunyan never uses the microcosm-macrocosm analogy that is Donne's stock-in-trade. For Donne, man is not only a little world, but, as I have already suggested, he frequently becomes the world, both in analogies (his veins are rivers, and so forth) and in importance. Metaphor unites and transforms. But for the Puritan the world is a more hostile place, more definitely allied with flesh and devil, and the individual is a pilgrim wayfarer or soldier passing through it.

In minor figures of speech, Bunyan makes constant and almost exclusive use of simile: "my heart . . . was as a clog on the leg of a Bird" (G.A., pp. 25-26); "they had as good have told me that I must reach the Sun with my finger" (G.A., p. 26); "I have found my unbelief to set as it were the shoulder to the door" (G.A., p. 26); "I found myself as on a miry bog" (G.A., p. 27). Donne is much more prone to use metaphors or symbols, eliminating "like" or "as" from the figure.

Yet the distinction which Bunyan consistently makes has nothing to do with a failure of the imagination or with the prissiness that we commonly call Puritanical. Donne is accustomed to dealing in ritual and symbol; for him, these unite world and spirit. For Bunyan, the particular symbols and rituals of Anglicanism are divisive, needlessly arbitrating for him between man and God. Therefore he wishes to dispense with the very tools upon which Donne relies for an orderly, coherent world. At the same time, Bunyan is less well-equipped than Donne, for a variety of reasons, to cope with a world that has not been ordered for him. He has less education and less familiarity with the printed word. He rejects various kinds of authority which Donne takes for granted and uses as boundaries or points of stability. His imagination thus is both unschooled and unbounded. He has to trust it, for through it comes his prized direct communication with the Almighty; but he cannot trust it, because it is itself unruled. These two factors—his need to accept the imagination and his unpreparedness to understand it—put him much more at the mercy of language and of the world than Donne is.

Simile is a simple way of controlling the imagination, and it is analogous here to the habit of breaking apart generalization and concrete detail, of substituting allegory and personal narrative for symbolism. If you say that one thing is like another, you can keep the two distinct and unconfused in your mind more easily than if you fuse them in metaphor.

The one place where Bunyan does not typically use simile is where he describes the power that thoughts and words are able to exert upon his mind—"this thought would when I stood and looked on, continually so shake my mind"; "these words broke in upon my mind." For here he speaks not in metaphor but in literal truth, insofar as such experiences can be literally described. And it is just when Bunyan begins to express himself in this way that Donne pulls back or finds himself at a loss. Donne wants to be ravished by God, struck by God's thunder, but he is too sophisticated and self-centered, too fully in control of his world to be able to open himself to such raw, direct experience. His religious experience, like Bunyan's, is formulated in language, but it is the ordered, disciplined language of Anglican ritual.

Unless he is careful to keep it in its place, Bunyan does not use language; it uses him. Donne modulates Scripture into his own imagination, and makes it speak in his voice. An apt example is this passage from his meditations on the tolling bell:

> The *voice, thy hand* is in this *sound,* and in this *one sound,* I heare this *whole Consort.* I heare thy *Jaacob* call unto his *sonnes,* and say; *Gather your selves together, that I may tell you what shall befall you in the last daies:* He saies, *That which I am now, you must bee then.* I heare thy *Moses* telling mee, and all within the *compasse* of this *sound, This is the blessing wherewith I blesse you before my death;* This, that before your death, you would consider your owne in mine. I heare thy *Prophet* saying to *Ezechias, Set thy house in order,*

for thou shalt die, and not live; Hee makes us of his *familie,*
and calls this a setting of *his* house in order, to compose *us* to
the *meditation* of *death.* I heare thy *Apostle* saying, *I thinke it
meet to put you in remembrance, knowing that shortly I must
goe out of this Tabernacle.* This is the *publishing* of his *will,*
& this *bell* is our *legacie,* the applying of *his present condition*
to our use. I heare that which makes al sounds *musique,* and
all *musique* perfit; I heare thy *Sonne* himselfe saying, *Let not
your hearts be troubled* . . . (*Dev.,* Expos. 17, pp. 421-23).

The perfect control of Scripture and of art which enables Donne to
"hear" these voices speaking in a concert that leads to a controlled
and beautiful climax in the words of Christ is typical of Donne's
imagination, as it is of Anglican ritual, which was thought to exemplify the beauty of holiness. Here also is manifest the "I" as cosmic
personality, in Donne's ability both to participate in time and to sur-
pass it. He hears the speakers, in their own times; he makes himself
one with them ("he makes us of his familie"), and at the same time
he compresses all these speakers and their occasions into a single moment when a bell tolls in London for all mankind.

Now compare these typical encounters between Bunyan and
Scripture:

Lord, thought I, if both these Scriptures would meet in my
heart at once, I wonder which of them would get the better of
me. So me thought I had a longing mind that they might come
both together upon me; yea, I desired of God they might.

Well, about two or three days after, so they did indeed; they
boulted both upon me at a time, and did work and struggle
strangly in me for a while; at last, that about *Esaus* birthright
began to wax weak, and withdraw, and vanish; and this about
the sufficiency of Grace prevailed, with peace and joy (*G.A.,*
pp. 66-67).

When I had with much deliberation considered of this
matter, and could not but conclude that the Lord had comforted me, and that too after this my wicked sin; then methought I durst venture to come nigh unto those most fearful
and terrible Scriptures, with which all this while I had been
so greatly affrighted, and on which indeed before I durst scarce

cast mine eye, (yea, had much ado an hundred times to forbear wishing of them out of the Bible, for I thought they would destroy me) but now, I say, I began to take some measure of incouragement, to come close to them, to read them, and consider them, and to weigh their scope and tendence.

The which when I began to do, I found their visage changed; for they looked not so grimly on me as before I thought they did: And first, I came to the sixth of the *Hebrews*, yet trembling for fear it should strike me . . . (*G.A.*, pp. 69-70).

Where Donne assimilates Scripture into himself—makes it speak Donne—Bunyan encounters it, or fragments of it, as if it were another person. We know that Donne is in control of his concert, because all the members of it speak in turn at his bidding. Bunyan describes his younger self as having no control over his conflicts, except to the extent that he has a part, which is sometimes active and sometimes passive, in the proceedings. Sometimes he becomes the arena in which the Scripture battle rages; sometimes he himself can take one part against another. He is never "enlarged" by the presence of these passages within him, though he may be liberated as a result of struggle with them.

Donne's whole experience of life is literary, and indissolubly connected with the experiences of scholars and other writers whose works he knew. All creation is God's book, and he applies this cliché even more widely than was common in the age.[23] To him, things are words, and life has reality only when it becomes verbal; it is only then, too, that it acquires order and discipline, for, as he says in colloquy with the Trinity, "If your consultation determine in writing, if you refer me to that which is written, you intend my recovery; for all the way, *O my God* (ever constant to thine owne wayes), thou hast proceeded *openly, intelligibly, manifestly by the book*" (*Dev.*, Expos. 9, p. 217).

God's works are to be *read*, all of them. They may also be translated: "Let me think no degree of this thy correction, *casuall*, or without *signification*; but yet when I have read it in that language, as it is a *correction*, let me translate it into another, and read it as a *mercy*; and which of these is the *Originall*, and which is the *Translation*; whether thy *Mercy*, or thy *Correction*, were thy primary and original intention in this sicknes, I cannot conclude, though death conclude me . . ." (*Dev.*, Prayer 7, pp. 173-74). The fever spots, in their final metamorphosis, become God's writing: "These *spots* are but the *letters,* in which thou hast written thine owne *Name,* and conveyed thy selfe to mee . . ." (*Dev.,* Prayer 13, pp. 329-30). Donne, in fact, is an example of God's writing, just as everything else is, and his creation of himself in language in this book is a sort of imitation of God's creation of him.

Always, for Donne, experience and its literary rendition are inseparable. Bunyan, in the midst of a moving episode, may long for a recording pen, but that wish passes as does the experience itself, because for him there *is* a vast difference between a ploughed field and a printed page:

> Yea, I was now so taken with the love and mercy of God, that I remember I could not tell how to contain till I got home; I thought I could have spoken of his Love, and of his mercy to me, even to the very Crows that sat upon the plow'd lands before me, had they been capable to have understood me, wherefore I said in my Soul with much gladness, Well, I would I had a pen and ink here, I would write this down before I go any further, for surely I will not forget *this* forty years hence; but alas! within less then forty days I began to question all again (*G.A.,* p. 30).

Desire to write down the experience, or to talk about it, *follows* the experience but is not a necessary part of it.

To say that to Donne things are words and to Bunyan words are things is stretching the truth just slightly. While Donne puts the whole world into language, Bunyan finds language acting a part in the world; words strike him with objective force. To him at times Scripture seems more a blank physical power than a printed book: "Then did that Scripture seize upon my soul" (*G.A.,* p. 56); "Then would the former sentence, as the conclusion of all, fall like a hot thunder-bolt again upon my Conscience" (*G.A.,* p. 50).

Again, Donne's greater ability and desire to create order is apparent. Bunyan, in relation to words, is subject to dreams, visions, and voices, which he takes seriously, putting himself at their mercy. Donne hears and sees nothing except what he wants to, and what he does hear is consciously ordered. Bunyan talks of reading the Bible less often than of hearing at crucial moments verses whose source he does not know. His world is more magical and arbitrary than Donne's, partly because it is a peasant world, partly because he has to allow it to be in order to free himself of certain constricting traditions of the establishment.

Their different views of language are closely related to another primary difference in sensibility between them—Donne's persistent wit and Bunyan's sobriety. Donne, thinking himself on his deathbed, puns as if his life depended on it: his puns have been so immense nowhere else except in the "Hymne to God the Father," also written in sickness. Bunyan, in much less desperate circumstances, rejects any opportunity to smile at his younger self, and explicitly refuses to indulge in any play with style:

> I could have enlarged much in this my discourse of my temptations and troubles for sin, as also of the merciful kindness and working of *God* with my Soul: I could also have stepped into a stile much higher then this in which I have here discoursed, and could have adorned all things more then here I have seemed to do: but I dare not: *God* did not play in convincing of me; the *Devil* did not play in tempting of me; neither did I play when I sunk as into a bottomless pit, when *the pangs of hell caught hold upon me*: wherefore I may not play in my relating of them, but be plain and simple, and lay down the thing as it was . . . (*G.A.,* pp. 3-4).

Naturally, Bunyan cannot "lay down the thing as it was"; the phrase suggests a complete bypassing of language, as does the phrase quoted earlier where he invites his people to "read God's work upon me." The *thing* cannot be laid down except by being put into words, and in order to do that, interpreter-Bunyan must make constant choices—between one episode and another, and between one word or phrase and another. Nevertheless, the aim—to submit language to reality—is important.

Whether presented in the form of words that "bolt in upon him" (words as things), or of more conventional experience, Bunyan's reality is recognizable partly by its seriousness. One way to get rid of sin and error is to give up games—cat, bell-ringing, dancing, all had to be forsaken. Conversion is an abandonment of the enticements of the world in favor of a sterner existence. One may suggest that in the Puritan's world there is no time for play because all energies are consumed in action. Analogously, there is no time for the play of art, but only for careful reporting of events.

Bunyan's God has no sense of humor, in his work or in his language. The messages Bunyan receives from him are brief, and sometimes cryptic, often seeming less like language than like physical blows. Donne's God, on the other hand, delights in play of words, as Donne points out here in justifying his own style:

> My *God,* my *God,* Thou art a *direct God,* may I not say, a *literall God,* a *God* that wouldest bee understood *literally,* and according to the *plaine sense* of all that thou saiest? But thou art also (*Lord* I intend it to thy *glory,* and let no *prophane misinterpreter* abuse it to thy *diminution*) thou art a *figurative,* a *metaphoricall God* too: A *God* in whose words there is such a height of *figures,* such *voyages,* such *peregrinations* to fetch remote and precious *metaphors,* such *extensions,* such *spreadings,* such *Curtaines* of *Allegories,* such *third Heavens* of *Hyperboles,* so *harmonious eloquutions,* so *retired* and so *reserved expressions,* so *commanding perswasions,* so *perswading commandements,* such *sinewes* even in thy *milke,* and such *things* in thy *words,* as all *prophane Authors,* seeme of the seed of the *Serpent,* that *creepes,* thou art the *dove,* that flies (*Dev.,* Expos. 19, pp. 479-81).

> This hath occasioned thine ancient *servants,* whose delight it was to write after thy *Copie,* to proceede the same way in their *expositions* of the *Scriptures,* and in their composing both of *publike liturgies,* and of *private prayers* to thee, to make their accesses to thee in such a kind of *language,* as thou wast pleased to speake to them, in a *figurative,* in a *Metaphoricall language;* in which manner I am bold to call the comfort which I receive now in this *sicknesse,* in the *indication* of the *concoction* and *maturity* thereof, in certaine *clouds,* and *recidences,* which the *Physitians* observe, a discovering of *land* from *Sea,* after a long and tempestuous *voyage* (*Dev.,* Expos. 19, pp. 486-87).

These passages are almost infinitely suggestive. Samuel Johnson might here find himself anticipated, in Donne's elegant comment on "remote and precious metaphors," and daringly refuted in the series of words that equate more literal writers, profane writers, and the devil. Opposed to the creeping serpent of literalism is the flying dove, conveyor of facility in tongues; and a high-flown style thus becomes a vehicle, even a sign of grace.

The opportunity for play of wit arises because Donne conceives of the purpose of Scripture differently than Bunyan does. For Bunyan, cryptic passages must be solved; there must be literal interpretations, literal solutions to the whole text of the Bible because the Bible is an instrument of edification, intended to be useful to men. And as God did not play in writing the Bible, Bunyan will not play in writing his own book.

For Donne, edification is of course the Bible's principal use. But Donne's God constantly runs the risk of being misunderstood through abundance of metaphor.[24] Obscurely magnificent passages, featuring, perhaps, "*extentions, . . . spreadings, . . . Curtaines of Allegories,*" are intended for admiration as well as for instruction. God here, as he is the Word of the Bible, makes himself an object of contemplation. He presents Himself in the Bible, and in the three faces of the Trinity, as a Being, mysterious, unknowable, delighting in "*third Heavens of Hyperboles.*" And Donne, made in God's image (who is made in whose image?), reflects back his own three faces in the triple stations of the *Devotions,* and his own "height of figures" in their metaphors and puns.

Bunyan's Bible plays a role in his life. It, and fragments of it, strike him like weapons, call upon him to do this or that, force him to respond, to move forward. Donne's Bible is something which one can enter "for our *satisfaction,* and for our *Inquisition,* for our *Instruction,* and for our *Admiration* too." Centuries of many-levelled exegesis had taught men, in a sense, how to write the Bible as they read it, to enter into an "inventive" (in the Renaissance sense) relationship with this text similar to that which Donne ideally establishes with his reader in the *Devotions.* It is a literary relationship.

The whole subject of the use of the Bible by Puritans and Anglicans is, of course, a book in itself. My intention here has been merely to suggest very briefly that Donne and Bunyan, in their different attitudes toward the Bible, and in their different concepts of its Author, naturally enough reveal the same attitudes that they have toward life, and to some extent the same concepts that they have of themselves.

These can now be briefly summarized. Donne's prose is analytical, psychological, subjective, meditative, private, self-centered, and literary. The "I" tends to make himself the center of things, the object of contemplation. He both insists upon and denies an audience. He rejects the opportunity to justify his writing in utilitarian terms. He is ambiguous, elusive, highly self-conscious, and creates his own reality. Constantly turning himself and experience into art, he absolves himself from time and reaches toward the limits of space, thus achieving a cosmic personality which sees itself as one with all men. The self-centeredness of the prose is qualified by the fact that "I" and "we" are so interchangeable, by the fact that the "I" symbolizes all men.

Bunyan's prose is reportorial, straightforward, apparently objective, taking place in public, and inviting the reader to see him as an instrument of use rather than an object of contemplation. He tries to describe himself as simply as possible, with a distant narrator correcting the earlier Bunyan's errors in vision. His only obvious distortions come as an attempt to answer the distortions of the Slanderer, who speaks for the conservative underworld. His prose is directly addressed to his congregation, and thereby to the reader, who consequently never feels like an eavesdropper. Writing autobiography, Bunyan submits himself to the demands of time and space, and so speaks as an isolated human being. His material is particularized and he rarely makes generalizations about Man. He chooses to submit language to life, showing himself at the mercy of experiences which are then described as accurately as possible.

Donne's prose encourages a reciprocal relationship with language. The writer creates and is created by his prose. The reader, experiencing meditation, is invited by Donne to become part of the "I" and so of all men, since time and space are obliterated. To some extent, Bunyan too is created by his book. But it is also clearly meant to be used as a guide, and in it Bunyan is an exemplum.

If we are sometimes annoyed with Donne's excessive artificiality, his excessive control, we may become bored with Bunyan's refusal to control his own destiny, with the extent to which he puts himself at the mercy of experience. Their strengths are one with their weaknesses, and alert us once more to the different emphases of their interests. Donne turns life into art, and thereby immeasurably enriches man's potential range of sensibility, duration, self-expression, communion with others. There can be no forward movement, but there can be the fullest possible use of what *is*. The Anglican "I" is obviously conducive to meditative literature, to poetry, and to the kind of symbolic (not allegorical) fiction that plays with space and time. As Donne employs it, its weakness is its unwillingness to take a fresh view of life. Its elaborate metaphors can obscure as well as illuminate reality. His personality can be cosmic because he is his world.

In reaction to this kind of artificiality, splendid as it is, there is bound to be a turning away from art toward life. Necessarily he who does this, like Bunyan, will be at the mercy of experience. His concentration is outward, and his role is subject to the limitations of a time-bound world. Less independent and disciplined than Donne's, his imagination lacks control and humor. But the freshness and vigor of his experience lend urgency and immediacy to a prose in which the techniques of "realistic" fiction are already being exercised.[25] In fact, the likeness of accurate reporting to documentary fiction provided England's strongest impulse to the rise of the novel, as is evident in the familiar progress of English fiction from Bunyan to Defoe and onward.

NOTES

1. I. A. Shapiro, "Watson and the Occasion of Donne's *Devotions*," *Review of English Studies*, N.S., IX (1958), 18-22.
2. Edward LeComte, *Grace to a Witty Sinner* (New York, 1965), p. 190.
3. See Mrs. Bunyan's testimony in "A Relation of the Imprisonment of Mr. John Bunyan," in John Bunyan, *Grace Abounding to the Chief of Sinners,* ed. Roger Sharrock (Oxford, 1962), pp. 127-28.
4. Henri Talon, *John Bunyan: The Man and His Works*, English translation London, 1951), p. 74.
5. It has been remarked that Bunyan's conversion experience falls into a standard Puritan pattern. William York Tindall asserts that "the details of Bunyan's conversion could be supplied by a diligent anthologist from the autobiographies of other preachers" (*John Bunyan, Mechanick Preacher*, New York, 1934, pp. 33-34). While Tindall's book has been much attacked, and this observation is surely exaggerated, Bunyan did want his conversion to conform to the rules. He had to have certain experiences in order to achieve approval among his co-religionists; the harder the conversion, the greater the assurance of God's favor. Donne in his own time was thought too fancy, a preacher of the wisdom of words rather than the Word of wisdom (an attack levelled at all the "witty" preachers), and in subsequent generations has been thought too melodramatic as well, too mindful of the effects he might be achieving, ex-

ploiting his own illness in order to create an interesting pose. (See, for example, on Donne's sermon "I," William R. Mueller, *John Donne: Preacher,* Princeton, 1962, pp. 248-50). If Bunyan was too imitative, Donne was too mannered: in both cases, such criticism really implies, there is a lack of spontaneity, a striving for effect at the expense of truth to experience.

6. For discussion of how-to books on the art of self-knowledge, see Paul A. Jorgenson, *Lear's Self-Discovery* (Berkeley and Los Angeles, 1967).

7. Isaiah 38.

8. See *Peake's Commentary on the Bible,* ed. Matthew Black (London, 1962), p. 515.

9. R. C. Bald, "Dr. Donne and the Booksellers," *Studies in Bibliography: Papers of the Bibliographical Society of the University of Virginia,* XVIII (1965), 79-80. Quoted by permission of the publisher.

10. Izaak Walton, *The Lives of John Donne, Sir Henry Wotton, Richard Hooker, George Herbert, and Robert Sanderson* (London, World's Classics, 1956), p. 78.

11. *Ibid.,* p. 74, citing in full a letter from Donne.

12. See Sharrock, p. xxxvi. Sharrock does point out that the Great Fire destroyed a number of copies, and adds that early editions of Bunyan are generally extremely rare; they were all read to pieces.

13. On this, see J. Paul Hunter, *The Reluctant Pilgrim: Defoe's Emblematic Method and Quest for Form in Robinson Crusoe* (Baltimore, 1966). Mr. Hunter calls the Puritan method emblematic, but I believe that his distinction between Puritan and Anglican technique is somewhat analogous to mine.

14. Substantiation of this is everywhere apparent in the literature. For modern commentators on the Puritan pilgrim, see William Haller, *The Rise of Puritanism* (New York, 1938), and Hunter, *The Reluctant Pilgrim;* for Puritan pilgrim and Anglican microcosm, see Michael Walzer, *The Revolution of the Saints: A Study in the Origins of Radical Politics* (Cambridge, Mass., 1965).

15. Bunyan does not always use this device for this purpose. The "as I thought" can be simply a distancing device, for separating the Bunyan who thought this way from interpreter-Bunyan. But in any event the distancing involves a detachment that allows for the possibility of errors on the part of Bunyan-in-process.

16. There was, from the thirteenth century, civil relief for defamation in local courts, and later in ecclesiastical courts, but slander was not a criminal offense until 1609, when the first criminal case was tried. See William F. Walsh, *Outlines of the History of English and American Law* (New York, 1926), pp. 399-400. See also W. S. Holds-

worth, *A History of English Law,* 7 vols., VI (Boston, 1927). Holdsworth points out that the relaxation of censorship under Parliamentary government made much more important the establishment and development of libel laws (p. 377).

Sir Francis Bacon speaks at length of the evils of scurrility, commenting as follows on the relative efficacy of Puritan and Anglican name-calling: "Nevertheless, I note, there is not an indifferent hand carried towards these pamphlets as they deserve; for the one sort flieth in the dark, and the other is uttered openly . . ." (*The Works of Francis Bacon, Lord Chancellor of England,* ed. Basil Montague, 3 vols., Philadelphia, 1884, II, 413). Walsh, *Outlines of the History of English and American Law,* points out that, according to precedent in Roman law linking defamation of character with breach of peace, truth of the libel was no defense for the speaker/ writer, since his remarks in any case could be said to create a breach of the peace (p. 400). An anti-establishment "libeller" would of course be in every way more vulnerable to such a charge than a member of the party in power.

17. In his sermons, Donne repeatedly comments on the fact that "that language in which God hath spoken in his written word, the Hebrew, [has] the least consideration of Time of any other language" (*The Sermons of John Donne,* ed. George R. Potter and Evelyn Simpson, 10 vols., Berkeley, 1953-61, IX, 335-36). See also *Sermons,* VIII, 76-77, and 144-45.

18. Directly influenced by St. Augustine, this passage reminds us of Augustine's influence upon Donne's consideration of time. See St. Augustine's *Confessions,* Book XI.

19. For a full analysis if the rhetorical evidence for this conclusion, see my *Contrary Music: The Prose Style of John Donne* (Madison, 1963), Ch. VII.

20.   . . . Spirante *columba*
                 Suppositâ pedibus, revocantur ad ima *vapores.* . . .
In this case, he is clearer about the treatment in the poem than he is in the meditation, although the added clarity does not inspire greater confidence in seventeenth-century medicine.

21. *Contrary Music,* Ch. VII.

22. For total contrast with Donne in this particular detail, see *The Journal of George Fox,* rev. John L. Nickalls (Cambridge, 1952). Fox hears voices commanding him to do things whose purpose he does not even understand—for example, to walk barefoot in the snow to the town at hand (whose name he does not know) and cry through the streets "Woe to the bloody city of Litchfield." After obeying, he devises an explanation having to do with ancient persecution of Christians in Litchfield. The founder of the Quakers, he represents

an extreme openness to visions and voices (direct communication with God), compared to which Bunyan's experiences seem almost ordinary.

23. See my *Contrary Music,* Ch. V.

24. On the literary mysteries and delights of the Bible as seen by Renaissance commentators, see Israel Barroway, "The Bible as Poetry in the English Renaissance," *Journal of English and Germanic Philology,* XXXIII (1933), 447-80.

25. For sources in Puritan homily of many of Bunyan's techniques, see Haller, *The Rise of Puritanism,* and Katherine Koller, "The Puritan Preacher's Contribution to Fiction," *Huntington Library Quarterly,* XI (August 1948), 321-40.

U. MILO KAUFMANN

⤶

The Analogy of Faith and the Unity of *The Pilgrim's Progress*

The Pilgrim's Progress opens with a distinction between outer and inner landscape. Bunyan says: "As I walk'd through the wilderness of this world, I lighted on a certain place, where was a Denn; And I laid me down in that place to sleep: And as I slept I dreamed a Dream." There is a significant difference between the world of Bunyan's waking life and the world of his dream. Whatever else the world of his dream is, it is *not* wilderness. Rather, it is an ordered spiritual realm in which good and evil, though in continual warfare, are in a strife where all battle lines are clearly drawn. Christian's universe is one of unambiguous meaning, of polarities which reduce every decision to a clear choice. The world indeed is one of such implicit meaning that right conduct is, with only rare exceptions (e.g. the episode with Flatterer), a function of the good will rather than of acute discernment.

Christian has more than a clear way, however. When first encountered, he is reading a book which convincingly predicts for him the whole future of his present course. Not long thereafter, he meets Evangelist, who has perfect counsel on what he must do to be saved.

From U. Milo Kaufmann, *The Pilgrim's Progress and Traditions in Puritan Meditation* (New Haven: Yale University Press, 1966), pp. 106-117. Copyright 1966 by Yale University.

This collaboration of book and Evangelist is the Word both in its convicting and instructive power and in its exemplification of an accessible body of truth wholly adequate to one's spiritual pilgrimage. Equipped with the Word and walking the way he does, Christian is without excuse, should he digress.

Not surprisingly, *The Pilgrim's Progress* presents a conspicuous superimposition of stasis and linear movement—a feature expected in allegory that develops a determinate structure of beliefs—and such a narrative appears to lack genuine contingency. Suspense grows out of the reader's interest in the varied guises or costumery which the anticipated terms of the shaping system assume when they appear in the action. The linear development, then, is a program of implementation answering the question "How?" rather than a course involving emergence of true novelty answering the question "What?" But even as we generalize upon the peculiar design *The Pilgrim's Progress* presents, on the assumption that it is not unique, we are obliged to admit that in the world of *belles lettres,* works which enjoy an intimacy of connection with a canon of truth believed entire, such as *The Pilgrim's Progress* enjoys with the Christian Scriptures, are rare. This intimacy is precarious: narrative so ordered is apt to be wholly assimilated to idea (in which case movement collapses into static structure) or to betray the informing truth by allowing the action to exercise its autonomous energies. Neither *The Divine Comedy* nor *The Faerie Queene* offers the kind of connections between canon and narrative that are present in Bunyan's allegory, and in neither do movement and resolution seem in some sense illusory.

Given its problematic dynamics, the unity of *The Pilgrim's Progress* is to a great extent a reflection of the unity of Puritan religious experience as it was wrought in the eminently practical struggle to define a body of practice that could assimilate and be assimilated to the Word while, at the same time, maintaining a coherence adequate to the variety of historical pressures exerted on it. In hermeneutical practice, this concern showed itself in the heavy stress upon the analogy, or proportion, of faith—that is, the Word that stood luminous and coherent behind the convolutions of the letter as the perfectly unified disclosure of the mind of God. The common assumption within Puritanism was that all Scripture could be reduced to a consistent body of doctrine. The susceptibility of Scripture to such a reduction meant that it could be seen simultaneously as a *fait accompli,* one complete thought in the mind of God, and as a dynamic unfolding, and this superimposition of statis and cursus is a paradigm for *The Pilgrim's Progress*. The fact, incidentally, that the analogy of faith, reflecting a supposed *a priori* unity of the Word as well as an achieved coherence of practice, proved itself a generally useful hermeneutical device suggests that Puritanism had early attained a fair measure of internal consistency, whatever judgments may be brought against the adequacy or stability of the synthesis.

William Perkins gives a succinct description of this strategic criterion in *The Arte of Prophecying*. It is, he says, "a certaine *abridgement* or *summe* of the Scriptures, collected out of most manifest & familiar places. The parts thereof are two. The first concerneth faith, which is handled in the Apostles Creede. The second concerneth charitie or love, which is explicated in the ten Commandements."[1] Among the several assumptions implicit in this practice the most important was the simple belief that scriptural doctrine *did* comprise a unity. If the import of a passage tugged in a direction opposite to the approved consensus, it was not allowed to qualify the consensus but was manipulated into agreement.[2] Furthermore the identity of the analogy of faith with the summary of beliefs held by the Puritan to be important was assumed to bear witness to the derivation of the latter from the former. The possibility that the analogy of faith simply represented a kind of exegetical gerrymandering, carried out to authorize practice, was not entertained. These primary assumptions are well illustrated in the following passages from John Owen. Speaking on the unity of the Word, Owen says: "In our search after truth our minds are greatly to be influenced and guided by the analogy of Faith. . . . There is a harmony, an answerableness, and a proportion, in the whole system of faith, or things to be believed. Particular places are so to be interpreted as that they do not break or disturb this order, or fall in upon their due relation to one another."[3] All the Scripture, he adds, "is from the same spring of divine inspiration, and is in all things perfectly consistent with itself." Regarding the second assumption implicit in this hermeneutical practice, Owen says: "And this *analogy* or 'proportion of faith' is what is taught plainly and uniformly in the whole Scripture as the rule of our faith and obedience."[4] Right conduct, or obedience, was conceived as consequent to the clear apprehension of the divine will, as stated in the proportion of faith. Yet it was quite possible, even if the possibility were overlooked, that favored modes of conduct—ritual, devotional, and the like—prompted the searching of Scripture for the doctrines that would confirm them.[5]

If the Reformation inspired a conception of the church universal as invisible rather than visible entity, it also encouraged a conception of the unity of doctrine in the Word which rested not so much on coerced sense as upon faith. Paul Baynes, who succeeded William Perkins in the pulpit of Great St. Andrews at Cambridge, put the profession in words which suggest its underpinnings in something other than direct observation. After declaring that the law and the gospel reveal a single "matter and substance," he affirms that "the true churches of God profess one and the self-same doctrine, and therefore must hold in spiritual concord one with another." This is the case since "There is but one Christian doctrine which the visible church can embrace and hold; for God and Christ were 'yesterday, to-day, and will be the same for ever,' Heb. xiii. 8. And as the church of God hath had one, so all the churches now have one and the same."[6]

With substantial motivations for assembling a body of doctrine that would be clear, harmonious, and authoritative, it is not surprising that the Puritan refined procedures for discerning latent doctrine, such as would dovetail to form the desired unity. Some attention has already been given to this in the discussion of the techniques of collection. Puritan hermeneutics never hesitated to go beyond the letter to the Word of doctrine. A representative utterance of Thomas Adams will clearly demonstrate how the freedom exercised in the quest of doctrine afforded ample opportunity to press literal meaning into a system predetermined according to the dictates of coherence. The Scripture, he says, "is the golden pot of *Manna;* the words, that is the golden pot: the sense, that is the *Manna.* It is not enough to take what offers it selfe at the first proposed; but to digge deepe. God that is rich in the veines of nature, is not poore in the veines of Scripture: excellent in the historic, more excellent in the mysterie."[7] Adams hints that a doctrinal richness in Scripture licenses a certain freedom of movement. Though his freedom was materially limited by the bias against *mythos,* the interpreter still had scope for synthesis, for pulling together compatible teachings, and the presence in Scripture of "mysterie," understood in this way, had weighty implications for mystery in human experience. If the mystery of the Word could in fact be articulated in an authoritative and coherent body of doctrine, such as Ames attempted in *The Marrow of Sacred Divinity* and Samuel Willard in his *Compleat Body of Divinity,* then the mysteries confronting man in daily experience were of no consequence. For practical purposes, the mystery of the Word cancelled the mystery of experience.

While this notion is basic to an appreciation of the dynamics of *The Pilgrim's Progress,* it runs so counter to many modern conceptions of man's relation to truth that it warrants amplification. When Christian at the story's opening asks "What must I do to be saved?" all answers which are not present in the book he holds in his hands are presumably accessible in the person of Evangelist. Christian is of course the ectype of his creator, who can sit in Bedford Jail and, without moving from his cell, go on pilgrimage in a static exploration of the meanings of the Christian vision of truth. Truth was for Christian, for Buynan, and for every Puritan, an *a priori* deliverance, at least in theory. And whereas the modern pilgrim sails his odyssey in the hopes of finding truth somewhere in his peregrinations, the Puritan pilgrim of the seventeenth century felt assured that truth was early and always seeking him, in the form of a revealed word. The modern reader can perhaps be forgiven for his impression that in a pilgrimage that is in large measure the exfoliation of a Word once and for all delivered, events only seem to be happening. Movement is paradoxically at once cursus and stasis. Behind event is discerned the Word, behind act the animating Truth, and the progress takes on the quality of illusion, while the static changeless truth is apprehended as reality.

We do not make this point at the expense of a commendation of Bunyan's mythic realism, but neither do we defend too simple a conception of Bunyan's relationship to Puritan practice. Bunyan knew well that the interpretive method that wrought doctrine from Scripture in Purtan hermeneutics, that delighted in reducing event to moral and action to statement, plainly undercut the dynamics of narrative. If unreduced action gave too much scope to the transient, to discrepancy, and plurality of viewpoint—the very features historical criticism, which takes the dynamic perspective for granted, does in fact discover—reduced action provided a perfected monolithic unimpeachable unity. But that unity was essentially static, devoid of the strengths as well as the weaknesses of the dynamic perspective. Bunyan is capable of qualifying this hermeneutics in his handling of scriptural event and metaphor, but it is necessary to point out that the peculiar dynamics of his narrative are indebted to the Puritan conception of reading the Word as static system. Not only is such a system present behind the action, but it is related to Christian and his pilgrimage as prevenient truth in the shape of Evangelist and the book.

This point is borne out by a nuance of Bunyan's characterization. The typical reader who, like Coleridge, finds himself following along with the characters of Christian's pilgrimage as human folk nicknamed by their neighbors is apt to be disturbed by the severity of Bunyan's handling of that "very brisk Lad" Ignorance. When Christian and Hopeful first meet him after they descend from the Hill Clear, not far from the Celestial City, it takes Christian only a moment to discover that there is little hope for the fellow. Ignorance falls behind but later rejoins the two before they reach Enchanted Ground. The conversation is heavy with remonstrance, to which Ignorance is impervious, and the last glimpse of the obtuse fellow is at the close, when Bunyan makes of him a final grim "example." The same King who receives Christian and Hopeful orders two shining ones to go out and "take *Ignorance* and bind him hand and foot, and have him away. Then they took him up, and carried him through the air to the door that I saw in the side of the Hill, and put him in there. Then I saw that there was a way to Hell, even from the Gates of Heaven, as well as from the City of *Destruction*" (p. 163). Such a summary disposition of Ignorance would certainly have occasioned no remorse for the Puritan reader, for his fate was in keeping with the Puritan conception of truth as so accessible to every man as to render inexcusable the ignorant. What is perhaps so startling in Bunyan's account is not his disposal of one deluded pilgrim named Ignorance, but the fact that he dares to disassociate his other pilgrims from this most human of traits, precipitating it out into one poor wretch and throwing it away at the last. Implicit in such a procedure is the understanding of truth, discussed above, that is integral to the unity of *The Pilgrim's Progress*. The shaping doctrine of the work has something of the imposing poise and weight of the timeless axiom or a heavenly Jerusalem delivered intact to an awed creaturedom, and such structures stand above the impeachments of time. The unity of such tranquil fabrications, is that impressive one of *a priori* deliverance. Plainly, the unity of *The Pilgrim's Progress* may be traced to its informing brief, which assumed the Word was a single structure of doctrine and religious experience a fitting witness to that structure.

The analogy of faith, of course, represented the fruitful corroboration of Word by way. The body of doctrine requiring acceptance was the Word as it had meaningfully addressed itself to the peculiar contours of Puritan life. Even if there was hesitation about admitting the reciprocal influence here, it was natural to associate ordered life with ordered doctrine. Baxter uses strong language in commenting on the association: "There are so few Christians that have a true method of faith or divinity in their understandings, even in the great points which they know disorderly, that it is no wonder if there by lamentable defectiveness and deformity, in those inward and outward duties, which should be harmoniously performed, by the light of this harmonious truth."[8] It must be apparent, however, that when ordered life and ordered doctrine were conjugate, the Word would be read as license and vindication. So in *The Pilgrim's Progress* it is impossible to disengage Word from Way, especially when the focus is the coherence of the entire work.

Whatever else it may be, the way Christian goes is a canonization of Puritan religious experience, and its unity is the historically refined wholeness of that experience. It is important to note that in Bunyan's allegory, way and wayfarer reciprocally define the other. If to be a Christian is to travel the way, it is equally true that the Way names the course which the Christian takes. The correct route to the Celestial City reflects, presumably, not only the *de jure* pronouncements of its King, but also the practical discoveries of pilgrims about the efficient ways to get from terminus to terminus. A review of the whole course of Christian's journey—the Slough of Despond, the Burning Mount, the little wicket gate, Interpreter's House, the two valleys, Vanity Fair, Doubting Castle, Enchanted Ground, Beulah Land, the river of death—cannot help but persuade one that in all features Bunyan sets forth the way canonized by consensus. It was the way that Puritan pilgrims did in fact travel, beset by the peculiar temptations of doubt, despair, legalism, and rationalism, encouraged by the Word, the sharing of experiences, the sweet breezes of Beulah (the land of the marriage covenant), and the vision of an eternal city discontinuous with the *civitas terrena*. The Way is as much descriptive as prescriptive.

I concede that it is natural and popular to take Christian as the classic paradigm of man the lonely voyager, the embattled individual, in contrast with Christiana of Part Two, who makes her pilgrimage as part of a churchly entourage.[9] But even as Wayfarer Christian is ingredient in tradition, one of a host whose wayfaring has helped inscribe in the landscape the road he walks. Indeed, he himself helps to define the road to be walked. To read the two parts of the allegory in close sequence is to be convinced of the multitude of ways Christian prepares the way for his wife and family. By instructive markers, by decisive victories over besetting enemies, by the impalpable influence of reputation, he transforms the way he covers. The reader can conjecture that it was the same with all pilgrims before him. Yet it is possible to fall into error here, since the basic outlines of the way were fixed before Christian came to it and endured after he left it behind. This general shape witnessed to the *a posteriori* achieved unity of Puritan experience, serving as a containing structure for individual pilgrimage and the natural correlate of the *a priori* unity of the Word. On the one hand, the coherent Word, implied in the analogy of faith, contributes to the impression of stasis in *The Pilgrim's Progress* by functioning as the prevenient knowledge undercutting the exigency in Christian's pilgrimage as well as by providing the timeless structure of idea standing behind the flickering play of action. On the other hand, coherent experience, similarly implied in the analogy of faith, is a unifying influence upon Bunyan's narrative insofar as it insures that the Way is coherent.

While the unity of the way is humanly achieved, it is important to indicate the way in which it is also presumably dictated by God. The features of this imposition offer a close analogy with the workings and consequences of prevenient knowledge. In view of Bunyan's Calvinism, we can scarcely avoid speaking of Christian the pilgrim as one of God's elect, whose willing must sooner or later be related to the fact of prevenient and sustaining grace. But prevenient grace, like prevenient knowledge, if too evident in the springs of narrative, is likely to destroy the illusion of a dynamic career.

As Christian, the elect, goes on pilgrimage, the reader is encouraged to see that the most important criterion for judging one's prospects on the way is the condition of the will, and the inner self of the pilgrim thus becomes the real locus of conflict. Christian's success will depend on the quality of his intent rather than the external challenges that he meets. But when the locus of conflict is the will, and that will is in fact fixed by divine grace, there can be no contingency. There is, however, sufficient novelty in the implementation of divine grace, and Christian's experimental exfoliation of the divine Word, to tug the reader onward. It must be admitted, too, that Bunyan is not at great pains to keep before the reader this element of his theological brief: Christian and the other pilgrims of the first and second parts spend no time worrying about the illusoriness of their freedom.

This scrutiny of the Word and the way and their relations to questions of coherence and dynamics in *The Pilgrim's Progress* discloses, we may observe, Bunyan's indebtedness to the Puritan understanding of the analogy of faith, which argued the unity of the Word and of the correlate Puritan experience which it illuminated and by which it was construed. An appreciation of the unity of Word and of way is basic to an understanding of the unity of Bunyan's allegory.

NOTES

1. Perkins, *The Arte of Prophecying, The Works*, 3, 737.
2. Cf. Perkins, p. 740. "*If the native (or naturall) signification of the words doe manifestly disagree with either the analogy of faith, or very perspicuous places of the Scripture: then the other meaning which is given of the place propounded, is naturall & proper, if it agree with contrarie and like places,*" etc. Cf. also John Owen, ΣΥΝΕΣΙΣ ΠΝΕΥΜΑΤΙΚΗ or, *The Causes, Ways, and Means of Understanding the Mind of God as Revealed in His Word, Works* (London, 1678) 4, 197. "The rule in this case is That we *affix no sense unto any obscure or difficult passage of Scripture but what is materially true and consonant unto other express and plain testimonies*" (p. 740).
3. Owen, *An Exposition of the Epistle to the Hebrews, Works*, 13, 315.
4. Owen, ΣΥΝΕΣΙΣ ΠΝΕΥΜΑΤΙΚΗ, *Works*, 4, 198.
5. Insensitivity to the reciprocal dependence of Word and practice led to the grave irony of invoking the analogy of faith when clearly it did not point to a résumé of belief which recommended itself to all men. We may make this point simply by juxtaposing a statement by Owen with one by George Tavard, a twentieth-century Catholic theologian. Says Owen, in *An Exposition of . . . Hebrews*: "Want of a due attendance unto this rule [the analogy of faith] is that which hath produced the most pestilent heresies in the church. Thus the Papists, taking up these words, 'This is my body,' without a due consideration of the analogy of faith about the human nature of Christ, the spirituality of the union and communion of believers with him, the nature of sacramental expressions and actions, which are elsewhere evidently declared, by which the interpretation, according to the apostle's rule, is to be regulated and squared, have from them fancied the monstrous figment of their transubstantiation, absolutely destructive of them all." The analogy of faith, however, says Tavard in his *Holy Writ or Holy Church* (New York, Harper and Brothers, 1959), p. 95, can be nothing less than a reflection of the consensus of believers, and it is less than clear how the Reformers paid heed to the issue of consensus. His position is in bold conflict

with Owen's. "In breaking through the analogy of faith, the Reformation became neither scriptural nor traditional. . . . Only the
totality of the Church's tradition, universal in time and space, guided
by the inspiring presence of the Paraclete, reflected in the consciences of believers, is adequate to the totality of Scripture" (p. 316).

6. Paul Baynes, *An Entire Commentary upon the Whole Epistle of
   St. Paul to the Ephesians* (Edinburgh, James Nichol, 1866), p. 246.
7. Adams, *A Commentary or, Exposition upon* . . . *St. Peter*, p. 287.
8. Baxter, *The Life of Faith, The Practical Works*, 12, 390.
9. Louis Martz, for one, points attention to this contrast in his introduction to the Rinehart edition of *The Pilgrim's Progress*.

IRÈNE SIMON

✍

Dryden's Prose Style[1]

By way of introduction I should like to examine briefly three passages of pre-Restoration prose. First, Sir Thomas Browne's preface to *Religio Medici* (1643), in which he explains that this is the authorized edition, the former being a surreptitious issue from a transcript that somehow arrived at the press.[2] But Browne tells us a good deal more than this, for instance: that he was not prompted by the wish to achieve immortality, for mortality being common in all things it would be foolish to repine at death. This may have little to do with the matter in hand, but it is characteristic of the man who was to write the fully orchestrated meditation on death at the end of *Urn-Burial*. Further, that but for the importunity of his friends and his own love of truth, the inactivity of his disposition might have made him bear this affront without protest, a detail which we prize for what it tells us about the author: his inactivity, his acceptance of what is beyond redress, his readiness to comply with his friends' wishes, and his decision to seek what reparation lies in his power. These revelations about himself prepare us for what he says in the second paragraph, namely: that this work is directed to himself, for his private exercise and satisfaction, a memorial unto him rather than an example or rule unto any other man; that there may be singulari-

From *Revue des Langues Vivantes*, 31 (1965), pp. 506-530. Reprinted with the permission of the author.

ties in it correspondent unto the private conceptions of some men, or dissentaneous thereunto; and finally, that many things in it are delivered rhetorically, many expressions merely tropical, and many to be taken in a soft and flexible sense, and not to be called unto the rigid test of reason. Thus in the preface no less than in the work itself, Browne is laying himself bare much in the way in which Montaigne announced: "Je me peins moi-même." Yet we have the impression that we are allowed to peep into his closet and to overhear meditations that were never meant for the public ear; that he has been brought against his will to allow us into his private study. It is characteristic that although this is a preface to the reader, Browne never addresses him directly. It is as though he were talking to himself rather than to us, the reader is merely "he that shall peruse that work."

Though Browne has moved a long way from the Ciceronian period, the style of the opening paragraph is highly patterned: the sense is held in suspense within the parts of the sentence, but the parts do not form a rounded whole, rather they develop along parallel lines without however moving to a climax; moreover the movement is repeatedly broken when the parallelism does not extend to the end of the syntactic unit and the asymmetrical second part moves in a new direction. Thus in:

> Certainly that man were greedy. . . , who . . . ;
> and he must needs be . . . , who . . .

both sense and movement are repeated, as again in:

> Had not almost every man . . .
> or were not the tyranny . . .
>   I had not wanted. . . .

This first part of the second sentence is followed by:

> but in times wherein I have lived to behold
>   the highest perversion . . .
>   the name of his Majesty defamed
>   the honour of Parliament depraved
>   the writings of both . . . imprinted
>   complaints may seem. . . .

The subordinate does not repeat the movement of the first part, and it accumulates objects which are also asymmetrical (*perversion, name defamed, honour depraved, the writings imprinted*), the last breaking the parallelism with the second and third by the insertion of three adverbs (*depravedly, anticipatively, counterfeitly*) which do not move in an ascending line. We notice the same difference between the two main clauses: *I had not wanted* in the first part, *complaints may seem . . . and men may be* in the second, the twofold division being repeated in *as incapable of affronts, as hopeless of their reparation.* This is studied asymmetry, and it is felt all the more for the use of parallel members inside the parts, or of parallel parts in the sentence. In spite of its looseness, the style of this paragraph is thus highly artificial, and the art is obvious at once.

In the second paragraph such patterning only appears at the end, thus in:

> and therefore also there are many things to be taken in a soft
> and flexible sense,
> and not to be called unto the rigid test of reason . . .

or in:

> under favour of which considerations I have made its secrecy
> public
> and committed the truth thereof to every ingenuous reader.

The rest of the paragraph is written in a loose style similar to that of the work itself: the syntactic structure seems to follow the thought as it emerges, not to be wholly shaped beforehand, e.g.:

> It was set down many years past,
> and was the sense of my conception at that time,
> not an immutable law unto my advancing judgement at all
> times,
> and therefore there might be many things therein plausible
> unto my passed apprehension,
> which are not agreeable unto my present self.

The stages in the development of the thought are marked by the two *and's,* joining members of unequal length and of different value.

Though less formal than in the first paragraph the style has none of
the clarity and directness of the plain prose style. It is as though
Browne were thinking of the effect in par. 1, and of himself in par.
2; but in neither does he seem to be much concerned with his reader.

Let us now consider the beginning of another preface,[3] Burton's
preface to *The Anatomy of Melancholy* (1621), or "Democritus Junior to the Reader." This is ostensibly addressed to the "gentle reader,"
but Burton treats him very offhandedly, not to say insolently, as is
only fit in such a "satirical preface" where he is playing the part of
Democritus Junior. Yet, the tone and style are characteristic of
Burton's relation to his public, they suggest the freedom and lack of
art of extemporaneous discourse, and the syntax is as free as in spoken
style. Again and again we are jolted by the abrupt change of rhythm,
as in the opening sentence with its sudden break after "another
man's name." Or, having promised something, Burton goes off at a
tangent as in: "And first of the name of Democritus; lest any man
. . . others. Besides, it has been. . . ," which finally leads, not to an
explanation of his assumed name, but to: "Thou thyself art the subject of this discourse." This rambling way has its counterpart in the
parentheses which are often inserted before the sense of the part is
clear, e.g.: "for thirty years I have continued (having the use of as
good libraries as ever he had) a scholar." The same unconcern for
the easy flow of the sentence appears in his many quotations, particularly when he does not translate, thus not only expecting his reader
to be equally at home in both languages, but making Latin words
express an important part of the meaning. He is surely right to compare himself to "a ranging spaniel, that barks at every bird he sees,
leaving his game." This "roving humour" of his and his habit of
catching at everything that falls within his reach make his style particularly quaint, and it is clear that he is merely indulging his humour.
There is more method in the madness of his cumulative sentences
than strikes the eye, but he clearly enjoys heaping up the parts, and
will not give over, even for the sake of his reader. A good example of
this at the beginning of the preface is the description of Democritus,
but he can have much longer lists than this without apparently need-
ing to take breath.

Though Burton heard the noise of the great world outside, of its
"plagues, fires, inundations, thefts, murders, massacres, meteors,
comets, spectrums, prodigies, apparitions, towns taken, cities be-

sieged," etc.; though he took more interest than most in his fellow-beings and noted their quirks and oddities no less than his own, we are not surprised to hear that Democritus "lived at last in a garden in the suburbs, wholly betaking himself to his studies and a private life," and that Burton himself has lived "a silent, sedentary, solitary life, *mihi et musis* in the university . . . *ad senectam fere.*" What the preface, as indeed the whole work, shows is that Burton lived among books, and had not learnt the art of polite conversation. This makes him no less attractive to us; indeed we enjoy his company and the strange ways in which his mind works; we enjoy his humour too, particularly when he tells us, in dealing with love melancholy, that he is a bachelor, but has heard it said that "an Irish sea is not so turbulent and raging as a litigious wife." But we feel that Dryden's remark about Jonson applies even better to Burton: "the best of his discourse is drawn, not from the knowledge of the town, but books, and, in short, he would be a fine gentleman in an university."

As appears from this preface, the looseness and freedom of extemporaneous writing, however much it may suggest the spoken style, is even further removed from plain style than is the Senecan amble of Sir Thomas Browne or of Montaigne. And this is mainly because Burton, even when ostensibly addressing a reader, is in fact speaking for his private satisfaction, and, like Sir Thomas Browne, exercising his mind in his closet, not in society, following his own quirks rather than suiting his discourse to a listener, whether real or imaginary.

The next passage I wish to examine is the opening paragraph of a book, or long pamphlet, written at about the same time as *Religio Medici*, Milton's *Of Reformation in England* (1641). This is not a preface to the reader since the whole is addressed to "a friend."[4] The opening sentence is certainly impressive, but I cannot help feeling that Cicero and his imitators were right to insist that in such elaborate sentences the rhythm should carry us along so that the relation of parts to parts should appear from the movement of the voice no less than from the meaning of the words. No doubt Bacon was also right when he denounced the orotundity that merely served to conceal the emptiness of meaning. But when we read any sentence of Hooker's, for instance, we at once realise that his periods give a clear outline of his thought, of the nice dependencies and subordination of the parts. Here, instead of sound and sense working together, we have an elabo-

rate sentence whose structure is all but obscured by the asymmetry of
the word-groups. Consider, for instance, the predicate of the first relative clause:

> which . . . ought to be of God
> and of his miraculous ways and works among men
> and of our religion and works, to be performed
> to him.

The second and third predicates consist of two units, but the third has
an adjunct after the second noun—*to be performed*—referring to it
alone, while the adjective before the first noun—*ours*—refers to both.

Consider next the relation between the adjuncts preceding the main
clause:

1. amidst those . . . thoughts (which . . .
2. after the story of . . . Christ suffering and . . . triumphing

to which is added a relative clause, as a kind of rider or afterthought:
which drew up his body also

3. till we . . . be united . . .

These adjuncts perform the same syntactical function, yet the first two
are nouns, while the third is a clause. It is therefore natural that on
first reading this we should not see the relation clearly. The logic binds
the parts to each other as the sentence proceeds, but it is not a firm
framework within which the sentence develops. Hence, though we enjoy following the thought as it emerges, we are not quite sure where
we are going. This is no doubt more interesting, but such open structure is a little baffling.

The first part of the sentence being so elaborate, the sentence will be
top-heavy unless the object of *I do not know* is given considerable
weight. And so it is, but the sentence comes to an abrupt end with the
weak ending: *in these latter days*. It is the more abrupt because the two
objects of *to consider* are of unequal length:

> first, the foul and sudden corruption
> then, . . . the long deferred but much more wonderful and
> happy reformation of the church . . .

so that the sentence seems to be gathering momentum, when it suddenly breaks off after a mere time adjunct, *in these latter days*.

The next sentence presents similar characteristics, though here the process is reversed:

> Sad it is to think how that. . . .

The object of *think* is developed in the rest of the sentence, first in parallel members—though again the parallelism is slightly broken by the many *and*'s—which lead on to a consecutive clause:

> to such a spiritual height . . . that the body. . . .

This relation, however, does not appear at once because of the three nouns linked by *and*'s. Moreover this is followed by an absolute clause inserted like a parenthesis:

> faith needing not . . . ordained,

which breaks the movement so completely that Milton repeats:

> that such doctrine should,

i.e. begins anew the object clause of the first verb:

> Sad it is to think. . . .

After another break to introduce an adjunct:

> through the grossness and blindness . . . and the fraud. . . ,

we at last get the verb:

> drag so downwards, as to. . . .

After several subordinate clauses, with subordinates inside some of them, the sentence comes to rest on:

> because they could not make themselves heavenly and spiritual.

Whether we give the semi-colon after this its modern value, and consider all that follows to the next full stop as part of the same sentence;

or whether we treat it as ending a unit of thought as it so often does in the seventeenth century, the change in syntax and rhythm is equally obvious. The passion that informs the first independent sentence issues is the staccato style of the next short sentences merely juxtaposed to each other:

> they hallowed it, they fumed it, they sprinkled it, they bedecked it . . .

until in his fury Milton resorts to invective and uses words more fitting for Billingsgate than for a tract written to a friend.

I hope I haven't given the impression that Milton is a poor stylist, for the style *is* the man. Surely it is of supreme interest to us to see how his thought shapes itself; how after starting with a rhetorical structure he then doffs his robe; how in the urgency of the denunciation he is carried away from the main stream, yet manages thereby to intensify the attack. This is extremely lively, even though it may occasionally be hard for us to follow. All I am trying to show is that the friend Milton addresses is a mere device, and felt to be such. For Milton is wholly oblivious of him, fired as he is by the urgent work of reformation. He is not talking to somebody, he is the prophet crying in the wilderness, or soon will be, since at the time he thought he could make common cause with the Presbyterians. As we know, he was not to give up the struggle and was to advocate "the Ready and Easy way to Establish a Free Commonwealth" even after it had become clear to all that it was only a matter of weeks before monarchy was restored in England.

Milton has not one but many styles, as we can see even from this short extract. He can be elaborate, or brief and direct. He can use invective of the lowest kind as well as oratory at its most magniloquent as he does when addressing the Parliament of England in *Areopagitica*. He can also state his views in a style that is close to the plain style of the Restoration, as when he defines the aim of education in his letter to Hartlib (1644), or when he defines temperance in the *Areopagitica*. What he does not, and perhaps cannot, do is to assume the gentlemanly tone of polite conversation or write in the simple epistolary style of friendly intercourse, even in the tract *Of Education*, which takes the form of a letter to Hartlib. He addresses Hartlib in a slightly formal tone, and indeed expresses his esteem for him in such a way that he has long been mistaken for a true disciple of

Comenius. But the letter is in a key altogether different from those of the next age. Perhaps he was too conscious of speaking, as he says of Hartlib, "by the definite will of God so ruling, or the peculiar sway of nature, which also is God's working." For a man to write the plain prose that emerged with the Restoration, it is perhaps necessary that he should not feel himself to be doing God's work.

We may now turn to Dryden, and to his best-known prose work, *An Essay of Dramatic Poesy* (1668). The *Essay* purports to relate a conversation between four "men of wit and quality," a friendly exchange in which each is given the opportunity to state his views on the drama. The essay is "problematical" not only because different views are expressed without the superiority of any being demonstrated —unless we consider that Neander has answered the objections of Crites because he has the last word—, but also because none of the speakers canvasses his own conception or tries to persuade the others: each merely sets forth the argument and allows for the others' different opinions. It is not a debate, but a friendly converse, each being tolerant of the others' views. The tolerant attitude—Dryden calls it sceptical—, the openness to other points of view, the courtesy of the rejoinders, all these unmistakably suggest the conversation of men of good breeding. And we do hear the talking voice, for instance when Eugenius says: "'Tis true, they have kept the continuity, or, as they call it, the *liaison des scènes* somewhat better" or "To go no further than Terence; you find in the *Eunuch* . . . ;" or: "I pass by this; neither will I insist on the care they take. . . ." Indeed, none of them insists, each only states his views, quietly and without emphasis.

The talking voice is heard from a little distance, like the noise of the battle they hear afar off. For the essay does not suggest the vivacity of dialogue: each speaker is given time to expound his views in a little set piece before another voice is heard. Thus, we are at a remove from actual conversation, the *Essay* being an imitation of nature, i.e. a slightly formalized version of it. This is also true of the style. Consider, for instance, the following paragraph:[5]

Is it not evident, in these last hundred years, when the study of philosophy has been the business of all the Virtuosi in Christendom, that almost a new nature has been revealed to us? That more errors of the school have been detected, more useful ex-

periments in philosophy have been made, more noble secrets
in optics, medicine, anatomy, astronomy, discovered, than in
all those credulous and doting ages from Aristotle to us?—so true
it is, that nothing spreads more fast than science, when rightly
and generally cultivated (p. 26).

The first sentence is slightly more formal than actual spoken style,
because of the when-subordinate between "Is it not evident" and
"that almost a new nature has been revealed to us." Dryden then proceeds to elaborate this point by beginning anew: "that more errors
. . . more useful experiments . . . more noble secrets. . . ." This is
nearer to spoken discourse than a period in which these members
would have been included in one ample movement. Yet it is linked to
the preceding by *that,* and develops the first statement in three members, the first two being parallel in structure and of almost equal
length while the third is longer and enumerates various fields in
which knowledge has improved, thus suggesting the opening of a new
nature in an ascending movement to be opposed to the last part of the
sentence "than in all those credulous and doting ages from Aristotle
to us," which in point of length stands midway between the first two
members and the third. Note also the careful use of the adjectives:
*more errors, more useful experiments, more noble secrets, those credu-
lous and doting ages; useful* is there for precision, but the movement
becomes more ample partly through the use of the adjective, *noble* is
an important qualification and stresses the parallelism, while "credulous and doting" neatly counterbalance the first two both by their
meaning and by the weight they give to the last part. This is more
neatly patterned than the first sentence, yet it sounds quite natural,
because the style follows the outline of the thought. And the paragraph ends with a shorter sentence, beginning like the first: "so true
it is" (cp. with "Is it not evident"), but reversing the order of the two
clauses: "*that* nothing spreads . . . *when* . . . cultivated" (cp. with
"in these . . . years *when* . . . *that* almost a new nature . . .").
Yet nothing could be simpler and more direct than this last sentence;
the two adverbs are not there merely for the sake of rhythm, they are
both necessary for the accurate rendering of the thought: science
rightly and *generally* cultivated defines the method of the new science
through which a new nature has been revealed, and this is given emphasis by coming at the end. For all this what strikes us when we
read this passage, is the ease and naturalness with which the thought

is expressed. The art is there, but it is hidden, the more obvious device—the three parallel *more*-members—suggesting the enthusiasm of the speaker rather than the careful patterning. In the tone of the voice as well as in the syntax there is both variety and parallelism. The last sentence, for instance, is barer than the preceding, and is pitched much lower. This variation of movement and tone makes Dryden's style particularly lively, and the right choosing and placing of words gives that impression of inevitability which is best described as "proper words in proper places." The speaking voice is heard distinctly, but it is slightly more "natural" than in actual speech. This is nature to advantage dressed, not in all the fineries of the fops nor in the magnificent robes fit only for ceremonies, but in the quiet style of gentlemen of good breeding.

The conversation reported in the *Essay of Dramatic Poesy* takes place on a barge on the Thames while the noise of battle is heard in the distance, and we know that Dryden wrote the *Essay* in Wiltshire, while the plague was raging in London. But this was only a temporary retreat; similarly, the four friends land amidst a crowd of French people dancing in the open air, and "nothing concerned for the noise of guns which had alarmed the town that afternoon." The friends are reluctant to part, and they stand "awhile looking back on the water, upon which the moonbeams play . . . and [make] it appear like floating quicksilver." But they do return to the town and the unconcern of the French people dancing reminds us of the friends' anxiety about the outcome of the battle. This last paragraph indirectly defines Dryden's attitude as an artist: both his distance from the business of the world and his interest in what is going on around him. It also suggests the very quality of his prose style, its basis in everyday speech and the slight formalization which dresses ordinary language to advantage, much as the moonbeams make the water appear like floating quicksilver.

The *Essay of Dramatic Poesy*, written in 1666, was published in August 1667 with a dedication to Lord Buckhurst, a member of the merry gang of Charles II. The most striking quality of his dedication is the tone in which Dryden addresses this young Lord: it is courteous but not formal. The ease with which he performs the difficult task of praising without flattering results from his ability to adapt his tone and style to the nature of the person he addresses, for instance when he says:

> Seeing our theatres shut up, I was engaged in these kind of thoughts with the same delight which men think upon their absent mistresses (p. 13).

Speaking to his social superior, he yet manages to give the impression that he can express himself freely; it is clear that he is not merely bowing before rank, and that for all his respect for Buckhurst he is also aware of his own merits. Thus:

> It is enough for me to have your lordship's example for my excuse in that little which I have done in it [i.e. for using rhyme in plays]; and I am sure my adversaries can bring no such arguments against verse, as those with which the fourth act of *Pompey* [i.e. by Buckhurst] will furnish me in its defence (p. 13).

If the praise sounds natural it is because his respect is counterbalanced by the sense of his own worth, which enables him to address Buckhurst almost as an equal. Almost, but not quite. The grace with which he rebukes him for having stopped writing is equally characteristic:

> Yet, my Lord, you must suffer me a little to complain of you, that you too soon withdraw from us a contentment, of which we expected the continuance, because you gave it us so early. It is a revolt, without occasion, from your party, where your merits had already raised you to the highest commands, and where you have not the excuse of other men, that you have been ill used, and therefore laid down arms. . . . I am almost of opinion, that we should force you to accept of the command, as sometimes the Praetorian bands have compelled their captains to receive the empire. . . . As for your own particular, my Lord, you have yet youth and time enough to give part of them to the divertisement of the public, before you enter into the serious and more unpleasant business of the world (pp. 13-14).

If the comparison with thinking upon absent mistresses is fitting for the young libertine, the military comparisons that follow are fitting for the young lord who will be called upon to play his part in the business of the world. And Dryden readily recognizes that the claims of this world are more serious than the divertisement of the public, to which Buckhurst might devote a few idle hours. Implicit in this is the notion of the gentleman of quality's negligence, of the ease with which he can dash off a piece of verse, of the effortlessness of his accomplishments, etc. Dryden is speaking as if he shared Buckhurst's attitude to life and grounded his behaviour on the same assumptions; he has keyed his style so as to speak like the person he addresses, without ceremony yet with deference.

The simplicity and grace of Dryden's style derive from this assumption of equality, or near equality, with persons of wit and quality: the freedom of converse implies both candour and civility, an easy familiarity between men of gentle breeding. This is the manner Dryden claims to have adopted in the *Essay,* and the style in which he says this is the best evidence of it:

> And yet, my Lord, this war of opinions, you well know, has fallen out among the writers of all ages, and sometimes betwixt friends. Only it has been prosecuted by some, like pedants, with violence of words, and managed by others, like gentlemen, with candour and civility (p. 15).

Except for "my Lord," we would forget that he is speaking to his social better, for he merely refers to what both of them, as educated gentlemen, know well. In this respect they are equals, sharing the same interests and the same tastes, i.e. preferring the candour and civility of gentlemen to the violence of pedants. He need do no more than state this, and he does it simply yet gracefully: the second adjunct in the first sentence ("and sometimes betwixt friends") not only refers to the controversy between Dryden and his friend Howard, it announces the twofold movement of the next sentence:

> by some, like pedants, with violence of words . . .
> by others, like gentlemen, with candour and civility.

The parallelism is not stressed, nor can it be without distorting the meaning; but "with violence of words" is paralleled and contrasted with "with candour and civility," and the weak ending here seems to suggest the unemphatic, quiet tone of this civil exchange.

The distinction between scholars and gentlemen, and their different ways of managing a dispute, was stressed by Robert Boyle in his

Introductory Preface to *The Sceptical Chymist* (1661), though he
himself never achieved the simple elegance of Dryden:

> If some morose readers shall find fault with my having made
> the interlocutors upon occasion compliment with one another,
> and that I have almost all along written these dialogues in a
> style more fashionable than that of mere scholars is wont to be,
> I hope I shall be excused by them that shall consider, that to
> keep a due decorum in the discourses it was fit that in a book
> written by a gentleman, and wherein only gentlemen are intro-
> duced as speakers, the language should be more smooth and the
> expressions more civil than is usual in the more scholastic way
> of writing. And indeed, I am not sorry to have this opportunity
> of giving an example how to manage even disputes with civility;
> whence perhaps some readers will be assisted to discern a dif-
> ference betwixt bluntness of speech and strength of reason, and
> find that a man may be a champion for truth without being an
> enemy to civility; and may confute an opinion without railing
> at them that hold it.

The civility of gentlemen, then, allies smoothness of expression to
strength of reason, their style "keeps a due decorum" and their tone
implies due respect for others, or modesty.

Dryden's model, he tells Buckhurst, is Tully's controversy with his
dear Atticus, the Ciceronian dialogue, where such qualities obtain.
In a later essay, on the *Dramatic Poetry of the Last Age* (1672) he
was to attribute the greater refinement of wit in his age to the influence of the Court and the conversation of gentlemen. Such a conversation, though slightly formalized, is mirrored in the *Essay,* and we
may infer that Dryden modelled his style on that of the young aristo-
crats and men of quality with whom he associated. Professor Sutherland has defined the characteristics of such conversation:

> The gentleman converses with ease, and with an absence of
> emphasis that may at times become a conscious and studied
> under-emphasis, but is more often the natural expression of his
> poise and detachment. He is imperturbable, nothing puts him
> out or leads him to quicken his pace; indeed, a certain noncha-
> lance and a casual way of making the most devastating remarks
> are characteristic of him, for if he is always polite he is never
> mealy-mouthed, and has no middle-class inhibitions. He will

never betray too great eagerness or ride his ideas too hard or
insist too absolutely, for that is to be a bore; he will not consciously exploit his own personality or indulge in eccentricity
or whimsies, for that is to be selfish, to think too much about
himself. On all occasions, like a good host, he will consult the
convenience and pleasure of those he is entertaining; and he
will therefore try to express himself clearly and politely and
unpedantically. If he can manage it (and if he can't he won't
try) he will make his points with a witty turn of thought and
phrase. He will not dogmatize, or proselytize, or appeal exclusively to the emotions; for to do so is the mark of the ignorant
zealot and the godly fanatic, of whom no Restoration gentleman
wished to be reminded.[6]

These qualities will appear more clearly if we compare the dedication
of the *Essay* with the account "of the ensuing poem," *Annus Mirabilis,* "in a letter to the Honourable Sir Robert Howard," written
shortly before the dedication to Buckhurst.[7] The opening sentences
are highly patterned, and the formal arrangement is at once obvious;
in the next sentences the careful balancing of the parts is also felt at
once, and the formality of the address is enhanced by the exaggerated
simile: Howard-martyr. Yet as soon as Dryden proceeds to the account
of the nature and manner of the poem, the stiffness disappears, as
though he were too much concerned with what he has to say to waste
any time on useless decoration:

I have called my poem historical. . . .

Most of this is written in simple, straightforward style, the style of
exposition; he expounds his views to Howard as to another man
equally interested in the problem, not to a patron before whom he
must humble himself. Note for instance his assumption of Howard's
approbation in:

I have chosen to write my poem in quatrains or stanzas of four
in alternate rhyme, because I have ever judged them more noble
and of greater dignity both for the sound and number than any
other verse in use amongst us; in which I am sure I have your
approbation (p. 95).

But at the end when he once more addresses Howard directly the tone and style become more formal. He is not above using a little conceit, one of these gaudy conceits he was himself to condemn: "I hope it will stir you up to make my poem fairer by many of your blots"; and he ends his dedication with a flourish, by attributing whatever merits the poem has to the judgment of his friend.

Now, it can hardly be argued that the ease with which Dryden addresses Buckhurst had been acquired between 10 Nov. 1666, the date affixed to the Account of *Annus Mirabilis,* and August 1667, when the *Essay* was published. The formality of the earlier piece must be related to the person he addresses there. Though Sir Robert Howard was Dryden's brother-in-law, the poet owed him a considerable debt; not only had he encouraged Dryden and helped him to correct the poem, but he "had helped to see it through the press."[8] This certainly accounts for Dryden's gratitude, for his humility towards his protector, and for the emphatic tone in which he praises and thanks him. The style is that of a complimentary address, not of friendly converse. But Dryden does not keep it up, and the main body of the piece is a clear exposition of his views, in which he felt more at home than in high eulogy.

Professor Pinto has recently drawn attention to the "vein of rather fulsome flattery" in which Dryden wrote to Rochester to thank him for his help with *Marriage à la Mode.* This private letter reveals his lack of ease, which issues in fulsome compliments. Yet the dedication of *Marriage à la Mode* to Rochester, though more formal and rhetorical than the dedication to Buckhurst, is far more natural than the opening of the letter to Howard. In 1673 Dryden still felt too much an inferior to the brilliant young Rochester to address him as an equal, but he no longer felt the need to humble himself as he had to his patron Howard in 1666. The discrepancy between the style of the private letter and that of the dedication to Rochester only goes to show that he had to learn how to speak with ease, and first of all to acquire the social poise which was natural to men like Rochester and Buckhurst. His best prose pieces, and the plain style that we have come to admire, were written when he spoke to his equals with perfect assurance, to expound his views to men of wit and quality. When trying to win approbation, or to engage his readers' sympathy, he could not resort to the style of friendly converse or of lucid exposition. As he himself was to say in the Preface to *Religio Laici* "A man is to be cheated into passions, but to be reason'd into truth." He had found the converse true when he dedicated his *Annus Mirabilis* "to the Metropolis of Great Britain, the most renowned and late flourishing city of London, in its Representatives The Lord Mayor and Court of Aldermen, the Sheriffs and Common Council of it." Here, as he knew, he could not count on the tolerant, open, friendly, attitude of his readers; he was more likely to encounter unfavourable prejudices and therefore he had to win their sympathies, if not by fulsome flattery at least by eulogy of their virtues, if they were to accept his view of the late events. Consequently the address to the metropolis is couched in rhetorical language, intended to "cheat into passion"; patterning, amplification, antithesis, figurative language, all play their part in order to win assent, and Dryden is not above turning to account the citizens' belief in the judgment of Heaven visited upon London for the sins of the time. Yet here also he can use the divers means at his disposal to vary his rhythms and effects, so as to lead his readers gradually from self-satisfaction in their righteousness to acceptance of the visitation as an incentive to Christian virtue, and to confidence in the happiness to come. Here Dryden is the good orator, and his address owes little to the conversation of gentlemen "speaking to their equals with perfect social assurance."[9]

In 1673 Dryden still lacked the self-assurance, or social poise, which his earlier dedication to Buckhurst had seemed to imply; but he was learning apace. In the dedication of *Aureng-Zebe* to the Earl of Mulgrave (1676) he no longer appears as the humble professional poet looking up to his social better. The bitterness with which he speaks of courtiers in general may owe something to Rochester's criticism of him in *An Allusion to Horace* (1675), and if so we may have to thank the satirist for forcing Dryden to a clearer realisation of his true worth and for making him speak with greater confidence. But his attack on courtiers "who make it their business to ruin wit" leads quite naturally to his praise of Mulgrave's retired virtue and true friendship, which in the context does not need to be heightened by any formal means. From this he can proceed to praise the valour of the earl, which he skillfully links to the sacrifice of his ancestor. However respectful the tone, however high the eulogy, the style is unemphatic, at one remove from familiar discourse yet also free of formality, e.g.:

> How much more great and manly in your lordship, is your contempt of popular applause, and your retired virtue, which shines

only to a few; with whom you live so easily and freely, that you make it evident, you have a soul which is capable of all the tenderness of friendship, and that you only retire yourself from those, who are not capable of returning it. Your kindness, when you have once placed it, is inviolable; and it is to that only I attribute my happiness in your love. This makes me more easily forsake an argument, on which I could otherwise delight to dwell; I mean your judgment in your choice of friends; because I have the honour to be one.[10]

Consider in this passage the variations in syntactic structure and in rhythm. First a complex sentence, yet with a pause between the main clause and the relative, which itself contains two consecutive clauses again separated by a shorter pause. These pauses not only allow us to stress "which shines only to *a few*," and "all the tenderness of *friendship*," they also make the style nearer to spoken discourse in spite of the subordination. On the other hand the near parallelism of the two consecutive clauses, with a relative in each, allows for the smooth development without yet emphasizing the pattern. The second sentence, on the contrary, consists of two shorter units, with a short pause between them, yet with *and* to link them. Finally in the third sentence the members are merely juxtaposed, which again varies the movement, and allows Dryden to bring in unobtrusively the fact that he has the honour of being one of these few privileged friends. The style images the relation between writer and patron, the ease of their intercourse, the speaker's respect for his noble friend, the value of the friendship, but also the self-assurance of the recipient of such valuable gift. If this is not the friendly converse of equals, it is much nearer to it than Dryden's praise of Rochester in the dedication of *Marriage à la Mode,* where the style tends to be more highly patterned as a consequence of Dryden's sense of inferiority. For instance:

But, my Lord, I ought to have considered, that you are as great a judge, as you are a patron; and that in praising you ill, I should incur a higher note of ingratitude, than that I thought to have avoided. I stand in need of all your accustomed goodness for the dedication of the play; which, though perhaps it be the best of my comedies, is yet so faulty, that I should have feared you for my critic, if I had not, with some policy, given you the trouble of being my protector.[11]

The roundabout way, the airs and graces of parallelism and antithesis, betray the insecurity of the speaker, and his praise inevitably sounds like flattery. Consider also the opening sentences of the dedication to Rochester:

> I humbly dedicate to your Lordship that poem, of which you were pleased to appear an early patron, before it was acted on the stage. I may yet go farther, with your permission, and say, that it received amendment from your noble hands ere it was fit to be presented. You may please likewise to remember, with how much favour to the author, and indulgence to the play, you commended it to the view of his Majesty, then at Windsor, and, by his approbation of it in writing, made way for its kind reception on the theatre.[12]

Dryden is asking permission, venturing to remind Rochester of his former favour, etc., in other words cringing before his noble patron. Compare with this the way in which he dedicates his tragedy to Mulgrave:

> In the meantime, my Lord, I take the confidence to present you with a tragedy, the characters of which are the nearest to those of an heroic poem. It was dedicated to you in my heart, before it was presented on the stage. Some things in it have passed your approbation, and many your amendment. You were likewise pleased to recommend it to the King's perusal, before the last hand was added to it, when I received the favour from him, to have the most considerable event of it modelled by his royal pleasure. It may be some vanity in me to add his testimony then, and which he graciously confirmed afterwards, that it was the best of all my tragedies; in which he has made authentic my private opinion of it; at least he has given it a value by his commendation, which it had not by my writing.[13]

This is a much more manly tone: the speaker knows his own worth, acknowledges the favour of Mulgrave and rejoices in the commendation of the king, but he adds that the king's praise merely authenticates his own opinion of the play, and slyly implies that the play's success owes more to the royal approval than to its own merits. This is a man capable of looking up to his betters, but in no way confusing rank and worth. This confidence is reflected in the style, which has the directness and simplicity of the earlier dedication to Buckhurst, as well as its graceful ease.

If we now turn to a later dedication, that of *The Spanish Friar* to Lord Haughton (1681), we shall see that Dryden simply skips the complimentary address, and writes, as he says, a preface rather than a dedication. Some critics have taken exception to his complacent tone in this piece. True, the compliment he offers Lord Haughton may seem unduly curt. Yet the very form of the dedication implies that this patron no more appreciates fulsome panegyrics than Dryden does, and prefers to be entertained with somewhat of the writer's own art:

And now, My Lord, I must confess, that what I have written looks more like a preface than a dedication; and truly it was thus far my design, that I might entertain you with somewhat of my own art which might be more worthy of a noble mind than the stale exploded trick of fulsome panegyrics. 'Tis difficult to write justly on anything, but almost impossible in praise. I shall there-fore waive so nice a subject; and only tell you, that, in recom-mending a Protestant play to a Protestant patron, as I do my-self an honour, so I do your noble family a right, who have been always eminent in the support and favour of our religion and liberties. And if the promises of your youth, your education at home, and your experience abroad, deceive me not, the princi-ples you have embraced are such as will no way degenerate from your ancestors, but refresh their memory in the minds of all true Englishmen, and renew their lustre in your person; which, My Lord, is not more the wish than it is the constant expectation of your Lordship's

Most obedient,

faithful Servant,

John Dryden (p. 279).

Except for the last sentence, the style of this passage is more concise than in any of the examples we have discussed so far. Dryden is mov-ing straight to the point; he has no time to waste on developments, but he makes each of his brief statements with graceful confidence. The last sentence, of course, has an ampler movement, as is only fitting for the close of the argument and for the compliment; yet here again Dryden confines himself to essentials, while neatly paralleling the example of Lord Haughton's ancestors with the promise of his future achievements. Moreover, the most obedient and faithful servant whose wish and expectation are here expressed, is talking to the young Lord as to an equal, who shares his interest in the writing of plays. Whether this was true or not, and it may be argued that Dryden's compliment is so short because he hardly knew the recipient of the dedication, the main thing is that Dryden envisages the man to whom he is speaking as of similar breeding and taste as himself. He therefore can expound his views to him as the speakers of the *Essay* do theirs, without emphasis or attempt to persuade or to "cheat into passion."

From this we can now return to an earlier piece which is a preface proper, the Preface to *All for Love* (1678). The style and tone hardly differ from those of the Dedication of *The Spanish Friar*. This is of interest in so far as it may help to define Dryden's attitude to his public when writing his prefaces. He is not writing for his own exercise and pleasure, as did Sir Thomas Browne, nor entirely oblivious of his public and barking at every bird he sees, like Burton, nor yet crying like a prophet in the wilderness, like Milton. This is a man speaking to men with the same tastes and interests as himself, "a gentleman speaking to his equals with perfect social assurance," as Professor Pinto says of Rochester's *Allusion to Horace*. Moreover, Dryden's confident tone derives from his assumption that those he addresses are reasonable men, ready to consider what he has to say dispassionately, to be reasoned into truth or at least to give his opinions a fair trial. He clearly assumes that his readers will grasp the point immediately, because they are educated men; he does not need to develop nor to insist, since his readers are expected to know what his statements imply. True, another reason why he speaks briefly and confidently is that he knows he is right; but he does not try to impress his readers, he contents himself with a clear exposition of his views. The readers are free to judge for themselves, to use their own sense. The underlying assumption is, of course, that they cannot but agree; yet if they do so it is as reasonable creatures assenting to truth: both the writer and his readers are reasonable men, and they can meet to discuss the merits of the play.

Consider, for instance, how much is implied in the two following sentences:

> All reasonable men have long since concluded, that the hero of
> the poem ought not to be a character of perfect virtue, for then
> he could not, without injustice, be made unhappy; nor yet al-
> together wicked, because he could not then be pitied. I have
> therefore steered the middle course; and have drawn the char-
> acter of Antony as favourably as Plutarch, Appian, and Dion
> Cassius would give me leave; the like I have observed in Cleo-
> patra (p. 222).

It took Bossu several chapters in his *Traité du Poème Epique* to explain that the hero of an epic poem should not be a character of perfect virtue. Dryden's reader is expected to be conversant with the
whole controversy as well as with Aristotle's theory of the end of
tragedy, and to grasp at once why a tragic hero should not be fault-
less. Further, the reference to ancient writers in sufficient to remind
the reader of the problem of historical truth in epic or tragic poetry;
but the reader is expected to be a gentleman, not a pedant, who would
insist on knowing the sources the dramatist has "observed in Cleopatra." I need hardly add that Dryden's statements, clear and simple
though they be, do not lack the graceful ease that results from the
right placing of words, both for the meaning and for the rhythm of
the sentences. Thus, the assumption which underlies the whole essay
appears at the beginning of the sentence and as such is given no
special stress: "All reasonable men have long since concluded . . .";
the parallel between the two extremes "could not be made unhappy"
—"could not be pitied" yet allows for variety, since "without injustice"
is merely recalled by "then." Note also, in the second sentence, the
pause before "and have drawn . . . ," which is equivalent to the
pause before the third clause: "the like I have observed. . . ." A less
careful writer might have said: "I have therefore steered the middle
course and drawn the character . . . give me leave; the like I have
observed in Cleopatra." This is a stylistic device which we have noted
before and which recurs repeatedly in Dryden: a pause before a
connective, whether in coordination or in subordination. The device
leads to greater clarity and smoothness, and gives more value to the
added clause. Similar examples occur in the same essay, and already
in the next sentence:

> That which is wanting . . . ; for the crimes . . . ; since our
> passions are, or ought to be, in our power . . .

or again:

> The fabric of the play is regular enough, as to the inferior parts
> of it; and the unities of Time . . .

or a little further down:

> The greatest error in the contrivance . . . which I reserved
> for Antony and Cleopatra; whose mutual love . . .

If we compare these sentences with the second paragraph of Browne's
preface, we shall see at once that Dryden's syntactic structure is similar to Browne's, yet also different. The first sentence in Browne's second paragraph also has a pause followed by a connective:

> . . . I had at leisurable hours composed; which being com-
> municated unto one, it became common unto many.

What comes after the pause is to all intents and purposes a new
sentence, and twentieth-century usage would prefer a full stop rather
than a colon before it. Not so with Dryden's "whose mutual love
being founded upon vice must lessen. . . ." The difference appears
even more clearly if we consider the second sentence of Browne's
paragraph:

> He that shall peruse . . . . and being a private exercise . . .

for here the movement begins anew, instead of being continued beyond the link-word. This gives the impression that the thought is
gradually being shaped, the various : and's in the sentence indicating
the stages at which it takes a new turn. In Dryden, on the other
hand, the connective does link, while the pause allows the reader to
grasp each member more easily. The effect is that of spoken style
because of the shorter units, but the relation between them is
indicated to the reader by means of the connectives and the sentence
reads more easily. That Dryden deliberately sought to create such
an effect appears from some of his revisions of the *Essay of Dramatic
Poesy* for the 1684 edition, "where he occasionally subordinated
clauses that were co-ordinated or merely juxtaposed"[14] in the first
version.

Dryden's later essays, whether dedications or prefaces, have the same stylistic qualities as the preface to *All for Love*. So had large parts of his earlier essays, but these were occasionally marred by a formality due to his lack of ease, either because he was addressing a superior, as in the dedications to Howard and to Rochester, or because he had not yet found the right natural style, as in parts of the *Essay of Dramatic Poesy*. As we saw in discussing the dedication to Buckhurst he seems to have modelled his tone and style on that of the men of quality whom he frequented in the sixties and seventies, on the conversation of gentlemen to which he refers in his dedication of *The Assignation* to Sedley (1673). Having spoken of the *eruditam voluptatem* of the Augustan poets, he goes on to say:

> We have, like them, our genial nights, where our discourse is neither too serious, nor too light, but always pleasant, and for the most part instructive: the raillery neither too sharp upon the present, nor too censorious upon the absent; and the cups only such as will raise the conversation of the night, without disturbing the business of the morrow (p. 186).

These sentences are more carefully patterned than in the preface to *All for Love,* as if to suggest the witty conversation of these gentlemen. In 1673 Dryden could count himself a member of such a witty group, and Sir Charles Sedley was a member of the merry gang; the 1678 preface to *All for Love* "marks his break with the Court wits, whose favours he had once sought,"[15] and from whom he had learned to converse with ease. His reply in this preface to Rochester's criticism of him in *An Allusion to Horace* may unduly belittle the talent of the young aristocrat (whom he does not name); but the criticism has clearly made him realise his strength and free himself from his excessive regard for his social betters. Though his reply is not quite fair, it reveals a social poise which his earlier reply to Howard, in the *Defence of the Essay,* completely lacked. While he there sneered at his adversary and resorted to low invective, he now admits his inferior social position and is not ashamed to confess that he writes for his living.[16] The value he attaches to the approbation of sober men, as contrasted with the flattery reaped by the young wits, is best evidenced by his attitude to his reader in this preface.

Dryden never forgot what he had learned from his association with the wits, their mode of easy converse, their graceful, unemphatic style. But he was never so dazzled by the brilliancy of his aristocratic friends as to forget that men of solid judgment also were capable judges of literature. This he seems to imply in his dedication to Buckhurst when he says:

> The court, which is the best and surest judge of writing, has generally allowed of verse; and in the town it has found favourers of wit and quality (p. 14).

His distinction as a prose-writer lies in the happy blend of the aristocratic virtues of ease and negligence with sense, in the alliance of grace and reasonableness. The later essays reveal his self-assurance and his readiness to speak to his readers as to reasonable men whose education makes them the equals of men of quality. Whether or not he addresses them directly, he is always talking to them, not to himself. And when, as in the 1700 preface to the *Fables*, he explains what he first intended to do and how he came to alter his plans, he is aware of the presence of his reader all along; this is no mere self-revelation as in the case of the introvert Sir Thomas Browne, as appears clearly from such remarks as: "But to return:", or "With this account of my present undertaking, I conclude the first part of this discourse." This is what Professor Sutherland has called the writer's "willingness to 'get together' with the reader."[17] Dryden had shown such willingness from the beginning of his career, in his prologues and epilogues; but this was the kind of familiarity that is apt to breed contempt. In his essays, on the other hand, he neither played down to his reader nor—except occasionally—tried to flatter him. Rather he spoke as an educated gentleman to another, and this is what distinguishes his prose style from the pertness of Rymer or the colloquial style of Lestrange.

APPENDIX

I. Sir Thomas BROWNE: *Religio Medici, The Works of Sir Thomas Browne,* edited by Geoffrey Keynes, Faber & Faber, London, 1964.*

TO THE READER

Certainly that man were greedy of life, who should desire to live when all the world were at an end; and he must needs be

* Printed by kind permission of Messrs. Faber & Faber, Ltd.

very impatient, who would repine at death in the societie of all things that suffer under it. Had not almost every man suffered by the presse; or were not the tyranny thereof become universall; I had not wanted reason for complaint: but in times wherein I have lived to behold the highest perversion of that excellent invention; the name of his Majesty defamed, the honour of Parliament depraved, the writings of both depravedly, anticipatively, counterfeitly imprinted; complaints may seeme ridiculous in private persons, and men of my condition may be as incapable of affronts, as hopelesse of their reparations. And truly had not the duty I owe unto the importunitie of friends, and the allegeance I must ever acknowledge unto truth prevayled with me; the inactivitie of my disposition might have made these sufferings continuall, and time that brings other things to light, should have satisfied me in the remedy of its oblivion. But because things evidently false are not onely printed, but many things of truth most falsly set forth; in this latter I could not but thinke my selfe engaged: for though we have no power to redresse the former, yet in the other the reparation being within our selves, I have at present represented unto the world a full and intended copy of that Peece which was most imperfectly and surreptitiously published before.

This I confesse about seven yeares past, with some others of affinitie thereto, for my private exercise and satisfaction, I had at leisurable houres composed; which being communicated unto me, it became common unto many, and was by transcription successively corrupted untill it arrived in a most depraved copy at the presse. He that shall peruse that worke, and shall take notice of sundry particularities and personall expressions therein, will easily discern the intention was not publick: and being a private exercise directed to my selfe, what is delivered therein was rather a memoriall unto me then an example or rule unto any other: and therefore if there bee any singularitie therein correspondent unto the private conceptions of any man, it doth not advantage them; or if dissentaneous thereunto, it no way overthrowes them. It was penned in such a place and with such disadvantage, that (I protest) from the first setting of pen unto paper, I had not the assistance of any good booke, whereby to promote my invention or relieve my memory; and therefore there might be many reall lapses therein, which others might

take notice of, and more than I suspected my selfe. It was set
downe many yeares past, and was the sense of my conceptions
at that time, not an immutable law unto my advancing judgement at all times, and therefore there might be many things
therein plausible unto my passed apprehension, which are not
agreeable unto my present selfe. There are many things delivered Rhetorically, many expressions therein meerely Tropicall,
and as they best illustrate my intention; and therefore also there
are many things to be taken in a soft and flexible sense, and not
to be called unto the rigid test of reason. Lastly all that is contained therein is in submission unto maturer discernments, and
as I have declared shall no further father them then the best
and learned judgements shall authorize them; under favour of
which considerations I have made its secrecie publike and committed the truth thereof to every ingenuous Reader.

                                                    Thomas BROWNE

II. Robert BURTON: *The Anatomy of Melancholy* (Bohn's Standard
Library, London, 1903).

DEMOCRITUS JUNIOR TO THE READER

Gentle Reader, I presume thou wilt be very inquisitive to
know what antick or personate actor this is, that so insolently
intrudes upon this common theatre to the world's view, arro-
gating another man's name, whence he is, why he doth it, and
what he hath to say. Although, as he said, *Primum si noluero,
non respondebo, quis coacturus est?* I am a free man born, and
may choose whether I will tell, who can compel me? If I be
urged, I will as readily reply as that *Egyptian* in *Plutarch*, when
a curious fellow would needs know what he had in his basket,
Quum vides velatam, quid inquiris in rem absconditam? It was
therefore covered, because he should not know what was in it.
Seek not after that which is hid; if the contents please thee,
and be for thy use, suppose the Man in the Moon, *or whom
thou wilt, to be the Author;* I would not willingly be known.
Yet in some sort to give thee satisfaction, which is more than I
need, I will shew a reason, both of this usurped name, title, and
subject. And first of the name of *Democritus*; lest any man by

reason of it should be deceived, expecting a pasquil, a satire, some ridiculous treatise (as I myself should have done) some prodigious tenent, or paradox of the Earth's motion, of infinite Worlds, *in infinito vacuo, ex fortuitâ atomorum collisione,* in an infinite waste, so caused by an accidental collision of Motes in the Sun, all which *Democritus* held, *Epicurus* and their Master *Leucippus* of old maintained, and are lately revived by *Copernicus, Brunus,* and some others. Besides it hath been always an ordinary custom, as *Gellius* observes, *for later Writers and impostors, to broach many absurd and insolent fictions, under the name of so noble a philosopher as* Democritus, *to get themselves credit, and by that means the more to be respected,* as artificers usually do, *novo qui marmori ascribunt Praxitelen suo.* 'Tis not so with me.

III. John MILTON: *Of Reformation in England, The Works of John Milton,* Columbia University Press, New York, 1931, III, pp. 1-3.*

* Printed by kind permission of Columbia University Press.

THE FIRST BOOK

Sir,—Amidst those deepe and retired thoughts, which with every man Christianly instructed, ought to be most frequent, of *God,* and of his miraculous *ways,* and *works,* amongst men, and of our *Religion* and *Worship,* to be perform'd to him; after the story of our Saviour *Christ,* suffering to the lowest bent of weaknesse, in the *Flesh,* and presently triumphing to the highest pitch of *glory,* in the *Spirit,* which drew up his body also, till we in both be united to him in the Revelation of his Kingdome: I do not know of any thing more worthy to take up the whole passion of pitty, on the one side, and joy on the other: then to consider first, the foule and sudden corruption, and then after many a tedious age, the long-deferr'd, but much more wonderfull and happy reformation of the *Church* in these latter dayes. Sad it is to thinke how that Doctrine of the *Gospel,* planted by teachers Divinely inspir'd, and by them winnow'd, and sifted, from the chaffe of overdated Ceremonies, and refin'd to such a Spirituall height, and temper of purity, and knowledge of the Creator, that the body, with all the circum-

stances of time and place, were purifi'd by the affections of the
regenerat Soule, and nothing left impure, but sinne; *Faith* need-
ing not the weak, and fallible office of the Senses, to be either
the Ushers, or Interpreters, of heavenly Mysteries, save where
our Lord himselfe in his Sacraments ordain'd; that such a Doctrine should through the grossenesse, and blindnesse, of her
Professors, and the fraud of deceivable traditions, drag so down-
wards, as to backslide one way into the Jewish beggery, of old
cast rudiments, and stumble forward another way into the new-
vomited Paganisme of sensuall Idolatry, attributing purity, or
impurity, to things indifferent, that they might bring the inward
acts of the *Spirit* to the outward, and customary ey-Service of
the body, as if they could make *God* earthly, and fleshly, because they could not make themselves *heavenly,* and *Spirituall*:
they began to draw downe all the Divine intercours, betwixt
God, and the Soule, yea, the very shape of *God* himselfe, into
an exterior, and bodily forme, urgently pretending a necessity,
and obligement of joyning the body in a formall reverence, and
Worship circumscrib'd, they hallow'd it, they fum'd it, they
sprincl'd it, they be deck't it, not in robes of pure innocency,
but of pure Linnen, with other deformed, and fantastick dresses
in Palls, and Miters, gold, and guegaw's fetcht from *Arons* old
wardrope, or the *Flamins vestry*: then was the *Priest* set to *con
his motions,* and his *Postures h*is *Liturgies,* and his *Lurries,* till
the Soule by this meanes of over-bodying her selfe, given up
justly to fleshly delights, bated her wing apace downeward: and
finding the ease she had from her visible, and sensuous collegue
the body in performance of *Religious* duties, her pineons now
broken, and flagging, shifted off from her selfe, the labour of
high soaring any more, forgot her heavenly flight, and left the
dull, and droyling carcas to plod on in the old rode, and drudg-
ing Trade of outward conformity.

NOTES

1. Lectures given at the University of Groningen, November, 1963.
2. See Appendix I.
3. See Appendix II.
4. See Appendix III.
5. Unless otherwise stated all references are to DRYDEN: *Of Dramatic*

Poesy and Other Critical Essays, ed. George Watson, London, Everyman's Library, 1962, 2 vols. Referred to hereafter as: Watson.
6. *On English Prose,* University of Toronto Press, 1960, pp. 67–8.
7. See Watson, I, 94–103.
8. Watson, p. 93.
9. V. DE S. PINTO: "Rochester and Dryden," *Renaissance and Modern Studies.* V (1961), p. 33.
10. The Mermaid Series, DRYDEN, ed. George Saintsbury (1949), I, 337.
11. *Ibid.,* p. 231.
12. Ibid., p. 229.
13. *Ibid.,* p. 341.
14. See my: "Dryden's Revision of the *Essay of Dramatic Poesy*," R.E.S., May 1963, p. 139.
15. Watson, I, 221.
16. I do not think that Professor Pinto is quite fair to Dryden when he interprets his argument as meaning that: "Poverty, apparently, is the only valid excuse for authorship" (*op. cit.,* p. 35). Dryden says, in fact, that only those who write "for a poor subsistence" can be excused for writing ill, i.e. for writing *and publishing.* Cp. with *Le Misanthrope,* Act I, sc. 2: "Si l'on peut pardonner l'essor d'un mauvais livre, Ce n'est qu'aux malheureux qui composent pour vivre." The play was first published in 1667.
17. *Op. cit.,* p. 69.